A Manual of Ugaritic

Linguistic Studies in Ancient West Semitic

edited by

M. O'Connor† and Cynthia L. Miller

The series Linguistic Studies in Ancient West Semitic is devoted to the ancient West Semitic languages, including Hebrew, Aramaic, Ugaritic, and their near congeners. It includes monographs, collections of essays, and text editions informed by the approaches of linguistic science. The material studied will span from the earliest texts to the rise of Islam.

1. *The Verbless Clause in Biblical Hebrew: Linguistic Approaches*, edited by Cynthia L. Miller
2. *Phonology and Morphology of Biblical Hebrew: An Introduction*, by Joshua Blau
3. *A Manual of Ugaritic*, by Pierre Bordreuil and Dennis Pardee
4. *Word Order in the Biblical Hebrew Finite Clause: A Syntactic and Pragmatic Analysis of Preposing*, by Adina Moshavi

A Manual of
Ugaritic

Pierre Bordreuil and Dennis Pardee

Winona Lake, Indiana
Eisenbrauns
2009

www.eisenbrauns.com

First published as *Manuel d'Ougaritique*

Library of Congress Cataloging-in-Publication Data

Bordreuil, Pierre.
[Manuel d'Ougaritique. English]
A manual of Ugaritic / Pierre Bordreuil and Dennis Pardee.
p. cm. — (Linguistic studies in Ancient West Semitic ; 3)
Includes bibliographical references and index.
ISBN 978-1-57506-153-5 (hardback : alk. paper)
1. Ugaritic language—Grammar. 2. Ugaritic language—Texts.
I. Pardee, Dennis. II. Title.
PJ4150.B5913 2009
492′.6782421—dc22

2009037311

The paper used in this publication meets the minimum requirements of the American National Standard for Information Sciences—Permanence of Paper for Printed Library Materials, ANSI Z39.48-1984. ♾™

Contents

Preface

Pierre Bordreuil and Dennis Pardee are eminently qualified to prepare a *Manual of Ugaritic* that takes into account the most recent advances in the field while at the same time honoring the pioneers of Ugaritological research, Edouard Dhorme and Charles Virolleaud, by publishing the first edition of this book in French. Both authors possess the primary qualification of having extensive teaching experience. Pierre Bordreuil inaugurated a position in Ugaritic at the *École des langues et civilisations orientales* of the *Institut catholique de Paris*, a language that is rightly considered indispensable for an establishment where biblical studies are held in such high esteem. Dennis Pardee teaches in the Department of Near Eastern Languages and Civilizations at the University of Chicago, where the study of the literatures of the ancient Near East has long been pursued at the highest level. Furthermore, and most importantly, they are the world's leading experts on the documents that their *Manual* treats. They have edited or newly reedited numerous tablets with exemplary attention to the slightest details of paleography and language. It is out of their concern for precision that they resume an American practice going back, I believe, to W. F. Albright and endeavor to reconstruct completely a plausible vocalization using, in some cases, the three distinctive *alif*-signs. The effort may appear bold, but it is predicated on an impeccable knowledge of Comparative Semitic grammar that augments the consonantal skeleton of the language and takes into account the fact that Ugaritic was a living, poetic language which was less restricted by rigid consonantal notation than was Sabaean or even Phoenician.

This expertise typifies Ras Shamra's epigraphic tradition which, since 1930, has inspired interest, even enthusiasm. As chance would have it, the Library of the High Priest was the first building excavated and, as a result, the religious literature reflecting Semitic mythology came immediately to be known from the tablets of Ilimilku, a mythology of which Renan had disputed the very existence. The myths, the recitation of which may have been thought necessary for the proper functioning of the world, presented gods and goddesses whose names were long familiar to those acquainted with the Bible and the other, unfortunately rare, relics of ancient Semitic thought. It thus became clear that the normative monotheism of Israelite religion had arisen out of a well-organized polytheism that distributed the necessary functions of natural and social life among different divine figures. Because of these similarities, Ugaritology ran the risk of developing into an auxiliary discipline to biblical exegesis. I have heard Charles Virolleaud complain with his customary discretion that the new discipline had broken away from Assyriology, which was his own field, only to fall into the hands of "Old Testament" specialists. Subsequent discoveries have allowed for a correction of this approach, though without ignoring the contributions of the religious texts, still to this day unique. The numerous collections of "practical documents," inventories, personnel lists, and international correspondence now provide the data necessary to reconstruct in some detail the life of a Syrian state at the end of the Bronze Age. Ras Shamra is one of the richest sites for understanding ancient Syria, which was not merely a "no man's land" between Mesopotamia and Egypt but home to an independent civilization whose legacy continues in our alphabet and our religions.

Ugaritology deserves to be considered an independant historical discipline, one to be mastered by itself and for itself, as distinct a field as Assyriology or Egyptology, even if it appears easier because of the profound affinities shown by Ugaritic with other long known Semitic languages. The authors of this *Manual*, I would judge, are motivated by a desire to promote this type of Ugaritic research. They cover the essential aspects of previous excavation and research, the alphabetic Ugaritic writing system and the problems it poses, the history of the Kingdom of Ugarit and its place in the concert of nations, its organization, administration, and resources. But it is in the selection of texts that their originality is displayed, for they do not omit a single genre represented at Ugarit—to the point of restricting the myths and legends to a reduced proportion. The lexicon, which is only intended to be one aid for students working on the texts and which omits comparative or etymological notes, may surprise its users by its imitation of the alphabetic order in use at Ugarit, as attested by the famous abecedaries discovered there (an order in which the voiceless palatal sibilant follows the voiced palatal stop because of graphic similarity). By refusing to adopt the order of Hebrew letters familiar to Semitists, Bordreuil and Pardee make of this unfamiliar element an excellent pedagogical tool for recalling the specificity of Ugaritic and of the civilization that this language has transmitted.

A. Caquot

Preface to the English Edition

The English edition of the *Manuel d'ougaritique* (2004) consists of an English version of the French original incorporating corrections, modifications of some of the grammatical presentations as well as of some of the interpretations of texts, and some updating of the bibliographical data. The only errors in the copies provided for the Selection of Texts of which we are aware were {n} for {r} in **3** RS 2.[003]$^{+}$ i 10, {w} for {r} in **19** RS 17.120:9, and {z} for {ḫ} in **35** RS [Varia 4]:10. Errors of other kinds, both in content and in form, were, however, more numerous; we hope to have caught most of the former and to have corrected them here. The most important of the modifications is in the presentation of the verbal system particular to poetry. The basic structure of the work, down to and including paragraph numbers, remains unchanged, and anyone familiar with the French original should be able to move to this new edition with little effort.

THE AUTHORS

Foreword, Including a Description of the Intended Audience

The object of this *Manual* is to put into the hands of persons who wish to learn the Ugaritic language a tool enabling them to acquire the rudiments of every aspect of the study of Ugaritic texts, from the decipherment of the tablet to an understanding of the deciphered text. But it is limited to the rudiments, and those who desire to become specialists should further their knowledge in three principal ways: (1) immerse themselves in the study of the Ugaritic texts; (2) consult a wide variety of secondary sources, some of which are indicated in the list of works cited; (3) learn at least one other Semitic language, preferably a language for which the (or a) vocalization is known, such as Arabic, Aramaic, or Hebrew. It appears obvious to us that a preliminary knowledge of another Semitic language and study under the direction of a capable professor or instructor who can explain the difficult aspects of the texts assigned here will facilitate the use of this *Manual*.

This *Manual* contains three parts: a grammar, a selection of texts, and a glossary.

1. The *grammar*, preceded by an introduction to the discovery of Ugarit and a brief description of the Kingdom of Ugarit, covers the traditional subjects (phonology, morphology, syntax) as well as the particulars of Ugaritic vocabulary and a very brief introduction to the basic features of poetry. Grammatical rules are copiously illustrated by examples, drawn wherever possible from the selection of texts. In these cases we indicate the reference according to this collection. If an example comes from a text that is not presented in the selection of texts, we cite it according to the RS/RIH number followed by the reference to the *editio princeps* or to *KTU/CAT*.

2. The goal of our *selection of texts* was to provide a representative range of attested literary genres, from the celebrated mythological texts to humble scribal exercises. In the introductions to each text there are bibliographic references that allow the reader to locate the *editio princeps*, principal collections, and one or two of our studies where ample explanations of our interpretation of the text can be consulted. The user should not expect to find here a complete bibliography but simply some basic and recent works from which the history of the study of the text in question may be traced. The text itself is reproduced in three forms: a facsimile of the tablet, a transcription of the cuneiform signs into Roman characters, and a vocalization. Generally, we have endeavored to add as little as possible in the transcription, compared with what is actually on the tablet. Also, the corrections are not typically shown in the text itself, but they are indicated in the notes, in the translation, and in the vocalized text. On the other hand, the restorations of important passages drawn from parallel texts are directly inserted into the transcribed text so as not to overload the notes. Of course, the third of these presentations, the vocalized text, reflects our conception of Ugaritic grammar, and it is to be considered an exercise in phonetic reconstruction; as such, it contains a degree of subjectivity not found in the copy or in the transcription. We consider the grammatical exercise that is the vocalization of a Ugaritic text to be a helpful one—not because it faithfully reproduces all the details of Ugaritic grammar, which is an impossible goal at the present stage of our knowledge of Ugaritic—but because it communicates our understanding of the texts according to the rules outlined in the grammar. For example, whether /ḫipānu/ is or is not the correct vocalization of the common noun written {ḫpn}, the ending with /-u/ conveys to the reader that we analyze it as a nominative-singular noun; or similarly, the vocalization of a verb with the form /yaQaTTiLu/ indicates its parsing as a D-stem imperfective indicative.

The user who wishes to learn all facets of Ugaritic will also take advantage of the facsimiles and the photographs along with the transcriptions, in order to learn the signs and their various forms. The vocalized text will serve, then, as a bridge between the text and the grammar. Contrary to the facsimile, which in principle conforms in every detail to the text as it appears on the tablet, the transcribed text is arranged according to the literary form of the text; the poetic texts are divided according to the poetic structure with the translation opposite it, while the presentation of the texts in prose depends more on the form of the tablet (i.e., it has been possible to place the translation of prose texts opposite the transcription only if the lines of the text on the tablet were short).

Lastly, one will find a "notes" section the purpose of which is to explain epigraphic difficulties and to aid the reader in the analysis of a word, a formula, or a text. It should be observed that these notes diminish in the course of the *Manual* because we offer such remarks only for the first attestation of a word or form. The inscribed objects themselves are presented in two forms—facsimile and photo—and may also be found, along with the photos, in digital form on a CD-ROM. This digital version is a complete PDF of the entire book, including the text, facsimiles, and photos (the latter in color). All references to texts have been hyperlinked in the PDF so that, for instance, one may move freely from a discussion of the text in the grammar to the facsimile, to a color photo of the tablet—and back. No tools other than the free Adobe Acrobat Reader® are needed in order to access this material; more information is found on the CD itself.

3. The *glossary* lists all of the attestations of each word in the selection of texts (with the exception of the conjunction *w*) and in rare instances is abridged for specific texts; for example, each attestation of the conjunction *ủ* in RS 1.002 is not listed in the glossary. The reason for this procedure is to permit the user to be certain to find our analysis of every word for each text; if at first the reference to a word is not located, then it is necessary to rethink the analysis and to continue the search. This glossary is organized by roots, but we include all the nominal forms which begin with a consonant other than the initial consonant of the root with a cross-reference to the principal entry (for example, "MDBḤT: see DBḤ"). For those who are interested in questions of etymology, we indicate the historical form of the root from which the Ugaritic one derives (for example, DBḤ "to sacrifice" comes from /ḎBḤ/, and ŠRP 'to burn' from /ŚRP/). Contrary to the majority of authors, who have opted for the West Semitic order of the first millennium (with the modifications necessary for Ugaritic) or the Latin order (with more significant modifications), we have judged it appropriate to adopt the sequence of the Ugaritic alphabet as known from the several abecedaries discovered at the site (for two examples, see the last texts in the selection of texts). This choice is all the more logical when one considers that the Ugaritic sequence is a variant of the order attested for the other Northwest-Semitic languages: see the comparative table in the grammar.

This work would not have been possible without the help of our colleagues responsible for Oriental antiquities at the museums where the tablets are kept: Mouna Moazzen and Muyassar Yabroudi in the Damascus Museum; Nasser Sharaf and Samer Abdel-Ghafour in the Aleppo Museum; Jamal Haïdar in the Lattakia Museum; Annie Caubet, Béatrice André-Salvini, and Norbeil Aouici in the Louvre. It goes without saying that the directors of antiquities in Damascus (Tammam Fakouch, then Bassam Jamous) and in Aleppo (Sakhr al-Olabi) have given us their full cooperation, as has the *Mission de Ras Shamra* (Yves Calvet and Bassam Jamous, then Jamal Haïdar) and the *Mission de Ras Ibn Hani* (Adnan Bounni and Jacques Lagarce). Lastly, many thanks also to Carole Roche and Robert Hawley for the hours they spent helping us photograph the inscribed objects. All these photographs are new and were taken under the sponsorship of the *Mission de Ras Shamra* and the *Mission de Ras Ibn Hani*, with the exception of the coverage of RS [Varia 14] (text 40) because this tablet is presently in a private Norwegian collection (the photographs reproduced here, taken when the tablet was still part of an American collection, were provided by the West Semitic Research Project).

Historical Introduction and Grammar

1. *Introduction to the History and Culture of Ugarit*

1.1. The Discovery of the Port and Village

The modern discovery of ancient Ugarit began in 1928 on the Mediterranean coast about a dozen kilometers to the north of Lattakia near the bay of Minet el-Beida. At the time, the region was administered by France under a mandate of the League of Nations. This is how Gabriel Saadé, a Lattakian authority on Ras Shamra–Ugarit, has described the discovery of this archaeological site by a farmer named Mahmoud Mella az-Zîr according to local tradition:

> . . . one morning early in March of 1928, as he was plowing with an ox-team, he noticed an area where the plow made only a shallow furrow and was bumping against something hard that made a ringing noise when struck. That evening he came back with some friends to the field. Only a few inches under the surface, they came upon a series of large flat stones. Moving these aside, they discovered a tomb made of hewn stone along with a great deal of pottery.
>
> For a week they worked at uncovering the tomb. Then a certain Bruno Michel, who owned a farm not far from there, happened to be passing by Minet el-Beida on horseback and saw the locals standing around the excavation with its numerous pottery vessels. He immediately informed Ernest Schaeffler, who was the governor of the territory of Lattakia under the Mandate. He in turn sent a report to the headquarters of the Service des Antiquités, located in Beirut and responsible for both Lebanon and Syria. The director, Charles Virolleaud, sent one of his men, Léon Albanèse, to investigate the discovery. . . . Soon thereafter, Pierre Delbès . . . began a small excavation near the tomb. . . . (translated from Saadé 1979: 38–39)[1]

---

1. ". . . un matin du mois de mars 1928, tandis qu'il poussait ses boeufs, il remarqua un endroit du terrain où le soc de sa charrue, au lieu de s'enfoncer dans le sol, heurtait quelque chose de dur en émettant un bruit sec. Le soir du même jour, il revint sur les lieux, accompagné de quelques camarades. A peine eurent-ils enlevé une mince couche de terre qu'ils aperçurent quelques dalles. Les ayant déplacées, ils virent un caveau funéraire construit en pierres de taille et renfermant une nombreuse poterie.

"Pendant une semaine ils se mirent à retourner le caveau. Puis, Bruno Michel, qui possédait une propriété non loin de là, passa à cheval près de Minet el Beida. Il vit alors les paysans entourant la fosse remplie de vases en terre cuite. Il en informa aussitôt M. Ernest Schaeffler qui était, sous le Mandat français, gouverneur du territoire de Lattaquié. Celui-ci avisa, à son tour, le Service des Antiquités dont le siège était alors à Beyrouth et qui était responsable aussi bien du Liban que de la Syrie. Charles Virolleaud, qui dirigeait ce service,

The *Service des Antiquités* sent pottery samples collected from the tomb as well as a plan of the tomb itself to the Louvre. René Dussaud, at that time in charge of the Oriental antiquities section, at once understood the promising nature of the discovery and obtained the funds necessary for an archaeological investigation. Claude F.-A. Schaeffer was named director, and he began excavations on April 2, 1929. He at first concentrated on the site of the accidental discovery at Minet el-Beida but soon, following the counsel of René Dussaud, he expanded his efforts to the summit of Tell Ras Shamra, situated less than a kilometer inland. On May 14, 1929, five days after the beginning of the excavations on the tell, the first tablet with cuneiform writing appeared (this initial discovery has been recounted in detail by the excavator himself [Schaeffer 1956]).

The discovery of cuneiform tablets along the Levantine coast was hardly surprising in and of itself, for half a century earlier the epigraphic discoveries of el-Amarna had revealed that the kings of the cities along the Syrian coast, from Gubla (Byblos) to Ṣur (Tyre), had in the 14th century couched their correspondence with the pharaohs Amenhotep IV/Akhenaten in Akkadian. And indeed some of the first tablets discovered at Ras Shamra were written in an Akkadian comparable to that of the Amarna Letters. This linguistic similarity led the first epigrapher of the French archaeological team, Charles Virolleaud, to place the new texts in the same time frame as that of the Amarna texts. So early a dating has, however, been shown by subsequent archaeological and epigraphic discoveries to be incorrect. Most of the Amarna texts date to a narrow time frame in the first third of the 14th century while only a small minority of the Akkadian texts from Ras Shamra date to later in that century—the vast majority are from the 13th and early 12th centuries, with the major concentration belonging to the last half-century or so of the history of the kingdom. This distribution of the Akkadian sources is confirmed by the historical and linguistic data now available from the cuneiform archives of other Syrian sites such as Alalakh, Emar, etc. Furthermore, it is generally the case that, anywhere one excavates the surface-level archaeological stratum, its artifacts represent the last few years of the occupation of the city, in round figures from ca. 1200 to 1185 B.C.

1.2. The Identification of Ugarit

The site of the city of Ugarit had not been identified previously, but there were good reasons to believe that it was located somewhere on the Levantine coast. Its name was known from the Amarna correspondence of Rib-Haddi,

---

envoya l'un de ses collaborateurs, Léon Albanèse, enquêter sur place. . . . Peu de temps après, Pierre Delbès . . . entreprit des fouilles à proximité du caveau. . . ."

king of Byblos in the 14th century B.C., who evoked its splendor in a letter addressed to the pharaoh Amenhotep IV/Akhenaten: "Look, there is no mayor's residence like that of the residence in Tyre. It is like the residence in Ugarit. Exceedingly [gr]eat is the wealth [i]n it" (EA 89:48–52, translation by Moran 1992: 162). Ugarit was also mentioned in the Egyptian geographical lists of Amenhotep III at the Temple of Soleb and among the allies of the Hittites in the poem of Pentaur, which relates the Egyptian version of the battle of Qadesh. A Hittite prayer addressed to the goddess Ishtar of Nineveh mentions Ugarit in the same context with Alalakh and Sidon. Before 1929, however, the location of this city was still entirely uncertain (de Langhe 1945: 1.32–37). As with the decipherment of the Ugaritic language, the identification of the newly discovered city was primarily the result of intuition. W. F. Albright (1931–32: 165) and C. Virolleaud (1931b: 351) were the first to express in writing that the ruins of Tell Ras Shamra represented the ancient city of Ugarit, but É. Forrer appears to have made the same suggestion a year earlier (Schaeffer 1932: 26). In his published remarks in 1931 that we have just cited, C. Virolleaud mentioned his decipherment of the name of a Niqmaddu, king of Ugarit (*nqmd mlk ủgrt*), on a tablet from 1931 (RS 3.347, *editio princeps* by Virolleaud 1932; cf. Bordreuil and Pardee 1989: 31). This reading was confirmed in 1933 thanks to the colophon on an alphabetic tablet written by "Ilimilku . . . scribe of Niqmaddu, king of Ugarit" (RS 5.155, *editio princeps* by Virolleaud 1934). In 1932, F. Thureau-Dangin accepted this identification (Schaeffer 1932: 26), which was definitively established two years later by an Akkadian letter from the Euphrates region in which the author expressed for his Ugaritian correspondent the wish "that the gods of the land of Ugarit guard you, my brother" (RS 6.198, *editio princeps* by Thureau-Dangin 1935).

1.3. The Decipherment of the Alphabetic Cuneiform Writing System

While the first epigraphic discoveries, including, as we have seen, tablets written in an Akkadian similar to that of the Amarna Letters, permitted a rapid and positive identification of the ancient city concealed by Tell Ras Shamra, the decipherment of the new cuneiform writing system and the language it represented was a much more complicated matter. More than a half-century after the rediscovery of cuneiform literature from Mesopotamia, this new writing system appeared on the Levantine coast with the peculiarity of being made up of cuneiform characters that did not, however, conform to the Mesopotamian logo-syllabic system. Since the number of signs was relatively small, the system was identified as alphabetic even before it had been completely deciphered. As a result of the geographic proximity between the Syrian coast and the nearby island of Cyprus, C. Virolleaud, who was entrusted with editing these new texts, initially wondered if it could be a Cypriot or Aegean writing system.

This line of inquiry soon proved to be a dead end, but the editor's observation of three phenomena of a graphic nature was certainly significant for the rapid decipherment that followed. He pointed out: (1) that the total number of signs in use was relatively small, an indication that the writing system was probably alphabetic in nature; (2) that words, rarely comprising more than four signs, were separated by a wedge or simple vertical stroke; (3) that an identical sequence of signs was found on five bronze blades discovered in 1929 (see Bordreuil and Pardee 1989: 20, numbers RS 1.[051] to RS 1.[055]) and at the beginning of a text on a clay tablet excavated in the same year (RS 1.018, see Bordreuil and Pardee 1989: 17). In this latter document, a sign preceding the sequence was interpreted as the Semitic preposition *l* meaning 'to', and the sequence itself was interpreted as the name of the owner of the bronze object (as we shall see, however, the term is to be analyzed as a title rather than as a proper name) and as the addressee of the text incised on the tablet. Admittedly, these common-sense observations were of limited value, for the linguistic identity of this new language remained unknown. Virolleaud later described in very lucid terms the preliminary obstacles to decipherment: "As we had at our disposition not the briefest of bilingual or trilingual inscriptions, the problem with which we were presented was particularly daunting. Indeed it could have gone without a solution, for it is obvious that an unknown language expressed in an unknown script is undecipherable" (Virolleaud 1936a: 68;[2] cf. Caquot, Sznycer, and Herdner 1974: 36). In sum, it was an equation with two unknown variables.

Another difficulty was the impossibility to derive the signs incised on these tablets from the Sumero-Akkadian syllabary, which had been known for decades. Perplexity followed the initial surprise, for the uncertainty obtained at three levels: the nature of the signs (logograms, syllables, or phonemes?), the identification of the individual signs, and the classification of the language represented by these signs. Virolleaud noted the presence of small vertical wedges separating sequences of signs that generally did not number more than four or five elements. One should not underestimate this preliminary observation, which was an important condition for decipherment, though not sufficient in itself. The total number of signs in the system was about 30, making it probable that they were letters of an alphabet. Yet each of the signs and their divergent forms still needed to be identified and each one assigned its precise value—no easy series of tasks. While this process was underway, Virolleaud's copies of the more important of the new texts appeared in mid-April of 1930 in

2. "Comme nous ne disposions d'aucune bilingue, ou trilingue, si courte fût-elle, le problème se posait dans des conditions particulièrement ingrates, et ce problème d'ailleurs eût très bien pu être insoluble, car il est évident qu'une langue inconnue exprimée par une écriture inconnue est indéchiffrable."

the journal *Syria* (a specialized periodical created at the initiative of René Dussaud), in vol. 10, bearing the imprint date of 1929 (see Virolleaud 1929). These reproductions immediately attracted the attention of Semitists and sparked intense activity in this new field of study among the experts.

Among them, H. Bauer, a Semitist at Halle, immediately sensed that the new language was Semitic, and this intuition, which he was the first to put in writing, turned out to be correct. Profiting from Virolleaud's observation regarding the use of word-dividers, he grouped into words those sequences that were marked off by separators and comprised four or five signs. The first and/or the last sign would correspond in Semitic morpho-syntax to prefixes or suffixes added to the tri-consonantal structure characteristic of the Semitic languages. As a result, the first sign (a preformative) and/or the last sign (an afformative) could be identified as /n/ or /t/, letters commonly used as prefixes and suffixes in other known Semitic languages. The sign indicating possession could be identified as the preposition *l*, and other isolated letters correlated with prepositions or conjunctions comprising only one letter: *b*, *w*, *k*, and *l*. In many texts, sequences of three to five letters repeatedly separated by the same two letters and situated between two small vertical wedges were interpreted as lists of proper names, where the patronym was followed by *bn*, 'son of', a common practice in the Semitic world (in actuality the sequence is {bˁl . bt.} + PN, repeated over several consecutive lines of the tablet RS 1.014). These devices enabled Bauer to propose identifications for seventeen letters.

É. Dhorme, while adopting some of Bauer's identifications, undertook his own research and improved on Bauer's results by correcting the reading of five signs. At the same time, Virolleaud identified a small tablet from the 1930 excavations as an administrative document that revealed the names of several numbers spelled out using letters. By comparing these with their counterparts found in other Semitic languages, he determined values for some letters that were still uncertain or unidentified. In July of 1931, just a little more than two years after the discovery of the first tablet, Virolleaud was able to present a full set of values for the signs of this first alphabet represented by wedges incised in clay, which at the time he thought numbered 28 signs (Virolleaud 1931a).

With 70 years of hindsight, we may describe the contributions of Bauer, Dhorme, and Virolleaud to the decipherment of Ugaritic as complementary. (The inscriptions on the hoe and the adze blades provide a good example of the *ad hoc* methods of the first decipherers—see Bordreuil 1998; on the history of decipherment, see Caquot, Sznycer, and Herdner 1974: 34–41, and, for more details on the role played by each of these decipherers, Day 2002). During the following years, the regular publication of new texts by Virolleaud not only made known this new Semitic language but also revealed that this cuneiform alphabet had been used at Ugarit to write Hurrian texts and some Akkadian texts. The remarkably rapid decipherment of the cuneiform alphabet resulted in the identification of a new language: Ugaritic was added to the West Semitic languages of the 1st millennium that were already known to exist (Phoenician, Hebrew, and Aramaic), and it provided vast numbers of new data on the roots of these 1st-millennium languages extending back into the last third of the 2nd millennium B.C. (de Langhe 1945: 1.221–34). Improvements were made on these initial results during the following decades, and it is still occasionally demonstrated that the best interpretations of new forms are not necessarily the first proposed (cf. Freilich and Pardee 1984).

1.4. Tablet Discoveries

It was primarily during the first three years of archaeological excavations, from 1929 to 1931, that the Library of the High Priest, adjacent to the Temple of Baal and situated in the upper part of the city in the northeastern sector of Tell Ras Shamra, yielded the major literary documents in alphabetic cuneiform—among others, the legends of Kirta (Keret) and Danilu (Danel), the various myths of the storm-god Haddu (better known by his title Baʿlu 'master')—as well as some Akkadian texts. Several alphabetic texts bore the signature of the scribe (and author?) Ilimilku, an upper-level official in the service of King Niqmaddu (III) (another tablet inscribed by this famous scribe was discovered 60 years later in the House of Urtenu, situated in the south-central section of the city [RS 92.2016, *editio princeps* by Caquot and Dalix 2001]). During the following years, until 1939, the greatest part of the archaeological effort was focused on this first area, which is traditionally called the acropolis, and, to a lesser extent, on the sections of the lower city that were located just to the west and to the east of the acropolis. The resemblances between the language of the first Akkadian texts discovered and the texts from el-Amarna, the only texts of Levantine origin known at that time, led Virolleaud to propose a date for the texts in the 14th century, and Schaeffer followed him in this dating, though he had at first preferred a 13th-century date.

Just before the interruption of excavations in 1939 owing to the outbreak of World War II, Schaeffer began excavating the Royal Palace and he continued in this area when archaeological activities resumed in 1948. One of the first finds from this area was a group of alabaster fragments bearing hieroglyphic inscriptions of Ramses II that provided an approximate chronology in the 13th century. Though new areas were opened, excavations in the Royal Palace continued until 1955 and yielded hundreds of texts written primarily in Akkadian that belonged to two principal groups: the southern archive, containing mostly legal documents (treaties, contracts, edicts, and verdicts), and the eastern archive, where some of the international correspondence in Akkadian was kept (Lackenbacher 2002: 42–45).

In the Residential Quarter, the House of Rapanu (excavated in 1953, 1956, 1958) contained another part of the international correspondence in Akkadian. There also were the House of Rashapabu (1953) and the House of the Lettered Gentleman (1953); in the South Acropolis trench, the House of Agapsharri (1962), the House of the Priest with Lung and Liver Models (1961, 1965), and the House with Magic Texts (1962). In 1954, then in 1964 and 1965, excavation took place in the South Palace, located across a street from the Royal Palace (today the identification of this large house as belonging to the royal family is widely abandoned and attribution to Yabninu is preferred: see Courtois 1990). Beginning in 1973, a fortuitous find (Bordreuil, ed. 1991: 7–9) led to the discovery of more than 600 tablets, known as the archive of the House of Urtenu, second in total number of tablets only to the archives of the Royal Palace. The principal publications of texts from this house may be found in Bordreuil, ed., 1991; Yon and Arnaud, eds., 2001.

The excavations continue and the *Mission de Ras Shamra–Ougarit*, successively led since 1971 by H. de Contenson, J. C. Margueron, M. Yon, and Y. Calvet (a clear and complete presentation may be found in Yon 1997, 2006), as well as the *Mission de Ras Ibn Hani*, led by A. Bounni and J. Lagarce (see Bounni, Lagarce, and Lagarce 1998), have discovered over the past quarter-century several hundred tablets that supply important information on the last years of life in this Bronze Age Syrian kingdom at the end of the 13th and the beginning of the 12th century B.C.

1.5. Abecedaries

In 1939, ten years after the first discoveries, the order as well as the number of letters according to the Ugaritic alphabetic tradition were provided by the find of a cuneiform abecedary consisting of 30 signs arranged roughly in the order of the Semitic alphabet as attested in the 1st millennium B.C. The five interdentals and velars that had disappeared in the 1st-millennium writing traditions were now seen to be interspersed throughout the Ugaritic alphabet (see below, §3 Phonology). Other examples have been unearthed since, and the number of complete abecedaries currently published is more than a dozen, inscribed on ten tablets found between the 10th and 24th campaigns: RS 10.081, RS 12.063, RS 19.031, two complete sequences on RS 19.040 and on RS 20.148 + 21.069, RS 23.492, two complete sequences on RS 24.281, and RS 24.288 (for details on the publications of these texts, see Bordreuil and Pardee 1989). R. Hawley (personal communication) has identified two additional fragmentary abecedaries: RS 5.274 and RS 19.174,[4], and a new exemplar containing two complete sequences has been included in our selection of texts (**55** RS 94.2440).

The original decipherment had been achieved brilliantly without the help of an abecedary, but 25 years later it was further confirmed by a damaged text discovered in the excavations of the Royal Palace in 1955 (RS 19.159, *editio princeps* by Virolleaud 1957, text 189). This synoptic table of signs originally contained the Ugaritic alphabet and its phonetic equivalents in the Akkadian syllabary arranged in parallel columns. The first ten letters (from {å} to {ṭ}) and the final ten (from {p} to {s̀}) of the alphabet are preserved. This table thus provides the vocalization of two-thirds of the Ugaritic cuneiform alphabet. This document certainly represents an attempt to set down the correspondences between the letters of the alphabet and certain signs of the traditional cuneiform repertory. With this table of equivalences may be compared to the Akkadian and Hurrian texts from the Library of the High Priest written in alphabetic characters. This discovery illustrates the extent to which Ugarit was a part of the broader cuneiform world, where Mesopotamian scribal practices were all pervasive. Perhaps the clearest indications of this cultural context are the adaptation of the alphabetic tradition to a system of cuneiform signs inscribed in clay and the fact that Ugaritic is written from left to right—in keeping with syllabic cuneiform practice but against the usage that prevailed in the other West Semitic traditions. Finally, we must keep in mind that the Ugaritic alphabet reflects a Semitic language with all that this implies for the importance of consonantal phonemes. It is thus properly termed a consonantal alphabet.

1.6. Languages in Use at Ugarit

Eight different languages are presently attested in the documents from Ugarit: Sumerian, Akkadian, Hittite, Luwian, Hurrian, Ugaritic, Egyptian, and Cypriot-Minoan. These languages were rendered using five distinctive writing systems. In most common use were the Sumero-Akkadian logo-syllabic system (also used to write Hittite and Hurrian) and the Ugaritic alphabetic system (also used to write Hurrian and, to a much lesser extent, Akkadian). In addition to these systems consisting of cuneiform signs inscribed on clay, Luwian hieroglyphs, Egyptian hieroglyphs, and the Cypriot-Minoan syllabic systems are attested in relatively limited corpora. The two principal corpora are the texts in the local "Ugaritic" language, which today number about 2,000, and the texts written in Akkadian (more than 2,500), the chancellery language of the period.

1.7. Bilingual and Multilingual Documents

Marginal notations or numbers written in Mesopotamian signs are sometimes found in administrative documents otherwise composed in alphabetic cuneiform (for example, RS 11.715+, *editio princeps* by Virolleaud 1940b). Less frequently attested are tablets with a Ugaritic text on one side, and on the other a text written in the syllabic writing system (for example, RS 18.102, Virolleaud 1965: text 34). Among the unpublished texts from the House of Urtenu, a new example of the latter has been found that contains two seemingly identical texts (RS 94.2519), as well as two texts in which the two writing systems are mixed in an irregular fashion (RS 94.2276 and RS 94.2411).

There are several ritual texts where Ugaritic and Hurrian, both written alphabetically, are mixed in a single text (see Pardee 1996). In one, a paragraph in Hurrian is clearly set off from the preceding and following Ugaritic texts by horizontal lines (**12** RS 24.643:13–17).

A great many lexical texts have been discovered at Ugarit. These consisted of columns of signs or words that apprentice scribes had to learn as part of their education. These lists were often bilingual (Sumerian and Akkadian), but they also were adapted to the multilingual milieu of Ugarit by the addition of one column in Hurrian and another in Ugaritic (the most complete text of this type is RS 20.123^{+}, *editio princeps* by Nougayrol 1968: text 137). For the contributions of this type of text to our understanding of Ugaritic, see Huehnergard 1987.

A trilingual document (Sumerian-Akkadian-Hurrian) discovered in 1994 has recently been published (André-Salvini and Salvini 1998a, 1999a, 1999b, 1999c, 2000). Its Sumerian and Akkadian columns contain the beginning of a large lexical list, the first terms of which were previously unattested at Ugarit. The last column, an important new source for the history of the Hurrian language, provides the meaning of several new words and confirms some older hypotheses that were based on comparative considerations.

1.8. Ugaritic Texts

There are approximately 50 mythological texts in poetry and some 1,500 texts in prose (including decipherable fragments). The primary types of prose texts are: religious (ritual, deity lists, votive), ominological (astral, malformed births, extispicy), medical (hippiatric), epistolary, administrative (contracts, lists of many sorts), and didactic (abecedaries, exercises).

The prose texts, the majority of which were discovered in the Royal Palace, excavated primarily after World War II when excavations resumed in 1948, originate largely from the royal administration. The administration was headed by a king, often in vassal position to a king of a larger political entity, the Hittite king in the period documented. Many of the letters emanate directly from the royal family; many of the ritual texts specifically mention the king; most of the administrative texts deal with one aspect or another of royal control of the resources of the kingdom (real estate, taxes, management of royal goods, working of raw materials, etc.). The 100-plus epistolary documents, in particular, reveal the Ugaritic that was in everyday use in the city.

The poetic texts have made the fame of Ugarit, because they provide a mythical and literary background for the Hebrew Bible. They are, however, comparatively few in number, and the poetic dialect presents many difficulties of interpretation. Several of the major mythological texts bear the signature of a scribe named Ilimilku, whom some now suspect to have lived near the end of the Kingdom of Ugarit (Dalix 1997b, 1998; Pardee 1997a: 241 n. 3; state of the question in Pardee 2007), rather than a century earlier, as the traditional position maintained. The poems that he and other scribes recorded had in all likelihood been passed down by oral tradition for centuries.

The nature of the corpus and of the writing system places limits on our ability to describe the language. The number of texts is relatively small and virtually all are damaged to some degree, leaving few long stretches of text for analysis. This is especially true of the prose texts, which were usually written on tablets smaller than those bearing the major mythological texts. No prose narrative texts are as yet attested on which to base a description of narrative prose syntax. The poetic texts are largely narrative rather than lyrical but are of little use, because of their archaic form, for projecting a prose syntax. The upshot is that phonology is described largely in terms of graphemes; morphology is to a significant degree reconstructed; reasonably comprehensive descriptions of morpho-syntax and of poetic syntax are possible; the prose discourse syntax particular to letters is reasonably well known, while narrative prose syntax is known primarily from narrative sections of letters.

1.9. The Archives of Ugarit and the History of the Kingdom

Traces of uninterrupted human occupation, from virgin soil in the middle of the 8th millennium until the beginning of the12th century B.C., are still visible in the baulks of the 20-meter-deep sounding that was undertaken on the western slope of the acropolis. C. F.-A. Schaffer began this project in 1934, and H. de Contenson reinitiated it in the early 1950s, concluding it in 1976 (de Contenson 1992).

Texts have been recovered only from the Late Bronze Age—the Middle Bronze Age levels, where Akkadian texts surely await discovery, have been reached only in limited soundings. Beginning in 1977, Ugaritic and Akkadian texts have been discovered at the neighboring site of Ras Ibn Hani, a suburb of Ugarit (Bordreuil et al. 1984, 1987; Bounni, Lagarce, and Lagarce 1998). Ugarit is occasionally mentioned in texts from other sites (Mari, el-Amarna). In these sources, Ugaritians belong to the "Amorite" element since they bear "Amorite" names and, in the 18th century B.C., they maintain cultural relations with other "Amorite" kingdoms. At present, the oldest texts discovered on the site of Ras Shamra–Ugarit go back to the 14th century (with the notable exeption of RS 16.145 [*PRU* III, p. 179]—see Arnaud 1998) and, thanks to the recent discoveries in the House of Urtenu, our knowledge of the political history of the last two centuries of this kingdom, which has gradually increased over the years, will continue to grow in the years to come as these texts are published. Nevertheless, many uncertainties remain, for the dates of many texts are still approximate. The Akkadian text known as "the General's letter" is a good example of this uncertainty (RS 20.033, *editio princeps* by Nougayrol 1968: text 20), for the writer's name is damaged and that of the recipient is no longer extant, with the result that various historical contexts have been proposed with dates ranging over nearly a cenury (see Lackenbacher 2002: 54–55, 66–69; Freu 2006: 81–86, 90, 94, 233–34).

The first important event in the history of the kingdom for which documentary evidence from Ugarit is preserved is reflected in the international treaty RS 19.068 (*editio princeps* by Nougayrol 1956: 284–86; cf. Lackenbacher 2002: 53–54, 64–66, 180 + n. 597, 289 n. 1029) which was concluded by Niqmaddu II with Aziru of Amurru in *ca.* 1360. The text evokes a conflict between Niqmaddu and Aziru for sovereignty over the buffer-state of Siyannu, located to the south and east of Ugarit and north of Amurru. It contains the agreement that Ugarit will pay Amurru a total of 5,000 shekels of silver in settlement of all outstanding matters. From that point on, military assistance would be required of Aziru against any potential enemy, although no reciprocal obligation was stipulated in the treaty. The unique character of this payment, the relative modesty of which is surprising, precludes the possibility that it was tribute. The image projected by this text is less that of a tributary state protected by Amurru than that of a state preferring to secure its peace rather than to use force. In other words, it appears to be an instance of preferring an expensive peace over a costly war.

Shortly thereafter, the invasion of Syria by Shupiluliuma I created a new situation that forced Ugarit to choose between, on the one hand, solidarity with a coalition of Syrian kingdoms (led by Mukish to the north and Nuḫashe and Nia in the Orontes Valley to the east and to the south) and, on the other, an alliance with Ḫatti that promised Ugarit substantial territorial gains. Niqmaddu II opted for the latter but was not able to withstand his neighbors' offensive, which devastated his territory before his new ally could arrive to force the invaders' departure. (It is difficult to evaluate the real military capabilities of Niqmaddu, since there are no direct data on the real number of his troops, but a letter of Shupiluliuma, RS 17.132 [*editio princeps* by Nougayrol 1956: 35–37], mentions a Ugaritic military force capable of subduing cities.) The net gains from this operation, however, were not insignificant, for Ugarit obtained (1) an assurance that its reigning dynasty should remain in place while the Hittites imposed their own kings in other Syrian polities, (2) a definitive stop to the expansion of Amurru to the north, (3) the assurance of protection by a great power, (4) the extension of Ugaritic territory, and (5) a privileged position in the administration of Hittite Syria—all this established by the treaty between Niqmepaʿ and Murshili II that was promulgated shortly after these military operations.

These two early examples illustrate and anticipate the political stance of the Kingdom of Ugarit during its last century and a half of existence. Between the options of an increasingly untenable isolationism or of collaboration with the Hittites, who were capable of ordering reprisals from a whole series of neighboring kingdoms, two policies of moderation were developed. The first, which consisted of forming alliances with the various Syrian polities, was preferred in the 14th century. In ca. 1340, Arḫalba of Ugarit joined a coalition against the Hittites that included the kingdoms of Nuḫashe and Qadesh that was supported by Egypt under Horemheb. But the coalition was defeated in Murshili II's ninth year and, among other detrimental consequences suffered by the Kingdom of Ugarit, this defeat led to decreased control of Ugarit over its southern neighbor, Siyannu-Ushnatu. The second policy, a sort of "passive resistance" (Liverani 1979: 1311), seems more accurately to describe the 13th century, and it was perhaps while walking this tightrope that the Ugaritians most clearly practiced politics as the art of the possible.

This strategy was, however, already perceptible in the 14th century: it is important not to overlook the likely presence in Ugarit of widespread anti-Hittite resentment following on the previous animosity to Egyptian domination. We have seen that such an attitude was not unknown in Ugarit, for the political choices of Arḫalba seem to have been based on this type of sentiment—but they had led to adverse consequences for the kingdom. This failure of Ugaritic politics toward the Hittites seems, however, not to have dampened the Ugaritic resolution to oppose Hittite domination nor to have stemmed the development of a popular opposition to Hittite domination. Thus Ugarit's support of Ḫatti is not to be characterized as loyal and unconditional but rather as that of an ally, whether willing or not. Niqmaddu II was not able to refuse the proposition of Shupiluliuma, whose armies were at his doors, but, after the death of this Hittite king, he clearly balked at continuing a policy that he had not chosen of his own free will. As a result, the attitude of Ugarit as a Hittite vassal was pragmatic, entirely contingent on circumstances.

From the beginning of the 13th century on, the official documentation provides a more solid chronological foundation. The majority of these texts were no doubt composed and kept until 1185 in the Royal Palace of Ugarit, in the South Palace, a mansion that is increasingly being identified as the dwelling of an important personage named Yabninu, and in various other private dwellings of important officials at the court of Ugarit. For the last 30 years, hundreds of new tablets discovered in the south-central region of Tell Ras Shamra have been grouped under the name "archives of the House of Urtenu," because the name Urtenu, a courtier contemporary with the last kings of Ugarit, appears frequently in these texts, some of which are of a private nature (see Bordreuil and Pardee 1995a; and, here below, text **18** RS 92.2014). This final period in the history of Ugarit is particularly interesting because it marks the beginning of a new geopolitical equilibrium. This new historical situation was the logical consequence of the battle of Qadesh in 1275 between Egypt and Ḫatti, which positioned Ugarit within the southern sphere of influence of the Hittite Empire.

The attitude of minimal cooperation with the Hittite overlord that had been put to the test in the 14th century became the norm in the first half of the 13th century. The Hittite king Tudḫaliya IV granted Ammistamru II a remarkable exemption given the previous treaty between Murshili II and Niqmepaʿ: in exchange for 50 minas of gold, Ugarit was not required to send troops to the aid of Ḫatti in a conflict with Assyria: "In the presence of Ini-Teššup, king of Charchemish . . . the Sun, Tudḫaliya, Great King, King of Ḫatti, has released Ammistamru, king of Ugarit. . . . Until the war with Assyria is over, the infantry and the chariotry of the king of Ugarit need not participate" (RS 17.059, *editio princeps* by Nougayrol 1956: 150–51).

Under the earlier treaty, Ugaritic participation in Hittite military operations was stipulated, and the presence of a Ugaritic contingent at the battle of Qadesh shows that this requirement was still in force some decades later. The text just quoted, written under Tudḫaliya IV at a moment when Ammistamru II was desirous of loosening his ties to the Hittites, may have been the first concrete manifestation of the Ugaritic policy of limiting political and military cooperation to the extent possible, of interpreting *a minima* the terms of the older treaty. Lines 9–19 reveal the precautions that Ammistamru II had inserted against possible Hittite reprisals:

> No suit shall be brought in the future against the king of Ugarit. When the war with Assyria has come to an end, if the Sun prevails over the king of Assyria and peace is established between them, no suit may be brought concerning the infantry and the chariotry of the king of Ugarit, and no suit against him shall be possible at a later point. The king of the land of Ugarit has paid to the Sun fifty minas of gold in ten shipments from the sealed storehouse.

As the editor saw, the context of this document cannot have been that of a major conflict with Assyria for, if this had been the case, the Hittite king would certainly not have exempted the king of Ugarit from his obligations, or even have allowed him to buy his way out—or, if he had, he would not have ratified the procedure by a formal document. If the Assyrian threat was still alive, it could not have been life-threatening. Expertly negotiating his way through his new-found freedoms, Ammistamru II arranged not to send troops but, the Hittite state being in some trouble, the maneuver required a large sum of money. This episode is no doubt a good illustration of the political choices traditionally made by Ugarit.

In the second part of the 13th century, "passive resistance" was still the policy of choice: particularly under Ibiranu, a ruler who stands out less clearly than those who preceded and followed him but whose government can be credited with the same ambiguous yet effective attitude. Lines from a letter addressed to the king of Ugarit clearly denounce this absence of pro-Hittite enthusiasm:

> Thus says the King of Karkemish: To Ibiranu, king of Ugarit, say: May it be well with you. The *kartappu*-official Talmiteshub will be coming to you to verify the numbers of your soldiers and of your chariots. You have been made responsible for these soldiers and chariots, and it is your duty to get them ready so that the Sun may carry out this census. May the Sun not be disappointed. (This is a matter of) life and death. (RS 17.289, *editio princeps* by Nougayrol 1956: 192)

Other letters reveal that Ugarit reduced to a minimum the troops furnished to Ḫatti via Karkemish, both as to number and as to quality: "Moreover, as regards the chariotry that you sent to me, the soldiers are mediocre and the horses are starving. . . . You have kept the best *maryannu*-forces while sending me mediocre troops" (RS 34.143, *editio princeps* by Malbran-Labat in Bordreuil, ed. 1991: text 6). The writer is again the king of Carchemish, and the Ugaritic king's willingness to take advantage of him demonstrates the relative strength of his position, for the king of Carchemish was unable to impose his interests on him and could only appeal to intervention from the Hittite sovereign. Another text, apparently addressed to the king of Ugarit by one of his officials, confirms that this lack of consideration was not unintentional but premeditated: "My lord, a messenger from the king of Carchemish has gone to Qadesh seeking chariotry and infantry. He will come next to Ugarit. My lord, do not show him any chariotry or infantry and do not allow him to take any away" (RS 34.150, *editio princeps* by Malbran-Labat in Bordreuil, ed. 1991: text 10; other examples: RS 34.140, Bordreuil, ed. 1991: text 11; RS 34.138, Bordreuil, ed. 1991: text 8; RS 20.237, *editio princeps* by Nougayrol 1968: text 31; RS 11.834, *editio princeps* by Nougayrol 1955: 17).

All of this evidence confirms how important the contributions from Ugarit were for the Hittites. The policy of minimum participation presented, however, certain risks, and it was necessary to calculate in advance how to proceed without going too far. A case in point is a military expedition to the south that was challenged by the king of Carchemish: "The king of Ushnatu has come and lodged the following complaint: 'The king of Ugarit has confiscated territory on my side of the border, including a town.' How could you have acted thus? He used to be one with you but now he is free. So refrain henceforth from invading his borders" (RS 20.174A, *editio princeps* by Nougayrol 1968: text 25).

Everything that we know about the political history of Ugarit—that is, essentially its foreign policy—indicates that it was predicated above all on a remarkable pragmatism. Abandoning the isolationist position from which it had for many years successfully negotiated peace for a price, Ugarit became a vassal to the Hittites when there was no other recourse. But it made the best of this misfortune, demonstrating great skill in opposing Hittite domination without provoking direct conflict. Its financial contributions and military aid earned it considerable advantages compared with other Syrian states. Within the bounds permitted by its position as a vassal, Ugarit continued to foster its own interests, and its army remained an important element of this policy. When it seemed appropriate or inevitable, Ugarit supplied precious military support and did not hesitate to profit from Ḫatti's moments of political weakness so as to enlarge its own sphere of activity.

On the other hand, Ugarit never failed to assist its Anatolian protector in decisive moments, such as when the enemy at the battle of Qadesh in the early 13th century came from the south or at the beginning of the 12th century when the invaders came from the sea. Particularly in the latter context, its military and naval contributions were increasingly important to the regional power with whose destiny its own was bound, as we know today to have been the case during the few years that remained before the disappearance of both Ugarit and Ḫatti from the historical scene.

1.10. The Geography of the Kingdom of Ugarit

The Kingdom of Ugarit was situated on the Syrian coast, in the northwestern corner of the Fertile Crescent, between Antioch to the north and Gaza to the south and bordered to the west by the Mediterranean Sea and to the east by the important geological fault that runs north and south, through which the Orontes flows north, while the Litani and the Jordan rivers flow south. The Kingdom of Ugarit is estimated to have covered about 2,000 km^2 (Saadé 1979: 33), nearly corresponding to the present province of Lattakia.

1.10.1. The Borders

It is possible to determine the frontiers of the Kingdom of Ugarit at the time of the archives discovered at Ras Shamra, capital of the Kingdom of Ugarit, situated a little more than ten kilometers north of present-day Lattakia and a few hundred meters inland of the best port along the Syrian coast, the modern bay of Minet el-Beida. Thanks to the text of a treaty concluded between the Hittite king and the king of Ugarit in the 14th century B.C. that set out the frontier with Mukish (the modern-day region of Antioch), we know that the border ran along the chain of mountains which reaches its highest point at the Gabal al-Aqraᶜ at an altitude of 1,800 m, a peak that the Ugaritians called *Ṣapunu*. On a clear day, this summit, on the Turkish side of the modern border, is visible from the site of Ugarit some 50 km to the south. The same treaty reveals that Ugarit was bounded to the north by a natural frontier running from Birziḫeh, near the Crusader castle of Burzeh in the mountainous area to the west of the Orontes Valley, to the Mediterranean. This northern region corresponded roughly to the drainage area of the Nahr al-Kebir and its tributaries.

The sources of this river, which in the Bronze Age was called *Raḫbanu* (literally, 'the wide one'), are located in the mountainous area to the east of the Gabal al-Aqraʿ, and it reaches the Mediterranean a few kilometers south of Lattakia. It provided an essential part of the communication system of the kingdom, for it served as the primary route from the coastland into its northern and northeastern sections.

The Mediterranean provided the western boundary while the eastern border followed the chain known today as the Alaouite Mountains or the Gabal al-Ansariyeh, which marks the western side of the Orontes Valley. It is possible that during certain periods Ugarit may have controlled some territories situated on the east bank of the Orontes. The southern border was situated to the south of the Gableh Plain, including at some periods the inland Kingdom of Siyannu, and was probably marked specifically by the Nahr es-Sinn, a short but abundant river that flows out of the rocky pass that separates the coastal plain from the plain and harbor of Banyas to the south.

These natural boundaries certainly contributed to a strong geographic, economic, even national identity for this Syrian kingdom, at least for the period from the Late Bronze Age when written sources are available (middle 14th–early 12th centuries B.C.). The Ugaritians exploited their exceptional geographic location within the haven formed by these boundaries. Maḫadu, the port of the capital, and the smaller ports of other coastal villages served as doors to the Aegean world, in particular via the island of Cyprus, only 70 km away. Regarding contacts with the east, Ugarit is situated at the same latitude as Emar, a city situated on the great bend of the Euphrates, where the river turns to the southeast after meandering southwest then south from its source in modern Turkey. It was between Ugarit and Emar that the overland distance to the Euphrates was the shortest and most advantageous for transporting merchandise. The activities of the Ugaritic merchants also contributed to relations with more distant regions, including the island of Crete (*kaptāru*), whence cereals, beverages, oil, and so on, were imported, and the mountains of Afghanistan, where lapis lazuli was mined.

1.10.2. Hydrography

The Fertile Crescent roughly follows the 250 mm isohyet—that is, an imaginary line setting off zones that receive more or less than 250 mm of rainfall per year. This average annual rainfall is important because it distinguishes regions where irrigation is called for during the summer months in the dry years from regions where irrigation is not necessary. These humid zones are called regions of "rain cultures" to distinguish them from regions where the digging of irrigation canals is essential for agriculture, as in southern Mesopotamia. The territory of the Kingdom of Ugarit is located within the region that receives a minimum of 250 mm and, in fact, the mountainous region around the Gabal al-Aqraʿ receives even more precipitation than this. This climatic factor played an important role in the development of the agrarian myths from Ugarit, one of which reports that *Haddu* (better known by his title *Baʿlu* 'Master'), the god of the storm and of rain, engaged in annual combat with *Môtu*, an entity personifying drought and death. One of the functions of this myth was to accompany the renewal of the agricultural year, and it is difficult to find a more apposite climatic context for such a myth than a "rain culture." The tale recounts that *Baʿlu* was defeated and then forced to descend into the heart of the earth by his rival. Thereafter, the goddess *ʿAnatu*, who controls the subterranean waters at their sources, and *Šapšu*, the sun-goddess, who controls the evaporation of the earthly waters, become involved. Together, the goddesses collect the body of *Baʿlu* and transport it to his palace on Mount *Ṣapunu* (the Gabal al-Aqraʿ) located north of the city of Ugarit. It is also at *Ṣapunu* that the god manifests himself in the autumn rains (*CTA* 6 V 1–6; see Caquot, Sznycer, and Herdner 1974: 265–66) after being brought back to life by the care of the goddesses *ʿAnatu* and *Šapšu*. The presence of the god in his mountain abode was felt particularly in autumn, when the desired rains returned after months of absence. This was the moment when storms, observable from great distances around the region of the Syrian interior, broke out on the Gabal al-Aqraʿ and vividly announced the return of the god to his palace.

Similarly, the myth of *Baʿlu* against *Yammu* ('Sea') would appear to find its provenance in this same region. The proximity of the sea to the Gabal al-Aqraʿ (the height of this peak is more than 1,800 m, and its distance from the sea is no more than 3 km as the crow flies) explains the appearance of a "mountain effect," well known in the Mediterranean. In this meteorological phenomenon, dense clouds gather around the summit of the Gabal al-Aqraʿ while, from the center of the spectacular storm, lightning is attracted to the sea. These autumn and winter tempests must have made a big impression on fishermen, mariners, and travelers who considered the region situated to the north of the bay of Ras al-Bassit to be the place *par excellence* of the conflict between the Sea and the storm-god and interpreted the appearance of billows and powerful waves as the Sea's response to the storm-god's blows. The geographical context of the two principal myths from Ugarit, therefore, is found in the interior of the kingdom: *Baʿlu*'s combat with the Sea is waged from his mountain residence on Ṣapunu, and *Baʿlu*'s battle with *Môtu* also victoriously concludes there with the return of the god to his palace.

1.10.3. The Regions of the Kingdom

The kingdom was divided into three large geographical regions that are mentioned in the lists enumerating the contributions of various kinds furnished by the villages. These regions were subdivided into several administrative districts. The first of these regions, called *Arru*, corresponded to the plain surrounding the present village of Gableh, known as Gabala in the Greco-Roman era. We know that the southern boundary of Ugarit was situated to the south of this city because Gibʿalaya (*gbʿly*) is mentioned among the port-villages of the kingdom, whereas the Nahr es-Sinn may preserve the memory of the Kingdom of Siyannu mentioned in the Ugaritic texts and in chapter 10 of Genesis. Several villages mentioned in the Ugaritic texts belonged to this region, such as Atalligu, Ushkenu, Mulukku, etc. The mountainous area that separates the coastal plain from the Orontes Valley seems to have constituted another region, Ǵuru, whose name means 'the Mountain'. The environs of the capital, including the ancient city on Ras Ibn Hani, probably constituted another district, named after the capital city itself. The city of Ḫalbu Ṣapuni, located in the vicinity of modern Kassab, was probably the administrative center of the northern region known as Ṣapunu.

1.10.4. The Landscape

As we have seen, the landscape of the area provides a backdrop for the divine exploits and quarrels described in the mythological texts from Ugarit. A fragmentary new mythological text discovered in 1992 (RS 92.2016, *editio princeps* by Caquot and Dalix 2001) refers to the activity of the goddess *ʿAṯtartu* in the *Raḫbanu*, modern Nahr al-Kebir, the river that probably delimited the northern border of the region of Arru, which extented from there to the southern border of the Kingdom of Ugarit. According to one mythological text, "the goddess *ʿAnatu* ascends over *Ǵuru*, *Arru*, and *Ṣapunu*." These three names gathered in a single phrase undoubtedly conveyed in mythological terms the principal regional components of the Kingdom of Ugarit (Bordreuil 1984).

A tablet discovered in the excavations of Ras Ibn Hani (RIH 84/13, preliminary edition by Bordreuil in Bordreuil et al. 1987: 299–301) enumerates diverse herds of bovines that were located, probably for the summer, in several villages of the kingdom. Some of these villages were located along the northern border of the kingdom, and this is certainly related to the pastoral activity characteristic of this region, where pastureland abounds. In addition to the numerous springs and grassy valleys that made the area ideal for the summer pasturing of bovines and ovines, the mountains were also covered with extensive forests. Not only is this evidenced by the name of a city from the northern region, *Ḫalbu Ṣapuni*, which literally means 'the forest of Ṣapon', which is probably situated near present-day Kassab, but the texts mention other towns with the word *ḫalbu* as a component in the Kingdom of Ugarit, two of which are located in the eastern mountain chain. These two mountain regions were covered with vast and dense forests, of which the only vestige today is the forest of Fourlloq not far from present-day Kassab. Thus the practice of forestry and pastoralism in the northern region was complementary to the agricultural activities in the southernmost region, which was rich in springs from the Alaouite chain and in fertile soil. The mention of the *ʾIlū bildāni* (*ỉl bldn*), 'the gods of the land', in a list including some of the principal divine actors in the Ugaritic myths (RS [Varia 20], *editio princeps* by Bordreuil and Pardee 1993b: 42–53; cf. Pardee 2000a: 894–97) suggests that the convergence of factors resulting from the physical geography (orography and climatology) and the economic geography encouraged the emergence of Ugaritic civilization and a specific national identity.

1.11. The Ugaritic Language

Ugaritic is the only well-attested example known today of the West Semitic languages spoken in the Levant during the 2nd millennium B.C. The place of Ugaritic in the Semitic languages has been a matter of dispute, in part because of a confusion of categories, viz., between literary and linguistic criteria. Literarily, the poetic texts show strong formal (poetic parallelism), lexical, and thematic affinities to Biblical Hebrew poetry. Linguistically, however, Ugaritic is considerably more archaic than any of the well-attested Northwest Semitic languages and probably descends directly from a Levantine "Amorite" dialect. All indications are that it is more directly related to West Semitic than to East Semitic (Akkadian). Within the former branch, it shares certain important isoglosses with Northwest Semitic as opposed to Arabic (e.g., roots I-*w* → I-*y*) and with Canaanite as opposed to Aramaic (e.g., /ḏ/ → /ṣ/). The isoglosses shared with Arabic (e.g., consonantal inventory) represent for the most part shared archaic features.

Ugaritic is a one-period language, attested only for the last part of the Late Bronze Age, approximately 1300–1190 B.C. This is because the writing system in which known Ugaritic texts are inscribed was not invented (at least according to present data) until sometime during the first half of the 13th century, whereas the city of Ugarit—virtually the only site where Ugaritic texts have been discovered—was destroyed early in the 12th century. In recent years it has become clearer that the greatest number of texts date from the last few decades of the site and there is, therefore, no basis on which to define a "late" Ugaritic over against the main body of texts (*contra* Tropper 1993b), for the main body of texts is late Ugaritic. The strata of the language that can be distinguished are not defined by the chronology of the texts but by the characteristics of the language: the poetic dialect of the mythological texts and the prose dialect of the administrative documents and everyday texts.

Until recently, it was commonly believed that Ugaritic was invented in the 14th century. Today, however, there are good reasons for believing that the invention of the cuneiform alphabet is to be situated in the first half of the 13th century (Dalix 1997a, 1997b, 1998; Pardee 1997a: 241 n. 3; 2001b; 2007). A mythological fragment in alphabetic cuneiform in the archive of Urtenu, the archaeological context of which is firmly dated to the end of the 13th century and the beginning of the 12th, bears the signature of Ilimilku and suggests that the mythological texts from the acropolis that also bear his name should be dated to this period. The absence of any royal name in alphabetic cuneiform before Ammistamru, the son of Niqmepa, whose reign extended for three decades in the middle of the 13th century, supports this hypothesis. At the same time, it should be noted that the royal names at Ugarit were frequently repeated (see Arnaud 1998), and this naming practice does not make it easy for the historian to distinguish the texts between Niqmaddu I (who died around 1350 B.C.) and Niqmaddu II (who died sometime during the last decade of the 13th century), between Ammistamru I (from the first half of the 14th century) and Ammistamru II (from the middle of the 13th century), or between Shupiluliuma I (who died in the middle of the 14th century) and Shupiluliuma II (who took the throne somewhere around 1200). Today it seems clearer that the names attested in the alphabetic texts are those of the kings who reigned in the 13th century: *ʿmyḏtmr*/*ʿmṯtmr* = Ammistamru II, *nqmd* = Niqmaddu III, *ṯpllm* = Shupiluliuma (either I or II, depending on the historical background of the only text where the name is found [**36** RS 11.772+ in the selection of texts]). As a result, though a number of texts from Ugarit date to the 14th century, it is becoming more and more likely that so early a date is to be attached only to texts written in Akkadian.

2. *Writing System*

The Ugaritic writing system is unique in that it adapts the cuneiform principle (wedges inscribed in clay) to represent graphemes of an alphabetic type for the purpose of writing a West Semitic language. (For several examples of the full repertory of consonants written out in the conventional order by scribes who were native speakers, see the abecedaries in the selection of texts, section VIII, texts **53–55**.) The alphabet had been invented somewhere between one century and half a millennium before the earliest attested Ugaritic texts (Sass 2004–5), and there is no particular reason to believe that the linear alphabet was unknown at Ugarit before the invention of the cuneiform alphabetic system. Indeed, it is not unlikely that the cuneiform system is a representation in clay of a linear alphabet (i.e., one written with ink), though presently available data do not allow a precise description of the origin of the cuneiform alphabet.

At present, three alphabetic systems are attested at Ugarit: (1) the "long" alphabet, well attested by abecedaries; (2) the "short" alphabet, very rarely attested and of uncertain composition (no abecedary has yet been discovered representing the "short" alphabet); (3) an alphabet of the South-Semitic type, presently attested at Ugarit by a single abecedary (RS 88.2215), arranged in South-Arabian order (i.e., {h, l, ḥ, m . . . } and with peculiar sign forms), very similar to an abecedary discovered in 1933 at Beth-Shemesh in Palestine but only recently deciphered (Loundine 1987; cf. Bordreuil and Pardee 1995b; 2001: text 32).

The long alphabet was clearly intended for writing Ugaritic because it is the means of graphic expression chosen for virtually all texts inscribed in that language, whether in prose, in poetry, or of a didactic nature. The short alphabet shows fusion of graphemes on the Phoenician model (e.g., /š/ and /ṯ/ written {ṯ}), and the few texts in alphabetic cuneiform discovered beyond the borders of Ugarit seem to be written in variants of the short alphabet (Dietrich and Loretz 1988; cf. Bordreuil 1981). It seems, therefore, to be an adaptation of the long alphabet to a Phoenician-type consonantal repertory. The language of at least one text written in this system, discovered in Lebanon at Sarafand-Sarepta, has been identified as Phoenician (Greenstein 1976; Bordreuil 1979). Though the abecedary in South Arabian order consists of the same number of signs as the basic consonantal repertory of the long alphabet, it shows several variant sign forms and was not, therefore, a simple reorganization of the Ugaritic alphabet along South Arabian lines. Because only abecedaries are attested in this version of the alphabet, one can only speculate as to the language that it was used to convey.

The epigraphic study of Ugaritic texts consists principally, then, of the examination of the texts written in the long alphabet. Signs are formed with three types of wedges: vertical, horizontal, and oblique. These wedges are used in various combinations, from a single wedge ({g, ʿ, t}) to seven wedges ({s̀}). The signs with multiple wedges may consist of one type of wedge (for example the {r} has five horizontal wedges), two ({q} has one vertical wedge followed by one oblique wedge), or all three (for example, {ṭ} has one horizontal wedge, one vertical wedge, and one oblique wedge). The reading of texts is complicated by the frequently damaged state of the tablets. It is also necessary for the beginner to learn to recognize the various forms of each sign. Those who are especially interested in Ugaritic paleography would do well to consult Ellison 2002 and to make their own table of signs based on the facsimiles and photos in the present *Manual*.

An important principle of variation encountered in Ugaritic texts is the addition of wedges to some signs, but only to those that are made up of the largest possible number of wedges for their formal type. For example, the {l}, which has as its standard form three vertical wedges, may also be inscribed with four or even five wedges, but the forms of the {ṣ} (two vertical wedges) and of the {g} (one vertical wedge) are immutable, since to add a wedge to the {ṣ} would made it a {l} and to add a wedge to the {g} would make it a {ṣ}. According to this principle, the signs allowing for supplementary wedges are {l, ḫ, y} (which consist of a combination of vertical wedges), {n, r, h, ỉ} (horizontal wedges), {s̀} (the oblique wedges on both sides of the vertical wedge may be supplemented), {ủ} (may have four or more vertical wedges), and {d} (either the row of vertical wedges, the row of horizontal wedges, or both may be supplemented) (see Pardee 2002c).

Because the Ugaritic writing system does not represent vowels, Ugaritic grammar represents an uneasy truce between description and reconstruction. It has this feature in common with all of the pre-Christian-era Northwest Semitic languages, but those attested in the 1st millennium either make use of *matres lectionis* and have later vocalization systems on the basis of which some retrojection may be done (Aramaic, Hebrew), or else have later congeners in which *matres lectionis* are used (Phoenician, Punic, Neo-Punic). The reconstruction of the Ugaritic vocalic system must rely, therefore, on two types of internal sources: (1) the "extra" *alif* signs in the Ugaritic alphabet; and (2) Ugaritic words in syllabically written texts. The latter appear in three distinct forms: (a) the so-called polyglot vocabularies (Ugaritic words written in ancient "dictionary" entries); (b) Ugaritic words in Akkadian texts; (c) proper names. For the first two types, see Nougayrol 1968: texts 130–42 and indices pp. 351–52; and Huehnergard 1987; the third type is more difficult to use for reliable results because of the presence of archaic elements in Ugaritic names and of the occurrence of non-Ugaritic names. If one wishes to reconstruct a form or a word where these internal sources are silent, one must rely on comparative Semitic considerations.

3. *Phonology*

The vocalization of Ugaritic is largely reconstructed, while the consonantal system is described primarily in terms of the graphemes rather than in phonetic terms. By comparison with the later West Semitic languages, and in comparison with other contemporary languages (Akkadian, Egyptian, Hurrian), the phonetic system can be approximated (e.g., {ṣ} and {ẓ} represent "emphatics").

Several examples of the consonantal alphabet written out partially or in full ("abecedaries") provide the oldest witnesses to the concept of a repertory of consonants recited in a fixed order, corresponding essentially to the later Northwest Semitic alphabets. The Ugaritic abecedary consists of 27 signs, corresponding to the consonantal repertory, to which three signs have been added: the first two, variant forms of *alif*; the third, a variant of /s/. These signs follow the order customary for the later Northwest Semitic alphabets, which contain 22 signs; the five supplementary signs are dispersed at apparent random within the order:

Northwest Semitic
ʾ b g d h w z ḥ ṭ y k l m n s ʿ p ṣ q r š t

Ugaritic
ả b g ḫ d h w z ḥ ṭ y k š l m ḏ n ẓ s ʿ p ṣ q r ṯ ǵ t ỉ ủ s̀

This dispersal has generally been assumed to indicate the invention of the Northwest Semitic alphabet for a language, such as Ugaritic, that had a larger consonantal inventory than the well-known 1st-millennium languages.

The origin of the three signs added to those of the standard consonantal inventory is in dispute. The patent similarity of form between sign 30, usually transliterated {s̀}, and the {s} in the later Northwest Semitic alphabet makes a common formal origin likely, but the reason for the addition of this sign to the Ugaritic alphabet is unclear. (Compare Segert 1983; Dietrich and Loretz 1988.) The most recent explanation suggests that the phonetic evolution of /s/ was caused by phonetic environment (Tropper 1995b). In function, sign 30 is like {s} but only in certain words; other {s}-words are never written with {s̀}.

The origin and the reason for the addition of the 2 extra *alif* signs are both uncertain. (Perhaps they were added for the purpose of writing a language such as Akkadian, or Hurrian, which permits syllables to begin with vowels. Akkadian texts written with the Ugaritic script have been found, but they are rare; Hurrian texts are more common.) In function, the 3 *alif* signs are used when writing Ugaritic to indicate /ʾ/ plus following vowel, with {ỉ} used for syllable-final *alif* (thus {ỉ} = /ʾi/ or /aʾ/, /iʾ/, and /uʾ/). The situation presents difficulties, however, for syllable-final *alif* appears sometimes to quiesce, sometimes to function consonantally, sometimes to function as a "guttural"—that is, to be followed by a very brief vowel (compare "secondary opening" in Biblical Hebrew). These three possibilities are encountered in the attested forms of the word meaning 'seal': {mỉšmn} = /maʾšamānu/ ({ỉ} = /ʾ/ without a following vowel), {mšmn} = /maš(a)mānu/ (loss of the /ʾ/) and {måšmn} = /maʾaš(a)mānu/ ({å}indicates a secondary vowel after the /ʾ/). For the texts that contain the word 'seal', see Bordreuil and Pardee 1984, 1987. On the problem of the three {ʾ}s, see Verreet 1983; another hypothesis is proposed by Tropper 1990b.

3.1. The Consonants

By comparison with other writing systems, the alphabet may be roughly arranged according to phonetic properties (Tropper 1994a; 2000: 90–133 [§32.1]). For paucity of Ugaritic data, the precise definition of each of the phonetic properties and places of articulation must be done by comparison with other Semitic languages and will not be attempted here.

	Bilabials	Dentals	Interdentals	Sibilants	Palatals	Velars	Pharyngeals	Laryngeals
Unvoiced	*p*	*t*	*ṯ*	*s* (*s̀*)	*k*	*ḫ*	*ḥ*	*h*
Voiced	*b*	*d*	*ḏ*	*z*	*g*	*ǵ*	ʿ	ʾ
Emphatic		*ṭ*	*ẓ*	*ṣ*	*q*			

In addition to these relatively clear two- or three-element sets, there is a series of continuants (*m* = bilabial, *n* = alveolar/palatal, *l* = lateral, *r* = apical or lateral, *š* = sibilant or lateral) and two semivowels (*w* = bilabial, *y* = palatal).

In comparison with Arabic, Ugaritic had one consonantal phoneme fewer, there being no sign for /ḍ/, which had shifted to /ṣ/. The Ugaritic writing system made no distinction between /š/ and /ś/ ({s̀}, sign 30, does not correspond to later /ś/!); indeed, there being no evidence from graphic confusions within Ugaritic for the survival of /ś/, we may assume that it had fused with /š/ (Blau 1977: 106; Tropper 1994a: 29–30).

The graphic system does not correspond precisely to the phonetic. {ẓ} is used for etymological /ẓ/, but certain words containing etymological /ẓ/ are regularly written with {ǵ}, e.g., *nǵr* 'guard' (← NẒR), probably expressing a phonetic shift, itself reflective of a double articulation of /ẓ/, i.e., dental and laryngeal (cf. Aramaic /ḏ/ ≈{q} → /ʿ/; Segert 1988). The use of {ẓ} for /ṭ/ is not nearly as widespread as has been claimed (see Freilich and Pardee 1984) appearing only in *CTA* 24 and probably in RIH 78/14 (Bordreuil and Caquot

1980: 352–53; Tropper 1994b; Pardee 2000a: 866, 870–71). Etymological /ḏ/ poses particular problems: it is sometimes written {ḏ}, but usually {d}. Apparent confusion of /ḏ/ and /z/ characterize certain roots, e.g., *nḏr*/*nzr* 'vow' (both in Ugaritic; cf. Hebrew NZR), *ḏmr*/*zmr* 'sing' (cf. Hebrew ZMR), *ḏrʿ*/*zrʿ* 'seed/arm' (cf. Hebrew ZRʿ). Though there is, therefore, certainly evidence for disparities between the graphic and phonetic systems, the situation was probably not as confused as some have thought: examination of the confusions claimed by Tropper 1994a reveals that the interpretations of the texts, and hence of the phoneto-semantic identifications, are sometimes either dubious or faulty (e.g., *šỉr* and *ṯỉr* are not the same word [1994a: 38]: the first is 'flesh, meat', while the second denotes a kinship status [see glossary]; the two terms only become homophonous in Hebrew with the coalescence of /š/ and /ṯ/).

In addition to these disparities between phonology and orthography, variations are encountered that reflect changes owing to phonetic environment, for example:

- {tmḫṣ} /tamaḫḫiṣu/ 'you strike' (**1** RS 3.367 iv 9′) or {mḫṣt} /miḫḫaṣat/ 'she struck' (RS 3.322 iv 58 [*CTA* 19:220]), but {mḫšt} /miḫḫaštu/ (**2** RS 2.[014]⁺ iii–iv 41′, 43′, 45′) (loss of the "emphatic" pronunciation in proximity to the /t/).
- *w ht hn bnš hw b gty ḫbṯ* /wa hatti hanna bunušu huwa bi gittiya ḫabaṯa/ 'and that servant worked on my farm' (**33** RS 96.2039:8–9), but *lm tlỉkn ḫpṯ hndn* /lêma talaʾʾikīna ḫupṯa hannadāna/ 'Why did you send this *ḫupṯu*(-soldier?)?' (**29** RS 34.124:10); also two common nouns are attested meaning 'garment', {lbš} and {lpš}, probably /labūšu/ and /lipšu/ (devoicing of the /b/ in proximity to the /ṯ/ and to the /š/).
- {špš} /šapšu/ 'sun' is unique to Ugaritic, for ŠMŠ is found in the other Semitic languages (devoicing of the /m/ in proximity to the /š/).

3.2. The Vowels

The Ugaritic vocalic system is assumed to have consisted of the six vocalic phonemes reconstructed for Proto-Semitic, /a/, /i/, /u/, /ā/, /ī/, /ū/, to which two secondary long vowels were added by monophthongization, /ê/ ← /ay/ and /ô/ ← /aw/. There is no evidence for secondary "lengthening" of the short vowels (e.g., /a/ → *qameṣ* in Biblical Hebrew) or for any shifts of the long vowels (e.g., the "Canaanite shift" /ā/ → /ō/). There also were long vowels created by contraction, which correspond to historically long vowels (for example, /iy/ → /î/, /uw/ → /û/). To indicate the different origin of these secondary vowels, we have marked them with a circumflex accent (e.g., /ê/ and /ô/). However, it should also be mentioned that this is solely a historical description, and there is no reason to believe that in Ugaritic the quality of /î/ (← /iy/) differed from that of /ī/ (the original "pure" long vowel). It may also be remarked that if the short vowels /e/ and /o/ existed in Ugaritic, it would only have been in the local pronunciation of foreign words, mostly proper names, that contained roughly corresponding vowels in closed syllables.

3.3. The Combination of a Consonant with a Vowel

Theoretically, each consonant was able to be followed by any vowel or no vowel. For example, the sign {b} could have the following values:

/ba/ : {bˤl} /baˤlu/ 'master'
/bi/ : {bt} /bittu/ 'daughter'
/bu/ : {bnš} /bunušu/ 'member of the (royal) personnel'
/bā/ : {bny} /bāniyu/ '(one who) builds'
/bī/ : {kbkbm} /kabkabīma/ 'stars (in the plural oblique)'
/bū/ : {zbl} /zabūlu/ 'prince'
/bê/ : {bt} /bêtu/ 'house'
/bô/ : [there are no examples with /b/; cf. with /t/, {tk} /tôku/ 'middle']
/bØ/ : {šby} /šabyu/ 'captive'

The uses of the three *alif*-signs are certainly more complex—but they are also more informative for vocalizing the language:

{ả} = /ʾa/ : {ảrṣ} /ʾarṣu/ 'earth'
/ʾā/ : {ảkl} /ʾākilu/ '(one who) eats'
{ỉ} = /ʾi/ : {ỉl} /ʾilu/ 'god'
/ʾī/ : {lbỉm} /labaʾīma/ 'lions (plural oblique)'
/ʾê/ : {ỉb} /ʾêbu/ 'enemy'
/aʾ/ : {mỉšmn} /maʾšamānu/ 'seal'
/iʾ/ : {qrỉt} /qāriʾtu/ '(one who) calls (fem.)'
/uʾ/ : {tbỉ} /tubuʾ/ 'you should enter'
{ủ} = /ʾu/ : {ủṣbˤ} /ʾuṣbaˤu/ 'finger'
/ʾū/ : {ủz} /ʾūzu/ 'goose'
/ʾô/ : {ủ} /ʾô/ 'or'

3.4. The Syllable

The syllable in the ancient Semitic languages always begins with a consonant. It is either "open," a term that traditionally means that the form of the syllable is /consonant + vowel/ (for example, the three syllables of /bu-nu-šu/), or "closed," a syllable with the form /consonant + vowel + consonant/ (for example, the first syllable of /kab-ka-bī-ma/).

3.5. Secondary Phenomena of the Vocalic System

- A characteristic of Proto–West Semitic, and one that is assumed for Ugaritic because it is a member of this family, is that long vowels are not found in closed syllables. As a result, some forms of a verbal paradigm will have a long vowel, while others will have a short vowel (for example,

/yaqūmu/ 'he will arise' and /yaqum/ 'may he arise'—see below, II-weak verbs §4.1.2.7).

- A vowel may be colored by a following long vowel if only one consonant intervenes between the two vowels (e.g., {i͗ẖy} /ʾiẖîya/ 'my brother' [genitive] ← /ʾaẖîya/ [**31** RS 94.2406:32]; *i͗ẖršp* /ʾiẖîrašap/ [personal name] ← /*ʾaẖīrašap/ [**40** RS [Varia 14]:18]). {a͗ẖy} is also found for /ʾaẖîya/ (**26** RS 18.031:2), which appears to indicate either that the different writings reflect complementary pronunciations (the word was pronounced either /ʾaẖîya/ or /ʾiẖîya/) or that the shift had occurred in all possible environments but the scribes sometimes used phonetic orthography, sometimes historical orthogaphy.
- Secondary vowels, which seem to have occurred occasionally after *alif* in a closed syllable, seem sometimes to be colored by the following vowel even if it is short (for example, *yu͗ẖd i͗b mlk* /yaʾuẖudu [← /yaʾẖudu/] ʾêba malki/ 'he will be seized by the enemy of the king' [**20** RS 24.247+:17]). See Sivan 1997: 45; Tropper 2000: 33–35 (§21.322.1); Pardee 2003–4: 26–27. On the other hand, since the writing with {u͗} is attested with at least one root that should not have had /u/ as stem vowel (the II-*h* root ʾHB 'to love' should have been /yiʾhab-/ but {yu͗hb} is attested [*CTA* 5 v 18]), this use of {u͗} may only represent the irregular use of that sign (in place of {i͗}) to note syllable-final /ʾ/.

4. Morphology

Like the other Semitic languages, Ugaritic morphology is of the inflecting (or fusional) type. The traditional view according to which a Semitic word consists of a consonantal "root" + internal vowel(s) + additional morphemes still has merit today. Though there are clearly nominal roots that include a vocalic element (e.g., *kalb-* 'dog') and verbal roots in which vocalic variation is the rule and which serve as the basis for nominal derivation (see below), both types of roots generate derivatives.

The morphology of a Ugaritic word will thus be made up of the following elements: (1) an abstract entity known as the root, which exists in concrete form as a set of consonants, usually two or three, which in a nominal root may include a vowel, (2) one or more vowels (semantic variation is expressed by internal vowel changes that specialists call *Ablaut*, as in German), with the possibility of longer forms produced (3) by affixation and/or (4) by prefixation. This is why a Ugaritic dictionary organized by roots (as traditional dictionaries of Semitic languages are) will begin with the simplest form, verb or noun, followed by the attested verbal forms (if they exist), then forms with suffixation, and conclude with forms including prefixes and/or suffixes (e.g., MLK 'to rule', *mlk* 'king', *mlkt* 'queen', **mmlkt* 'kingdom').

4.1. Morphological Categories

Though it is not without value to analyze an old West Semitic text according to the grammatical categories commonly used for the modern languages of scholarship, a descriptive analysis of these languages gives three primary categories of words: nouns, verbs, and particles. There is, nonetheless, a significant degree of overlap within these categories (e.g., verbal nouns and particles derived from nouns), and there are clearly definable subcategories (e.g., adjectives and adverbs). The three-element description is nevertheless important, for the elements belonging to overlapping categories and to subcategories are clearly definable according to one or another of the primary categories (e.g., verbal nouns will have nominal morphology along with certain syntactic and lexical features of verbs, adjectives will have nominal morphology not verbal morphology, verbal adjectives will have nominal morphology along with certain syntactic and lexical features of verbs, etc.).

Nouns and **adjectives** are marked for gender, number, and case but not for definiteness and only partially for state. These grammatical categories are expressed by affixation. Internal vowel variation and prefixation function primarily in nouns to mark lexical categories rather than grammatical ones.

Verbs are marked for aspect/tense, for person, for voice, and for mood. There are two aspects, perfective and imperfective, the first marked only by suffixation, the second by prefixation and suffixation; three voices, active, middle, and passive, marked by internal vowel change and by prefixed consonantal morphemes; and five moods, all marked by suffixation to the imperfective verb. The position of the person markers indicates aspect/tense—i.e., person is expressed by suffixation in the perfective, by prefixation in the imperfective.

Particles are characterized by the absence of the morphological markers of nouns and verbs. This is completely true, however, of only the most basic particles, for many are secondarily derived from nouns or pronouns and may thus include markers characteristic of the nominal system.

The following presentation of the morphological categories will follow this three-way division, with an attempt to delineate clearly the overlapping categories and the subcategories. In the following discussions and tables, ∅ is used to indicate forms that are expected to exist but that are not attested in the texts presently extant, while -∅ is used for forms without a consonantal indicator of a morpheme otherwise indicated consonantally in the paradigm or for a form ending with a hypothetical "zero" vowel.

4.1.1. Nominal Categories

4.1.1.1. Categories of Nominal Inflection

4.1.1.1.1. Grammatical Case

Case markers are suffixed and consist of a combination of vocalic and consonantal elements. A triptotic case system (nominative, genitive, accusative) is used in the singular, a diptotic system (nominative, oblique) in the dual and plural. This system is consistent with case systems known from fully vocalized languages and is demonstrated internally by the reasonably consistent use of the appropriate *alif* sign in writing nouns of which /ʾ/ is the final consonant, e.g., s.m.nom. {ksủ} = /kussaʾu/, s.m.gen. {ksỉ} = /kussaʾi/, s.m.acc. {ksả} = /kussaʾa/; pl.m.nom. {rpủm} = /rapaʾūma/, pl.m.obl. {rpỉm} = /rapaʾīma/.

There is not a separate case for the expression of the vocative. There are two lexical vocative markers that are placed before the noun, *l* and *y* (cf. Arabic *ya*; see also below, "Particles"), but a noun may be vocative without the use of a lexical marker. There is some evidence that the oblique case was used in the plural (Singer 1948) and one datum (*ksỉ* 'O throne' [**13** RS 34.126:13]) for the genitive in the singular, perhaps by analogy with the case that normally follows the preposition *l* (Bordreuil and Pardee 1991: 158). But because of a dearth of data pertaining to the case used in vocative expressions, this matter remains largely unresolved.

There are some nouns, particularly proper names with a nominal suffix containing a long vowel (e.g., /-ān/, /-īt/), that have a diptotic singular system: /-u/ nominative, /-a/ oblique (Liverani 1963; Huehnergard 1987: 299). Therefore, in the vocalization of proper nouns, the genitive will be marked by /-a/ if the penultimate syllable has a long vowel.

Certain divine names are attested only in the "absolute" case, i.e., without a case-vowel, such as *Dagan*, while others are declined for case, such as *Šapšu*. Regarding the difficulties of vocalizing divine names as well as other proper nouns, see below, "Vocabulary" (§8).

The genitive case expresses not only origin (e.g., *l bn ảdm* /lê bini ʾadami/ 'the son of the man' [**17** RIH 78/20:15]), possession in the economic sense (*ḫmš ảlp ṯlṯ l ḫlby* /ḫamišu ʾalpu ṯalṯu lê ḫalbiyyi/ 'five thousand (shekels) of copper for the Ḫalbean' [**43** RS 18.024:6]), or in the physical sense (*hlm ktp zbl ym* /hulum katipa zabūli yammi/ 'strike the head of Prince *Yammu'* [**1** RS 3.367 iv 14′]), but many other relationships (e.g., *tqḥ mlk ʿlmk* /tiqqaḥu mulka ʿālamika/ 'you will take your eternal kingship', lit., 'you will take kingship of your eternity' [**1** RS 3.367 iv 10′]). As in other Northwest Semitic Languages, a genitival formula frequently is used where we would use an adjective (e.g., *ảṯṯ ṣdqh l ypq* /ʾaṯṯata ṣidqihu lā yapūqu/ 'his rightful wife he does not obtain' [**3** RS 2.[003]⁺ i 12]). One notes examples of the traditional categories of "subjective genitive" (*tḥm ảliyn bʿl* /taḥmu ʾalʾiyāna baʿli/ 'message of Mighty *Baʿlu*', that is, the message that *Baʿlu* sent, not that which he received [**2** RS 2.[014]⁺ iii 13′]) and "objective genitive" (e.g., *mdd il ym* /môdada ʾili yamma/ 'the beloved of ʾIlu, Yammu', that is, the one whom *ʾIlu* loves and not the one who loves *ʾIlu* [**2** RS 2.[014]⁺ iii 38′–39′]). The "genitive of identification" is also used (*ksp ḥbl rišym* /kaspu ḥābilī raʾšiyyīma/ 'the silver of the mariners of *Raʾšu* [lit.: the mariners of the Raʾšians]' [**52** RIH 83/22:3] — cf. Biblical Hebrew /nᵊhar pᵊrāt/ 'the Euphrates', lit., 'the river of the Euphrates'). Lastly, the demonstrative/relative pronoun could be used to express a genitive and was, itself, followed by a genitive (e.g., *tqḥ mlk ʿlmk drkt dt dr drk* /tiqqaḥu mulka ʿālamika darkata dāti dāri dārika/ 'you will take your eternal kingship, your sovereignty (which endures) from generation to generation [lit.: the one of generation of generation]' [**1** RS 3.367 iv 10′]). For additional uses of *d*(*t*), see below, "Pronouns" (§4.1.1.5) and "Particles" (§4.1.3).

The accusative case was used for the direct object(s) of transitive verbs (e.g., *yʿdb ksả* /yaʿdubu kussaʾa/ 'he draws up a chair' [**6** RS 24.244:7]) and for various adverbial expressions (e.g., *ʿz mỉd* /ʿazzu maʾda/ 'very strong' [**21** RS 4.475:13]; *ảrṣ rd w špl ʿpr* /ʾarṣa rid wa šapal ʿapara/ 'descend to the earth and fall to the dust' [**13** RS 34.126:21–22]).

4.1.1.1.2. Grammatical Gender

Gender is marked by suffixed morphemes: s.m. by -Ø, s.f. by *-t* = /-(a)t-/, pl.m. by lengthening of the case-vowel (lengthened genitive singular = plural oblique), pl.f. by *-t* = /-āt-/. The dual morpheme was probably attached to the singular stem, masculine or feminine.

Several nouns that take feminine agreement do not bear the /-(a)t-/ morpheme (e.g., *ủm* 'mother'), while the plural morphemes do not correspond in every case to the sex/gender of the entity involved (e.g., *grnt* [pl. of *grn*, 'threshing-floor', a masculine noun]).

4.1.1.1.3. Grammatical Number

Singular, dual, and plural are productive number categories, marked by variations in the case-vowel, with affixation of *-m* to the dual and plural (for the problem of the quality of the vowel after this *-m* on the dual, see Huehnergard 1987: 298, who posits that it was originally /i/ on the dual, /a/ on the plural; pending future data, we have consistently indicated it as /-ma/). For certain nouns, the base is not the same in the singular and the plural (e.g., /binu/ 'son [s.]', /banūma/ 'son [pl.]'). The dual morpheme is attached to the singular stem, masculine or feminine (see the table on p. 32).

4.1.1.1.4. Definiteness

There is no quasi-lexical marker of definiteness in Ugaritic (cf. *h-* in Hebrew), though the unusually frequent use of *hn* in one text may be a precursor of such a development (*w ht hn bnš hw ʿmm ảṯth btk ṯb* /wa hatti hanna bunušu huwa ʿimmama ʾaṯṯatihu bêtaka ṯāba/ 'but that servant returned to his wife at your house' [**33** RS 96.2039:10–12]). Definiteness was thus not a marked grammatical category in Ugaritic and must be expressed in modern translation according to context. Some cases nevertheless exist, although they are rare, where a noun or a pronoun was preceded by *h-*, which should be analyzed as the demonstrative particle /ha(n)/ from which the Hebrew and Phoenician definite article develop (*w ảnk ḥrš lqḥt w ḥwt hbt* /wa ʾanāku ḥarrāša laqaḥtu wa ḥiwwêtu habbêta/ 'Here is what I have done: I have hired a workman and had this house repaired' [**28** RS 29.093:14–16]). These instances where *h-* and *hn-* have this deictic (demonstrative) function, however, are presently too rare to qualify them as examples of the "definite article."

4.1.1.1.5. Grammatical State

State is the fifth category according to which the grammatically expressed relationship between two or more nouns in ancient Semitic languages (i.e., their morpho-syntax) is described. There are two primary states, absolute and construct; a third, the pronominal state, is useful in describing some of the later Northwest Semitic languages where vowel reduction is prevalent and will be referred to briefly here. "Absolute" describes a noun in unbound form (/malku/ 'king'), "construct" a noun bound to a following noun in the genitive relationship (/malku qarîti/ 'king of the city'); this construction is less frequently formed with a verb *šmʿt ḫti nḫtủ* /šamaʿtu ḫataʾī naḫtaʾū 'I have heard that they have suffered a defeat' = 'I have received a report about the blows with which they were struck' [**21** RS 4.475:7–8]). The "pronominal" state is that of a noun bound to a suffixed pronoun in the genitive relationship (/malkuhu/ 'his king' ≈ 'the king of him').

In Ugaritic, the case-vowel is preserved in the first word(s) of genitive phrases. (In traditional grammar, the head noun is called the *nomen regens*, the second noun the *nomen rectum*.) Thus, in the singular, the genitive relationship is marked only by the genitive case-vowel on the second element of the phrase. This feature is shared with, for example, Classical Arabic, whereas in other Semitic languages the first word also shows some form of modification (e.g., Akkadian /šarru/ → /šar/ in construct, Hebrew /dāḇār/ → /dᵊḇar/ in construct; see Huehnergard 1987: 300–301). In the dual and the plural, the *-m* of the *nomen regens* is usually dropped in construct.

The case-vowel is also preserved in the pronominal state, again in contrast with Akkadian, where the case-vowel drops in most forms (/šarratu + šu/ → /šarrat + šu/ → /šarrassu/); here Hebrew shows remnants of a system similar to the Ugaritic one (/dᵊbārᵊkā/ ← /*dabar + V + ka/).

4.1.1.1.6. Examples of Typical Masculine and Feminine Nouns indicating the markers of case, gender, number, and (absolute) state:

Absolute State

<table>
<tr><td>s.m.Nom.</td><td>/malku/</td><td>Du.m.Nom.</td><td>/malkāma/
or
/malkāmi/</td><td>Pl.m.Nom.</td><td>/malakūma/†
or
/malkūma/†</td></tr>
<tr><td>s.m.Gen.</td><td>/malki/</td><td rowspan="2">Du.m.Obl.</td><td rowspan="2">/malkêma/*
or
/malkêmi/*</td><td rowspan="2">Pl.m.Obl.</td><td rowspan="2">/malakīma/†
or
/malkīma/†</td></tr>
<tr><td>s.m.Acc.</td><td>/malka/</td></tr>
<tr><td>s.f.Nom.</td><td>/malkatu/</td><td>Du.f.Nom.</td><td>/malkatāma/
or
/malkatāmi/</td><td>Pl.f.Nom.</td><td>/malakātu/†
or
/malkātu/†</td></tr>
<tr><td>s.f.Gen.</td><td>/malkati/</td><td rowspan="2">Du.f.Obl.</td><td rowspan="2">/malkatêma/*
or
/malkatêmi/*</td><td rowspan="2">Pl.f.Obl.</td><td rowspan="2">/malakāti/†
or
/malkāti/†</td></tr>
<tr><td>s.f.Acc.</td><td>/malkata/</td></tr>
</table>

* /ê/ ← /ay/

† on the difference between singular/dual and plural nominal formation, see below.

Below are examples of the construct state. The first noun (the *nomen regens*) varies in its case (nominative, genitive, or accusative), but the second (the *nomen rectum*) is always in the genitive.

/malku qarîti/	'The/A king (Nom.) of the/a city'
/malki qarîti/	'The/A king (Gen.) of the/a city'
/malka qarîti/	'The/A king (Acc.) of the/a city'
/malkā qarîti/	'(The) two kings (Nom.) of the/a city'
/malkê qarîti/	'(The) two kings (Obl.) of the/a city'
/malakū qarîti/	'(The) kings (Nom.) of the/a city'
/malakī qarîti/	'(The) kings (Obl.) of the/a city'

Pronominal State:

/malkuhu/	'his king' (Nom.)
/malkihu/	'his king' (Gen.)
/malkahu/	'his king' (Acc.)
/malkāhu/	'his two kings' (Nom.)
/malkêhu/	'his two kings' (Obl.)
/mal(a)kūhu/	'his kings' (Nom.)
/mal(a)kīhu/	'his kings' (Obl.)

4.1.1.2. Nominal Forms

Nominal forms may consist of:

- ROOT + internal vowel(s) (e.g., /MaLK-/ 'king', /DaKaR-/ 'male')
- nominal prefix + ROOT + internal vowel(s) (e.g., /maLʾaK-/ 'messenger')
- ROOT + internal vowel(s) + nominal suffix (e.g., /ʾuLMān-/ 'widowhood')
- combinations of the last two (e.g., /ʾaLʾiYān-/ 'mighty')
- reduplicated (e.g., *qdqd* 'top of head' [complete], *ysmsm* 'beauteous' [partial, √YSM])
- quadriconsonantal forms (e.g., /ʿiRGuZu/ 'walnut'?).

Certain forms of the first category have specific semantic ranges: the /QuTL-/ type regularly expresses abstract nouns (e.g., *šbʿ* /šubʿu/ 'satiety' [**7** RS 24.258:3], *mlk* /mulku/ 'kingship' [**1** RS 3.367 i 10′]); nouns of the /QaTTāL-/ type express a social or civil position (the *nomen professionis* in traditional grammars, e.g., *ḥrš* /ḥarrāšu/ 'workman, artisan' [**28** RS 29.093:14], *kšp* /kaššāpu/ 'sorcerer' [**17** RIH 78/20:9]).

The most common nominal prefixes are *m-* (concrete entities, e.g., *mgdl* /magdalu/ 'tower') and *t-* (abstract entities, e.g., *tʿḏr* /taʿḏiru/ 'assistance'). *ʾ-* and *y-* (both best attested in nouns expressing concrete entities) are much rarer (the example of *ủṣbʿ* /ʾuṣbaʿu/ 'finger' is attested in our selection of texts).

The most common nominal suffixes are:

- *-n* (/-ān-/ [e.g., *ủlmn* /ʾulmānu/ 'widowhood'], more rarely /-an-/ [e.g., *ṯlḥn* /ṯulḥanu/ 'table']);
- *-t* (perhaps as in the later Northwest Semitic languages, /-īt-/ [as in the name of the city of Ugarit, *ủgrt* /ʾugārit/, see below, "Vocabulary," §8] and /-ūt-/ for other abstracts);
- *-y* is used with feminine nouns in the absolute state, typically without a case-vowel (e.g., the divine names *ảrṣy* /ʾarṣay/, *ṭly* /ṭallay/, and *pdry* /pidray/, all daughters of *Baʿlu*, the divine title *ḫbly* /ḫablay/ that expresses a manifestation of the god *ʿAnatu*, and the common noun *mrḥy* /murḥay/ 'weapon'). On the adjectival suffix *-y*, see below, §4.1.1.3.

The available data are equivocal on whether nouns of the *qatl/qitl/qutl* type have monosyllabic or bisyllabic bases in the plural (as in Hebrew: /melek/ ← /malk/, /mᵊlākīm/ ← /malak-/). Either the bisyllabic plural base was developing from a monosyllabic one (Sivan 1992), or the plural was already bisyllabic in proto-Ugaritic, and the second vowel was eventually elided in Ugaritic (Huehnergard 1987: 304–7). Another explanation is that this second vowel was not always indicated in the syllabic writing, which is the primary source of data available. Above, in the table of noun inflections (p. 32), the nominal pattern for the noun *malku* is indicated as bisyllabic in the plural (*malak* + inflected ending).

4.1.1.3. Adjectives

Adjectival morphology is identical to that of nouns. An adjective used independently ("substantivally," according to the traditional grammatical term), i.e., not as a modifier of a noun, functions as a noun (e.g., *k gr ʿz ṯǵrkm* /kī gāra ʿazzu ṯaǵrakumu/ 'When a strong one attacks your gate . . .' [**11** RS 24.266:26′]). When an adjective modifies a noun, it agrees in gender, number, and case with the noun. It is by this morphosyntactic feature that adjectives are most clearly differentiated from nouns, for a noun used to modify another noun does not vary in gender (e.g., the phrase 'the woman is a man' in Ugaritic would be *ảṯt mt hy*, '(the) woman, a man (is) she', where *ảṯt* retains its feminine marker and *mt* its masculine marker).

Attributive adjectives normally follow the noun they modify (e.g., *ḫswn ḫrb* /ḫaswannu ḫaribu/ 'dried thyme' [**48** RS 94.2600:13]). Attested predicate adjectives follow the noun they modify (e.g., *šptḥm mtqtm* /šapatāhumā matuqatāma/ 'their lips are sweet' [**5** RS 2.002:50]) though in theory they may precede it (there are no extant examples in Ugaritic).

The primary adjectival suffix is the so-called gentilic or *nisbe* ending consisting of vowel + *-y* (/-yy-/) + case-vowel. The quality of the first vowel is uncertain. The only apparently explicit indication shows /u/, *qnủym* 'people who work with royal purple dye' (RS 17.434:39′ [Caquot 1978; cf. Pardee 1983–84]). In syllabic writing, both /i/ and /u/ are found (e.g., {u-ga-ar-ti-yu} in RS 19.042:15 [Nougayrol 1970: text 79] and {a-ta-li-gu-yu} two lines later in the same text). These meager data force us to leave the matter unresolved, but we have adopted /-iyy-/ (or /-īy-/) as a conventional form for the morpheme. The function of the morpheme is to transform a noun into an adjective, which is most frequently seen in gentilics (e.g., *rỉš* /raʾšu/ '[the city of] *Raʾšu*' → *rỉšy* /raʾšiyyu/ 'a person from the city of *Raʾšu*'), but is also found in common adjectives (e.g., *qdmy* /qadmiyyu/ 'ancient' ← /*qadmu/ 'East, the remote past', *tḥty* /taḥtiyyu/ 'lower' ← /taḥta/ 'under').

Comparative and superlative adjectival markers do not exist, and such notions must thus be expressed lexically (e.g., by forms of the root MʾD 'much') or syntactically (e.g., *nˁmt šnt il* /naˁīmāti šanāti ʾili/ 'the best years of El' [RS 24.252: 27 (Virolleaud 1968: text 2)], a substantival adjective in construct with a noun, literally, 'the good ones of the years of El').

A nominal genitive formation is often used in place of an adjectival one, e.g., *ảṯt ṣdqh* /ʾaṯṯatu ṣidqihu/ 'the wife of his legitimacy' = 'his legitimate wife' (**3** RS 2.[003]⁺ i 12 [cf. Gordon 1965: 113, §13.22]).

4.1.1.4. Numbers

Numerals are nominal categories: cardinal numbers are nouns, ordinals adjectives. Numbers in texts may either be fully written out or expressed symbolically, using the same system as is used in Akkadian texts (a single vertical wedge = '1', a single oblique wedge = '10', etc.).

The Ugaritic repertory of numerals is largely similar to the standard West Semitic inventory:

	Cardinals	Ordinals (where different)
1	*ảḥd*/*ảḥt* and *ˁšty*	?
2	*ṯn*/*ṯt*	
3	*ṯlṯ*/*ṯlṯt*	
4	*ảrbˁ*/*ảrbˁt*	*rbˁ*
5	*ḫmš*/*ḫmšt*	
6	*ṯṯ*/*ṯṯt*	*ṯdṯ*
7	*šbˁ*/*šbˁt*	
8	*ṯmn(y)*/*ṯmnt*	
9	*tšˁ*/*tšˁt*	
10	*ˁšr*/*ˁšrt*	
11	*ˁšty ˁšr*/*ˁšrh*	
12	*ṯn ˁšr*/*ˁšrh*	
etc.		
20	*ˁšrm*	
etc.		
100	*mỉt* (Sg.)/*mảt* (Pl.)	
1,000	*ảlp*	
10,000	*rbt*	

With the exception of words containing an *alif* sign, the vocalization may only be reconstructed from comparative data: /ʾaḥḥadu/, /ṯinâ/ (the case-vowel is that of the dual), /ṯalāṯu/, /ʾarbaʿu/, /ḫamišu/, /ṯiṯṯu/ (← /*ṯidṯu/, by assimilation), /šabʿu/, /ṯamānû/ (or /ṯamāniyu/), /tišʿu/, /ʿašru/. The ordinal numbers are typically reconstructed either according to the Hebrew and Aramaic stem forms, where the *nisbe* suffix is added (e.g., Hebrew /šiššī/ or Aramaic /šᵊtītāy/, to which the corresponding Ugaritic form, which manifestly does not bear the *nisbe* ending, would be /ṯadīṯu/ 'sixth'), or according to Arabic (in which case the form would be *ṯādiṯu*).

The distinctive feature of the Ugaritic numbers is their morpho-syntax: as opposed to the other ancient Semitic languages, where the numerals 3 through 10 observe "chiastic concord" (i.e., incongruent gender agreement, feminine-looking numbers with masculine nouns and vice versa), the distribution of numbers marked with -∅ versus -(*a*)*t* shows less regularity. The primary difference, however, is the occasional absence of the terminative *-t* on the number noun when preceding a masculine noun (e.g., *ṯlṯ ủṭbm* /ṯalāṯu ʾuṭbūma/ 'three *ʾuṭbu*-garments' [**43** RS 18.024:11] and *ṯlṯ ktnt* /ṯalāṯu kutunātu/ 'three *kutunu*- garments' [ibid., line 18], where the number noun is invariable before a noun of the opposite grammatical gender). See Tropper 2000: 392–96 (§69.133).

Other features deserving special comment:

• *ʿšty* is attested with the meaning '1' (*ʿšty w ṯ*⸢ʿ⸣[*y*] /ʿaštaya wa ṯaʿaya/ 'Once and perform the *ṯaʿû*-sacrifice' [**13** RS 34.126:27]), as in Akkadian, not just in the number '11' as in Hebrew.

• The only attested forms of the absolute case of the number '2' are *ṯn* and *ṯt* (*ṯnm* is adverbial, 'twice', in RS 3.340 iv 22, 33 [*CTA* 18]; RS 3.322⁺ ii 78 [*CTA* 19]; RS 24.248:18, 20 [Herdner 1978a: 39–41]). Examples: *ṯn b gt mzln* 'Two in (the village) *gt mzln*' (RS 17.384:1 [Virolleaud 1957: text 61]) and *ṯn l ʿšrm*, '22' (on this use of *l*, see below). This form constitutes an isogloss with Akkadian (*šine*) against the other West Semitic languages (e.g., Hebrew *šnayim*). See Pardee 2000a: 195; Tropper 2000: 345–46 (§62.121).

• The alternate form with *-h* of the word for 'ten' in the cardinal numbers for the teens is not used only to modify feminine nouns as in Hebrew. Moreover, the presence of the {h} in the Ugaritic writing system shows that the origin of the element was consonantal, though its form (i.e., the vowel[s] with which the consonant was associated) and its function are uncertain. We vocalize /ʿašrih/ on the model of Hebrew /ʿeśrēʰ/, but the origin of the vowel in question remains a mystery.

• Multiples of 'ten' end in *-m* and probably are in the plural ('30' = many '3s' /ṯalāṯūma/) except in the case of '20', where this notion is plausibly expressed correctly by the dual (/ʿašrāma/ = 2 '10s'—contrast Hebrew /ʿeśrīm/).

• The ordinals had a long vowel between the second and third radicals, though their quality is unknown; hence the difference between '6' and '6th', respectively /ṯiṯṯu/ (←/ṯidṯu/) versus /ṯadīṯu/, or the like. The ordinals were certainly not formed with the *nisbe* suffix (as in Hebrew), for that morpheme appears in Ugaritic as {-y}.

Fractions are very poorly known: *ḫṣt* appears in prose in the meaning 'half' of a given quantity (**8** RS 1.001:10) while *nṣp* apparently means 'half' of a (shekel-)weight in administrative texts (*b ṯql w nṣp ksp* /bi ṯiqli wa naṣpi kaspi/ 'for a shekel and a half of silver' [**43** RS 18.024:13] and *b šbʿt w nṣp ksp* /bi šabʿati wa naṣpi kaspi/ 'for seven and half shekels of silver' [ibid., line 27]—this interpretation is certain since it is the only way to incorporate the data from these two lines with the rest of the entries so that the sum corresponds to the total indicated at the end of the text). In recently discovered texts, *mṯlṯ* is used with the sense of 'one-third' (e.g., *mṯlṯm*, 'two-thirds', where the *-m* is the dual morpheme [**48** RS 94.2600:2, 6]).

Multiplicatives are expressed by the addition of a morpheme written {-ỉd}, perhaps related historically to deictic/enclitic {-d}: *ṯnỉd*, '2 times', *ṯlṯỉd*, '3 times', šbʿid, '7 times' (usually contracted to {šbʿd}: Tropper 2000: 150 [§33.116.2]; Pardee 2003–4: 79), *ṯmnỉd*, '8 times' (in the unpublished text RS 94.2273:4.), and *ʿšrỉd*, '10 times', are currently attested.

In a mythological text (**3** RS 2.[003]$^+$ i 16–20), one finds a series of D-stem passive feminine participles of denominative verbs formed from numbers, designating a series of women: *mṯlṯt*, *mrbʿt*, *mḫmšt*, *mṯdṯt*, *mšbʿt* 'the third one . . . the seventh one'. From context, these forms refer back to *mtrḫt* (line 13) 'the married one', namely, 'the third woman (taken in marriage)', 'the fourth . . .', etc. These words are thus neither fractions nor multiplicatives, as has often been claimed.

In the number phrase (e.g., *ṯlṯ lbšm* '3 garments'), the noun denoting the counted entity may be either in the same case as the number (*/ṯalāṯu labūšūma/*, i.e., the numeral and the noun are in apposition) or in the genitive case (*/ṯalāṯu labūšīma/*; see Blau 1972: 78–79).

In poetry, several cases are found of the ordinal number preceding the noun it modifies, in apparent contradiction to the rule that attributive adjectives follow the noun they modify (Gordon 1965: 48–49, §7.44; Blau 1972: 79). It is likely that such constructions were genitival (i.e., the adjective was in construct with the noun) rather than appositional (as is the case when the attributive adjective follows the noun it modifies). The precise semantic nuance of this genitival construction is, however, unknown. One encounters, for example, *b šbʿ ymm* (**4** RS 2.[004] i 15′), probably /bi šabīʿi yamīma/ 'on the seventh of days'). Rarer is a prepositional formulation: *hn šb*[ʿ] *b ymm* (RS 2.[004] v 3′–4′ [*CTA* 17]), probably /hanna šabīʿa bi yamīma/, literally, 'Behold on the seventh among days'. Lastly, one finds instances where two nouns are in the singular (e.g., *hn ym w ṯn . . . ṯlṯ rbʿ ym . . . ḫmš ṯdṯ ym . . . mk b šbʿ ymm* 'A day [even two . . .]. A third, even a fourth day. . . . A fifth, even a sixth day. . . . Then, on the seventh day' (**4** RS 2.[004] i 5′–15′). It is likely that all these formulae are adverbial, the first six in the accusative case (e.g., /hanna yôma wa ṯanâ/), while the last one is appropriately in the genitive because preceded by the preposition *b*.

The preposition *l* is often used to join the unit to the 10 in compound numbers involving one of the decades, as in *ṯn l ʿšrm* '22' (e.g., *ṯṯ l ʿšrm* /ṯiṯṯu lê ʿašrêma/ '26': **44** RS 19.016:49 [cf. Pardee 1976: 302]).

The adverbial noun /kubda/ with a possible literal meaning of 'plus' appears often as a linking device in compound numbers, usually to be omitted from the translation: **43** (RS 18.024):2–5 {ḫmš- . kkrm . ảlp- ⸢.⸣ kb⸢d⸣ (3) ṯlṯ . l . nskm . bỉrtym (4) bd . ủrtn . w . ṯṯ . mảt . brr (5) b . ṯmnym . ksp ṯlṯt . kbd} /ḫamišu kakkarūma ʾalpu kubda ṯalṯu lê nāsikīma biʾirātiyyīma bîdê ʾurtēna wa ṯiṯṯu miʾāti barūru bi ṯamāniyīma kaspi ṯalāṯati kubda/ '5 talents, 1,000 (shekels) (3) of copper for the founders of *Biʾirātu*, (4) entrusted to *ʾUrtēnu*, and 600 (shekels) of tin, (5) for 83 (shekels) of silver'. Here *kbd* appears at the end of two number phrases to mark the link between the larger number or amount and the following smaller number or amount: after *ảlp* '1,000 (shekels)', to mark the link with *ḫmš kkrm* '5 talents', and after *ṯlṯt* '3', to mark the link with *ṯmnym ksp* '80 (shekels) of silver'.

4.1.1.5. Pronouns

Pronouns in their function as replacing nouns share features with nouns, though they are not as consistently marked for case, gender, and number as are nouns and adjectives.

4.1.1.5.1. Personal Pronoun

4.1.1.5.1.1. Independent Personal Pronoun

The primary function of independent personal pronouns is to express the grammatical concept of person on the noun side of the grammar (person is expressed grammatically in verbs but not in nouns); this function entails the marking for gender. Case is also marked, apparently diptotically, though the oblique forms are rarely attested.

Nominative Case

S.1c.	*ảnk/ản*	Du.1c.	Ø	Pl.1c.	Ø
2m.	*ảt*	2m.	*ảtm*	2m.	*ảtm*
2f.	*ảt*	2f.	Ø	2f.	Ø
3m.	*hw*	3m.	*hm*	3m.	Ø
3f.	*hy*	3f.	Ø	3f.	Ø

Oblique case: separate forms are attested for the 3m.s. (*hwt*), 3f.s. (*hyt*), 3m.du. (*hmt*), and 3m.pl. (*hmt*). These forms function both as accusatives (i.e., direct object of a transitive verb: [*kbd hyt* /kabbidā hiyati/ 'honor her' (**2** RS

2.[014]+ iii 10′), *kbd hwt* /kabbidā huwati/ 'honor him' (RS 1.[014]+ vi 20, *CTA* 3)] and as genitives (*t̠br dỉy hwt* /t̠abara dāʾiyī huwati/ 'he broke the pinions of him', *t̠br dỉy hyt* /t̠abara dāʾiyī hiyati/ 'he broke the pinions of her' [RS 3.322 iii 37 = *CTA* 19:143]).

The 1st- and the 2nd-person forms consist, as in most of the Semitic languages, of a deictic element *ản* followed by the pronominal element proper (the /n/ assimilates to the following consonant except in the 1st person). The vocalization of these forms may thus be approximated as:

1st- and 2nd-Person Pronouns

Sg.	Du.	Pl.
/ʾanāku/ (← /ʾan + āku/)		
/ʾatta/ (← /ʾan + ta/)	*/ʾattumā/ (← /ʾan + tumā/)*	*/ʾattumu/ (← /ʾan + tumu/)*
/ʾatti/ (← /ʾan + ti/)		

The optional 1st-person-singular form, *ản*, already shows the dropping of the consonantal element -*k*-, though its vocalization is unknown (/ʾanā/, as in Aramaic, or /ʾanī/, by analogy with other 1st-person pronominal forms, as in Hebrew?).

The 3rd-person-singular forms consist of an augmented form of the primitive pronouns, /hu/ → /huwa/, /hi/ → /hiya/.

4.1.1.5.1.2. Proclitic and Enclitic Personal Pronouns

Proclitic and enclitic pronouns, clearly related historically to the independent forms just cited, are also attested. Historically speaking, finite verbal forms are made up of a pronominal element providing the notion of "person," plus the verbal element. These pronominal elements were suffixed in the perfective, essentially prefixed in the imperfective:

Pf.	Sg.	Du.	Pl.	Impf.	Sg.	Du.	Pl.
1c.	*-t*	*-ny*	*-n*	1c.	*ʾ*	*n-*	*n-*
2m.	*-t*	*-tm*	*-tm*	2m.	*t-*	*t-*	*t-*
2f.	*-t*	∅	*-tn*	2f.	*t-*	*t-*	*t-*
3m.	-∅ /-a/	-∅ /-ā/	-∅ /-ū/	3m.	*y-*	*y-/t-*	*y-/t-*
3f.	*-t*	*-t*	-∅ /-ā/	3f.	*y-*	*t-*	*t-*

Because it is absent in the other Semitic languages while being attested in Egyptian, the 1c.du. *-ny* (also attested as a genitive enclitic) is apparently an archaic retention in Ugaritic. Other dual forms indicated were apparently differentiated from identically written plural forms (or singular in the case of the 3f. pf.) by vocalic pattern.

The data for the vowel of the 1c.pl. in the other Semitic languages are too disparate to propose a Ugaritic form using comparative data. Huehnergard (1997: 219) thinks he has found support for the form /-nū/. It is possible on account of the presence of the {y} in the 1c.du. pronoun that the characteristic vowel for this form was /ā/ (likely /-nāyā/), and this form was originally that of the oblique case.

Enclitic pronouns were also attached to nouns, with a genitival function, and to verbs, with primarily an accusative function (rarely dative). Here, the 2nd person is not marked by *-t-*, but by *-k-*:

	Sg.	Du.	Pl.
1c.	*-y/-Ø/-n*	*-ny*	*-n*
2m.	*-k*	*-km*	*-km*
2f.	*-k*	Ø	*-kn*
3m.	*-h*	*-hm*	*-hm*
3f.	*-h*	*-hm*	*-hn*

The forms indicated for the 1st person are distributed according to function: *-y/-Ø* is genitive (i.e., attached to nouns), *-n* accusative (i.e., attached to transitive verbs). The first set is distributed according to the case of the singular noun to which the genitive suffix is attached (nom. = -Ø; gen./acc. = *-y*); the -Ø form is assumed to have arisen through syncope (/-uya/ → long vowel usually reconstructed as /-î/). This distribution differs from early Phoenician, where the suffix on nominative/accusative nouns in the pronominal state is identical (i.e., orthographic -Ø), *-y* only appearing in the genitive.

As with the independent and prefixed pronominal elements, most of the dual forms were apparently differentiated from identically written plural forms by vocalic pattern.

Accusative pronouns on imperfect verbs show a great deal of variation because of assimilation to *-n* verbal forms (see below) and apparent reanalysis. The 3m.s. suffix, for example, can appear on nouns and verbs as:

- *-h* = /-hu/ (e.g., *bˁlh* /baˁluhu/ 'his lord' [**36** RS 11.772⁺:12′]);
- *-n* = /-annu/(← /-an/ + /hu/; e.g., *ylmn* /yallumannu/ 'he struck him' [**7** RS 24.258:8]);
- *-nh* = /-annahu/ (← /-anna/ + /hu/; e.g., *štnnh* /šattinannahu/ 'deliver him over' [**33** RS 96.2039:16]);
- *-nn* = /-annannu/ (apparently /-anna/ + /nnu/ through reanalysis of the latter as a pronominal suffix; e.g., *tbrknn* /tabarrikannannu/ 'you should bless him' [**4** RS 2.[004] i 23′]);

- *-nnn* (if this analysis is correct, this form should be = /-annannannu/, through double reanalysis; see {ttnn ⌜.⌝ nn} /tatinannannannu/ 'you must give it' [new reading of RS 15.174:17 (Virolleaud 1957: text 16) and *tšknnnn* /tašakīnannannannu/ '(someone) will establish him' [RS 1.026⁺:12 = *KTU* 2.7]).

For this hypothesis on the origin of these forms, see Pardee 1984b: 244–45 n. 14. Tropper (2000: 222–23 [§41.221.52c], 501–4 [§73.62]) believes that the form written {-nn} reveals the existence of the a third "energic" ending (on /YQTL/ forms, see below), a hypothesis that is not supported by parallels from other Northwest Semitic languages (see Pardee 2003–4: 245–50).

4.1.1.5.2. Relative Pronoun

The relative pronoun is **ḏ* + vowel, nearly always written with {d}, marked for gender and number, though the forms are not used consistently. This particle is directly related to the *ḏū/ḏā/ḏī* series in Arabic and to the *zeʰ/zōʾt* series in Hebrew (used sporadically as a relative pronoun there), and its basic function is therefore deictic, as is shown in Ugaritic by the enclitic use of *-d* in demonstrative pronouns and adjectives and in adverbials. The masculine singular is attested only in the form of *d*, while the other grammatical persons and numbers are written with or without *-t*. By comparison with the other Semitic languages, one may conclude that only the masculine singular was marked for all three grammatical cases, while the other forms were invariable for case but able either to have the enclitic *-t* or not:

Masculine Singular	Feminine Singular	Plural of both Genders
/dū/, /dā/, /dī/	/dā(ti)/	/dū(ti)/

For examples of forms and usages of various demonstrative pronouns and adjectives containing this basic element, see below, "Syntax: Agreement" (§7.3).

The other primary function of *d* is as a determinative: in these formulae, the pronoun defines an entity as belonging to another category. The absolute usage is still not attested in Ugaritic (cf. *zeʰ sînay* in Biblical Hebrew, 'he of [Mount] Sinai') but one finds examples of genitive expressions (see above, "Nouns," §4.1.1.1.1).

4.1.1.5.3. The Demonstrative Pronoun

The primary demonstrative pronouns and adjectives are compounds consisting of the deictic particle *hn* (probably essentially the same particle as the Hebrew definite article and as the deictic particle *hēn/hinnēʰ* in that language), to which expanding elements are joined: either the relative pronoun *d* (cf. Arabic *ʾallaḏī*) in the case of the proximal demonstrative, or *k*, of uncertain origin, in the distal. The forms are identical to those of the demonstrative adjectives and the two categories are defined, therefore, by their syntactic characteristics. Forms with and without *-t* occur (*hndt*/*hnkt*), but they are rare and it is therefore likely that the *-t* is the enclitic particle rather than the feminine morpheme.

Though the usage is rare and to date attested primarily in the oblique case, the 3rd-person independent personal pronouns could also be used as demonstrative adjectives, apparently, as in Hebrew, with a distal connotation (*mlk hwt* /malku huwati/ 'that king' [**20** RS 24.247⁺:43], *ḥwt hyt* /ḥuwwat- hiyati/ 'that land' [ibid., 45′, 55′, 56′; for the reading of line 45′, see Pardee 1986: 119, 124]). In a recently discovered text, *hw* is attested as a demonstrative adjective in the nominative: *w yủḫd hn bnš hw* /wa yuʾuḫad hanna bunušu huwa/ 'so this servant must be seized' (**33** RS 96.2039:14–15). The demonstrative pronoun m. pl.ob. is attested with the expanding element *-t* functioning as an adjective: *b šdm hnmt* /bi šadîma hannamati/ 'for these fields' (**39** RS 94.2965:20).

4.1.1.5.4. Other Pronouns

The other pronominal elements do not show the primary morphological characteristics of nouns and thus overlap with the category of particles. They are included here in order to provide a complete picture of pronouns:

• The attested interrogative pronouns are: *my* 'who?', *mh* 'what?'. Comparing *mh*, of which the *-h* is consonantal, with Biblical Hebrew {mah} leads to the conclusions that (1) the gemination following the Hebrew pronoun represents assimilation of the *-h* and (2) the presence of the {h} in the orthography is therefore historical writing. (This solution appears more likely than positing a proto-Hebrew form *man* and identifying the {h} in the orthography as a secondary *mater lectionis*.)

• The indefinite pronouns and adjectives are *mn*/*mnk*/*mnm*/ 'whoever/whatever'. As presently attested, *mn* and *mnk* denote human entities, *mnm* inanimate ones. The basic particle was plausibly /mV(n)/ with the distinction between human and nonhuman referents expressed by *Ablaut* (e.g., /mīn-/ for humans, /man-/ for nonhumans); *-k* and *-m* are expanding elements of uncertain semantic content. Because "enclitic" *-m* may be attached to any part of speech, it is not surprising to encounter the form *mnm* applied to an animate entity (**2** RS 2.[014]⁺ iv 4); it would have been distinguished from the nonhuman reference by its characteristic vowels (*mnm ỉb ypʿ l bʿl* /mīnama ʾêbu yapaʿa lê baʿli/ 'What enemy has arisen against *Baʿlu*?').

4.1.1.6. Adverbs

Adverbials may be expressed by adverbial lexemes or by adverbialization of a noun—that is, by prefixing a preposition (e.g., *b ym* /bi yammi/ 'in the sea' [**1** RS 3.367 iv 3′]), by suffixation of an adverbial morpheme (e.g., *ttlh* /tuttulaha/ 'to [the city of] Tuttul' [**6** RS 24.244:15]; see below, "Particles,"

§4.1.3), or by using a particular form of the noun (e.g., *bt bˁl* /bêta baˁli/ 'in the temple of *Baˁlu*' [**4** RS 2.[004] i 31′]).

Adverbial lexemes are either etymological nouns of which the derivation is clear (e.g., *ˁt* /ˁatta/ 'now', *ˁln* /ˁalâna/ 'above' [= *ˁl*+-*n*]) or particles (e.g., *ṯm* /ṯamma/ 'there').

The accusative case was the primary case used for adverbialization of nouns, e.g., *qdqd* /qudquda/ 'on the head', *ym* /yôma/ 'for a day', *šmm* /šamîma/ 'to the heavens'. The existence of a specific adverbial case is uncertain (see Pardee 2003–4: 80–82, 192–96).

4.1.1.7. Verbal Nouns and Adjectives

On the infinitive and the participle, see the following section on verbs (§4.1.2.8).

4.1.2. Verbs

The verbal system represents an archaic form of West Semitic, one with an N-stem, a D-stem (characterized by the doubling of the middle radical), a causative stem in Š, t-stems built off the G-, D-, and Š-stems, as well as some less well-attested stems.

4.1.2.1. Semantic Categories

As in the other Semitic languages, the basic verbal form can itself express various sorts of action. The primary division is transitive : intransitive. Within the latter division, there are two primary types: verbs of motion and stative verbs. Within the verbs of motion, there are again two primary types: verbs that express only motion and those that express either the motion or the state achieved (e.g., *qm* 'arise' or 'be standing'). Stative verbs can also denote either the state itself or the attainment thereof (e.g., *qrb* 'be near' or 'become near' [i.e., 'approach']). These distinctions are reflected in the verbal system: only transitive verbs can be passivized, and they tend to take double accusatives in the causative and single accusatives in the D-stem. Stative verbs are factitivized in the D-stem, cannot be passivized in the G-stem, and have a stative participial form rather than the active one. Verbs of motion cannot be passivized in the G-stem, appear rarely in the D-stem, and are transitivized in the Š-stem, where they take the single accusative construction. There are, of course, a certain number of verbs that cross categories or that defy classification.

4.1.2.2. Attested Verbal Stems

G-stem (base stem, or simple stem; active and passive voices)
Gt-stem (-*t*- infixed after first radical; middle/reflexive in function)
D-stem (doubled middle radical; factitive in function; active and passive voices)
tD-stem (*t*- prefixed to D-stem [see Huehnergard 1986]; middle/reflexive in function)

N-stem (preformative *n*-; middle/passive in function)
Š-stem (preformative *š*-; causative in function; active and passive voices)
Št-stem (-*t*- infixed after *š*- of causative stem; middle/reflexive in function; the few forms attested indicate that the form may no longer have been productive)
L-stem (lengthened vowel after first radical and reduplicated second/third radical; intensive or factitive in function [for a preliminary description of the distribution of these functions, see Pardee 2003–4: 279–85])
R-stem (reduplication of both radicals of biconsonantal root, of second and third radicals of triconsonantal root; factitive in function)
tR- or Rt-stem (*t* prefixed to first root consonant or infixed after first root consonant of R-stem; factitive-reflexive in function)

The following examples are given with the vocalization of the 3m.s. in order to illustrate the phonetic distinctions between the forms (see below). Many details of the vocalizations are, however, still uncertain. An asterisk before a G-stem form indicates that the verb is only attested in Ugaritic in the following derived stem.

LḤM 'to eat (something)' (G-stem transitive, /laḥama/), LḤM 'to provide (someone) with food' (D-stem, /liḥḥama/), ŠLḤM 'to cause (someone) to eat (something)' (Š-stem, /šalḥima/)
QRʾA 'to call' (G-stem transitive, /qaraʾa/), QRʾA 'to be called' (G-stem passive, /quraʾa/ or /quriʾa/ [Tropper 2000: 514 (§74.223.1)])
RḤṢ 'to wash' (G-stem transitive, /raḥaṣa/), (ʾI)RTḤṢ 'to wash oneself' (Gt-stem, /ʾirtaḥiṣa/)
NTK 'to pour out' (G-stem transitive, /nataka/), NTK 'to pour forth' (N-stem, /nattaka/ ← /nantaka/)
ʾAHB 'to love' (G-stem active, /ʾahiba/), ʾIHB 'to love intensely' (D-stem, /ʾihhaba/)
*BKR 'to be the firstborn' (G-stem stative, /bakura/), BKR 'to promote (someone) to the status of firstborn' (D-stem, /bikkara/)
*KMS 'to squat' (G-stem intransitive, /kamasa/), TKMS 'to collapse' (tD-stem, /takammasa/)
ʿRB 'to enter' (G-stem verb of movement, /ʿaraba/), ŠʿRB 'to cause (someone) to enter' (Š-stem, /šaʿriba/)
RḤQ 'to be far off or to move far off' (G-stem stative, /raḥuqa/), ŠRḤQ 'to cause to be far off' (Š-stem, /šarḥiqa/)
QL 'to fall' (G-stem intransitive, /qāla/), ŠQL 'to cause (something) to fall' (Š-stem, /šaqīla/), (ʾI)ŠTQL 'to cause oneself to fall → to arrive' (Št-stem, /ʾištaqāla/)
RM 'to be or become high' (G-stem stative, /rāma/), RMM 'to raise' (L-stem, /rāmama/)

*KR(R) 'to turn' (G-stem verb of movement, /karra/); KRKR 'to turn, twist, snap' (said of what one does with the fingers) (R-stem, /karkara/); cf. the adjectival form YSMSM 'beautiful' ← YSM (G-stem stative, /yasuma/ 'to be beautiful')

*YPY 'to be beautiful' (G-stem stative, /yapiya/), TTPP 'she makes herself beautiful' (only form attested of Rt- or tR-stem, /tîtapêpû/ ← /tiytapaypiyu/ or /titêpêpû/ ← /titaypaypiyu/)

4.1.2.3. Verbal Aspect

There are two verbal conjugations marked for person, gender, and number: one is characterized by STEM + PRONOMINAL ELEMENT and expresses acts viewed as complete ("perfective," often called the "perfect" though the term is technically incorrect); the other is characterized by PRONOMINAL ELEMENT + STEM (+ AFFIX in some forms) and expresses acts not viewed as complete ("imperfective," often called the "imperfect"). The pronominal elements were joined to the verbal elements in an archaic stage of the language (see above at proclitic and enclitic pronouns, §4.1.1.5.1.2, p. 39). This description of the form and function of the two verbal conjugations is valid for the prose texts.

In poetry, however, the ambiguities of the writing system have compounded the ambiguities of usage, and no broad agreement exists on the correlation between form and function in the verbal system. Usage may reflect an older stage of the language, when the zero-ending /YQTL/ form (see below, §4.1.2.5.2, p. 48) functioned as a perfective/preterite, like Akkadian *iprus*. In the West Semitic verbal system, the permansive (corresponding to Akkadian *paris*) came to function as perfective and the imperfective /YQTLu/ (corresponding to the Akkadian "subjunctive," *iprusu*) as an imperfective. The /YQTL/ form without a vowel at the end (corresponding to Akkadian *iprus*) retained its old jussive function but also that of a perfective/preterite. (This is the form that, particularly in Biblical Hebrew, was retained as a frozen perfective/preterite after *wa-*, as in *wayyiktōb* 'he wrote'.)

In spite of the problems of description and categorization of the verbal system in the poetic texts, many scholars (e.g., Tropper 1995a) have preferred to classify the Ugaritic verbal system on the basis of poetic usage, rather than on that of the prose texts (similar attempts, of course, have been made in the classification of Biblical Hebrew). It is legitimate to see in the poetic texts remnants of a previous stage of the language (plausibly closer to East Semitic), remnants that seem not to be used consistently because they are no longer representative of the spoken language, while the prose texts reflect spoken Ugaritic in the 13th–12th centuries B.C. Only in these texts is a reasonably consistent system visible (cf. Mallon 1982), although Tropper (2000) has attempted to explain all verbal forms in poetry as conforming to the rules of a verbal system that expresses aspect.

More recently, Greenstein (2006) has argued that the /YQTLØ/ perfective/preterite cannot be isolated in poetic narrative, that the lack of discernible pattern in /YQTL/ forms of III-*y* roots (i.e., with and without {y}) coupled with the almost exclusive attestion of /YQTLu/ forms of III-ʾ roots may be taken as showing that the /YQTLØ/ perfective/preterite was no longer used with this function but in free variation with the /YQTLu/ forms. We find these arguments convincing and, in contrast with the first edition of this work, where Tropper's views were reflected, have adopted Greenstein's basic perspective (with some modifications) in vocalizing the poetic texts in our Selection of Texts.

The Ugaritic verbal system is here classified as aspectual, that is, as reflecting the perspective of the speaker or author of the action in question, which is expressed as either complete or incomplete. This classification is owing to the similarity between the Ugaritic verbal system and the prose system of Biblical Hebrew (Pardee 1993a, 1993b, 1995). It is not, then, a temporal system that expresses past, present, and future. While tense is a real-world phenomenon (past-present-future), aspectual systems include a greater degree of subjectivity; that is, the speaker may express a situation as complete or incomplete according to several criteria. Because of the nature of tense, aspectual systems cannot ignore temporal considerations, and a language may not, therefore, be classed as a tensed language merely because it reflects real-world temporal considerations.

On the other hand, a language may be classed as aspectual if it ignores real-world temporality, as in the use of the imperfect in Biblical Hebrew prose to express past-tense iteratives (e.g., *yišmaʿ* 'he used to hear'). Because of the simplicity of the verbal systems in the Northwest Semitic languages, where there are only two basic finite forms, with modal variation expressed as a subsystem of the /YQTL/ form, it is not likely that both aspect and tense were marked categories—as may be the case in languages with more complex systems. We conclude that the Ugaritic verbal system was primarily marked for aspect and that tense was expressed as appropriate within this perspective and by various lexical and discourse markers.

The perfective may have been characterized by internal *Ablaut* for active (/QaTaL-/) versus stative (/QaTiL-/, /QaTuL-/), but the only internal evidence is for the /QaTiL-/ type (writings of the middle radical with {ỉ}: {lỉk} = /laʾika/ 'he sent', {šỉl} = /šaʾila/ 'he asked'). Syllabic writings attest some /QaTaL-/ forms (Huehnergard 1987: 319–20).

There are three types of imperfective forms characterized by internal *Ablaut*: active (/yaQTuL-/) versus stative (/yiQTaL-/); the third form (/yaQTiL-/) seems to follow other rules, as in Biblical Hebrew, for, as far as we can tell, it is only attested in weak roots: I-weak (e.g., /ʾaṯibu/ 'I sit', /ʾatinu/ 'I give'), II-weak (e.g., /ʾabīnū/ 'I understand', /ʾaṣīḥu/ 'I call out'), and III-weak (e.g.,

/ʾabkiyu/ 'I weep', /ʾamǵiyu/ 'I arrive'). There are few data for these differentiations, but what there are tend to agree with the data from the later West Semitic languages, making reconstruction of Ugaritic along the same lines plausible. In addition, the imperfective is also marked, by affixation to the stem, for mood (see below). The "Barth-Ginsberg" law of /a/ dissimilation (/yaQTaL-/ → /yiQTaL-/) was operative in Ugaritic.

No certain evidence exists for a present-future form corresponding to Akkadian *iparras* (Fenton 1970; Tropper 2000: 460–61 [§73.28]).

4.1.2.4. Grammatical Voice

Active verbs are of two primary types, transitive and intransitive (e.g., /maḫaṣa ʾêba/ 'he smote the enemy' and /halaka/ 'he went'). The concept of transitivity is not a useless one in Semitics, for not only do certain verbs take complements that correspond to what in other languages would be direct objects, but distinctively marked passive forms, used almost exclusively for verbs that in other languages would be qualified as transitive, are common. Though lack of vocalization in Ugaritic makes identification difficult, it is likely that all transitive forms—that is, G-stem transitive verbs, D-stem, and Š-stem—had passive forms that were differentiated from the active by *Ablaut* (for a contrary view on the G-passive finite forms, see Verreet 1986: 324–30; brief refutation in Tropper 1993a: 478–79; more details are in Tropper 2000: 509–18 [§74.22 for the Gp], 567–70 [§74.42 for the Dp], 604–6 [§74.63 for the Šp]). In addition, the N-stem, basically an intransitivizing and deagentifying stem, can be used as a passive. (This usage of the t-stems, which became common in Hebrew, is not clear in Ugaritic.) Passive forms are attested for finite forms (e.g., *tšt ỉšt b bhtm* /tušātu ʾišatu bi bahatīma/ 'fire is placed in the palace' [RS 2.[008]$^{+}$ vi 22 = *CTA* 4]) as well as for participles. There is as yet no evidence for *Ablaut*-passive imperatives, though there was almost certainly an N-stem imperative (**13** RS 34.126:13 *ỉbky* and line 18 *ỉšḫn*, the first of which appears to function as a passive 'be bewept'). On the basis of comparative data, one would not expect a passive infinitive necessarily to have existed.

Between the two extremes marked by the clearly transitive and passive forms, there is a whole middle range of forms denoting reflexivity, reciprocity, advantage or disadvantage to actor, etc. These notions are clearest in the t-stems (Gt, tD, and Št). The primary function of the N-stem in Ugaritic, as in several of the Semitic languages, was for patient-oriented expressions, and it is thus used for both the middle and the passive, the latter encountered mostly in prose (e.g., nḫtů /naḫtaʾū/ 'they were struck' [**21** RS 4.475:8, 10]).

4.1.2.5. Mood

Mood in Ugaritic was marked, as in the other West Semitic languages, by variations to the imperfective stem.

4.1.2.5.1. Imperative

The imperative in Ugaritic does not have the preformative element characteristic of the imperfective, but the fact that its stem vowel is identical to that of the imperfective leaves no doubt as to the historical linkage of the imperative to the imperfective. Its form is thus ROOT + stem vowel (+ additional PRONOMINAL ELEMENT). The question of an additional vowel between the first two radicals is unresolved: impf. = /yaQTuL-/, imper. = /QVTuL-/ or /QTuL-/. In the first case, the quality of the first vowel is unknown: always identical to the stem vowel or sometimes different? The comparative and internal indications best support the dissyllabic reconstruction /QuTuL-/. To the basic imperative element may be added the /-a(n)(na)/ elements listed below in this section. The imperative existed only in the second person and was used only for positive commands (negative commands are expressed by *ủl* + jussive).

4.1.2.5.2. The Expression of Mood in the /YQTL/ Forms

The moods are marked by affixation to the full imperfective stem (the forms *YQTL* /yaQTuL-/ will be used below for STEM):

YQTL + Ø	= jussive	/yaQTuL/
YQTL + /u/	= indicative	/yaQTuLu/
YQTL + /a/	= volitive	/yaQTuLa/
YQTL + /anna/	= energic 1	/yaQTuLanna/
YQTL + /(a)n/	= energic 2	/yaQTuLVn/

The morpho-semantic values are largely derived from comparison with other Semitic languages, for the forms are not used consistently in the poetic texts, and the prose texts have not yet furnished sufficient material to establish usage with certainty. Because of the absence of vowel indicators, the use of one mood or another can only be determined when the root ends in /ʾ/ or, perhaps, /y/: the form of /ʾ/ will indicate the quality of the following vowel (e.g., *ảšṣỉ* /ʾašôṣiʾ/ 'I will certainly cause to go out'). A phrase from the incantation RIH 78/20 (**17**, line 18) illustrates the interplay between the indicative and the jussive: *bt ủbủ ảl tbỉ* /bêta ʾubūʾu ʾal tubuʾ/tubūʾī/ 'the house that I enter, you will not enter' (the indicative ends with /-u/ in the first phrase, an unmarked relative clause; in the negative phrase, a 2m.s. form would not have /-u/ in the jussive while the 2f.s. would not have /-n/).

According to Tropper's reconstructions, the presence or absence of the {y} should indicate the presence or absence of a following vowel (/yabkiyu/ = {ybky}, /yabkiy/ → /yabki/ = {ybk}). For example, the {-y} of *ykly* in the following phrase may show that it is either /YQTLu/ or /YQTLa/: *ykly ṯpṭ nhr* /yakalliya ṯāpiṭa nahara/ 'he sets about finishing off Ruler Naharu' (**1** RS 3.367 iv 27′), while the absence of the {-y} may reveal the presence of a

/YQTLØ/ form: *hlm ʿnt tph ỉlm* which, according to this view, would be vocalized /hallima ʿanatu tipha ʾilêma/ 'when *ʿAnatu* sees the two deities' (/tipha/ ← /*tiphay/, **2** RS 2.[014] iii 32′). These III-weak roots have been thought to provide us with the primary internal data on the aspectual and modal systems in Ugaritic, but inconsistency of usage, particularly in the case of III-*y* roots, also creates a significant degree of uncertainty (see Pardee 2003–4: 341).

Greenstein's arguments (2006) have convinced us that the level of uncertainty is too high to continue taking /YQTL/ forms of III-*y* roots in poetry that are written without the third radical as /YQTLØ/ perfectives; in his view, the /YQTLØ/ perfective/preterite was no longer operative in poetic narrative, and the two principal forms were /QTLa/ and /YQTL/—according to his hypothesis, the /YQTLu/ and /YQTLØ/ forms would have lost distinctive functions, and both would have been used as "historical futures."

We believe, on the other hand, that the III-*y* forms written without {-y} may not always be formally identical to historical /YQTLØ/ forms, e.g., /yabki/ ← /yabkiyØ/, but that they may perhaps be taken as contracted /YQTLu/ forms—that is, vocalized /yabkû/ ← /yabkiyu/ (Pardee 2003–4: 323–24). The data on the question are very few, but there is one relatively clear form: *tlủ* /tilʾû/ ← /*tilʾayu/ or /*tilʾawu/ 'it is weak' (**6** RS 24.244:68). Regarding the evidence from III-ʾ roots, there is one clear /YQTLØ/ form in the narrative section of an incantation: *tspỉ* /tissapiʾ/ 'it devours' (RS 22.225:3 [Virolleaud 1960: 182–84]). Because Greenstein's study dealt only with the principal mythological texts, an exhaustive investigation might reveal a few more forms of this type, but they cannot be numerous. Because the /YQTLØ/ perfective/preterite is clearly absent from prose (Pardee 2003–2004: 221, 339–42, 351–52), accepting Greenstein's theory that it is also absent from poetic narrative requires the conclusion that the productive /YQTLØ/ perfective/preterite has disappeared from the language and that such forms appear only as archaisms and in essentially free variation with /YQTLu/ forms.

The /YQTLa/ form does not function primarily as a marker of syntactic dependency (Verreet 1988) but as a volitive (Tropper 1991; 1993a: 473–74; Pardee 1993b), and its traditional classification, namely, the "subjunctive," borrowed from Arabic, is thus not appropriate. This may be observed clearly in the example of RIH 78/20 cited agove, this section: *bt ủbủ* /bêta ʾubūʾu/ 'the house that I enter', where the form appropriate for a subordinate clause is seen to be /YQTLu/. Tropper (2000: 455–56 [§73.26]) has proposed that the /YQTLa/ form is used only for the 1st person, as in the Hebrew cohortative. However, while the number of forms in the 2nd and 3rd persons that unequivocally indicate the final vowel by the use of {ả} are limited, its attestation assures that the form was in use in the poetic language (e.g., *w ymẓả ʿqqm* /wa yimẓaʾa ʿāqiqīma/ 'that he might find the devourers' [RS 2.[012] i 37 = *CTA* 12]).

The presentation of the two energic forms indicated above is that of Arabic grammar. The two energic forms are only distinguishable when followed by a suffix (see above at "Pronouns," §4.1.1.5.1.2, p. 41) and their semantic import is uncertain. The distribution of these suffixed forms clearly indicates the existence of two energic forms, /-an/ and /-anna/ (as in Arabic); whether there also existed a similar form built off the "indicative" (/-u+n(a)/), as apparently in old Canaanite (Rainey 1996: 2.234–44; Tropper 2000: 497–506 [§73.6]), has not been determined. Finally, Tropper's hypothesis that a third energic form existed in Ugaritic perhaps does not provide the best explanation of the data (see also above at "Pronouns").

Mood distinction in forms containing a suffixed pronominal subject element (e.g., 3m.pl. /Y/TQTL+ū/) is variable in the later languages and impossible to determine in Ugaritic (except where the distinction was marked by consonantal *-n*, and there the problem is the precise function of the *-n*). It appears permissible, however, to think that in standard Ugaritic the indicative was distinguished from the jussive by this {-n}: /taQTuLūna/ 'they will do X', /taQTuLū/ 'let them do X'. In Greenstein's theory (2006), the /-ū/-ūna/ forms are distributed in poetic narrative in a manner analogical to the /YQTLØ/ YQTLu/ forms, namely, that the /YQTLū/ perfective/preterite has disappeared from the language, and the /YQTLū/ and /YQTLūna/ forms are used in stylistic/prosodic variation. In prose, {-n} plural forms are well established as having an indicative function (Tropper 2000: 459 [§73.273.3]), but there is no explicit evidence for the function of /YQTLū/ (which one would in any case expect to function uniquely as a jussive in prose, not as a perfective/preterite).

4.1.2.6. Verbal Inflection

The large amount of reconstruction in the Ugaritic verbal system makes a long set of examples unnecessary (particularly doubtful reconstructions in the following table are indicated with one or more question marks). It is largely a question of the interplay between the elements that were originally pronominal or properly verbal in the morphology of the verb. A table of pronominal elements can be found in §4.1.1.5.1.2 (p. 39). We provide here a complete set of forms for the G-stem /qatala/ and the /yaqtul-/. The /qatila/qatula/ and /yiqtal-/yaqtil-/ represent *Ablaut* variation. More complete sets, with proposed vocalizations, may be found in Segert 1984.

4.1.2.6.1. G-Stem of Strong Verbs

	perfective	*imperfective*	*jussive*	*imperative*
S.3m.	/QaTaLa/	/yaQTuLu/	/yaQTuL/	
3f.	/QaTaLat/	/taQTuLu/	/taQTuL/	
2m.	/QaTaLta/	/taQTuLu/	/taQTuL/	/QuTuL(a)/
2f.	/QaTaLti/	/taQTuLīna/	/taQTuLī/	/QuTuLī/
1c.	/QaTaLtu/	/ʾaQTuLu/	/ʾaQTuL/	
Du. 3m.	/QaTaLā/?	/yaQTuLā(na)/ or /taQTuLā(na)/	/yaQTuLā/ or /taQTuLā/	
3f.	/QaTaLtā/?	/taQTuLā(na)/	/taQTuLā/	
2m.	/QaTaLtumā/	/taQTuLā(na)/	/taQTuLā/	/QuTuLā/
2f.	∅	∅	∅	∅
1c.	/QaTaLnāyā/?	/naQTuLā/?	/naQTuLā/?	
Pl.3m.	/QaTaLū/	/taQTuLūna/ or /yaQTuLūna/	/taQTuLū/ or /yaQTuLū/	
3f.	/QaTaLā/	/taQTuLna/?	/taQTuLna/?	
2m.	/QaTaLtum(u)/	/taQTuLū(na)/	/taQTuLū/	/QuTuLū/
2f.	/QaTaLtin(n)a/	/taQTuLna/?	/taQTuLna/??	/QuTuLā/?
1c.	/QaTaLnū/	/naQTuLu/	/naQTul/??	

The standard 3rd-person dual and plural imperfective has preformative *t*-, rather than *y*- (Verreet 1988; Tropper 2000: 432–41 [§73.223.3–42]). The interplay of forms occasionally indicates that the groups indicated by the same term may vary in number: *tʿrbn gṯrm* 'the *gṯrm* [pl.] will enter' (RS 1.005:9 [*CTA* 33]) and *yrdn gṯrm* [du., not pl.] 'the *gṯrm* will descend' (RS 24.256:18 [Herdner 1978a: 21–26]; cf. *tʿln ỉlm* 'the gods ascend', ibid., line 8).

Second-person feminine dual forms are not attested, but the graphic identity of 3rd-person masculine and feminine pronominal forms (see above) indicates that a distinction would, in any case, have been vocalic and thus indeterminable from the consonantal orthography.

4.1.2.6.2. N-Stem

The internal evidence is insufficient to determine the internal vowels of the /QTLa/ form in the N-stem, which may have been /naQTaLa/ as in proto-Hebrew; it is known from the 1st-person singular that the preformative vowel of the imperfective was /i/ (*ỉlḥmn* /ʾillaḥiman(na)/ ← /*ʾinlaḥim-/ 'I will continue to fight' [RIH 78/12:20, Bordreuil and Caquot 1980: 359–60]). The N-stem imperative had /i/ in the preformative syllable (*ỉšḫn* /ʾiššaḫin-/ ← /*ʾinšaḫin-/ 'be hot!' [**13** RS 34.126:18; cf. *ỉbky* 'be bewept!' in ibid., line 13; Bordreuil and Pardee 1991: 157–58]).

Abbreviated table of the N-stem:

	perfective	*imperfective*	*jussive*	*imperative*
3m.s.	/naQTaLa/	/yiQQaTiLu/ ← /*yinQaTiLu/	/yiQQaTiL/ ← /*yinQaTiL/	
2m.s.				/ʾiQQaTil/ ← /*ʾinQaTiL/

4.1.2.6.3. D-Stem

The vocalization of the first syllable of the D-stem /QTLa/ forms seems to be demonstrated by *ỉhb* /ʾihhaba/ 'he loved' (**38** RS 94.2168:11). There are no data establishing the second vowel, and the comparative evidence is equivocal. Huehnergard (1987: 182, 321) cites {ša-li-ma} in RS 20.012 (Nougayrol 1968: text 96) in favor of the vocalization /QaTTila/, but the new data from RS 94.2168 show that this analysis of this Akkadian form is to be reconsidered. This analysis of {ša-li-ma} and the presence of /QaTTiLa/ in proto-Aramaic led Huehnergard (1992) to propose /QaTTiLa/ for proto-Northwest Semitic. One may, however, think that /QaTTaLa/ in Arabic and Ethiopic shows that this was the Proto-Semitic form and that the Northwest Semitic languages followed two principal lines of development: /QaTTiLa/ in Aramaic and /QiTTaLa/ in Canaanite. /QiTTiLa/, which appears in the final phase of proto-Hebrew (one finds /bērēk/ as well as /bērak/ in Biblical Hebrew) and in Phoenician, would then be a later evolution. The vowel of the preformative syllable of the /YQTL/ form was /a/, at least in the 1st-person singular, for one finds {ả} in these forms (e.g., *ảnšq*/ʾanaššiq/ 'I will assault' [**1** RS 3.367 iv 4′]). It is legitimate to think that this vowel did not vary for other persons. For Tropper (2000: 544–46 [§74.412.1]), the vowel would have been /u/ everywhere except for the 1st-person singular, where the variation was due to the influence of the /ʾ/. The vowel of the stem syllable was /i/: compare G-stem *ỉlảk* (/ʾilʾaku/ 'I will send' [**25** RS 16.379:20]) with the D-stem form *tlỉkn* (/talaʾʾikīna/ 'you send' [**29** RS 34.124:10]).

Abbreviated table of the D-stem:

	perfective	*imperfective*	*jussive*	*imperative*
3m.s.	/QiTTaLa/	/yaQaTTiLu/	/yaQaTTiL/	
2m.s.				/QaTTiL/

4.1.2.6.4. Gt- and tD-Stems

The /QTLa/ form of the Gt-stem has /i/ in the preformative syllable (note {ỉtdb}, which is typically considered to be a metathesis error for *ỉtbd* /ʾîtabida/ ← /ʾiʾtabida/ 'he has perished' [**3** RS 2.[003]+ i 8]) as does the stem syllable (*ỉštỉr* /ʾištaʾira/ 'it remains' [RS 17.297:3 = Virolleaud 1957: text 83]). The forms of the tD-stem are not well attested, but it has been proposed that the Gt and tD were characterized by different stem vowels in the imperfect, /i/ versus /a/: *yštỉl* (Gt) versus *yštảl* (tD) 'ask, importune' (Huehnergard 1986): the latter would be /yištaʾʾal-/ ← /*yitšaʾʾal-/ by metathesis (as in similar forms in the Hebrew Hithpael). It is necessary, however, to keep in mind that only the second form is clearly attested: *hlny bn ʿyn yštảl ʿm ảmtk* /halliniya binu ʿayāna yištaʾʾalu ʿimma ʾamatika/ 'here *Binu-ʿAyāna* keeps making demands on your maidservant' (**28** RS 29.093:11–12).

Abbreviated table of the Gt- and tD-stems:

		perfective	*imperfective*	*jussive*
Gt-stem	3m.s.	/ʾiQtaTiLa/	/yiQtaTiLu/	/yiQtaTiL/
tD-stem:	3m.s.	/taQaTTaLa/	/yitQaTTaLu/	/yitQaTTaL/

4.1.2.6.5. Š-Stem

No form is attested at present that establishes the vocalization of the /QTLa/ form for the Št-stem, /šaQTala/ or /šaQTila/. Tropper (2000: 596, §74.624) thinks that the orthography of *šʿly* and *šʿlyt*, where the /y/ is not lost, indicates that the /šaQTila/ form is to be preferred. It can also be reasoned by analogy that, if the D-stem has already taken the form /QiTTaLa/, known to have existed in proto-Hebrew, /šaQTaLa/ may also have undergone a development characteristic of Northwest Semitic, where the second vowel changes from /a/ to /i/ (cf. /ʾaQTēL/ in Aramaic, /yiQTiL/ in Phoenician-Punic, /hiQTīL/ ← /*hiQTiL/ in Hebrew, /ī/ by analogy with II-weak verbs). The situation of the /YQTL/ form is similar to that of the D-stem: the data furnished by the forms of the 1st-person singular unanimously support an /a/ vowel in the prefix syllable (e.g., *ảšspr* /ʾašaspiru/ 'I will make [you] count' [RS 2.[004] vi 28′ = *CTA* 17]; *ảšld* /ʾašôlidu/ ← /*ʾašawlidu/ 'I have begot' [**5** RS 2.002:65]). Here also Tropper (2000: 587–88, §74.622.1) thinks that other grammatical persons had /u/ in their preformative syllable. The existence of a H-causative ("Hiphil/Haphel") or of an ʾ-causative ("Aphel") alongside the Š-causative (Merrill 1974; Tropper 1990a) is improbable.

Abbreviated table of the Š-stem:

	perfective	*imperfective*	*jussive*	*imperative*
3m.s.	/šaQTiLa/	/yašaQTiLu/	/yašaQTiL/	
2m.s.				/šaQTil/

4.1.2.6.6. Št-Stem

The examples of the Št-stem are not numerous, but the 1st-person singular is found in our selection of texts, where it can be observed that the Št-stem has /i/ in the preformative vowel of the /YQTL/ form: *ptḥ bt w ủbả hkl w ỉštql* /pataḥī bêta wa ʾubūʾa hēkala wa ʾištaqīla/ 'open the house that I may enter, the palace that I may come in' (**6** RS 24.244:72). The primary forms of the Št-stem are:

	perfective	*imperfective*	*jussive*
3m.s.	/ʾištaQTiLa/	/yištaQTiLu/	/yištaQTiL/

4.1.2.7. Peculiarities of Weak Roots

Some I-*alif* roots show orthographic variations which suggest that some form of mutation of the *alif* had occurred (quiescence, "secondary opening"?): *yỉḫd* versus *yủḫd*, both meaning 'he seizes' (see Verreet 1983; Tropper 1990b). The hypothesis that best accounts for these varying orthographies is to posit secondary opening in the first syllable and vowel harmony with the theme vowel: /yaʾḫud-/ → /yaʾuḫud-/. It should be noted that the presence of variant orthographies indicates that the second form is relatively recent and that the scribes tended to preserve historical spellings, which would have been part of the writing tradition.

I-*y*/*w* roots have all (with very rare exceptions) become I-*y* in the perfective. Most imperfectives show a bisyllabic stem, with /a/ in the prefix syllable: *ảrd* /ʾarid-/ 'I descend'. YDʿ 'to know' has /i/ in the prefix syllable, *ỉdʿ* /ʾidaʿ-/ 'I know', reflecting stem-vowel /a/ because of the final guttural and the Barth-Ginsberg law (/*yadaʿ-/ → yidaʿ-/). By analogy with Hebrew, historically I-*w* roots in the causative were formed before the shift of I-*w* → I-*y* (e.g., {ảšṣỉ} /ʾašôṣiʾ/ ← /*ʾašawṣiʾ/ 'I will certainly make them leave' [**1** RS 3.367 iv 2′]; {ảšld} /ʾašôlid/ ← /*ʾašawlid/ 'I beget' [**5** RS 2.002:65]). As in other Northwest Semitic languages, the imperfective of the verb HLK 'to go' is formed like I-*y* verbs (*ảlk* /ʾalik-/ 'I go'); the absence of {h} in the Gt-stem should also be noted (*ntlk* /nitaliku/ 'we will go' [**11** RS 24.266:34′]), although it is present in the Š-stem (*ảšhlk* /ʾašahliku/ 'I will cause to go' [RS 2.[014]⁺ v 24 = *CTA* 3 v 32]).

The verb YTN 'to give' poses particular problems because it is a I-*y* verb (as in Phoenician), but comparative data for the vocalization come from languages where the root is NTN (Hebrew, Aramaic) or NDN (Akkadian). Believing that these comparative data indicate that the I-y form originates at a later date, we vocalize the forms where the /y/ is not written as if they derive from the biradical root TN. {ảtn} 'I give' is attested, which is not derived from YTN (/*ʾaytin-/ should become /ʾêtin-/, which would be written {ỉtn}) or from WTN (/*ʾawtin-/ should become /ʾôtin-/, which would be written {ủtn}). The two remaining options are /ʾattin-/ (← /*ʾantin-/ by analogy with Hebrew and Akkadian) or simply /ʾatin-/, following the pattern of /ʾarid-/ 'I descend'. If the form YTN is relatively late, the Š-stem should not be /šôtina/ (← /*šawtina/) nor /šêtina/ (← /*šaytina/), but /šatina/ or /šattina/. Because there are no indications that the root NTN existed in proto-Ugaritic, the first option is preferable.

In the /QTLa/ form, this root presents the following difficulties: sometimes the /n/ assimilated to the following consonant (e.g., {ytt} /yatattu/ ← /*yatantu/ 'I gave' [**6** RS 24.244:75]), as in Hebrew, but other times it did not (e.g., {štnt} /šatinātu/ 'I delivered' [**32** RS 94.2479:21]), with apparently an /ā/ between the verbal stem and the pronominal element as in II-weak verbs (see the paragraph below). The currently available data are insufficient to determine if one form was the result of scribal error ({ytt} would be a mistake for {ytnt}) or if both forms were used side by side.

Hollow roots (*mediae infirmae*, "second weak radical" according to traditional terminology) have no consonantal element in the slot occupied by consonant II in triconsonantal roots. Numerous indicators may be observed in other Semitic languages that show that this radical was originally /w/ or /y/, but the consonantal element has disappeared in Ugaritic, leaving a long vowel in its place when the syllable is open (/qāma/ 'he rose', /yaqūmu/ 'he will rise', but /yaqum/ 'let him rise' [/u/ short in the final syllable because it is closed]). It is clear that in the /QTLa/ conjugation a vowel was inserted between the verbal root and the pronominal element (e.g., *i͗qnả štt bhm* /ʾiqnaʾa šātātu bihumu/ 'I will certainly put (some of the purple wool) with them' [**34** RS 94.2284:21]). This vowel was undoubtedly /ā/, corresponding to /ō/ in Biblical Hebrew (/hᵃqīmōtā/ 'you raised') and to /ā/ in Akkadian, where this vowel, which originally was that of the 1st-person singular, spread throughout the *paris* paradigm (e.g., *parsāku/parsāta*). Most attested imperfectives have the preformative vowel /a/: *ảbn* /ʾabīn-/ 'I understand' or /ʾabin/ 'let me understand'. Bʾ 'to enter' is written with {ủ}, apparently representing /u/, which is explained by vowel harmony: *ủbủ* /ʾubūʾu/ ← /*ʾabūʾu/ 'I enter' (indicative [**17** RIH 78/20:18]), *ủbả* /ʾubūʾa/ ← /*ʾabūʾa/ 'that I might enter' (/YQTLa/-optative [**6** RS 24.244:72]).

III-*y*/*w* roots have shifted almost entirely to III-*y* (exceptions are attested for *ảšlw* 'I relax' [RS 2.[003]⁺ iii:45 = *CTA* 14:149] and *ảtwt* 'you have come' [RS 2.[008]⁺ iv:32 = *CTA* 4]). The /YQTLØ/ form (jussive) has apparently monophthongized (/*yaʿniy/ → /yaʿni/), since this is the form found in Arabic and in proto-Hebrew (/yáʿan/ ← /*yaʿn/ ← /*yaʿni/). As noted above, usage is not consistent in the poetic texts, and the {yʿn}/{yʿny} writings either represent contraction versus noncontraction (/yaʿnû/yaʿniyu/) or else nonfunctional retention of the old /YQTLØ/ perfective/preterite (/yaʿni/yaʿniyu/) (see Verreet 1988 and Sivan 1982 for III-weak nominal forms). As seen above, Tropper

(2000: 682–701, §76.1–4) explains all forms according to aspectual interplay and poetic variation. Thus, he takes, as do we, forms such as *tlủ* /tilʾû/ ← /*tilʾayu/ or /tilʾawu/ 'it is weak' (**6** [RS 24.244]:68) or *ykl* /yiklû/ ← /*yikl-ayu/ 'it will be consumed' (**41** [RS 19.015]:1) as contractions (on the contrasting views of Tropper and Greenstein regarding the usage of these forms in poetry, see above, §§4.1.2.3 and 4.1.2.5.2).

Geminate roots are not well attested. However, it is clear that the D-stem was factitive (*ỉlm tšlmk tǵrk tʿzzk* /ʾilūma tašallimūka taǵǵurūka taʿazzizūka/ 'may the gods keep you well, may they protect you, may they strengthen you' [RS 1.018:4–6 = *CTA* 55, with restorations]), whereas the L-stem was intensive (*mlkn yʿzz ʿl ḫpṯh* /malkuna yaʿāzizu ʿalê ḫupṯihu/ 'the king will become more powerful than his *ḫupṯu*-troops' [**20** RS 24.247⁺:57′]). Roots of this type are not well attested for the G-stem, but the tendency toward simplification is evident: in our Selection of Texts, see *rš* /ruššа/ ← /rušaša/ or /rušiša/ (G-passive) 'it was crushed' (**3** [RS 2.[003]⁺ i]:10), *zb* /zabbu/ (verbal adjective) or /zabba/ (G-stem perfective, **18** [RS 92.2014:1]), and perhaps *l ymk* /lā yamukku/ 'he does not collapse', if it is from a geminate root (**1** [RS 3.367 iv]:17′).

4.1.2.8. Verbal Nouns and Participles

There are two productive forms, the infinitive and the participle, that are associated with the verb but not marked for aspect or person. These forms belong by their morphology to the noun side of the grammar and by their syntax to both the noun and the verb—that is, complementation can be either accusatival or genitival.

The paradigmatic verbal noun expressing abstractly the basic notion of the verb is known as the infinitive. The pattern in the G-stem does not seem to have been fixed (Huehnergard 1987: 320), though it is likely that /QaTāL-/ was the most common for strong roots (cf. *b šả1* [preposition *b* + infinitive] /bi šaʾāli/; [**3** RS 2.[003]⁺ i:38]). The infinitive in the derived stems was formed by *Ablaut*; no *m*-preformative infinitives are attested. The nominal character of the infinitive will, of course, have appeared also in the case morphology and morpho-syntax characteristic of nouns.

Though there is a syntactic usage corresponding to the formula known as the "infinitive absolute" construction in the grammars of later West Semitic languages, in Ugaritic there does not seem to have been a productive separate form so used in contradistinction to the standard verbal noun. It is nevertheless worth noting that it is the /QaTāL-/ form that became the "infinitive absolute" in Biblical Hebrew, and this form functions frequently as a verbal noun in Ugaritic. Where discernible—that is, in III-ʾ roots—the infinitive in "absolute" usage ends in /u/, homophonous with the nominative, though its origin may be different: *hm ǵmủ ǵmỉt* /himma ǵamāʾu ǵamiʾti/ 'If you are indeed thirsty' (RS 2.[008]⁺ iv 34 [*CTA* 4]; cf. Gordon 1965: 79, 121, §§9.27; 13.57).

Each verbal stem has at least one corresponding verbal adjective (participle). If the stem is transitive, there will be a participle for each voice, the active and the passive. In addition, it is likely that the G-stem had two stative verbal adjectives, for a total of four: /QāTiL-/ = active, /QaTiL-/ and /QaTuL-/ = statives, /QaTūL-/ = passive (the second vowel is known from the form *l'uk* /laʾūku/ 'sent' [RS 15.098:11 = Virolleaud 1957: text 21:4]).

All the derived stems except the N-stem form the participle with a prefixed *m-*. The D-stem had /u/ in the preformative of the participle, as is known from {mu-na-aḫ-ḫi-mu}, the syllabic writing of the personal name *mnḥm*, 'the one who brings comfort'.

The morphology of the verbal adjectives is like that of the other adjectives, and the nominal case system could in most cases indicate a participle where there was potential ambiguity (e.g., *raḥuqu*, with final *-u*, could only be a stative participle, while *raḥuqa* could be either verbal or adjectival—but only the latter if the word could be construed as in the accusative case).

Several nouns, nonparticipial in form, are formed from the Š-stem, e.g., *šʿtqt* /šaʿtiq(a)tu/ 'she who causes to pass on', *šmrr* /šamriru/ 'that which causes bitterness (i.e., venom)' (**6** RS 24.244:4 et passim).

4.1.3. Particles

As indicated above, particles differ from nouns and verbs by the absence of a system of declension or inflection. They are fundamentally unchangeable, although many varieties exist on account of the diverse origins of the particles and their tendency to join together to form new, longer forms (e.g., *mhk*, formed from *m* + *h* + *k*, and which is also attested in the form *mhkm* and *hmhkm*).

4.1.3.1. Deictics

The standard presentative particle is *hn* 'behold' (e.g., *hn š* /hanna šû/ 'here is the ram' (**9** RS 1.002:17′, 25′), *hn ʿr* /hanna ʿêru/ 'here is the donkey' (lines 34′, 43′). The basic element is *h-*; *hn* is the long form, perhaps /han-/, or /hanna/ (← /ha + n + na/). Compared with the definite article in Hebrew (*ha* + gemination), the rarity of {h-} probably reflects a form /han-/, where the /n/ has assimilated to the following consonant (*ḥwt hbt* /ḥiwwêtu habbêta/ 'I have . . . had this house repaired' [**28** RS 29.093:15–16]). Alongside *hn*, one finds *hl*, *hln*, *hlny* (on expanding particles, see below). It is likely that this particle *hn* is at the origin of the Phoenician/Hebrew definite article (*ha* + gemination), while variant forms thereof appear in other West Semitic languages (e.g., Arabic *ʾil-* and the Aramaic postpositive article, if from *hʾ* or the like).

In epistolary usage, the functions of *hn-* and *hl-* are distinct in that only the latter is used in a clearly local sense ('here' [cf. **28** RS 29.093:11]), whereas both function deictically ('behold'). This analysis of previously known texts is reinforced by the following unpublished examples in which *hl-* appears immediately before *hn-*: *hln hn ʿmn* /hallina hanna ʿimmānī/, 'here, behold with me . . .' (RS 92.2005:9 [RSO XIV 49]), *hlny hnn b bt mlk* /halliniya hannana bi bêti malki/, 'Here, behold in the house of the king . . .' (**32** RS 94.2479:5–6).

Rhetorical 'now' is expressed by a form of this deictic particle with affixed *-t* (see next section).

The deictic element *-d-* (← /-d̲/) was quite productive, functioning independently as a relative/determinative pronoun and enclitically as part of the demonstrative pronoun and adjective (see above on these two categories) and as an adverbial (see §4.1.3.5 below, at "Enclitic Particles," p. 60).

There are two vocative particles, *l* (e.g., *l rgmt lk l zbl bʿl* /la ragamtu lêka lê zabūli baʿli/ 'I hereby announce to you, Prince *Baʿlu*' [**1** RS 3.347 iv 7′–8′]) and *y* (e.g., *y mt mt* /yā muti muti/ 'O man, man' [**5** RS 2.002:40]). The former is likely a specific use of the preposition *l*.

4.1.3.2. Adverbs

As noted above (§4.1.1.6), adverbials may be expressed by adverbial lexemes or by adverbialization of a noun—that is, by prefixing a preposition, by use of the accusative case, or by suffixation of an adverbial morpheme.

Examples of adverbial particles: *hn* /hanna/, *hnn* /hannana/ and *hnny* /hannaniya/ 'here', *hl* /halli/, *hlh* /halliha/, *hlny* /halliniya/ 'here', *t̲m* /t̲amma/, *t̲mn /t̲ammāna/*, *t̲mny* /t̲ammāniya/ 'there', *ht* /hatti/ 'now' (probably *hn* + *-t*), and *ảp* /ʾapa/ 'also' (this particle functioned mostly at the level of the paragraph and is defined as an adverb rather than as a conjunction; it is very likely that it derives from the conjunction *p* with a prefixed /ʾ/). The vocalization of most of these forms is hypothetical, but that of *hlny* is indicated by {al-li-ni-ya} in a polygot vocabulary (Nougayrol 1968: text 138:5′).

Interrogative adverbs are *ỉy* /ʾêya/ 'how' (which consists of /ʾê/ [← /*ʾay/] + the enclitic particle *-ya*), *ản* /ʾana/ 'where?', *ỉk*(*y*) /ʾêka(ya)/ (← /ʾê/ [← /*ʾay/] + ka + ya) 'how (is it that?)', and *lm* (probably *l* 'to/for' + *m* 'what?') 'why?'. *ỉk* is often used as a rough equivalent of *lm*, e.g., *ỉk mǵy gpn w ủgr* 'how is it that *gpn-w-ủgr* have come?' (not: 'how have *gpn-w-ủgr* come?') (**2** RS 2.[014]⁺ iii:36′). The interrogative particles normally come at the head of the sentence. Judging from passages that are difficult to interpret if taken as declarative, it is likely that interrogation could also be indicated by voice inflection. (There is no interrogative particle in Ugaritic, like Hebrew *hă-*, which marks a following phrase as a question.)

Negative adverbs are *l* /lā/ (primarily indicative) and *ảl* /ʾal/ (primarily volitive). *ỉn* /ʾênu/ is, as in Hebrew, used primarily to negativize nominal phrases. *bl* /balû/ is rare, attested primarily in poetry and only with nouns.

The primary asseveratives and negatives were identical in writing but probably had different vocalizations: *l* = /lā/ 'not' and /la/ 'indeed' (Huehnergard 1983: 583–84); *ảl* = /ʾal/ 'must not' and /ʾallu/? 'must'.

Prepositional adverbialization is extremely common, e.g., *l* (preposition) + *ʿlm* /lê ʿālami/ (noun) = 'for a long time'.

The two most common adverbial suffixes attached to nouns are *-m* and *-h*. The first cannot be defined precisely, for it appears on virtually all parts of speech. One common occurrence is on adverbial nouns, perhaps only augmenting the adverbial accusative (e.g., *ṯm ḥrbm ỉts* /ṯamma ḥarbama ʾittasi/ 'There with the sword I will lay waste' [**1** RS 3.367 iv 4′]). The second corresponds to the locative/directive *hê* in Biblical Hebrew and is used both locally and temporally, e.g., *šmmh* /šamîmaha/ 'to the heavens', *ʿlmh* /ʿālamaha/ 'for a long time'. Note that, in contrast to Hebrew, where the *hê* is written without *mappīq*, the Ugaritic *-h* is consonantal. The vocalization of the particle is unknown, but it could be attached to the accusative/oblique forms of common nouns (/šamîmaha/ 'to the heavens') and to the uninflected form of proper nouns (/bibittaha/ 'at Bibitta' [**6** RS 24.244:31], /mariha/ 'to Mari', ibid., line ⟨34b⟩ = line 78). It should therefore be assumed that it contained a vocalic element after the /h/, as in the vocalization that we have proposed, for it may be doubted that the consonant /h/ was itself sufficient to express the notion of direction—this is most clearly the case for the cited proper nouns that do not bear a case-vowel.

4.1.3.3. Conjunctions

The most common coordinating conjunction is *w-* /wa/, capable of linking phrases at all levels (word, clause, sentence, paragraph). *p* /pa/ (cf. Arabic *fa*) occurs more rarely, usually with a notion of cause-and-effect linkage. (On the derived form *ảp*, see above, "Adverbs"). *ủ* functions both independently and correlatively (*ủ* . . . *ủ* 'either . . . or') and probably represents two lexemes: (1) /ʾū/ 'and' (e.g., *qrả ủ nqmd mlk* /quraʾa ʾū niqmaddu malku/ 'king *Niqmaddu* has been called as well' [**13** RS 34.126:12]); (2) /ʾô/ (← /*aw/) 'either/or' (see **9** RS 1.002 passim).

The most common subordinating conjunction is *k* /kī/ 'because, when, if' (comparable to Hebrew *kī*), expanded with *-y* /kīya/ and with *-m* /kīma/ (all with the same meaning), and rarely with *d* /kīdā/ (the same particle as the relative pronoun), with no appreciable change of meaning. Both *ỉm* (/ʾimma/) and *hm* (/himma/) are attested as conditional conjunctions ('if').

4.1.3.4. Prepositions

Ugaritic overlaps significantly with the other West Semitic languages in its prepositional system. Some of these are primitive particles (e.g., *b* /bi/, 'in'; *k* /ka/, 'like'; *l* /lê/ ← /lay(a)/, 'at'—for this explanation of the form, see Pardee 2003–4: 37–38, 371), others are derived from clearly identifiable verbal or nominal roots (e.g., *ʿl* /ʿalê/ ← /ʿalay(a)/ 'upon', *tḥt* /taḥta/ 'under', *ảḫr* /ʾaḫḫara/ 'after'), others are combinations of these two categories (e.g., *l* + *pn* /lê panî/ 'in front of'; *b* + *yd* /bi yadi/ or /bi yadê/ 'in the hand/control of';

b + *tk* /bi tôki/ 'in the midst of'). One also finds similarities in nuances and translation values (e.g., *b* = 'in, within, through, by the intermediary of, by the price of', etc.). The status of compound prepositions—that is, those formed of two primary prepositions—is as yet uncertain: the only example attested to date is *l* + *b*, apparently meaning something like 'within', though the identity of the first element is uncertain (Rainey 1973: 56; Freilich 1986).

The primary peculiarity of Ugaritic is the absence of a prepositional lexeme expressing the ablative 'from, away from'. This absence is compensated by a complex system of verb + preposition combinations, where the translation value of the preposition can only be determined by usage and by context (Pardee 1975, 1976, with a discussion of prepositional semantic ambiguity). The prepositional system as a whole appears to function primarily to denote position rather than direction, a stative notion rather than a motional one. Directionality and motion were supplied primarily by the verb. What this means in practice is that virtually any preposition may appear in expressions of the ablative, and the modern reader must depend on elements other than the preposition itself to reach a proper interpretation of a passage. The following passage is instructive, for it includes a preposition with "opposite meanings" in the expression of a 'from . . . to' situation, but along standard Ugaritic lines—that is, by means of different verb + preposition combinations (*yrd l* 'descend from', *yṯb l* 'sit upon'): *yrd l ksỉ yṯb l hdm w l hdm yṯb l ảrṣ* /yaridu lê kussaʾi yaṯibu lê hidāmi wa lê hidāmi yaṯibu lê ʾarṣi/ 'he descends from the throne, he sits upon the footstool, and (he descends) from the footstool, he sits upon the earth' [RS 2.[022]+ vi 12–14 = *CTA* 5]). This "ablative" usage may be clearly observed when the verb explicitly expresses directionality (e.g., *b ph rgm l yṣả* /bi pīhu rigmu lā yaṣaʾa/ 'hardly has the word left his mouth' = 'with respect to his mouth, the word had not left' [**1** RS 3.367 iv 6′]).

There are also certain functional differences between Ugaritic and the other Semitic languages (e.g., the increased use of *ʿm* /ʿimma/ 'with' to denote the end-point of a trajectory; *l* /lê/, used to form compound numbers) as well as different lexemes (e.g., *ẓr* /ẓûru/ 'back' → *l ẓr* /lê ẓûri/ 'on top of').

Substantives that follow a preposition are, insofar as we can tell, always in the genitive case (as in Akkadian, Arabic, etc.). For Ugaritic, this is demonstrated by nominal phrases that end in *alif*, e.g., *l ksỉ* /lê kussaʾi/ 'to the throne/chair'; *b nšỉ* /bi našāʾi/ 'when he arises'.

Because the case system remained in force, no particle developed in Ugaritic to introduce the direct object of a transitive verb (e.g., as *ʾyt* in Phoenician and in Old Aramaic, *ʾōt-* and *ʾet*/*ʾēt* in Hebrew, *yāt-* in Aramaic).

4.1.3.5. Enclitic Particles

Ugaritic makes use of a baroque array of enclitic particles (Aartun 1974, 1978), the disentanglement of which is made all the more difficult by the absence of vocalized texts. These particles are joined to all parts of speech and are capable of accretion one to another (e.g., *h+n+n+y*). Particles that apparently have little more than an "emphatic" function may develop a paradigmatic function alongside particles of more precisely definable origin (e.g., *hnd* 'this' = *h* [deictic particle] + *n* [particle] + *d* [relative/determinative pronoun] alongside *hnk* 'that' = *h* [deictic particle] + *n* [particle] + *k* [particle]).

The principal enclitic particles are:

• *-d* /dū/dī/dā/ = relative pronoun that can function as a compounding element with other particles (e.g., *hnd* /hannadū/ 'this') and can itself be expanded (e.g., the adverb *ỉd* /ʾida/ 'at this moment' [we indicate the final vowel as short since it has fallen off in Hebrew *ʾāz*], also attested as a multiplicative morpheme: in the Selection of Texts, one will encounter *ṯnỉd* /ṯinêʾida/ 'two times' and *šbʿỉd* /šabʿaʾida/ 'seven times', but more often *šbʿd* /šabʿida/, with the dropping of the case-vowel and the /ʾ/ because of the proximity of the latter to the /ʿ/).

• *-h* /-ha/ = afformative particle with an adverbial function (see immediately above).

• *-y* /-ya/ = enclitic particle attached to all forms of speech, particularly as expander to another particle (e.g., *hn+n+y*); it is frequently used after the vowels /i/ī/ê/ (e.g., *by* /biya/ 'in' [**26** RS 18.031:13, 25], *ky* /kīya/ 'that' [**24** RS 15.008:7], *ly* /lêya/ 'at' [**29** RS 34.124:5]), which has led some to believe that it was used as a *mater lectionis* (Tropper 2000: 37–38 [§21.322.5]), an analysis that is rendered doubtful by the presumed use of {y} as a *mater lectionis* for short /i/ and by the absence of other consonants used in this manner (in writing systems that employ *matres lectionis*, one also finds {w} for /ū/ô/ and often {h} and/or {ʾ} for various vowels); as with enclitic *-m*, this particle could be attached to nouns in the construct, as may be observed in the formula *ỉly ủgrt* /ʾilūya ʾugārit/ 'the gods of Ugarit' (**24** RS 15.008:4–5).

• *-k* /ka/ = enclitic particle, particularly as expander to another particle (e.g., *hnk* 'that' and *mhk*, *mhkm* 'anything').

• *-l* /li/ = enclitic particle, used especially in *hl*, *hln*, *hlny*.

• *-m* = enclitic particle attached to many particles and used on all parts of speech (see above, §4.1.1.6, p. 42, for occurrence with adverbials).

— attached to an independent pronoun (*ảnkm ỉlảk* /ʾanākuma ʾilʾaku/ 'I'll send a(nother) message' [**31** RS 94.2406:25]);

— attached to a pronominal suffix (*ʿmkm lỉkt* /ʿimmakama laʾiktu/ 'to you (m.s.) I have sent' [**33** RS 96.2039:21]);

— attached to a noun in the vocative (*bʿlm* /baʿlima/ 'O *Baʿlu*' [**1** RS 3.367 iv 9′]);

— attached to the first noun in a genitival construction (*yzbrnn zbrm gpn yṣmdnn ṣmdm gpn* /yazburanannu zābiruma gapna // yaṣmudanannu ṣāmiduma gapna/ 'the pruner of the vine prunes it, the binder of the vine binds it' [**5** RS 2.002:9–10]);

— attached to the second noun in a genitival construction (*mdd ỉlm* /môdada ʾilima/ 'the Beloved of *ʿIlu*' [**2** RS 2.[014] iii 43′]);

— attached to a noun that follows a first token of the noun in a list (*bʿl ṣpn ảlp w š bʿlm ảlp w š* /baʿli ṣapuni ʾalpu wa šû baʿlima ʾalpu wa šû/ 'for *Baʿlu* of *Ṣapāni* a bull and a ram; also for *Baʿlu* (no. 2) a bull and a ram' [**12** RS 24.643:2–3]);

— attached to a noun that is repeated to express the superlative (*bnš bnšm* /bunušu bunušuma / '(no) member of the (royal) personnel' [**37** RS 16.382:16]);

— attached to an imperative (*ảtm* /ʾatîma/ 'come' [**2** RS 2.[014] iii 28′]);

— attached to a /YQTL/ form (*tlkm rḥmy* /talikuma raḥmay/ 'off goes *Raḥmay*' [**5** RS 2.002:16]);

— attached to the infinitive (*lảkm ỉlảk* /laʾākuma ʾilʾaku/ 'I will certainly send (you a message)' [**25** RS 16.379:19–20]);

— attached to the other particles (e.g., *bm bkyh* /bima bakāyihu/ 'as he wept' [**3** RS 2.[003]:31]);

— this particle is found in many fixed expressions, such as *mrḥqtm* /marḥaqtama/ 'from afar' (an epistolary formula), *bn ỉlm mt* /binu ʾilima môtu/ '*Môtu*, son of *ʾIlu*' (title of the god *Môtu* in the mythological texts), *ybmt lỉmm* /yabamatu liʾmima/ 'sister-in-law of (the god) *Liʾimu*' (title of the goddess *ʿAnatu* in the mythological texts);

— see above concerning its attachment to nouns that function adverbially (§4.1.1.6, p. 42).

• *-n* /na/ni/ = enclitic particle used on all parts of speech. One particularly striking usage is the '*n* of apodosis' (Hoftijzer 1982); in certain omen texts characterized by a repetitive protasis-apodosis structure, the first word in the apodosis, if a singular noun in the absolute state, has enclitic *-n* (e.g., *w ʿnh b lṣbh mlkn yʿzz ʿl ḫpṯh* /wa ʿênāhu bi liṣbihu malkuna yaʿāzizu ʿalê ḫupṯihu/ 'and if its eyes are [in] the forehead, the king will become more powerful than his *ḫupṯu*-troops' [**20** RS 24.247+:57′]; Pardee 1986: 126, 129; Tropper 1994b: 466–69).

• *-t* /ti/ = enclitic particle, particularly as expander of another particle (e.g., *ht* ← *hn* + *t* with assimilation; *hn* + *d* + *t; hn* + *m* + *t*).

5. *Derivational Processes*

Because Ugaritic is a poorly attested, one-period language, it is hardly possible to describe synchronic derivational processes. Viewing the language comparatively, however, it appears clear that the known state of the language reflects a number of processes of this sort, for one can spot certain morphemes the function of which is best described as derivational.

Within categories, the generating of new particles by particle accretion is perhaps the clearest derivational process (better so termed than as compounding), though the semantics of the process are unclear in most cases.

Across categories, the nominal system, particularly the *m-* and *t-* prefixes and the *-n* suffix already described above, as well as certain *Ablaut* forms (e.g., /QaTTāL/ to express a *nomen professionis*) usually reflect a deverbal notion rather than an inner-nominal process. The suffixing of particles to nominal elements (e.g., *w mlk bʿly ydʿ* /wa malku baˁlî-ya yidaˁ/ 'The king, my master, must know this!' [**27** RS 18.040:18–19]), to the extent that these particles were not perceived by native speakers as lexical items, also represents a form of derivation.

Across subcategories, the case of the *nisbe* ending, by which nouns are transformed into adjectives, is the clearest case of a derivational morpheme.

6. Compounding

Compound verbs are virtually unknown in old West Semitic, and compound nouns are rare (the primary case cited for Ugaritic is *bl mt* /balû môti/, 'not death' used in parallel with *ḥym* /ḥayyūma/ 'life' in RS 2.[004] vi 27′ [*CTA* 17]). Complex prepositional phrases, made up of a preposition and a common noun, are certainly well attested (see above and the list and discussion in Pardee 1976: 306–10), but in most cases it is doubtful that the complex phrase had evolved as a lexical entity of which the compositional elements were no longer perceived. The example of *bdn* (*lqḥ kl d̠rʿ bdnhm* /laqaḥa kulla d̠arʿi bîdênahumu/ 'he removed the entire (cargo of) grain in their possession' [**26** RS 18.031:17–18]) may be cited to show that the expansion of *bd* by means of *n* indicates that the complex preposition (*b* + *d* [← *yd*]) was perceived as a lexical unit.

7. Syntax

The relative dearth of prose texts, mentioned in the introduction, makes it difficult to ascertain a normative prose syntax, while the lack of vocalized texts makes some aspects of morpho-syntax difficult to ascertain precisely.

7.1. Word Order

7.1.1. Nominal Constructions

On the phrase level, there are two primary nominal phrases: the genitival and the adjectival.

The genitival phrase is the common Semitic "construct state": X of Y (e.g., *mlk ḥwt* /malku ḥuwwati/ 'king of the land'). The first element is in the case required by context, the second in the genitive. It can denote the various relationships well known to grammarians (subjective genitive, objective genitive, genitive of identification, genitive of material, etc.). No lexical or pronominal element may intervene between the members of a construct chain—only enclitic particles (e.g., *ỉly ủgrt* /ʾilū-ya ʾugārit/ 'the gods of Ugarit' [**24** RS 15.008:4–5]).

The adjectival phrase is of two types: (1) the phrase-level or attributive, in which the adjective follows the noun and agrees in gender, number, and case; and (2) the sentence-level or predicative, in which the adjective may either precede or follow the noun and agrees in gender, number, and case (see above, §4.1.1.3, "Adjectives," p. 34). An attributive adjective modifying any member of a construct chain must come at the end of the chain (e.g., *ḥbr kṯr ṭbm* 'the companions of Kothar, the good ones' [RS 24.252:5; Virolleaud 1968: text 2]). Apparent attributive adjectives preceding the noun they modify are most frequently substantives in construct with the noun (*nʿmt šnt ỉl* /naʿīmāti šanāti ʾili/ 'the excellent ones of the years of El' = 'the most excellent years of El' [Virolleaud 1968: text 2, line 27]). The most-often-cited exception to this word-order rule is in ordinal numbers, which occur several times in poetry preceding the noun (for an explantion of these phrases in terms of standard morpho-syntactic categories, see above, §4.1.1.4, "Numbers," p. 35).

In nominal sentences, word order is essentially free, with fronting used for topicalization. Thus *hw mlk* (/huwa malku/) will denote 'he, not someone else, is king' (an "identifying" sentence), *mlk hw* (/malku huwa/) 'he is king, he is not something else' (a "classifying" sentence). Here is an example of the first construction: *ảt ảḫ* /ʾatta ʾaḫû/ 'you are a brother (to me)' (RS 3.340 i 24 = *CTA* 18). A clear example of the second construction comes from the Selection of Texts: *dbḥn ndbḥ hw ṯʿ nṯʿy hw* /dabḥuna nidbaḥu huwa ṯaʿû niṯʿayu huwa/ 'The sacrifice, it is sacrificed, the *ṯaʿû*-sacrifice, it is offered' (**9** RS 1.002: 23′–24′ and parallels from this text).

7.1.2. Verbal Phrases

In the simplest verbal phrase, consisting of verb + pronoun, the subject pronoun is part of the verbal form itself, suffixed in the perfective (QTLa) and prefixed in the imperfective (YQTL). The primary variation occurs through addition of an independent pronoun for "emphasis," creating a formal *casus pendens* (e.g., *ảtm bštm w ản šnt* /ʾattumā bāšātumā wa ʾanā šanîtu/ 'as for you, you may tarry, but as for me, I'm off' [RS 2.[014]⁺ iv 33 = *CTA* 3 iv 77]). The independent pronoun may precede or follow the verbal unit. The simple verbal phrase is by definition a sentence: SUBJECT + PREDICATE (imperfective) or PREDICATE + SUBJECT (perfective).

In verbal sentences, one finds fronting for topicalization as in, for example, *ybnn hlk ʿm mlk ảmr wybl hw mỉt ḫrṣ* /yabninu halaka ʿimma malki ʾamurri wa yabala huwa miʾta ḫurāṣi/ 'Yabninu (not someone else) went to the king of Amurru, and he took, did he, one hundred (pieces of) gold' (SUBJECT : VERB :: VERB : SUBJECT) (RS 34.124: 25–28 [Bordreuil and Pardee 1991: 148]).

According to one study, there is a strong tendency in poetry to place the object phrase close to the verb, either before it or after it (Wilson 1982: 26).

The verb is usually fronted in subordinate clauses where the subject is known (*ủmy tdʿ ky ʿrbt l pn špš* /ʾummiya tidaʿī kīya ʿarabtu lê panî šapši/ 'My mother, know that I have entered before the "Sun"' [**24** RS 15.008: 6–8]).

The word order subject – verb – direct object – modifier is regular in the first clause of apodoses in texts of the omen and hippiatric genres (the basic structure of sentences in both genres is protasis-apodosis). This order cannot be proved to be the result of influence from another language (Pardee 1986: 128–29) and probably reflects, therefore, systematized topicalization (Tropper 1994b: 469–71), though the general absence of *w* of apodosis and the presence of *-n* of apodosis in these texts must be included in an explanation of the phenomenon.

On the basis of present evidence, therefore, it is impossible to say that Ugaritic is a primarily VSO language (namely, if verb – subject – direct object was normative) though, as in Biblical Hebrew, this is certainly the case in subordinate clauses.

7.1.3. Phrases in the Administrative Texts

In the administrative texts, including the ritual texts but not the letters, one encounters many brief nominal phrases that can be understood only in light of the sense of the whole passage. For example, in the ritual texts, offerings for divinities were expressed by a nominal phrase that may contain the preposition *l* (*š l ỉl* /šû lê ʾili/ 'a ram for *ʾIlu*' [**8** RS 1.001:2]) or that may consist of nonprepositional formulas that do not show a fixed order (*gdlt ỉlhm ṯkmn w šnm dqt ršp dqt šrp* /gadulatu ʾilāhīma ṯukamuni wa šunami daqqatu rašap daqqatu šurpu/ 'A cow for the *ʾIlāhūma*; for *Ṯukamuna-wa-Šunama* a ewe; for

Rašap a ewe as a burnt offering' [**8** RS 1.001:3–4]—the sense of these words is established from the formulas in the preceding and following context; in the translations in the Selection of Texts, we put in brackets the words that have been added to make the English translation comprehensible).

In the economic texts, where verbal phrases are rare, a wide range of expressions is attested, from true verbal phrases to the simplest of nominal phrases with no expression of the function of a given entry or of an entire text:

- *l ytn ksphm* /la yatanū kaspahumu/ 'they have indeed given their sum' (**52** RIH 83/22:4): true verbal phrase;
- *yn d ykl* /yênu dū yiklû/ 'wine which is to be consumed' (**41** RS 19.015:1): nominal phrase that incorporates a verbal phrase in a relative clause;
- *ṯṯ mảt ksp ḥṯbn ybnn* /ṯiṯṯu miʾāti kaspu ḥiṯbānu yabnini/ 'Six hundred (shekels) of silver: the *Yabninu* account' (**42** RS 15.062:1–2): nominal phrase used as title for the following text;
- *tgmr ksp ṯlṯ mảt* /tagmaru kaspi ṯalāṯu miʾāti/ 'total silver: three hundred (shekels)' (**43** RS 18.024:28); nominal sentence used as conclusion for the text that precedes;
- *bn glʿd—5* /binu galʿadi ḫamišu/ '*Binu-Galʿadi*: five' (**46** RS 94.2050+:1): a nominal phrase as individual entry in a text; the relationship between the proper name and the number is deduced from the continuation of this text and its comparison with another (RS 94.2064 [unpublished]).

7.2. Coordinate and Subordinate Clauses

Coordination is indicated most commonly by *w-* /wa/; by *p-* /pa/ when effect is expressed (see §4.1.3.3). Asyndeton (i.e., the association of words or phrases without linking particles) is fairly frequent at the sentence (and paragraph) level, common at the phrase level (e.g., *l pʿn ảdtny mrḥqtm qlny ỉlm tǵrk tšlmk* /lê paʿnê ʾadattināyā marḥaqtama qālānāyā ʾilūma taǵǵurūki tašallimūki/ 'At the feet of our lady (from) afar we fall. May the gods guard you, may they keep you well' [**22** RS 8.315:5–9]).

The principal types of subordinate clauses are (1) relative, (2) conditional, and (3) a variety of temporal/circumstantial, causal, resultative, and completative (object) clauses most commonly introduced by *k* /kī/ when lexically marked (the conjunction is written both {k} and {ky}).

The whole concept of "subordinate" clause is rendered murky by the frequent use of the so-called *w* (or more rarely *p*) of apodosis—that is, heading the main clause with *w* or *p* when it follows the "subordinate" clause. The details have not been worked out for Ugaritic, and the state of the corpus renders a comprehensive view difficult; points of similarity with Biblical Hebrew indicate that the overall situation in Ugaritic may not have been dissimilar (cf. Gross 1987). For example, the epistolary formula of well-being often has the *w* of apodosis (*ṯmny ʿm ủmy mnm šlm w rgm ṯṯb ly* /ṯammāniya ʿimma ʾummiya mannama šalāmu wa rigma ṯaṯībī layya/ 'there with my mother, whatever is well, send word (of that) back to me' [**23** RS 11.872:11–13]), but it is sometimes omitted (*ṯmny ʿm ảdtny mnm šlm rgm ṯṯb l ʿbdk* /ṯammāniya ʿimma ʾadattināyā mannama šalāmu rigma ṯaṯībī lê ʿabdêki/ 'there with our lady, whatever is well, return word of that to your servants' [**22** RS 8.315:14–18]).

Explicit relative clauses are preceded by *d*/*dt* (e.g., *ỉl d ydʿnn yʿdb lḥm lh* /ʾilu dū yidaʿannannu yaʿdubu laḥma lêhu/ 'Any god who knows him gives him food' [**7** RS 24.258:6–7]; *l pn ỉl mṣrm dt tǵrn npš špš mlk* /lê panī ʾilī miṣrêma dūti taǵǵurūna napša šapši malki/ 'before the gods of Egypt, that they might protect him' [RS 16.078+:21–23 = Virolleaud 1957: text 18]). Relative adverbials are usually marked (e.g., *ảdrm d b grn* /ʾadurīma dī bi gurni/ 'the leaders who are at the threshing floor' [RS 2.[004] v 7′ = *CTA* 17]).

Unmarked relative verbal clauses are difficult to spot because the notion of person is marked in the verb and SUBJECT is by definition included in both verbs. An example upon which there is general agreement is *yd mḫṣt ảqht ǵzr tmḫṣ ảlpm ỉb* /yadu miḫḫaṣat ʾaqhata ǵazra timḫaṣu ʾalapīma ʾêbi/ 'the hand (that) struck Hero Aqhat will strike the enemy by thousands' (RS 3.322 iv 58–59 [*CTA* 19: 220–21]).

The relative pronoun functions at both the phrase level (*ỉl d pỉd* /ʾilu dū piʾdi/ 'god of mercy' [RS 2.[008] ii 10 = *CTA* 4, etc.]) and at the sentence level (subject: *ỉl . . . d yšr* /ʾilu . . . dū yašīru/ 'the god . . . who sings' [RS 24.252: 2–3 = Virolleaud 1968: text 2]; object: *skn d šʿlyt ṯryl* /sikkannu dū šaʿliyat ṯarriyelli/ 'sacred stone which Ṯarriyelli offered' [**14** RS 6.021:1–2]; adverbial: *ảnḫ ǵzr mt hrnmy d ỉn bn lh* /ʾanāḫa ǵazri muti harnamiyyi dī ʾênu binu lêhu/ 'the groaning one, the Harnamite man to whom there is no son = who has no son' [**4** RS 2.[004] i 17′–18′]). Note the relative genitive construction *ḥry . . . d k nʿm ʿnt nʿmh* /ḥurray . . . dā ka nuʿmi ʿanati nuʿmuha/ 'Ḥurraya . . . who like the beauty of *ʿAnatu* is her beauty = whose beauty is like *ʿAnatu*'s' (RS 2.[003] vi 24–27 = *CTA* 14: 289–92).

The relative pronoun either may have an explicit antecedent, as in the examples just cited, or be used "absolutely" (*p d ỉn b bty ttn* /pa dū ʾênu bi bêtiya tatin/ 'for what is not in my house shall you give' [RS 2.[003]+ iii 38 = *CTA* 14:142]).

The conjunction *k*(*y*) does not function as a relative particle (see the epistolary formula *lḥt* X *k*[*y*], below).

Conditions may be marked by *hm* or (less frequently) *ỉm* and tend to precede the main clause. Conditional clauses may be unmarked. A lexical distinction between real and irreal conditions is as yet unknown. The main clause following the conditional clause may or may not be preceded by the so-called *w* or *p* of apodosis. An example of each conjunction: *hm ymt w ỉlḥmn ảnk* /himma yamūtu wa ʾillaḥiman(na) ʾanāku/ 'if he should die, I will go on fighting on my own' (RIH 78/12: 19–22 [Bordreuil and Caquot 1980: 359–60; Pardee 1984a: 222]); *ỉm ht l b mṣqt yṯbt qrt p mn lỉkt ảnk lḥt bt mlk ảmr* /ʾimma hatti lê bi maṣūqati yāṯibatu qarîtu pa manna laʾiktu ʾanāku lūḥata bitti malki ʾamurri/ 'so if the city remains undecided, then for what reason did I send a letter regarding the daughter of the king of Amurru?' (**29** RS 34.124:20–24 [Bordreuil and Pardee 1991: 147]). In texts whose structure indicates that the clauses are of the same general type as the conditional phrase, the condition is introduced by *k* (e.g., *k ygʿr s̀s̀w št ʿqrbn ydk* /kī yigʿaru s̀ūs̀awu šūta ʿuqrubāni yadūku/ 'if the horse has a bad cough, one should bray a ŠT(-measure) of "scorpion-plant" ' [**19** RS 17.120:2–3]).

Temporal/circumstantial phrases may be expressed as a true clause—that is, conjunction + finite verb (*k tdbr* /kīya tadabbiru/ 'concerning the fact that she is to speak' [**29** RS 34.124:18]), or as a prepositional phrase consisting of preposition + infinitive (*b šảl* /bi šaʾāli/ 'in (his) asking' = 'when he asks' [**3** RS 2.[003]⁺ i 38]). In poetry, these constructions are found parallel to one another: *ảḫd ydh b škrn mʿmsh k šbʿ yn* /ʾāḫidu yadahu bi šikkarāni muʿammisuhu kī šabiʿa yêna/ 'someone to take his hand when (he is) drunk, to bear him up when (he is) full of wine' (**4** RS 2.[004] i 30′–31′)—the *-n* indicates that *škrn* is a verbal noun but not an infinitive.

Causal and resultative clauses are not nearly so frequent as in Biblical Hebrew. Causal clauses, particularly, are often difficult to distinguish from temporal/circumstantial clauses. A reasonably clear example of each: *tšmḫ . . . ảṯrt . . . k mt ảlỉyn bʿl* /tišmaḫ . . . ʾaṯiratu . . . kī mīta ʾalʾiyānu baʿlu/ 'may *ʾAṯiratu* rejoice because Mighty *Baʿlu* is dead' (RS 2.[009]⁺ i 39–42 [*CTA* 6]); *w yd ỉlm p k mtm ʿz mỉd* /wa yadu ʾilima pā kī môtuma ʿazzu maʾda/ 'pestilence is (at work) here, for death is very strong' (**21** RS 4.475:11–13). In the formula *mn*! *krt k ybky ydmʿ nʿmn ǵlm ỉl* /mīna kirta kī yabkiyu yidmaʿu naʿmānu ǵalmu ʾili/ 'Who/what is Kirta that he should weep? Should shed tears, the goodly lad of *ʾIlu*?' (**3** RS 2.[003]⁺ i 38–41), the particle *k* introduces a condition implied by the question: 'Is Kirta that type of person who weeps?'

k(*y*) is the principal marker of completive (object) clauses (i.e., it functions as the verbal equivalent of a direct object): *w dʿ k yṣảt ảp mlkt* /wa daʿ kī yaṣaʾat ʾapa malkatu/ 'You must recognize that the queen also has left' (**31** RS 94.2406:38). As in other Semitic languages, one finds cases where some verbs take two types of complements, verbal and nominal: *tp ảḫh k nʿm ảḫh k ysmsm* /tippa ʾaḫâhu kī naʿīmu ʾaḫâhu kī yasumsumu/ 'she sees her brother, (sees) that he is good, (sees) her brother, (sees) that he is handsome' (RS 22.225:2–3 [Virolleaud 1960: 182–84]). A similar construction is also found without *k*: *yʿn ḥtkh krt yʿn ḥtkh rš mỉd grdš ṯbth* /yaʿīnu ḥatkahu kirta yaʿīnu ḥatkahu rušša maʾda gurdaša ṯibtahu/ 'Kirta sees his family, he sees his family crushed, his dwelling utterly destroyed'; that is, 'Kirta saw his family (and in doing so, saw that his family was) crushed, (he saw that his dwelling was) utterly destroyed' (**3** RS 2.[003]⁺ i 21–23).

A particularly common word order in letters is a construction in which a *casus pendens* is followed by a subordinate clause marked by *k*(*y*), with the main clause coming only after these two clauses (for this structural interpretation, see Pardee 1977: 7–8, where the analysis of *k*(*y*) as a relative pronoun is refuted). One encounters a fairly simple example in an otherwise badly damaged text: *lḥt šlm k lỉkt ủmy ʿmy ht ʿmny kll šlm* /lūḥata šalāmi kī laʾikat ʾummîya ʿimmaya hatti ʿimmānîya kalīlu šalima/ 'as for the letter of greeting, as for the fact that my mother sent [it] to me, behold with me everything is fine' (RS 17.139:5–7 [Virolleaud 1965: text 9]). A more complicated example is found in our selection of texts: *w lḥt bt mlk ảmr ky tdbr ủmy l pn qrt ỉm ht l b mṣqt yṯbt qrt p mn lỉkt ảnk lḥt bt mlk ảmr* /wa lūḥatu bitti malki ʾamurri kīya tadabbiru ʾummîya lê panî qarîti ʾimma hatti lê bi maṣūqati yāṯibatu qarîtu pa manna laʾiktu ʾanāku lūḥata bitti malki ʾamurri/ 'Concerning my mother's (= your) upcoming presentation to the city(-council) of the correspondence relative to the daughter of the king of Amurru: if the city remains undecided, then why have I sent letters (to them) on the topic of the daughter of the king of Amurru?' (**29** RS 34.124:17–24). The structure of this phrase may be delineated in the following way:

w lḥt bt mlk ảmr: a *casus pendens* stating the general subject of what will follow, 'correspondence relative to the daughter of the king of Amurru'
ky tdbr ủmy l pn qrt: a subordinate clause expressing what is known about the subject that has just been introduced
ỉm ht l b mṣqt yṯbt qrt: the comment in the form of a conditional clause, here the protasis expressing the complexity of the situation
p mn lỉkt ảnk lḥt bt mlk ảmr: the apodosis of the conditional clause conveying the frustration of the writer on account of this condition.

7.3. Agreement

Personal pronouns agree in person, gender, and number with an appositional verbal form (*ảnk ảḥwy* /ʾanāku ʾaḥawwiyu/ 'I give life' [RS 2.[004] vi 32′ = *CTA* 17]); in gender, number, and case with an appositional or predicate noun (*ảt ủmy*, /ʾatti ʾummiya/ 'you, my mother' [**25** RS 16.379:20–21]; *ảt ảḫ* /ʾatta ʾaḫû/ 'you are a brother (for me)' [RS 3.340 i 24 = *CTA* 18]) and with predicate adjectives (*dbḥn ndbḥ hw* /dabḥuna nidbaḥu huwa/ 'the sacrifice [-*n* of apodosis], sacrificed is it' [*ndbḥ* = N-stem participle] [*CTA* 40:9]).

The adjective agrees in gender, number, and case with the modified noun:

- m.s.: *by gšm ảdr* /biya gišmi ʾaduri/ 'in a powerful storm' (**26** RS 18.031:13–14);
- f.s.: *dblt yṯnt . . . yṣq* /dabilata yaṯanata . . . yaṣuqu/ 'an aged bunch of figs . . . ⟨one should bray⟩ (and) pour' (**19** RS 17.120:31–32);
- m.du.: *ỉqrả ỉlm nʿmm* /ʾiqraʾa ʾilêma naʿīmêma/ 'I would call on the gracious gods' (**5** RS 2.002:1);

- f.du.: *špthm mtqtm* /šapatāhumā matuqatāma/ 'their lips are sweet' (**5** RS 2.002:50);
- m.pl.: *qrủ rpỉm qdmym* /qaraʾū rapaʾīma qadmiyyīma/ 'they have called the ancient *Rapaʾūma*' (**13** RS 34.126:8);
- f.pl.: *ảrbʿ ủzm mrảt* /ʾarbaʿu ʾūzūma marīʾātu/ 'four fattened geese' (RS 16.399:21 [Virolleaud 1957: text 128]).

Demonstrative pronouns agree in gender and number with the antecedent, while demonstrative adjectives agree in gender, number, and case with the modified noun.

Demonstrative pronoun:

- f.s. *ảnykn dt lỉkt mṣrm hndt b ṣr mtt* /ʾanayyukana dāti laʾikta miṣrêma hannadāti bi ṣurri mêtatu/ 'your ships that you dispatched to Egypt have wrecked off Tyre' (**26** RS 18.031:10–13);
- absolute usage (no explicit antecedent): *w mlk bʿly ht lm škn hnk l ʿbdh* /wa malku baʿlîya hatti lêma šakkana hannaka lê ʿabdihu/ 'Now (as for) the king, my master, why has he assigned this (responsibility) to his servant . . . ? (RS 16.402:22–24 [Virolleaud 1957: text 12]).

Demonstrative adjective (*hnd*):

- m.s. nom.: *w mspr hnd hwm* /wa masparu hannadū huwama/ 'now this document, it . . .' (RS 92.2016:41′ [RSO XIV 53]);
- m.s. acc.: *hlny ảnk b ym k ytnt spr hnd ʿmk* /halliniya ʾanāku bi yammi kī yatanātu sipra hannadā ʿimmaka/ 'I was on the sea when I gave this document (to be delivered) to you' (**31** RS 94.2406:3–5);
- m.s. gen.: *l ym hnd ʿmṯtmr . . . ytn* /lê yômi hannadī ʿammiṯtamru yatana/ 'On this day *ʿAmmiṯtamru* . . . has given' (**37** RS 16.382:1–4);
- m.pl. nom.: *tmǵyy hn ảlpm s̀s̀wm hnd* /tamǵiyūya huna ʾalpāma s̀ūs̀awūma hannadū/ 'those 2,000 horses must arrive here' (RS 16.402:31–32 [Virolleaud 1957: text 12]).
- there are no examples for the feminine form.

Demonstrative adjective (*hw/hy*):

- adj. m.s. nom.: *ht hn bnš hw b gty ḫbṯ* /hatti hanna bunušu huwa bi gittiya ḫabaṯa/ 'that servant worked on my farm' (**33** RS 96.2039:8–9);
- adj. m.s. obl.: *b ym hwt ảnk b mlwm* /bi yômi huwata ʾanāku bi MLWM/ 'today I lodged at MLWM . . .' (**31** RS 94.2406:5–6);
- There are no examples of the feminine adjective in the nominative;
- adj. f.s. obl.: *ỉlm tbʿrn ḥwt hyt* /ʾilūma tabaʿʿirūna ḥuwwata hiyati/ 'the gods will destroy that land' (**20** RS 24.247⁺:56);
- this use of corresponding plural pronouns is not yet attested.

The relative pronoun agrees in gender and number with its antecedent, though whether the case of the relative pronoun itself is decided by the case of the antecedent or by the function of the relative pronoun in the following clause cannot yet be determined from internal data—in Arabic, case agreement is decided as for any adjective, i.e., by agreement with the antecedent. Assuming this to be the case in Ugaritic, the passage *bt mlk ỉtdb d šbʿ ảḫm lh* should be vocalized /bêtu malki ʾîtabida! dī šabʿu ʾaḫḫīma lêhu/ if *malki* was the antecedent ('the house of the king perished, who had seven brothers'), but /bêtu malki ʾîtabida! dū šabʿu ʾaḫḫīma lêhu/ if *bêtu* was the antecedent ('the house of the king perished, which had seven brothers') (**3** RS 2.[003]+ i 7–9).

Interrogatives and indefinite pronouns do not show agreement.

8. Vocabulary/Lexicon

8.1. Common Nouns and Verbs

Ugaritic fits the common Semitic and common West Semitic pattern in kinship terms (*ảb* /ʾabû/ 'father', *ủm* /ʾummu/ 'mother', etc.), tree names (*ảrz* /ʾarzu/ 'cedar', etc.), geographical terms (*nhr* /naharu/ 'river', etc.), with some notable peculiarities, e.g., *ḥwt* /ḥuwwatu/ 'land (geographical-political entity)' alongside *ảrṣ* /ʾarṣu/ 'earth, ground' and *bld* /bilādu/ 'homeland', or *ảdn* /ʾadānu/, which in prose means 'father' (not 'master/lord').

When deciphering a Ugaritic text, one finds points of lexical contact with all of the Semitic languages. Because of the small number of texts, the image of the Ugaritic scholar deciphering a text on the basis of various Semitic dictionaries is not totally false, though with the increase in number of reasonably well-understood texts, inner-Ugaritic lexicography is becoming more practicable. The apparent heterogeneity of the Ugaritic lexicon may be explained in two ways: (1) the archaic nature of the language (cognates with other Semitic languages will thus be largely with retentions in those languages); (2) the relatively poor corpus of texts in the languages with which Ugaritic appears most closely related linguistically—if Hebrew and Phoenician were attested more extensively, there would be fewer isoglosses between Arabic and Ugaritic.

The principal motion verbs are useful language/dialect isoglosses (e.g., for all the similarities between Hebrew and Aramaic, the systems of motion verbs are quite different in the two languages). Here Ugaritic falls directly in the Hebrew/Phoenician group: *hlk* 'go', *yrd* 'descend', *ʿly* 'ascend', *bʾ* 'enter' (alongside *ʿrb*), *yṣʾ* 'exit', *ṯb* 'return'. Some verbs of movement that can also denote the state attained are: *qm* 'arise', *škb* 'lie down', *ʿmd* 'stand', *rkb* 'mount'.

Primary motion verbs peculiar to Ugaritic are the following: *tbʿ* 'go away', *mǵy* 'go to, arrive at' (apparently ← MẒY), and *ql* Št-stem (or *šql*, Gt-stem) used only in poetry, in the imperfective, *yštql* 'he arrives'.

Expressions of existence resemble most closely the later Northwest Semitic pattern: there are positive and negative quasi-verbs, *ỉṯ* and *ỉn*, respectively, corresponding, e.g., to Hebrew *yēš* and *ʾayin*/*ʾēʸn*, as well as the verb *kn* (*nʿmn ykn* /nuʿmānu yakūnu/ 'there will be prosperity' [RIH 78/14:3; Bordreuil and Caquot 1980: 352–53]), which corresponds to the regular verb 'to be' in Phoenician (and Arabic) and to the more strongly marked verb 'to be stable' in Hebrew.

In spite of the cosmopolitan nature of the city of Ugarit, there are relatively few readily identifiable loanwords: *ḥṯṯ* /ḥattuṯu/ 'silver' is an apparent example from Hittite, *kḥṯ* /kaḫṯu/ 'chair, throne' an example from Hurrian. More words of non–West Semitic origin are found in the economic vocabulary, e.g., *sbrdn* /sabardennu/ 'bronze worker' (**43** RS 18.024:1), plausibly a loanword from Hurrian; the first element of the word appears to correspond to the Sumerian

ZABAR or to the Akkadian *siparru* 'bronze', and the second to the Hurrian suffix *tn/dn* 'maker'.

8.2. Onomastics

8.2.1. Personal Names

Since the Kingdom of Ugarit was open to the world of its day, names of many different origins are found, including Ugaritic (these being defined by the status of the language as it is known from the end of the Late Bronze Age), old Amorite, Hurrian, and Anatolian. Less frequently attested are Canaanite, Akkadian, and Egyptian names. Gröndahl (1967) provided an excellent treatment of the onomastics of Ugarit, but it needs to be redone to include the new names and to incorporate the advances of the past half-century in the knowledge of the various languages that are attested.

A proper name may only be vocalized according to the same principles employed for other vocabulary: the presence of one of the three /ʾ/-signs, attestations in syllabic writing, or comparative Semitics. This enterprise is, however, complicated by the diverse origins of these names. One expects, for example, the consonantal orthography of most Ugaritic, Canaanite, or old Amorite names to be identical, and only attestation in syllabic writing will reveal a vocalized form for any given name. It is necessary, therefore, always to consider the matter carefully before proposing a vocalization for a name attested only in consonantal orthography. Some examples of the difficulties that one may encounter:

• The name *kṯrm* is attested for the first time in RS 2002.3000.01:11 (unpublished). It is known that many names begin with {kṯr}, e.g., *kṯrmlk* or *kṯrn*. The only vocalization of the element *kṯr* known from syllabic writing is for the god *Kôṯaru*, e.g., {ARAD-ku?-ša-ri} (RS 20.007:9 [Nougayrol 1968: text 98]) or {[DUMU]-ku-ša-ri[. . .]} (RS 17.242:20 [Nougayrol 1970: text 82], where what followed the theophoric element is lost). From the entry for *kṯrmlk*, its form is probably /kôṯarumalku/ '(the god) *Kôṯaru* is king'. But without a vocalized form, it is impossible to know if *kṯrn* is an abridged form of a name of this type or if it is formed on an entirely different pattern—nominal, adjectival, or verbal. The same applies to the new name, *kṯrm*.

• Sometimes one consonantal orthography represents two different names: for example, the name *ʿzỉlt* is first attested in RS 92.2005:4 (RSO XIV 49), and it is only the mention of this person's father that allows him to be to identified with the person whose name is written {a-zi-il-tù} /ʿazziʾiltu/ '(this child represents) the strength of the goddess' (i.e., 'that which is strong and belongs to the goddess') (RS 34.134:18 [RSO VII 31]) rather than with the person whose name was spelled syllabically {uz-zi-DINGIR-ti} /ʿuzzîʾiltu/ 'my force is the goddess' (RS 34.133:2 [RSO VII 36]).

• Sometimes it is impossible to know the origin of a name if the vocalic structure is unknown; for example, *pdn* could be West Semitic or Anatolian.

• There are examples of names attested in two very different forms: the royal name Ammistamru is attested in Ugaritic in the form *ʿmṯtmr*, which corresponds to *ʿAmmistamru* in syllabic writing (with several attested spellings: Nougayrol 1955: 239); but, on the personal seal of this king, the name appears in Ugaritic in the form {ʿmyḏtmr} (Bordreuil and Pardee 1984). Undoubtedly, the latter reflects the name in its historical form (/ʿammîyiḏtamar/ 'my (divine) uncle protects [me]'). This name thus illustrates two stages in the evolution of the old Amorite form of the name *ʿmyḏtmr*; *ʿmṯtmr* was the result of two phonetic evolutions: /-iyî-/ → /-î-/ and devoicing of /ḏ/ in proximity to /t/. The question remains how King *ʿAmmiṯtamru*, who lived in the middle of the 13th century B.C., knew the ancient form of his name and why he chose to put this form on his seal.

Four aspects of personal names are particularly important for understanding their structure:

(1) According to the syllabic representations of Ugaritic personal names and according to the data from Northwest Semitic languages of the 1st millennium B.C., it is known that an /i/ vowel often separated the two elements of personal names: e.g., /ʿabdibaʿlu/ 'servant of (the god) *Baʿlu*' or /ʾilîmilku/ '(the god) *Milku* is my god'. The second example illustrates that this vowel can express the 1st-person-singular pronominal suffix; but this cannot be the case in the first example—this name cannot mean 'my servant is (the god) *Baʿlu*'—and this vowel therefore must serve to connect the two elements of the name (Layton 1990: 107–54). For Ugaritic, the quantity of the vowel that connects the two elements of personal names (and does not represent the pronominal suffix) is not known but, as a convention and so that the user of our vocalizations can distinguish it from the pronominal suffix, we have indicated it as /i/.

(2) The data currently available preclude the possibility of determining when and how case endings were attached to proper names. Ugaritic personal names often do, however, bear a case-vowel that properly corresponds to the grammatical function of the name in the sentence and not necessarily to the internal structure of the name itself (e.g., *ʿbdrpủ* /ʿabdirapaʾu/ 'servant of [the god] *Rapaʾu*' [**44** RS 19.016:33], where the nominative case-vowel expected in this context is used, rather than the genitive that the internal structure of the name requires; Gröndahl 1967: 33–34).

(3) Liverani's thesis (1963) that names with a final syllable containing a long vowel show a diptotic inflection relies mainly on syllabic writings of proper names. Although scribal practices at Ugarit are not completely uniform in this respect, it seems fair to assess the length of the penultimate vowel

according to the case system used for the name: e.g., {gln} (**49** RIH 84/04:25) will be /gallānu/ because one finds {gal-la-na} in the genitive in RS 17.430 iv 10 (Nougayrol 1970: text 83).

(4) Last, it should be noted that there are many foreign names of which the form is invariable.

8.2.2. Divine Names

Religious exclusivism was probably not present at Ugarit. Divinities from every corner of the world as it was known at the time are attested there. The forms of these names obviously reveal their place and language of origin, but the exact form by which these names were known and used at Ugarit remains uncertain. Some divine names appear in the polyglot vocabularies with a nominative case ending (e.g., *Šapšu* in RS 20.123+ IVa 31 {ša-ap-šu} [Nougayrol 1968: text 137]), whereas others are only known in syllabic writing (in personal names of the pattern 'servant of theophoric element') in the absolute form, namely, without a final vowel: e.g., *Dagan* (RS 16.273:4 {am-mi-ni-da-ga-an} [Nougayrol 1955: 44–45]). The vocalization of the theophoric element may be complicated or made impossible by the fact that divine names are rarely written syllabically in the Akkadian texts, most often with logograms (e.g., *Šapšu* is written with the Sumerogram {UTU}, which means 'sun', preceded by the sign indicating 'divinity', {DINGIR}). In certain cases it can be determined from the Ugaritic form that the theophoric element bears the case ending, e.g., {hd} must be /haddu/ because the absolute form would be /hadad/ and would be written {hdd}. The convention that we use to vocalize these elements is as follows: if the divine name is attested for one or the other of these forms, absolute or with case ending, we reproduce it; if not, we indicate the case-vowel (e.g., {yrḫ}, which is attested only in the syllabic texts in logographic form, is vocalized *Yariḫu*). This convention is based on the fact that the Ugaritic divine names that appear in the polyglot vocabularies (which are unfortunately very few) always carry the nominative ending.

8.3. Toponomy

Toponyms present a different sort of problem. They often occur in the Akkadian administrative texts, where they are generally written syllabically rather than logographically, and the phonetic structure of many of these names is thus well known. On the other hand, as van Soldt has shown (1996: 653–54), several names in Ugaritic that end with either {-y} or {-∅} are represented in the Akkadian texts sometimes with final /-â/ and sometimes with /-āy + case-vowel/ (e.g., {ḫpty} and {ḫbt [= ḫpt!]} would correspond to {ḫu-pa-ta-ú} and {ḫu-pa-ta}, the first reflecting /ḫupatāyu/, the second /ḫupatâ/ or /ḫubatâ/). Van Soldt's thesis is based, however, on a limited number of examples, in which the syllabic orthography formally establishes the presence of the case-vowel, and one wonders whether orthographic variation in Ugaritic always corresponds to this grammatical explanation or whether the {y} may not constitute a historical spelling (the ending of these names in an earlier period would have been /-āyu/ but would have become /-â/ in 13th-century pronunciation).

As with personal names (see previous section), place-names with a long vowel in the penultimate syllable tend to be inflected diptotically. Thus, the river name *Raḫbānu* is attested with both /-i/ and /-a/ when the noun is in the genitive (van Soldt 1996: 685); the name in all likelihood consists of the base form /raḥb-/ 'wide', to which the derivational ending /-ān/ has been attached. On the other hand, the vowel in the penultimate syllable of the town name *ʾUškanu* was probably short because /-i/ is well attested as the genitive ending (van Soldt 1996: 662); this name is not, therefore, derived from /ʾušk-/ 'testicle', which would in any event be a rather strange point of departure for a place-name, but is based on the root ŠKN 'settle', to which prothetic /ʾ/ has been attached.

The name of the city of Ugarit poses a particular problem. According to the etymology that is typically cited, it is based on the common noun /ʾugār-/ 'field', to which the suffix /-īt-/ was been added. Van Soldt (1996: 657 n. 21), however, has observed that the syllabic spelling of the gentilic form of this toponym ({u-ga-ar-ti-yu} in RS 19.042:15 [Nougayrol 1970: text 79]) suggests the vocalization /ʾugartiyyu/, where the vowel between the /r/ and the /t/ has elided. Since long vowels are not prone to disappear by syncope, van Soldt (followed by Tropper 1997: 670) concluded that this vowel was short. These two scholars do not, however, agree on the vocalization of the second vowel: Tropper thinks that it was short because this syllable was closed in the gentilic form, whereas van Soldt (1999: 775) believes this vowel was long in the toponym but secondarily shortened in the gentilic form (or even maintained in its long form). The etymology cited by a Ugaritic scribe indicates /ʾugāru/ 'field' as the basis of the name ({A.GÀR-ít} in RS 16.162:23 [Nougayrol 1955: 126], which means 'the field + {ít}'), and neither van Soldt nor Tropper has proposed a different etymology for the name. However, it is known that toponyms can reflect a linguistic layer that precedes the Amorite period, which may be the case for Ugarit as well. But the presence of /ʾ/ in this name and the etymology indicated by RS 16.162:23 suggest that, for the Ugaritians (whatever the true origin of the name may have been), it was a noun associated with the word /ʾugāru/ and it was pronounced (regardless of the original pronunciation) by Ugaritians according to the current pronunciation of this word. Since a morpheme /-it-/ is not known in West Semitic, it is likely that the noun was historically /ʾugārīt-/ (with a dash instead of the case-vowel to leave that question open for a moment). The syllabic spelling of the name in the 14th and 13th centuries indicates that the typical form was in the "absolute" case—that is, without a case-vowel: one finds only a very few instances where a vowel follows the /t/, (twice /i/, once /e/, and twice /a/; see van Soldt 1996: 657). Since Ugaritic did not tolerate long vowels in closed syllables, the pronunciation of this "absolute" form would have been /ʾugārit/, and the pronunciation of the gentilic, after syncope of the short /i/, would have been /ʾugartiyyu/ with short /a/ in the secondarily closed syllable.

9. Particularities of Poetic Texts

To appreciate the poetry that appears in the Selection of Texts, the user of this manual should keep in mind three principal characteristics of the language of these texts that distinguish it from Ugaritic prose.

(1) The morpho-syntax of the verb in poetry is peculiar in that the old perfective /YQTLØ/ has largely disappeared as a form marked for perfectivity, and it is either replaced by /YQTLu/ or used in free variation with /YQTLu/ forms. These forms are thus used in a manner comparable to the use of the "historical present" in tensed languages and in constant interplay with /QTLa/ perfective forms (for some of the rules of the game, see Greenstein 2006). We propose grammatical analyses for the forms where the consonantal orthography is ambiguous, but these are often hypothetical and the presently available data do not allow them to be corroborated or to be contradicted. It also appears likely that the jussive of the 1st person (*ảšṣỉ* /ʾašôṣiʾ/ 'I will certainly cause to leave') and the /YQTLa/ volitive in the 2nd and 3rd persons is distinctive of poetry, but the data are insufficient to define the use of these forms with precision.

(2) The basic structure of Ugaritic poetry resembles that of Biblical Hebrew; namely, it is not metric but founded on the parallelism of lexical and syntactic elements organized into groups of two or more statements (called bicola and tricola or distichs and tristichs). Some examples of these processes:

(a) **1** RS 3.367 iv 5′ (bicolon):

Text	*Translation*	*Semantic Parallelism*	*Syntactic Parallelism*
l ảrṣ ypl ủlny	The powerful one will fall to the earth,	a b c	A V S
w l ʿpr ʿẓmny	the mighty one to the dust.	a′ c′	A S

The sigla "a" and "a′" designate common nouns with a similar meaning, "b" the verb that is not paralleled in the second colon, and "c" and "c′" the two substantival adjectives that also have approximately the same meaning.

A = adverbial locution (*l ảrṣ // l ʿpr*), V = verb, S = subject.

(b) **1** RS 3.367 iv 8′–9′ (tricolon):

Text	*Translation*	*Semantic Parallelism*	*Syntactic Parallelism*
ht ỉbk bʿlm	As for your enemy, O *Baʿlu*,	a b c	I O S^{voc}
ht ỉbk tmḫṣ .	as for your enemy, you'll smite (him),	a b d	I O V
ht tṣmt ṣrtk	you'll destroy your adversary.	a d′ b′	I V O

The combination of repetitive parallelism here (a = a = a and b = b), of semantic parallelism (b ≅ b′ and d ≅ d′), and the organization of these last two elements in chiasm are noteworthy. This form of tricolon is called a "staircase" because of its particular structure: repetitive parallelism at the beginning of the first two cola, a vocative or another form of the subject in the first colon (replaced here by the verb in the second colon), and semantic parallelism between the second and third cola (Greenstein 1977).

The syntactic analysis stresses the importance of the particle *ht* in the verse (I = interjection).

(c) **2** RS 2.[014]$^+$ = iii 19′–25′ (a larger structure composed of a bicolon and a tricolon):

Text	*Translation*	*Semantic Parallelism*	*Syntactic Parallelism*
Bicolon:			
dm rgm iṯ ly w ảrgmk	For I have something to tell you,	a b a	S P+A V
hwt w ảṯnyk	a matter to recount to you:	a′ a″	S V
Tricolon:			
rgm ʿṣ w lḫšt ảbn	Words regarding wood, whisperings regarding stones,	a b a′ b′	S² S²
tảnt šmm ʿm ảrṣ	conversations of heaven with earth,	a″ c d	S² A
thmt ʿmn kbkbm	of the deep with the stars.	d′ c′	S A

This analysis of the parallelism of this passage reflects the presence of two well-delimited verses—even if they are syntactically dependent ("enjambment"); this is demonstrated by the fact that the first element b expresses possession, while the second expresses one of the two elements that this subject comprises. It should be noted that the structure of these two verses is much more complicated than either of the first two examples. Comparing the two parallel structures demonstrates that the poet intended to use a limited semantic range but avoided monotony by varying the morpho-syntactic structures and by means of interplay of the semantically parallel terms within these structures. Particularly noteworthy are:

- the complicated interplay of nouns and verbs that follow the first *rgm* (a noun and verb from the root RGM in the first colon ["internal parallelism" of words derived from the same root], semantic parallelism of the noun and the verb in the second, repetition of the noun at the beginning of the second verse, followed by two semantic parallels);

- the interplay of the terms designating parts of the cosmos in the second verse (*ʿṣ* and *ảbn* in one colon ["internal semantic parallelism"]; *šmm* closer to *kbkbm* than to the other two terms in spite of the existence of a divinity *ảrṣ w šmm* [**12** RS 24.643:5, 24]). The syntactic analysis reveals three levels of structure in these verses: the presence of a nominal predicator of existence (P) along with a verb in the first colon of the first verse, the significant number of subjects that consist of two elements in the second verse, and the interplay of subjects and adverbial formulae that diversify the already sophisticated use of semantic parallelism.

(d) **3** RS 2.[003]⁺ i 12–21 (a larger structure consisting of several substructures, all bicola except the last):

Text	*Translation*	*Semantic Parallelism*	*Syntactic Parallelism*
Bicolon:			
ảṯṯ ṣdqh l ypq	His rightful wife he does not obtain,	a b c	O^2 V
mtrḫt yšrh	even his legitimate spouse.	a′ b′	O^2
Bicolon:			
ảṯṯ trḫ w tbʿt	A(nother) woman he marries but she disappears,	a b c	O V V
ṯảr ủm tkn lh	even the kinswoman who was to be his.	a'^2 d	O^2 V
Bicolon:			
mṯlṯt kṯrm tmt	A third spouse dies in good health,	a b c	S A V
mrbʿt ẓblnm	a fourth in illness.	a′ b′ (≠b$^{!}$)	S A
Tricolon:			
mḫmšt yỉtsp ršp	A fifth *Rašap* gathers in,	a b c	O V S
mṯdṯt ǵlm ym	a sixth the lad(s) of Yammu,	a′ c'^2	O S^2
mšbʿthn b šlḥ ttpl	the seventh of them falls by the sword.	a″ d e	S A V

The identification of this longer structure is based on the series of participles formed from denominal verbs from number nouns (*mṯlṯt* ← *ṯlṯ* 'three'), which take their contextual meaning from *mtrḫt* 'she who is given in marriage' at the beginning of the structure. As in the preceding example, the analysis of parallelism starts over for each verse, but the verses are all related to one another at the semantic level by the words designating 'the wife' and the participles that refer back to this feminine noun.

(3) The third characteristic is to be identified at the lexical level, and a link with the phenomenon of parallelism is often apparent. Indeed, to create a lexicon according to usage in prose or poetry would show that words may appear:

- in one or the other of these (e.g., *yštql* 'arrive' is attested only in poetry, whereas the root ḤLL 'to be clear, clean, to glitter' is presently attested only in prose),
- most commonly in only one of these forms of discourse (for example, *ḥwt* 'country' is frequent in prose but only attested once in poetry),
- regularly in both (e.g., *mǵy* 'to arrive'). Moreover, it is not uncommon for a word only attested in poetry to occur in parallel with a better-known term but in second position (e.g., *brlt* following *npš* in **4** RS 2.[004]+ I 36′–37′ or *yštql* following *mǵy* in **6** RS 24.244:67–68). In poetry, parallelism can help to determine the meaning of obscure terms (e.g., the etymology of *brlt* is unknown, but its general meaning is clear on account of its parallelism with *npš* 'throat, neck, etc.'). On the other hand, because prosaic speech makes only infrequent use of parallelism, one must generally do without this aid when interpreting the vocabulary of prose texts.

Abbreviations and Sigla

Abbreviations:

Parts of speech: pron[oun], [common] noun, adj[ective]; conj[unction], prep[osition]
Grammatical person: 1, 2, 3
Grammatical gender: m[asculine], f[eminine], c[ommon gender]
Grammatical number: s[ingular], du[al], pl[ural]
Grammatical case: n[ominative], a[ccusative], g[enitive], obl[ique]
Grammatical state: abs[olute], con[struct]
Verbal stems: G, Gp[assive], Gt; N; D Dp[assive], tD; Š, Šp[assive]; L, Lt; R, Rt
Verbal forms: imper[ative], inf[initive], part[icipal], pf. = perfect; impf. = imperfect

Sigla:

[x]	=	completely restored
[-]	=	number of restorable sign(s)
[. . .]	=	restoration of unknown length
[ ]	=	lacuna of known length but for which the number of signs may not be estimated
⸢x⸣	=	damaged sign of which the epigraphic reading is uncertain but of which the contextual reading is likely or even certain; sign of which the reading is uncertain for some reason other than damage
⸢-⸣	=	unidentifiable trace(s) of writing
-	=	erased sign (text); unknown vowel (vocalized text)
. . . . . .	=	lacuna of a line or more
⟨ x ⟩	=	scribal omission
⟨⟨ x ⟩⟩	=	scribal error
{x}	=	reading
/x/	=	phonetic transcription
x!	=	corrected reading

Works Cited and Bibliographical Abbreviations

Aartun, K.

1974 *Die Partikeln des Ugaritischen. 1. Teil.* Alter Orient und Altes Testament 21/1. Kevelaer: Butzon & Bercker / Neukirchen-Vluyn: Neukirchener Verlag.

1978 *Die Partikeln des Ugaritischen. 2. Teil.* Alter Orient und Altes Testament 21/2. Kevelaer: Butzon & Bercker / Neukirchen-Vluyn: Neukirchener Verlag.

Albright, W. F.

1931–32 "The Syro-Mesopotamian God Šulmân-Ešmûn and Related Figures." *Archiv für Orientforschung* 7: 164–69.

André-Salvini, B., and M. Salvini

1998 "Un nouveau vocabulaire trilingue sumérien-akkadien-hourrite de Ras Shamra." Pp. 3–40 (photos 32–40) in D. I. Owen and G. Wilhelm, eds., *General Studies and Excavations at Nuzi* 10/2. Studies on the Civilization and Culture of Nuzi and the Hurrians 9. Bethesda, Maryland: CDL.

1999a "A New Trilingual Vocabulary from Ras Shamra and the Relationship between Hurrian and Urartian." Pp. 267–75 in D. I. Owen and G. Wilhelm, eds., *Nuzi at Seventy-Five.* Studies on the Civilization and Culture of Nuzi and the Hurrians 10. Bethesda, Maryland: CDL.

1999b "Additions and Corrections to *SCCNH* 9 3–40." Pp. 434–35 in D. I. Owen and G. Wilhelm, eds., *Nuzi at Seventy-Five.* Studies on the Civilization and Culture of Nuzi and the Hurrians 10. Bethesda, Maryland: CDL.

1999c "Le vocabulaire trilingue." *Le Monde de la Bible* 120: 52.

2000 "Le liste lessicali e i vocabolari plurilingui di Ugarit: Una chiave per l'interpretazione della lingua hurrica." *La parola del passato* 55: 321–48.

Arnaud, D.

1998 "Prolégomènes à la rédaction d'une histoire d'Ougarit II: Les bordereaux de rois divinisés." *Studi Micenei ed Egeo-Anatolici* 41: 153–73.

Blau, J.

1972 "Marginalia Semitica II." *Israel Oriental Studies* 2: 57–82.

1977 "'Weak' Phonetic Change and the Hebrew *śîn*." *Hebrew Annual Review* 1: 67–119.

Bordreuil, P.

1979 "L'inscription phénicienne de Sarafand en cunéiformes alphabétiques." *Ugarit-Forschungen* 11: 63–68.

1981 "Cunéiformes alphabétiques non canoniques. I) La tablette alphabétique sénestroverse RS 22.03." *Syria* 58: 301–11.

1982 "Quatre documents en cunéiformes alphabétiques mal connus ou inédits (*U.H.* 138, *RS* 23.492, *RS* 34.356, *Musée d'Alep M.* 3601)." *Semitica* 32: 5–14.

1984 "Arrou Ǵourou et Ṣapanou: Circonscriptions administratives et géographie mythique du royaume d'Ougarit." *Syria* 61: 1–10.

1990 "Recherches ougaritiques I: Où Baal a-t-il remporté la victoire contre Yam?" *Semitica* 40: 17–28.

1995 "Les tablettes alphabétiques de Ras Shamra et de Ras Ibn Hani (1986–1992)." Pp. 1–5 in M. Dietrich and O. Loretz, eds., *Ugarit: Ein ostmediterranes Kulturzentrum im Alten Orient. Ergebnisse und Perspektiven der Forschung. Band I: Ugarit und seine altorientalische Umwelt.* Abhandlungen zur Literatur Alt-Syrien-Palästinas 7. Münster: Ugarit-Verlag.

1998 "Le premier mot de l'herminette découverte à Ras Shamra en 1929: outil ou personnage?" Pp. 127–32 in M. Dietrich and I. Kottsieper, eds., *Und Mose schrieb dieses Lied auf. Studien zum Alten Testament und zum Alten Orient: Festschrift für Oswald Loretz zur Vollendung seines 70. Lebensjahres mit Beiträgen von Freunde, Schülern und Kollegen.* Alter Orient und Altes Testament 250. Münster: Ugarit-Verlag.

1999 "L'armée d'Ougarit au XIIIe siècle: Pour quoi faire?" Pp. 33–40 in L. Nehmé, ed., *Guerre et conquête dans le Proche-Orient ancien.* Antiquités sémitiques 4. Paris: Maisonneuve.

Bordreuil, P., ed.

1991 *Une bibliothèque au sud de la ville (Quartier "Sud-Centre"): Les textes de la 34e campagne (1973). Deuxième partie: Les textes ougaritiques.* Ras Shamra–Ougarit VII. Paris: Éditions Recherche sur les Civilisations.

Bordreuil, P., A. Bounni, E. Lagarce, J. Lagarce, and N. Saliby

1984 "Les découvertes archéologiques et épigraphiques de Ras Ibn Hani (Syrie) en 1983: Un lot d'archives administratives." *Académie des Inscriptions et Belles-Lettres, Comptes Rendus*: 398–438.

1987 "Les dixième et onzième campagnes de fouilles (1984 et 1986) à Ras Ibn Hani (Syrie)." *Académie des Inscriptions et Belles-Lettres, Comptes Rendus*: 274–301.

Bordreuil, P., and A. Caquot

1980 "Les textes en cunéiformes alphabétiques découverts en 1978 à Ibn Hani." *Syria* 57: 343–73.

Bordreuil, P., R. Hawley, and D. Pardee

forthcoming "Lettres." *Les textes ougaritiques des campagnes de 1994 à 2002.* Paris: Éditions Recherche sur les Civilisations.

Bordreuil, P., and D. Pardee

1982 "Le rituel funéraire ougaritique RS. 34.126." *Syria* 59: 121–28.

1984 "Le sceau nominal de *ʿAmmīyiḏtamrou*, roi d'Ougarit." *Syria* 61: 11–14.

1987 "Le sceau en cunéiformes alphabétiques RS 7.088 (= AO 18.576)." *Syria* 64: 309–10.

1989 *La trouvaille épigraphique de l'Ougarit.* 1: *Concordance.* Ras Shamra–Ougarit 5/1. Paris: Éditions Recherche sur les Civilisations.

1991 "Les textes ougaritiques." Pp. 139–72, 199, 208 in Bordreuil, ed., 1991.

1993a "Le combat de *Baʿlu* avec *Yammu* d'après les textes ougaritiques." *MARI* 7: 63–70.

1993b "Textes ougaritiques oubliés et 'transfuges.'" *Semitica* 41–42: 23–58.

1995a "L'épigraphie ougaritique: 1973–1993." Pp. 27–32 in M. Yon, M. Sznycer, P. Bordreuil, eds., *Le pays d'Ougarit autour de 1200 av. J.-C.* Ras Shamra–Ougarit 11. Paris: Éditions Recherche sur les Civilisations.

1995b "Un abécédaire du type sud-sémitique découvert en 1988 dans les fouilles archéologiques françaises de Ras Shamra–Ougarit." *Académie des Inscriptions et Belles-Lettres, Comptes Rendus*: 855–60.

2001 "Textes alphabétiques en ougaritique." Pp. 341–92, 411–14, in M. Yon and D. Arnaud, eds., 2001.

forthcoming *Les textes ougaritiques des campagnes de 1994 à 2002.* Paris: Éditions Recherche sur les Civilisations.

Bounni, A., E. Lagarce, and J. Lagarce

1998 *Ras Ibn Hani, I: Le palais nord du Bronze récent, fouilles 1979–1995, synthèse préliminaire.* Bibliothèque Archéologique et Historique 151. Beirut: Institut Français d'Archéologie du Proche-Orient.

Caquot, A.

1978 "La lettre de la reine Puduḫepa." Pp. 121–34 in *Ugaritica VII.* Mission de Ras Shamra 18. Bibliothèque Archéologique et Historique 99. Paris: Mission Archéologique de Ras Shamra and Geuthner.

1989 "Textes religieux." Pp. 17–123 in Caquot, de Tarragon, and Cunchillos 1989.

Caquot, A., and A.-S. Dalix

2001 "Un texte mythico-magique." Pp. 393–405 in M. Yon and D. Arnaud, eds., 2001.

Caquot, A., M. Sznycer, and A. Herdner

1974 *Textes ougaritiques.* Tome I: *Mythes et légendes.* Littératures Anciennes du Proche-Orient 7. Paris: Cerf.

Caquot, A., J.-M. de Tarragon, and J.-L. Cunchillos

1989 *Textes ougaritiques.* Tome II: *Textes religieux, rituels, correspondance.* Littératures Anciennes du Proche-Orient 14. Paris: Cerf.

CAT = Dietrich, M., O. Loretz, and J. Sanmartín 1995

Cohen, C.

1996 "The Ugaritic Hippiatric Texts: Revised Composite Text, Translation and Commentary." *Ugarit-Forschungen* 28: 105–53.

Contenson, H. de

1992 *Préhistoire de Ras Shamra: Les sondages stratigraphiques de 1955 à 1976.* Ras Shamra–Ougarit 8/1–2. Paris: Éditions Recherche sur les Civilisations.

Courtois, J.

1990 "Yabninu et le palais sud d'Ougarit." *Syria* 67: 103–42.

CTA = Herdner 1963

Cunchillos, J.-L

1989 "Correspondance." Pp. 239–421 in Caquot, de Tarragon, and Cunchillos, 1989.

Cunchillos, J.-L., and J.-P. Vita

1993 *Banco de datos filológicos Semíticos Noroccidentales. Primera Parte: Datos Ugaríticos. I. Textos Ugaríticos.* Madrid: Instituto de Filología.

1995 *Banco de datos filológicos Semíticos Noroccidentales. Primera Parte: Datos Ugaríticos. II/1–3. Concordancia de palabras Ugaríticas en morfología desplegada.* Madrid: Instituto de Filología.

Dalix, A.-S.

1997a *Iloumilkou, scribe d'Ougarit au XIIIe siècle avant J.C.* Thèse Institut Catholique de Paris and Université de Paris IV.

1997b "Ougarit au XIIIe siècle av. J.-C.: Nouvelles perspectives historiques." *Académie des Inscriptions et Belles-Lettres, Comptes Rendus*: 819–24.

1998 "Šuppiluliuma (II?) dans un texte alphabétique d'Ugarit et la date d'apparition de l'alphabet cunéiforme: Nouvelle proposition de datation des 'Archives Ouest.'" *Semitica* 48: 5–15.

Day, P.

2002 "*Dies diem docet*: The Decipherment of Ugaritic." *Studi epigrafici et linguistici* 19: 37–57.

Dhorme, E.

1933 "Deux tablettes de Ras-Shamra de la campagne de 1932." *Syria* 14: 229–37.

1938 "Nouvelle lettre d'Ugarit en écriture alphabétique." *Syria* 19: 142–46.

Dietrich, M., and O. Loretz

1978 "Die keilalphabetische Krugaufschrift RS 25.318." Pp. 147–48 in *Ugaritica VII.* Mission de Ras Shamra 18. Bibliothèque Archéologique et Historique 99. Paris: Mission Archéologique de Ras Shamra and Geuthner.

1988 *Die Keilalphabete: Die phönizisch-kanaanäischen und altarabischen Alphabete in Ugarit.* Abhandlungen zur Literatur Alt-Syrien-Palästinas 1. Münster: Ugarit-Verlag.

1997 "Mythen und Epen in ugaritischer Sprache." *Texte aus der Umwelt des Alten Testaments*, vol. 3. Gütersloh: Gütersloher Verlagshaus.

2000 *Studien zu den ugaritischen Texten I: Mythos und Ritual in KTU 1.12, 1.24, 1.96, 1.100, 1.114.* Alter Orient und Altes Testament 269/1. Münster: Ugarit-Verlag.

Dietrich, M., O. Loretz, and J. Sanmartín

1976 *Die keilalphabetischen Texte aus Ugarit einschließlich der keilalphabetischen Texte außerhalb Ugarits*, Teil 1: *Transkription.* Alter Orient und Altes Testament 24/1. Kevelaer: Butzon & Bercker / Neukirchen-Vluyn: Neukirchener Verlag.

1995 *The Cuneiform Alphabetic Texts from Ugarit, Ras Ibn Hani and Other Places (KTU: Second, Enlarged Edition).* Abhandlungen zur Literatur Alt-Syrien-Palästinas und Mesopotamiens 8. Münster: Ugarit-Verlag.

Dussaud, R.

1935 "Deux stèles de Ras Shamra portant une dédicace au dieu Dagan." *Syria* 16: 177–80.

EA = text from el-Amarna

Ellison, J. L.

2002 *A Paleographic Study of the Alphabetic Cuneiform Texts from Ras Shamra/Ugarit.* Ph.D. diss., Harvard University, Cambridge, MA.

Fenton, T. L.

1970 "The Absence of a Verbal Formation **yaqattal* from Ugaritic and North-West Semitic." *Journal of Semitic Studies* 15: 31–41.

Ford, J. N.

2002a "The New Ugaritic Incantation against Sorcery RS 1992.2014." *Ugarit-Forschungen* 34: 119–52.

2002b "The Ugaritic Incantation against Sorcery RIH 78/20 (KTU² 1.169)." *Ugarit-Forschungen* 34: 153–211.

Freilich, D.

1986 "Is There an Ugaritic Deity *Bbt*?" *Journal of Semitic Studies* 31: 119–30.

Freilich, D., and D. Pardee

1984 "{ẓ} and {ṭ} in Ugaritic: A Re-examination of the Sign-Forms." *Syria* 61: 25–36.

Freu, J.

2006 *Histoire politique du royaume d'Ugarit.* Collection Kubaba, Série Antiquité. Paris: L'Harmattan.

Friedman, R. E.

1979–80 "The *mrzḥ* Tablet from Ugarit." *Maarav* 2: 187–206, pls. 1–12.

Ginsberg, H. L.

1950 "Ugaritic Myths, Epics, and Legends." Pp. 129–55 in J. B. Pritchard, ed., *Ancient Near Eastern Texts Relating to the Old Testament.* Princeton: Princeton University Press.

Gordon, C. H.

1965 *Ugaritic Textbook: Grammar, Texts in Transliteration, Cuneiform Selections, Glossary, Indices.* Analecta Orientalia 38. Rome: Pontifical Biblical Institute.

Greenstein, E. L.

1976 "A Phoenician Inscription in Ugaritic Script?" *Journal of the Ancient Near Eastern Society of Columbia University* 8: 49–57.

1977 "One More Step on the Staircase." *Ugarit-Forschungen* 9: 77–86.

1997 "Kirta." Pp. 9–48 in Parker, ed., 1997.

2006 "Forms and Functions of the Finite Verb in Ugaritic Narrative Verse." Pp. 75–101 in S. E. Fassberg and A. Hurvitz, eds., *Biblical Hebrew in Its Northwest Semitic Setting: Typological and Historical Perspectives.* Jerusalem: Magnes / Winona Lake, IN: Eisenbrauns.

Gröndahl, F.

1967 *Die Personennamen der Texte aus Ugarit.* Studia Pohl 1. Rome: Pontifical Biblical Institute.

Gross, W.

1987 *Die Pendenskonstruktion im Biblischen Hebräisch.* Arbeiten zu Text und Sprache im Alten Testament 22. St. Ottilien: EOS.

Hallo, W. W., and K. L. Younger, eds.
1997 *The Context of Scripture*. Vol. I: *Canonical Compositions from the Biblical World*. Leiden: Brill.
2002 *The Context of Scripture*. Vol. III: *Archival Documents from the Biblical World*. Leiden: Brill.

Hawley, R., and D. Pardee
2002–7 "Le texte juridique RS 16.382: Nouvelle étude épigraphique." *Semitica* 52–53: 15–35.

Herdner, A.
1963 *Corpus des tablettes en cunéiformes alphabétiques découvertes à Ras Shamra–Ugarit de 1929 à 1939*. Mission de Ras Shamra 10. Bibliothèque Archéologique et Historique 79. Paris: Imprimerie Nationale / Geuthner.
1978a "Nouveaux textes alphabétiques de Ras Shamra: XXIVe campagne, 1961." Pp. 1–74 in *Ugaritica VII*. Mission de Ras Shamra 18. Bibliothèque Archéologique et Historique 99. Paris: Mission Archéologique de Ras Shamra and Geuthner.
1978b "Lettre de deux serviteurs à leur maître." Pp. 75–78 in *Ugaritica VII*. Mission de Ras Shamra 18. Bibliothèque Archéologique et Historique 99. Paris: Mission Archéologique de Ras Shamra and Geuthner.

Hoftijzer, J.
1979 "Une lettre du roi de Tyr." *Ugarit-Forschungen* 11: 383–88.
1982 "Quodlibet Ugariticum." Pp. 121–27 in G. van Driel et al., eds., *Zikir Šumim: Assyriological Studies Presented to F. R. Kraus on the Occasion of His Seventieth Birthday*. Nederlands Instituut voor het Nabije Oosten, Studia Francisci Scholten Memoriae Dicata 5. Leiden: Brill.

Huehnergard, J.
1983 "Asseverative **la* and Hypothetical **lu/law* in Semitic." *Journal of the American Oriental Society* 103: 569–93.
1986 "A Dt Stem in Ugaritic?" *Ugarit-Forschungen* 17: 402.
1987 *Ugaritic Vocabulary in Syllabic Transcription*. Harvard Semitic Studies 32. Atlanta: Scholars Press. Rev. ed.: Winona Lake, IN: Eisenbrauns, 2008.
1992 "Historical Phonology and the Hebrew Piel." Pp. 209–29 in W. R. Bodine, ed., *Linguistics and Biblical Hebrew*. Winona Lake, IN: Eisenbrauns.
1997 "Notes on Ras Shamra–Ougarit VII." *Syria* 74: 213–20.

Izre'el, S., and I. Singer
1990 *The General's Letter from Ugarit: A Linguistic and Historical Reevaluation of RS 20.33 (Ugaritica V, no. 20)*. Tel Aviv: Tel Aviv University.

KTU = Dietrich, Loretz, and Sanmartín 1976

Lackenbacher, S.
2002 *Textes akkadiens d'Ugarit: Textes provenant des vingt-cinq premières campagnes*. Littératures Anciennes du Proche-Orient 20. Paris: Cerf.

Lam, J.
2006 "The Hurrian Section of the Ugaritic Ritual Text RS 24.643 (KTU 1.148)." *Ugarit-Forschungen* 38: 399–414.

Langhe, R. de
1945 *Les textes de Ras Shamra–Ugarit et leurs rapports avec le milieu biblique de l'Ancien Testament*. Universitas Catholica Lovaniensis, Dissertationes

ad gradum magistri in Facultate Theologica vel in Facultate Iuris Canonici consequendum conscriptae, Series II, Tomus 35. Gembloux: Duculot; Paris: Desclée de Brouwer.

Layton, S. C.
1990 *Archaic Features of Canaanite Personal Names in the Hebrew Bible.* Harvard Semitic Monographs 47. Atlanta: Scholars Press.

Lewis, T. J.
1997a "The Birth of the Gracious Gods." Pp. 205–14 in Parker, ed., 1997.
1997b "El's Divine Feast." Pp. 193–96 in Parker, ed., 1997.

Liverani, M.
1963 "Antecedenti del diptotismo arabo nei testi accadici di Ugarit." *Rivista degli Studi Orientali* 38: 131–60.
1964 "Elementi innovativi nell'ugaritico non letterario." *Atti della Accademia Nazionale dei Lincei, Rendiconti della Classe di Scienze morali, storiche e filologiche* 8/19: 173–91.
1979 "Ras Shamra: Histoire." Cols. 1295–1348 in vol. 9 of *Supplément au dictionnaire de la Bible.* Paris: Loutouzey & Ané.

Loundine, A. G.
1987 "L'abécédaire de Beth Shemesh." *Le Muséon* 100: 243–50.

Mallon, E. D.
1982 *The Ugaritic Verb in the Letters and Administrative Documents.* Ph.D. dissertation, The Catholic University of America.

Merrill, E. H.
1974 "The Aphel Causative: Does It Exist in Ugaritic?" *Journal of Northwest Semitic Languages* 3: 40–49.

Miller, P. D., Jr.
1971 "The *mrzḥ* Text." Pp. 37–49 in L. R. Fisher, ed., *The Claremont Ras Shamra Tablets.* Analecta Orientalia 48. Rome: Pontifical Biblical Institute.

Moran, W. L., with the collaboration of V. Haas and G. Wilhelm
1987 *Les lettres d'el-Amarna: Correspondance diplomatique du pharaon.* Translated by D. Collon and H. Cazelles. Littératures Anciennes du Proche-Orient 13. Paris: Cerf.
1992 *The Amarna Letters Edited and Translated.* Baltimore: Johns Hopkins University Press.

Nougayrol, J.
1955 *Le palais royal d'Ugarit III: Textes accadiens et hourrites des archives est, ouest et centrales.* Mission de Ras Shamra 6. Paris: Imprimerie Nationale / Klincksieck.
1956 *Le Palais Royal d'Ugarit IV: Textes accadiens des archives sud (Archives internationales).* Mission de Ras Shamra 9. Paris: Imprimerie Nationale / Klincksieck.
1968 "Textes suméro-accadiens des archives et bibliothèques privées d'Ugarit." Pp. 1–446 in J.-C. Courtois, ed., *Ugaritica V.* Bibliothèque Archéologique et Historique 80. Mission de Ras Shamra 16. Paris: Imprimerie Nationale.

1970 *Le palais royal d'Ugarit VI: Textes en cunéiformes babyloniens des archives du Grand Palais et du Palais Sud d'Ugarit.* Mission de Ras Shamra 12. Paris: Imprimerie Nationale / Klincksieck.

Olmo Lete, G. del

1999 *Canaanite Religion according to the Liturgical Texts of Ugarit.* Translated by W. G. E. Watson. Bethesda, Maryland: CDL.

Pardee, D.

1975 "The Preposition in Ugaritic." *Ugarit-Forschungen* 7: 329–78.

1976 "The Preposition in Ugaritic." *Ugarit-Forschungen* 8: 215–322, 483–93.

1977 "A New Ugaritic Letter." *Bibliotheca Orientalis* 34: 3–20.

1983–84 "The Letter of Puduḫepa: The Text." *Archiv für Orientforschung* 29–30: 321–29.

1984a "Further Studies in Ugaritic Epistolography." *Archiv für Orientforschung* 31: 213–30.

1984b "Three Ugaritic Tablet Joins." *Journal of Near Eastern Studies* 43: 239–45.

1985 *Les textes hippiatriques.* Ras Shamra–Ougarit II. Paris: Editions Recherche sur les Civilisations.

1986 "The Ugaritic *šumma izbu* Text." *Archiv für Orientforschung* 33: 117–47.

1987 "'As Strong as Death'." Pp. 65–69 in J. H. Marks and R. M. Good, eds., *Love and Death in the Ancient Near East: Essays in Honor of Marvin H. Pope.* Guilford, CT: Four Quarters.

1988 *Les textes para-mythologiques de la 24ᵉ campagne (1961).* Ras Shamra–Ougarit IV. Paris: Editions Recherche sur les Civilisations.

1993a Review. *Journal of Near Eastern Studies* 52: 313–14.

1993b Review. *Journal of Near Eastern Studies* 52: 314–17.

1995 Review. *Journal of Near Eastern Studies* 54: 64–66.

1996 "L'ougaritique et le hourrite dans les textes rituels de Ras Shamra—Ougarit." Pp. 63–80 in F. Briquel-Chatonnet, ed., *Mosaïque de langues, mosaïque culturelle. Le bilinguisme dans le Proche-Orient ancien: Actes de la Table-Ronde du 18 novembre 1995 organisée par l'URA 1062 "Études Sémitiques."* Antiquités Sémitiques 1. Paris: Maisonneuve.

1997a "The Baʿlu Myth." Pp. 241–74 in Hallo and Younger, eds., 1997.

1997b "Dawn and Dusk: The Birth of the Gracious and Beautiful Gods." Pp. 274–83 in Hallo and Younger, eds., 1997.

1997c "Ugaritic Prayer for a City under Siege (RS 24.266)." Pp. 283–85 in Hallo and Younger, eds., 1997.

1997d "Ugaritic Birth Omens (RS 24.247⁺, RS 24.302)." Pp. 287–89 in Hallo and Younger, eds., 1997.

1997e "Ugaritic Liturgy against Venomous Reptiles (RS 24.244)." Pp. 295–98 in Hallo and Younger, eds., 1997.

1997f "ʾIlu on a Toot (RS 24.258)." Pp. 302–5 in Hallo and Younger, eds., 1997.

1997g "A Ugaritic Incantation against Serpents and Sorcerers (1992.2014)." Pp. 327–28 in Hallo and Younger, eds., 1997.

1997h "The Kirta Epic." Pp. 333–43 in Hallo and Younger, eds., 1997.

1997i "The ʾAqhatu Legend." Pp. 343–56 in Hallo and Younger, eds., 1997.

1999 "Les hommes du roi propriétaires de champs: Les textes ougaritiques RS 15.116 et RS 19.016." *Semitica* 49: 19–64.

2000a *Les textes rituels*. Ras Shamra—Ougarit 12. Paris: Éditions Recherche sur les Civilisations.

2000b "Trois comptes ougaritiques: RS 15.062, RS 18.024, RIH 78/02." *Syria* 77: 23–67.

2001a "Ugaritic Science." Pp. 223–54 in M. Daviau et al., eds., *The World of the Aramaeans: Studies in Language and Literature in Honour of Paul-E. Dion*, vol. 3. Journal for the Study of the Old Testament Supplement 326 Sheffield: Sheffield Academic Press.

2001b "Le traité d'alliance RS 11.772+." *Semitica* 51: 5–31.

2002a *Ritual and Cult at Ugarit*. Society of Biblical Literature Writings from the Ancient World 10. Atlanta: Society of Biblical Literature.

2002b "Ugaritic Letters." Pp. 87–116 in Hallo and Younger, eds., 2002.

2002c "RIH 77/27, RIH 77/12, RIH 78/26 et le principe de l'écriture cunéiforme alphabétique." *Syria* 79: 51–63.

2003 "Une formule épistolaire en ougaritique et accadien." Pp. 446–75 in *Semitic and Assyriological Studies Presented to Pelio Fronzaroli by Pupils and Colleagues*. Wiesbaden: Harrassowitz.

2003–4 Review of Tropper 2000. *Archiv für Orientforschung online version* 50, http://orientalistik.univie.ac.at/publikationen/archiv-fuer-orientforschung/

2007 "The Ugaritic Alphabetic Cuneiform Writing System in the Context of Other Alphabetic Systems." Pp. 181–200 in C. L. Miller, ed., *Studies in Semitic and Afroasiatic Linguistics Presented to Gene B. Gragg*. Studies in Ancient Oriental Civilization 60. Chicago: The Oriental Institute of the University of Chicago.

forthcoming "Two Epigraphic Notes on the Ugaritic *Šaḥru-wa-Šalimu* Text (RS 2.002 = *CTA* 23)."

Parker, S. B.

1997a "Aqhat." Pp. 49–80 in Parker, ed., 1997.

1997b "The Mare and the Horon." Pp. 219–23 in Parker, ed., 1997.

Parker, S. B., ed.

1997 *Ugaritic Narrative Poetry*. Writings from the Ancient World 9. Atlanta: Society of Biblical Literature.

PRU II = Virolleaud 1957

PRU III = Nougayrol 1955

PRU V = Virolleaud 1965

Rainey, A. F.

1973 "Gleanings from Ugarit." *Israel Oriental Studies* 3: 34–62.

1996 *Canaanite in the Amarna Tablets: A Linguistic Analysis of the Mixed Dialect Used by the Scribes from Canaan*. Handbuch der Orientalistik, Erste Abteilung: Der Nahe und Mittlere Osten 25/1–4. Leiden: Brill.

RIH = text from Ras Ibn Hani

RS = text from Ras Shamra

RSO = Ras Shamra–Ougarit. Publications de la Mission Française Archéologique de Ras Shamra–Ougarit. Paris: Éditions Recherche sur les Civilisations, 1983–

Saadé, G.
1979 *Ougarit: Métropole cananéenne*. Beirut: Imprimerie Catholique.

Sass, B.
2004–5 "The Genesis of the Alphabet and Its Development in the Second Millennium B.C. Twenty Years Later." *De Kemi à Birît Nari* 2: 147–66.

Schaeffer, C. F. A.
1932 "Note additionnelle à propos du nom ancien de la ville de Ras-Shamra." *Syria* 13: 24–27.
1956 "La première tablette." *Syria* 33: 161–68.
1978 "Contexte archéologique et date du rhyton léontocéphale de la maison d'Agaptarri (RS 25.318)." Pp. 149–54 in C. F.-A. Schaeffer-Forrer et al., eds., *Ugaritica* VII. Mission de Ras Shamra 18. Bibliothèque Archéologique et Historique 99. Paris: Mission Archéologique de Ras Shamra / Geuthner.

Segert, S.
1983 "The Last Sign of the Ugaritic Alphabet." *Ugarit-Forschungen* 15: 201–18.
1984 *A Basic Grammar of the Ugaritic Language*. Berkeley: University of California Press.
1988 "The Ugaritic Voiced Postvelar in Correspondence to the Emphatic Interdental." *Ugarit-Forschungen* 20: 287–300.

Singer, A. D.
1948 "The Vocative in Ugaritic." *Journal of Cuneiform Studies* 2: 1–10.

Sivan, D.
1982 "Final Triphthongs and Final *yu/a/i - wu/a/i* Diphthongs in Ugaritic Nominal Forms." *Ugarit-Forschungen* 14: 209–18.
1992 "Notes on the Use of the Form *qatal* as the Plural Base for the Form *qatl* in Ugaritic." *Israel Oriental Studies* 12: 235–38.
1997 *A Grammar of the Ugaritic Lanauage*. Handbuch der Orientalistik, Erste Abteilung: Der Nahe und Mittlere Osten 28. Leiden: Brill.

Smith, M. S.
1997 "The Baal Cycle." Pp. 81–180 in Parker, ed., 1997.

Soldt, W. H. van
1996 "Studies in the Topography of Ugarit (1): The Spelling of the Ugaritic Toponyms." *Ugarit-Forschungen* 28: 653–92.
1999 "Studies in the Topography of Ugarit (4): Town Sizes and Districts." *Ugarit-Forschungen* 31: 749–84.

Tarragon, J.-M. de
1989 "Les rituels." Pp. 125–238 in Caquot, de Tarragon, and Cunchillos 1989.

TO I = Caquot, Sznycer, and Herdner 1974

TO II = Caquot, de Tarragon, and Cunchillos 1989

Thureau-Dangin, F.
1935 "Une lettre assyrienne à Ras Shamra." *Syria* 16: 188–93.

Tropper, J.

1990a *Der ugaritische Kausativstamm und die Kausativbildungen des Semitischen. Eine morphologisch-semantische Untersuchung zum Š-Stamm und zu den umstrittenen nichtsibilantischen Kausativstämmen des Ugaritischen.* Abhandlungen zur Literatur Alt-Syrien-Palästinas 2. Münster: Ugarit-Verlag.

1990b "Silbenschließendes Aleph im Ugaritischen: Ein neuer Versuch." *Ugarit-Forschungen* 22: 359–69.

1991 "Finale Sätze und *yqtla*-Modus im Ugaritischen." *Ugarit-Forschungen* 23: 341–52.

1993a "Auf dem Weg zu einer ugaritischen Grammatik." Pp. 471–80 in M. Dietrich and O. Loretz., eds., *Mesopotamica—Ugaritica—Biblica: Festschrift für Kurt Bergerhof zur Vollendung seines 70. Lebensjahres am 7. Mai 1992.* Alter Orient und Altes Testament 232. Kevelaer: Butzon & Bercker / Neukirchen-Vluyn: Neukirchener Verlag.

1993b "Morphologische Besonderheiten des Spätugaritischen." *Ugarit-Forschungen* 25: 389–94.

1994a "Das ugaritische Konsonanteninventar." *Journal of Northwest Semitic Languages* 20/2: 17–59.

1994b "Zur Grammatik der ugaritischen Omina." *Ugarit-Forschungen* 26: 457–72.

1995a "Das altkanaanäische und ugaritische Verbalsystem." Pp. 159–70 in M. Dietrich and O. Loretz, eds., *Ugarit: Ein ostmediterranes Kulturzentrum im Alten Orient: Ergebnisse und Perspektiven der Forschung.* Band I: *Ugarit und seine altorientalische Umwelt.* Abhandlungen zur Literatur Alt-Syrien-Palästinas 7. Münster: Ugarit-Verlag.

1995b "Das letzte Zeichen des ugaritischen Alphabets." *Ugarit-Forschungen* 27: 505–28.

1997 "Aktuelle Probleme der ugaritischen Grammatik." *Ugarit-Forschungen* 29: 669–74.

2000 *Ugaritische Grammatik.* Alter Orient und Altes Testament 273. Münster: Ugarit-Verlag.

Tsumura, D. T.

2007 "Revisiting the 'Seven' Good Gods of Fertility in Ugarit." *Ugarit-Forschungen* 39: 629–41.

Ugaritica V = *Ugaritica* V. J.-C. Courtois, ed. Bibliothèque Archéologique et Historique 80. Mission de Ras Shamra 16. Paris: Imprimerie Nationale, 1968.

Ugaritica VII = *Ugaritica* VII. C. F.-A. Schaeffer-Forrer et al., eds. Mission de Ras Shamra 18. Bibliothèque Archéologique et Historique 99. Paris: Mission Archéologique de Ras Shamra and Geuthner, 1978.

Umwelt = Bordreuil 1995

Verreet, E.

1983 "Das silbenschliessende Aleph im Ugaritischen." *Ugarit-Forschungen* 15: 223–58.

1986 "Beobachtungen zum ugaritischen Verbalsystem II." *Ugarit-Forschungen* 17: 319–44.

1988 *Modi Ugaritici: Eine morpho-syntaktische Abhandlung über das Modalsystem im Ugaritischen.* Orientalia Lovaniensia Analecta 27. Leuven: Peeters.

Virolleaud, C.

1929 "Les inscriptions cunéiformes de Ras Shamra." *Syria* 10: 304–310, pl. LXI–LXXX.

1931a "Le déchiffrement des tablettes alphabétiques de Ras-Shamra." *Syria* 12: 15–23.

1931b "Note complémentaire sur le poème de Môt et Aleïn." *Syria* 12: 350–57.

1932 "Un nouveau chant du poème d'Aleïn-Baal." *Syria* 13: 113–63.

1933 "La naissance des dieux gracieux et beaux: Poème phénicien de Ras-Shamra." *Syria* 14: 128–51.

1934 "Fragment nouveau du poème de Môt et Aleyn-Baal (I AB)." *Syria* 15: 226–43.

1935 "La révolte de Košer contre Baal: Poème de Ras-Shamra (III AB, A)." *Syria* 16: 29–45.

1936a *La légende phénicienne de Danel. Texte cunéiforme alphabétique avec transcription et commentaire, précédé d'une introduction à l'étude de la civilisation d'Ugarit.* Mission de Ras Shamra 1. Bibliothèque Archéologique et Historique 21. Paris: Geuthner.

1936b *La légende de Keret roi des Sidoniens publiée d'après une tablette de Ras-Shamra.* Mission de Ras Shamra 2. Bibliothèque Archéologique et Historique 22. Paris: Geuthner.

1938 *La déesse ʿAnat, poème de Ras Shamra publié, traduit et commenté.* Mission de Ras Shamra 4. Bibliothèque Archéologique et Historique 28. Paris: Geuthner.

1940a "Lettres et documents administratifs provenant des archives d'Ugarit." *Syria* 21: 247–76.

1940b "Un état de solde provenant d'Ugarit (Ras-Shamra)." Pp. 39–49 in *Mémorial Lagrange: Cinquantenaire de l'École Biblique et Archéologique Française de Jérusalem (15 novembre 1890–15 novembre 1940).* Paris: Gabalda.

1951 "Les nouvelles tablettes de Ras Shamra (1948–1949)." *Syria* 28: 22–56.

1957 *Textes en cunéiformes alphabétiques des archives est, ouest et centrales.* Palais Royal d'Ugarit II. Mission de Ras Shamra 7. Paris: Imprimerie Nationale / Klincksieck.

1960 "Un nouvel épisode du mythe ugaritique de Baal." *Académie des Inscriptions et Belles-Lettres, Comptes Rendus*: 180–86.

1965 *Textes en cunéiformes alphabétiques des archives sud, sud-ouest et du petit palais.* Palais Royal d'Ugarit V. Mission de Ras Shamra 11. Paris: Imprimerie Nationale / Klincksieck.

1968 "Les nouveaux textes mythologiques et liturgiques de Ras Shamra (XXIVe Campagne, 1961)." Pp. 545–95 in C. F.-A. Schaeffer et al., eds., *Ugaritica* V. Mission de Ras Shamra 16. Bibliothèque Archéologique et Historique 80. Paris: Imprimerie Nationale / Geuthner.

Wilson, G. H.
1982 "Ugaritic Word Order and Sentence Structure in KRT." *Journal of Semitic Studies* 27: 17–32.

Wyatt, N.
1998 *Religious Texts from Ugarit: The Words of Ilimilku and His Colleagues.* Sheffield: Sheffield Academic Press.

Yon, M.
1997 *La cité d'Ougarit sur le tell de Ras Shamra.* Guides Archéologiques de l'Institut Français d'Archéologie du Proche-Orient 2. Paris: Éditions Recherche sur les Civilisations.
2006 *The City of Ugarit on Tell Ras Shamra.* Winona Lake IN: Eisenbrauns.

Yon, M., and D. Arnaud, eds.
2001 *Études ougaritiques*, I: *Travaux 1985–1995.* Ras Shamra–Ougarit 14. Paris: Éditions Recherche sur les Civilisations.

Hand Copies

RS 3.367 IV

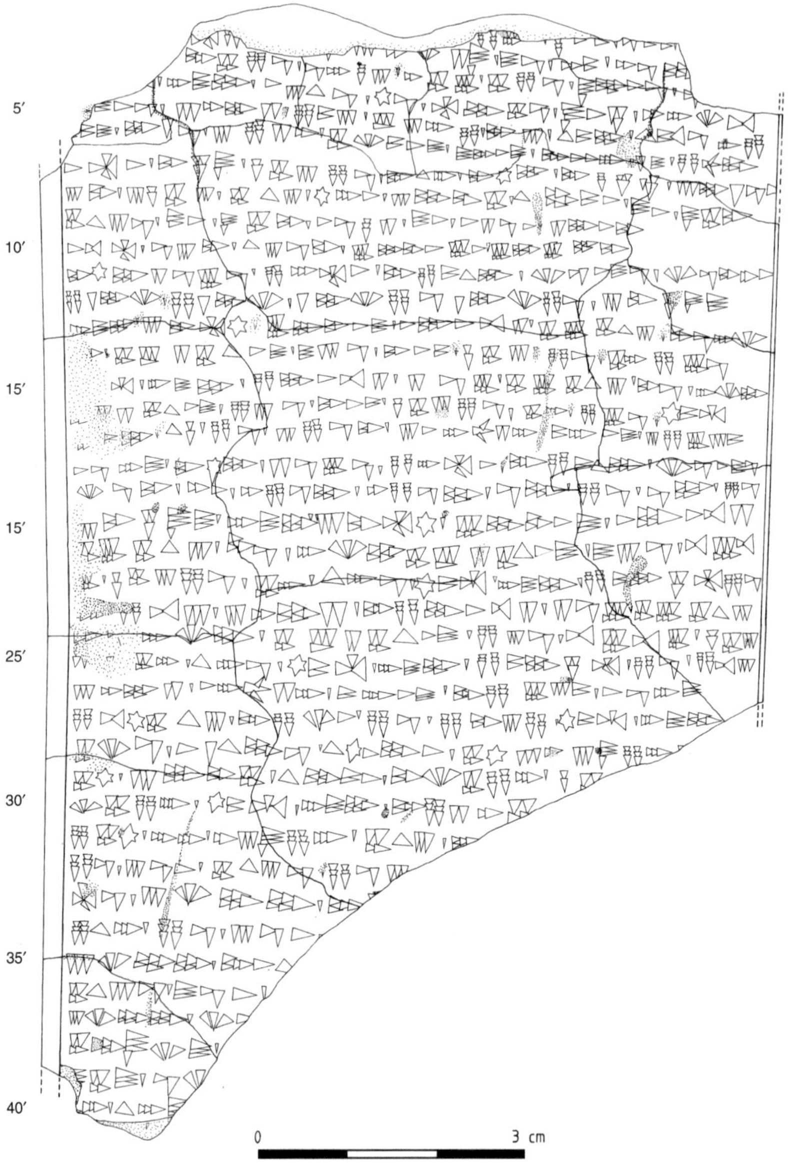

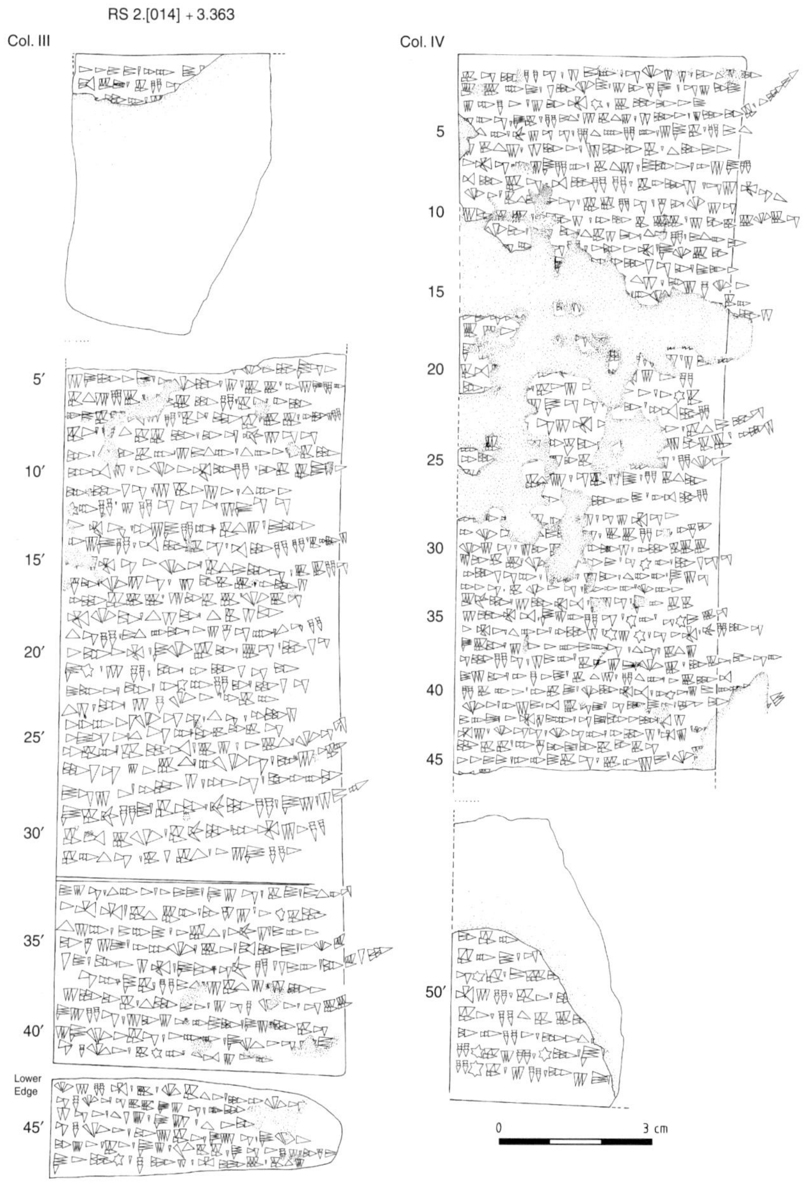
RS 2.[014] + 3.363
Col. III
Col. IV
Lower Edge
0
3 cm

RS 2.[003]+

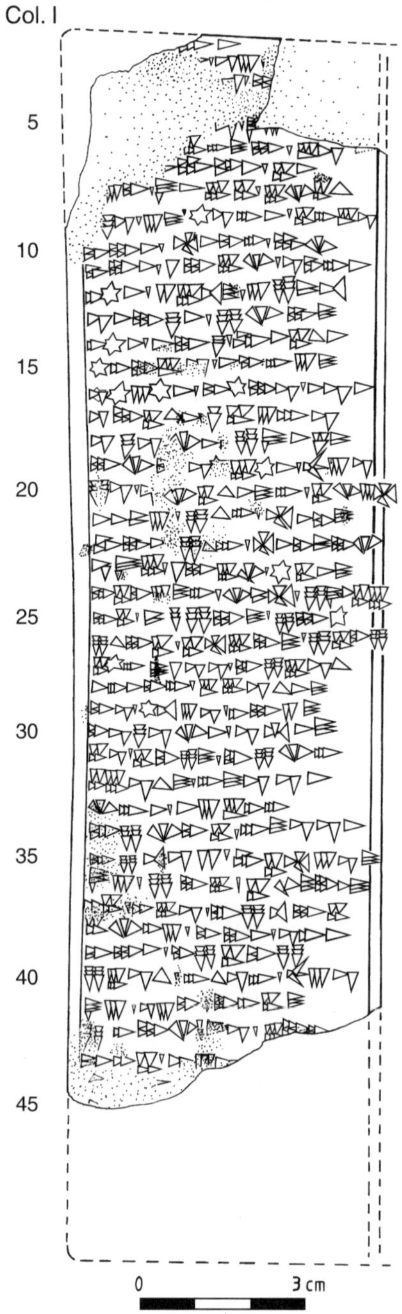

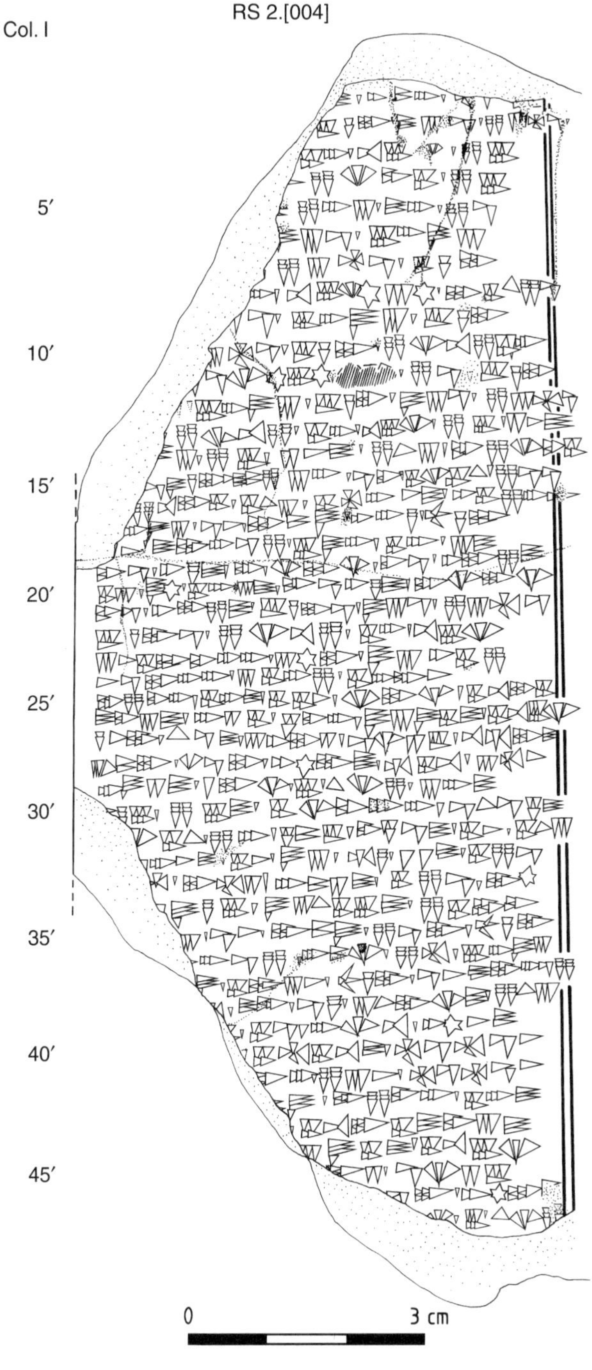
RS 2.[004]
Col. I
5′
10′
15′
20′
25′
30′
35′
40′
45′
0
3 cm

RS 2.002

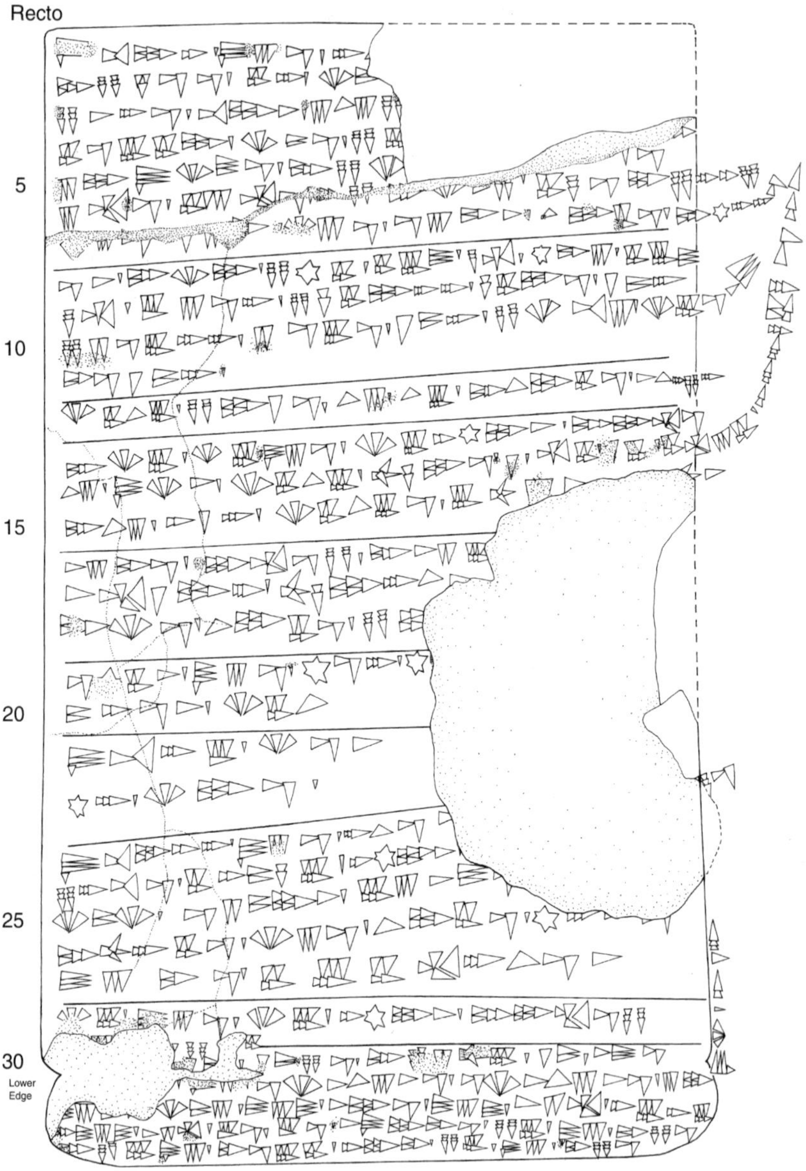

Verso

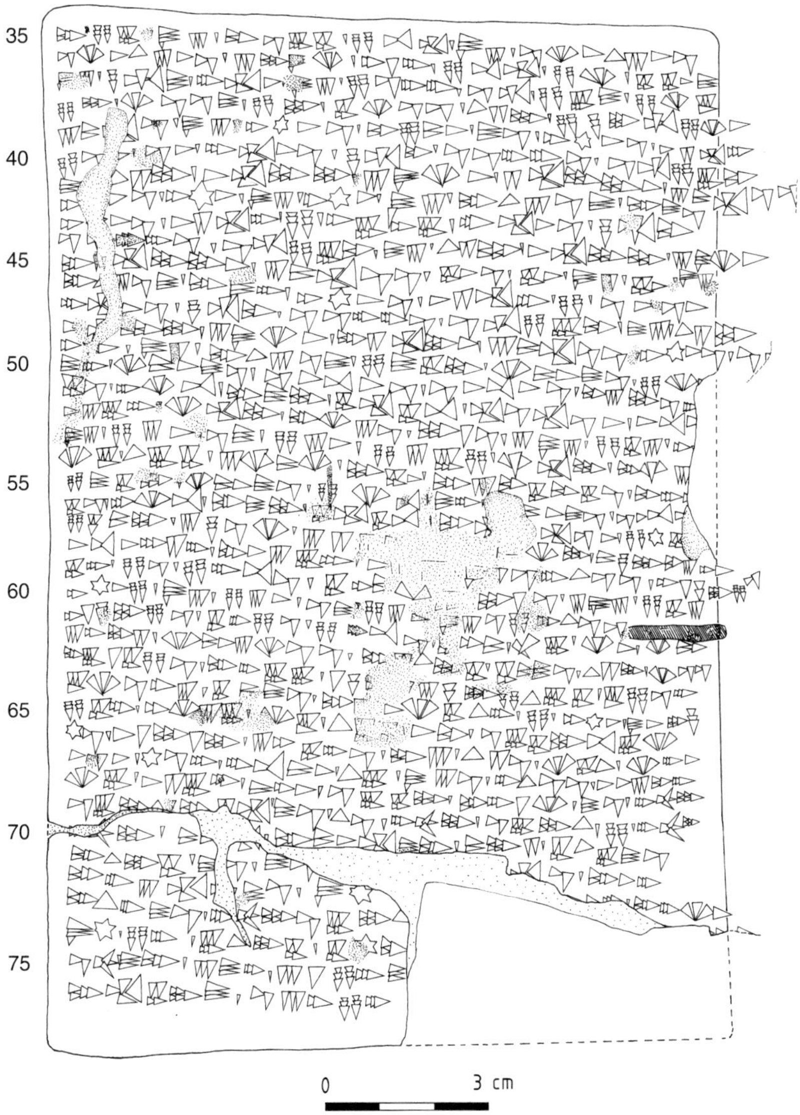

RS 24.244

Recto

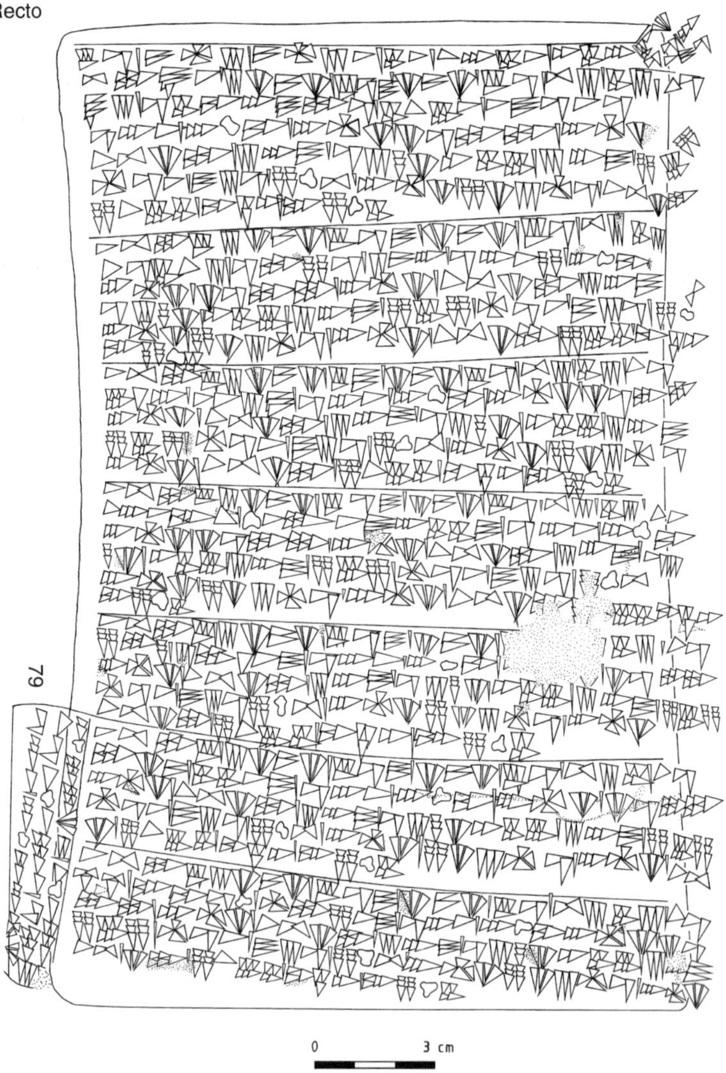

Lower Edge

Verso

RS 24.258

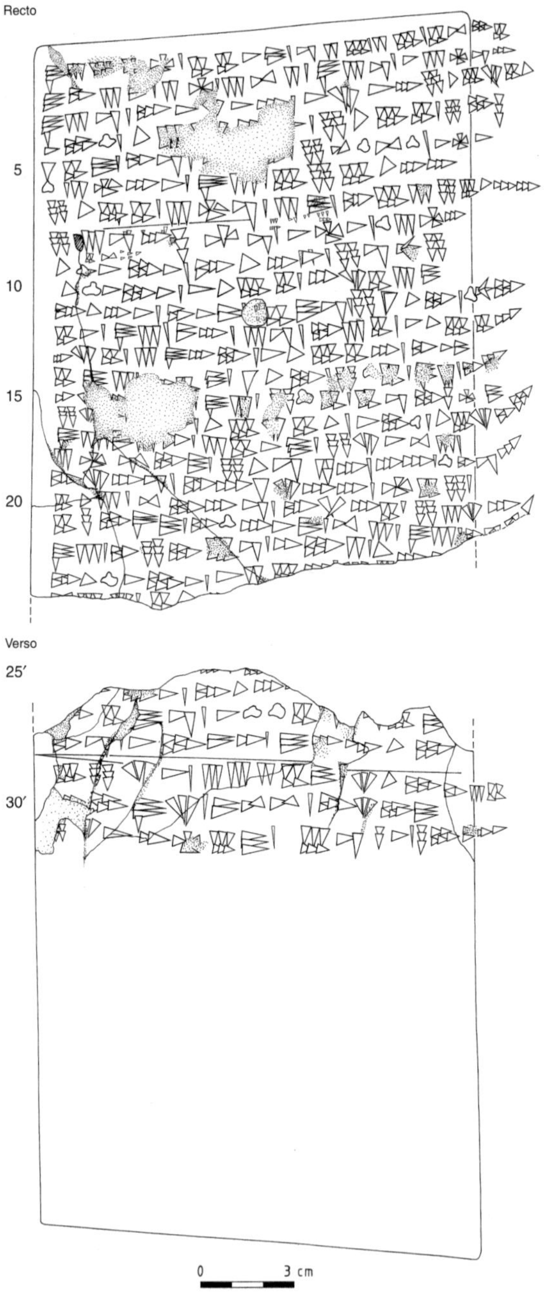

RS 1.001

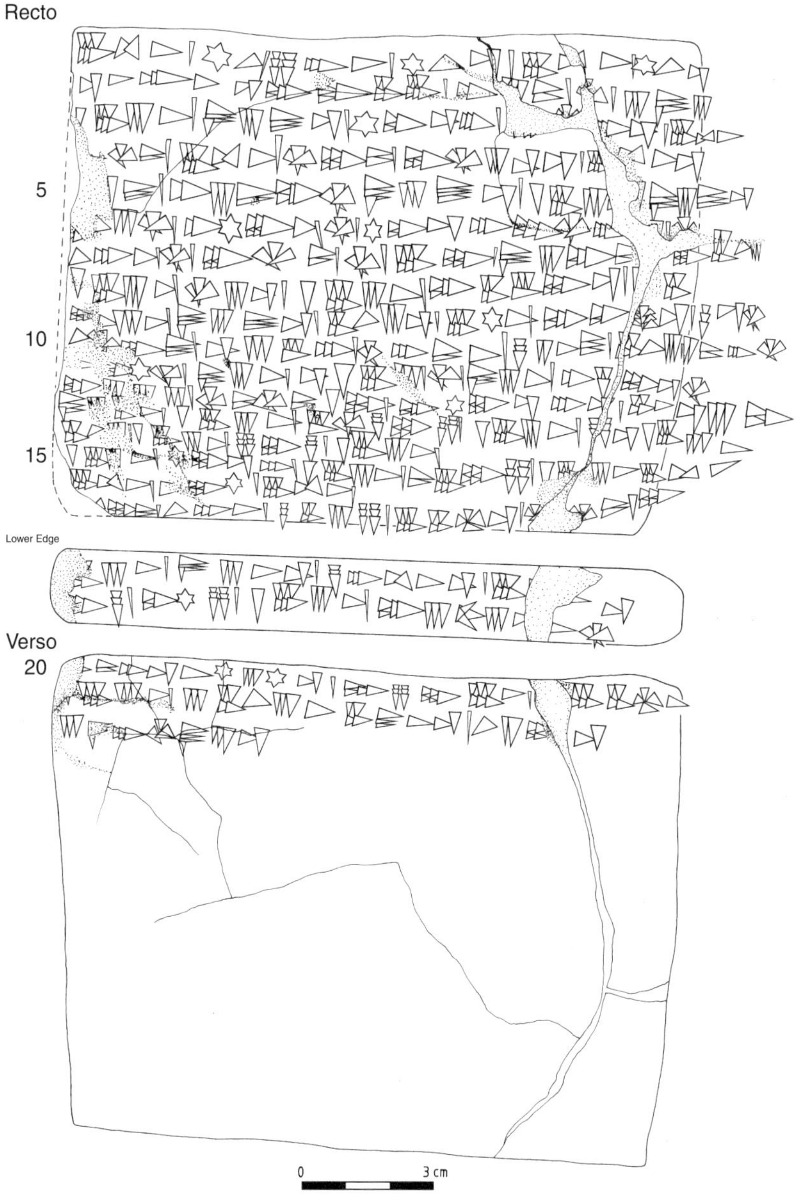

RS 1.002

Recto

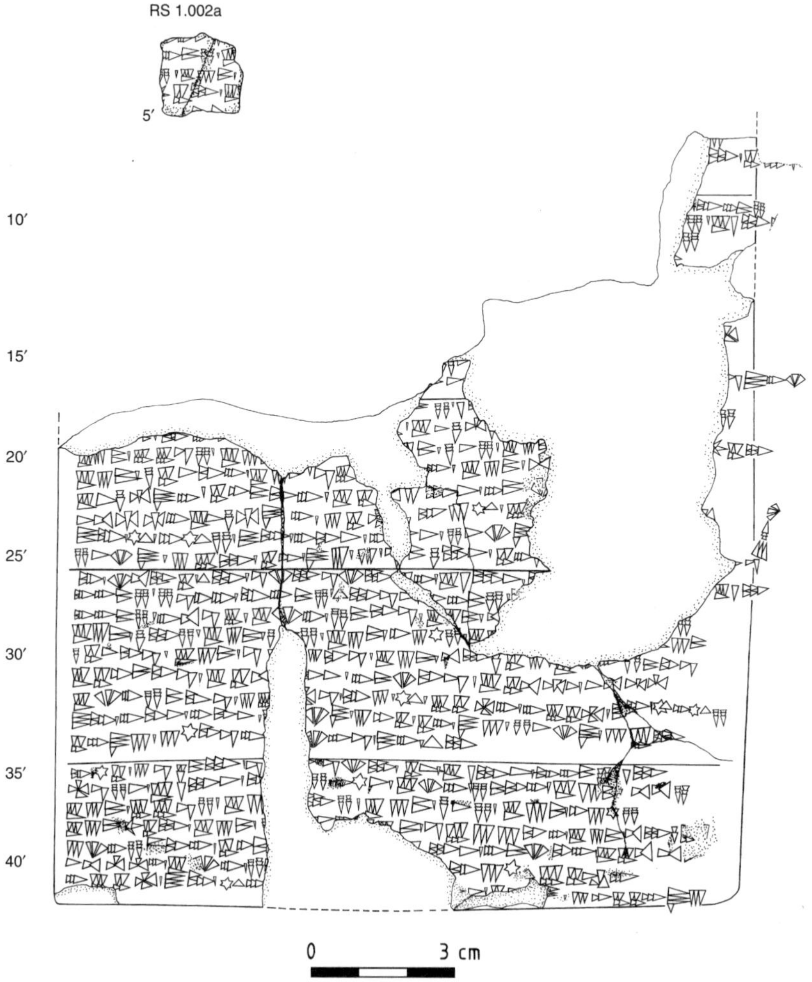

Verso

42′

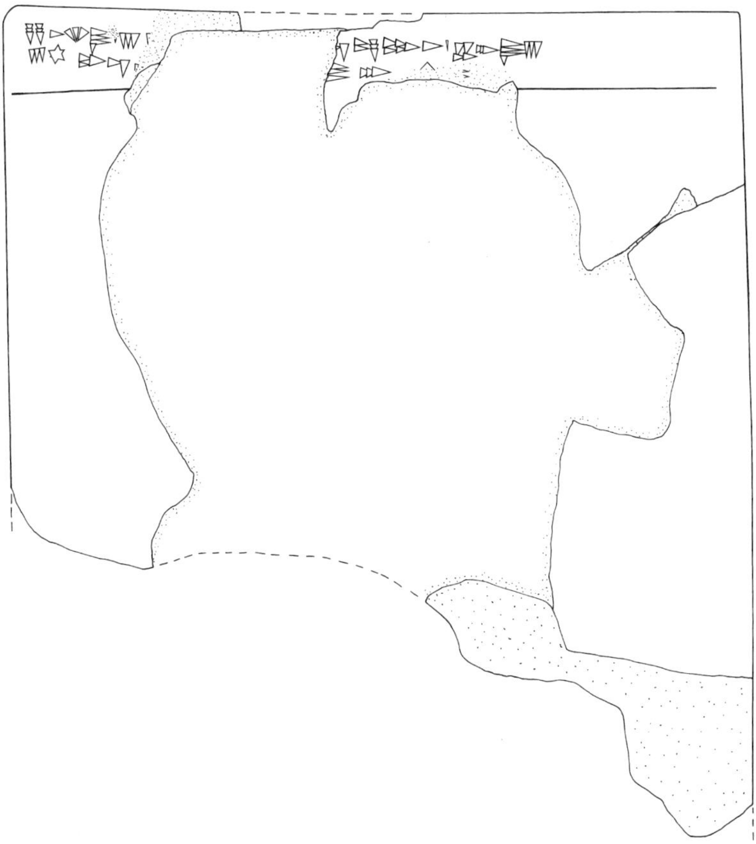

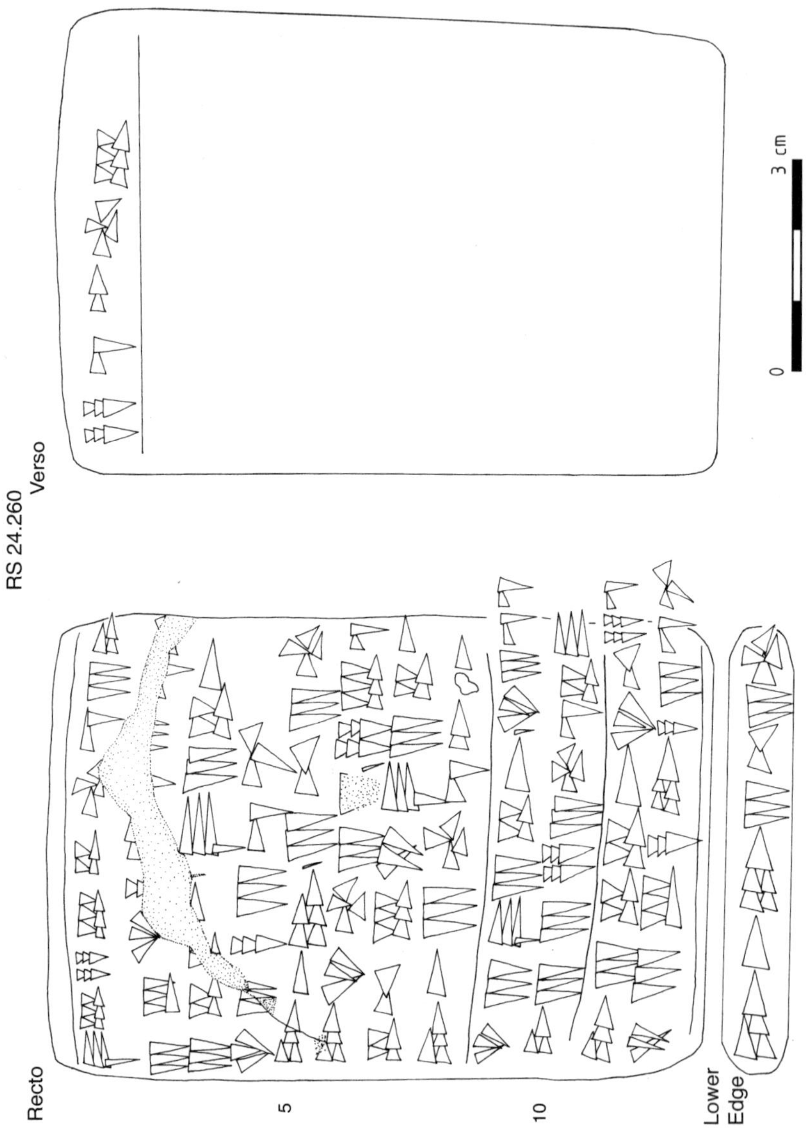
RS 24.260
Verso
Recto
5
10
Lower Edge
0
3 cm

RS 24.266

Recto

Verso

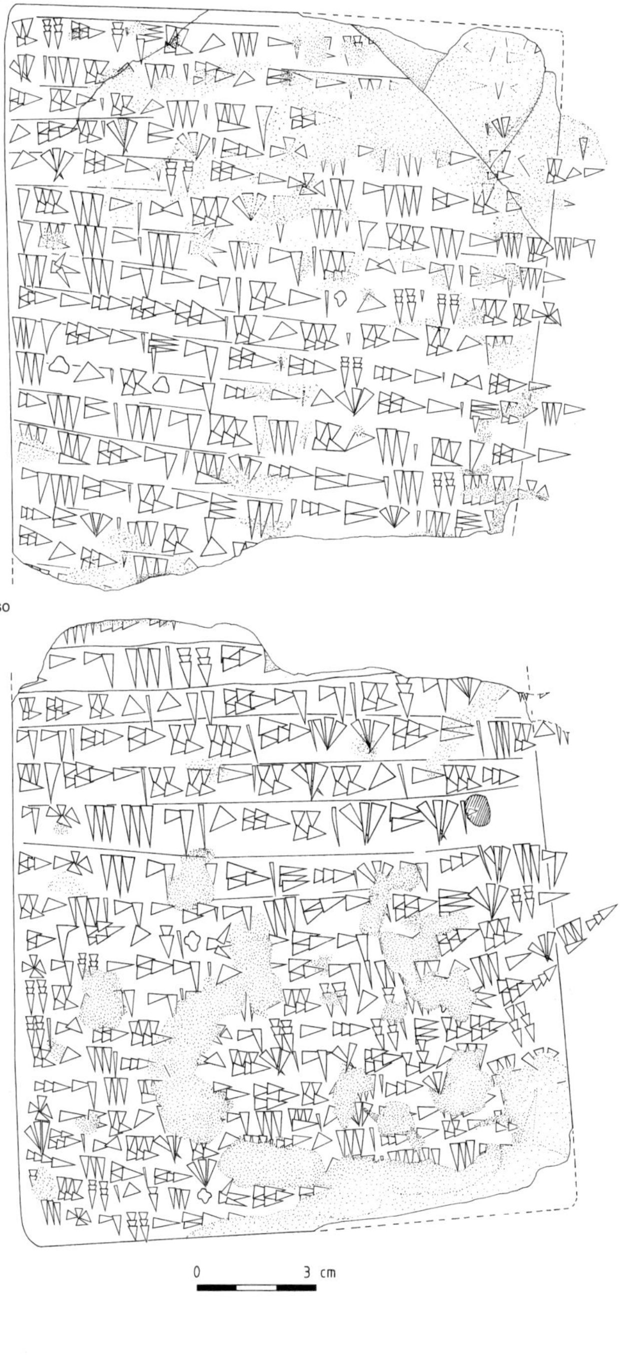

RS 24.643

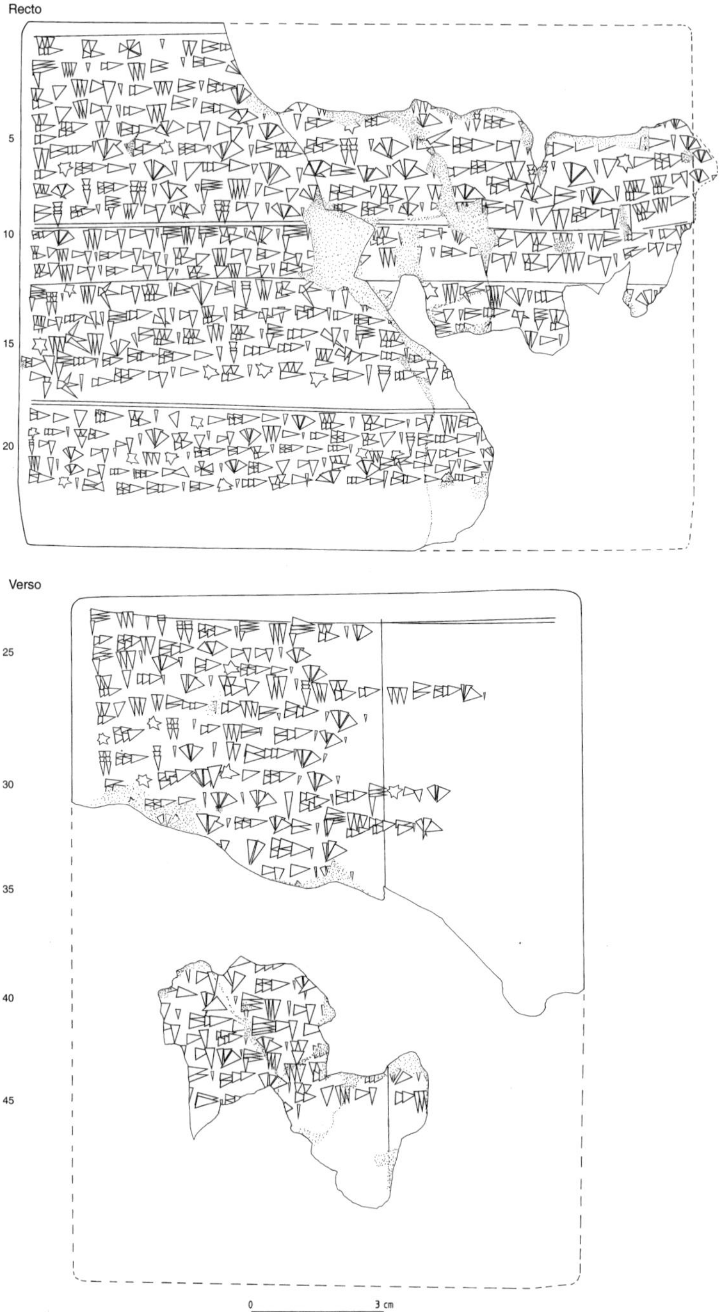

RS 34.126

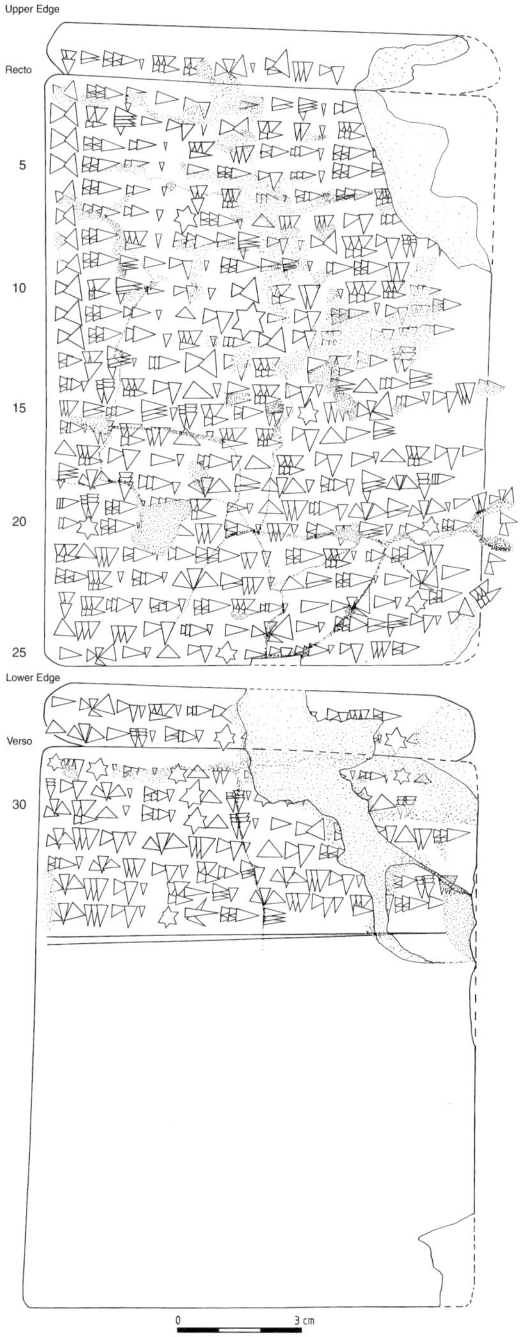

RS 6.021

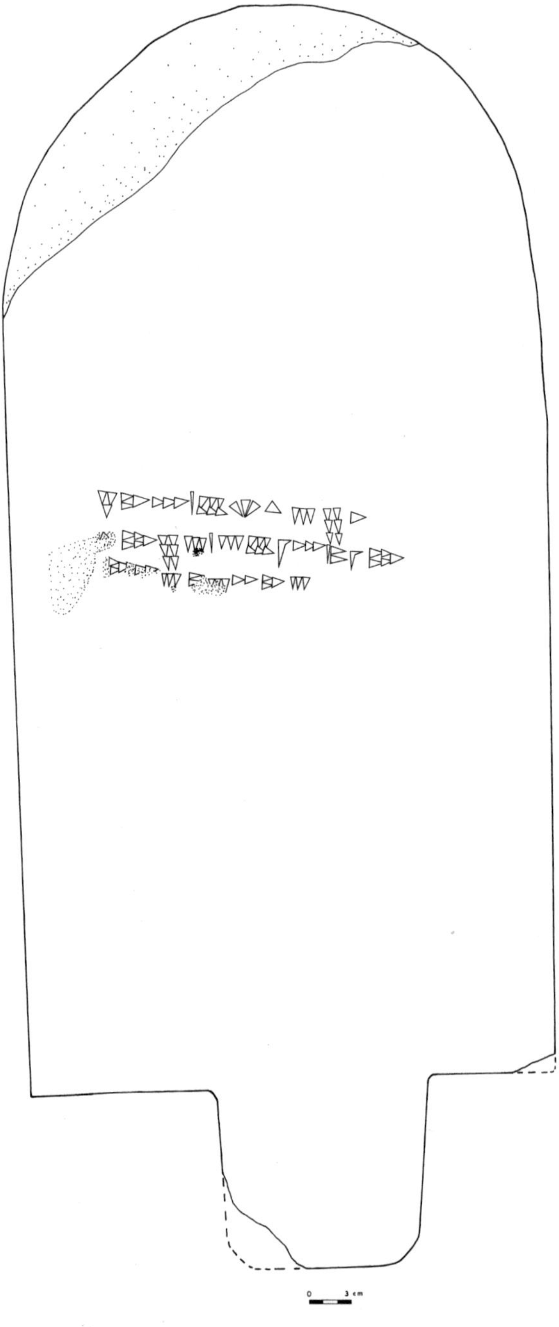

RS 6.028

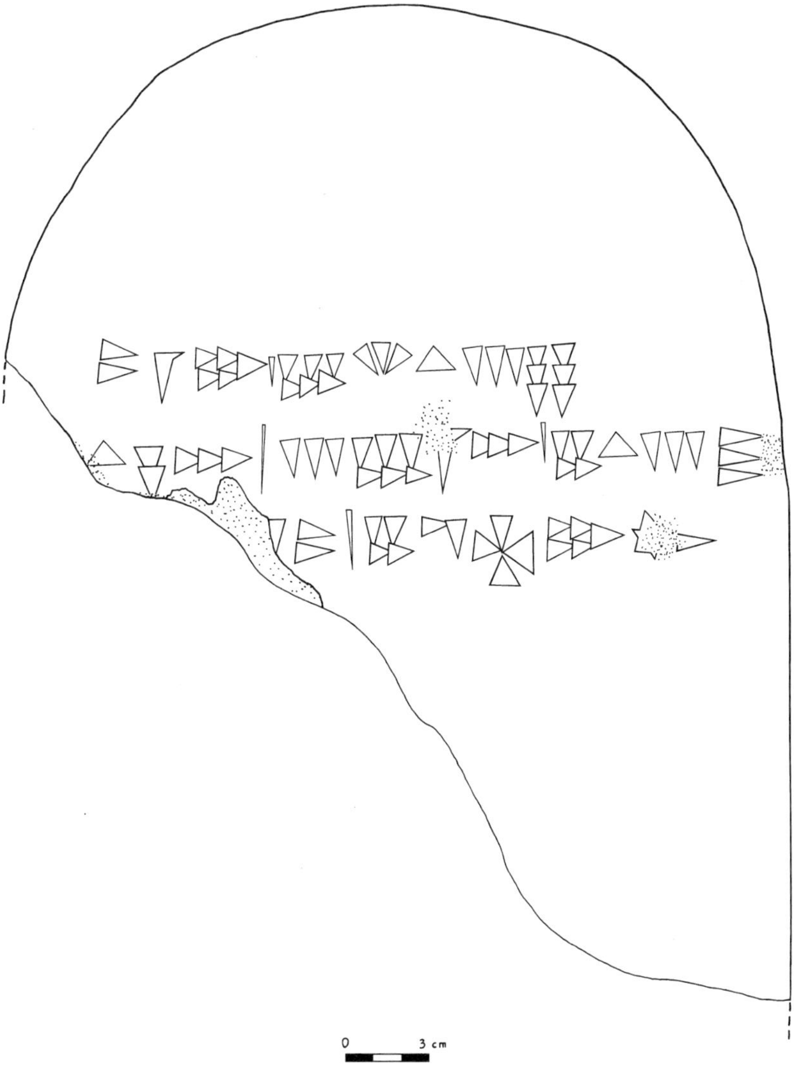

RS 25.318

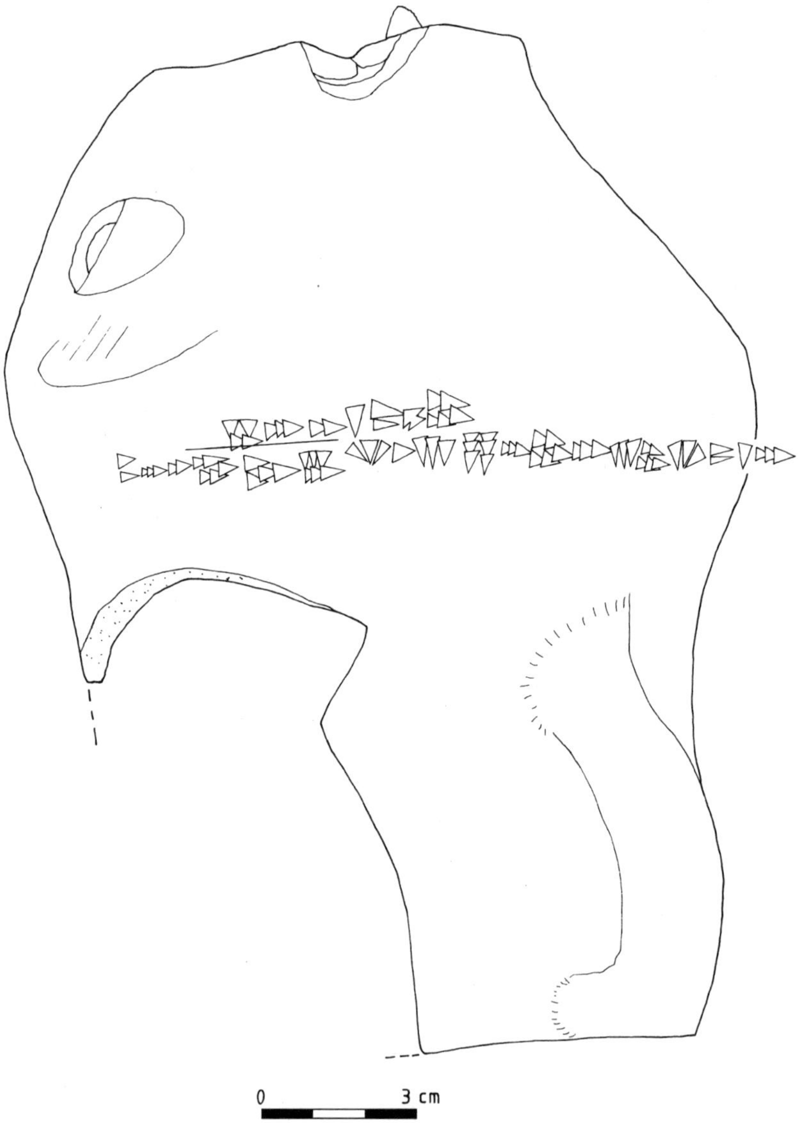

RIH 78/20

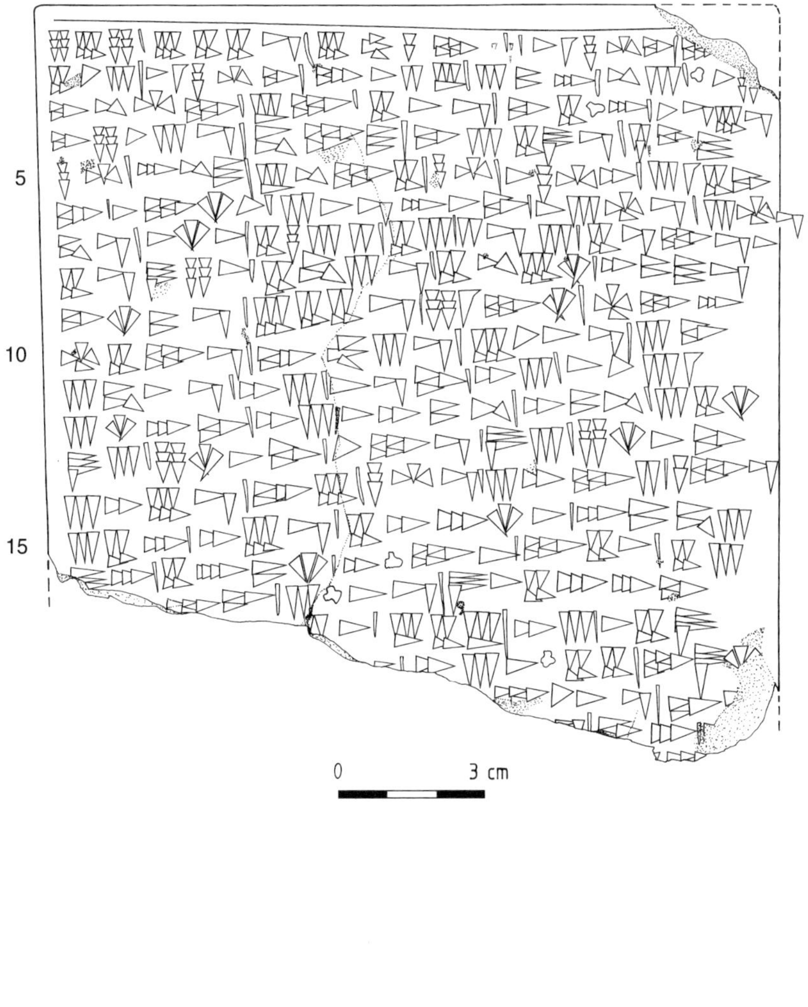

RS 92.2014

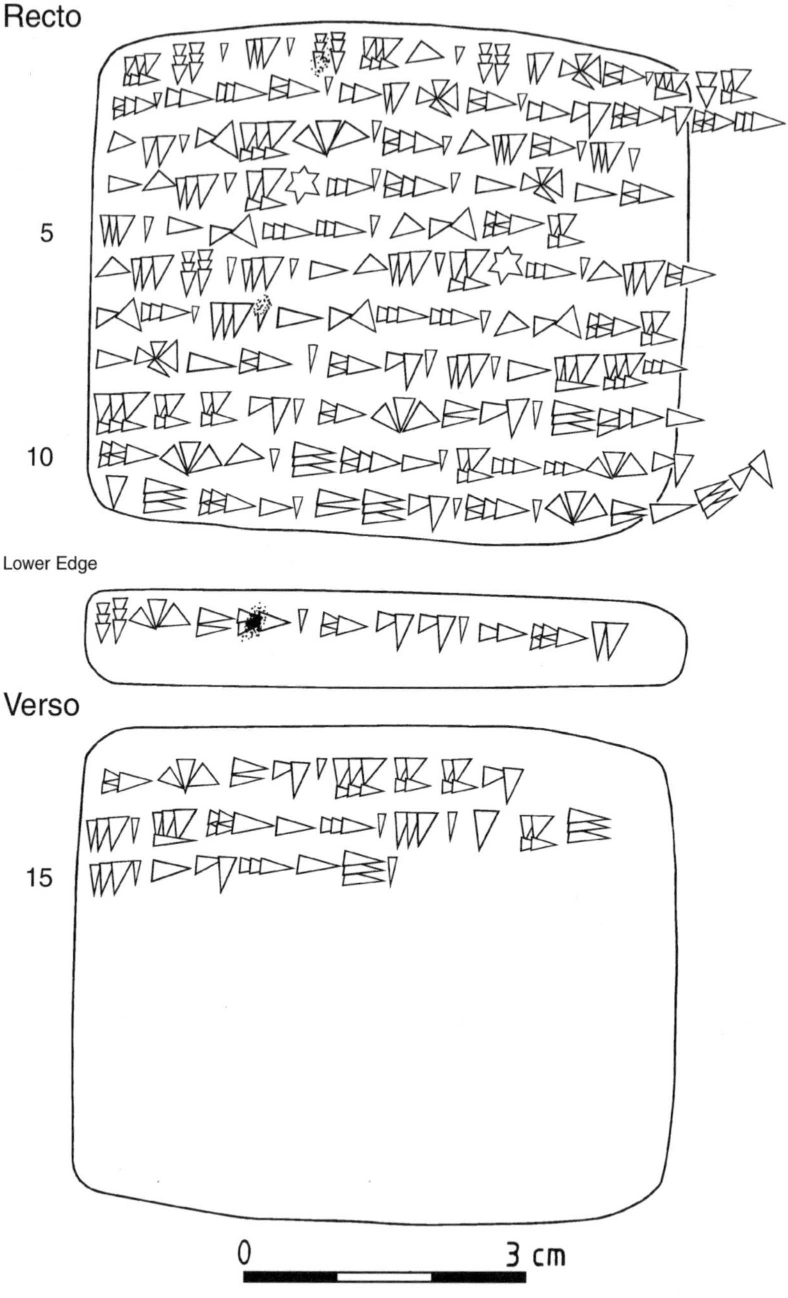

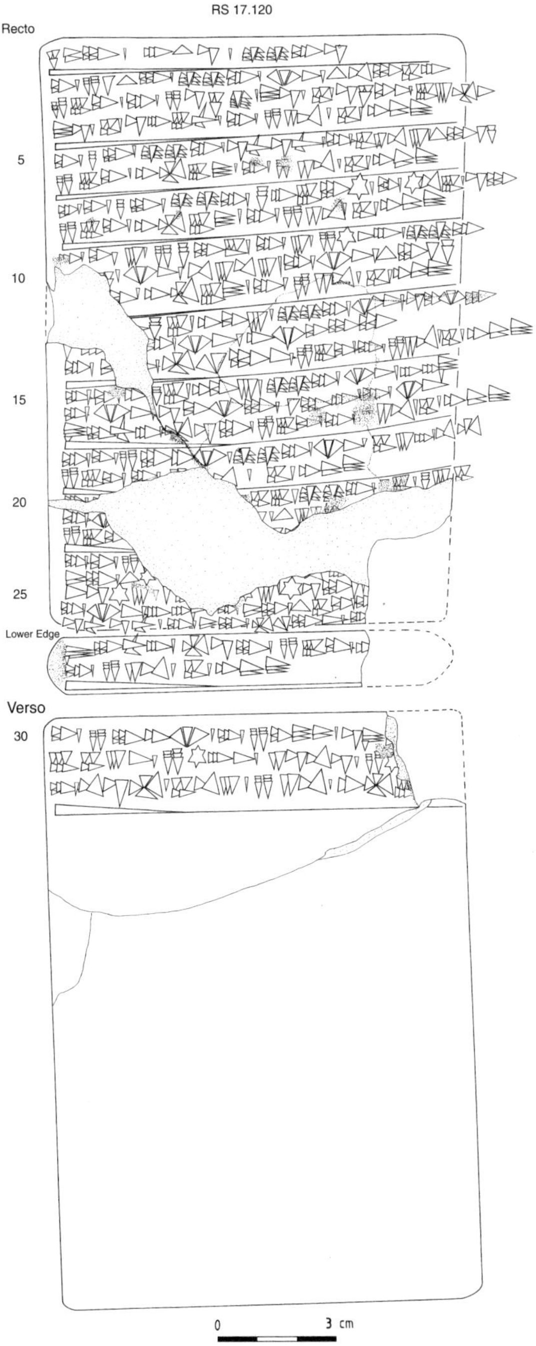
RS 17.120
Recto
Lower Edge
Verso
0
3 cm

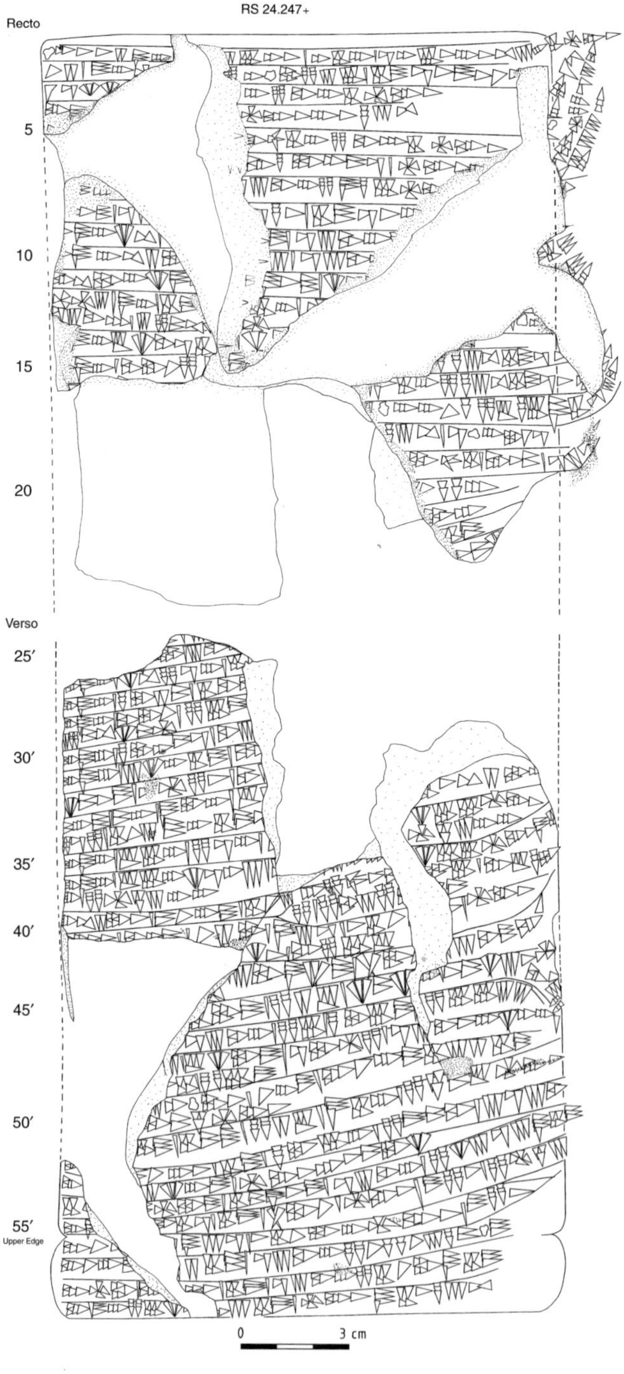
RS 24.247+
Recto
Verso
Upper Edge
0
3 cm

RS 4.475

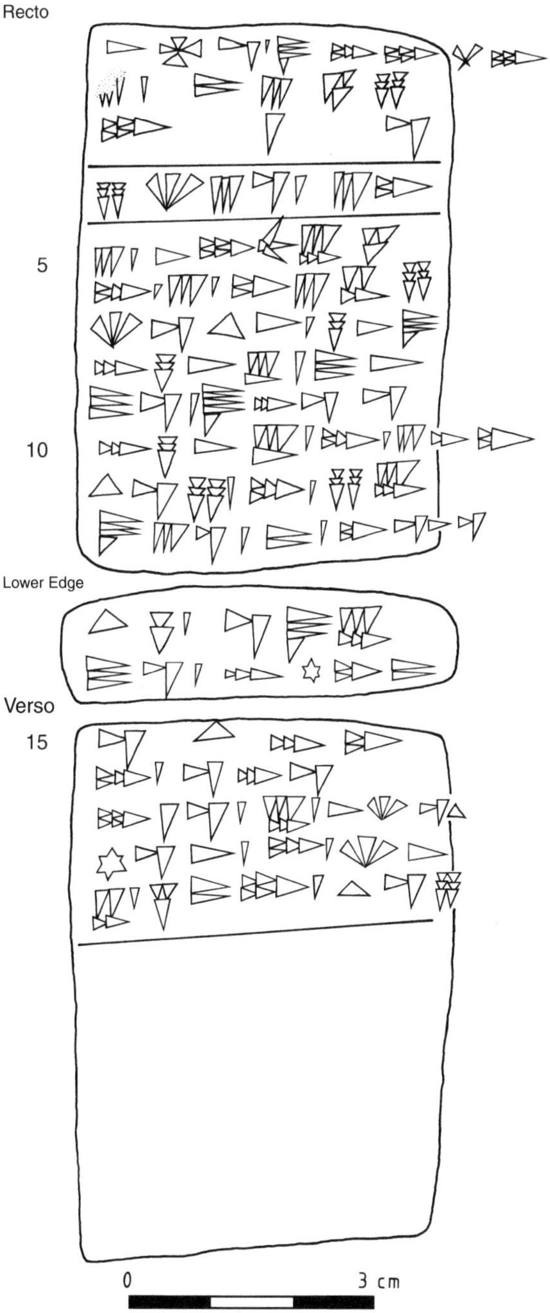

RS 8.315

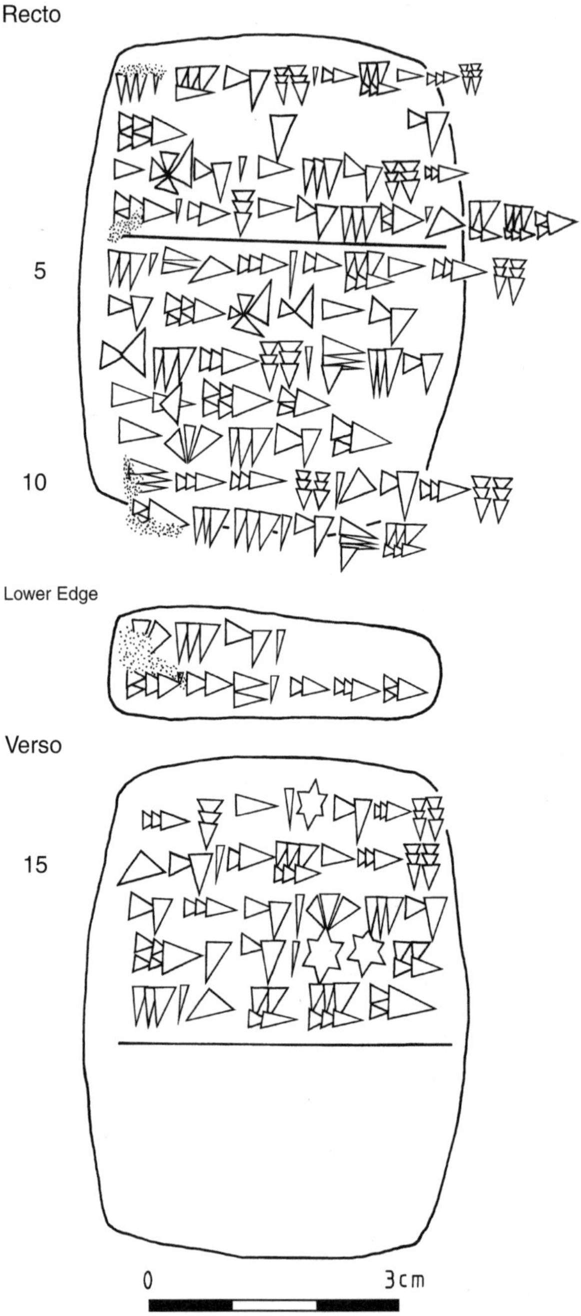

RS 11.872

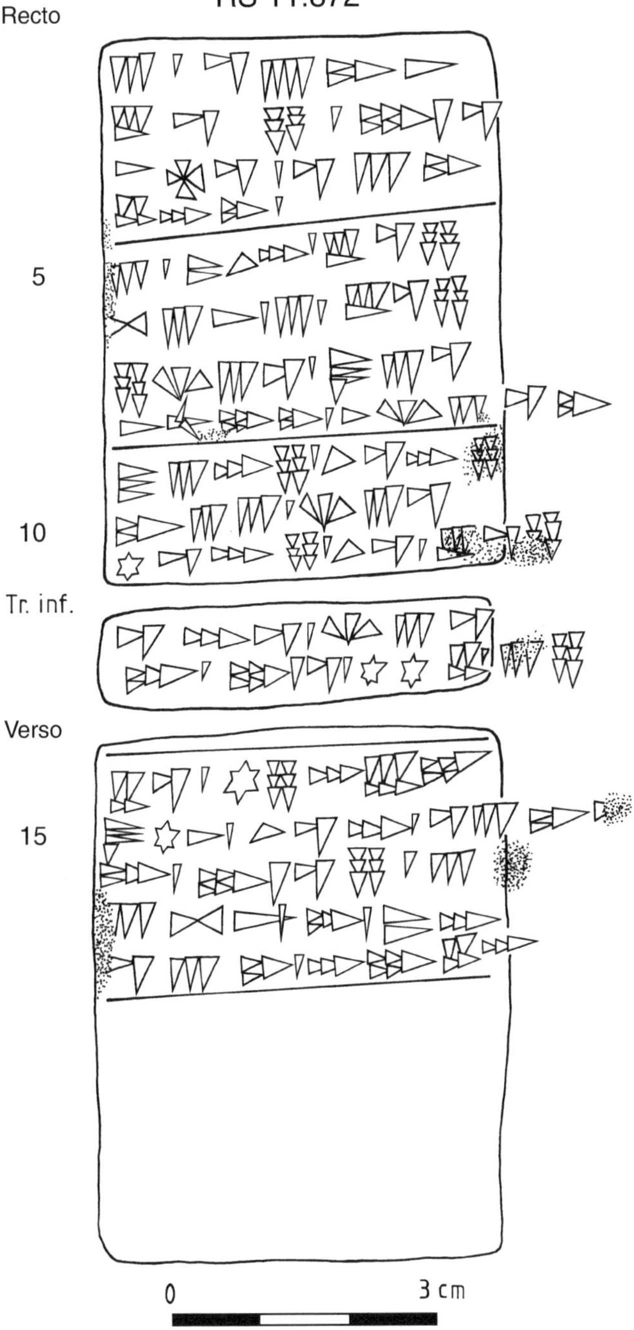

RS 15.008

Recto

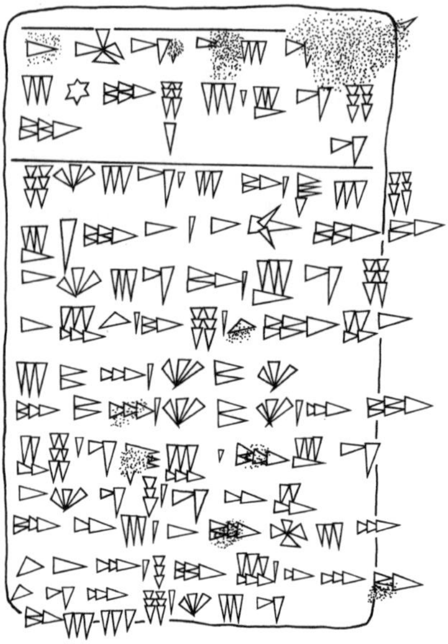

Lower Edge

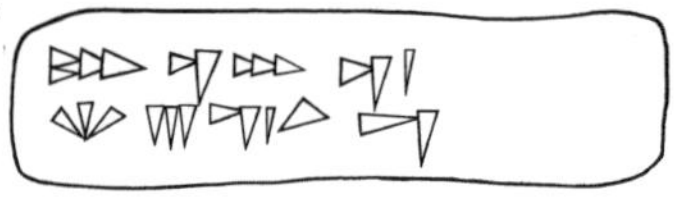

Verso

RS 16.379

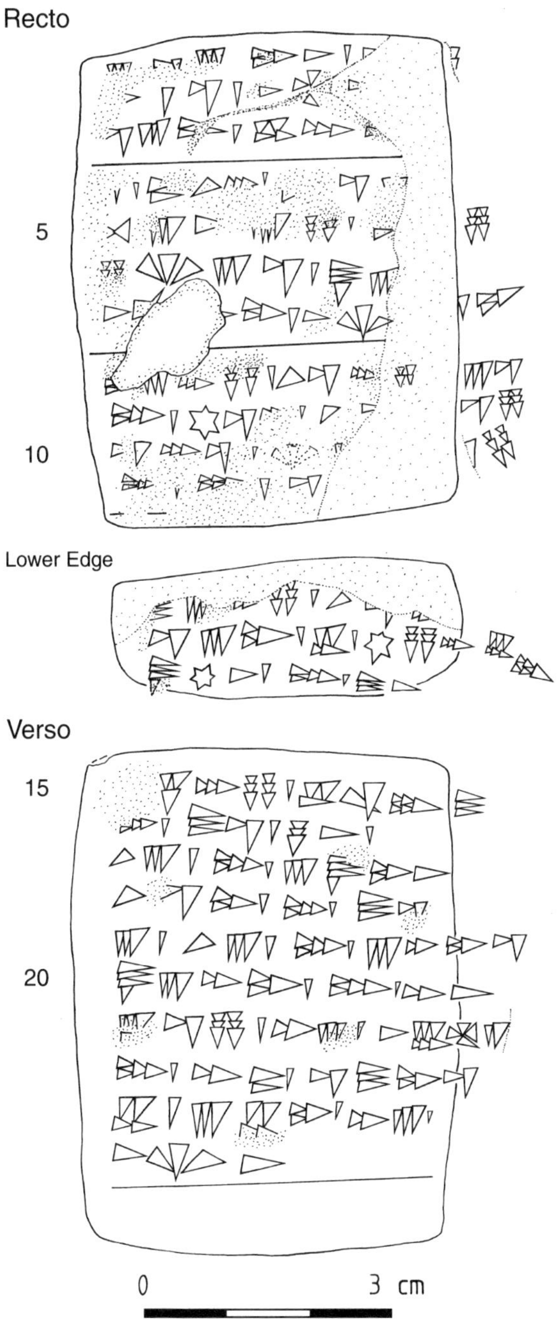
Recto
5
10
Lower Edge
Verso
15
20
0
3 cm

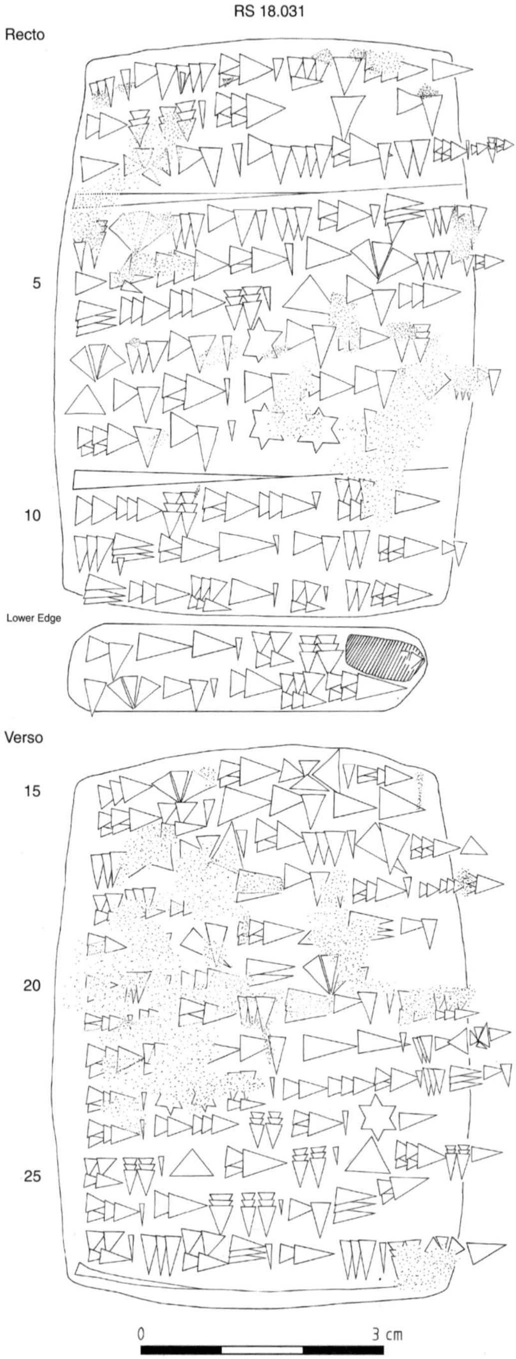
RS 18.031
Recto
5
10
Lower Edge
Verso
15
20
25
0
3 cm

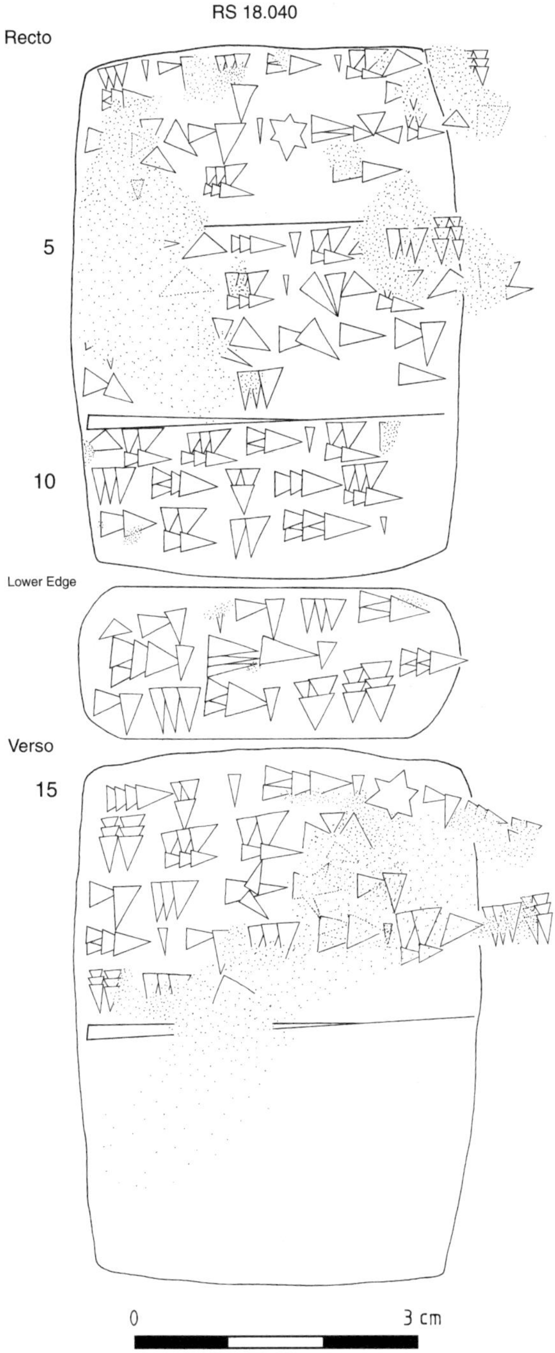
RS 18.040
Recto
5
10
Lower Edge
Verso
15
0
3 cm

RS 29.093

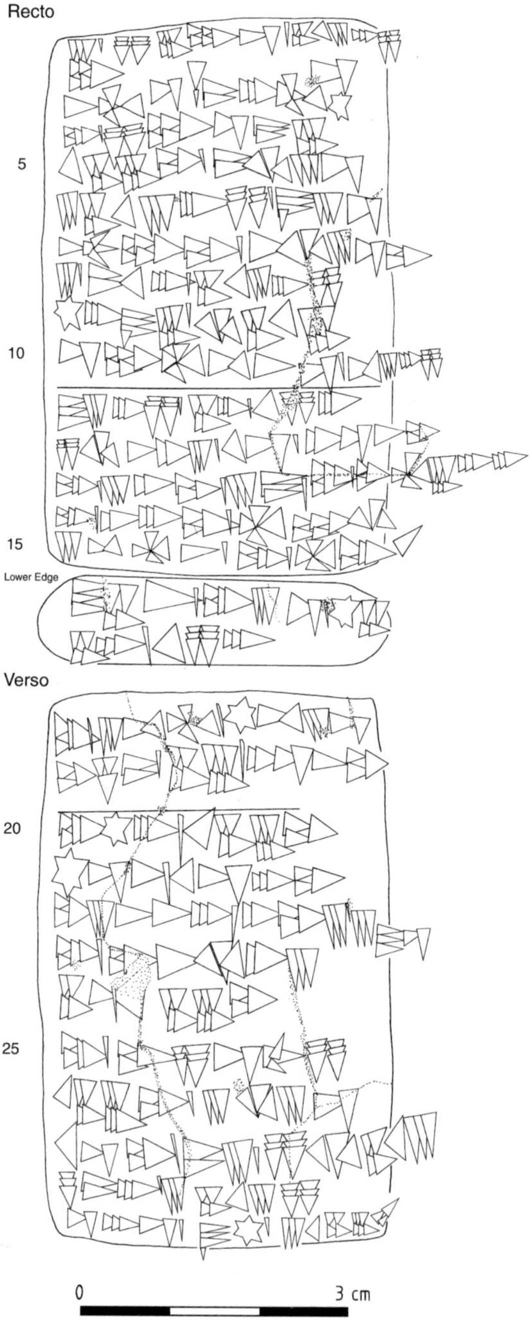

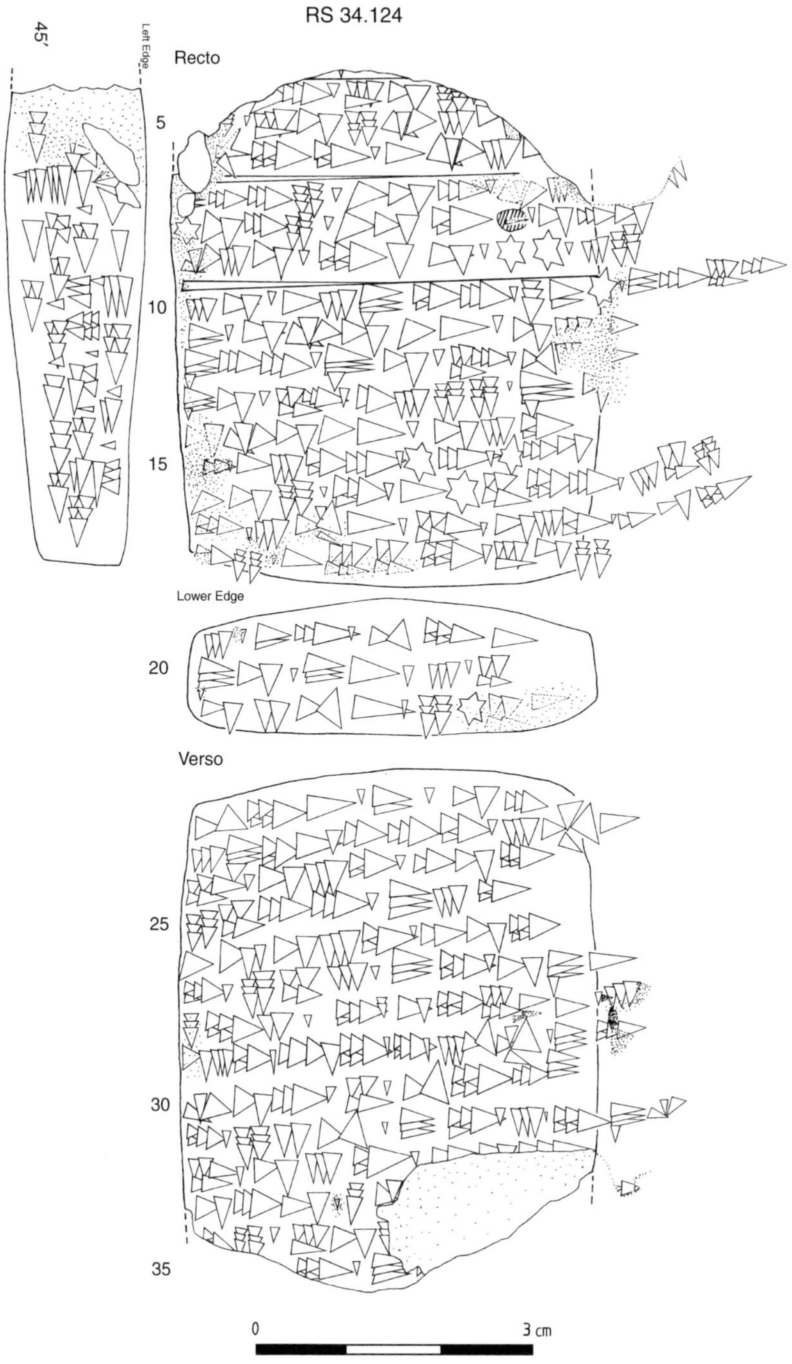
RS 34.124
Recto
Left Edge
45′
5
10
15
Lower Edge
20
Verso
25
30
35
0
3 cm

RS 92.2010

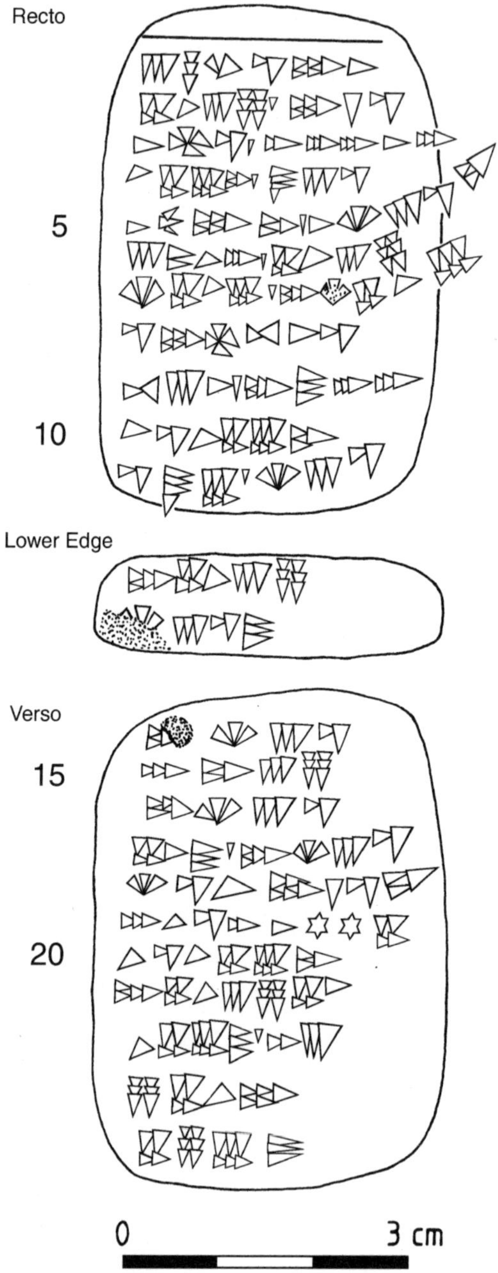

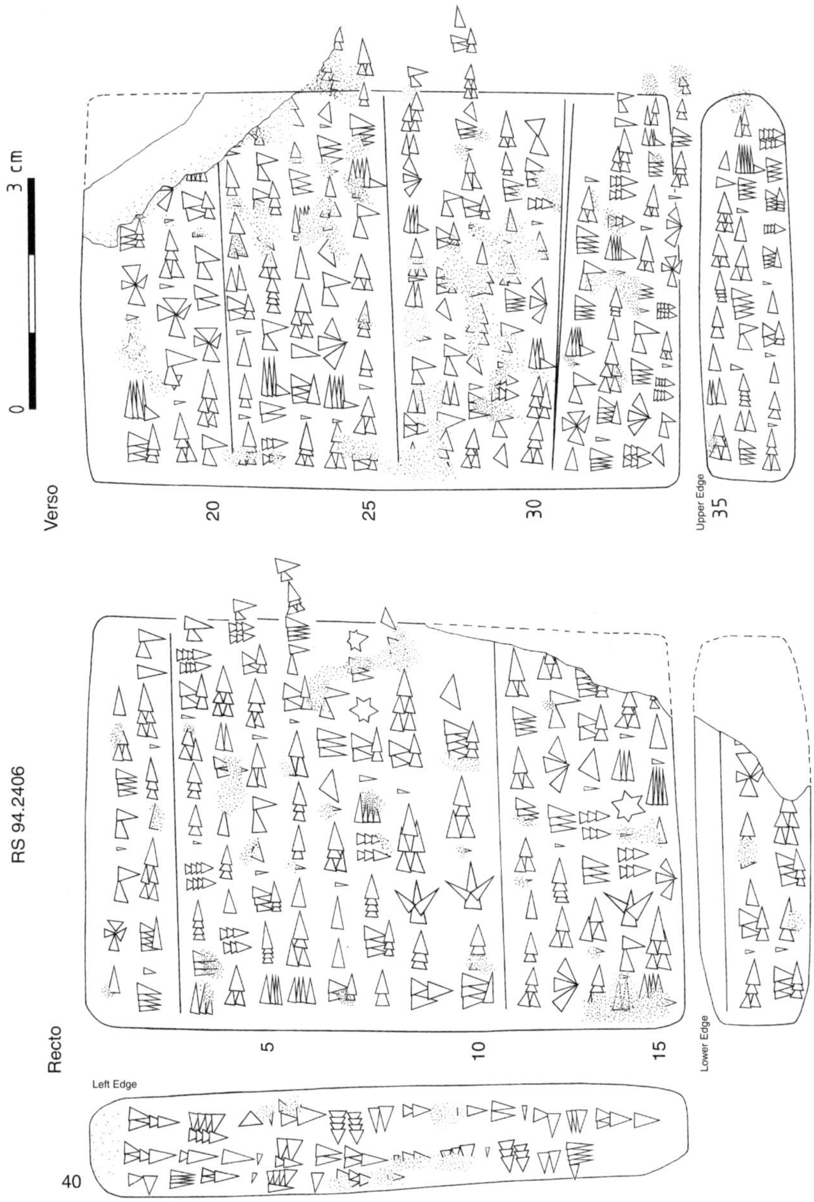
RS 94.2406
3 cm
0
Recto
Verso
Left Edge
Lower Edge
Upper Edge
5
10
15
20
25
30
35
40

RS 94.2479

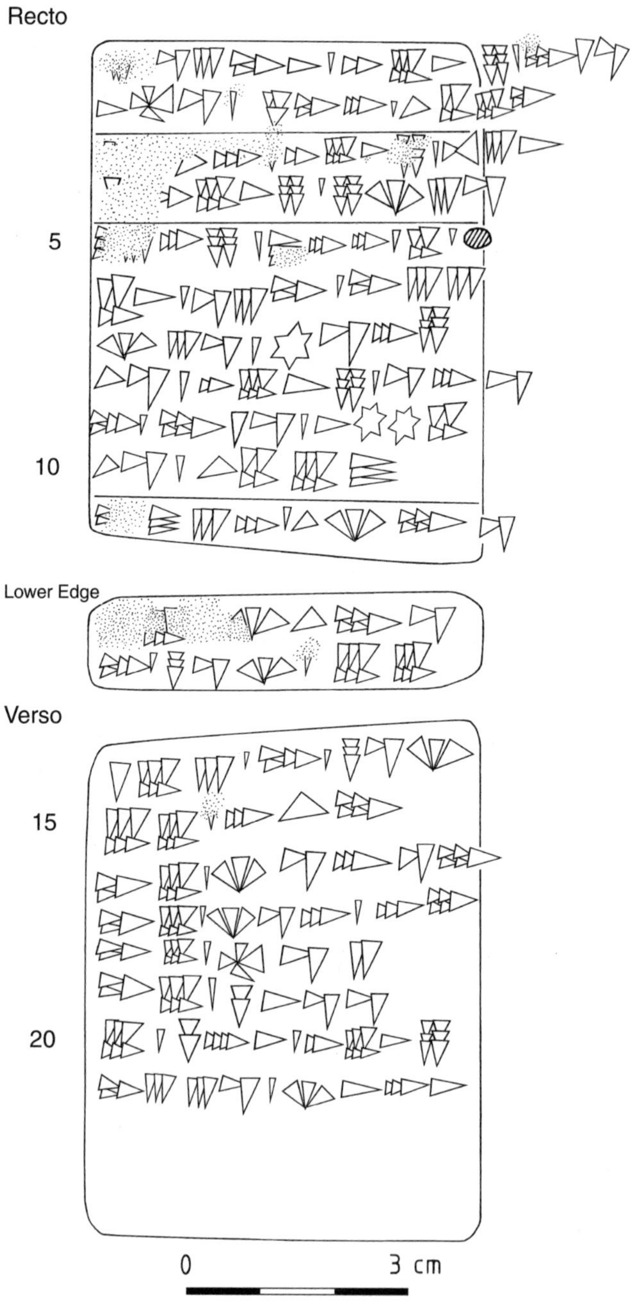

RS 96.2039

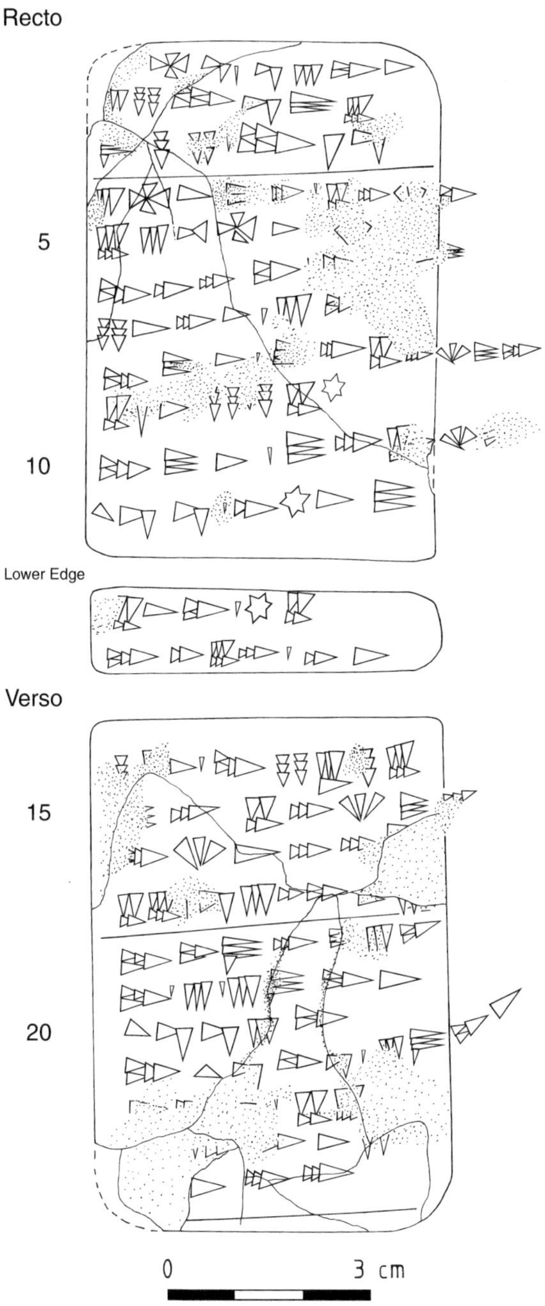

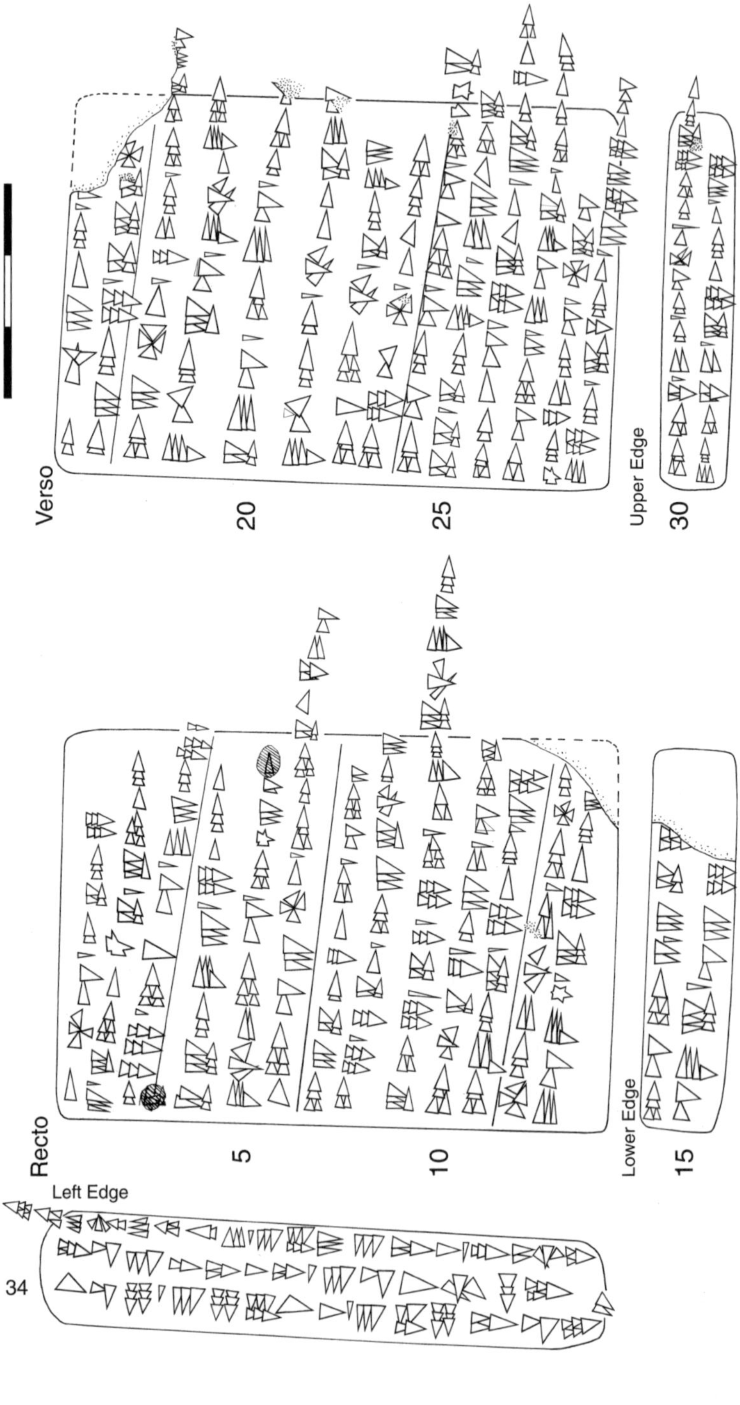
RS 94.2284
0
3 cm
Verso
20
25
Upper Edge
30
Recto
5
10
Lower Edge
15
Left Edge
34

RS [Varia 4]

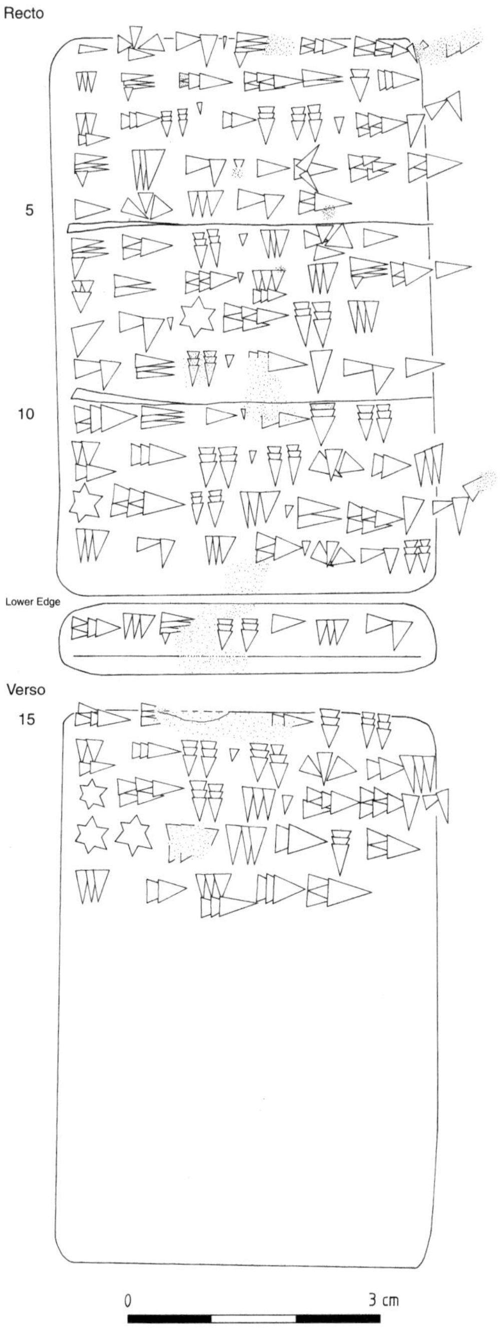

RS 11.772 + 11.780 + 11.782 + 11.802

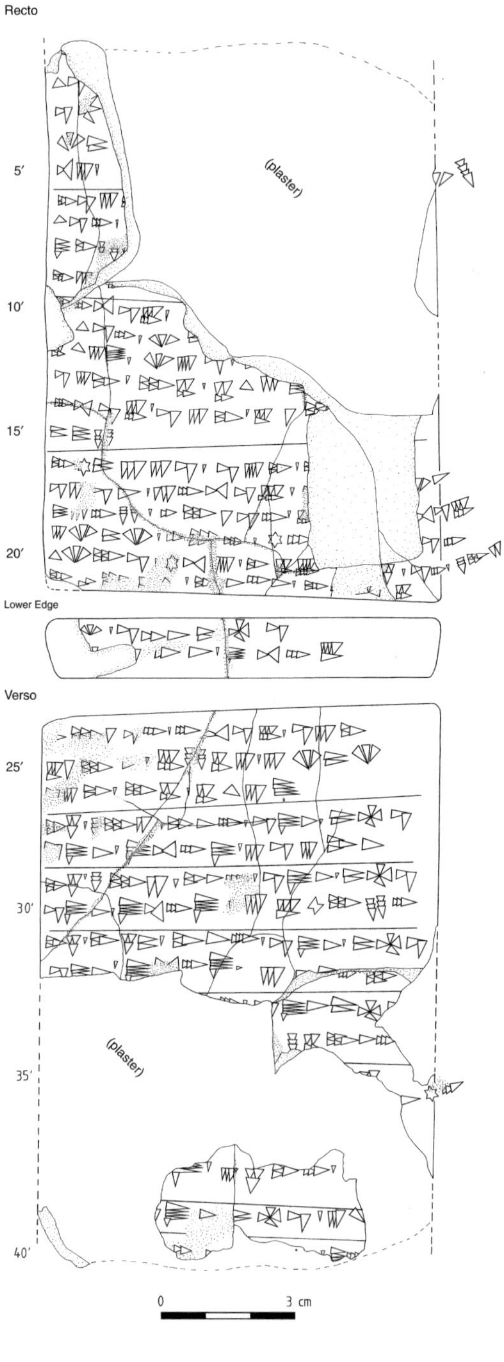

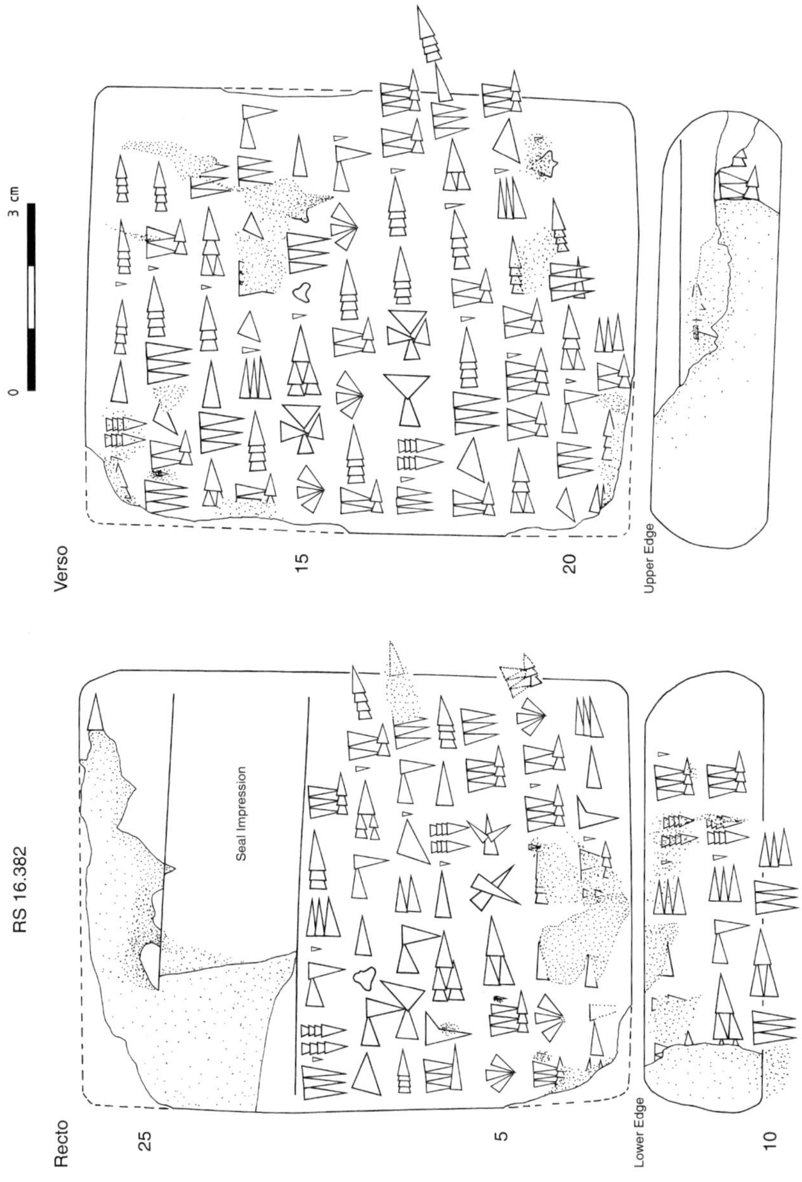

RS 16.382
0
3 cm
Verso
15
20
Upper Edge
Recto
25
Seal Impression
5
Lower Edge
10

RS 94.2168

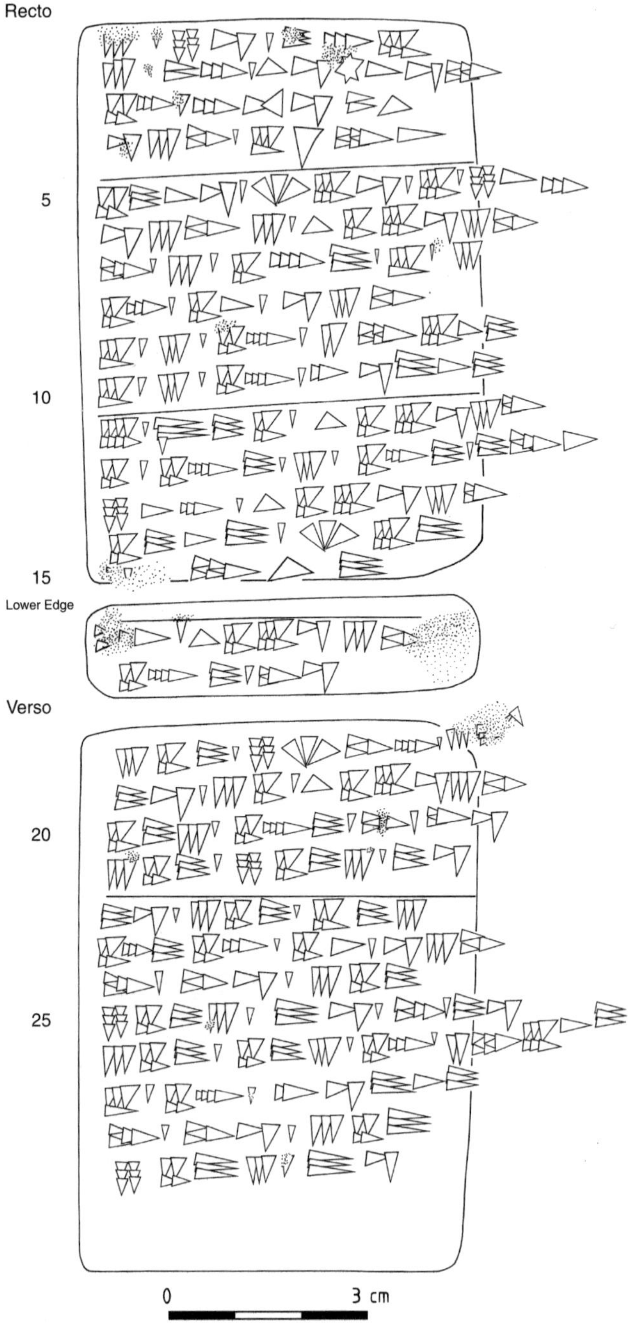

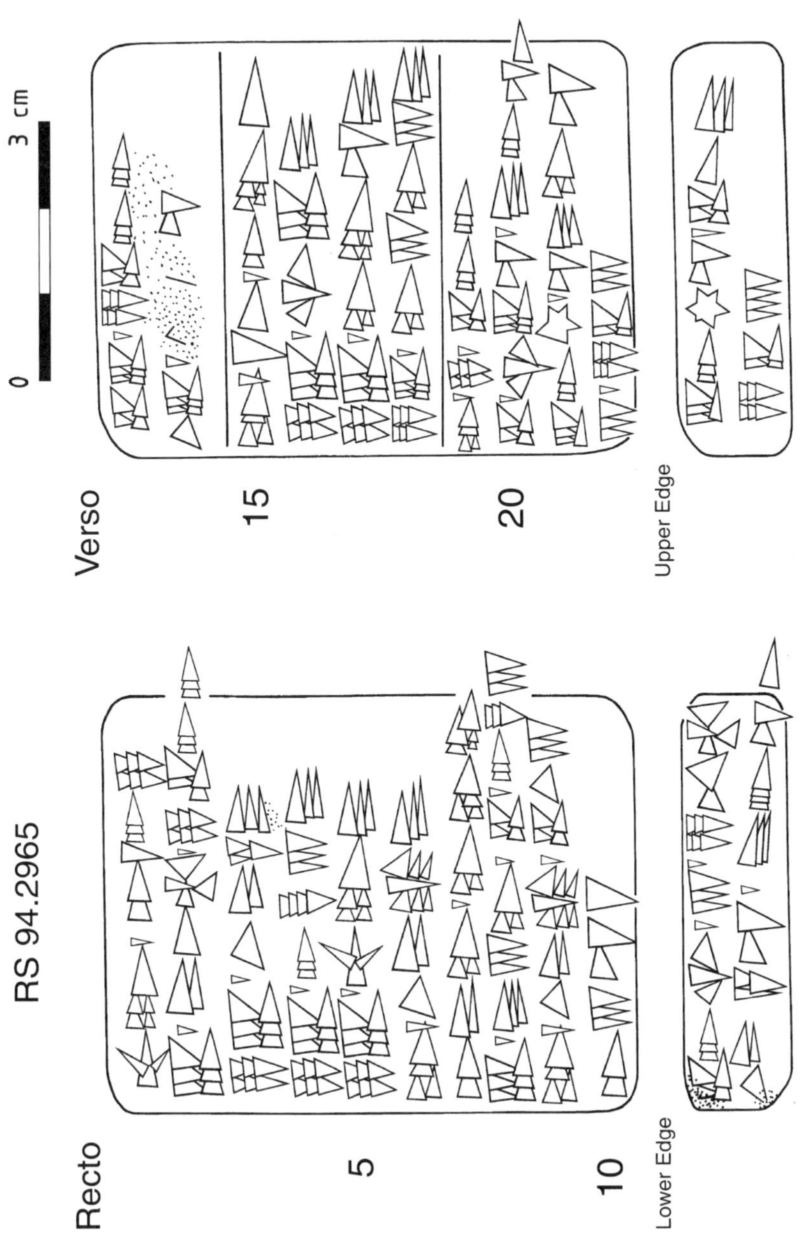
RS 94.2965
0
3 cm
Recto
Verso
Lower Edge
Upper Edge

RS [Varia 14]

Recto

Lower Edge

Verso

Upper Edge

RS 19.015

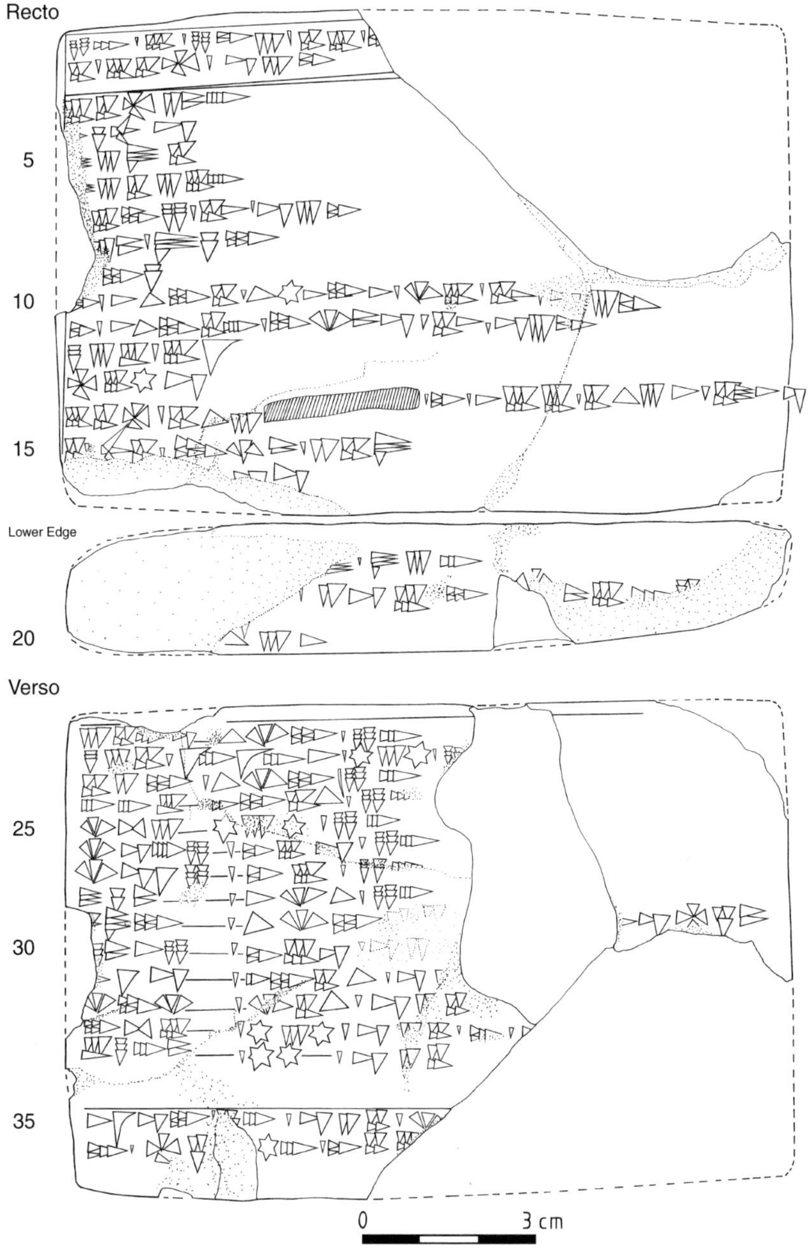

RS 15.062

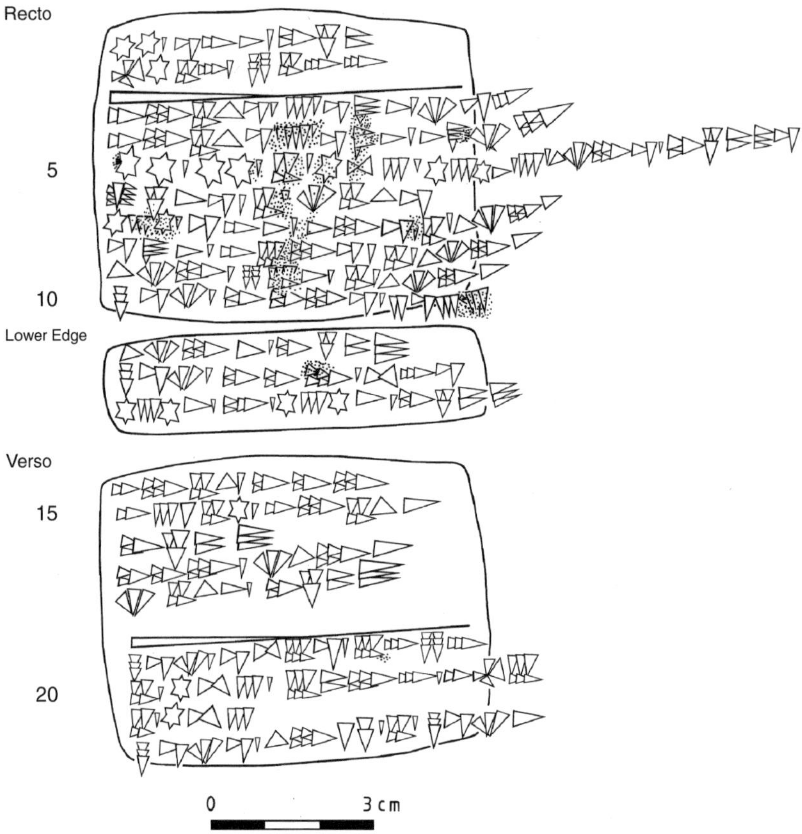

RS 18.024

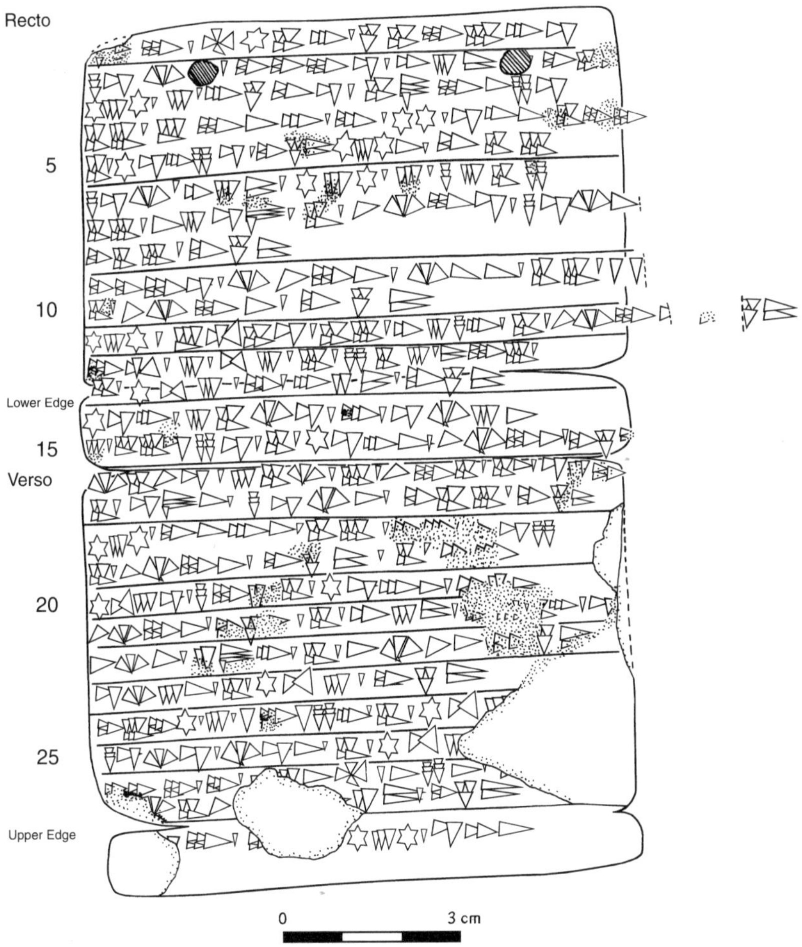
Recto
5
10
Lower Edge
15
Verso
20
25
Upper Edge
0
3 cm

RS 19.016

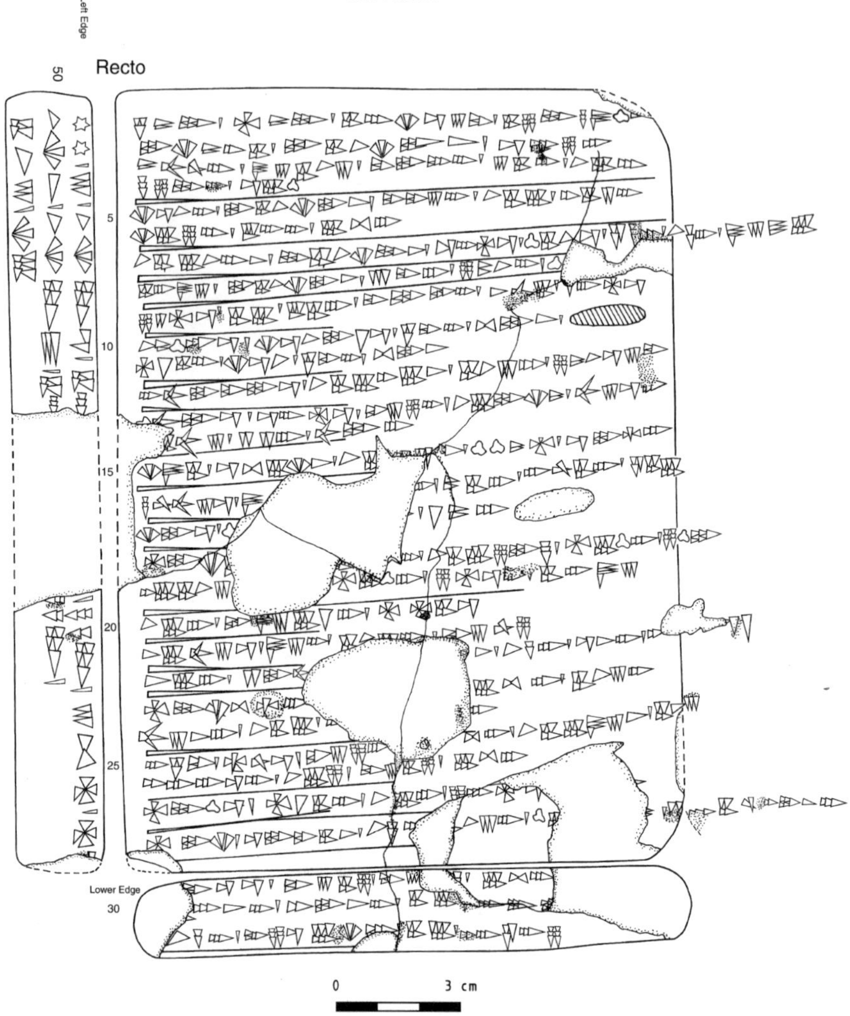

RS 19.016

Verso

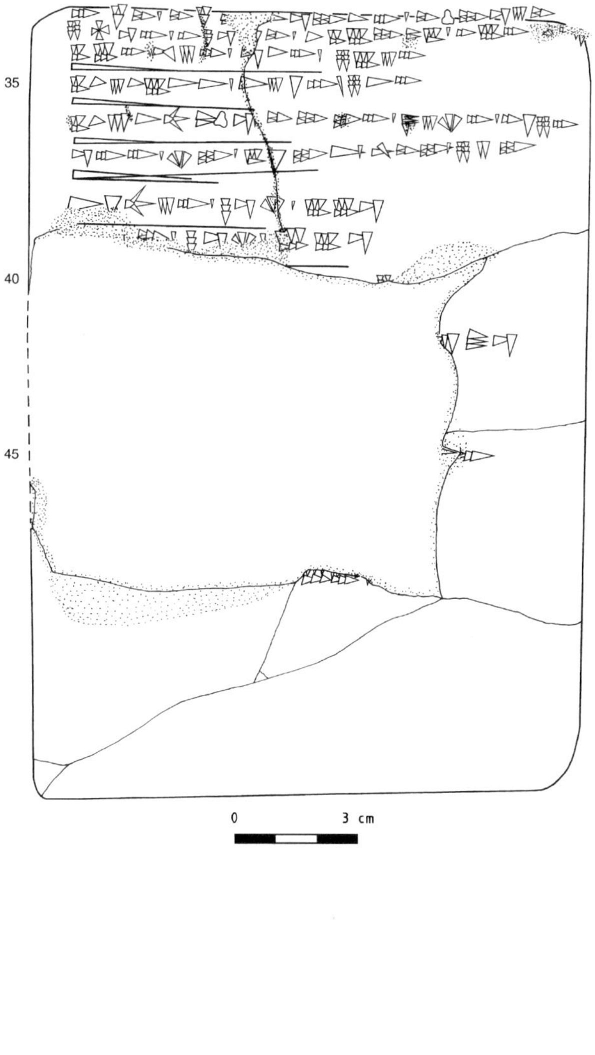

RS 86.2213

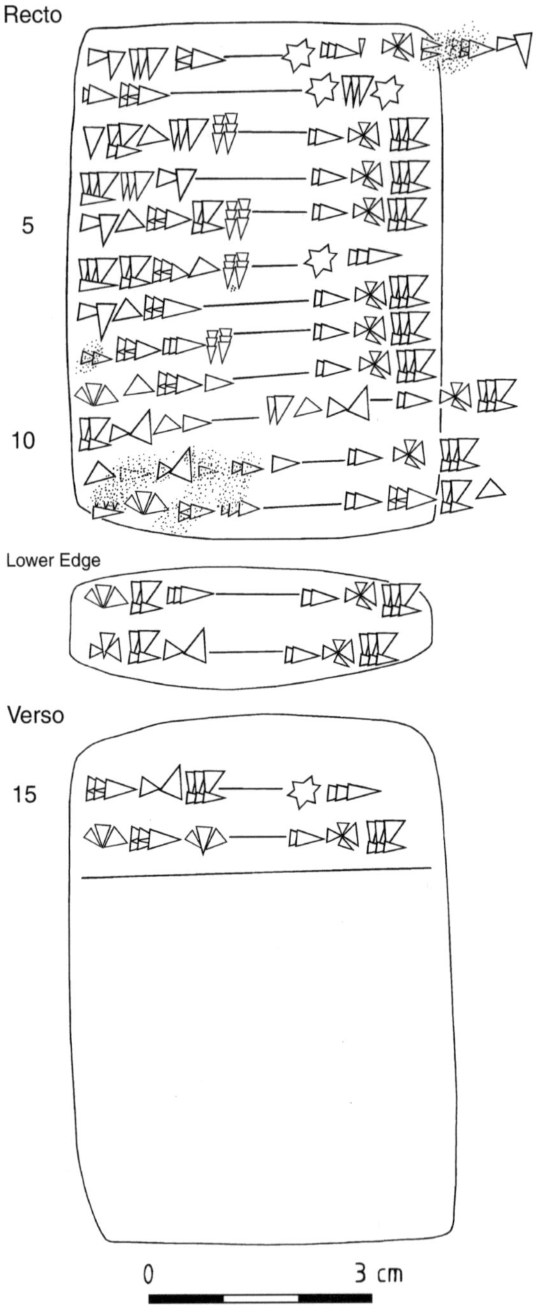
Recto
5
10
Lower Edge
Verso
15
0
3 cm

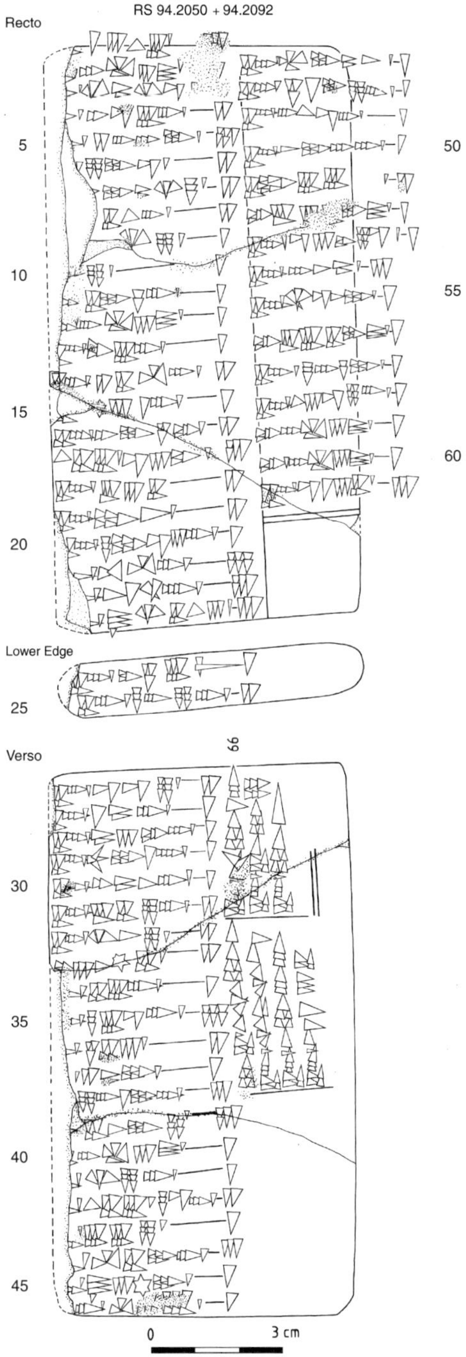
RS 94.2050 + 94.2092
Recto
Lower Edge
Verso
0
3 cm

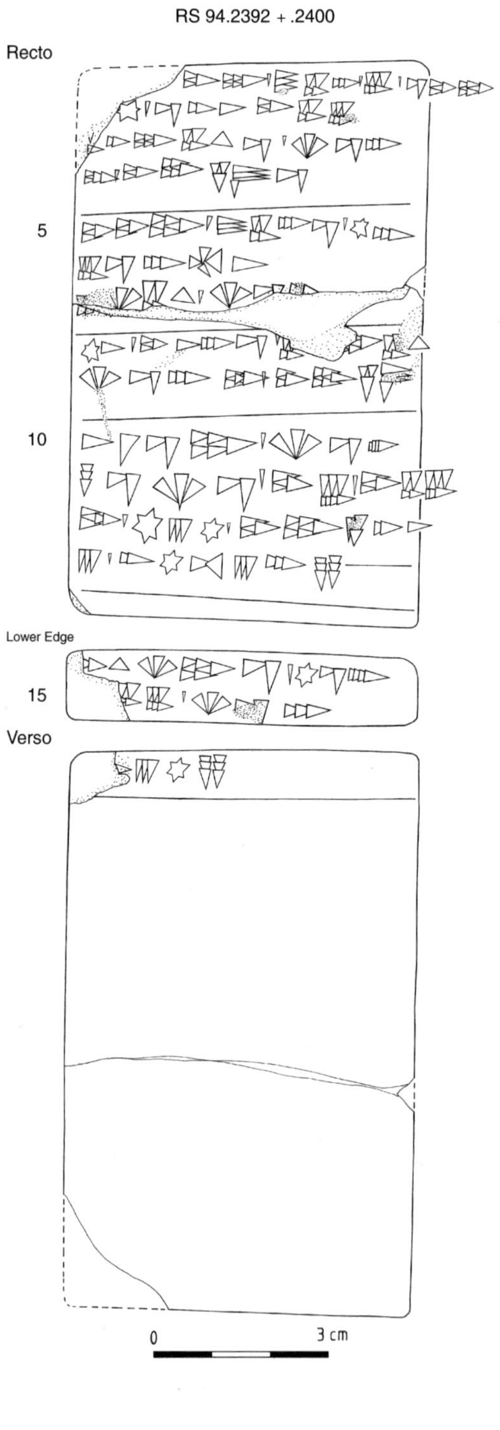
RS 94.2392 + .2400
Recto
5
10
Lower Edge
15
Verso
0
3 cm

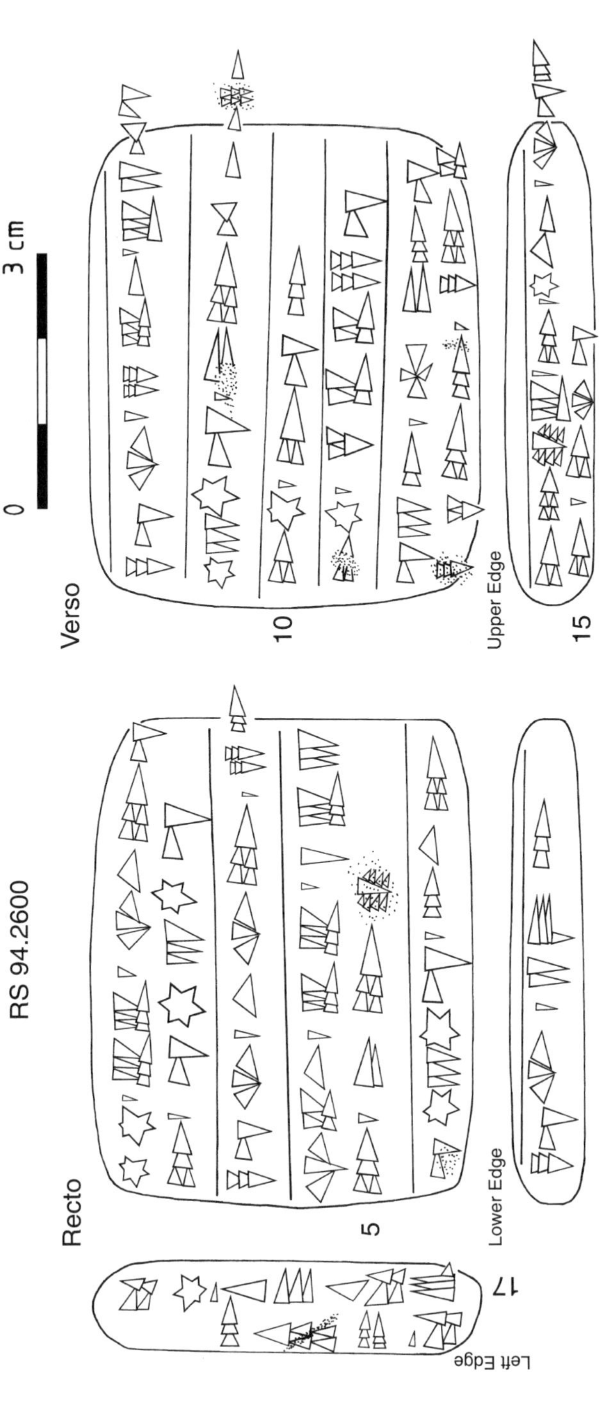
RS 94.2600
Recto
Verso
0
3 cm
5
10
15
17
Lower Edge
Upper Edge
Left Edge

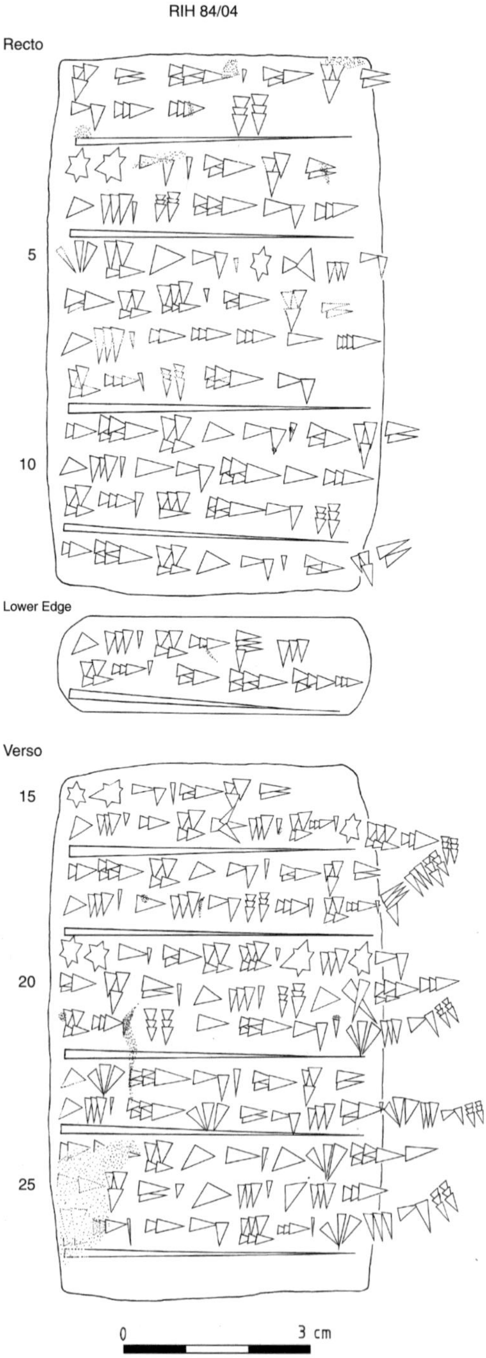
RIH 84/04
Recto
5
10
Lower Edge
Verso
15
20
25
0
3 cm

RIH 84/06

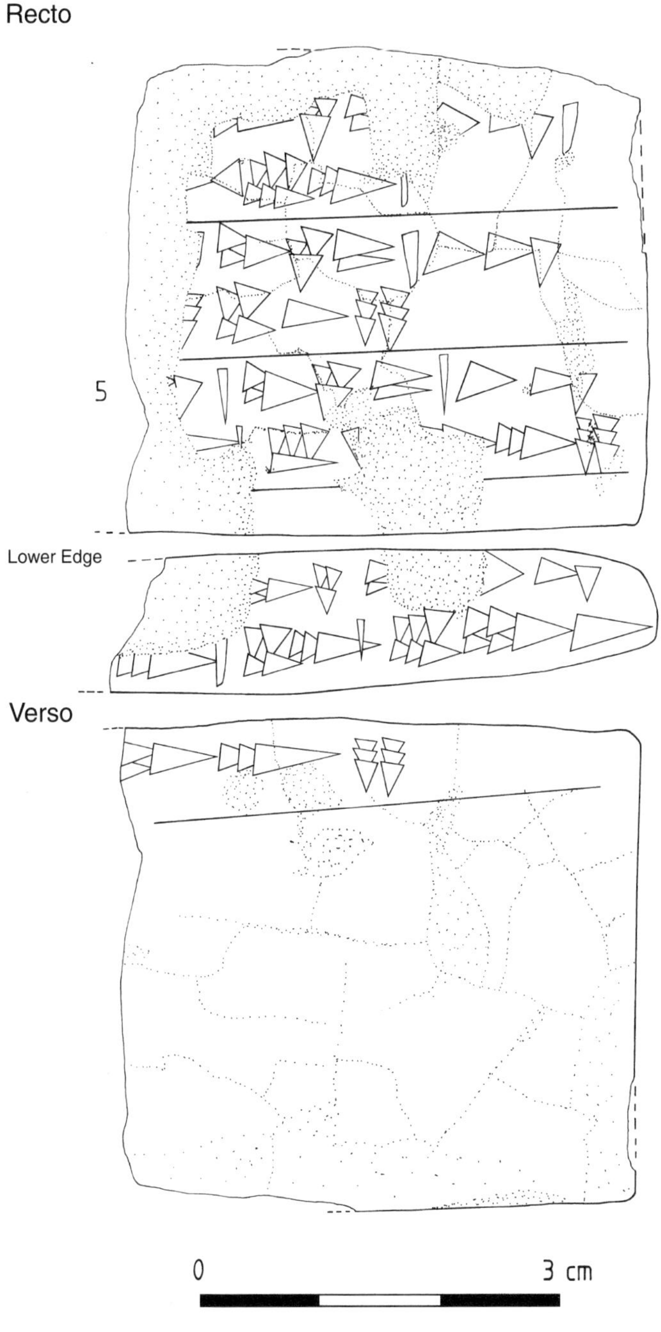

RIH 84/33

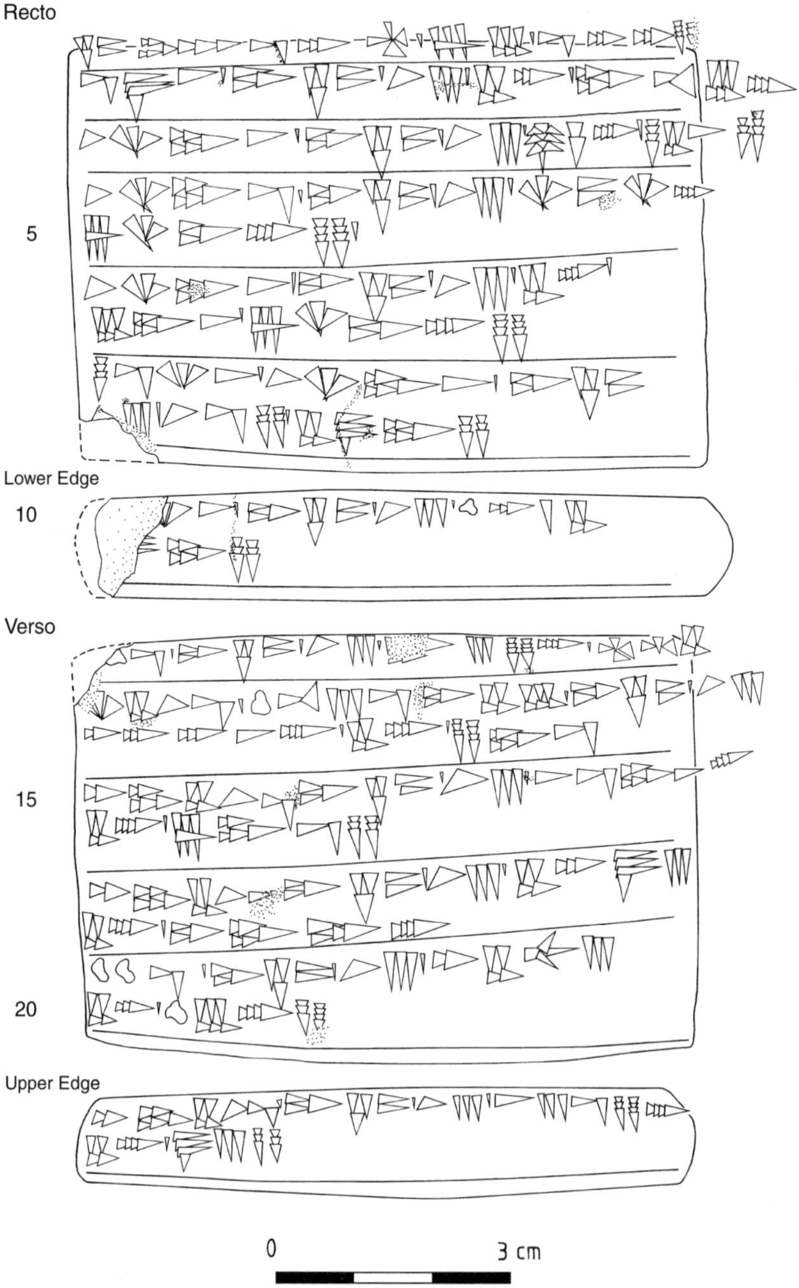

RIH 83/22

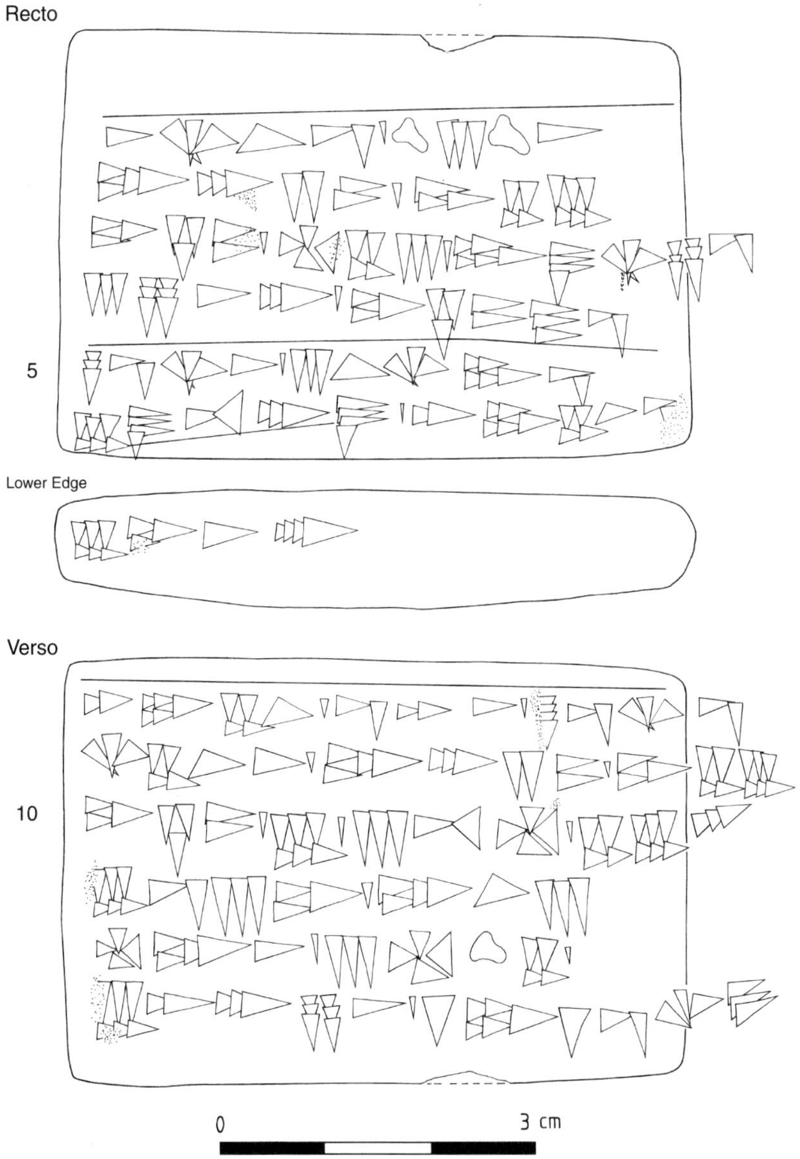

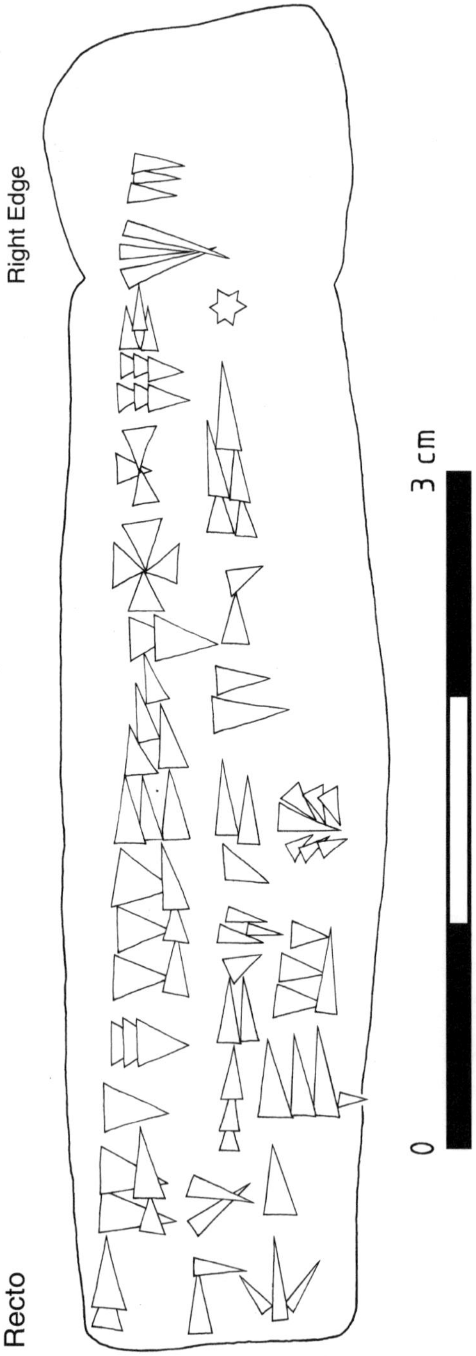
Right Edge
RS 12.063
Recto
3 cm
0

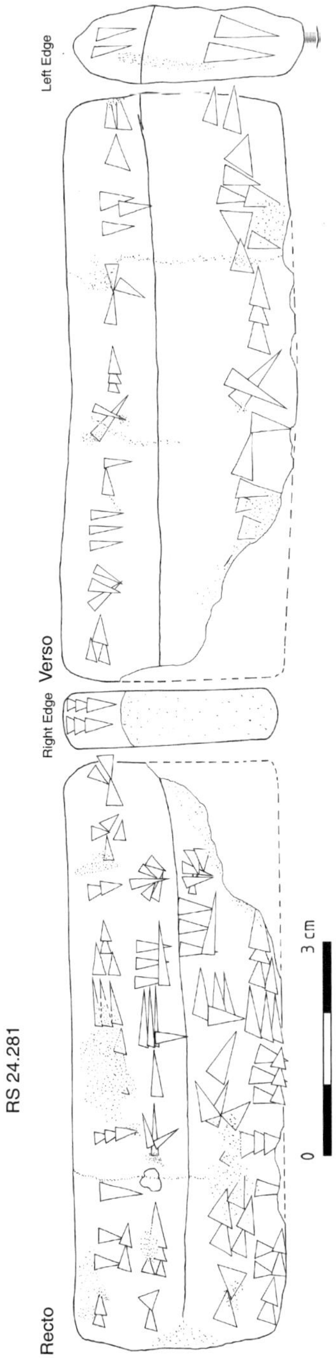
RS 24.281
Left Edge
Verso
Right Edge
Recto
3 cm
0

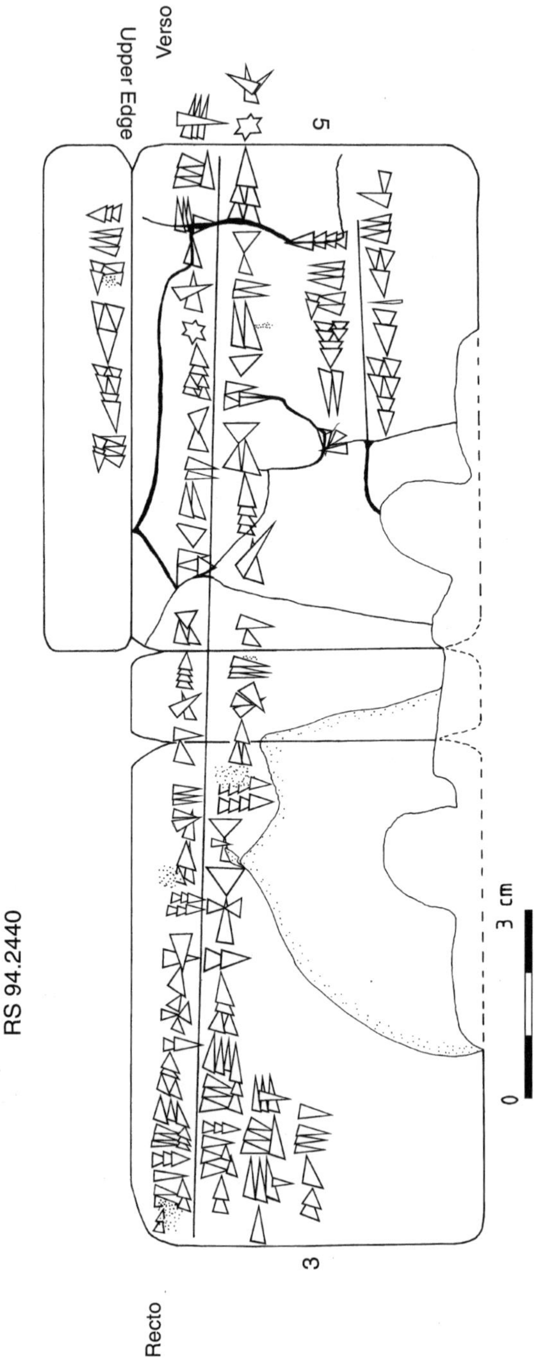
RS 94.2440
Recto
Verso
Upper Edge
3
5
0
3 cm

Selection of Texts

List

I. Mythological Texts

The *Baʿlu* Myth: (1) *Baʿlu*'s Battle with *Yammu* (RS 3.367 i)
(2) *Baʿlu* and *ʿAnatu* (RS 2.[014]+ iii–iv)

(3) *Kirta*: *Kirta*'s Seven Wives (RS 2.[003]+ i)
(4) *ʾAqhatu*: The Promise of a Son (RS 2.[004] i)
(5) *Šaḥru-wa-Šalimu*: The Birth of the Gracious and Beautiful Gods (RS 2.002)
(6) *Ḥôrānu* and the Serpents (RS 24.244)
(7) The Drunkenness of *ʾIlu* (RS 24.258)

II. Ritual Texts

(8) A Sacrificial Ritual for a Day and a Night (RS 1.001)
(9) A Sacrificial Ritual for National Unity (RS 1.002)
(10) A Sacrificial Ritual for *ʾUšḫarâ Ḫulmiẓẓi* (RS 24.260)
(11) A Sacrificial Ritual with a Prayer (RS 24.266)
(12) A Sacrificial Ritual for the Gods of the "Pantheon" (RS 24.643)
(13) A Royal Funerary Ritual (RS 34.126)
(14) Commemoration of the Mortuary Offering of *Ṯarriyelli* (inscribed stela RS 6.021)
(15) Commemoration of the Mortuary Offering of *ʿUzzīnu* (inscribed stela RS 6.028)
(16) An *Ex Voto* Inscription (inscribed lion-headed vase RS 25.318)

III. Incantations

(17) An Incantation against Male Sexual Dysfunction (RIH 78/20)
(18) An Incantation against Snakes and Scorpions (RS 92.2014)

IV. "Scientific" Texts

(19) Hippiatric Prescriptions (RS 17.120)
(20) Manual of Teratology (RS 24.247+)

V. Letters

(21) A Military Situation (RS 4.475)
(22) *Talmiyānu* and *ʾAḫâtumilki* to Their Lady (RS 8.315)

(23) The King to the Queen-Mother (RS 11.872)
(24) *Talmiyānu* to His Mother, *Ṯarriyelli* (RS 15.008)
(25) The King Meets His Hittite Sovereign (RS 16.379)
(26) The King of Tyre to the King of Ugarit (RS 18.031)
(27) *Ṯipṭibaʿlu* to the King (RS 18.040)
(28) Two Servants to Their Master (RS 29.093)
(29) The King to the Queen-Mother in the Matter of the Amurrite Princess (RS 34.124)
(30) *ʾAnantēnu* to His Master, *Ḫiḏmiratu* (RS 92.2010)
(31) A Double Letter: The Queen to *ʾUrtēnu* and *ʾIlîmilku* to the Same (RS 94.2406)
(32) A Business Letter: The Governor to the Queen (RS 94.2479)
(33) The Queen to *Yarmihaddu* on the Matter of a Missing Slave (RS 96.2039)
(34) *ʾABNY* to *ʾUrtēṯub*/*ʾUrtēnu* (RS 94.2284)
(35) *ʾIwriḏēnu* Asks to Be Named before the King (RS [Varia 4])

VI. Legal Texts

(36) A Suzerainty Treaty between *Ṯuppiluliuma* and *Niqmaddu* (RS 11.772^{+})
(37) A Real-Estate Transfer (RS 16.382)
(38) How *ʿAbdimilku* May Bequeath His Property (RS 94.2168)
(39) *Yabninu* Acquires Real Estate (RS 94.2965)
(40) A *marziḥu*-Contract (RS [Varia 14])

VII. Administrative Texts

(41) Wine for Royal Sacrificial Rites (RS 19.015)
(42) An Account Text for *Yabninu* (RS 15.062)
(43) An Account Text for Bronzeworkers (RS 18.024)
(44) A Ration List for Royal Workers (RS 19.016)
(45) A Ration List with Village Names (RS 86.2213)
(46) Leaders of Ten and Their Men (RS 94.2050^{+})
(47) A Sale of Ebony-Wood (RS 94.2392^{+})
(48) Provisions for a Month (RS 94.2600)
(49–51) Debit Accounts Owing to *Muninuya*
(49) RIH 84/04
(50) RIH 84/06
(51) RIH 84/33
(52) Boats to Carchemish (RIH 83/22)

VIII. Abecedaries

(53) An Abecedary (RS 12.063)
(54) A Double Abecedary (RS 24.281)
(55) A Double Abecedary with Place Names (RS 94.2440)

I. Mythological Texts

Text 1: The *Baʿlu* Myth: *Baʿlu*'s Battle with *Yammu* (RS 3.367 i)

Virolleaud 1935; *CTA* 2 iv; *KTU* 1.2 iv; Ginsberg 1950: 130–31; Bordreuil and Pardee 1993a; Pardee 1997a: 248–49; Dietrich and Loretz 1997: 1129–34; Smith 1997: 102–5; Wyatt 1998: 63–69.

	Text	***Translation***
(1′)	[. . .]yd[-]ḫtt . mtt ˹.˺[. . .]	
(2′)	[-----]ḥy[---]˹-˺[-] l ảšṣỉ . hm .	[. . .] I will indeed force them to leave,
	ảp . ảmr [ ] (3′) [----]	moreover I will drive out [. . .].
	w b ym . mnḫ l ˹.˺ ảbd .	In *Yammu* I will indeed destroy the resting place,
	b ym . ỉrtm . m[. . .]	in *Yammu*, at (his) very heart, (I will destroy) the M[. . .],
	(4′) [b ṯp]˹ṭ˺ . nhr . tlʿm .	[(as for) Rule]r *Naharu*, (I will destroy) (his) neck.
	ṯm . ḥrbm . ỉts .	There with the sword I will lay waste,
	ảnšq (5′) ˹b˺htm .	I will burn down (his) house:
	l ảrṣ . ypl . ủlny .	The powerful one will fall to the earth,
	w l . ʿpr . ʿẓmny	the mighty one to the dust.
(6′)	˹b˺ ph . rgm . l yṣả	Hardly has the word left his mouth,
	b špth . hwth .	the utterance his lips,
	w ttn ˹.˺ gh .	when she pronounces:
	yǵr (7′) tḥt . ksỉ . zbl ym .	Under the throne with Prince *Yammu*!
	w ʿn . kṯr . w ḫss .	*Kôṯaru-wa-Ḫasīsu* speaks up:
	l rgm˹t˺ (8′) lk . l zbl . bʿl .	I hereby announce to you, Prince *Baʿlu*,
	ṯnt . l rkb . ʿrpt .	and I repeat, Cloud-Rider:
	ht . ỉbk (9′) bʿlm .	As for your enemy, O *Baʿlu*,
	ht . ỉbk . tmḫṣ .	as for your enemy, you'll smite (him),
	ht . tṣmt ˹.˺ ṣrtk	you'll destroy your adversary.
(10′)	tqḥ . mlk . ʿlmk .	You'll take your eternal kingship,
	drkt dt ˹.˺ dr drk	your sovereignty (that endures) from generation to generation.
(11′)	kṯr ṣmdm . ynḥt .	(Then) *Kôṯaru* prepares two maces
	w ypʿr . šmthm .	and proclaims their names:
	šmk ảt (12′) ygrš ˹.˺	You, your name is *Yagrušu*:
	ygrš . grš ym	O *Yagrušu*, drive out *Yammu*;
	grš ym . l ksỉh	drive *Yammu* from his throne,
(13′)	nhr ˹.˺ l kḥṯ ˹.˺ drkth .	*Naharu* from his seat of sovereignty.
	trtqṣ . bd bʿl ˹.˺	You'll whirl in *Baʿlu*'s hand,

	km nš(14′)⸢r⸣ . b ủṣbʿth .	like a hawk in his fingers.
	hlm . ktp ⸢.⸣ zbl ⸢.⸣ ym ⸢.⸣	Strike Prince *Yammu* on the shoulder,
	bn ydm (15′) [ṯp]ṭ . nhr .	Ruler *Naharu* on the chest.
	yrtqṣ . ṣmd . bd bʿl .	(So) the mace whirls in *Baʿlu*'s hand,
	km . nšr (16′) ⸢b ủ⸣ṣbʿth .	like a hawk in his fingers.
	ylm . ktp . zbl ym .	It strikes Prince *Yammu* on the shoulder,
	bn ⸢.⸣ ydm ⸢.⸣ ṯpṭ (17′) ⸢nh⸣r ⸢.⸣	Ruler *Naharu* on the chest.
	ʿz . ym . l ymk .	(But) *Yammu* is strong, he does not collapse,
	l tnǵṣn [.] pnth .	his joints do not go slack,
	l ydlp (18′) tmnh .	his body does not slump.
	kṯr . ṣmdm . ynḥt ⸢.⸣	(So) *Kôṯaru* prepares two maces
	w ypʿr . šmthm .	and proclaims their names:
(19′)	šmk . ảt . ảymr .	You, your name is *ʾAyamiri*:
	ảymr . mr . ym .	O *ʾAyamiri*, drive out *Yammu*;
	mr . ym (20′) l ksỉh .	drive out *Yammu* from his throne,
	nhr . l kḥṯ . drkth .	*Naharu* from his seat of sovereignty.
	trtqṣ (21′) bd bʿl .	You'll whirl in *Baʿlu*'s hand,
	km . nšr b ủṣbʿth .	like a hawk in his fingers.
	hlm . qdq(22′)⸢d⸣ . zbl ym .	Strike Prince *Yammu* on the head,
	bn . ʿnm . ṯpṭ . nhr .	Ruler *Naharu* on the forehead.
	yprsḥ ym	*Yammu* will go groggy
(23′)	w yql . l ảrṣ .	and will fall to the ground.
	w yrtqṣ . ṣmd⸢.⸣bd bʿl	So the mace whirls in *Baʿlu*'s hand,
(24′)	⸢km⸣ [.] nšr . b ủṣbʿth .	like a hawk in his fingers.
	ylm . qdqd . zbl (25′) ⸢ym⸣ [.]	It strikes Prince *Yammu* on the head,
	bn . ʿnm . ṯpṭ . nhr .	Ruler *Naharu* on the forehead.
	yprsḥ . ym .	*Yammu* goes groggy,
	yql (26′) l ảrṣ .	falls to the ground;
	tnǵṣn . pnth .	his joints go slack,
	w ydlp . tmnh	his body slumps.
(27′)	yqṯ bʿl . w yšt . ym .	*Baʿlu* grabs *Yammu* and sets about dismembering (him),
	ykly . ṯpṭ . nhr	sets about finishing off Ruler *Naharu*.
(28′)	b šm . tgʿrm . ʿṯtrt .	By name *ʿAṯtartu* reprimands (him):
	bṯ l ảlỉyn ⸢b⸣[ʿl]	Scatter (him), O Mighty *B*[*aʿlu*],
(29′)	bṯ . l rkb . ʿrpt .	scatter (him), O Cloud-Rider,
	k šbyn . zb[l . ym .	For Prin[ce *Yammu*] is our captive,
	k] (30′) šbyn . ṯpṭ . nhr	[for] Ruler *Naharu* is our captive.
	w yṣả b[. . .]	And EXIT from [. . .]

(31′)	ybṯ . nn . ảlỉyn . bˁl .	Mighty *Baˁlu* disperses him
	w[. . .]	and[. . .]
(32′)	ym . l mt .	*Yammu* is indeed dead,
	bˁlm . yml[k . . .]	*Baˁlu* will rei[gn . . .]
	[. . .] (33′) ḥm . l šrr .	[. . .] certainly true
	w[. . .]	and [. . .]
	[. . .] (34′) yˁn .	[. . .] speaks up:
	ym . l mt[. . .]	*Yammu* is indeed dead [. . .]
	[. . .] (35′) l šrr .	[. . .] certainly true.
	w tˁ[n . . .]	And she respon[ds . . .]
(36′)	bˁlm . hmt .[. . .]	*Baˁlu* . . . them [. . .]
(37′)	l šrr . š⸢-⸣[. . .]	certainly true [. . .]
(38′)	b rỉšh . [. . .]	on his head [. . .]
(39′)	⸢ỉ⸣bh . mš[. . .]	his enemy [. . .]
(40′)	[-]n . ˁn⸢h⸣[. . .]	his forehead [. . .]

Vocalized Text

(2′) [. . .] la ʾašôṣiʾhumā // ʾapa ʾamri[humā . . .] (3′) [----]
wa bi yammi manūḫa la ʾabbid
// bi yammi ʾirtama M[ ]
// (4′) [bi ṯāpiṭ]i nahari talaˁama
ṯamma ḥarbama ʾittasi // ʾanaššiq (5′) bahatīma
lê ʾarṣi yappulu ʾūlāniyyu // wa lê ˁapari ˁaẓūmāniyyu
(6′) bi pîhu rigmu lā yaṣaʾa // bi šapatêhu huwātuhu // wa tatinu gâha
yaǵur (7′) taḥta kussaʾi zabūlu yammu
wa ˁanû kôṯaru wa ḫasīsu
la ragamtu (8′) lêka lê zabūli baˁli // ṯanîtu lê rākibi ˁurpati
hatti ʾêbaka (9′) baˁlima // hatti ʾêbaka timḫaṣu // hatti taṣammitu ṣarrataka
(10′) tiqqaḥu mulka ˁālamika // darkata dāti dāri dārika
(11′) kôṯaru ṣimdêma yanaḥḥitu // wa yipˁaru šumātihumā
šumuka ʾatta (12′) yagrušu // yagruši guruš yamma
guruš yamma lê kussaʾihu // (13′) nahara lê kaḥṯi darkatihu
tirtaqiṣu bîdi baˁli // kama naš(14′)ri bi ʾuṣbaˁātihu
hulum katipa zabūli yammi // bêna yadêma (15′) [ṯāpi]ṭi nahari
yirtaqiṣu ṣimdu bîdi baˁli // kama našri (16′) bi ʾuṣbaˁātihu
yallumu katipa zabūli yammi // bêna yadêma ṯāpiṭi (17′) nahari
ˁazzu yammu lā yamūku // lā tinnaǵiṣna pinnātuhu // lā yadlupu (18′) tamūnuhu
kôṯaru ṣimdêma yanaḥḥitu // wa yipˁaru šumātihumā
(19′) šumuka ʾatta ʾāyamiri // ʾāyamiri miri yamma

miri yamma (20′) lê kussaʾihu // nahara lê kaḥṯi darkatihu
tirtaqiṣu (21′) bîdi baʿli // kama našri bi ʾuṣbaʿātihu
hulum qudqu(22′)da zabūli yammi // bêna ʿênêma ṯāpiṭi nahari
yipparsiḥu yammu // (23′) wa yaqīlu lê ʾarṣi
wa yirtaqiṣu ṣimdu bîdi baʿli // (24′) kama našri bi ʾuṣbaʿātihu
yallumu qudquda zabūli (25′) yammi // bêna ʿênêma ṯāpiṭi nahari
yipparsiḥu yammu // yaqīlu (26′) lê ʾarṣi
tinnaǵiṣna pinnātihu // wa yadlupu tamūnuhu
(27′) yaquṯṯu baʿlu wa yašittu yamma // yakalliyu ṯāpiṭa nahara
(28′) bi šumi tigʿaruma ʿaṯtartu
buṯ lê ʾalʾiyāna [baʿli] // (29′) buṯ lê rākibi ʿurpati
kī šabyunū zabū[lu yammu] // [kī] (30′) šabyunū ṯāpiṭu naharu
wa YṢʾA bi[. . .]
(31′) yabuṯṯannannu ʾalʾiyānu baʿlu // wa [. . .]
(32′) yammu la mīta // baʿluma yamlu[ku . . .]
[. . .] (33′) ḤM la šarrīru
wa [. . .]
[. . .] (34′) yaʿnû
yammu la mêta
[. . .] (35′) la šarrīru
wa taʿnû [. . .]
(36′) baʿluma humati[. . .]
(37′) la šarrīru Š⌈-⌉[. . .]
(38′) bi raʾšihu [. . .]
(39′) ʾêb-hu MŠ[. . .]
(40′) [bê]na ʿênêhu [. . .]

Notes

(2′) {l} asseverative particle; {ảšṣi} 1c.s. jussive, Š-stem (the {i} shows that the form is /YQTLØ/), √YṢʾ ← √WṢʾ 'to exit → to cause to exit' /ʾašôṣiʾ/ ← /ʾašawṣiʾ/; {hm} either the conditional particle or a pronominal suffix expressing the direct object; if a pronominal suffix it may be either in the plural, referring to all the enemies of Baʿlu, or in the dual expressing the duality of the following combat (two arms, two battles, the adversary bears two names); {ảmr} 1c.s. jussive, G-stem of √MRY; perhaps restore {hm} with or without a word-divider after this verb, as in the case of the preceding verb.

(3′) {mnḫ} *m*- preformative common noun, m.s.a. √NḪ; {ảbd} 1c.s. jussive, D-stem, √ʾBD 'perish → destroy' /ʾabbid/ ← /ʾaʾabbid/; {ỉrtm} common noun, f.s.a. + *m*-enclitic; {tlʿm} common noun, m.s.a. + *m*-enclitic.

(4′) {ḥrbm} common noun, f.s.a. + *m*-enclitic; {ỉts} 1c.s. jussive, Gt-stem, √NSY /ʾittasi/ ← /*ʾintasiy/; {ảnšq} 1c.s. jussive, D-stem, √NŠQ ← *NŚQ.

(5′) {ypl} 3m.s. imperfective, G-stem, √NPL 'to fall' /yappulu/ (or, if the jussive mood continues, /yappul/ 'may he fall'); {ủlny} common noun, m.s.n. + *n*-enclitic + *y*-enclitic √ʾL; {ʿẓmny} common noun, m.s.n. + *n*-enclitic + *y*-enclitic √ʿẒM.

(6′) {yṣả} 3m.s. perfective, G-stem, √YṢʾ; {ttn} form uncertain, perhaps either a 3f.s. /YQTLu/-imperfective, G-stem, √YTN (subject *ʿAṯtartu*—see line 28′) or a verbal noun, 'the fact of giving', here of 'the voice'; {yǵr} 3m.s. jussive, G-stem, √ǴR.

(7′) {ʿn} either the infinitive of √ʿNY /ʿanû/ or 3m.s. perfective, G-stem, same root /ʿana/ (though the deity bears two names, this verb is probably not in the dual for, in the following speech, he speaks in the 1st person).

(9′) {bʿlm} divine name m.s. vocative + *m*-enclitic.

(10′) {tqḥ} 2m.s. imperfective, G-stem, √LQḤ /tiqqaḥu/ ← /tilqaḥu/; {mlk ʿlmk} lit., 'the kingship of your perpetuity'; {drkt dt dr drk} the genitive is here expressed by the relative/determinative pronoun with repetition of the second noun functioning as an elative, lit., 'the sovereignty of the generation of your generation'.

(11′) {ynḥt} 3m.s. imperfective, D-stem, √NḤT (the {n} precludes analysis as a G-stem); {ypʿr} 3m.s. imperfective, G-stem, √PʿR; {šmthm} common noun m.pl.a. + pronoun 3c.du.

(12′) {ygrš . . . grš} proper noun and m.s. imperative, G-stem, both √GRŠ.

(13′) {trtqṣ} 2m.s. imperfective, Gt-stem, √RQṢ.

(14′) {hlm} m.s. imperative, G-stem, √HLM; {bn ydm} lit., 'between the two hands/arms' (the {-m} must be enclitic because the noun is in the construct state).

(15′) {yrtqṣ} 3m.s. imperfective, Gt-stem, √RQṢ.

(16′) {ylm} 3m.s. imperfective, G-stem, √HLM.

(17′) {ymk} 3m.s. imperfective, G-stem, √MK /yamūku/ (√MWK) or /yamukku/ (√MKK); {tnǵṣn} 3f.pl. imperfective, N-stem, √NǴṢ.

(19′) {ảymr . . . mr} same type of expression as {ygrš . . . grš} but here the proper name includes the particle {ảy} (either the verbal element is in the imperative or else the /y/ of the particle assimilated to the /y/ of the verb: /ʾāya + yamrû/ → /ʾayyamrû/).

(22′) {bn . ʿnm} lit., 'between the two eyes', common noun f.du.obl.con. + *m*-enclitic; {yprsḥ} 3m.s. imperfective, N-stem, of the quadriliteral root PRSḤ.

(23′) {yql} 3m.s. imperfective, G-stem, √QL.

(27′) {yqṯ} 3m.s. imperfective, G-stem, √QṮṮ; {yšt} 3m.s. imperfective, G-stem, √ŠTT; {ykly} 3m.s. imperfective, D-stem, √KLY.

(28′) {tgʿrm} 3f.s. imperfective, G-stem, √GʿR + *m*-enclitic; {bṯ} m.s. imperative, G-stem, √BṮṮ /buṯ/ or /buṯṯa/; {ảliyn} substantivized adj.,

m.s.obl. √LʾY (vocalized as diptotic because of the long vowel in the penultimate syllable).
(29′) {šbyn} common noun, m.s.n. + pronoun 1c.pl.
(30′) {yṣả} either 3m.s. perfective, G-stem, /yaṣaʾa/, 'he exited', or 3m.s. optative, G-stem, /yaṣiʾa/ 'may he exit'.
(31′) {ybṯ . nn} 3m.s. imperfective-energic, G-stem, √BṮṮ, + pronoun 3m.s.
(33′) {ḥm} if the word is complete as preserved, the idea is that of 'heat' /ḥummu/; or it might be the last two signs of *tḥm*, 'message' (the {t} would have been the last sign of the preceding line).
(34′, 35′) {yʿn . . . tʿ[n]} 3m./f.s. imperfective (contracted), G-stem, √ʿNY.
(40′) The restoration of {[b]n} is based on the presence of the same phrase in line 22′.

Text 2: The *Baʿlu* Myth: *Baʿlu* and *ʿAnatu* (RS 2.[014]⁺ iii–iv)

Virolleaud 1938: 29–59; *CTA* 3 iii–iv; *KTU* 1.3 iii–iv; Ginsberg 1950: 136–37; Dietrich and Loretz 1997: 1140–46; Pardee 1997a: 251–52; Smith 1997: 109–15; Wyatt 1998: 76–84.

Text	***Translation***
(1) ttpp . ảnh⸢b⸣[. . .]	She beautifies herself with ʾANHBM,
[. . .] (2) ẓủ⸢h⸣ . bym[. . .]	that range [a thousand furlongs] in the sea.
(3) ⸢-⸣[-]rn . ⸢l⸣[. . .]	
. . . .	
(4′) [. . .]	[. . .]
⸢m⸣št rỉmt (5′) l ỉrth .	the pulling of the lyre to (her?) breast:
mšr . l . dd . ảlỉyn (6′) bʿl .	A song for the love of Mighty *Baʿlu*,
yd ⸢.⸣ pdry . bt . ảr	the affection of Pidray, daughter of *ʾArû*,
(7′) ảhb⸢t . ṭ⸣ly . bt . rb .	the love of *Ṭallay*, daughter of Rabbu,
dd . ảrṣy (8′) bt . yʿbdr .	the ardor of *ʾArṣay*, daughter of *Yaʿībudāru*.
km . ǵlmm (9′) w . ʿ⸢r⸣bn .	Then, lads, enter,
l pʿn . ʿnt ⸢. h⸣br (10′) w ql .	at *ʿAnatu*'s feet bow and fall,
tštḥwy . kbd hyt	do homage, honor her.
(11′) w ⸢.⸣ rgm . l btlt . ʿnt	Say to Girl *ʿAnatu*,
(12′) ṯny . l ymmt . lỉmm	repeat to the sister-in-law of *Liʾmu*:
(13′) tḥm . ảlỉyn . bʿl .	"Message of Mighty *Baʿlu*,
hwt (14′) ảlỉy . qrdm .	word of the mightiest of heroes:
qryy . b ảrṣ (15′) ⸢ml⸣ḥmt	Present bread offerings in the earth,
št . b ʿprm . ddym	place love-offerings in the dust;
(16′) sk ⸢.⸣ šlm . l kbd ⸢.⸣ ảrṣ	pour well-being out into the earth,

(17′)	ảrbdd . l kbd . šdm	calmness into the fields.
(18′)	ḥšk . ʿṣk . ʿbṣk	Hurry, press, hasten,
(19′)	ʿmy . pʿnk . tlsmn .	to me let your feet run,
	ʿmy (20′) twtḥ . ỉšdk .	to me let your legs hasten;
	dm . rgm (21′) ỉṯ . ly . w . ảrgmk	For I have something to tell you,
(22′)	hwt . w . ảṯnyk .	a matter to recount to you:
	rgm (23′) ʿṣ . w . lḫšt . ảbn	words regarding wood, whisperings regarding stone,
(24′)	tảnt . šmm . ʿm . ảrṣ	conversings of heaven with earth,
(25′)	thmt . ʿmn . kbkbm	of the deep with the stars;
(26′)	ảbn . brq . d l . tdʿ . šmm	I understand lightning which not even the heavens know,
(27′)	rgm l tdʿ . nšm .	a matter (which) men do not know,
	w l tbn (28′) hmlt . ảrṣ .	(which) the hordes of the earth do not understand.
	ảtm . w ảnk (29′) ỉbǵyh .	Come and I will explain it (to you)
	b tk . ǵry . ỉl . ṣpn	in my mountain, Divine *Ṣapunu*,
(30′)	b qdš . b ǵr . nḥlty	in the holy place, in the mountain that is my personal possession,
(31′)	b nʿm . b gbʿ . tlỉyt	in the goodly place, the hill of my victory."

(32′)	hlm . ʿnt . tph . ỉlm .	When *ʿAnatu* sees the two deities,
	bh . pʿnm (33′) tṭṭ .	her legs shake,
	bʿdn . ksl . ṯṯbr	behind, her back muscles snap,
(34′)	ʿln . pnh . tdʿ .	above, her face sweats,
	tǵṣ . pnt (35′) kslh .	her vertebrae rattle,
	ảnš . dt . ẓrh .	her spine goes weak.
	tšủ (36′) gh . w ⸢.⸣ tṣḥ .	She raises her voice and says aloud:
	ỉk . mǵy . gpn . w ủgr	"How is it that you have come, *Gapnu-wa-ʾUgāru*?
(37′)	mn . ỉb . ypʿ ⸢.⸣ l bʿl ⸢.⸣	Who is the enemy (who) has arisen against *Baʿlu*,
	ṣrt (38′) l rkb . ʿrpt .	the adversary against Cloud-Rider?
	l mḫšt . mdd (39′) ỉl ym .	I have surely smitten *ʾIlu*'s beloved, *Yammu*,
	l klt . nhr . ỉl . rbm	have finished off the great god *Naharu*,
(40′)	l ỉštbm . tnn . ỉštm⸢dh⸣	proceeding to bind the dragon's jaws so as to destroy it.
(41′)	mḫšt . bṯn . ʿqltn	I have smitten the twisting serpent,
(42′)	šlyṭ . d . šbʿt . rảšm	the close-coiled one with seven heads.

(43′)	mḫšt . mdd ⸢.⸣ ỉlm. ⸢-⸣r[. . .]	I have smitten ʾ*Ilu*'s beloved ʾ*Arišu* (Demander),
(44′)	ṣmt . ʿgl . ỉl . ʿtk	have wreaked destruction on ʾ*Ilu*'s calf ʿ*Atiku* (Binder).
(45′)	mḫšt . klbt . ỉlm . ỉšt	I have smitten ʾ*Ilu*'s bitch ʾ*Išatu* (Fire),
(46′)	klt . bt . ỉl . ḏbb .	have finished off ʾ*Ilu*'s daughter *Ḏabibu* (Flame),
	ỉmtḫṣ . ksp (47′) ỉtrṯ . ḫrṣ .	proceeding to smite for silver, to take possession of the gold of
	ṭrd . bʿ⸢l⸣ (IV 1) b mrym . ṣpn .	him who would have driven *Baʿlu* from the heights of *Ṣapunu*,
	mšṣṣ ⸢.⸣ k ⸢.⸣ ʿṣr (2) ủdnh .	him who would have caused (him) to flee like a bird (from) (the seat of) his power,
	gršh . l ksỉ . mlkh	him who would have banished him from his royal throne,
(3)	l nḫt . l kḥṯ . drkth	from (his) resting-place, from the seat of his dominion.
(4)	mnm . ỉb . ypʿ . l bʿl .	So, who is the enemy who has arisen against *Baʿlu*,
	ṣrt . l rkb . ʿrpt	the adversary against Cloud-Rider?"
(5)	⸢m⸣ʿn . ǵlmm . yʿnyn .	The lads answer up:
	l ỉb . ypʿ (6) l bʿl .	"No enemy has arisen against *Baʿlu*,
	ṣrt . l rkb . ʿrpt	(no) adversary against Cloud-Rider.
(7)	tḥm . . .	(Rather we have a) message. . . ."

Vocalized Text

(1) tîtapêpû ʾanhabī[ma] // [dū ʾalpi šiddi] (2) ẓiʾuhu bi yammi
(3) ⸢-⸣[-]RN . ⸢L⸣[. . .]
. . . .
(4′) [. . .]mašītu riʾmata (5′) lê ʾiratiha // mašīru lê dādi ʾalʾiyāna (6′) baʿli
// yaddi pidray bitti ʾarî
// (7′) ʾahbati ṭallay bitti rabbi
// dādi ʾarṣay (8′) bitti yaʿībudāri
kama ǵalmêma (9′) wa ʿarabāna
lê paʿnê ʿanati habarā (10′) wa qīlā // tištaḥwiyā kabbidā hiyati
(11′) wa rugumā lê batūlati ʿanati // (12′) ṯiniyā lê yabˡimti liʾmima
(13′) taḥmu ʾalʾiyāna baʿli // huwātu (14′) ʾalʾiyi qarrādīma
qarriyīya bi ʾarṣi (15′) malḥamāti // šītī bi ʿaparima dādāyīma
(16′) sukī šalāma lê kabidi ʾarṣi // (17′) ʾarbadāda lê kabidi šadîma
(18′) ḥāšuki ʿaṣûki ʿabāṣuki
// (19′) ʿimmaya paʿnāki talsumāna

// ʿimmaya (20′) tawattiḥā ʾišdāki
dāma rigmu (21′) ʾiṯu layya wa ʾargumakki // (22′) huwātu wa ʾaṯniyakki
rigmu (23′) ʿiṣi wa laḫaštu ʾabni //
(24′) taʾanatu šamîma ʿimma ʾarṣi // (25′) tahāmati ʿimmānu kabkabīma
(26′) ʾabīnu baraqa dā lā tidaʿū šamûma
// (27′) rigma lā tidaʿū našūma
// wa lā tabīnu (28′) hamullatu ʾarṣi
ʾatîma wa ʾanāku (29′) ʾibǵayuhu // bi tôki ǵūriya ʾili ṣapuni
(30′) bi qudši bi ǵūri naḥlatiya // (31′) bi naʿīmi bi gabʿi talʾiyati

---

(32′) hallima ʿanatu tiphû ʾilêma
biha paʿnāma (33′) taṭṭuṭā // baʿdāna kisla tuṯbaru // (34′) ʿalâna panûha tidaʿū
taǵǵuṣ pinnāti (35′) kisliha // ʾanišū dāti ẓûriha
tiššaʾu (36′) gâha wa taṣīḥu
ʾêka maǵayā gapnu wa ʾugāru
(37′) mīna ʾêbu yapaʿa lê baʿli // ṣarratu (38′) lê rākibi ʿurpati
la maḫaštu môdada (39′) ʾili yamma
// la killêtu nahara ʾila rabbama
// (40′) la ʾištabimu tunnana ʾištamiduhu
(41′) maḫaštu baṯna ʿaqallatāna // (42′) šalyaṭa dā šabʿati raʾašīma
(43′) maḫaštu môdada ʾilima ʾāri[ša] // (44′) ṣimmattu ʿigla ʾili ʿātika
(45′) maḫaštu kalbata ʾilima ʾišta // (46′) killêtu bitta ʾili ḏabība
ʾimtaḫiṣu kaspa (47′) ʾîtariṯu ḫurāṣa // ṭāridi baʿla (IV 1) bi maryamī ṣapuni
mušaṣṣiṣi ka ʿuṣṣūri (2) ʾudānihu
// gārišihu lê kussaʾi mulkihu
// (3) lê nāḫati lê kaḥṯi darkatihu
(4) mīnama ʾêbu yapaʿa lê baʿli // ṣarratu lê rākibi ʿurpati
(5) maʿnâ ǵalmāma yaʿniyāna
lā ʾêbu yapaʿa (6) lê baʿli // ṣarratu lê rākibi ʿurpati
(7) taḥmu . . .

Notes

(1) {ttpp} 3f.s. imperfective, Rt-stem, √YPY /tîtapêpû/ ← /tiytapaypiyu/; the end of the line is to be restored on the basis of col. iv 45 as {ånh⸢b⸣[m . d ålp .šd]}.

(4′) {mšt} analysis uncertain, perhaps a common noun meaning 'putting'—this noun and {mšr} in the following line are vocalized here as nominatives, but their grammatical case is in fact unknown because of the loss of the beginning of the verse.

(9′) {w} is pleonastic, i.e., it can precede a verb at the end of a sentence; {ʿrbn} 2c.du. imperative, G-stem.
(10′) {tšthẖwy} 2c.du. jussive, Št-stem, √ḤWY.
(12′) {ymmt} scribal error for {ybmt}; {li͗mm} divine name Liʾmu + *m*-enclitic.
(14′) {qryy} f.s. imperative, D-stem, + *y*-enclitic.
(15′) {ʿprm} either a common noun m.s.g.abs. + *m*-enclitic (// {årṣ} in the singular) or a common noun m.pl.g.abs.
(16′) {sk} f.s. imperative, G-stem, √NSK.
(18′) {ḥšk . ʿṣk . ʿbṣk} inf. + 2f.s. pronoun, lit., 'your haste', etc.
(19′) {tlsmn} 3c.du. energic, G-stem, √LSM.
(20′) {twtḥ} 3c.du. jussive, D-stem, √YTḤ ← WTḤ.
(21′) {årgmk} the following verb being in the energic mood, this one probably is also (/ʾargumakki/ ← /ʾarguman + ki/); the pronoun expresses a dative notion, lit., 'I will tell (it to) you'.
(22′) {åṯnyk} the {y} is perhaps preserved because this is an energic form {ʾaṯniyakki} ← /ʾaṯniyan + ki/; as in the preceding line, the pronoun expresses a dative notion.
(24′) {tånt} the {å} appears to reflect the secondary opening of the syllable /taʾnatu/ ≈ [taʾᵃnatu].
(26′) {åbn} 1c.s. imperfective, G-stem, √BN.
(26′, 27′) {tdʿ} 3m.pl. imperfective without {-n} or /YQTLØ/-perfective, G-stem, √YDʿ.
(27′) {tbn} 3f.s. imperfective or /YQTLØ/-perfective (/tabin/), G-stem, √BN.
(28′) {åtm} f.s. imperative, G-stem, √ʾTY, + *m*-enclitic /ʾatîma/ ← /ʾatayī + ma/ (or inf. /ʾatâma/ ← /ʾatāyu + ma/).
(32′–35′) The subject of the verb in these five lines alternates as follows: body part, person, body part, person, body part.
(33′) {tṯṭ} 3c.du. imperfective, G-stem, √NṮṬ /taṯṭuṭā/ ← /tanṭuṭā/; {tṯbr} 3f.s. imperfective, Gp-stem, √ṮBR.
(34′) {tdʿ} 3m.pl. imperfective, G-stem, √YDʿ ← WḎʿ; {tǵṣ} 3f.s. imperfective, G-stem, √NǴṢ.
(35′) {ånš} 3f.pl. perfective, G-stem, √ʾNŠ; {tšů} 3f.s. imperfective, G-stem, √NŠʾ (the imperfective expresses the forward movement of the story).
(38′–46′) most of the verbs are 1c.s. du. perfectives expressing past complete acts.
(38′–39′) {l} either the asseverative particle or the negative particle in rhetorical questions.
(38′, 41′, 43′, 45′) {mẖšt} ← MẖṢ (/maẖaštu/ ← /maẖaṣtu/ (deaffricativization of the /ṣ/ before /t/).
(39′) {rbm} adj. m.s.a.abs. + *m*-enclitic.

(40′) {ỉštbm} 1c.s. imperfective, Gt-stem, √ŠBM; {ỉštmdh} 1c.s. imperfective, Gt-stem, √ŠMD (these two imperfectives preceded and followed by perfectives appear not to be simple "historical presents" but to express another register in the narrative—see the similar structure in lines 46′–47′, also with Gt forms).

(42′) {šlyṭ} common noun, {š}-preformative, 'the one that produces coils'.

(43′–46′) nothing is known of the place in Ugaritic mythology of any of the divine beings named in these verses.

(43′) the preserved remnants of the first sign permit the restoration {⸢ả⸣r[š]}.

(44′) {ṣmt} 1c.s. perfective, D-stem, √ṢMT /ṣimmattu/ ← /ṣimmat + tu/.

(46′–47′) {ksp}, {ḫrṣ} the accusative expresses the goal of the action, not the direct object.

(47′) {ỉtrṯ} 1c.s. perfective, Gt-stem, √YRṮ /ʾîtariṯ/ ← /ʾiytariṯ/.

(47′–IV 1) {ṯrd}, {mšṣṣ}, {ksp} either in the genitive, expressing the owner of the silver and gold, or in the accusative, expressing the direct object of the verbs in the preceding line.

(1) {mšṣṣ} Š-stem part., m.s.g.abs. √NṢṢ.

(2) {gršh} the absence of {m-} shows that the form is G-stem.

Text 3: *Kirta*: *Kirta*'s Seven Wives (RS 2.[003]$^{+}$ i)

Virolleaud 1936b: 34–37, 52–63; *CTA* 14 i; *KTU* 1.14 i; Ginsberg 1950: 143; Dietrich and Loretz 1997:1216–19; Pardee 1997h: 333–34; Greenstein 1997: 12–13; Wyatt 1998: 179–84.

	Text	***Translation***
(1)	[l k]⸢r⸣t	[(Belonging) to (the) *Ki*]*rta*(-cycle).
(2)	[ ]⸢-⸣ . ml⸢-⸣[. . .]	[ ]KINGSH[IP$^{?}$ . . .]
(3)	[ ]m . r[. . .]	
(4)	[. . .]	
(5)	[ ]m . ỉl[. . .]	
(6)	[ ]d nhr . ủm⸢-⸣	[ ]RIVER MOTHER
(7)	[ ]⸢-⸣r⸢w⸣t .	[ ]
	bt (8) [m]lk . ỉtdb .	The house of the king has perished,
	d šbʿ (9) [ả]ḫm . lh .	who had seven brothers,
	ṯmnt . bn ủm	eight siblings.
(10)	krt . ḥtkn . rš	*Kirta*—(his) family is crushed,
(11)	krt . grdš . mknt	*Kirta*—(his) home is destroyed.
(12)	ảṯt . ṣdqh . l ypq	His rightful wife he has not obtained,
(13)	mtrḫt . yšrh	even his legitimate spouse.
(14)	ảṯt . trḫ . w tbʿt	A(nother) woman he marries but she disappears,

(15)	ṯảr ủm . tkn lh	even the kinswoman who was to be his.
(16)	mṯlṯt . kṯrm . tmt	A third spouse dies in good health,
(17)	mrbʿt . zblnm	a fourth in illness;
(18)	mḫmšt . yỉtsp (19) rš⸢p⸣ [.]	A fifth *Rašap* gathers in,
	mṯdṯt . ǵlm (20) ym .	a sixth the lad(s) of *Yammu*,
	mšbʿthn . b šlḥ (21) ttpl .	the seventh of them falls by the sword.
	yʿn . ḥtkh (22) krt [.]	*Kirta* sees his family,
	yʿn . ḥtkh rš	he sees his family (and) is crushed,
(23)	mỉd . grdš . ṯbth	(that) he is utterly destroyed in (the loss of) his dwelling.
(24)	w b klhn . špḥ . yỉtbd	Completely has the family perished,
(25)	w b . pḫyrh . yrṯ	in their entirety the heirs.
(26)	yʿrb . b ḥdrh . ybky	He enters his room, he weeps,
(27)	b ṯn⸢h⸣ gmm . w ydmʿ	as he speaks forth (his) grief, he sheds tears.
(28)	tntkn . ủdmʿth	His tears pour forth
(29)	km . ṯqlm . ảrṣh	like shekel(-weights) to the earth,
(30)	km ḫmšt . mṭth	like five(-shekel-weights) to the bed.
(31)	bm . bkyh . w yšn	As he weeps, he falls asleep,
(32)	b dmʿh . nhmmt	as he sheds tears, he slumbers.
(33)	šnt . tlủản (34) w yškb .	Sleep overcomes him and he lies down,
	nhmmt (35) w yqmṣ .	slumber and he curls up.
	w b ḥlmh (36) ỉl . yrd .	In a dream *ʾIlu* descends,
	b ḏhrth (37) ảb ⸢.⸣ ảdm .	in a vision, the father of mankind.
	w yqrb (38) b šảl . krt .	He comes near, asking *Kirta*:
	mảt (39) krt . k ybky	"Who is *Kirta* that he should weep?
(40)	ydmʿ . nʿmn . ǵlm (41) ỉl .	should shed tears, the goodly lad of *ʾIlu*?
	mlk ⸢ṯ⸣r ảbh (42) yảrš .	Would he request the kingship of the Bull, his father,
	⸢h⸣m . drk[t] (43) k ảb . ả⸢dm⸣	or dominion like (that of) the father of mankind?"
	[. . .]	

Vocalized Text

(1) lê kirta

. . .

(7) . . . bêtu (8) [ma]lki ʾîtabida! // dī šabʿu (9) [ʾa]ḫḫîma lêhu // ṯamānatu banī ʾummi

(10) kirta ḥatkāna ruššа // (11) kirta gurdaša makānata

(12) ʾaṯṯata ṣidqihu lā yapūqu // (13) mutarraḫata yušrihu

(14) ʾaṯṯata taraḫa wa tabaʿat // (15) ṯaʾara ʾummi takūnu lêhu

(16) muṯallaṯatu kiṯrama tamūtu // (17) murabbaʿatu zabalānama
(18) muḫammašata yiʾtasipu (19) rašap
// muṯaddaṯata ǵalamū (20) yammi
// mušabbaʿatuhini bi šilḥi (21) tittapilu
yaʿīnu ḥatkahu (22) kirta // yaʿīnu ḥatkahu ruššа // (23) maʾda gurdaša ṯibtahu
(24) wa bi kullihuna šupḥu yiʾtabidu // (25) wa bi puḫayyirihu yurṯu
(26) yiʿrabu bi ḥudurihu yabkiyu // // (27) bi ṯanîhu gâmama wa yidmaʿu
(28) tinnatikna ʾudmaʿātuhu // (29) kama ṯiqalīma ʾarṣaha // (30) kama ḫamišāti maṭṭâtaha
(31) bima bakāyihu wa yîšanu // (32) bi damāʿihu nahamāmatu
(33) šinatu talaʾʾunna[!]nnu // (34) wa yiškabu // nahamāmatu (35) wa yaqmuṣu
wa bi ḥulumihu (36) ʾilu yaridu // bi ḏahratihu (37) ʾabû ʾadami
wa yiqrabu (38) bi šaʾāli kirta
mīna[!] (39) kirta kī yabkiyu // (40) yidmaʿu naʿmānu ǵalmu (41) ʾili
mulka ṯôri ʾabîhu (42) yaʾarriša // himma darka[ta] (43) ka ʾabî ʾadami

---

Notes

(1) {krt} the vocalization of the name is uncertain.
(2) {ml⌈-⌉} the restoration of a form of the root MLK is possible but not certain.
(8) {ỉtdb} either 3m.s. perfective, Gt-stem √ʾDB, 'to be afflicted' or, preferably, correct to {ỉtbd} 3m.s. perfective, Gt-stem √ʾBD, 'perish' (cf. line 24); {d} the vocalization of {d} as in the genitive indicates the analysis as agreeing with /malki/ rather than with /bêtu/.
(9) {bn ủm} lit., 'sons of a mother', that is, of the same mother as she who had given birth to the 'brothers'.
(10–11) the subject of the verbs, which are in the passive, is Kirta, and the two common nouns are in the accusative, lit., 'Kirta, as regards (his) family, he is crushed . . .'.
(10) {krt} in the French edition, the copy incorrectly read {knt}.
(12–15) these two verses describe the first two wives: the first is the eldest cousin on the father's side, the second is from the mother's side.
(13) {mtrḫt} passive participle, D-stem, f.s. √TRḪ, 'she who is given in marriage'; the adjectives formed from number nouns in the following lines are all in this same form.
(18) {yỉtsp} 3m.s. imperfective, Gt-stem, √ʾSP, lit., 'takes her for himself'.
(21) {ttpl} 3f.s. imperfective, Gt-stem, √NPL.
(24) {klhn} the {n} is enclitic as is shown by the parallel form {pḫyrh}.
(27) {gmm} common noun *g*, 'voice' + double *m*-enclitic?

(29–30) {ṯqlm}, {ḫmšt} the terms express weights, not coins; the meaning of {ḫmšt} is either ‘five (shekels)’ and the image is that of an increase in weight or ‘one-fifth (of a shekel)’ and the image is that of an increase in the number of tiny weights (1/5 shekel = about 2 grams).

(32) {nhmmt} lit., ‘(there is) sleep’.

(33) {šnt tlủản} the reading is certain but the interpretation of the spelling is not: is the root Lʾʾ, a by-form of √LʾY, 3f.s. energic, G-stem transitive + pron. suff. 3m.s. /talʾuʾannu/ ‘overpowered him’? or should the {ả} be corrected to {n} and the root be identified as III-*y* with disappearance of the third radical /talaʾʾunnannu/ ← /talaʾʾiyunnannu/ (according to the analysis as a D-stem)? Because the form /yaQLuL/ is unknown in Ugaritic for geminated roots (/yaQLuL/ normally becomes /yaQuLL/) and because the G-stem form {tlủ} is attested in the meaning ‘it becomes feeble’ (**6** [RS 24.244]:68), we prefer the explanation by scribal error (the first {n} would have been inscribed with two wedges rather than three). Yet another possibility is as an imperfective of a root LʾW, ‘overcome’ /talʾuʾannanu/ ← /talʾuwannannu/ (cf. Tropper 2000: 427, 448, 617, 660)—this explanation of the form has the advantage of reflecting the better attested /-annannu/ pronominal ending.

(38) {mảt} plausibly to be corrected to {mn!}: the error would have consisted in writing two horizontal wedges followed by a separate third wedge rather than grouping the three together. Some take the reading at face value and as reflecting the interrogative pronoun followed by the 2m.s. independent pronoun /maʾʾatta/, ‘What’s wrong with you?’. The difficulty with this analysis is that the following verb is in the 3rd person.

Text 4: *ʾAqhatu*: The Promise of a Son (RS 2.[004] i)

Virolleaud 1936a: 186–96; *CTA* 17 i; *KTU* 1.17 i; Ginsberg 1950: 149–50; Dietrich and Loretz 1997: 1258–64; Pardee 1997: 343–44; Parker 1997a: 51–54; Wyatt 1998: 250–62.

	Text	***Translation***
(0′)	[. . . ảpnk] (1′) [dnỉl . mt . rp]⸢ ỉ⸣ .	Thereupon, as for *Dānîʾilu*, the man of *Rapaʾu*,
	ảpn . ǵ⸢zr⸣ (2′) [mt . hrnmy .]	thereupon, as for the valiant Harnamite man,
	ủzr ⸢.⸣ ỉlm . ylḥm .	girded, he gives the gods food,
(3′)	[ủzr . yšqy .] bn . qdš .	girded, he gives the Holy Ones drink.
	yd (4′) [ṣth . yʿl .] ⸢w⸣ yškb .	He casts off his cloak, goes up, and lies down,
	yd (5′) [mỉzrth] . ⸢p⸣ ynl .	casts down his girded garment so as to pass the night (there).

	hn . ym (6′) [w ṯn .	A day, even two,
	ủzr .] ỉlm . dnỉl	he who has girded himself (for) the gods, *Dānîʾilu*,
(7′)	[ủzr . ỉlm] ⸢.⸣ ylḥm .	girded, he gives the gods food,
	ủzr (8′) [yšqy . b]n . qdš	girded, he gives the Holy Ones drink.
	ṯlṯ . rbʿ ym	A third, even a fourth day,
(9′)	[ủzr . ỉ]⸢l⸣m . dnỉl .	he who has girded himself (for) the gods, *Dānîʾilu*,
	ủzr (10′) [ỉlm . y]lḥm .	girded, he gives the gods food,
	ủzr ⸢.⸣ yšqy bn (11′) [qdš .]	girded, he gives the Holy Ones drink.
	⸢ḫ⸣mš . ṯdṯ ⸢.⸣ --- ⸢.⸣ ym .	A fifth, even a sixth day,
	ủzr (12′) [ỉl]⸢m⸣ . dnỉl .	he who has girded himself (for) the gods, *Dānîʾilu*,
	ủzr . ỉlm . ylḥm	girded, he gives the gods food,
(13′)	[ủzr] . yšqy . bn . qdš .	girded, he gives the Holy Ones drink.
	yd . ṣth (14′) [dn]⸢ỉ⸣l .	*Dānîʾilu* casts off his cloak,
	yd . ṣth . yʿl . wyškb	he casts off his cloak, goes up, and lies down,
(15′)	[yd .] mỉzrth p yln .	casts down his girded garment so as to pass the night (there).
	mk ⸢.⸣ b šbʿ . ymm	Then on the seventh day,
(16′)	[w] yqrb . bʿl . b ḥnth .	*Baʿlu* approaches, having mercy on
	ảbyn⸢n⸣ (17′) [d]nỉl . mt . rpỉ ⸢.⸣	the destitute one, on *Dānîʾilu*, the man of *Rapaʾu*,
	ảnḫ . ǵzr (18′) ⸢m⸣t . hrnmy .	the groaning one, the valiant Harnamite man,
	d ỉn . bn . lh (19′) km . ảḫh .	who has no son like his brothers,
	w . šrš . km . ảryh	no scion like his kinsmen.
(20′)	bl . ỉṯ . bn . lh . wm ảḫh .	"May he not, like his brothers, have a son,
	w šrš (21′) km . ảryh .	like his kinsmen, a scion?
	ủzrm . ỉlm . ylḥm	(For,) girded, he gives the gods food,
(22′)	ủzrm . yšqy . bn . qdš	girded, he gives the Holy Ones drink.
(23′)	l tbrknn . l ṯr . ỉl ảby	O Bull *ʾIlu*, my father, please bless him,
(24′)	tmrnn . l bny . bnwt	please work a blessing for him, O creator of creatures,
(25′)	w ykn . bnh . b bt .	so that he may have a son in his house,
	šrš . b qrb (26′) hklh .	a scion within his palace:
	nṣb . skn . ỉlỉbh .	someone to raise up the stela of his father's god,
	b qdš (27′) ztr . ʿmh .	in the sanctuary the votive emblem of his clan;
	l ảrṣ . mšṣủ . qṭrh	to send up from the earth his incense,

(28′)	l ʿpr . ḏmr . åṯrh .	from the dust the song of his place;
	ṭbq . lḥt (29′) nỉṣh .	to shut up the jaws of his detractors,
	grš . d . ʿšy . lnh	to drive out anyone who would do him in;
(30′)	⸢å⸣ḫd . ydh . b šk⸢r⸣n .	to take his hand when (he is) drunk,
	mʿmsh (31′) [k] šbʿ . yn .	to bear him up when he is full of wine;
	spủ . ksmh . bt . bʿl	to supply his grain(-offering) in the Temple of *Baʿlu*,
(32′)	[w] ⸢m⸣nth . bt . ỉl .	his portion in the Temple of *ʾIlu*;
	ṭḫ . ggh . b ym (33′) [ṯỉ]ṭ .	to roll his roof when rain softens it up,
	rḥṣ . npṣh . b ym . rṯ	to wash his outfit on a muddy day.”
(34′)	[ks .] ⸢y⸣ỉḫd . ỉl ‹. bdh	A cup *ʾIlu* takes ‹in his hand,
	krpn . bm . ymn	a goblet in his right hand.
	brkm . ybrk .› ʿbdh .	He does indeed bless› his servant,
	ybrk (35′) [dnỉ]l . mt . rpỉ .	blesses *Dānîʾilu*, the man of *Rapaʾu*,
	ymr . ǵzr (36′) [mt . h]⸢r⸣nmy ⸢.⸣	works a blessing for the valiant Harnamite [man]:
	npš . yḥ . dnỉl (37′) [mt . rp] ỉ .	“May *Dānîʾilu*, the man of *Rapaʾu*, live indeed,
	brlt . ǵzr . mt hrnmy	may the valiant Harnamite man live to the fullest!
(38′)	[. . .]⸢-⸣ . hw . mḫ .	[. . .] may he be successful:
	l ʿršh . yʿl (39′) [w yšk]⸢b⸣ .	to his bed he shall mount and lie down.
	bm . nšq . åṯth (40′) [w hrt .]	As he kisses his wife there will be conception,
	b ḥbqh . ḥmḥmt	as he embraces her there will be pregnancy!
(41′)	[hr . tš]⸢k⸣n . ylt .	She will attain pregnancy, she who is to bear,
	ḥmḥmt (42′) [l mt . r]pỉ .	pregnancy for the man of *Rapaʾu*!
	w ykn . bnh (43′) [b bt .	He will have a son in his house,
	šrš] ⸢.⸣ b qrb hklh	a scion within his palace:
(44′)	[nṣb . skn . ỉ]lỉbh .	someone to raise up the stela of his father’s god,
	b qdš (45′) [ztr . ʿmh .	in the sanctuary the votive emblem of his clan;
	l å]⸢r⸣ṣ . mšṣủ (46′) [qṭrh .	to send up from the earth his incense,
	l ʿpr . ḏ]mr . åṯr⸢h⸣	from the dust the song of his place;
(47′)	[ṭbq . lḥt . nỉṣh .	to shut up the jaws of his detractors,
	gr]š . d . ʿšy (48′) [lnh .]	to drive out anyone who would do [him] in. . . .”

Vocalized Text

(0′) [ʾapanaka] (1′) [dānîʾilu mutu rapa]ʾi // ʾapana ǵaz[ru] (2′) [mutu harnamiyyu]
ʾuzūru ʾilīma yalaḥḥimu // (3′) [ʾuzūru yašaqqiyu] banī qudši
yaddû (4′) [ṣītahu yaʿlû] wa yiškabu // yadû (5′) [maʾzaratahu]pa yalīnu!
hanna yôma (6′) [wa ṯanâ] //
[ʾuzūru] ʾilīma dānîʾilu
// (7′) [ʾuzūru ʾilīma] yalaḥḥimu
// ʾuzūru (8′) [yašaqqiyu ba]nī qudši
ṯalīṯa rabīʿa yôma //
(9′) [ʾuzūru ʾi]līma dānîʾilu
// ʾuzūru (10′) [ʾilīma ya]laḥḥimu
// ʾuzūru yašaqqiyu banī (11′) [qudši]
[ḫa]mīša ṯadīṯa yôma //
ʾuzūru (12′) [ʾilī]ma dānîʾilu
// ʾuzūru ʾilīma yalaḥḥimu
// (13′) [ʾuzūru] yašaqqiyu banī qudši
yaddû ṣītahu (14′) [dānî]ʾilu
// yaddû ṣītahu yaʿlû wa yiškabu
// (15′) [yaddû] maʾzaratahu pa yalīnu
maka bi šabīʿi yamīma // (16′) [wa] yiqrabu baʿlu bi ḥunnatihu //
ʾabyānana (17′) [dā]nīʾila muta rapaʾi // ʾāniḫa ǵazra (18′) [muta] harnamiyya
dā ʾênu binu lêhu (19′) kama ʾaḫḫîhu // wa šuršu kama ʾaryihu
(20′) balâ ʾiṯu binu lêhu kama ʾaḫḫîhu // wa šuršu (21′) kama ʾaryihu
ʾuzūruma ʾilīma yalaḥḥimu // (22′) ʾuzūruma yašaqqiyu banī qudši
(23′) la tabarrikannannu lê ṯôri ʾili ʾabîya // (24′) tamīrannannu lê bāniyi bunuwwati
(25′) wa yakūnu binuhu bi bêti // šuršu bi qirbi (26′) hēkalihu
nāṣibu sikkanna ʾiluʾibîhu // bi qidši (27′) zittara ʿammihu
lê ʾarṣi mušôṣiʾu quṭrahu // (28′) lê ʿapari ḏamāra ʾaṯrihu
ṭābiqu laḥata (29′) nāʾiṣihu // gārišu dā ʿāšiya lênahu
(30′) ʾāḫidu yadahu bi šikkarāni // muʿammisuhu (31′) [kī] šabiʿa yêna
sāpiʿu kussumahu bêta baʿli // (32′) [wa ma]natahu bêta ʾili
ṭāḫu gaggahu bi yômi (33′) [ṯaʾ]ṭi // rāḥiṣu nipṣahu bi yômi raṯṯi
(34′) [kāsa ya]ʾḫudu ʾilu ⟨bîdihu // karpāna bima yamīni
barrākuma yabarriku⟩ ʿabdahu
// yabarriku (35′) [dānîʾi]la muta rapaʾi
// yamīru ǵazra (36′) [muta har]namiyya

napša yaḥî dānîʾilu (37′) [mutu rapa]ʾi
// būrālata ǵazru mutu harnamiyyu
// (38′) [. . .] huwa muḫḫa
lê ʿaršihu yaʿlû (39′) [wa yiškab]u
// bima našāqi ʾaṯṯatahu (40′) [wa haratu]
// bi ḥabāqihu ḥamḥamatu
(41′) [harâ taša]kīnu yālittu // ḥamḥamata (42′) [lê muti ra]paʾi
wa yakūnu binuhu (43′) [bi bêti // šuršu]bi qirbi hēkalihu
(44′) [nāṣibu sikkanna ʾi]luʾibîhu // bi qudši (45′) [zittara ʿammihu]
[lê ʾa]rṣi mušôṣiʾu (46′) [quṭrahu // lê ʿapari ḏa]māra ʾa[ṯ]rihu
(47′) [ṭābiqu laḥata nāʾiṣihu // gāri]šu dā ʿāšiya (48′) [lênahu]

Notes

(2′) the word-divider at the end of this line in fact marks the division between this word, which extended into the space occupied by the second column, and the first word of the facing line in that second column.

(2′–3′) {ylḥm} . . . {yšqy} 3m.s. imperfective, D-stem (expressing the repetition of the act).

(2′) {ủzr} passive participle, G-stem, m.s.n. abs. √ʾZR.

(3′) {yd} 3m.s. imperfective, G-stem √NDY.

(4′) {yʿl} 3m.s. imperfective, G-stem √ʿLY.

(5′) {ynl} scribal error for{yln} (see line 16′).

(5′–6′) {ym} . . . {ṯn} the noun and the ordinal number are in the accusative functioning as a temporal adverbial; ditto for the following number phrases.

(6′) {ủzr ỉlm} lit., 'the girded one of the gods'.

(8′) the scribe forgot the {š} of *qdš* and subsequently he corrected his error by placing a {š} on top of the word-divider by which he had first indicated the division between this word and the following.

(10′) the scribe erroneously wrote *šbʿ* after *ṯdṯ* and did not notice the mistake until some time later, at the least after the line was completely inscribed, at which point he simply erased the intrusive word.

(15′) the scribe forgot the last sign of *mỉzrth* and, as in the similar case of line 8′, he corrected the error by placing the {h} on top of the word-divider and without bothering to erase the small vertical wedge first.

(16′) {ḥnth} verbal noun √ḤNN, /ḥunnatu/ + pron. suff. 3m.s. with reference to Baʿlu as the subject of the nominal phrase; {ảbyn⌜n⌝} if the reading is correct, it apparently reflects the adjective *ảbyn* to which *n*-enclitic has been attached.

(20′) {wm} error for {km}.

(21′, 22′) {ủzrm} *m*-enclitic attached to the word otherwise written {ủzr} where extant.

(25′) lit., 'so his son may be in the house'.

(26′–28′) the first verse alludes to the ancestral cult in a sanctuary, the second to the same type of cult as practiced at the family tomb situated under the dwelling.

(27′) {mšṣủ} active participle, Š-stem, m.s.n. abs. √YṢʾ.

(32′–33′) lit., 'on a day of mud . . . on a day of dirt'.

(34′) the restitution is based on the text of *CTA* 15 ii 16–18.

(36′–37′) lit., 'as to his throat, may he live!'.

(38′) the partially preserved sign to the left is clearly {ṭ} or {ḥ}, but there is no extant parallel text on which to base a restoration of the beginning of the line.

(39′) {w yškb} a hypothetical restitution based on the traces of the last sign.

(40′) the restoration of a verbal noun from the root HRY is indicated by the term {ḥmḥmt}, a parallelism that is attested elsewhere, but the precise restoration is hypothetical.

(40′–41′) {[hr tš]kn} also a hypothetical restoration; the conception appears to be expressed by verbal nouns, {[hr]} and {ḥmḥmt} functioning as direct objects of {tškn} 3f.s. jussive, Š-stem, √KN, lit., 'may she cause conception, pregnancy, to be'.

(41′) {ylt} active participle, G-stem, f.s.n. abs. /yālittu/ ← /yālidtu/.

Text 5: *Šaḥru-wa-Šalimu*: The Birth of the Gracious and Beautiful Gods (RS 2.002)

Virolleaud 1933; *CTA* 23; *KTU* 1.23; *TO* I, pp. 353–79; Lewis 1997a; Pardee 1997b; Wyatt 1998: 324–35.

	Text	***Translation***
	Obverse	
(1)	⸢ỉ⸣qrả . ỉlm . n⸢ʿ⸣[mm .	I would call on the gr[acious] gods
	. . .] (2) w ysmm .	[. . .] and beautiful,
	bn . š⸢p⸣[. . .]	sons of [. . .],
(3)	ytnm . qrt . l ʿly	who have provided a city on high,
	[. . .]	[. . .]
(4)	b mdbr . špm . yd[	in the steppe-land, on the barren hilltops [. . .]
	. . .]⸢-⸣ (5) l rỉšhm .	[. . .] on their heads,
	w yš[ ]⸢-⸣m	and [. . .].
(6)	lḥm . b lḥm ⸢. ả⸣y [.]	Eat the food, yes do!
	⸢w⸣ š⸢t⸣y . b ḫmr yn ảy	Drink the foaming wine, yes do!

(7)	šlm [.] ⸢mlk⸣ .	Give well-being to the king!
	šlm . mlkt .	Give well-being to the queen,
	ˤrbm . w ṯnnm	to those who enter and to those who stand guard!

(8)	mt . w šr . yṯb .	*Mutu-wa-Šarru* takes a seat,
	bdh . ḫṭ . ṯkl .	in his hand the staff of bereavement,
	bdh (9) ḫṭ . ủlmn .	in his hand the staff of widowhood.
	yzbrnn . zbrm . gpn	The pruner of the vine prunes it,
(10)	yṣmdnn . ṣmdm . gpn .	the binder of the vine binds it,
	yšql . šdmth (11) km gpn .	he causes (it) to fall to the-field-of-a-man like a vine.

(12)	šbˤd . yrgm . ˤl . ˤd .	Seven times (these verses) are pronounced by the ˤD-room
	w ˤrbm . tˤnyn	and those who enter respond.

(13)	w šd . šd ⸢.⸣ ỉlm .	The field is the field of the gods,
	šd ảṯrt . w rḥm	the field of *ʾAṯiratu* and *Raḥmu*.
(14)	ˤl . ỉšt . šbˤd . ǵzrm . ⸢g⸣ . ṭb ⸢.⸣	Over the fire, seven times the sweet-voiced youths (chant):
	⸢g⸣d . b ḥlb .	Coriander in milk,
	ảnnḫ b ḫmảt	mint in melted butter.
(15)	w ˤl . ảgn .	And over the jar
	šbˤdm . dǵ⸢-(-)-⸣[--]⸢ǵ⸣t	seven times again (they chant): The *dǵ*[*ṯ*-sacrifices have been sacri]ficed.

(16)	tlkm . rḥmy . w tṣd [. . .]	Off goes *Raḥmay* and hunts, [. . .]
(17)	tḥgrn . ǵzr n⸢ˤ-⸣[. . .]	she/they gird; the goodly youth [. . .]
(18)	w šm . ˤrbm . yr[. . .]	and those who enter pronounce the name [. . .].

(19)	mṯbt . ỉlm . ṯmn . ṯ⸢m⸣[n . . .]	Dwellings of the gods: eight (here), eig[ht (there) . . .]
(20)	pảmt . šbˤ [. . .]	seven times [. . .].

(21)	ỉqnủ . šmt [. . .]	Blue, carnelian(-colored) [. . .]
(22)	ṯn . šrm . [. . .]	two singers.

(23)	ỉqrản . ỉlm . nˤm⸢m⸣[.	I would call on the gracious gods,
	ảgzr ym . bn .] ym	[who delimit one day from] another,

(24)	ynqm . b ảp zd . ảṯrt ⸢.⸣	who suck the nipples of the breasts of *ʾAṯiratu*.
	[. . .] (25) špš . mṣprt . dlthm	[. . .] *Šapšu*, who cares for their feebleness
	[. . .] (26) w ǵnbm .	[(with) X] and (with) grapes.
	šlm . ʿrbm . ṯ⸢nnm⸣	Give well-being to those who enter and to those who stand guard,
(27)	hlkm . b dbḥ nʿmt	to those who form a procession with sacrifices of prosperity!

---

(28)	šd . ⸢ỉ⸣lm .	The field of the two gods,
	šd . ảṯrt . w rḥmy	(is) the field of *ʾAṯiratu-wa-Raḥmay*,
(29)	[ỉ]⸢l⸣[m] . y[ṯ]b	(the field where) the [two go]ds d[we]ll.

---

(30)	[---(-)]⸢--⸣ . gp ym .	[*ʾIlu* goes] to the seashore,
	w yṣǵd . gp . thm	strides along the shores of the Great Deep.

Lower Edge

(31)	[ ]⸢. ỉl .⸣ mštʿltm .	*ʾIlu* [spies] two females presenting (him with) an offering,
	mštʿltm . l rỉš . ảgn	presenting (him with) an offering from the jar.
(32)	⸢h⸣l⸢h⸣ . [t]špl .	One gets down low,
	hlh . trm .	the other up high.
	hlh . tṣḥ . ảd ảd	One cries out: "Father, father,"
(33)	w hlh . tṣḥ . ủm . ủm .	the other cries out: "Mother, mother."
	tỉrkm . yd . ỉl . k ym	"May *ʾIlu*'s hand stretch out as long as the sea,
(34)	w yd ỉl . k mdb .	(may) *ʾIlu*'s hand (stretch out as long) as the flowing waters.
	ảrk . yd . ỉl . k ym	Stretch out, (O) hand of *ʾIlu*, as long as the sea,

Reverse

(35)	w yd . ỉl . k mdb .	(stretch out, O) hand of *ʾIlu*, (as long) as the flowing waters."
	yqḥ . ỉl . mštʿltm	*ʾIlu* takes the two females presenting an offering,
(36)	mštʿltm . l rỉš . ảgn .	presenting an offering from the jar;
	yqḥ . yš . b bth	he takes (them), estab<lish>es (them) in his house.
(37)	ỉl . ḫṭh . nḥt .	*ʾIlu* prepares his staff,

ỉl . ymnn . mṭ . ydh .	*ʾIlu* grasps his rod in his right hand.
yšủ (38) yr . šmmh .	He raises (it), casts (it) into the sky,
yr . b šmm . ʿṣr .	casts (it at) a bird in the sky.
yḫrṭ yšt (39) l pḥm .	He plucks (the bird), puts (it) on the coals,
ỉl . ảṯtm . k ypt .	(then) *ʾIlu* sets about enticing the women.
hm . ảṯtm . tṣḥn	"If," (says he,) "the two women cry out:
(40) y m⸢t .⸣ mt .	'O man, man,
nḥtm . ḫṭk .	you who prepare your staff,
mmnnm . mṭ ydk	who grasp your rod in your right hand,
(41) h[l .] ʿṣr . tḫrr . l ỉšt .	a bird is roasting on the fire,
ṣḥrrt . l pḥmm	has roasted golden brown on the coals,'
(42) ả[ṯ]⸢t⸣m . ảṯt . ỉl .	(then) the two women (will become) the wives of *ʾIlu*,
ảṯt . ỉl . w ʿlmh .	*ʾIlu*'s wives forever.
w hm (43) ả⸢ṯ⸣tm . tṣḥn .	But if the two women cry out:
y . ảd ảd .	'O father, father,
nḥtm . ḫṭk	you who prepare your staff,
(44) mmnnm . mṭ ydk .	who grasp your rod in your right hand,
hl . ʿṣr . tḫrr . l ỉšt	a bird is roasting on the fire,
(45) w ⸢ṣ⸣ḥrrt . l pḥmm .	has roasted golden brown on the coals,'
btm . bt . ỉl .	(then) the two daughters (will become) the daughters of *ʾIlu*,
bt . ỉl (46) w ʿlmh .	*ʾIlu*'s daughters forever."
w hn . ảṯtm . tṣḥn .	The two women do (in fact) cry out:
y . mt mt	"O man, man,
(47) nḥtm . ḫṭk .	you who prepare your staff,
mmnnm . mṭ ydk .	who grasp your rod in your right hand,
hl . ʿṣr (48) t⸢ḫ⸣rr . l ỉšt .	a bird is roasting on the fire,
w ṣḥrt . l pḥmm .	has roasted golden brown on the coals."
ảṯtm . m⸢t⸣[. ỉl]	(Then) the two women (become the wives) of 'the man' [*ʾIlu*],
(49) ả⸢ṯ⸣t . ỉl . w ʿlmh .	*ʾIlu*'s wives forever.
yhbr . špthm . yš⸢q⸣	He bends down, kisses their lips,
(50) hn . špthm . mtqtm .	their lips are sweet,
mtqtm . k lrmn[m]	sweet as pomegranates.
(51) bm . nšq . w hr .	With the kisses (comes) conception,
b ḥbq . ḥmḥmt .	with the embraces, pregnancy.
tq⸢t⸣[nṣn] (52) tldn .	The two (women) squat and give birth
šḥr . w šlm .	<give birth to> *Šaḥru-wa-Šalimu*.
rgm . l ỉl . ybl .	Word is brought to *ʾIlu*:
ả⸢ṯ⸣[t] (53) ỉl . ylt ⸢.⸣	"The two wives of *ʾIlu* have given birth."
mh . ylt .	"What have they borne?"
yldy . šḥr . w šl[m]	"Two boys, *Šaḥru-wa-Šalimu*."

(54)	šủ . ʿdb . l špš . rbt .	"Take up a gift for great *Šapšu*
	w l kbkbm . kn⸢m⸣	and for the imutable stars."
(55)	yhbr . špthm . yšq .	(Again) he bends down, kisses their lips,
	hn ⸢.⸣ [š]pthm . mtq⸢t⸣[m .	their lips are sweet,
	mtqtm . k lrmnm]	sweet as pomegranates.
(56)	bm . nšq . w hr .	With the kisses (comes) conception,
	b ḥbq . w ḥ[m]ḥmt .	with the embraces, pregnancy.
	yṯb[. . .] (57) yspr .	He sits[. . .], he counts
	l ḫmš . l ṣ⸢b-⸣[-]	to five for the [bulge to appear],
	[-]⸢-⸣šr . pḫr klảt	[to t]en, the completed double.
(58)	tqtnṣn . w tldn .	The two (women) squat and give birth,
	t⸢ld⸣ [.] ⸢ỉl⸣m nʿmm .	they give birth to the gracious gods,
	ảgzr ym (59) bn . ym .	who delimit one day from another,
	ynqm . b ảp ḏ⸢d⸣ [.]	who suck the nipples of the breasts (of *ʾAṯiratu*).
	rgm . l ỉl . ybl	Word is brought to *ʾIlu*:
(60)	ảṯty . ỉl . ylt .	"The two wives of *ʾIlu* have given birth."
	mh . ylt [.]	"What have they borne?"
	ỉlmy [.] nʿmm --[-]--	"The gracious gods,
(61)	ảgzr ym . bn ym .	who delimit one day from another,
	ynqm . b ảp . ḏd . št .	who suck the nipples of the breasts of the Lady."
	špt (62) l ảrṣ .	(One) lip to the earth,
	špt l šmm .	(the other) lip to the heaven,
	w ⸢y⸣ʿrb . b phm .	into their mouths enter
	ʿṣr . šmm	bird of heaven
(63)	w dg b ym .	and fish in the sea.
	w ndd . gz⸢r⸣ . l zr	They stand, delimitation to 〈deli〉mitation,
	yʿdb . ủ ymn (64) ủ šmảl .	they prepare (food for themselves) on right and left,
	b phm . w ⸢l⸣ [.] ⸢b⸣ tšbʿn ⸢.⸣	into their mouth (it goes) but not with satiety.
	y . ảṯt . ỉtrḫ	"O women whom I have wedded,
(65)	y bn . ảšld .	O sons whom I have begot:
	šủ . ʿdb . tk . mdbr qdš	Take a gift to the steppe-land of Qadeš,
(66)	ṯm . tgr	where you must dwell as aliens;
	gr . l ảbnm .	dwell among the stones
	w l . ʿṣm .	and among the trees
	šbʿ . šnt (67) tmt .	seven full years,
	ṯmn . nqpt . ʿd .	eight revolutions of time."
	ỉlm . nʿmm . ttlkn (68) šd .	The gracious gods range through the field,
	tṣdn . pảt . mdbr .	hunt along the fringes of the steppe-land.

	w ngš . hm . nǵr (69) mdrʿ .	They meet the guardian of the sown land
	w ṣḥ . hm . ʿm . nǵr . mdrʿ .	and they call out to the guardian of the sown land:
	y . nǵr (70) ⸢n⸣ǵr . p⸢tḥ⸣ .	"O guard, guard, open up!"
	w ptḥ hw . prṣ .	He makes an opening (in the fence):
	bʿdhm (71) w ʿrb . hm .	'Tis (there) for them and they enter.
	hm[.i͗ṯ . lk . l]⸢ḥ⸣m .	"If [you have b]read,
	w tn (72) w nlḥ⸢m⸣ .	then give (us some) that we might eat.
	hm . i͗ṯ[. lk . yn.]	If [you] have [wine],
	⸢w tn⸣ w nšt	then give (it to us) that we might drink."
(73)	w ʿn hm . nǵr mdrʿ	The guardian of the sown land answers them:
	[ ]⸢-(-)-⸣	["There is bread that has . . .]
(74)	i͗ṯ . yn . d ʿrb . b ṯk[. . .	There is wine that has arrived in/from [. . .]."
	. . .] (75) mǵ . hw .	[. . .] he arrives,
	lhn . lg ynh[. . .	he serves a *luggu*-measure of his wine
	. . .]	[. . .]
(76)	w ḥbrh . mla͗ yn	and his companion fills (it) with wine [. . .].

Vocalized Text

(1) ʾiqraʾa ʾilêma naʿī[mêma] // [. . .] (2) wa yasīmêma // banī Š⸢P⸣[. . .]
(3) yātinêma qarîta lê ʿalliyi // [. . .]⸢-⸣
(4) bi madbari šapîma YD[. . .] // [. . .]⸢-⸣ (5) lê raʾšihumu // wa [. . .]
(6) laḥamā bi laḥmi ʾāya // wa šatayā bi ḫamri yêni ʾāya
(7) šallimā malka // šallimā malkata // ʿāribīma wa ṯannānīma

(8) mutu wa šarru yaṯibu // bîdihu ḫaṭṭu ṯukli // bîdihu (9) ḫaṭṭu ʾulmāni
yazburanannu zābiruma gapna
// (10) yaṣmudannannu ṣāmiduma gapna
// yašaqīlu šadûmutaha (11) kama gapni

(12) šabʿida yargumu ʿalê ʿādi wa ʿāribūma taʿniyūna

(13) wa šadû šadû ʾilīma // šadû ʾaṯirati wa raḥmi
(14) ʿalê ʾišti šabʿida ǵazarūma gâ ṭāba
giddu bi ḥalabi // ʾananiḫu bi ḫimʾatu
(15) wa ʿalê ʾaganni šabʿidama DǴ[. . .]⸢Ǵ⸣T

(16) talikuma raḥmay wa taṣūdu[. . .] (17) taḥguruna ǵazru Nʿ⸢-⸣[. . .]
(18) wa šuma ʿāribūma YR[. . .]

---

(19) môṯabātu ʾilīma ṯamānû ṯam[ānû . . .] (20) paʾamāti šabʿa

---

(21) ʾiqnaʾu šamtu [. . .] (22) ṯinâ šārāma [. . .]

---

(23) ʾiqraʾanna ʾilêma naʿīmêma
// [ʾagzarê yômi bina] yômi
// (24) yāniqêma bi ʾappi zadî ʾaṯirati
(25) [. . .] šapša muṣappirata dullatahumā // [. . .] (26) [. . .] wa ǵanabīma
šallimā ʿāribīma ṯannānīma // (27) hālikīma bi dabaḥī nuʿmati

---

(28) šadû ʾilêma // šadû ʾaṯirati wa raḥmay // (29) [ʾil]ā[ma] ya[ṯa]bā

---

(30) [---(-)]⌜--⌝ gīpa yammi // wa yiṣǵadu gīpa tahāmi
(31) [. . .] ʾilu muštaʿilatêma // muštaʿilatêma lê raʾši ʾaganni
(32) halliha [ti]špalu // halliha tarīmu
halliha taṣīḥu ʾadi ʾadi // (33) wa halliha taṣīḥu ʾummi ʾummi
tiʾrakma yadu ʾili ka yammi // (34) wa yadu ʾili ka madūbi
ʾarakī yadi ʾili ka yammi // (35) wa yadi ʾili ka madūbi
yiqqaḥu ʾilu muštaʿilatêma
// (36) muštaʿilatêma lê raʾši ʾaganni
// yiqqaḥu yašī⟨tu⟩ bi bêtihu
(37) ʾilu ḫaṭṭahu naḥata // ʾilu yamnana maṭṭâ yadihu
yiššaʾu (38) yarû šamîmaha // yarû bi šamîma ʿuṣṣūra
yaḫruṭu yašītu (39) lê paḥmi // ʾilu ʾaṯṯatêma kī yapattû
himma ʾaṯṯatāma taṣīḥāna
(40) yā muti muti // nāḥitima ḫaṭṭaka // mêmaninima maṭṭâ yadika
(41) ha[lli] ʿuṣṣūru taḥāriru lê ʾišti // ṣaḥrarat lê paḥamīma
(42) ʾa[ṯṯa]tāma ʾaṯṯatā ʾili // ʾaṯṯatā ʾili wa ʿālamaha
wa himma (43) ʾaṯṯatāma taṣīḥāna
yā ʾadi ʾadi // nāḥitima ḫaṭṭaka // (44) mêmaninima maṭṭâ yadika
halli ʿuṣṣūru taḥāriru lê ʾišti // (45) wa ṣaḥrarat lê paḥamīma
bittāma bittā ʾili // bittā ʾili (46) wa ʿālamaha
wa hanna ʾaṯṯatāma taṣīḥāna
yā muti muti // (47) nāḥitima ḫaṭṭaka // mêmaninima maṭṭâ yadika
halli ʿuṣṣūru (48) taḥāriru lê ʾišti // wa ṣaḥra⟨r⟩at lê paḥamīma
ʾaṯṯatāma muti [ʾili] // (49) ʾaṯṯatā ʾili wa ʿālamaha
yihbaru šapatêhumā yaššuqu
// (50) hanna šapatāhumā matuqatāma
// matuqatāma ka lurmānī[ma]
(51) bima našāqi wa harû // bi ḥabāqi ḥamḥamatu
tiqt[aniṣāna] (52) talidāna // ⟨talidā⟩ šaḥra wa šalima

rigma lê ʾili yabilu
ʾaṯṯa[tā] (53) ʾili yalattā
maha yalattā
yaldêya šaḥri wa šali[mi]
(54) šaʾū ʿadūba lê šapši rabbati // wa lê kabkabīma kīnīma
(55) yihbaru šapatêhumā yaššuqu
// hanna šapatāhumā matuqatā[ma
// matuqatāma ka lurmānīma]
(56) bima našāqi wa harû // bi ḥabāqi wa ḥa[m]ḥamatu
yaṯibu [ʾilu] (57) yisparu //lê ḫamiši lê Ṣ⸢B-⸣[-] //[-]ʿašri puḫri kilʾati
(58) tiqtaniṣāna wa talidāna // talidā ʾilêma naʿīmêma
ʾagzarê yômi (59) bina yômi // yāniqêma bi ʾappi ḏadî
rigma lê ʾili yabilu
(60) ʾaṯṯatāya ʾili yalattā
maha yalattā
ʾilêmaya naʿīmêma
// (61) ʾagzarê yômi bina yômi
// yāniqêma bi ʾappi ḏadî šitti
šapatu (62) lê ʾarṣi // šapatu lê šamîma
wa yiʿrabu bi pîhumā // ʿuṣṣūru šamîma // (63) wa dagu bi yammi
wa nadāda gazara lê ⟨ga⟩zari
// yaʿdubu ʾô yamīna (64) ʾô šamʾala
// bi pîhumā wa lā bi šabʿāni
yā ʾaṯṯatê ʾitraḫu // (65) yā binê ʾašôlidu
šaʾū ʿadūba // tôka madbari qidši
(66) ṯamma tagūrū // gūrū lê ʾabanīma // wa lê ʿiṣīma
šabʿa šanāti (67) tammāti // ṯamānâ niqpāti ʿadî
ʾilāma naʿīmāma titalikāna (68) šadâ // taṣūdāna piʾāti madbari
wa nagāšu humā nāǵira (69) madraʿi // wa ṣāḥu humā ʿimma nāǵira madraʿi
yā nāǵiri (70) nāǵiri pataḥ
wa patāḥu huwa parṣa // baʿdahumā (71) wa ʿarābu humā
himma [ʾiṯu lêka la]ḥmu // wa tin (72) wa nilḥamā
himma ʾiṯu [lêka yênu] // wa tin wa ništâ
(73) wa ʿanahumā nāǵiru madraʿi // [. . .]⸢-(-)-⸣
(74) ʾiṯu yênu dū ʿaraba bi ṮK[. . .] // [. . .] (75) maǵâ huwa
lihhana lugga yênihu[. . .]
(76) wa ḥabiruhu millaʾa yêna

Notes

(1) {ilm nʿmm} are vocalized as duals according to the hypothesis that the reference is to *Šaḥru-wa-Šalimu.*

(5) {ri̊šhm} the pronominal suffix is in the plural if the antecedent is {špm}, in the dual if it is the gracious gods.

(6–7, 26) the imperatives are vocalized as duals, but the lacuna makes it uncertain whether the addressees are indeed the gracious gods.

(9–10) {yzbrnn zbrm}, {yṣmdnn ṣmdm} imperfective + substantivized participle m.s. + *m*-enclitic (or imperfective + common noun m.s., perhaps of the /QaTTāL-/ type).

(10) {yšql} 3m.s. imperfective, Š-stem, √QL.

(15) the restoration at the end of the line is uncertain; many exegetes have proposed the presence here of the word *dǵṯ* '(a type of offering)'.

(21) the two words preserved in this line designate either textiles tinted blue and red or else precious stones of the same colors.

(22) {ṯn} may designate scarlet textile, the number 'two', or the verb ṮNY, 'say'.

(23–27) all the terms in these lines that refer to divinities are in the dual, for the deities in question are *Šaḥru-wa-Šalimu*, as the phrase *ảgzr ym bn ym* shows.

(25) apparently an allusion to *Šaḥru-wa-Šalimu* during both the daylight and the night-time hours, when 'dawn' and 'dusk' are invisible.

(27) {dbḥ nˁmt} lit., 'sacrifices of goodness'.

(30) the beginning of this line probably once contained a verb parallel with {yṣǵd}.

(31) probably restore a verb at the beginning of the line, a verb expressing *ʾIlu*'s perception of the two women; {mštˁltm} active participle, Št-stem, f.du.obl.abs. √ˁLY 'the two females who present (a gift, an offering)'; {ri̊šagm} 'the top of the the jar'.

(32) {hlh . . . trm} lit., 'here she is low, here she is high'.

(32–33) imperfective verbs to express repeated acts.

(33, 34) {ti̊rk}, {ảrk} 3f.s. jussive G-stem, and f.s. imperative, G-stem, subject {yd} (a feminine noun).

(36) read {yš‹t›}.

(37) {ymnn} 3m.s. perfective, L-stem, of a denominative verb from YMN, 'right hand'.

(40, 44, 47) {mmnnm} active participle, L-stem, m.s.gen. of YMNN (see preceding note) + *m*-enclitic (/mêmaninima/ ← /*maymanin + i + ma/).

(42, 46) {w ˁlmh} 'pleonastic' or 'emphatic' *w*, lit., 'they (will be) the wives of *ʾIlu* and (they will remain so) forever'.

(48) read {ṣḥr‹r›t} as in line 41′.

(49–54, 55–61) the two birth narratives refer either to (1) two distinct birthings, first *Šaḥru-wa-Šalimu* then the gracious gods, with the latter not being identified by name, or to (2) two accounts of the birth of *Šaḥru-wa-Šalimu* (the reason for this presentation would be to reflect the fact of two wives, each of whom gave birth; compare the literary presentation of the two weapons in *CTA* 2 iv [text 1], where the two weapons are mentioned at the beginning of each pericope).

(52) probably restore {⟨tld⟩} after {tldn}on the model of line 58; {yld} either 3m.s., indefinite subject ('someone brings') or Gp; perhaps restore {å⸢ṯ⸣[ty]} at the end of the line (cf. line 60, where *y*-enclitic is attached to *åṯt*).

(53, 60) {ylt} 3f.du. perfective, G-stem, /yalattā/ ← /yaladtā/.

(53) {yldy} in the construct state + *y*-enclitic (in the oblique case as the object of the verb YLD—in spite of the change of speaker—as a genitive of identification of the common noun to the personal names that follow), or a scribal error for {yldm} /yaldêma/ (the common noun and the proper names would be in apposition), or a verbal form, 3m.du. perfective, Gp-stem, /yuladāya/ 'they (the gods to be named) have been born'; the nominal structure of lines 60–61 makes the first interpretation preferable.

(56) perhaps restore only {ỉl} at the end of the line.

(56–57) perhaps an allusion to the ten months of pregnancy, counting inclusively, divided into two five-month periods; this assumes the restoration of {⸢ʿ⸣šr} 'ten' at the beginning of line 57, but the preceding restorations are uncertain.

(58) {ỉlm nʿmm ågzr ym} vocalized as duals on the basis of the hypothesis that the gods would be *Šaḥru-wa-Šalimu* (cf. lines 1, 23), the only ones who set the limits of the day.

(60) {åṯty}, {ỉlmy} the {y} is enclitic.

(62) {yʿrb} the {-y} indicates a singular, and the agreement was thus marked with the first subject ({ʿṣr}).

(63) {zr} read {⟨g⟩zr}; {yʿdb} . . . {tšbʿn} unless the poet is playing with the two possible preformatives of the dual, {y-} or {t-}, {yʿdb} is a singular emphasizing the fact that each of the divinities, situated at the western or the eastern extremities of the horizon, is devouring all about him ({ndd} is thus parsed as a singular, like {yʿdb}, lit., 'he stands at the extremity with respect to the (other) ⟨ext⟩remity').

(64) For the new reading of this line as compared with the French edition, see Pardee forthcoming, inspired by Tsumura 2007.

(64–65) {åṯt}, {bn} asyndetic constructions; {ỉtrḫ}, {åšld} /YQTLu/-imperfectives expressing the double birth structure of the narrative or examples of /YQTLØ/-perfectives?

(72) {nlḥ⸢m⸣}, {nšt} 1c.du. jussive or optative, G-stem, ← /nilḥamā (+ a)/, /ništayā (+ a)/.

(76) {mlå yn} may mean 'is full of wine' (the antecedent of the pronominal suffix on *ḥbr* is unknown).

Text 6: *Ḥôrānu* and the Serpents (RS 24.244)

Virolleaud 1968, text 7; *KTU* 1.100; Pardee 1988: 193–226; 1997e; 2002a: 172–79; Parker 1997b; Wyatt 1998: 378–87; Dietrich and Loretz 2000: 263–402.

Text	***Translation***
Obverse	
I. (1) ủm . pḥl . pḥlt .	The mother of the stallion, the mare,
bt . ˤn . bt . ảbn .	the daughter of the spring, the daughter of the stone,
bt . šmm . w thm	the daughter of the heavens and the abyss,
(2) qrỉt . l špš . ủmh .	calls to her mother, *Šapšu*:
špš . ủm . ql . bl .	"Mother *Šapšu*, take a message
ˤm (3) ỉl . mbk nhrm .	to *ʾIlu* at the headwaters of the two rivers,
b ˤdt . thmtm	at the confluence of the deeps:
(4) mnt . nṯk . nḥš .	My incantation for serpent bite,
šmrr . nḥš (5) ˤqšr .	for the scaly serpent's poison:
lnh . mlḫš ảbd .	'From it, O charmer, destroy,
lnh . ydy (6) ḥmt .	from it cast out the venom.' "
hlm . yṯq . nḥš .	Then he binds the serpent,
yšlḥm . ˤqšr	feeds the scaly ‹serpent›,
(7) yˤdb . ksả . w yṯb	draws up a chair and sits.
II. (8) tqrủ . l špš . ủmh .	She again calls to her mother, *Šapšu*:
špš . ủm . ql bl	"Mother *Šapšu*, take a message
(9) ˤm . bˤl . mrym . ṣpn .	to *Baˤlu* on the heights of *Ṣapunu*:
mnty . nṯk (10) nḥš .	My incantation for serpent bite,
šmrr . nḥš . ˤqšr .	for the scaly serpent's poison:
lnh (11) mlḫš . ảbd .	'From it, O charmer, destroy,
lnh . ydy . ḥmt .	from it cast out the venom.' "
hlm . yṯq (12) nḥš .	Then he binds the serpent,
yšlḥm . nḥš . ˤqšr .	feeds the scaly serpent,
ydb . ksả (13) w yṯb	‹dr›aws up a chair and sits.
III. (14) tqrủ l špš . ủh .	She again calls to her mo‹th›er, *Šapšu*:
špš . ủm . ql . bl .	"Mother *Šapšu*, take a message
ˤm (15) dgn . ttlh .	to *Dagan* in Tuttul:
mnt . nṯk . nḥš .	My incantation for serpent bite,
šmrr (16) nḥš . ˤqšr .	for the scaly serpent's poison:
lnh . mlḫš . ảbd .	'From it, O charmer, destroy,
lnh (17) ydy . ḥmt .	from it cast out the venom.' "

hlm . yṯq . nḥš .	Then he binds the serpent,
yšlḥm (18) nḥš . ʿqšr .	feeds the scaly serpent,
yʿdb . ksả . w yṯb	draws up a chair and sits.

IV. (19) tqrủ l špš . ủmh .	She again calls to her mother, *Šapšu*:
špš . ủm . ql . bl .	"Mother *Šapšu*, take a message
ʿt (20) ʿnt w ʿ.ṯtrt ỉnbbh .	to! *ʿAnatu-wa-ʿAṯtartu* on (Mount) *ʾInbubu*:
mnt . nṯk (21) nḥš .	My incantation for serpent bite,
šmrr . nḥš . ʿqšr .	for the scaly serpent's poison:
lnh . ml(22)ḫš . ảbd .	'From it, O charmer, destroy,
lnh . ydy . ḥmt .	from it cast out the venom.'"
hlm . yṯq (23) nḥš .	Then he binds the serpent,
yšlḥm . nḥš . ʿqšr .	feeds the scaly serpent,
⸢yʿ⸣db ksả (24) w yṯb	draws up a chair and sits.

V. (25) tqrủ . l špš . ủmh .	She again calls to her mother, *Šapšu*:
špš . ⸢ủ⸣[m . q]⸢l⸣ bl .	"Mother *Šapšu*, take a message
ʿm (26) yrḫ . lrgth .	to *Yariḫu* in *Larugatu*:
mnt . nṯk . ⸢n⸣[ḥ]⸢š⸣ .	My incantation for serpent bite,
šmrr (27) nḥš . ʿqšr .	for the scaly serpent's poison:
lnh . mlḫš . ảbd .	'From it, O charmer, destroy,
lnh . ydy (28) ḥmt .	from it cast out the venom.'"
hlm yṯq . nḥš .	Then he binds the serpent,
yšlḥm . nḥš (29) ʿqšr .	feeds the scaly serpent,
yʿdb . ksả . w yṯb	draws up a chair and sits.

VI. (30) tqrủ . l špš . ủmh .	She again calls to her mother, *Šapšu*:
špš . ủm . ql b .	"Mother *Šapšu*, ta⟨ke⟩ a message
ʿm (31) ršp . bbth .	to *Rašap* in *Bibitta*:
mnt . nṯk . nḥš .	My incantation for serpent bite,
šmrr (32) nḥš . ʿqšr .	for the scaly serpent's poison:
lnh . mlḫš ảbd .	'From it, O charmer, destroy,
lnh . ydy (33) ḥmt .	from it cast out the venom.'"
hlm . yṯq . nḥš .	Then he binds the serpent,
yšlḥm . nḥš . ʿq(34)š .	feeds the scal⟨y⟩ serpent,
yʿdb . ksả . w yṯb	draws up a chair and sits.

⟨———

VII. (34a) tqrủ . l špš . ủmh .	⟨She again calls to her mother, *Šapšu*:
špš . ủm . ql bl .	"Mother *Šapšu*, take a message
ʿm (34b) ʿṯtrt . mrh .	to *ʿAṯtartu* in Mari:
mnt . nṯk . nḥš .	My incantation for serpent bite,

šmrr (34c) nḥš . ʿqšr .	for the scaly serpent's poison:
lnh . mlḫš ảbd .	'From it, O charmer, destroy,
lnh . ydy (34d) ḥmt .	from it cast out the venom.'"
hlm . yṯq . nḥš .	Then he binds the serpent,
yšlḥm . nḥš (34e) ʿqšr .	feeds the scaly serpent,
yʿdb . ksả . w yṯb⟩	draws up a chair and sits.⟩

VIII. (35) tqrủ l špš . ủmh .	She again calls to her mother, *Šapšu*:
špš . ủm . ql bl .	"Mother *Šapšu*, take a message
ʿm (36) ẓẓ . w kmṯ . ḥryth .	to *Ẓiẓẓu-wa-Kamāṯu* in ḤRYT:
mnt . nṯk nḥš .	My incantation for serpent bite,
šm(37)rr . nḥš . ʿqšr .	for the scaly serpent's poison:
lnh . mlḫš ảbd .	'From it, O charmer, destroy,
lnh (38) ydy . ḥmt .	from it cast out the venom.'"
hlm . yṯq . nḥš	Then he binds the serpent,
yšlḥm . nḥš (39) ʿq . šr .	feeds the scaly serpent,
yʿdb . ksả . w yṯb	draws up a chair and sits.

Lower edge

IX. (40) ⌜t⌝qrủ l špš . ủmh .	She again calls to her mother, *Šapšu*:
špš . ủm ql . bl .	"Mother *Šapšu*, take a message
ʿm (41) mlk . ʿṯtrth .	to *Milku* in *ʿAṯtartu*:
mnt . nṯk . nḥš .	My incantation for serpent bite,
šmrr (42) ⌜n⌝ḥš . ʿqšr .	for the scaly serpent's poison:
lnh . mlḫš ảbd .	'From it, O charmer, destroy,
lnh . ydy (43) ḥmt .	from it cast out the venom.'"
hlm yṯq . nḥš .	Then he binds the serpent,
yšlḥm . nḥš (*Reverse*) (44) ʿqšr .	feeds the scaly serpent,
yʿdb . ksả . w yṯb	draws up a chair and sits.

X. (45) tqrủ l špš . ủmh .	She again calls to her mother, *Šapšu*:
špš . ủm . ql bl .	"Mother *Šapšu*, take a message
ʿm (46) kṯr w ḫss . kptrh .	to *Kôṯaru-wa-Ḫasīsu* in Crete:
mnt . nṯk . nḥš	My incantation for serpent bite,
(47) šmrr . nḥš . ʿqšr .	for the scaly serpent's poison:
lnh . mlḫš . ảbd	'From it, O charmer, destroy,
(48) lnh . ydy . ḥmt .	from it cast out the venom.'"
hlm yṯq . nḥš	Then he binds the serpent,
(49) yšlḥm . nḥš . ʿqšr .	feeds the scaly serpent,
yʿdb . ksả (50) w yṯb	draws up a chair and sits.

XI. (51) tqrủ l špš . ủmh .	She again calls to her mother, *Šapšu*:
špš . ủm ql . bl .	"Mother *Šapšu*, take a message
ʿm (52) šḥr . w šlm šmmh .	to *Šaḥru-wa-Šalimu* in the heavens:
mnt . nṯk . nḥš	My incantation for serpent bite,
(53) šmrr . nḥš ʿqšr .	for the scaly serpent's poison:
lnh . mlḫš (54) ảbd .	'From it, O charmer, destroy,
lnh . ydy ḥmt .	from it cast out the venom.' "
hlm . yṯq (55) nḥš .	Then he binds the serpent,
yšlḥm . nḥš . ʿqšr .	feeds the scaly serpent,
yʿdb (56) ksả . w yṯb	draws up a chair and sits.

XII. (57) tqrủ . l špš . ủmh .	She again calls to her mother, *Šapšu*:
špš . ủm . ql . bl	"Mother *Šapšu*, take a message
(58) ʿm ḥrn . mṣdh .	to *Ḥôrānu* in MṢD:
mnt . nṯk nḥš	My incantation for serpent bite,
(59) šmrr . nḥš . ʿqšr .	for the scaly serpent's poison:
lnh . mlḫš (60) ảbd .	'From it, O charmer, destroy,
lnh . ydy . ḥmt .	from it cast out the venom.' "

XIII. (61) b ḥrn . pnm . trǵnw .	She (the mare) turns (her) face to *Ḥôrānu*,
w tṯkl (62) bnwth .	for she is to be bereaved of her offspring.
ykr . ʿr . d qdm	He (*Ḥôrānu*) returns to the city of the East,
(63) ỉdk . pnm . l ytn .	he heads
tk ảršḫ . rbt	for Great *ʾAraššiḫu*,
(64) w ảršḫ . ṯrrt .	(for) well-watered *ʾAraššiḫu*.
ydy . b ʿṣm . ʿrʿr	He casts a tamarisk (from) among the trees,
(65) w b šḥt . ʿṣ . mt .	the "tree of death" (from) among the bushes.
ʿrʿrm . ynʿrảh	With the tamarisk he expels it (the venom),
(66) ssnm . ysynh .	with the fruit stalk of a date palm he banishes it,
ʿdtm . yʿdynh .	with the succulent part of a reed he makes it pass on,
yb(67)ltm . yblnh .	with the "carrier" he carries it away.
mǵy . ḥrn . l bth .	Then *Ḥôrānu* goes to his house,
w (68) yštql . l ḥẓrh .	arrives at his court.
tlủ . ḥt . km . nḫl	The ve<no>m is weak as though (in) a stream,
(69) tplg . km . plg	is dispersed as though (in) a canal.

XIV. (70) bˁdh . bhtm . mnt .	Behind her the house of incantation,
bˁdh . bhtm . sgrt	behind her the house she has shut,
(71) bˁdh . ˁdbt . ṯlṯ .	behind her she has set the bronze (bolt?).
ptḥ . bt . mnt	"Open the house of incantation,
(72) ptḥ . bt . w ủbả .	open the house that I may enter,
hkl . w ỉštql	the palace that I may enter."
(73) tn . km . nḥšm .	"Give as ⟨my bride-price⟩ serpents,
yḥr . tn . km (74) mhry .	give poisonous lizards as my bride-price,
w bn . bṯn . ỉtnny	adders as my wife-price."
(75) ytt . nḥšm . mhrk .	"I hereby give serpents as your bride-price,
bn bṯn (76) ỉtnnk	adders as your wife-price."
Left edge	
(77) ảṯr ršp . ˁṯtrt	After *Rašap*, *ˁAṯtartu*:
(78) ˁm ˁṯtrt . mrh	". . . to *ˁAṯtartu* in Mari:
(79) mnt . nṯk nḥš	My incantation for serpent bite . . .

Vocalized Text

I. (1) ʾummu paḥlu paḥlatu // bittu ˁêni bittu ʾabni // bittu šamîma wa tahāmi
(2) qāriʾtu lê šapši ʾummiha
šapši ʾummi qāla bilī // ˁimma (3) ʾili mabbakê naharêma // bi ˁidati tahāmātima
(4) minûtî niṯka naḥaši // šamrira naḥaši (5) ˁaqšari
lênahu mulaḫḫiši ʾabbida // lênahu yidiya (6) ḫimata
hallima yaṯuqu naḥaša // yašalḥimu ⟨naḥaša⟩ ˁaqšara // (7) yaˁdubu kussaʾa wa yaṯibu

---

II. (8) tiqraʾu lê šapši ʾummiha
šapši ʾummi qāla bilī // (9) ˁimma baˁli maryamī ṣapuni
minûtîya niṯka (10) naḥaši // šamrira naḥaši ˁaqšari
lênahu (11) mulaḫḫiši ʾabbida // lênahu yidiya ḫimata
hallima yaṯuqu (12) naḥaša // yašalḥimu naḥaša ˁaqšara // ya⟨ˁ⟩dubu kussaʾa (13) wa yaṯibu

---

III. (14) tiqraʾu lê šapši ʾu⟨mmi⟩ha
šapši ʾummi qāla bilī // ˁimma (15) dagan tuttulaha
minûtî niṯka naḥaši // šamrira (16) naḥaši ˁaqšari
lênahu mulaḫḫiši ʾabbida // lênahu (17) yidiya ḫimata
hallima yaṯuqu naḥaša // yašalḥimu (18) naḥaša ˁaqšara // yaˁdubu kussaʾa wa yaṯibu

---

IV. (19) tiqraʾu lê šapši ʾummiha
šapši ʾummi qāla bilī // ʿimma[!] (20) ʿanati wa ʿaṯtarti ʾinbubaha
minûtî niṯka naḥaši // šamrira naḥaši ʿaqšari
lênahu mula(22)ḫḫiši ʾabbida // lênahu yidiya ḥimata
hallima yaṯuqu (23) naḥaša // yašalḥimu naḥaša ʿaqšara // yaʿdubu
kussaʾa (24) wa yaṯibu

V. (25) tiqraʾu lê šapši ʾummiha
šapši ʾu[mmi qā]la bilī // ʿimma (26) yariḫi larugataha
minûtî niṯka naḥaši // šamrira (27) naḥaši ʿaqšari
lênahu mulaḫḫiši ʾabbida // lênahu yidiya (28) ḥimata
hallima yaṯuqu naḥaša // yašalḥimu naḥaša (29) ʿaqšara // yaʿdubu
kussaʾa wa yaṯibu

VI. (30) tiqraʾu lê šapši ʾummiha
šapši ʾummi qāla bi⟨lī⟩ // ʿimma (31) rašap bibittaha
minûtî niṯka naḥaši // šamrira (32) naḥaši ʿaqšari
lênahu mulaḫḫiši ʾabbida // lênahu yidiya (33) ḥimata
hallima yaṯuqu naḥaša // yašalḥimu naḥaša ʿaq(34)ša⟨ra⟩ // yaʿdubu
kussaʾa wa yaṯibu

VII. (34a) tiqraʾu lê šapši ʾummiha
šapši ʾummi qāla bilī // ʿimma (34b) ʿaṯtarti mariha
minûtî niṯka naḥaši // šamrira (34c) naḥaši ʿaqšari
lênahu mulaḫḫiši ʾabbida // lênahu yidiya (34d) ḥimata
hallima yaṯuqu naḥaša // yašalḥimu naḥaša (34e) ʿaqšara // yaʿdubu
kussaʾa wa yaṯibu⟩

VIII. (35) tiqraʾu lê šapši ʾummiha
šapši ʾummi qāla bilī // ʿimma (36) ẓiẓẓi wa kamāṯi ḤRYT-ha
minûtî niṯka naḥaši // šam(37)rira naḥaši ʿaqšari
lênahu mulaḫḫiši ʾabbida // lênahu (38) yidiya ḥimata
hallima yaṯuqu naḥaša // yašalḥimu naḥaša (39) ʿaqšara // yaʿdubu
kussaʾa wa yaṯibu

IX. (40) tiqraʾu lê šapši ʾummiha
šapši ʾummi qāla bilī // ʿimma (41) milki ʿaṯtartaha
minûtî niṯka naḥaši // šamrira (42) naḥaši ʿaqšari
lênahu mulaḫḫiši ʾabbida // lênahu yidiya (43) ḥimata
hallima yaṯuqu naḥaša // yašalḥimu naḥaša (44) ʿaqšara // yaʿdubu
kussaʾa wayaṯibu

X. (45) tiqraʾu lê šapši ʾummiha
šapši ʾummi qāla bilī // ʿimma (46) kôṯari wa ḫasīsi kaptāraha
minûtî niṯka naḥaši // (47) šamrira naḥaši ʿaqšari
lênahu mulaḫḫiši ʾabbida // (48) lênahu yidiya ḥimata
hallima yaṯuqu naḥaša // (49) yašalḥimu naḥaša ʿaqšara // yaʿdubu kussaʾa (50) wa yaṯibu

---

XI. (51) tiqraʾu lê šapši ʾummiha
šapši ʾummi qāla bilī // ʿimma (52) šaḥri wa šalimi šamîmaha
minûtî niṯka naḥaši // (53) šamrira naḥaši ʿaqšari
lênahu mulaḫḫiši (54) ʾabbida // lênahu yidiya ḥimata
hallima yaṯuqu (55) naḥaša // yašalḥimu naḥaša ʿaqšara // yaʿdubu (56) kussaʾa wa yaṯibu

---

XII. (57) tiqraʾu lê šapši ʾummiha
šapši ʾummi qāla bilī // (58) ʿimma ḥôrāna MṢD-ha
minûtî niṯka naḥaši // (59) šamrira naḥaši ʿaqšari
lênahu mulaḫḫiši (60) ʾabbida // lênahu yidiya ḥimata

XIII. (61) bi ḥôrāna panîma tarūǵan // wa tiṯkalu (62) bunuwwataha
yakurru ʿīra dā qidmi // (63) ʾidaka panîma la yatinu
tôka ʾaraššiḫi rabbati // (64) waʾaraššiḫi ṯarīrati
yadiyu bi ʿiṣīma ʿarʿara // (65) wa bi šīḥāti ʿiṣa môti
ʿarʿarama yanaʿʿirannʾaha // (66) sissinnama yassiyannaha //
ʿadattama yaʿaddiyannaha // yābi(67)latama yabilannaha
māǵiyu ḥôrānu lê bêtihu // wa (68) yištaqīlu lê ḥaẓirihu
tilʾû ḥi<ma>tu kama naḫali // (69) tippaligu kama palgi

XIV. (70) baʿdaha bahatīma minûti
// baʿdaha bahatīma sāgiratu
// (71) baʿdaha ʿādibatu ṯalṯa
pataḥī bêta minûti // (72) pataḥī bêta wa ʾubūʾa // hēkala wa ʾištaqīla
(73) tin kama <muhriya> naḥašīma // yaḥara tin kama (74) muhriya // wa bina baṯni ʾitnāniya
(75) yatattu naḥašīma muhraki // bina baṯni (76) ʾitnānaki
(77) ʾaṯra rašap ʿaṯtartu (78) ʿimma ʿaṯtarti mariha (79) minûtî niṯka naḥaši

---

Notes

(2) {bl} f.s. imperative, G-stem, √YBL.
(5–6) {ảbd} . . . {ydy} vocalized as /QTLa/-imperatives because of the writing of the second with {y}.

(6) read {yšlḥm . ⟨nḥš⟩ ʿqšr} as in the other paragraphs.
(9) {mnty} either an error for {mnt} or /minûtī/ + *y*-enclitic.
(12) {ydb} read {y⟨ʿ⟩db}.
(14) {ủh} read {ủ⟨m⟩h}.
(19) {ʿt} read {ʿm!}.
(20) Word-divider misplaced in {wʿ.ṯtrt}.
(30) {qlb} read {ql b⟨l⟩}.
(33–34) {ʿqš} read {ʿqš⟨r⟩}.
(34a–e) this paragraph is reconstructed on the basis of the indications in lines 77–79.
(39) {ʿq.šr} read {ʿqšr}.
(61) {trǵnw} read {trǵn} (dittography of the first sign in the next poetic line).
(63) {pnm l ytn} lit., 'give/put the face'.
(64) {ʿrʿr} the small vertical line after the {r} appears too small to be an intentional word-divider; it is perhaps simply the result of an inadvertent stroke of the stylus.
(65) {ynʿrảh} read {ynʿrn!h}.
(66) {ysynh} 3m.s. imperfective, G-stem, √NSY.
(66–67) {ybltm} identification uncertain, perhaps active participle, G-stem, f.s.a. √YBL + *m*-enclitic.
(68) {yštql} 3m.s. imperfective, Št-stem, √QL; {tlủ} 3f.s. imperfective, G-stem, √LʾY (← *LʾW?) /tilʾû/ ← /tilʾayu/ ou /tilʾawu/; {ḥt} read {ḥ⟨m⟩t}.
(69) {km} to the left of the {m} is the head of a wedge inscribed by mistake.
(71–72) *Ḥôrānu* is speaking, (73–74) the mare is speaking, (75–76) *Ḥôrānu* is again speaking.
(73) perhaps restore {tn . km . ⟨mhry⟩ nḥšm}.
(75) {ytt} 1c.s. perfective, G-stem, √YTN (/yatattu/ ← /yatantu/).
(77–79) the scribe, having forgotten to inscribe the paragraph dealing with *ʿAṯtartu*, placed an abbreviated version thereof on the left edge of the tablet, exactly at the spot where this paragraph should have been.

Text 7: The Drunkenness of *ʾIlu* (RS 24.258)

Virolleaud 1968, text 1; *KTU* 1.114; Pardee 1988: 13–74; 1997f; 2002a: 167–70; *TO* II, pp. 71–78; Lewis 1997b; Wyatt 1998: 404–13; Dietrich and Loretz 2000: 403–523.

Text	***Translation***
Obverse	
(1) ỉl dbḥ . b bth . mṣd .	*ʾIlu* slaughters game in his house,
ṣd . b qrb (2) hkl⌜h⌝ .	prey within his palace;

ṣḥ . l qṣ . ìlm .	he invites the gods to partake.
tlḥmn (3) ìlm . w tštn .	The gods eat and drink,
tštn y ʿd šbʿ	they drink wi<ne> to satiety,
(4) trṯ . ʿd ⸢škr⸣ .	new wine to drunkenness.
yʿdb . yrḫ (5) gbh .	*Yariḫu* prepares his goblet,
km . ⸢k⸣[l]⸢b⸣ . yqṯqṯ .	like a dog he drags it
tḥt (6) ṯlḥnt	under the tables.
ìl . d ydʿnn	Any god who knows him
(7) yʿdb . lḥm . lh .	prepares him a portion of food;
w d l ydʿnn	but one who does not know him
(8) ylmn . ḫṭm .	strikes him with a stick
tḥt . ṯlḥn	under the table.
(9) ʿṯtrt . w ʿnt . ymǵy	He goes up to *ʿAṯtartu* and *ʿAnatu*;
(10) ʿṯtrt . tʿdb . nšb lh	*ʿAṯtartu* prepares him a NŠB-cut of meat,
(11) w ʿnt . ktp .	*ʿAnatu* a shoulder-cut.
bhm . ygʿr . ṯǵr (12) bt . ìl .	The doorman of *ʾIlu*'s house yells at them
pn . lm . rlb . tʿdbn (13) nšb .	that they should not prepare a NŠB-cut for a dog!,
l ìnr . tʿdbn . ktp	not prepare a shoulder-cut for a hound.
(14) b ìl . åbh . gʿr .	He also berates *ʾIlu*, his father;
yṯb . ìl . k⸢r⸣ (15) å⸢šk⸣[rh] .	*ʾIlu* takes a seat and calls together his drinking [group],
ìl . yṯb . b mrzḥh	*ʾIlu* takes his seat in his drinking club.
(16) yš⸢t⸣ . [y]⸢n⸣ . ʿd šbʿ .	He drinks wine to satiety,
trṯ . ʿd škr	new wine to drunkenness.
(17) ìl . h⸢l⸣k . l bth .	*ʾIlu* heads off to his house,
yštql . (18) l ḥẓrh .	arrives at his court.
yʿmsn . nn . ṯkmn (19) w šnm .	*Ṯukamuna-wa-Šunama* bear him along;
w ngšnn . ḥby .	ḤBY meets him,
(20) bʿl . qrnm . w ḏnb .	he who has two horns and a tail.
ylšn (21) b ḫrìh . w ṯnth .	He knocks him over in his feces and his urine;
ql . ìl . km mt	*ʾIlu* falls as though dead,
(22) ìl . k yrdm . årṣ .	*ʾIlu* falls like those who descend into the earth.
ʿnt (23) w ʿṯtrt . tṣdn .	*ʿAnatu* and *ʿAṯtartu* go off on the hunt,
⸢š---⸣[. . .] (24) q⸢d⸣š .	
bʿ⸢-⸣[. . .]	[. . .]

. . . .

Reverse

(25′)	[ ]⸢n⸣ . d[. . .]	[. . .]
(26′)	[ˁṯ]⸢t⸣rt . w ˁn⸢t⸣[. . .] [. . .]	*ˁAṯtartu* and *ˁAnatu* [. . .]
(27′)	⸢w⸣ bhm . tṯṯb . ⸢-m⸣dh[. . .]	and in them she brings back [. . .].
(28′)	km . trpả . hn nˁr	When she would heal him, he awakes.
(29′)	d yšt . l lṣbh . šˁr klb	What is to be put on his forehead: hairs of a dog.
(30′)	⸢w⸣ rỉš . pqq . w šrh	And the head of the PQQ and its shoot
(31′)	yšt ảḥdh . dm zt . ḫr⸢p⸣ảt	he is to drink mixed together with fresh! olive oil.

Vocalized Text

(1) ʾilu dābiḥu bi bêtihu maṣūda // ṣêda bi qirbi (2) hēkalihu // ṣāḥu lê quṣṣi ʾilīma
tilḥamūna (3) ʾilūma wa tištûna // tištûna yê<na> ˁadê šubˁi // (4) tirāṯa ˁadê šukri
yaˁdubu yariḫu (5) gūbahu // kama k[al]bi yaqaṭqiṭu // taḥta (6) ṯulḥanāti
ʾilu dū yidaˁannannu // (7) yaˁdubu laḥma lêhu
wa dū lā yidaˁannannu // (8) yallumannu ḫaṭṭama // taḥta ṯulḥani
(9) ˁaṯtarta wa ˁanata yamǵiyu // (10) ˁaṯtartu taˁdubu NŠBa lêhu // (11) wa ˁanatu katipa
bihumā yigˁaru ṯāǵiru (12) bêti ʾili
// pana lêma k!albi taˁdubāna (13) NŠBa
// lê ʾināri taˁdubāna katipa
(14) bi ʾili ʾabîhu gāˁiru // yāṯibu ʾilu karû (15) ʾaška[rahu] // ʾilu yāṯibu bi marziḥihu
(16) yištû [yê]na ˁadê šubˁi // tirāṯa ˁadê šukri
(17) ʾilu hāliku lê bêtihu // yištaqīlu (18) lê ḥaẓirihu
yaˁammisānannannu ṯukamuna-(19)-wa-šunama
// wa nāgišunnannu ḤBY
// (20) baˁlu qarnêma wa ḏanabi
yalaššinnu (21) bi ḫurʾihu wa ṯênātihu // qālu ʾilu kama mêti // (22) ʾilu ka yāridīma ʾarṣi
ˁanatu (23) wa ˁaṯtartu taṣūdāna // ⸢Š---⸣[. . .] (24) Q⸢D⸣Š . B⸢ˁ-⸣[. . .]

. . . .

(25′) [ ]⸢N⸣ . D[. . .]
(26′) [. . .] ˁaṯtartu wa ˁanatu [. . .]
(27′) wa bihumu taṯaṯību [. . .]
(28′) kīma tirpaʾa hanna naˁāru

(29′) dū yašītu lê liṣbihu šaˁarī kalbi (30′) wa raʾša PQQi wa šurrahu
(31′) yištû ʾaḥḥadaha dama zêti ḫurpāni!

Notes

(3) {tštn y} read {tštn y⟨n⟩}.

(7–9) signs smaller in size than those of the main text are visible between these lines.

(12) {rlb} read {k!lb}.

(16) {yšt} 3m.s. imperfective, G-stem, /yištû/ ← /yištayu/.

(20) {ylšn} 3m.s. energic, D-stem, √LŠY + suffix 3m.s. (/yalaššinnu/ ← /yalaššiyan + hu/).

(22) because it is smaller than the other word-dividers in this text, the vertical line between {k} and {yrdm} is probably accidental.

(24) {q⸢d⸣š} the meaning of this form of √QDŠ may not be determined because of the damaged state of the text (the original may, however, have contained a reference to the 'desert of QDŠ').

(28′) {nʿr} m.s. participle, N-stem, √ʿR.

(31′) {ḫr⸢p⸣ảt} read {ḫr⸢p⸣n!}.

II. Ritual Texts

Text 8: A Sacrificial Ritual for a Day and a Night (RS 1.001)

Virolleaud 1929: pl. LXI; *CTA* 34; *KTU* 1.39; *TO* II, pp. 135–39; del Olmo Lete 1999: 215–17; Pardee 2000a: 15–91; 2002a: 67–69.

Text

Obverse

(1) dqt . ṯʿ . ynt . ṯʿm . dqt . ṯʿm (2) mtntm w kbd . ảlp . š . l ỉl (3) gdlt . ỉlhm . ṯkmn . ⸢w⸣ šnm . dqt (4) ⸢r⸣šp . dqt . šrp . w šlmm . dqtm (5) [ỉ]⸢l⸣h . ảlp w š ỉlhm . gdl⸢t⸣ . ỉlhm (6) ⸢b⸣ʿl š . ảṯrt . š . ṯkmn w šn⸢m⸣ . š (7) ʿnt . š . ršp . š . dr . ỉl w p[ḫ]r bʿl (8) gdlt . šlm . gdlt . w b ủrm . ⸢l⸣b (9) rmṣt . ỉlhm . bʿlm . dṯt . w kŝm . ḫmš (10) ʿ⸢š⸣rh . mlủn . šnpt . ḫṣth . bʿl . ṣpn š (11) ⸢tr⸣ṯ š . ỉlt . mgdl . š . ỉlt . ảsrm š (12) w l ll . špš pgr . w ṯrmnm . bt mlk (13) ỉ⸢l b⸣t . gdlt . ủšḫry . gdlt . ym gdlt (14) bʿ⸢l⸣ . gdlt . yrḫ . gdlt . (15) gdlt . ṯrmn . gdlt . pdry . gdlt dqt (16) dqt . ⸢t⸣rṯ . dqt . (17) ⸢š⸣rp . ʿnt . ḫbly . dbḥm . š[p]š pgr (*Lower edge*) (18) [g]⸢d⸣lt . ỉltm . ḫnqtm . d⸢qt⸣m (19) [y]rḫ . kṯy . gdlt . w l ǵl⸢mt⸣ š (*Reverse*) (20) ⸢w⸣ pảmt ṯlṯm . w yrdt . ⸢m⸣dbḥt (21) ⸢g⸣dlt . l bʿlt bhtm . ʿṣrm (22) l ỉnš ỉlm

Translation

I. (At some time during the daylight hours.)
A. (1) A ewe as a *ṯaʿû*-sacrifice;
a dove, also as a *ṯaʿû* -sacrifice;
a ewe, also as a *ṯaʿû* -sacrifice;
(2) two kidneys and the liver (of?) a bull and a ram for *ʾIlu.*
B. (3) A cow for the *ʾIlāhūma*;
for *Ṯukamuna-wa-Šunama* a ewe;
(4) for *Rašap* a ewe as burnt-offering.
C. And as a peace-offering: two ewes (5) for [*ʾI*]*lāhu*;
a bull and a ram for the *ʾIlāhūma*;
a cow for the *ʾIlāhūma*;
(6) for *Baʿlu* a ram;
for *ʾAṯiratu* a ram;
for *Ṯukamuna-wa-Šunama* a ram;
(7) for *ʿAnatu* a ram;
for *Rašap* a ram;
for the-Circle-of-*ʾIlu*-and-the-As[sem]bly-of-*Baʿlu* (8) a cow;
for *Šalimu* a cow;

and in the flames the heart (9) as a roast-offering for the *ʾIlāhūma* and for the *Baʿalūma*;
dṯt-grain and emmer, (10) fifteen full measures of each (also for the *ʾIlāhūma* and the *Baʿalūma*[?]);

D. As a presentation-offering, half of this (also for the *ʾIlāhūma* and the *Baʿalūma*[?]);
for *Baʿlu* of *Ṣapunu* a ram;
(11) for *Tirāṯu* a ram;
for *ʾIlatu-Magdali* a ram;
for *ʾIlatu*-ʾASRM a ram.

IIA. (12) And at night, *Šapšu-Pagri* and the *Ṯarrumannūma* being in the royal palace, (13) for *ʾIlu-Bêti* a cow;
for *ʾUšḫaraya* a cow;
for *Yammu* a cow;
(14) for *Baʿlu* a cow;
for *Yariḫu* a cow;
for ⟨*Kôṯaru*⟩ (15) a cow;
for *Ṯarrummannu* a cow;
for *Pidray* a cow;
for *Daqqītu* (16) a ewe;
for *Tirāṯu* a ewe;
for ⟨*Rašap* a ewe⟩ (17) as burnt-offering.

B. For *ʿAnatu Ḫablay* two *dabḫu*-sacrifices (animal *ad libitum*[?]);
for *Ša*[*p*]*šu-Pagri* (18) a cow;
for *ʾIlatāma Ḫāniqatāma* two ewes;
(19) for Kassite [*Ya*]*riḫu* a cow;
and for *Ǵalmatu* a ram;
(20) and thirty times (is this set of offerings to be performed).

C. Then you will descend from the altars: (21) A cow for *Baʿlatu-Bahatīma*;
two birds (22) for the *ʾInāšu-ʾIlīma* (as burnt-offering[?]).

Vocalized Text

(1) daqqatu ṯaʿû yônatu ṯaʿûma daqqatu ṯaʿûma (2) matunatāma wa kabidu ʾalpi šû lê ʾili

(3) gadulatu ʾilāhīma ṯukamuni wa šunami daqqatu (4) rašap daqqatu šurpu

wa šalamūma daqqatāma (5) [ʾi]lāhi ʾalpu wa šû ʾilāhīma gadulatu ʾilāhīma (6) baʿli šû ʾaṯirati šû ṯukamuni wa šunami šû (7) ʿanati šû rašap šû dāri ʾili wa pu[ḫ]ri baʿli (8) gadulatu šalimi gadulatu wa bi ʾūrīma libbu (9) ramaṣati ʾilāhīma baʿalīma daṯâtu wa kuššumu ḫamišu (10) ʿašrihu malāʾuna šanūpatu ḫaṣâtuhu baˁli ṣapuni šû (11) tirāṯi šû ʾilati magdali šû ʾilati ʾASRM šû

(12) wa lê lêli šapšu pagri wa ṯarrummannūma bêta malki (13) ʾili bêti gadulatu ʾušḫaraya gadulatu yammi gadulatu (14) baˁli gadulatu yariḫi gadulatu 〈 kôṯari 〉 (15) gadulatu ṯarrummanni gadulatu pidray gadulatu daqqīti (16) daqqatu tirāṯi daqqatu 〈 rašap daqqatu 〉 (17) šurpu

ˁanati ḫablay dabḥāma ša[p]ši pagri (18) [ga]dulatu ʾilatêma ḫāniqatêma daqqatāma (19) [ya]riḫi kaṯṯiyyi gadulatu wa lê ǵalmati šû (20) wa paʾamāti ṯalāṯīma wa yaradta madbaḥāti

(21) gadulatu lê baˁlati bahatīma ˁuṣṣūrāma (22) lê ʾināši ʾilīma

Notes

For the divisions indicated in the translations of the ritual texts included here, see Pardee 2002a (explanation on pp. 6–7).

(3) {ỉlhm} proper noun m.pl.g.abs.—the attribution of a particular sacrifice is often indicated by the case-vowel alone in these texts.

(14) {〈kṯr〉} for the following reasons, the divine name *Kôṯaru* is to be inserted at the end of this line: (a) there is no divine name between the two sacrificial terms; (b) the scribe placed a word-divider after the last word inscribed, then left the rest of the line blank; (c) this divine name is situated between {yrḫ} and {ṯrmn} in RS 24.246:4–6, a list of divine names (Virolleaud 1968: text 14).

(16) {ršp dqt} it appears that both the divine name and the term designating the sacrifice are to be inserted here: (a) as in line 14, the scribe placed a word-divider after the last word inscribed, then left the rest of the line blank; (b) {ršp} follows {trṯ} in RS 24.246:9–10 (Virolleaud 1968: text 14).

(10) {mlủn} common noun m.s.n.abs. + *n*-enclitic.

Text 9: A Sacrificial Ritual for National Unity (RS 1.002)

Virolleaud 1929: pl. LXII; *CTA* 32; *KTU* 1.40; *TO* II, pp. 140–49; del Olmo Lete 1999: 146–60; Pardee 2000a: 92–142; 2002a: 77–83.

Text

Obverse

Section? (I or II)

(1′) [. . .] ⸢w⸣ n⸢py⸣[. . .]
(2′) [. . .] npy . ủ[. . .]
(3′) [. . .]y . ủ l p . [. . .]
(4′) [. . .]⸢ǵ⸣br . ủ ⸢l⸣[p . . .]
(5′) [. . .]⸢--⸣[. . .]

. . . .

Section II

(6′) [ṯʿ nṯʿ]⸢y⸣
(7′) [d]r . b⸢n⸣ ⸢ỉ⸣[l]
(8′) [ ]

Section III

(9′) [ ] ⸢.⸣ w npy
(10′) [ ]y . ủgr⸢t⸣
(11′) [ ]y
(12′) [ ]⸢-⸣
(13′) [ ]
(14′) [ ]
(15′) [ndb]ḥ
(16′) [ ]⸢yt⸣[šỉ]
(17′) [mpḫ]⸢r⸣t . [ṯkmn w šn]m hn š

Section IV

(18′) [w n]py . g⸢r⸣[. ḥmyt . ủgrt . w np]y
(19′) [ ]⸢-⸣ . w n⸢p⸣[y]⸢-⸣ . ủ tḫṭ⸢ỉ⸣[n . ủ l p . qṭy]
(20′) ủ l p . ddmy . ủ l ⸢p⸣ [. ḫry . ủ]⸢l⸣ p . ḫty . ủ l p [. ảlṯy . ủ l p .] ǵbr
(21′) ủ l p . ḫbtkn . ủ l ⸢p⸣ . md[llk]n . ủ l p . q[rzbl]
(22′) ủ tḫṭỉn . b ảpkn . ủ b ⸢q⸣ṣrt . npš[kn . ủ b qṭt]
(23′) tqṭṭn ủ tḫṭỉn . l bḥ⸢m⸣ w l ṯʿ . d[bḥn . ndb]⸢ḥ⸣
(24′) hw . ṯʿ . nṯʿy . hw . nkt . n⸢k⸣t . ytšỉ [. l ảb . bn ỉl]
(25′) ytšỉ . l dr . bn . ỉl . l . ⸢m⸣pḫrt . bn ⸢ỉ⸣[l . l ṯkmn . w š]nm hn š

Section V

(26′) w . šqrb . ʿr . mšr mšr [.] ⸢b⸣n . ủgrt . ⸢w⸣ [npy] ủgr
(27′) w npy . ymản . w npy . ʿrmt ⸢. w⸣ npy . ⸢-⸣[ ]
(28′) w npy . nqmd . ủ šn . ypkm . ủ l p . q[ṭy . ủ l p . ddm]y
(29′) ủ l p . ḫry . ủ l p . ḫ⸢t⸣y . ủ l p . ảlṯy . ủ ⸢l⸣ [p ǵbr .] ⸢ủ⸣ l p
(30′) ḫbtkm . ủ l p . m⸢d⸣[l]lkm . ủ l p . qrzbl . ủ ⸢šn⸣ [.] ypkm
(31′) ủ b ảpkm . ủ b q[ṣ]⸢r⸣t . npškm . ủ b qṭt . tqṭṭ
(32′) ủ šn ypkm . l d[b]ḥm . w l . ṯʿ . dbḥn . ndbḥ . hw . ṯʿ nṯʿy
(33′) hw . nkt . nkt . ⸢y⸣[t]šỉ . l ảb . bn . ỉl . ytšỉ . l dr
(34′) bn ỉl . l ṯkmn [. w] šnm . hn . ʿr

Section VI

(35′) w ṯb . l mspr . m[š]⸢r⸣ mšr . bt . ủgrt . w npy ⸢.⸣ gr

(36′) ḥmyt . ủgrt . w [np]y ⸢. ả⸣ṯt . ủ šn . ypkn . ủ l p ⸢.⸣ qṭy
(37′) ủ l p . ddmy . ủ l [p . ḫ]ry . ủ l p . ḫty . ủ l p . ảlṯy
(38′) ủ l p [.] ǵbr . ủ l p . ⸢ḫ⸣[bt]⸢kn . ủ l⸣ p . mdllkn . ủ l p ⸢.⸣ qrz⸢bl⸣
(39′) l šn ypkn . b ảp⸢k⸣[n . ủ b q]⸢ṣ⸣rt . npškn ⸢.⸣ ủ b q⸢ṭt⸣
(40′) tqṭṭn . ủ šn . y⸢p⸣[kn . l dbḥm .] w l ṯʿ dbḥn
(41′) ndbḥ . hw . ṯʿ n[ṯʿy . hw . nkt . n]⸢k⸣t . ⸢yt⸣[š]⸢ỉ .⸣ l ảb bn ỉl

Reverse

(42′) ytšỉ . l ⸢d⸣[r . bn ỉl . l] mpḫrt . bn ỉl
(43′) l ṯkm⸢n⸣ [. w šnm .] hn ⸢ʿr⸣

Translation

Section? (I or II)

(1′) [. . .] and well-being [. . .]
(2′) [. . . well-being of U[garit . . .]
(3′) [. . .]Y; be it according to the statement of [. . .]
(4′) [. . .] ǴBR, be it according to the state[ment of . . .]
(5′) [. . .] [. . .]

. . . .

Section II

(6′) [the *ṯaʿû*-sacrifice, it is offer]ed
(7′) [to the Circl]e-of-the-Sons-of-*ʾI*[*lu*]
(8′) [ ]

Section III

(9′) [ ] and well-being
(10′) [and well-be]ing of Ugarit
(11′) [Qaṭ]ian
(12′) [ ]
(13′) [ ]
(14′) [ ]
(15′) [. . . is sacrific]ed
(16′) [ ] May it be bor[ne]
(17′) [assemb]ly [of the sons of *ʾIlu*, to *Ṯukamuna-wa-Šuna*]*ma*: here is the ram.

Section IV

(18′) [we]ll-being of the foreigner [(within) the walls of Ugarit, and well-be]ing of (19′) [ ] and well[-being of];

whether you si[n:
be it according to the statement of the Qaṭian],
(20′) be it according to the statement of the DDMY,
be it according to the statement [of the Hurrian,
be it] according to the statement of the Hittite,
be it according to the statement [of the ʾAlashian,
be it according to the statement of] ǴBR,
(21′) be it according to the statement of your oppressed ones,
be it according to the statement of yo[ur] impo[verished ones],
be it according to the statement of Q[RZBL];
(22′) whether you sin:
be it in your anger,
be it in your [i]mpatience,
[be it in some turpitude] (23′) that you should commit;
whether you sin:
as concerns the ‹sa›crifices
or as concerns the *ṯaʿû*-sacrifice.
[The] sacrifice, it [is sacrific]ed,
(24′) the *ṯaʿû*-sacrifice, it is offered,
the slaughtering is done.
May it be borne [to the father of the sons of *ʾIlu*],
(25′) may it be borne to the Circle-of-the-Sons-of-*ʾIlu*,
to the Assembly-of-the-Sons-of-*ʾI*[*lu*,
to *Ṯukamuna-wa-Šu*]*nama*:
here is the ram.

Section V

(26′) Bring near the donkey of "re[cti]tude": rectitude of the son of Ugarit:
and [well-being of the foreigner within the walls] of Ugar‹it›,
(27′) and well-being of YMʾAN,
and well-being of ʿRMT,
and well-being of [. . .]
(28′) and well-being of *Niqmaddu*;
whether your "beauty" be altered:
be it according to the statement of the Qa[ṭian,
be it according to the statement of DDM]Y,
(29′) be it according to the statement of the Hurrian,
be it according to the statement of the Hittite,
be it according to the statement of the ʾAlashian,
be it according to the sta[tement of ǴBR,]
be it according to the statement of (30′) your oppressed ones,

be it according to the statement of your im[pov]erished ones,
be it according to the statement of QRZBL;
whether your 'beauty' be altered:
(31′) be it in your anger,
be it in your im[pa]tience,
be it in some turpitude that you should commit;
(32′) whether your 'beauty' be altered:
as concerns the sa[cr]ifices
or as concerns the *ṯaʿû*-sacrifice.
The sacrifice, it is sacrificed,
the *ṯaʿû*-sacrifice, it is offered,
(33′) the slaughtering is done.
May it be b[or]ne to the father of the sons of *ʾIlu*,
may it be borne to the Circle-of-(34′)the-Sons-of-*ʾIlu*,
⟨to the Assembly-of-the-Sons-of-*ʾIlu*⟩,
to *Ṯukamuna-wa-Šunama*:
here is the donkey.

Section VI

(35′) And return to the recitation of "rec[tit]ude": rectitude of the daughter of Ugarit:
and well-being of the foreigner (36′) (within) the walls of Ugarit,
and [well-be]ing of the woman/wife;
whether your "beauty" be altered:
be it according to the statement of the Qaṭian,
(37′) be it according to the statement of DDMY,
be it according to the sta[tement of the Hu]rrian,
be it according to the statement of the Hittite,
be it according to the statement of the ʾAlashian,
(38′) be it according to the statement of ǴBR,
be it according to the statement of your o[ppressed ones],
be it according to the statement of your impoverished ones,
be it according to the statement of QRZBL;
(39′) whether (!) your "beauty" be altered:
be it in yo[ur] anger,
[be it in] your [impa]tience,
be it in some turpitude (40′) that you should commit;
whether [your] "beauty" be altered:
[as concerns sacrifices]
or as concerns the *ṯaʿû*-sacrifice.
The sacrifice, (41′) it is sacrificed,
the *ṯaʿû*-sacrifice, it is [offered,

the slaughtering] is done.
May it be borne to the father of the sons of *ʾIlu*,
(42′) may it be bor[n]e to the C[ircle-of-the-Sons-of-*ʾIlu*,
to] the Assembly-of-the-Sons-of-*ʾIlu*,
(43′) to *Ṯukamuna*-[*wa-Šunama*:]
here is the donkey.

Vocalized Text

(26′) wa šaqrib ʿêra mêšari mêšaru bini ʾugārit wa [nôpayu gêri ḥāmiyāti] ʾugāri<t>
(27′) wa nôpayu YMʾAN wa nôpayu ʿRMT, wa nôpayu [. . .]
(28′) wa nôpayu niqmaddi ʾô šanâ yupûkumu ʾô lê pî qa[ṭiyyi ʾô lê pî dadmi]yyi
(29′) ʾô lê pî ḫurriyyi ʾô lê pî ḫattiyyi ʾô lê pî ʾalaṯiyyi ʾô lê [pî ǴBR] ʾô lê pî
(30′) ḫabūtīkumu ʾô lê pî muda[lla]līkumu ʾô lê pî QRZBL ʾô šanâ yupûkumu
(31′) ʾô bi ʾappikumu ʾô bi qu[ṣ]rati napšikumu ʾô bi quṭṭati taqāṭiṭū<na>
(32′) ʾô šanâ yupûkumu lê da[ba]ḥīma wa lê ṯaʿî dabḥuna nidbaḥu huwa ṯaʿû niṯʿayu
(33′) huwa nakatu nakkatu yi[tta]šiʾ lê ʾabî banī ʾili yittašiʾ lê dāri
(34′) banī ʾili < lê mapḫarti banī ʾili > lê ṯukamuna [wa] šunama hanna ʿêru

---

(35′) wa ṭub lê maspari mê[ša]ri mêšaru bitti ʾugārit wa nôpayu gêri
(36′) ḥāmiyāti ʾugārit wa [nôpa]yu ʾaṯṯati ʾô šanâ yupûkini ʾô lê pî qaṭiyyi
(37′) ʾô lê pî dadmiyyi ʾô lê [pî ḫu]rriyyi ʾô lê pî ḫattiyyi ʾô lê pî ʾalaṯiyyi
(38′) ʾô lê pî ǴBR ʾô lê pî ḫa[būtī]kini ʾô lê pî mudallalīkini ʾô lê pî QRZBL
(39′) ʾô! šanâ yupûkini bi ʾappiki[ni ʾô bi qu]ṣrati napšikini ʾô bi quṭṭati
(40′) taqāṭiṭna ʾô šanâ yupû[kini lê dabaḥīma] wa lê ṯaʿî dabḥuna
(41′) nidbaḥu huwa ṯaʿû ni[ṯʿayu huwa nakatu na]kkatu yitta[ši]ʾ lê ʾabî banī ʾili
(42′) yittašiʾ lê dā[ri banī ʾili lê] mapḫarti banī ʾili
(43′) lê ṯukamuna [wa šunama] hanna ʿêru

Notes

A vocalization is offered only for lines 26′–43′, the only part of the text that is preserved well enough to make the effort worthwhile.
(23′) {l bḥ⌜m⌝} read {l <d>bḥ⌜m⌝}.
(26′) {ủgr} read {ủgr<t>}.
(31′) {tqṭṭ} is plausibly to be corrected to {tqṭṭ<n>} (as in lines 23′, 40′).
(33′, 41′, 42′) {ytšỉ} 3m.s. jussive, Gt-stem, √NŠʾ.
(34′) after {bn ỉl .} insert {l mpḫrt bn ỉl }, as in the other sections.
(39′) {l šn} read {ủ! šn}.

Text 10: A Sacrificial Ritual for *ʾUšḫarâ Ḫulmiẓẓi* (RS 24.260)

Virolleaud 1968: text 11; *KTU* 1.115; *TO* II, pp. 200–202; del Olmo Lete 1999: 265–71; Pardee 2000a: 643–51; 2002: 66–67a.

Text

Obverse

(1) ỉd ydbḥ mlk (2) l ủš⸢ḫr ḫ⸣lm⸢ẓ⸣ (3) l b bt ⸢.⸣ ỉl bt (4) š l ḫlmẓ (5) w tr . l qlḥ (6) w šḥl⸢l⸣ . ydm (7) b qdš ỉl bt (8) w tlḥm ảṯt

---

(9) š l ỉl bt . šlmm (10) kl l ylḥm bh

---

(11) w l b bt šqym (12) š l ủḫr ḫlmẓ

(*Lower edge*) (13) w tr l qlḥ (*Reverse*) (14) ym ảḥd

Translation

IA. (1) At that time, the king is to sacrifice (2) to *ʾUšḫarâ Ḫulmiẓẓi* (3) inside the Temple of *ʾIlu-Bêti*: (4) a ram for *Ḫulmiẓẓi*
(5) and a turtle-dove for QLḤ.
(6) Purify the hands (of the participants) (7) in the sanctuary of *ʾIlu-Bêti*;
(8) the woman/women may eat (of the sacrificial meal).

B. (9) A ram for *ʾIlu-Bêti* as a peace-offering; (10) all may eat of it.

C. (11) (Again) within the temple: libations;
(12) a ram for *ʾU⟨š⟩ḫarâ Ḫulmiẓẓi*.

D. (13) And a turtle-dove for QLḤ.
One day.

Vocalized Text

(1) ʾida yidbaḥu malku (2) lê ʾušḫarî ḫulmiẓẓi (3) lê bi bêti ʾili bêti (4) šû lê ḫulmiẓẓi (5) wa turru lê QLḤ (6) wa šaḥlil yadêma (7) bi qidši ʾili bêti (8) wa tilḥamu ʾaṯṯatu
(9) šû lê ʾili bêti šalamūma (10) kullu la yilḥamu bihu
(11) wa lê bi bêti ŠQYM (12) šû lê ʾu⟨š⟩ḫarî ḫulmiẓẓi
(13) wa turru lê QLḤ (14) yômu ʾaḥḥadu

Notes

(3) {l b} two prepositions forming a complex preposition with the meaning 'on the inside of'.

(12) {ủḫr} read {ủ⟨š⟩ḫr}.

(14) {ym ảḥd} the formula is both brief and obscure; it may mean that the rite is to be carried out in the course of a single day.

Text 11: A Sacrificial Ritual with a Prayer (RS 24.266)

Herdner 1978a: 31–39; *KTU* 1.119; *TO* II, pp. 206–11; del Olmo Lete 1999: 292–306; Pardee 2000a: 661–85; 2002: 50–53a.

Text

Obverse

(1) b yrḫ . ỉbʿlt ⸢. b⸣ y⸢m⸣ [.] ⸢šbʿ⸣ (2) š . l bʿl . r⸢ʿk⸣t ⸢. b-⸣[-(-)]⸢---⸣[. . .] (3) w bt . bʿl . ủgr[t] . š[--]⸢-⸣ (4) ʿrb . špš . w ḥ⸢l mlk⸣ [.]

b ⸢š⸣bʿt (5) ʿšrt . yrtḥṣ mlk b⸢rr⸣ (6) gdlt . qdš ỉl ⸢.⸣ gdlt ⸢.⸣ l bʿlm (7) gdlt . l ǵlm . dqtm . w glt (8) l ǵlmtm . bt . ṯʿy ⸢.⸣ ydbḥ (9) w tnrr . b ʿd . bt bʿl (10) lgrt . ỉmr . w ynt . qrt (11) l ṯʿ .

b ṯmnt ⸢.⸣ ʿšrt . ỉbʿlt (12) ảlp . l md⸢g⸣l ⸢.⸣ bʿl . ủgrt (13) ⸢ủ⸣ ủrm . ủ šnpt . l ydbḥ (14) mlk . bt ỉl . npš . l ỉ⸢-⸣[. . .] (15) npš . l b⸢ʿl⸣[. . .] (16) w ʿr . ⸢l -⸣[. . .] (17) ⸢---⸣[. . .] . . .

(*Reverse*) . . . (18′) [--]l . ⸢---⸣[. . .] (19′) ⸢-⸣tml . yk⸢-⸣[. . .]

(20′) b rbʿ . ʿṣrmm . b ḫmš [.] ⸢ʿṣr⸣(21′)mm . w kbd . w . š šrp . l b⸢ʿl⸣ (22′) ủgrt . b bt .

b šbʿ . tdn (23′) mḫllm . ʿrb . špš . (24′) w ḥl m⸢l⸣k . hn . šmn . šlm (25′) bʿl . mtk . mlk⸢m .⸣ rỉšyt

(26′) k gr ʿz . ṯǵ⸢r⸣km .
⸢q⸣rd (27′) ḥmytkm .
ʿ⸢n⸣km . l ⸢bʿ⸣l tšủn

(28′) y b⸢ʿl⸣m ⸢. hm . t⸣dy
ʿz l ⸢ṯ⸣ǵrn(29′)y .
qrd [l] ḥmytny .
ỉbr y (30′) bʿl . n⸢š⸣qdš .
mḏr bʿl (31′) nmlủ [.
b]kr b⸢ʿ⸣l . nš[q]dš
(32′) ḥtp b⸢ʿl⸣ [.] ⸢n⸣mlủ .
ʿ⸢šr⸣t . ⸢bʿl⸣ [.] ⸢n⸣[ʿ](33′)šr .
qdš b⸢ʿl .⸣ nʿl .
ntbt b[ʿl] (34′) ntlk .
w š[mʿ . b]⸢ʿl .⸣ l ⸢. ṣ⸣l⸢tk⸣[m]

(35′) ⌈y⌉dy . ʿz l ṯǵrk[m .
qrd] (36′) l ḥmytk⌈m⌉ [. . .]

Translation

IA. (1) In the month of *ʾIbʿalatu*, on the seventh day: (2) a ram for *Baʿlu*-RʿKT [. . .]
B. (3) and in the Temple of *Baʿlu* of Ugari[t . . .].
C. (4) When the sun sets, the king will be free (of further cultic obligations).
IIA. On the seven(5)teenth day, the king will wash himself clean.
B. (6) A cow in the sanctuary of *ʾIlu*;
a cow for the *Baʿlu*-deities;
(7) a cow for *Ǵalmu*;
two ewes and a c⟨o⟩w (8) for ǴLMTM—the preceding beasts are to be sacrificed at the house of the *ṯaʿʿāyu*-priest.
C. (9) Next you shall illumine the ʿD-room of the Temple of *Baʿlu* of (10) Ugarit: a lamb and a city-dove; (11) these belong to the category of the *ṯaʿû*-sacrifice.
IIIA. On the eighteenth of *ʾIbaʿlatu*, (12) a bull for the MDGL of *Baʿlu* of Ugarit.
B. (13) A flame-sacrifice and a presentation-offering the king (14) must sacrifice at the Temple of *ʾIlu*: a neck for ʾ⌈-⌉[. . .];
(15) a neck for *Baʿlu*[. . .];
(16) and a donkey for [. . .]
(17) [. . .]

. . .

(18′–19′) [. . .]
IV.(20′) On the fourth day: birds.
V. On the fifth day: bir(21′)ds and a liver and a ram as a burnt-offering for *Baʿlu* of (22′) Ugarit in the temple.
VIA. On the seventh day: you shall bring (23′) the purifiers near.
B. When the sun sets, (24′) the king will be free (of further cultic obligations).
C. Behold the oil of well-being of (25′) *Baʿlu*, libation-offering for the benefit of the *Malakūma*, of the best quality.
D. (26′) When a strong foe attacks your gate,
a warrior (27′) your walls,
You shall lift your eyes to *Baʿlu* and say:
(28′) O *Baʿlu*, if you drive the strong one from our gate,
(29′) the warrior [from] our walls,
A bull, (30′) O *Baʿlu*, we shall sanctify,
a vow, O *Baʿlu*, (31′) we shall fulfill;
[a first]born, O *Baʿlu*, we shall sa[nc]tify,

(32′) a *ḥtp*-offering, O *Baʿlu*, we shall fulfill,
a feast, O *Baʿlu*, we shall (33′) [of]fer;
to the sanctuary, O *Baʿlu*, we shall ascend,
that path, O *Ba*[*ʿlu*], (34′) we shall take.
And *Baʿ*[*lu* will h]ear [your] prayer:
(35′) He will drive the strong foe from yo[ur] gate,
[the warrior] (36′) from your walls.

Vocalized Text

(1) bi yarḫi ʾibʿalati bi yômi šabīʿi (2) šû lê baʿli Rʿ⸢K⸣T ⸢B-⸣[-(-)]⸢---⸣[. . .] (3) wa bêta baʿli ʾugāri[t] Š[--]⸢-⸣ (4) ʿarābu šapšu wa ḥallu malku

bi šabʿati (5) ʿašrati yirtaḥiṣu malku barūra (6) gadulatu qidša ʾili gadulatu lê baʿalīma (7) gadulatu lê ǵalmi daqqatāma wa ga‹du›latu (8) lê ǵalmatêma bêta ṯaʿʿāyi yidbaḥu (9) wa tanāriru bi ʿādi bêti baʿli (10) ʾu!gārit ʾimmiru wa yônatu qarîti (11) la ṯaʿû

bi ṯamānâti ʿašrati ʾibʿalati (12) ʾalpu lê MD⸢G⸣L baʿli ʾugārit (13) ʾū ʾūrīma ʾū šanūpata la yidbaḥu (14) malku bêta ʾili napšu lê ʾI⸢-⸣[. . .] (15) napšu lê baʿli[. . .] (16) wa ʿêru lê ⸢-⸣[. . .] (17) ⸢---⸣[. . .]

. . .

(18′) [--]L . ⸢---⸣[. . .] (19′) ⸢-⸣TML . YK⸢-⸣[. . .]

(20′) bi rabīʿi ʿuṣṣūrūmama

bi ḫamīši ʿuṣṣūrū(21′)mama wa kabidu wa šû šurpu lê baʿli (22′) ʾugārit bi bêti

bi šabīʿi tadanni (23′) muḥallilīma ʿarābu šapšu (24′) wa ḥallu malku hanna šamnu šalāmi (25′) baʿli mattaku malakīma raʾšiyyata

(26′) kī gāra ʿazzu ṯaǵrakumu
qarrādu (27′) ḥāmiyātikumu
ʿênêkumu lê baʿli tiššaʾūna

(28′) yā baʿlima himma tadiyu
ʿazza lê ṯaǵrinū(29′)ya
qarrāda [lê] ḥāmiyātinūya
ʾibbīra yā (30′) baʿli našaqdišu
maḏḏara baʿli (31′) namalliʾu
[bi]kāra baʿli naša[q]dišu

(32′) ḥitpa baʿli namalliʾu
ʿašrata baʿli na[ʿa](33′)šširu
qidša baʿli naʿlû
natībata ba[ʿli] (34′) nitaliku
wa ša[maʿa ba]ʿlu lê ṣalîti[kumu]

(35′) yadiyu ʿazza lê ṯaǵriku[mu
qarrāda] (36′) lê ḥāmiyātikumu

Notes

(1–25′) there is a horizontal line between each of these lines; they are not indicated in the transcription because they have no text-structuring function.

(7) {glt} read {g⟨d⟩lt}.

(10) {lgrt} read {ủ!grt}.

(15) {bˁl[. . .]} the word *Baˁlu* may have been followed by one of the terms designating a distinct hypostastis of the deity.

(20′, 20′–21′) {ˁṣrmm} common noun m.pl.n.abs. + *m*-enclitic.

(28′) {⸢hm⸣} the reading {⸢ỉm⸣} is also possible; {tdy} 2m.s. imperfective, G-stem, √YDY.

(28′–29′) (⸢ṯ⸣ǵrny}, {ḥmytny} the {-y} is enclitic.

(31′) {[b]kr} the restitution of {b} is not certain but is preferable to {d} for reasons of space.

(34′) {ntlk} 1c.pl. imperfective, Gt-stem, √HLK.

Text 12: A Sacrificial Ritual for the Gods of the "Pantheon" (RS 24.643)

Virolleaud 1968, text 9; *KTU* 1.148; *TO* II, pp. 224–28; del Olmo Lete 1999: 129–38; Pardee 2000a: 779–806; 2002a: 12–16, 17–19, 44–49.

Text

Obverse

---

(1) dbḥ . ṣp⸢n⸣[. ỉlỉb . ảlp . w š] (2) ỉl . ảlp . k š [. dgn . ảlp . w š . bˁl . ṣpn . ảlp . w š] (3) bˁlm . ảlp . w š [. bˁlm . ảlp . w š . bˁlm . ảlp . w š] (4) bˁlm . ảlp . w š ⸢. bˁl⸣[m . ả]⸢lp⸣[. w š . bˁlm . ảlp . w š] (5) ảrṣ . w šmm . š . kṯr[t .] š . yr⸢ḫ⸣[. š . ˁṯt]⸢r . š⸣ (6) ṣpn . š ⸢.⸣ kṯr . š . pdry . š . ǵrm . ⸢w thm⸣t . š (7) ảṯrt . š . ˁnt . š . špš . š ⸢. ả⸣rṣy . š . ˁṯtr⸢t⸣ š (8) ủšḫry . š . ỉl . tˁ⸢ḏ⸣r . bˁ⸢l⸣ . š ršp . š . ddmš ⸢š⸣ (9) pḫr . ỉlm . š . ym . š . [k]⸢n⸣r . š . ⸢ảl⸣pm . ˁṣrm [.] gdlt ⸢š⸣[rp]

---

(10) w šlmm . ỉlỉb . š . ỉ⸢l⸣[. š .] d⸢gn⸣ . ⸢š⸣ [.] ⸢b⸣ˁb⸢l⸣ . ṣpn . ảl[p . w š] (11) bˁlm . kmm . bˁlm km⸢m⸣[. b]ˁl⸢m⸣ . kmm . bˁlm . kmm (12) bˁlm . kmm . bˁlm . k⸢m⸣[m]

---

(13) ỉy . ṯlǵmd . pḏp . ḫlbǵ . ḫ⸢bt⸣ [.] ṯlǵlḏ . n[ ]⸢ḏ⸣ḏ . ⸢-⸣[. . .] (14) ủmnḏ . ỉnḏ . md . kḏmr . ảr⸢-⸣[-]⸢-⸣ˁ . pnṯḫb[. . .] (15) ṯlǵlḏ . pd . dld . ỉnḏ . ỉd[d]⸢ ỉn-⸣[-]⸢š⸣t . [. . .] (16) ⸢?⸣t⸢g⸣ỉn . kwrt ⸢.⸣ ḫnn . ủštn . ⸢-⸣[. . .] (17) tzǵ . ảrm . ṯṯb . ṯủṯk ⸢.⸣ ḫnz⸢r⸣[. . .]

---

(18) k tʿrb . ʿṯtrt . šd . bt . mlk[. . .] (19) ṯn . skm . šbʿ . mšlt . ảrbʿ . ḫpnt . ⸢-⸣[. . .] (20) ḫmšm . ṯlṯ . rkb . rtn . ṯlṯ . mảt . ⸢š⸣[. . .] (21) lg . šmn . rqḥ . šrʿm . ủšpǵtm . p⸢l⸣[. . .] (22) kṯ . ẓrw . kṯ . nbt . šnt . w t⸢ṯ⸣n⸢-⸣[. . .]

Reverse ?

---

(23) ỉl . ḫyr . ỉlỉb . š (24) ảrṣ w šmm . š (25) ỉl . š . kṯrt . š (26) dgn . š . bʿl . ḫlb ảlp w š . (27) bʿl ṣpn . ảlp . w . š . (28) ṯrṯy . ảlp . w . š . (29) yrḫ . š . ṣpn . š . (30) kṯr š ⸢.⸣ ʿṯtr . š . (31) [ả]⸢ṯ⸣rt . š . šgr . w ỉṯm š (32) [šp]š [.] š . ršp . ỉdrp . š (33) [----]⸢mṣ⸣r . š (34) [ddmš . š . -(-)]mt . ⸢š⸣ . (35) [ ]⸢-⸣[. . .] (36) [. . .] (37) [ủšḫry . š] (38) [gṯr ? . š . ʿṯ]⸢tr⸣[t . š] (39) [trṯ . š] . mḏr . š (40) [ỉl q]⸢r⸣t š . ỉl . m⸢-⸣[. . . š] (41) [ǵr]⸢m⸣ . w ⸢t⸣hmt [. š . ym . š] (42) [--]⸢m⸣mr ⸢.⸣ š . s⸢r⸣[--- . š . . . . . š . ỉl] (43) [dd]⸢m⸣m š . ỉl lb[-]⸢n⸣ š ⸢. ủ⸣[ṯḫt . š . (knr . š .) bʿlm] (44) [ảl]p . w š . bʿlm ảl[p . w . š . bʿlm . ảlp . w . š . bʿlm] (45) [ả]⸢l⸣p . w [.] ⸢š⸣ .

Translation

IA. (1) Sacrifice (for the gods of Mount) *Ṣapunu*: [for *ʾIluʾibî* a bull and a ram];
(2) for *ʾIlu* a bull and! a ram;
[for *Dagan* a bull and a ram;
for *Baʿlu* of *Ṣapunu* a bull and a ram];
(3) also for *Baʿlu* (no. 2) a bull and a ram;
[also for *Baʿlu* (no. 3) a bull and a ram;
also for *Baʿlu* (no. 4) a bull and a ram];
(4) also for *Baʿlu* (no. 5) a bull and a ram;
[also] for *Baʿlu* (no. 6) [a bu]ll [and a ram;
also for *Baʿlu* (no. 7) a bull and a ram];
(5) for *ʾArṣu-wa-Šamûma* a ram;
for the *Kôṯarā*[*tu*] a ram;
for *Yariḫu* [a ram];
for [*ʿAṯta*]*ru* a ram;
(6) for *Ṣapunu* a ram;
for *Kôṯaru* a ram;
for *Pidray* a ram;
for Mountains-and-the-Waters-of-the-Abyss a ram;
(7) for *ʾAṯiratu* a ram;
for *ʿAnatu* a ram;
for *Šapšu* a ram;
for *ʾArṣay* a ram;
for *ʿAṯtartu* a ram;
(8) for *ʾUšḫaraya* a ram;
for the Auxiliary-Gods-of-*Baʿlu* a ram;

for *Rašap* a ram;
for *Dadmiš* a ram;
(9) for the Assembly-of-the-Gods a ram;
for *Yammu* a ram;
for [*Kin*]*nāru* a ram;
two bulls, two birds, a cow: as a b[urnt-offering].

B. (10) And as a peace-offering: for *ʾIluʿibî* a ram;
for *ʾI*[*lu* a ram];
for *Dagan* a ram;
for *Baʿlu*! of *Ṣapunu* a bul[l and a ram];
(11) also for *Baʿlu* (no. 2) the same;
also for *Baʿlu* (no. 3) the same;
also for [*B*]*aʿlu* (no. 4) the same;
also for *Baʿlu* (no. 5) the same;
(12) also for *Baʿlu* (no. 6) the same;
also for *Baʿlu* (no. 7) the sa[me].

C. (13) O *Eya*, hear (me, namely) my mouth; let the Aleppian *Ḫebat* hear . . . (14) for the gods of the lands, wisdom, with KḎM . . . give(s) your *penušḫu*-vessel . . . (15) may (t)he(y) listen to you, the poor one; [f]or/[con]cerning the gods . . . (16) *Tagi*, the god(dess), . . . me, an old man; a hero was given birth(?) . . . (17) the giftly (thing?) . . . give(s) . . . *Teššub*; *Šauška* . . . .

D. (18) When *ʿAṯtartu-Šadî* enters the royal palace: [. . .] (19) two SK-garments, seven MŠLT-garments, four ḪPN-garments [. . .], (20) fifty-three RKB (of?) RTN, three hundred units of w[ool . . .], (21) a LG-measure of perfumed oil, two/some ŠRʿ, two ʾUŠPǴT-garments, [two] *pali*[*du*-garments . . .], (22) a KṮ-measure of gum, a KṮ-measure of liquid honey.
E. And you will reci[te . . .].

II. (23) The gods of the month *Ḫiyyāru*: for *ʾIluʾibî* a ram;
(24) for *ʾArṣu-wa-Šamûma* a ram;
(25) for *ʾIlu* a ram;
for the *Kôṯarātu* a ram;
(26) for *Dagan* a ram;
for *Baʿlu* of Aleppo a bull and a ram;
(27) for *Baʿlu* of *Ṣapunu* a bull and a ram;
(28) for *Ṯarraṯiya* a bull and a ram;
(29) for *Yariḫu* a ram;

for *Ṣapunu* a ram;
(30) for *Kôṯaru* a ram;
for *ʿAṯtaru* a ram;
(31) for [*ʾA*]*ṯiratu* a ram;
for *Šaggar-wa-ʾIṯum* a ram;
(32) for [*Šap*]*šu* a ram;
for *Rašap-ʾIdrippi* a ram;
(33) [for ----]⌜MṢ⌝R a ram;
(34) [for *Dadmiš* a ram;
for -(-)]MT a ram;
(35) [for . . . a ram];
(36) [for . . . a ram];
(37) [for *ʾUšḫaraya* a ram];
(38) [for *Gaṯaru* a ram;
for *ʿAṯ*]*tar*[*tu* a ram;
(39) for *Tirāṯu* a ram];
for *Maḏ*(*ḏ*)*ara* a ram;
(40) [for the Gods-of-the-Ci]ty a ram;
for the Gods-of-M[en-and-of-Women a ram];
(41) [for Mountain]s-and-the-Waters-of-the-Abyss [a ram;
for *Yammu* a ram];
(42) [for --]⌜M⌝MR a ram;
for S⌜R⌝[. . . a ram;
for Door-bolt a ram;
for the Gods-of-](43) [the-La]nd-of-Aleppo a ram;
for the Gods-of-*Lab*[-]*na* a ram;
for *ʾU*[*ṯḫatu* a ram;
for *Kinnāru* a ram;
also for *Baʿlu* (no. 4)] (44) [a bul]l and a ram;
also for *Baʿlu* (no. 5) a bul[l and a ram;
also for *Baʿlu* (no. 6) a bull and a ram;
also (for) *Baʿlu*] (no. 7) (45) [a bu]ll and a ram.

Vocalized Text

(1) dabḥu ṣapuni[ʾiluʾibî ʾalpu wa šû] (2) ʾili ʾalpu wa! šû [dagan ʾalpu wa šû baʿli ṣapuni ʾalpu wa šû] (3) baʿlima ʾalpu wa šû [baʿlima ʾalpu wa šû baʿlima ʾalpu wa šû] (4) baʿlima ʾalpu wa šû baʿli[ma ʾa]lpu [wa šû baʿlima ʾalpu wa šû] (5) ʾarṣi wa šamîma šû kôṯarā[ti] šû yariḫi [šû ʿaṯtar]i šû (6) ṣapuni šû kôṯari šû pidray šû ǵūrīma wa tahāmāti šû (7) ʾaṯirati šû ʿanati šû šapši šû ʾarṣay šû ʿaṯtarti šû (8) ʾušḫaraya šû ʾilī taʿḏiri baʿli šû rašap šû dadmiš šû (9) puḫri ʾilīma šû yammi šû [kin]nāri šû ʾalpāma ʿuṣṣūrāma gadulatu š[urpu]

---

(10) wa šalamūma ʾiluʾibî šû ʾili [šû] dagan šû baʿ⟨⟨b⟩⟩li ṣapuni ʾal[pu wa šû] (11) baʿlima kamāma baʿlima kamāma [ba]ʿlima kamāma baʿlima kamāma (12) baʿlima kamāma baʿlima kam[āma]

(13–17) [*Hurrian text*]

---

(18) kī tiʿrabu ʿaṯtartu šadî bêta malki[. . .] (19) ṯinâ sakkāma šabʿu mašallātu ʾarbaʿu ḫipânātu ⸢-⸣[. . .] (20) ḫamišūma ṯalāṯu RKB RTN ṯalāṯu miʾāti š[aʿarāti . . .] (21) luggu šamni ruqḫi ŠRʿM ʾušpaǵǵatāma pal[idāma . . .] (22) kīṯu ẓurwi kīṯu nūbati šannati wa T⸢Ṯ⸣N⸢-⸣[. . .]

---

(23) ʾilī ḫiyyāri ʾiluʾibî šû (24) ʾarṣi wa šamîma šû (25) ʾili šû kôṯarāti šû (26) dagan šû baʿli ḫalbi ʾalpu wa šû (27) baʿli ṣapuni ʾalpu wa šû (28) ṯarraṯiya ʾalpu wa šû (29) yariḫi šû ṣapuni šû (30) kôṯari šû ʿaṯtari šû (31) [ʾaṯ]irati šû šaggar wa ʾiṯum šû (32) [šap]ši šû rašap ʾidrippi šû (33) [----]⸢MṢ⸣R šû (34) [dadmiš šû -(-)]MT šû (35) [ ]⸢-⸣[. . .] (36) [. . .] (37) [ʾušḫaraya šû] (38) [gaṯari$^{?}$ šû ʿaṯ]tar[ti šû] (39) [tirāṯi šû] madara šû (40) [ʾilī qar]îti šû ʾilī M⸢-⸣[. . . šû] (41) [ǵūrīm]a wa tahāmāti [šû yammi šû] (42) [--m]amēri šû sur[a--- šû . . . šû ʾilī] (43) [dadm]ima šû ʾilī lab[-]na šû ʾu[ṯḫ]ati šû (kinnāri šû) baʿlima] (44) [ʾal]pu wa šû baʿlima ʾal[pu wa šû baʿlima ʾalpu wa šû baʿlima] (45) [ʾa]lpu wa šû

Notes

(1–12) the restorations of the divine names lost through damage to the tablet are included here in the main text because they are certain, based as they are on the lists of divine names attested in multiple copies, in both Ugaritic and Akkadian.

(2) for {k} (the sixth sign) read {w$^{!}$}.

(3–4, 11–12) {bʿlm} divine name m.s.g.abs. + *m*-enclitic, translated as "*Baʿlu* (no. 2)," etc., following the lists of divine names in syllabic script, where these different manifestations of the weather deity are numbered (e.g., RS 20.024:5 {^{d}IM II}).

(9) the last three offerings, with no indication of the divinities for whom they are intended, may have been for the deities {ủṯḫt}, {mlkm}, and {šlm}, the three divine names missing here from near the end of the deity list as known from RS 1.017 and RS 24.264^{+} (Ugaritic) and RS 20.024 (Akkadian).

(10) {⸢b⸣ʿb⸢l⸣} read {⸢b⸣ʿ⟨⟨b⟩⟩⸢l⸣}.

(13–17) the translation of the Hurrian passage is from Lam 2006, whom we thank for his reading and interpretation, including four corrections in the text (the remnants of {⸢bt⸣} in line 13 were previously copied as the tips of two vertical wedges and as an only vaguely horizontal form; {pnṯẖb} was previously read as {pnḏỉb—if the first corrected sign remains formally ambiguous, the second conforms much better to the reading as a four-wedged {h} than to that of {ỉ}). N.B. the vocabulary of this Hurrian paragraph is not included in the glossary.

(21) {šrʿm} no word of this form is known in Ugaritic—perhaps correct to {ʿšrm} 'twenty'; probably restore {p⸢l⸣[d]}.

(43) {lb[-]⸢n⸣} The Ugaritic form of the place name attested in syllabic script as {la-ab-a-na} is still unknown; {knr . š} is in parentheses because we cannot be certain that the divine name was present here (it is indicated in the restoration because of its presence in line 9 of this text, an offering sequence based on another divine list).

Text 13: A Royal Funerary Ritual (RS 34.126)

Bordreuil and Pardee 1982; idem, RSO IX 90; Pardee 2000: 816–25; 2002a: 85–88; *TO* II, pp. 103–10; *CAT* 1.161; Wyatt 1998: 430–41; del Olmo Lete 1999: 192–98.

Text	***Translation***
Obverse	
(1) spr . dbḥ . ẓlm	Document of the sacrificial liturgy of the Shades.
(2) qrỉtm [.] ⸢r⸣pỉ . ả[rṣ . . .]	You have been called, O *Rapaʾūma* of the Earth,
(3) qbỉtm . qbṣ . d[dn . . .]	you have been summoned, O Assembly of *Didānu*;
(4) qrả . ủlkn . r⸢p⸣[ủ . . .]	ʾULKN the *Rapaʾu* has been called,
(5) qrả . trmn . rp[ủ . . .]	TRMN the *Rapaʾu* has been called,
(6) qrả . sdn . w ⸢.⸣ rd[n . . .]	SDN-*wa*-RDN has been called,
(7) qrả . ṯr . ʿllmn[. . .]	ṮR ʿLLMN has been called—
(8) qrủ . rpỉm . qdmym[. . .]	they (in turn) have called the Ancient *Rapaʾūma*.
(9) qrỉtm . rpỉ . ảrṣ	You have been called, O *Rapaʾūma* of the Earth,
(10) qbỉtm . qbṣ . dd⸢n⸣	you have been summoned, O Assembly of *Didānu*;
(11) qrả . ʿmṯtm⸢r .⸣ m⸢l⸣k	King *ʿAmmiṯtamru* has been called,
(12) qrả . ủ . nqm⸢d⸣ [.] ⸢mlk⸣	King *Niqmaddu* has been called as well.
(13) ksỉ . nqmd [.] ⸢ỉbky⸣	O Throne of *Niqmaddu*, be bewept,
(14) w . ydmʿ . ⸢h⸣dm . ⸢p⸣ʿnh	and may tears be shed over the footstool of his feet.

(15) l pnh . ybky . ṯlḥn . ml⸢k⸣	Before him they must beweep the king's table,
(16) w . ⸢y⸣blˁ . ủdmˁth	each must swallow down his tears:
(17) ˁdmt . w . ˁdmt . ˁdmt	Desolation and desolation of desolations!
(18) ỉšḫn . špš .	Be hot, O *Šapšu*,
w . ỉšḫn (19) nyr . ⸢r⸣bt .	yea, be hot, O Great Light!
ˁln . špš . tṣ⸢ḥ⸣	On high *Šapšu* cries out:
(20) ảṯr ⸢.⸣ [b]ˁlk . l . ks⸢ỉ⸣ .	"After your lords, from the throne,
ảṯr (21) bˁlk . ảrṣ . rd .	after your lords descend into the earth,
ảrṣ (22) rd . w . špl . ˁpr .	into the earth descend and lower yourself into the dust:
tḥt (23) sdn . w . rdn .	under SDN-*wa*-RDN,
tḥt . ṯr (24) ˁllmn .	under ṮR ˁLLMN,
tḥt . rpỉm . qdm⸢y⸣m	under the Ancient *Rapaʾūma*;
(25) tḥt . ˁmṯtmr . mlk	under King *ˁAmmiṯtamru*,
Lower edge	
(26) tḥm . ủ . nq[md] . mlk	under[!] King *Niqmaddu* as well."
(27) ˁšty . w . ṯ⸢ˁ⸣[y .	Once and perform the *ṯaˁû*-sacrifice,
ṯn .] ⸢w .⸣ ṯˁ[y]	twice and perform the *ṯaˁû*-sacrifice,
Reverse	
(28) ṯlṯ . w . ṯˁy [.]	thrice and perform the *ṯaˁû*-sacrifice,
⸢ả⸣[rb]⸢ˁ⸣ . w . ṯˁ[y]	four times and perform the *ṯaˁû*-sacrifice,
(29) ḫmš . w . ṯˁy .	five times and perform the *ṯaˁû*-sacrifice,
ṯ⸢ṯ .⸣ [w .] ⸢ṯ⸣ˁy	six times and perform the *ṯaˁû*-sacrifice,
(30) šbˁ . w . ṯˁy .	seven times and perform the *ṯaˁû*-sacrifice.
tq⸢d⸣m ˁṣr (31) šlm .	You shall present bird(s) of well-being:
šlm . ˁmr[pỉ] (32) w . šlm . bảh .	Well-being for *ˁAmmurāpiʾ*, well-being for his house[!];
šlm . [ṯ]ry⸢l⸣ (33) šlm . bth .	well-being for *Ṯarriyelli*, well-being for her house;
šlm . ủ⸢g⸣rt (34) šlm . ṯǵrh	well-being for Ugarit, well-being for her gates.

Vocalized Text

(1) sipru dabḥi ẓillīma
(2) quraʾtumu rapaʾī ʾarṣi // (3) qubaʾtumu qibūṣi didāni
(4) quraʾa ʾULKN rapaʾu // (5) quraʾa TRMN rapaʾu //
(6) quraʾa SDN wa RDN // (7) quraʾa ṮR ˁLLMN //
(8) qaraʾū rapaʾīma qadmiyyīma
(9) quraʾtumu rapaʾī ʾarṣi (10) qubaʾtumu qibūṣi didāni

(11) qura'a ˤammitamru malku // (12) qura'a 'ū niqmaddu malku
(13) kussa'i niqmaddi 'ibbakiyī (14) wa yidmaˤ hidāma paˤnêhu
(15) lê panêhu yabkiya ṯulḫana malki
// (16) wa yiblaˤa 'udmaˤātihu
// (17) ˤudmatu wa ˤudmatu ˤudamāti
(18) 'iššaḫinī šapši // wa 'iššaḫinī (19) nayyāri rabbati
ˤalâna šapši taṣīḥī
(20) 'aṯra [ba]ˤalīka lê kussa'i
// 'aṯra (21) baˤalīka 'arṣa rid
// 'arṣa (22) rid wa šapal ˤapara
taḥta (23) SDN wa RDN // taḥta ṮR (24) ˤLLMN
// taḥta rapa'īma qadmiyyīma //
(25) taḥta ˤammiṯtamri malki
// (26) taḥta! 'ū niq[maddi] malki
(27) ˤaštaya wa ṯaˤa[ya] // [ṯinâ] wa ṯaˤa[ya] //
(28) ṯalāṯa wa ṯaˤaya // 'a[rba]ˤa wa ṯaˤa[ya] //
(29) ḫamiša wa ṯaˤaya // ṯiṯṯa [wa] ṯaˤaya // (30) šabˤa wa ṯaˤaya
taqaddim ˤuṣṣūrī (31) šalāmi
šalāmu ˤammurā[pi'] // (32) wa šalāmu bêti!hu //
šalāmu [ṯa]rriyelli // (33) šalāmu bêtiha //
šalāmu 'ugārit // (34) šalāmu ṯaǵarīha

Notes

(1) {spr dbḥ ẓlm} lit., 'document of the sacrifice of the shades', that is, 'for the shades (of the ancestors)'.

(12, 13, 26) the {nqmd} named in lines 12 and 26 is one of the ancestors (perhaps Niqmaddu "II") of the king who has just died, who was in all likelihood *Niqmaddu* "III," the next-to-the-last king of Ugarit.

(19) {nyr rbt} lit., "O source of light, O great one."

(21, 22) {rd} m.s. imperative, G-stem, √YRD.

(26) {tḥm} read {tḥt!}.

(30) {ˤṢR} is in the construct state, and we thus have no way of determining whether it is singular, dual, or plural (we vocalize as a dual because the offering of two birds is typical of offerings to those who have passed on to the afterlife).

(32) {bảh} read either {bt!h} 'his house' or {bn!h} 'his sons'.

Text 14: Commemoration of the Mortuary Offering of *Ṯarriyelli* (inscribed stela RS 6.021)

Dussaud 1935; *KTU* 6.13; Bordreuil and Pardee 1993b; Pardee 2000a: 386–95; 2002a: 123–25.

Text	*Translation*
(1) skn . d šʿlyt	Sacred stela that *Ṯarriyelli*
(2) ⸢ṯ⸣ryl . l dgn . pgr	offered to *Dagan*: mortuary sacrifice;
(3) ⸢w⸣ ålp l åkl	and a bull for food.

Vocalized Text

(1) sikkannu dū šaʿliyat (2) ṯarriyelli lê dagan pagrû (3) wa ʾalpu lê ʾakli

Text 15: Commemoration of the Mortuary Offering of *ʿUzzīnu* (inscribed stela RS 6.028)

Dussaud 1935; *KTU* 6.14; Bordreuil and Pardee 1993b; Pardee 2000a: 396–99; 2002a: 123–25.

Text	*Translation*
(1) pgr . d šʿly	Mortuary sacrifice that *ʿUzzīnu*
(2) ⸢ʿ⸣zn . l dgn . bʿlh	offered to *Dagan* his lord;
(3) [- å]⸢l⸣p . b mḥrṯt	[and a b]ull with the plow.

Vocalized Text

(1) pagrû dū šaʿliya (2) ʿuzzīnu lê dagan baʿlihu (3) [wa ʾa]lpu bi maḥraṯati

Text 16: An *Ex Voto* Inscription (inscribed lion-headed vase RS 25.318)

KTU 6.62; Dietrich and Loretz 1978; Schaeffer 1978; Pardee 2000a: 813–15; 2002a: 126.

Text	*Translation*
(1) bn ågpṯr	*Binu-ʾAgapṯarri.*
(2) pn årw d šʿly nrn l ršp gn	Lion's head (lit., 'face') that *Nūrānu* offered to *Rašap-Guni*.

Vocalized Text

(1) binu ʾagapṯarri (2) panū ʾarwi dū šaʿliya nūrānu lê rašap guni

III. Incantations

Text 17: An Incantation against Male Sexual Dysfunction (RIH 78/20)

Bordreuil and Caquot 1980: 346–50; *TO* II, pp. 53–60; *CAT* 1.169; Pardee 2000a: 875–93; Ford 2002b; Pardee, 2002a: 159–61.

Text	***Translation***
Obverse	
(1) ydy . dbbm . d ǵzr . .	(This recitation) casts out the tormenters of a young man:
tg ḫṭk . r[ḥq]	the pain of your rod it has ba[nished,]
(2) bʿl . tg ḫṭk .	the producers of the pain of your rod.
w tṣủ . l pn . ql . ṯʿy[(-)]	They go forth at the voice of the *ṯaʿʿāyu*-priest,
(3) k qṭr . ủr.btm .	like smoke from a window,
k bṯn . ʿmdm	like a serpent from a pillar,
(4) k yʿlm . ẓrh .	like mountain-goats to a summit,
k lbỉm . skh	like lions to the lair.
(5) ḫṭ . nqh .	The rod has recovered,
ủ qrb . ḫṭ .	yea the rod has approached.
tḫṭả . l gbk	Should you sin against your body,
(6) w ⸢.⸣ tršʿ . l tmntk .	should you commit evil against your members,
tlḥm . lḥm (7) ẓm .	you must eat hard bread,
tšt . b ḫlṣ . bl . ṣml .	in oppression drink a concoction of figs,
b mrmt (8) b mỉyt .	on the heights, in the well-watered valleys,
b ẓlm . b qdš .	in the shadows, even at the sanctuary.
ảphm (9) kšpm . dbbm .	Then, as for the sorcerers, the tormenters,
ygrš . ḥrn	*Ḥôrānu* will drive (them) out,
(10) ḥbrm . w ǵlm . dʿtm .	even the companions and the familiars.
lk (11) lẓtm . ảl . tmk .	You, with respect to heat, do not sag,
ảl . tʿlg (12) lšnk .	may your tongue not stutter,
ảl . tảpq . ảpq .	may your canal not be decanalized!
lbš (13) ỉl . yštk .	The god can clothe you,
ʿrm . ỉl . yštk	the god can make you naked.
(14) l ảdm . wd . ḫṭm .	For the man, descend[!] from the rod
l ảrṣ . zrm	to the earth, O flow;

(15) l bn . ảdm . b ảnšt . npẓl	for the son of man, from illness he is delivered.
(16) ⸢h⸣n . b npš . ảṯrt . rbt . bl (17) [--(-)]rk . l ṯtm . ỉtbnnk (18) [-----]	Behold, in the throat of Lady *ʾAṯiratu* do X with juice to regale her. I will recognize you [. . .]
⸢b⸣t . ủbủ . ảl . tbỉ	The house I enter you must not enter!
(19) [. . .]⸢-⸣ . ảl tṯbb . rỉš	[. . .] Do not turn your head
(20) [. . .]rʿtm . k⸢-⸣[-]	[. . .] disasters$^{?}$ K⸢-⸣[-]
(21) [. . .]⸢m⸣ . kn ⸢. -⸣[. . .]	[. . .]⸢M⸣ KN ⸢-⸣[. . .]
(22) [. . .]⸢-⸣r[. . .]	[. . .]⸢-⸣R[. . .]

Vocalized Text

(1) yadiyu dābibīma dī ǵazri
tôgâ ḫaṯṯika ri[ḥḥaqa] // (2) baʿalī tôgî ḫaṯṯika // wa taṣiʾū lê panî qāli ṯaʿʿāyi
(3) ka quṭri ʾurubbatama // ka baṯni ʿammūdama //
(4) ka yaʿalīma ẓûraha // ka labaʾīma sukkaha
(5) ḫaṯṯu naqaha // ʾū qaraba ḫaṯṯu
tiḫṭaʾa lê gabbika // (6) wa tiršaʿa lê tamūnātika
tilḥamu laḥma (7) ẓumî // tištû bi ḫulṣi billa ṣamli
bi marāmāti (8) bi māʾiyyāti // bi ẓillīma bi qidši
ʾapahama (9) kaššāpīma dābibīma // yagrušu ḥôrānu // (10) ḥabirīma wa ǵalamī daʿtima
lêka (11) luẓatama ʾal tamuk // ʾal tiʿlag (12) lašānuka // ʾal tiʾʾapiq ʾapīqu
labūša (13) ʾilu yašītuka // ʿaruma ʾilu yašītuka
(14) lê ʾadami r$^{!}$id ḫaṯṯama // lê ʿarṣi zarmi // (15) lê bini ʾadami bi ʾanašati napẓala
(16) hanna bi napši ʾaṯirati rabbati // billu (17) [--(-)]RK lê ṯâtima
ʾitbāninuka/i (18) [-----] // bêta ʾubūʾu ʾal tubuʾ/tubūʾī
(19) [. . .]⸢-⸣ ʾal taṯābib raʾša
(20) [. . .]raʿʿāt-ma . K⸢-⸣[-]
(21) [. . .]⸢M⸣ . KN ⸢. -⸣[. . .]
(22) [. . .]⸢-⸣R[. . .]

Notes

(3) {ủr.btm} read ủr⟨⟨.⟩⟩btm.
(6) there seems to be a small word-divider after the first sign (new reading as compared with the French edition, where this indentation in the clay was represented as damage).
(10) ‘familiars’, lit., ‘lads of knowledge’.
(14) {wd} read {r$^{!}$d}.

(15) lit., '(being) in weakness/sickness, he is delivered'.
(17) {ỉtbnnk} 1c.s. imperfective, Lt-stem, √BN.
(18) the subject is unknown and there is thus no way of knowing whether the jussive form is masculine (/tabuʾ/) or feminine (/tabūʾī/), for the writing with {ỉ} is appropriate for both.
(19) {ảl tṯbb rỉš} 2m.s. jussive, L-stem, √ṮB—the signs should perhaps be divided to give the reading {ảl tṯb b rỉš} /ʾal taṯib bi raʾšu/ 'do not dwell in the head' (2m.s. jussive, G-stem, √YṮB).

Text 18: An Incantation against Snakes and Scorpions (RS 92.2014)

Pardee 2000a: 829–33; Bordreuil and Pardee 2001: text 52; Ford 2002a; Pardee 2002a: 158–59.

Text	***Translation***
Obverse	
(1) dy . l . ydʿ . yṣḥk . ủ zb	When the unknown one calls you and begins foaming,
(2) w . ảnk . ảṣḥk .	I, for my part, will call you.
ảmrmrn (3) ʿṣ . qdš .	I will shake pieces of sacred wood,
w . ʿlk . l . (4) tʿl . bṯn .	so that the serpent does not come up against you,
w . tḥtk (5) l . tqnn . ʿqrb	so that the scorpion does not stand up under you.
(6) ʿly . l . tʿl . bṯn . ʿlk	The serpent will indeed not come up against you,
(7) qn . l . tqnn . ʿqrb (8) tḥtk .	the scorpion will indeed not stand up under you!
km . l . tủdn	So may they not give ear,
(9) dbbm . kšpm .	the tormenters, the sorcerers,
hwt (10) ršʿ .	to the word of the evil man,
hwt . bn nšm	to the word of any man (lit., 'son of the people'):
(11) ghrt . phm . w . špthm	When it sounds forth in their mouth, on their lips,
Lower edge	
(12) yšp⸢k⸣ . kmm . ảrṣ	so may they be poured out to the earth,
Reverse	
(13) kšpm . dbbm	the tormenters, the sorcerers!
(14) l . ủrtn . l . gbh (15) l . tmnth .	For *ʾUrtēnu*, for his body, for his members.

Vocalized Text

(1) dūya lā yadūʿu yaṣīḥuka ʾū zabbu
(2) wa ʾanāku ʾaṣīḥuka // ʾamarmiran (3) ʿiṣa qudši
wa ʿalêka lā (4) taʿlû baṯnu // wa taḥtêka (5) lā taqāninu ʿaqrabu
(6) ʿalāyu lā taʿlû baṯnu ʿalêka // (7) qannu lā taqāninu ʿaqrabu
(8) taḥtêka
kāma lā taʾudunū // (9) dābibūma kaššāpūma
huwāta (10) rašaʿi // huwāta bini našīma
(11) gahurat pâhumu wa šapatêhumu
(12) yašpuk kamāma ʾarṣa // (13) kaššāpīma dābibīma
(14) lê ʾurtēna lê gabbihu (15) lê tamūnātihu

Notes

(1) {dy} determinative pronoun + *y*-enclitic; {zb} either a verbal adjective (/zabbu/ ← /*zabibu/) or the perfective (/zabba/).

(4, 6) {tʿl} either contracted indicatives, as vocalized here (/taʿlû/ ← /taʿliyu/), or jussives irregularly negativized with /lā/, which would be a very strong volitive expression (this structure appears in line 8).

(4) {tḥtk} in Hebrew the corresponding preposition takes suffixes as though the stem were dual/plural—we have followed this pattern in vocalizing the form, but it may have been simply /taḥtaka/.

(7) {qn} a verbal noun.

(12) {yšpk} 3m.s. jussive, indefinite subject (lit., 'may someone pour'); {kmm} either an adverb, correlative with {km} line 8, or the preposition *k* + common noun *mm*, 'water' (/ka mêma/), 'may (someone) pour them out like water to the earth'.

IV. "Scientific" Texts

Text 19: Hippiatric Prescriptions (RS 17.120)

Pardee 1985; 2001a: 244–48; *KTU* 1.85; Cohen 1996.

Text

Obverse

(1) spr . nʿm . s̀s̀wm

---

(2) k . ygʿr . s̀s̀w . št . ʿqrbn (3) ydk . w . yms̀s̀ . hm . b . mskt . d lḥt (4) hm . b . mndǵ . w . yṣq . b . ảph

---

(5) k . ḫr . s̀s̀w . mǵmǵ . w . bṣql . ʿrgz (6) ydk . ảḥdh . w . yṣq . b . ảph

---

(7) w . k . ḫr . s̀s̀w . ḫndrṯ . w . ṯqd . mr (8) ydk . ảḥdh . w . yṣq . b . ảph

---

(9) w . k . l . yḫrủ . w . l . yṯtn . s̀s̀w (10) [ms]s . št . qlql . w . št . ʿrgz (11) [yd]k . ảḥdh . w . yṣq . b . ảph

---

(12) [w . k .]⸢ả⸣ḫd . ảkl . s̀s̀w . št . mkšr (13) ⸢gr⸣[n .] w . št . ảškrr (14) w . ⸢pr⸣ . ḥḏrt . ydk . w . yṣq . b . ảph

---

(15) w . k . ảḫd . ảkl . s̀s̀w . št . nnỉ (16) w . št . mkšr . grn . w . št (17) ỉrǵn . ḥmr . ydk . w ⸢. y⸣ṣq . b . ảph

---

(18) w . k . yrảš . s̀s̀w . št . bln . qṭ (19) ydk . w . ⸢y⸣[ṣ]q . b . ảph

---

(20) w . ⸢k⸣[ ]⸢-⸣bd . s̀s̀w . ⸢g⸣d . ḫlb (21) w . š[ ]⸢-⸣ . ʿl⸢- . -⸣[ ] (22) ydk[. ảḥdh . w. y]⸢ṣq⸣ [. b . ảph]

---

(23) w . k . y⸢g⸣[ʿr . s̀s̀w . ⸢--(-)⸣ . dprn . w] (24) pr . ʿṯ[rb . drʿ . w . ṯ]⸢qd⸣[. mr . w] (25) tmṯl . g⸢d⸣[. w . tm]ṯl . ṯmrg ⸢.⸣[w . mǵmǵ] (26) w . št . nn⸢ỉ?⸣ [.] w ⸢.⸣ pr . ʿbk . ⸢w⸣[. št . ʿqrb . w] (27) mǵmǵ . w . pr . ḥḏrt . w[. tmṯl] (*Lower edge*) (28) ỉrǵn . ḥmr . ydk . ả[ḥdh] (29) w . yṣq . b . ảph

---

(*Reverse*) (30) k . yrảš . w . ykhp . mỉ⸢d⸣ (31) dblt . yṯnt . ṣmqm . yṯ[nm] (32) w . qmḥ . bql . yṣq . ảḥd[h . b . ảph]

Translation

(1) Document of horse cures.

(2–4) If the horse has a bad cough, one should bray a ŠT(-measure) of "scorpion-plant" and dissolve it either in a mixture of natural juices or in MNDǴ and administer it through its nostrils.

(5–6) If the horse whinnies (unnaturally), one should bray MǴMǴ and green walnuts together and administer it through its nostrils.

(7–8) If the horse whinnies (unnaturally), one should bray Ḫ̮NDRṮ and bitter almond together and administer it through its nostrils.

(9–11) If the horse does not defecate and does not urinate, a ŠT(-measure) of cardamom [having been red]uced to a liquid (or: a powder?), one should then bray it together with a ŠT(-measure) of walnuts and administer it through its nostrils.

(12–14) [If] the horse seizes its food (unnaturally), one should bray a ŠT(-measure) of chopped grain from the threshing floor, a ŠT(-measure) of henbane, and the fruit of ḤḎRT and administer it through its nostrils.

(15–17) If the horse seizes its food (unnaturally), one should bray a ŠT(-measure) of ammi, a ŠT(-measure) of chopped grain from the threshing floor, and a ŠT(-measure) of fennel of the ḤMR-type and administer it through its nostrils.

(18–19) If the horse suffers in the head, one should bray a ŠT(-measure) of BLN from Qaṭi and [. . .] together and admi[nis]ter it through its nostrils.

(20–22) If the horse [does X], one should bray coriander from Aleppo and [. . . together and admin]ister it [through its nostrils].

(23–29) If [the horse] has a b[ad cough], one should bray [. . . of juniper], the fruit of ʿṮ[RB, (i.e., its) seed(s), bitter al]mond, a TMṮL(-vessel/amount) of coriander, [a TM]ṮL(-vessel/amount) of ṮMRG, [MǴMǴ], a ŠT(-measure) of ammi, the fruit of ʿBK, [a ŠT(-measure) of ʿQRB (a Heliotrope = scorpion?)], MǴMǴ, the fruit of ḤḎRT, and [a TMṮL(-vessel/amount)] of fennel of the ḤMR-type to[gether] and administer it through its nostrils.

(30–32) If ⟨the horse⟩? suffers in the head and is utterly prostrate, ⟨one should bray⟩ an aged bunch of figs, aged raisins, and flour of groats togeth[er] (and) administer it [through its nostrils].

Vocalized Text

(1) sipru nuʿʿami s̀ūs̀awīma

(2) kī yigʿaru s̀ūs̀awu šūta ʿuqrubāni (3) yadūku wa yamassis̀u himma bi maskati dī liḥḥāti (4) himma bi MNDǴ wa yaṣṣuqu bi ʾappêhu

(5) kī ḫ̮āra s̀ūs̀awu maǵmaǵa wa biṣqala ʿirguzi (6) yadūku ʾaḥḥadaha wa yaṣṣuqu bi ʾappêhu

(7) wa kī ḫ̮āra s̀ūs̀awu ḫ̮undurata wa ṯuqda marra (8) yadūku ʾaḥḥadaha wa yaṣṣuqu bi ʾappêhu

(9) wa kī lā yiḫraˀu wa lā yiṯṯānu s̀ūs̀awu (10) [mussa]sū šūtu qulqulli wa šūtu ˁirguzi (11) [yadū]ku ˀaḫḫadaha wa yaṣṣuqu bi ˀappêhu

(12) [wa kī]ˀaḫada ˀakla s̀ūs̀awu šūta makšari (13) gur[ni] wa šūta ˀaškurari (14) wa pirâ ḥadrati yadūku wa yaṣṣuqu bi ˀappêhu

(15) wa kī ˀaḫada ˀakla s̀ūs̀awu šūta nīniˀi (16) wa šūta makšari gurni wa šūta (17) ˀirǵāni ḤMR yadūku wa yaṣṣuqu bi ˀappêhu

(18) wa kī yirˀašu s̀ūs̀awu šūta billāni qaṭi (19) yadūku wa ya[ṣṣu]qu bi ˀappêhu

(20) wa kī [ ]⸢-⸣BD s̀ūs̀awu gidda ḫalbi (21) wa Š[ ]⸢-⸣. ˁL⸢-. -⸣ [ ] (22) yadūku [ˀaḫḫadaha wa ya]ṣṣuqu [bi ˀappêhu]

(23) wa kī yig[ˁaru s̀ūs̀awu ⸢--(-)⸣ diprāni wa] (24) pirâ ˁT[RB darˁa wa ṯu]qda [marra wa] (25) tamṯīla giddi [wa tam]ṯīla ṮMRG [wa maǵmaǵa] (26) wa šūta nīniˀi wa pirâ ˁBK wa [šūta ˁuqrub⟨ān?⟩i wa] (27) ⟨⟨maǵmaǵa⟩⟩? wa pirâ ḥadrati wa [tamṯīla] (28) ˀirǵāni ḤMR yadūku ˀa[ḫḫadaha] (29) wa yaṣṣuqu bi ˀappêhu

(30) kī yirˀašu ⟨s̀ūs̀awu⟩? wa yikhapu maˀda (31) dabilata yaṯanata ṣimmūqīma yaṯa[nīma] (32) wa qamḥa buqli yaṣuqu ˀaḫḫada[ha bi ˀappêhu]

Notes

(1) {nˁm} vocalized as an infinitive, D-stem ('the act of making good')—or it may be a common noun.

(3) {ydk} either /yadūku/ (middle-weak root) or /yadukku/ (geminate root).

(4) {yṣq} 3m.s. imperfective, G-stem, √YṢQ (the vocalization is patterned on the Hebrew /yiṣṣōq/ ← /yaṣṣuq-/).

(9) {yṯtn} 3m.s. imperfective, Gt-stem, √ṮN.

(14, 27) {pr ḥdrṯ} if *pr* here means 'seeds', as seems to be stated explicitly in line 24 for another vegetal product, the phrase may mean 'lettuce-seeds' (i.e., the result of letting some type of lettuce go to seed).

(23–29) the restorations of complete words are based on parallel passages in other hippiatric texts.

(26) RS 5.300:22 has {[. . . ˁ]qr⸢b⸣}—should this form {ˁqrb} be corrected to {ˁqrb⟨n⟩} on the basis of the occurrence of that word in line 2 of RS 17.120? (It must in any case be a vegetal product.)

(27) might the second occurrence of {mǵmǵ} in a single prescription be a mistake?

(30) the text is plausibly to be corrected by the addition of {⟨s̀sw⟩}.

(32) it appears necessary to add {⟨ydk⟩} here, which might in turn require the phrase to be rearranged to read {ydk ảḥdh w yṣq} as in the other paragraphs.

Text 20: Manual of Teratology (RS 24.247⁺)

Herdner 1978a: 44–60; *KTU* 1.103 + 1.145; Pardee 2000a: 532–64; 2002a: 135–40.

Text

Obverse

(1) ṯảtt ṣỉn ⸢-⸣[--]⸢-⸣dảt . ảbn . mảdtn tqln b ḥwt

(2) ʿṣ . hn⸢-⸣[--(-)]⸢y⸣ ảṯr yld . bhmth tʿ⸢--⸣[. . .]

(3) gmš š[ ]n ykn b ḥwt

(4) w ⸢ỉ⸣[n]ḥwtn tẖlq

(5) ⸢-⸣[ ]rǵbn ykn b ḥwt

(6) [ ]⸢-.⸣ w ẖr ảpm . ḥwt⸢n⸣ [tẖlq?] ⸢m⸣ṯn rgm

(7) [w] ⸢ỉn⸣[ ]⸢m⸣lkn yỉẖd ḥw[t ỉbh w?] mrḥy mlk ⸢t⸣dlln

(8) [-]⸢-⸣h . m⸢-⸣[----]⸢-m⸣ẖt . bhmtn[-------]⸢-⸣

(9) ⸢w⸣ ỉn šq . [šmảl] ⸢b⸣h . mlkn ⸢y⸣[-----(-)]⸢ỉ⸣bh

(10) ⸢w⸣ ỉn qṣr[t šm]⸢ả⸣l . mlk⸢n⸣[------(-) ỉ]⸢b⸣h

(11) w qrn šỉ⸢r⸣ [. b] ⸢p⸣ỉth . š⸢mả⸣[l]n

(12) ṭḥl . ỉn . bh[--]⸢-⸣dn . ⸢-⸣[ ] ⸢m⸣ṯ⸢n⸣ [. . .]
(13) mlkn . l ypq ⸢š⸣[p]ḥ

(14) [w] ỉn ʾuškm b⸢h .⸣ ḏ⸢r⸣[ʿ]⸢-⸣

(15) ⸢w⸣ ỉn . krʿ y⸢d⸣h ⸢-⸣[ ] ⸢y⸣ẖlq bhmt [--]⸢-⸣

(16) [-]⸢-⸣[-]⸢-⸣[ ] . ỉbn yẖlq bhmt ⸢ḥw⸣t

(17) [ ]⸢-⸣ . ṯnn ʿz yủẖd ỉb mlk

(18) [ ]ẖlq . mṯn rgm

(19) [ ]rǵb . w tp . mṣq⸢t⸣

(20) [ ]⸢y⸣ˁzzn

(21) [ ]rn

(22) [ ]bh
(23) [ ]⸢t⸣p⸢š⸣[. . .]

. . . .

Reverse

. . . .

(24′) [ ]⸢- . l⸣[. . .]

(25′) [ ]⸢ỉ⸣r . lk⸢-⸣[. . .]

(26′) w ỉn . šq ymn . b⸢h⸣[. . .]

(27′) w ỉn . ḫrṣp . b k⸢-⸣[. . .]

(28′) w ỉn . krˁ . ydh[. ymn ?]
(29′) ⸢l⸣ ypq špḥ

(30′) w ỉn . ḫr ảpm . kl[. . .]

(31′) w ỉn . lšn bh . r[. . .]

(32′) špth . tḥyt . k⸢-⸣[. . .]

(33′) pnh . pn . ỉrn . ủ⸢-⸣[ ]⸢-⸣tqṣrn[. . .]
(34′) ymy . bˁl hn bhm[t . . .]

(35′) w ỉn . ủdn . ymn . ⸢b⸣[h ỉbn y]šdd ḥwt
(36′) [w y]ḥslnn

(37′) w ỉn . ủdn šmảl . ⸢b⸣[h .]⸢mlkn⸣[y]šdd ḥwt ỉ⸢b⸣[h . . .]
(38′) w . yḥslnn

(39′) w qṣrt . pˁnh . bˁln yǵt⸢r⸣ [. ḫ]rd . w ủḫr
(40′) y . ykly ⸢rš⸣p

(41′) ⸢w⸣ ả⸢ph⸣ . k ảp . ˁṣr . ỉlm . tbˁ⸢rn⸣ . ḥwt

(42′) [ ]⌈-⌉št . w ydů

(43′) [ ]⌈.⌉ l rìšh . d̲r⌈ʿ⌉ [.] ⌈m⌉lk hwt
(44′) [-------]⌈ḥ⌉

(45′) [------]⌈d⌉rh . yṣů . špšn . tpšlt ḥ
wt hyt

(46′) [------]mlkn . yd . ḫrdh . yddll

(47′) [-----]⌈l⌉ . ůšrh . mrḫy . mlk tnšån
(48′) [-----]⌈-⌉b . ydh

(49′) [----]⌈-⌉ åt̲rt . ʿnh . w ʿnh b lṣbh
(50′) [ìbn y]rps ḥwt

(51′) [---]bh . b ph . yṣů . ìbn . yspů ḥwt

(52′) w [ìn] pʿnt . bh . ḫrdn . yhpk . l mlk

(53′) w [--] lšnh . ḥwtn tprš

(54′) b⌈-⌉[--]⌈-⌉ḫrh . b pìth . mlkn . yšlm l ìbh

(55′) w ì [n -]⌈k⌉bm . bh . d̲rʿ . ḥwt . hyt . yḥsl

Upper edge

(56′) w ʿ⌈-⌉[-] . ìlm . tbʿrn ḥwt . hyt

(57′) w ʿnh [b] ⌈l⌉ṣbh . mlkn yʿzz ʿl ḫpt̲h

(58′) w ḥr . ⌈w -⌉r . bh . mlkn ybʿr ìbh

(59′) w ìn yd š⌈må⌉l bh . ḥwt ìb tḫlq

Translation

(1) As for the ewes of the caprovids, [when t]hey give birth[!]: If it is a stone, many will fall in the land.
(2) If it is a piece of wood, behold [ ]⌈Y⌉ ʾAT̲R YLD, its cattle will be destroyed.
(3) If the fetus is smooth, without h[air[?]], there will be [. . .] in the land.

(4) And if i[t has no], the land will perish.
(5) [ ] there will be famine in the land.
(6) [ ] nor nostrils, the land [will perish[?];] ditto.
(7) [And] if it has no [ ], the king will seize the lan[d of his enemy and[?]] the weapon of the king will lay the land low.
(8) [ ] [ ] cattle [will peri]sh.[?]
(9) And if it has no [left] thigh, the king will [ ] his enemy.
(10) And if there is no lower [lef]t leg, the king [will] his enemy.
(11) And if there is a horn of flesh [in] its lef[t te]mple, [ ].
(12) If it has no spleen [ ] [;] di[tto;] (13) the king will not obtain off[sp]ring.
(14) [And] if it has no testicles, the (seed-)gra[in].
(15) And if the middle part of its foreleg is missing, [ ] will destroy the cattle [ ].
(16) [ ] the enemy will destroy the cattle of the land.
(17) [ ] the mighty archers will seize the enemy of the king.
(18) [ ] perish/destroy; ditto.
(19) [ ] famine, hard times will disappear.
(20) [ ]will become powerful/strengthen him.
(21) [ ]
(22) [ ] his [?]
(23) [ ]
(24′) [ ] [. . .]
(25′) [ ] [. . .]
(26′) And if it has no right thigh [. . .].
(27′) And if there is no ḪRṢP in [its?] K[. . .].
(28′) And if it has no middle part of the [right[?]] foreleg [. . .] (29′) will not obtain offspring.
(30′) And if [it has] no nostrils [. . .].
(31′) And if it has no tongue [. . .].
(32′) If its lo‹w›er lip [. . .].
(33′) If its face is that of a ʾIRN, [ ] will shorten/be shortened (34′) the days of our lord; behold, the catt[le . . .].
(35′) And if it has no right ear, [the enemy will] devastate the land
(36′) [and will] consume it.
(37′) And if [it] has no left ear, the king [will] devastate the land of [his] enemy (38′) and will consume it.
(39′) And if its (rear[?]) legs are (abnormally) short, our lord will confront the *ḫurādu*-troops and (40′) *Rašap* will consume the progeny.
(41′) And if its nose is like the "nose" of a bird, the gods will destroy the land
(42′) [ ] will fly (away[?]).
(43′) [ ]to/on its head, the (seed-)grain of that king (44′) [will . . .].
(45′) [ ] its [-]DR protrudes, the Sun/*Šapšu* will abase[!] that land.

(46′) [ ] the king will lay low! the power (lit., 'hand') of the *ḫurādu*-troops.

(47′) [ ] its penis, the weapon of the king will indeed be raised (48′) [. . .] his hand.

(49′) [ ] in place of (?) its eyes and its eyes are in its forehead, (50′) [the enemy will] tread the land under.

(51′) [And if] its [--]B protrudes from its mouth, the enemy will devour the land.

(52′) And if it has [no] (rear?) legs, the *ḫurādu*-troops will turn against the king.

(53′) And if it has [two?] tongue(s?), the land will be scattered.

(54′) If [its?] B-[(-) and?] its ḪR are in its temples, the king will make peace with his enemy.

(55′) And if it has n[o] [-]KB, the (seed-)grain of that land will be consumed.

(56′) And if ʿ-[-(-)], the gods will destroy that land.

(57′) And if its eye(s) is/are [in] the forehead, the king will become more powerful than his *ḫupṯu*-troops.

(58′) And if it has ḪR and? [-]R, the king will destroy his enemy.

(59′) And if it has no left (fore?)leg, the land of the enemy will perish.

Vocalized Text

(1) ṯuʾatātu ṣaʾni ⸢-⸣[kī ta]lidnā ! ʾabna maʾadatuna taqīlūna bi ḥuwwati

(2) ʿiṣa hanna ⸢-⸣[--(-)]⸢Y⸣ ʾAṮR YLD bahimatuha T⸢ʿ⸢--⸣[. . .]

(3) gamīšu ša[ʿiri ?]N yakūnu bi ḥuwwati

(4) wa ʾê[nu] ḥuwwatuna tiḫlaqu

(5) ⸢-⸣[ ] raǵabuna yakūnu bi ḥuwwati

(6) [ ]⸢-⸣ wa ḫurru ʾappêma ḥuwwatuna [tiḫlaqu?] maṯnû rigmi

(7) [wa] ʾênu[ ] malkuna yaʾḫudu ḥuwwa[ta ʾêbihu wa ?] murḥay malki tadallilanna

(8) [-]⸢-⸣hu M⸢-⸣[----]⸢-M⸣ḪT bahimatuna [---- tiḫla]qu

(9) waʾ ênu šāqu [šamʾala] bihu malkuna ⸢Y⸣[-----(-)] ʾêbahu

(10) wa ʾênu qiṣra[tu šam]ʾala malkuna [------(-)ʾê]bahu

(11) wa qarnu šiʾri [bi] piʾtihu šamʾa[la]N

(12) ṭiḥālu ʾênu bihu [--]⸢-⸣DN ⸢-⸣[ ] maṯnû [rigmi ?] (13) malkuna lā yapūqu ša[p]ḥa

(14) [wa] ʾênu ʾuškāma bihu ḏar[ʿu]⸢-⸣

(15) wa ʾênu karaʿu yadihu ⸢-⸣[ ] yaḫalliqu bahimata [--]⸢-⸣

(16) [-]⸢-⸣[-]⸢-⸣[ ] ʾêbuna yaḫalliqu bahimata ḥuwwati

(17) [ ]⸢-⸣ ṯannānu ʿuzzi yaʾuḫudu ʾêba malki

(18) [ ]ḪLQ maṯnû rigmi

(19) [ ]RǴB wa tuppû maṣūqatu

(20) [ ]yaˁazzizunnu
(21) [ ]RN
(22) [ ]B-hu
(23) [ ]⌜T⌝P⌜Š⌝[. . .]

. . . .

(24′) [ ]⌜- L⌝[. . .]
(25′) [ ]⌜ˀI⌝R LK⌜-⌝[. . .]
(26′) wa ˀênu šāqu yamīna bihu[. . .]
(27′) wa ˀênu ḫarṣuppu ? bi K⌜-⌝[. . .]
(28′) wa ˀênu karaˁu yadihu [yamīna?] (29′) lā yapūqu šapḥa
(30′) wa ˀênu ḫurrā ˀappêma KL[. . .]
(31′) wa ˀênu lašānu bihu R[. . .]
(32′) šapatuhu taḫ<ti>yyatu ka⌜-⌝[. . .]
(33′) panûhu panû ˀIRN ˀU⌜-⌝[ ]⌜-⌝taqaṣṣirūna [. . .] (34′) yamīya baˁli hanna bahima[tu . . .]
(35′) wa ˀênu ˀudnu yamīna bi[hu ˀêbuna ya]šaddidu ḥuwwata (36′) [wa ya]ḥsulannanna
(37′) wa ˀênu ˀudnu šamˀala bi[hu] malkuna [ya]šaddidu ḥuwwata ˀêbi[hu] (38′) wa yaḥsulannanna
(39′) wa qaṣirtā<ma>? paˁnāhu baˁluna yiǵtāru [ḫu]rāda wa ˀuḫrā(40′)ya yakalliyu rašap
(41′) wa ˀappuhu ka ˀappi ˁuṣṣūri ˀilūma tabaˁˁirūna ḥuwwata (42′) [ ] ⌜-⌝ŠT wa yidˀû
(43′) [ ] lê raˀšihu d̠arˁu malki huwati (44′) [ ]⌜Ḥ⌝
(45′) [ ]⌜D⌝R-hu yaṣiˀu šapšuna tapašillu(na)! ḥuwwati hiyati
(46′) [ ] malkuna yada ḫurādi yadallilu !
(47′) [ ]⌜L⌝ ˀušar-hu murḥay malki tinnašiˀanna (48′) [ ]⌜-⌝ bi yadihu
(49′) [ ] lê ˀat̠rati ? ˁênêhu wa ˁênāhu bi liṣbihu (50′) [ˀêbuna ya]rpusu ḥuwwata
(51′) [wa --]Buhu bi pîhu yaṣiˀu ˀêbuna yissapiˀu ḥuwwata
(52′) wa [ˀênu] paˁanātu bihu ḫurāduna yihhapiku lê malki
(53′) wa [--] lašān-hu ḥuwwatuna tipparišu
(54′) B⌜-⌝[--]⌜-⌝ḤR-hu bi piˀtêhu malkunu yišlamu lê ˀêbihu
(55′) wa ˀê[nu -]⌜K⌝B-ma bihu d̠arˁu ḥuwwati hiyati yiḥḥasilu
(56′) wa ˁ⌜-⌝[-] ˀilūma tabaˁˁirūna ḥuwwata hiyati
(57′) wa ˁênāhu (*or*: ˁênuhu) [bi] liṣbihu malkuna yaˁāzizu ˁalê ḫupt̠ihu
(58′) wa ḤR wa ⌜-⌝R bihu malkuna yabaˁˁiru ˀêbahu
(59′) wa ˀênu yadu šamˀala bihu ḥuwwatu ˀêbi tiḫlaqu

Notes

"Teratology": the study of monstrous phenomena, in the case of this text, of malformed animal fetuses.

(1) correct {ảt} to {n} and restore {ṯảtt ṣỉn ⌜.⌝ [k t]⌜l⌝dn!}; {ṯảtt} either an irregular plural (the feminine plural morpheme would be attached to the feminine singular stem) or a mistake for {ṯảt} /ṯuʾātu/; {mảdtn} the {-n} is enclitic (as in all cases in this text of a common noun which is the first word of an apodosis and is singular absolute).

(3) perhaps restore {[rǵb]n}.

(12) restore {[rgm]} after {mṯn}, as in lines 7 and 18?

(19) {tp} 3f.s. imperfective, Gp-stem, √NPY /tuppû/ ← /*tunpayu/.

(32′) {tḥyt} read {tḥ⟨t⟩yt}.

(33′) {tqṣrn} either 3m.pl. imperfective, D-stem, (subject lost in the break) or 3m.pl. imperfective, G-stem or Dp-stem, subject {ymy} 'the days of the master will be short/shortened').

(34′) {ymy} common noun m.pl. n. or a. (depending on how the preceding line is restored) + *y*-enclitic.

(39′) {qṣrt pʿnh} the second word should be in the dual (because the plural is *pʿnt* and, if it were singular, it should be specified as to 'right' or 'left') and it appears necessary to emend the adjective to agree in number; {yǵtr} 3m.s. imperfective, Gt-stem, √ǴR.

(44′–49′) the number of signs missing at the beginning of lines 44′–49′, 51′ may only be estimated approximately.

(45′) {tpšlt} correct either to {tpšl⟨⟨t⟩⟩} or to {tpšln!} and analyze as a verb—or analyze as a nominal predicate (/tapšilatu/ '*Šapšu* (will be) the debasing of that land').

(46′) {yddll} probably correct to {yd⟨⟨d⟩⟩ll}.

V. Letters

Text 21: A Military Situation (RS 4.475)

Dhorme 1933: 235–37; *CTA* 53; *KTU* 2.10; Pardee 1987; 2002b: 107–8; *TO* II, pp. 275–80.

Text

Obverse

(1) tḥm . ỉwrd̲r (2) l . plsy (3) rgm

---

(4) yšlm . lk

---

(5) l . trǵds (6) w . l . klby (7) šmʿt . ḫtỉ (8) nḫtů . ht (9) hm . ỉnmm (10) nḫtů . w . lắk (11) ʿmy . w . yd (12) ỉlm . p . k mtm (*Lower edge*) (13) ʿz . mỉd (14) hm . nt̲kp (*Reverse*) (15) mʿnk (16) w . mnm (17) rgm . d . tšmʿ (18) t̲mt . w . št (19) b . spr . ʿmy

---

Translation

(1) Message of *ʾIwrid̲arri*: (2) To *Pilsiya*, (3) say:
(4) May it be well with you.
(5) Regarding *Targ̀udassi* (6) and *Kalbiya*, (7) I have heard that they have (8) suffered defeat. (9) Now if such is not (10) the case, send (11) me a message (to that effect).
Pestilence (12) is (at work) here, for death (13) is very strong.
(14) If they have been overcome, (15) your reply (16) and whatever (else) (17) you may hear (18) there put (19) in a letter to me.

Vocalized Text

(1) taḥmu ʾiwrid̲arri (2) lê pilsiya (3) rugum
(4) yišlam lêka
(5) lê tarǵuddassi (6) wa lê kalbiya (7) šamaʿtu ḫataʾī (8) naḫtaʾū hatti
(9) himma ʾênumama (10) naḫtaʾū wa laʾak (11) ʿimmaya wa yadu
(12) ʾilima pā kī môtuma (13) ʿazzu maʾda (14) himma nat̲kapū (15) maʿnûka (16) wa mannama (17) rigmu dū tišmaʿu (18) t̲ammati wa šit (19) bi sipri ʿimmaya

Notes

(7–8) {ḫtỉ nḫtů} a common noun in construct with the following verbal phrase.
(9) {ỉnmm} particle {ỉn} + double *m*-enclitic.
(12) {mtm} common noun + *m*-enclitic.

Text 22: *Talmiyānu* and *ʾAḫâtumilki* to Their Lady (RS 8.315)

Dhorme 1938; *CTA* 51; *KTU* 2.11; *TO* II, pp. 281–84; Pardee 2002b: 90; 2003: 447.

Text

Obverse

(1) l . ủmy . ảdtny (2) rgm (3) tḥm . tlmyn (4) w . ảḫtmlk . ʿbdk

---

(5) l . pʿn . ảdtny (6) mrḥqtm (7) qlny . ỉlm (8) tǵrk (9) tšlmk (10) hnny . ʿmny (11) kll . mỉd (*Lower edge*) (12) šlm . (13) w ⸢.⸣ ảp . ảnk (*Reverse*) (14) nḫt . ṯmny (15) ʿm . ảdtny (16) mnm . šlm (17) rgm . ṯṯb (18) l . ʿbdk

---

Translation

(1) To my mother, our lady, (2) say: (3) Message of *Talmiyānu* (4) and *ʾAḫâtumilki*, your servants:

(5) At the feet of our lady (6) (from) afar (7) we fall. May the gods (8) guard you, (9) may they keep you well. (10) Here with the two of us (11) everything is very (12) fine. (13) And I, for my part, (14) have got some rest. There (15) with our lady, (16) whatever is well, (17) return word (of that) (18) to your servants.

Vocalized Text

(1) lê ʾummiya ʾadattināyā (2) rugum (3) taḥmu talmiyāna (4) wa ʾaḫâtimilki ʿabdêki

(5) lê paʿnê ʾadattināyā (6) marḥaqtama (7) qālānāyā ʾilūma (8) taǵǵurūki (9) tašallimūki (10) hannaniya ʿimmānāyā (11) kalīlu maʾda (12) šalima (13) wa ʾapa ʾanāku (14) nāḫātu ṯammāniya (15) ʿimma ʾadattināyā (16) mannama šalāmu (17) rigma ṯaṯībī (18) lê ʿabdêki

Notes

(1) {ảdtny} common noun f.s.g. + pronominal suffix 1c.du.

(6) {mrḥqtm} common noun + *m*-enclitic.

(8) {tǵrk} 3m.pl. imperfective, G-stem, √NǴR.

Text 23: The King to the Queen-Mother (RS 11.872)

Virolleaud 1940a: 250–53; *CTA* 50; *KTU* 2.13; Pardee 1984a: 223–25, 229–30; 2002b: 92; 2003: 447; *TO* II, pp. 287–90.

Text

Obverse

(1) l . mlkt (2) ủmy . rgm (3) tḥm . mlk (4) bnk .

---

(5) l . pʿn . ủmy (6) qlt . l . ủmy (7) yšlm . ỉlm (8) tǵrk . tšlmk

---

(9) hlny . ʿmny (10) kll . šlm (11) ṯmny . ʿm . ủmy (*Lower edge*) (12) mnm . šlm (13) w . rgm . t̳t̳b . ly

Reverse

---

(14) bm . ṯy ndr (15) ỉṯt . ʿmn . mlk⌜t⌝ (16) w . rgmy . l [?] (17) lqt . w . pn (18) mlk . nr bn

---

Translation

(1) To the queen, (2) my mother, say: (3) Message of the king, (4) your son.
(5) At my mother's feet (6) I fall. With my mother (7) may it be well! May the gods (8) guard you, may they keep you well.
(9) Here with me (10) everything is well. (11) There with my mother, (12) whatever is well, (13) send word (of that) back to me.
(14) From the tribute they have vowed (15) a gift to the queen. (16) My words she did indeed (17) accept and the face of (18) the king shone upon us.

Vocalized Text

(1) lê malkati (2) ʾummiya rugum (3) taḥmu malki (4) biniki
(5) lê paʿnê ʾummiya (6) qālātu lê ʾummiya (7) yišlam ʾilūma (8) taǵǵurūki tašallimūki
(9) halliniya ʿimmānîya (10) kalīlu šalima (11) ṯammāniya ʿimma ʾummiya (12) mannama šalāmu (13) wa rigma ṯaṯībī layya (14) bima ṯayyi nadarū (15) ʾit̳t̳ata ʿimmānu malkati (16) wa rigamīya la (17) laqa⟨ḥ⟩at wa panū (18) malki nārū binū

Notes

(9) {ʿmny} prep. + pron. 1c.s. + *y*-enclitic (/ʿimmān + î + ya/).
(17) {lqt} the translation is based on a text corrected to {lq⟨ḥ⟩t}

Text 24: *Talmiyānu* to His Mother, *Ṯarriyelli* (RS 15.008)

Virolleaud 1957: text 15; *KTU* 2.16; Pardee 1984a: 219–21, 229; 2002b: 89; 2003: 447–48; *TO* II, pp. 297–302.

Text

Obverse

(1) tḥm . ⸢t⸣lm[y]⸢n⸣ (2) l ṯryl . ủmy (3) rgm

(4) yšlm . lk . ỉly (5) ủgrt . tǵrk (6) tšlmk . ủmy (7) tdʿ . ky . ʿrbt (8) l pn . špš (9) w pn . špš . nr (10) by . mỉd . w ủm (11) tšmḫ . mảb (12) w ảl . twḥln (13) ʿtn . ḫrd . ảnk (14) ʿmny . šlm (15) kll (*Lower edge*) (16) w mnm . (17) šlm . ʿm (*Reverse*) (18) ủmy (19) ʿmy . tṯṯb (20) rgm

Translation

(1) Message of *Talmi*[*yā*]*nu*: (2) To *Ṯarriyelli*, my mother, (3) say:
(4) May it be well with you. May the gods of (5) Ugarit guard you, (6) may they keep you well. My mother, (7) you must know that I have entered (8) before the Sun (9) and (that) the face of the Sun has shone (10) upon me brightly. So may my mother (11) cause *Maʾʾabû* to rejoice; (12) may she not be discouraged, (13) (for) I am the guardian of the army. (14) With me everything (15) is well. (16) Whatever (17) is well with (18) my mother, (19) may she send word (of that) (20) back to me.

Vocalized Text

(1) taḥmu talmi[yā]na (2) lê ṯarriyelli ʾummiya (3) rugum
(4) yišlam lêki ʾilūya (5) ʾugārit taǵǵurūki (6) tašallimūki ʾummiya (7) tidaʿī kīya ʿarabtu (8) lê panî šapši (9) wa panû šapši nārū (10) biya maʾda wa ʾummī (11) tašammiḫ maʾʾabâ (12) wa ʾal tiwwaḥilan (13) ʿātinu ḫurādi ʾanāku (14) ʿimmānîya šalima (15) kalīlu (16) wa mannama (17) šalāmu ʿimma (18) ʾummiya (19) ʿimmaya taṯaṯib (20) rigma

Notes

(4) {ỉly} common noun m.pl.n.abs. + *y*-enclitic.

(6–7) {ủmy tdʿ} either a common noun f.s.g. functioning as a vocative + 1c.s. pronominal suffix followed by a jussive, G-stem, √YDʿ 2f.s. (this analysis is reflected in the translation and vocalization indicated here, lit., ‘O my mother, may you know’), or a common noun f.s.n. + 1c.s. pronominal suffix + *y*-enclitic followed by a jussive, G-stem, √YDʿ 3f.s. (/ʾummîya tidaʿ/, ‘may my mother know’).

(7) {ky} conj. {k} + *y*-enclitic.
(12) {twḥln} 3f.s. imperfective, N-stem, √WḤL (→ YḤL) + *n*-enclitic.

Text 25: The King Meets His Hittite Sovereign (RS 16.379)

Virolleaud 1957: text 13; *KTU* 2.30; Pardee 1984a: 225–26, 230; 2002b: 92; 2003: 448; *TO* II, pp. 321–24.

Text

Obverse

(1) ⸢l⸣ mlkt . ⸢ủ⸣[m]⸢y⸣ (2) ⸢r⸣gm . tḥ⸢m⸣[ ] (3) mlk . bn⸢k⸣[ ]

---

(4) ⸢l⸣ . pʿn . ⸢ủ⸣m⸢y⸣ (5) qlt ⸢. l⸣y . ⸢ủ⸣[m]y (6) yšlm . ỉl[m] (7) tǵ⸢r⸣k . tš[l]⸢m⸣k

---

(8) ⸢h⸣lny . ʿmn⸢y⸣ [. š]lm (9) w . ṯm⸢n⸣ . ʿ⸢m⸣ [. ủ]my (10) mnm . š⸢l⸣[m] (11) w . rgm [. ṯṯb .] ⸢l⸣y

---

(*Lower edge*) (12) hl⸢n⸣y . ʿm⸢n⸣ (13) mlk . b . ṯy ndr (14) ỉṯt . w . ht (*Reverse*) (15) [-]sny . ủ$^{!?}$ḏrh (16) w . hm . ḫt . (17) ʿl . w . lỉkt (18) ʿmk . w . hm (19) l . ʿl . w . lảkm (20) ỉlảk . w . ảt (21) ủmy . ảl . tdḥ⸢ṣ⸣ (22) w . ảp . mhkm (23) b . lbk . ảl . (24) tšt

---

Translation

(1) To the queen, my mo[ther], (2) say: Message of (3) the king, your son.
(4) At my mother's feet (5) I fall. With my mo[ther] (6) may it be well. May the god[s] (7) guard you, may they k[ee]p you well.
(8) Here with me it is [w]ell. (9) There with my [mo]ther, (10) whatever is we[ll], send (11) word (of that) back to me.
(12) Here to the (13) king from the tribute they have vowed (14) a gift and (15) [h]e (as a result has agreed to) augment his 'vow'?. (16) Now if the Hittite (forces) (17) go up, I will send you a (18) message; and if they (19) do not go up, I will certainly (20) send one. Now you, (21) my mother, do not be agitated (22) and do not allow (23) yourself to be distressed (24) in any way.

Vocalized Text

(1) lê malkati ʾu[mmi]ya (2) rugum taḥmu (3) malki biniki
(4) lê paʿnê ʾummiya (5) qālātu lêya ʾu[mmi]ya (6) yišlam ʾilū[ma] (7) taǵǵurūki taša[lli]mūki
(8) halliniya ʿimmānîya [ša]lima (9) wa ṯammāna ʿimma [ʾu]mmiya (10) mannama šalā[mu] (11) wa rigma [ṯaṯībī] layya

(12) halliniya ʿimmānu (13) malki bi ṭayyi nadarū (14) ʾiṯṯata wa hatti (15) [ya]sanniyu ʾuḏḏarahu (16) wa himma ḫatti (17) ʿalâ wa laʾiktu (18) ʿimmaki wa himma (19) lā ʿalâ wa laʾākuma (20) ʾilʾaku wa ʾatti (21) ʾummiya ʾal tidḫaṣī (22) wa ʾapa mahakama (23) bi libbiki ʾal (24) tašītī

Notes

(12–13) {ʿm⸢n⸣ mlk} the king of Ugarit was with the Hittite king when he dictated this letter.
(15) restore {[y]sny} ?
(22–24) lit., 'do not place anything in your heart'.

Text 26: The King of Tyre to the King of Ugarit (RS 18.031)

Virolleaud 1965: text 59; *KTU* 2.38; Hoftijzer 1979; *TO* II, pp. 349–57; Pardee 2002b: 93–94; 2003: 448.

Text

Obverse

(1) l . mlk . ủgrt (2) ảḫy . rgm (3) tḥm . mlk . ṣr . ảḫk

---

(4) yšlm . lk . ỉlm (5) tǵrk . tšlmk (6) hnny . ʿmn (7) šlm . ṯmny (8) ʿmk . mnm ⸢.⸣ šlm (9) rgm . ṯṯ⸢b⸣

---

(10) ảnykn . dt (11) lỉkt . mṣrm (12) hndt . b . ṣr (*Lower edge*) (13) mtt . by -⸢-⸣ (14) gšm . ảdr (*Reverse*) (15) nškḥ . w (16) rb . tmtt (17) lqḥ . kl . ḏrʿ (18) bd⸢nh⸣m . w . ản⸢k⸣ (19) k[l] ⸢.⸣ ḏrʿ⸢h⸣m (20) ⸢k⸣l ⸢. n⸣pš . (21) w ⸢. ả⸣klhm . bd (22) r⸢b⸣ [.] tmtt . lqḥt (23) w . ṯṯb . ảnk . lhm (24) w . ảnyk . ṯt (25) by . ʿky . ʿryt (26) w . ảḫy . mhk (27) b . lbh . ảl . yšt

---

Translation

(1) To the king of Ugarit, (2) my brother, say: (3) Message of the king of Tyre, your brother.
(4) May it be well with you. May the gods (5) guard you, may they keep you well. (6) Here with me (7) it is well. There (8) with you, whatever is well, (9) send word (of that) back (to me).
(10) Your ships that (11) you dispatched to Egypt (12) have wrecked (13) off Tyre (14) when they found themselves (15) caught in a bad storm. (16) The salvage master, however, (17) was able to remove the entire (cargo of) grain (18) in their possession. (Then) I took over (19) the ent[ire] (cargo of) grain, (20) as well as all the people (21) and their food, from the (22) salvage master (23) and I returned (all these things) to them. (24) Now your boats

have been able to moor (25) at Acco, stripped (of their rigging). (26) So my brother (27) should not worry.

Vocalized Text

(1) lê malki ʾugārit (2) ʾaḫîya rugum (3) taḥmu malki ṣurri ʾaḫîka (4) yišlam lêka ʾilūma (5) taǵǵurūka tašallimūka (6) hannaniya ʿimmānî (7) šalima ṯammāniya (8) ʿimmaka mannama šalāmu (9) rigma ṯaṯib (10) ʾanayyukana dāti (11) laʾikta miṣrêma (12) hannadāti bi ṣurri (13) mêtatu biya (14) gišmi ʾaduri (15) naškaḥū wa (16) rabbu tamūtati (17) laqaḥa kulla ḏarʿi (18) bîdênahumu wa ʾanāku (19) ku[lla] ḏarʿihumu (20) kulla napši (21) wa ʾaklahumu bîdê (22) rabbi tamūtati laqaḥtu (23) wa ṯaṯābu ʾanāku lêhumu (24) wa ʾanayyuka ṯit (25) biya ʿakkāyi ʿarīyatu (26) wa ʾaḫûya mahaka (27) bi libbihu ʾal yašit

Notes

(10) {ånykn} common noun + pronominal suffix + *n*-enclitic (this noun is grammatically feminine, as may be seen from the feminine verbal forms of which it is the subject in the continuation of the text).

(12–15) lit., ‘that (group of ships) in Tyre were dying (when) in a strong storm they found themselves’ (‘were dying’ = ‘were dead in the water’).

(13) the two signs erased at the end of the line appear to have been {gš}, that is, the first two signs of the word *gšm*; the scribe began to write the word here, then seeing that the space was too short for the entire word on the lower edge, he erased what he had written and moved down to the next line and began the word again.

(23) {w ṯṯb ånk} the verbal form is plausibly the infinitive (this explanation appears preferable to correcting the text to read {ṯṯbt}).

(24) {ṯt} 3f.s. perfective √ṮWY, /ṯawiyat/ → /ṯit/ or /ṯat/.

Text 27: *Ṯipṭibaʿlu* to the King (RS 18.040)

Virolleaud 1965: text 63; *KTU* 2.40; Pardee 2002b: 104.

Text

Obverse

(1) l . mlk . bʿ⸢l⸣y (2) rgm (3) ⸢t⸣ḥm . ṯpṭbʿ⸢l⸣ (4) [ʿ]⸢b⸣dk

---

(5) [l .]⸢p⸣ʿn . bʿly (6) [šb]⸢ʿ⸣d . šbʿ⸢d⸣ (7) ⸢m⸣[r]ḥqtm (8) qlt

---

(9) ʿbdk . b . (10) lwsnd (11) ⸢å⸣bṣr . (*Lower edge*) (12) ʿm . mlk (13) w . ht . (14) mlk . syr (*Reverse*) (15) ns . w . ṯm⸢ny⸣ (16) ydbḥ (17) mlǵ⸢ǵm⸣ (18) w . mlk . bʿly (19) y⸢dʿ⸣

Translation

(1) To the king, my master, (2) say: (3) Message of *Ṯipṭibaʿlu*, (4) your [se]rvant:
(5) [At] the feet of my master, (6) [seve]n times, seven times, (7) (from) a[f]ar (8) do I fall.
(9) As for your servant, in (10) *Lawasanda* (11) I am keeping an eye (on the situation) (12) along with the king. (13) Now (14) the king has just left in haste to (Mount) Sēyēra, (15) where (16) he is sacrificing (17) MLǴ⌜ǴM⌝.
(18) The king, my master, (19) must know (this).

Vocalized Text

(1) lê malki baʿliya (2) rugum (3) taḥmu ṯipṭibaʿli (4) [ʿa]bdika
(5) [lê] paʿnê baʿliya (6) [šab]ʿida šabʿida (7) ma[r]ḥaqtama (8) qālātu
(9) ʿabduka bi (10) lawasanda (11) ʾabṣuru (12) ʿimma malki (13) wa hatti (14) malku Sēyēra (15) nāsa wa ṯammāniya (16) yidbaḥu (17) MLǴǴM (18) wa malku baʿlîya (19) yidaʿ

Note

(12, 13) {mlk} the reference is to the Hittite king.

Text 28: Two Servants to Their Master (RS 29.093)

Herdner 1978b; *KTU* 2.70; Pardee 2002b: 110–11.

Text

Obverse

(1) l . ydrm . bʿlny (2) rgm (3) tḥm . pnḥṯ (4) w . yrmhd (5) ʿbdk . p šlm (6) l bʿlny . ỉlm (7) tǵrk . tšlmk (8) l . pʿn . bʿlny (9) ṯnỉd . šbʿd (10) mrḥqtm . qlny

---

(11) hlny . bn . ʿyn (12) yštảl . ʿm . ảmtk (13) w . lảk . lh . w . kḥdnn (14) w . ảnk . ḫrš (15) lqḥt . w . ḫwt (*Lower edge*) (16) hbt . w lm . ṯb (17) bn . ʿyn (*Reverse*) (18) w . lqḥ . ṯqlm (19) ksp . bd . ảmtk

---

(20) w ṯn . ʿbdk (21) ṯmt . ʿmnk (22) klt tn . ảkl . lhm (23) w . k tšảl (24) bt . ʿbdk (25) w . k ymǵy (26) ʿbdk . l šlm (27) ʿmk . p l . yšbʿl (28) ḫpn . l bʿly (29) mnm . ỉṯ . l ʿbdk

Translation

(1) To *Yadurma*, our master, (2) say: (3) Message of *Pinḥaṯu* (4) and *Yarmihaddu*, (5) your servants. May it be well (6) with our master. May the gods (7) guard you, may they keep you well. (8) At the feet of our master

(9) twice seven times (10) (from) afar we fall.
(11) Here *Binu-ʿAyāna* (12) keeps making demands on your maidservant. (13) So send him a message and put a stop to this. (14) Here is what I have done: a workman (15) I engaged and had (16) this house repaired. So why did (17) *Binu-ʿAyāna* come back (18) and take two shekels (19) of silver from your maidservant?
(20) Now as for your two servants, (21) there with you (22) is all (one could need), so you must give food to them. (23) Moreover, thus must the (24) (members of) the house(hold) of your two servants ask. (25) And when your servant comes (26) to tender to you his formal greetings, (27) he will be sure to have (28) a *ḫipânu*-garment made for my master, (29) of whatever (is required) from your servant's own goods.

Vocalized Text

(1) lê yadurma baʿlināyā (2) rugum (3) taḥmu pinḥaṯi (4) wa yarmihaddi (5) ʿabdêka pa šalāmu (6) lê baʿlināyā ʾilūma (7) taǵǵurūka tašallimūka (8) lê paʿnê baʿlināyā (9) ṯinêʾida šabʿida (10) marḥaqtama qālānāyā
(11) halliniya binu ʿayāna (12) yištaʾʾalu ʿimma ʾamatika (13) wa laʾak lêhu wa kaḥḥidannannu (14) wa ʾanāku ḥarrāša (15) laqaḥtu wa ḥiwwêtu (16) habbêta wa lêma ṯāba (17) binu ʿayāna (18) wa laqaḥa ṯiqlêma (19) kaspa bîdê ʾamatika
(20) wa ṯinâ ʿabdāka (21) ṯammati ʿimmānuka (22) kullatu tin ʾakla lêhumā (23) wa kā tišʾalū (24) bêtu ʿabdêka (25) wa kī yamǵiyu (26) ʿabduka lê šalāmi (27) ʿimmaka pa la yašabʿilu (28) ḫipâna lê baʿliya (29) mannama ʾiṯu lê ʿabdika

Notes

(12) {åmtk} the use of the word designating a female servant indicates that just one of the two authors is speaking.
(20) {w ṯn ʿbdk} the phrase marks the return to a message of the two writers.
(23) {tšål} 3m.pl. jussive, G-stem, expressing the necessity for the habitants of the household to ask for provisions when their present supply has run out.
(26) {ʿbdk} that this form is singular is shown by the form {bʿly} in line 28 and this portion of the message was thus spoken by the male servant.

Text 29: The King to the Queen-Mother in the Matter of the Amurrite Princess (RS 34.124)

Bordreuil and Pardee 1991: text 88; Pardee 2002b: 90–92; 2003: 450; *TO* II, pp. 363–421; *CAT* 2.72.

Text

Obverse

(1) [l . mlkt . ủmy] (2) [rgm] (3) [tḥm .] ⸢m⸣[lk . bnk]

---

(4) [l p]ʿn . ủmy ⸢.⸣ [qlt] (5) [l]⸢y⸣ . ủmy šlm ⸢.⸣ [ỉlm] (6) [t]ġrk . tšl⸢m⸣[k]

---

(7) ⸢h⸣nny . ʿmn . šl[m . kl]⸢l⸣ (8) ṯmny . ʿmk- . mnm (9) šlm . rgm . ṯṯ . ly

---

(10) lm . tlỉkn . ḫpṯ . hndn (11) p . mšmʿt . m⸢lk⸣ (12) ỉnn . ỉm . bn . q⸢l-⸣ (13) ỉm . bn . ảlyy . ỉm (14) mšmʿt . mlk (15) ⸢w .⸣ tlkn . ṯn . ṯnm (16) ʿmy . w . tṯbrn . lby (17) w . lḥt . bt . mlk . ảmr (18) ⸢k⸣y ⸢.⸣ tdbr . ủmy (*Lower edge*) (19) l . pn . qrt (20) ỉm . ht . l . b (21) mṣqt . yṯ⸢bt⸣ (*Reverse*) (22) qrt . p. mn (23) lỉkt . ảnk . lḥt (24) bt . mlk . ảmr (25) ybnn . hlk (26) ʿm . mlk . ảmr (27) w . ybl . hw . mỉt (28) ḫrṣ . w . mrdtt . l (29) mlk . ảmr . w . lqḥ . hw (30) šmn . b . qrnh (31) w . yṣq . hw . l . rỉš (32) bt . mlk . ả⸢mr⸣ (33) mnm ⸢.⸣ ḫ⸢ṭ⸣[. . .]⸢-⸣ (34) ⸢k⸣y . ủm⸢y⸣[. . .] (35) [ ]r . h⸢w⸣[. . .] (36′–38′ [. . .]) (*Upper edge*) (39′–41′ [. . .]) (*Left edge*) (42′) [. . .]štỉr . p . ủ (43′) [. . .]⸢-⸣t . kly . b . kpr (44′) [. . .]hbk . w . ảnk (45′) [. . .]nỉtk

Translation

(1) [To the queen, my mother, (2) say: (3) Message of the] k[ing, your son.] (4) [At] my mother's [f]eet [I fall]. (5) [Wi]th my mother ⟨may⟩ it be well! [May the gods] (6) [g]uard you, may they keep [you] well.
(7) Here with me [everythi]ng is we[ll]. (8) There with you, whatever (9) is well, sen⟨d⟩ word (of that) back to me.
(10) Why do you send this *ḫupṯu*(-soldier?) (11) and not the royal guard? (12) If *Binu*-QL⸢-⸣, (13) *Binu-ʾAlliyaya*, and (14) the royal guard (15) go (elsewhere), inform (16) me, and you will disappoint me severely.
(17) As regards the correspondence relative to the daughter of the king of Amurru (18) (and the fact) you are to speak (about it) (19) to the city (-council): (20) if the city (21) remains undecided, (22) then why (23) have I sent a letter (to them) (24) (on the topic of) the daughter of the king of Amurru? (25) Now *Yabninu* has left (26) for the court of Amurru (27) and he has taken with him one hundred (28) (shekels of) gold and *mardatu*-cloth for (29) the king of Amurru. He has also taken (30) oil in a horn (31) and poured it on the head of (32) the daughter of the king of Amurru. (33) Whatever si[n? . . .] (34) because my mother [. . .].

[. . .]
(42′) [. . .] is left and moreover (43′) [. . .] brought to an end by expiating (44′) [. . .] your (male) ally/allies. And I, for my part, (45′) [. . .] your (female) enemy.

Vocalized Text

(1) [lê malkati ʾummiya] (2) [rugum] (3) [taḥmu] ma[lki biniki]
(4) [lê pa]ʿnê ʾummiya [qālātu] (5) [lê]ya ʾummiya ⟨yi⟩šlam [ʾilūma]
(6) [ta]ǵǵurūki tašallimū[ki]
(7) hannaniya ʿimmānî šali[ma kalī]lu (8) ṯammāniya ʿimmaki mannama
(9) šalāmu rigma ṯaṯī⟨bī⟩ layya
(10) lêma talaʾʾikīna ḫupṯa hannadāna (11) pa mašmaʿtu malki (12) ʾênuna ʾimma binu QL⌜-⌝ (13) ʾimma binu ʾalliyaya ʾimma (14) mašmaʿtu malki (15) wa talikūna ṯinî ṯanûma (16) ʿimmaya wa taṯburīna libbaya (17) wa lūḥatu bitti malki ʾamurri (18) kīya tadabbiru ʾummīya (19) lê panî qarîti (20) ʾimma hatti lê bi (21) maṣūqati yāṯibatu (22) qarîtu pa manna (23) laʾiktu ʾanāku lūḥata (24) bitti malki ʾamurri (25) yabninu halaka (26) ʿimma malki ʾamurri (27) wa yabala huwa miʾta (28) ḫurāṣi wa mardêta! lê (29) malki ʾamurri wa laqaḥa huwa (30) šamna bi qarnihu (31) wa yaṣaqa huwa lê raʾši (32) bitti malki ʾamurri (33) mannama ḪṬ[. . .] (34) kīya ʾumm-ya [. . .] (35–41′) [. . .] (42′) [. . .]ŠTʾIR pa ʾū (43′) [. . .] killaya bi kapāri (44′) [. . . ʾā]hib-ki wa ʾanāku (45′) [. . . šā]niʾt-ki

Notes

(1–3) the restoration of the address is based on epistolary usage, the space available, and the trace of a {⌜m⌝} in line 3.
(5) {ủmyšlm} probably correct to read {ủmy ⟨. y ⟩šlm}.
(9) {ṯṯ} certainly correct to read {ṯṯ⟨b⟩}.
(20) {l . b} either two prepositions forming a complex prepositional phrase (as is indicated in the vocalized text) or else asseverative /la/ + the preposition /bi/.
(28) {mrdtt} a mistake for {mrdt} or an irregular plural?
(33) {ḫṭ[. . .]} perhaps restore a form derived from the root ḪṬʾ, ‘to commit an error, to sin’.
(42′) {[. . .]štỉr} should be an imperfective, Gt-stem, from √ŠʾR, but the grammatical person is unknown.
(44′, 45′) {[. . .]hbk}, {[. . .]nỉtk} plausibly restore {[. . . ả]hbk} and {[. . . š]nỉtk} (in the first case, the grammatical number is unclear whereas in the second it must be singular [the plural would be written {šnảtk} for /šāniʾāt-ki/]; the grammatical case of both words is unknown because the context is lost).

Text 30: *ʾAnantēnu* to His Master, *Ḫid̲miratu* (RS 92.2010)

Bordreuil and Pardee 2001: text 50; Pardee 2002b: 112.

Text

Obverse

---

(1) l ḫd̲mrt (2) bʿly . rgm (3) tḥm . ånntn (4) ʿbdk . ỉlm (5) tǵrk . tšlmk (6) l pʿn . bʿly (7) šbʿd . w šbʿd (8) mrḥqtm (9) qlt . w hnn (10) ʿm ʿbdk (11) mỉd . šlm (*Lower edge*) (12) w bʿly (13) šlm⸢h⸣ (*Reverse*) (14) w šlm (15) nkly (16) w šlm (17) bth . w šlm (18) šmʿ rgmk (19) nʿm åt t̲t̲b (20) ʿm ʿbdk (21) w bʿly bt (22) ʿbdh . ål (23) ybʿr (24) b ydh

Translation

(1) To *Ḫid̲miratu*, (2) my master, say: (3) Message of *ʾAnantēnu*, (4) your servant. May the gods (5) guard you, may they keep you well. (6) At the feet of my master (7) seven times and seven times (8) (from) afar (9) do I fall. Here (10) with your servant (11) it is very well. (12) As for my master, (13) (news of) his well-being, (14) (of) the well being (15) of *Nikkaliya*, (16) (of) the well-being (17) of his household, (of) the well-being of (18) those who listen to your (19) good word(s), you, (O master,) you must send back (20) to your servant. (21–23) Now may my master not destroy his servant's house(hold) (24) by his (own) hand.

Vocalized Text

(1) lê ḫid̲mirati (2) baʿliya rugum (3) taḥmu ʾanantēna (4) ʿabdika ʾilūma (5) taǵǵurūka tašallimūka (6) lê paʿnê baʿliya (7) šabʿida wa šabʿida (8) marḥaqtama (9) qālātu wa hannana (10) ʿimma ʿabdika (11) maʾda šalima (12) wa baʿlîya (13) šulmahu (14) wa šulma (15) nikkaliya (16) wa šulma (17) bêtihu wa šulma (18) šāmiʿi/ī rigmika (19) naʿīmi ʾatta t̲at̲ib (20) ʿimma ʿabdika (21) wa baʿlîya bêta (22) ʿabdihu ʾal (23) yabaʿʿir (24) bi yadihu

Note

(13) {šlm⸢h⸣} the lower wedge of the last sign is extended downwards, making difficult the epigraphic distinction between {h} and {ỉ}; the meaning of the formula requires the reading of {h}.

Text 31: A Double Letter: The Queen to *ʾUrtēnu* and *ʾIlîmilku* to the Same (RS 94.2406)

Bordreuil, Hawley, and Pardee forthcoming: text 60; Pardee 2002b: 102–3.

Text

Obverse

(1) tḥm . mlkt (2) l . ủrtn . rgm

---

(3) hlny . ảnk . b ym (4) k ytnt [.] spr (5) hnd . ʿmk . w b ym (6) hwt . ảnk . b mlwm (7) btt . w . ʿlm (8) ảdnyh . b ṯlṯ (9) snǵr . b r⌜b⌝ʿ (10) ủnǵ . w dʿ

---

(11) w ảt ⌜.⌝ klklk[. . .] (12) škn . l šmk[. . .] (13) w . kly . ʿbd[. . .] (14) ⌜p .⌝ mǵy . ṯh . w[. . .] (15) ỉršth . t⌜-⌝[. . .]
(*Lower edge*)

---

(16) w . bt . ảḥ⌜d⌝[. . .] (17) d . ảdr[. . .] (*Reverse*) (18) d ỉ⌜ṯ⌝ . ḥd⌜-⌝[. . .] (19) w . ⌜-(-)⌝ḥ . w . ⌜š⌝[. . .] (20) mrḥṣm . bh[. . .]

---

(21) w . ảt . b pk ⌜.⌝ ả⌜l⌝[. . .] (22) yṣỉ mnk ⌜ʿ⌝d m⌜ǵ⌝[. . .] (23) w . ủgrt . ⌜ỉ⌝lả⌜k⌝[. . .] (24) w . ỉšmʿ . ⌜k⌝ . l . ʿ⌜rb⌝[. . .] (25) bk . ảnkm . ỉlảk

---

(26) ⌜-⌝sp m⌜-⌝p . w ỉšprm (27) ⌜w⌝ g⌜p⌝m . ʿdbm (28) w l . ʿ⌜rb⌝t . bk . l ʿrbt (29) ʿmy . mlk ⌜. t⌝lảk (30) w rỉš⌜k⌝ . ẖlq

---

(31) tḥm . ỉlmlk . (32) l . ủrtn . ỉẖy rgm (33) yšlm . lk . k lỉk[-] (34) ʿmy . ky ḥš . w lả⌜k⌝ (*Upper edge*) (35) w ht ảnk rgt (36) l pn . mlkt . lỉk[?] (37) w . ảt . bt . ủẖd ly (*Left edge*) (38) w dʿ . k yṣả[-] ⌜. ả⌝p . mlkt (39) w ảt . b pk . ảl . yṣỉ (40) mhk . ủgrt

Translation

(1) Message of the queen: (2) To *ʾUrtēnu*, say:
(3) I was on the sea (4) when I gave this document (5) (to be delivered) to you. To(6)day at MLWM I lodged, tomorrow (8) (it will be) at *ʾAdaniya*, the third (day) (9) at *Sunnaǵara*, and the fourth at (10) *ʾUnuǵu*. You are now informed.
(11) As for you, all that belongs to you [. . .] (12) ESTABLISH for your name [. . .] (13) and FINISH SERVANT [. . .] (14) for (some) disaster has arrived and [. . .] (15) his/her request [. . .].
(16) Now a house [. . .] (17) that ʾADR [. . .] (18) that is [. . .] (19) and [. . .] and [. . .] (20) those who cleanse BH[. . .].
(21) As for you, not a word must (22) escape your mouth until [X] arrives. (23) Then I will send a message to Ugarit [. . .]. (24) Should I hear that [she]

has not agreed to guarantee (25) you, then I'll send a(nother) message. (26) Now a SP-vessel (or: two SP-vessels) of M⌈-⌉P, two ʾIŠPR, (27) and two GP are ready. (28) (If) she does not guarantee you, does not (agree to) come (29) to me, she will send a message to the king (30) and you can kiss your head good-bye.
(31) Message of *ʾIlîmilku*: (32) To *ʾUrtēnu*, my brother, say: (33) May it be well with you.
Concerning the fact that [you] sent (34) me the message, "Send me a message quickly," (35) now I have dictat[ed] (this) message! (that I am sending to you) (36) in the presence of the queen. (37) What you must do is to seize the house for me. (38) Moreover, you must recognize that the queen also [has] left. (39) But you must keep (40) absolutely quiet (about all of this) at Ugarit.

Vocalized Text

(1) taḥmu malkati (2) lê ʾurtēna rugum
(3) halliniya ʾanāku bi yammi (4) kī yatanātu sipra (5) hannadā ʿimmaka wa bi yômi (6) huwati ʾanāku bi MLWM (7) bātātu wa ʿalâma (8) ʾadaniyaha bi ṯalīṯi (9) sunnaǵara bi rabīʿi (10) ʾunuǵi wa daʿ
(11) wa ʾatta kulkul-ka[. . .] (12) ŠKN lê šumika[. . .] (13) wa KLY ʿBD[. . .] (14) pa maǵaya ṮH wa[. . .] (15) ʾiršt-h- T⌈-⌉[. . .]
(16) wa bêtu ʾaḥḥadu[. . .] (17) dū ʾADR[. . .] (18) dū ʾiṯu ḤD⌈-⌉[. . .] (19) wa ⌈-(-)⌉Ḥ wa Š[. . .] (20) muraḥḥiṣ-ma BH[. . .]
(21) wa ʾatta bi pîka ʾal (22) yaṣiʾ mannaka ʿadê maǵā[yi--] (23) wa ʾugārit ʾilʾaku [. . .] (24) wa ʾišmaʿu kī lā ʿarab[at] (25) bika ʾanākuma ʾilʾaku (26) ⌈-⌉SP M⌈-⌉P wa ʾIŠPRM (27) wa G⌈P⌉M ʿadūbūma (28) wa lā ʿarabat bika lā ʿarabat (29) ʿimmaya malka tilʾaku (30) wa raʾšuka ḫaliqu
(31) taḥmu ʾilîmilki (32) lê ʾurtēna ʾiḫîya rugum (33) yišlam lêka kī laʾik[ta] (34) ʿimmaya kīya ḥuš wa laʾak (35) wa hatti ʾanāku rigma! (36) lê panî malkati laʾik[tu] (37) wa ʾatta bêta ʾuḫud layya (38) wa daʿ kī yaṣaʾa[t] ʾapa malkatu (39) wa ʾatta bi pîka ʾal yaṣiʾ (40) mahaka ʾugārit

Notes

(3–10) according to the epistolographic conventions followed at Ugarit, the author expresses acts associated with the writing of the letter in the perfective, adopting thus the perspective of the recipient, for whom these acts will have been in the past when the letter arrives; the day apparently began at sundown and thus the queen had lodged 'this day', i.e., the night before, in the first city named, written the letter during the daylight hours of that 'day', and indicated where she was planning on spending that night (the next 'day') and the two nights thereafter; this outline of her plans probably means that the messenger carrying the tablet RS 94.2406 took a ship back to Ugarit from the port serving *ʾAdanya*, the town on the Anatolian mainland from which the queen intended to head inland.

(10) {w dʿ} one of the epistolary formulae based on the root YDʿ (m.s. imperative) by which the sender emphasizes the need for the recipient to pay close attention to the message.

(19) {⸢-(-)⸣ḥ} the wedges that precede the {ḥ} may be read either as a {m} with the horizontal written over an oblique wedge or as {ṯg} (less likely).

(20) perhaps restore {bh[tm]} '(those who purify) hou[ses]'.

(24) probably restore {ʿrb[t]} and take the form as referring to the female personage mentioned below in this and the following paragraphs.

(26) the first sign is probably{⸢w⸣} ({⸢w⸣ sp} 'and *sappu*-containers') or {⸢k⸣} ({⸢k⸣sp} 'silver of').

(30) {rìšk ḫlq} lit., 'your head is dead, will disappear, perish, be destroyed'.

(32) {ìḫy} in the first syllable, /a/ has become /i/ through vowel harmony (/ʾaḫîya/ → /ʾiḫîya/).

(33) probably restore {lìk[t]}, analyze as 2m.s. perfective, and see it as part of the epistolary formula by which the sender of the present message refers to a message from the addressee of this letter.

(35–36) {rgt . . . lìk[?]} correct to {rgm} 'word' and restore {lìk[t]}, 1c.s. perfective, the author of the present letter referring to its sending, lit., 'Now, as for me, (this) word! I [have] sent (when) in the presence of the queen', i.e., with the queen's knowledge and authorization.

(38) restore {yṣà[t]} with {mlkt} as subject.

Text 32: A Business Letter: The Governor to the Queen (RS 94.2479)

Bordreuil, Hawley, and Pardee forthcoming: text 61; Pardee 2002b: 107.

Text

Obverse

(1) ⸢l⸣ [.] mlkt . àdty. rgm (2) tḥm . skn . ʿbdk

---

(3) ⸢l⸣ [. p]ʿn . àdty . qlt (4) ⸢l⸣ [.] àdty . yšlm

---

(5) hlny . hnn . b .—(6) bt . mlk . kll (7) šlm . ṯmny (8) ʿm . àdty . mnm (9) w . rgm . ṯṯb (10) ʿm . ʿbdh

---

(11) ⸢w⸣ [.] hln . ʿšrm (*Lower edge*) (12) [d]d [.] šʿrm (13) w . ḫmš . dd (*Reverse*) (14) gdl . w . ḫmš (15) dd . nʿr (16) kd . šmn mr (17) kd . šmn . nr (18) kd . ḥmṣ (19) kd . zt mm (20) d . znt . àdty (21) kllm . štnt

Translation

(1) To the queen, my lady, say: (2) Message of the governor, your servant. (3) [A]t the [f]eet of my lady I fall. (4) With my lady may it be well. (5) Here in (6) the king's palace, everything (7) is fine. There (8) with my lady, whatever 〈is fine〉, (9) may she return word (of that) (10) to her servant. (11) (From) here twenty (12) *[dū]du*-measures of barley (13) and five *dūdu*-measures of (14) GDL and five (15) *dūdu*-measures of NʿR, (16) (one) *kaddu*-measure of oil (perfumed with) myrrh, (17) (one) *kaddu*-measure of lamp-oil, (18) (one) *kaddu*-measure of vinegar, (19) (one) *kaddu*-measure of olives (in) water, (20) (from) my lady's food provisions, (21) all (of this) I herewith cause to be delivered (to you).

Vocalized Text

(1) lê malkati ʾadattiya rugum (2) taḥmu sākini ʿabdiki
(3) lê [pa]ʿnê ʾadattiya qālātu (4) lê ʾadattiya yišlam
(5) halliniya hannana bi (6) bêti malki kalīlu (7) šalima ṭammāniya (8) ʿimma ʾadattiya mannama 〈šalāmu〉 (9) wa rigma taṯaṯib (10) ʿimma ʿabdiha
(11) wa hallina ʿašrāma (12) [dū]du šiʿārīma (13) wa ḫamišu dūdū (14) GDL wa ḫamišu (15) dūdū NʿR (16) kaddu šamni murri (17) kaddu šamni nīri (18) kaddu ḥumṣi (19) kaddu zêtī mêma (20) dū zānati ʾadattiya (21) kalīlama šatinātu

Notes

(8) probably restore {〈šlm〉} at the end of the line.
(13–15) the numbers from 'three' to 'ten' are normally followed by a noun in the plural.
(17) {šmn nr} 'oil of fire, of light = lamp oil'.
(19) {zt mm} 'olives of water', perhaps olives in brine (more plausible than 'purified olive-oil' of the French edition because *zt* normally denotes the olive itself rather than the oil drawn therefrom).
(21) {kllm} given the abstract meaning of this noun, it is probably singular + *m*-enclitic rather than plural.

Text 33: The Queen to *Yarmihaddu* on the Matter of a Missing Slave (RS 96.2039)

Bordreuil, Hawley, and Pardee forthcoming: text 65; Pardee 2002b: 103.

Text

Obverse

(1) [t]ḥm . mlkt (2) l yrmhd (3) ỉḫy . rgm

(4) lḥt [.] ⸢h⸣n . bnšk (5) d lqḥt [.] ⸢-⸣[-(-)] (6) w ảnk ⸢.⸣ ⸢ả⸣[ṯ]⸢th⸣ (7) ytnt . lk[?] (8) w ht . hn bnš hw (9) b gty ⸢.⸣ ḫbṯ (10) w ht . hn bnš ⸢h⸣[w] (11) ʿmm . ảṯth (*Lower edge*) (12) btk . ṯb (13) w ảdn . ảt (*Reverse*) (14) ⸢ḫ-(?)⸣ . w yủḫd (15) hn bnš hw (16) w štnn⸢h⸣ (17) bd . mlảk⸢ty⸣

---

(18) w k ỉn ⸢h⸣lk (19) w . l . lỉkt (20) ʿm mlk (21) w ʿmkm . lỉkt (22) ⸢w⸣ [.] ⸢ảt⸣ . bd (23) [m]⸢lảk⸣t⸢y⸣ (24) [š]tnn

---

Translation

(1) [Me]ssage of the queen: (2) To *Yarmihaddu*, (3) my brother, say:
(4) (As for) the (message)-tablet (in which I said) "Your servant (5) whom I took [. . .]; (6) and I, for my part, gave his w[if]e (7) to you; (8) and that servant (9) worked on my farm; (10) but t[hat] servant returned (11) to his wife (12) at your house; (13) and you are the 'father' (14) Ḫ⸢-(?)⸣; so this servant must be (15) seized, (16) and deliver him (17) over to my messenger-party":
(18) Now, seeing that he has not moved, (19) and (that) I have not sent a message (20) to the king, (21) but to you have I sent (this message), (22–24) so now, you [must] deliver him over to my [mes]senger-party.

Vocalized Text

(1) [ta]ḥmu malkati (2) lê yarmihaddi (3) ʾiḫîya rugum
(4) lūḥatî hanna bunušuka (5) dū laqaḥtu . . . (6) wa ʾanāku ʾa[ṯṯa]tahu
(7) yatanātu lêka (8) wa hatti hanna bunušu huwa (9) bi gittiya ḫabaṯa
(10) wa hatti hanna bunušu hu[wa] (11) ʿimmama ʾaṯṯatihu (12) bêtaka ṯāba
(13) wa ʾadānu ʾatta (14) ⸢Ḫ-(?)⸣ wa yuʾuḫad (15) hanna bunušu huwa
(16) wa šatinannahu (17) bîdê malʾakatiya
(18) wa kī ʾênu hāliku (19) wa lā laʾiktu (20) ʿimma malki (21) wa ʿimmakama laʾiktu (22) wa ʾatta bîdê (23) [ma]lʾakatiya (24) [ša]tinannu

Notes

(11) {ʿmm} preposition + *m*-enclitic.
(14) {yủḫd} either G-stem, active voice (indefinite subject, 'may (someone) seize (him)') or Gp (for the various ways of explaining the writing with {ủ}, see §3.5 in the Grammar, p. 27).
(19–21) a thinly veiled threat to take the case to the king if *Yarmihaddu* should ignore the queen's repeated demand to return her slave.
(21) {ʿmkm} preposition + pronominal suffix 2m.s. + *m*-enclitic.

Text 34: *ʾABNY* to *ʾUrtēṯub*/*ʾUrtēnu* (RS 94.2284)

Bordreuil, Hawley, and Pardee forthcoming: text 67; Pardee 2002b: 113–14.

Text

Obverse

(1) tḥm . åbny (2) l . ủrtṯb . ủrtn (3) åḫy . rgm . hlny :

---

(4) bdnỉl . ytnt (5) ỉšprm . w ṯlṯ- (6) ʿrmlḥt . w årbʿ spm

---

(7) w lb åḫtk . mrṣ (8) ky . ḫbt w l ủšål (9) ủ ky . b ḫ . yr . k ỉnd šỉln (10) w ṭbḫ . ålp . mrủ (11) w ỉnd . ytn . ly

---

(12) ḥ npšk . w ḥ n[. . .] (13) hm ỉṯ . d ytn ⸢l⸣ [. . .] (*Lower edge*) (14) w mrṣ . lby [. . .] (15) mỉd . mly[. . .] (*Reverse*) (16) åǵltn . ⸢-⸣[. . .] (17) ålny . b dbḥ[. . .]

---

(18) w lḥt . ḫpn . w kblm (19) ỉqnủm . ỉštỉr (20) bhm . w hm . åk⸢ǵ⸣ (21) ỉqnå . štt bhm (22) w grš . bnỉl (23) w yqḥ . tʿnk

---

(24) w mnm . rgm . w ṯṯb (25) bb . bnỉl . hl ʿkd (26) w åtm . ydʿt . lb åḫtk (27) k mrṣ . hm ỉbt . w åtn (28) ṯn ḫpnm . ḥdm (29) hyn . d znt . ly l ytn (*Upper edge*) (30) w ks . på . åmḥt . åkydnt (31) hn ksp . d ytnt . ly (*Left edge*) (32a) låkh åšhkr (32b) . l d hlkt . npšk (33) w mlåktk . lm tšḫr (34) ʿmy . l ydʿt . lby k mrṣ

Translation

(1) Message of ʾABNY: (2) To *ʾUrtēṯub*, *ʾUrtēnu*, (3) my brother, say: Here . . .
(4) With ⟨*Bi*⟩*niʾilu* I (herewith) send (you) (5) two ʾIŠPR and three (6) ʿRMLḤT and four jars (of wine).
(7) Now, the heart of your sister is sick (8) because they have treated me ill and I was never consulted. (9) In the month of *Ḫiyyāru*—when nobody consulted me— (10) a fattened bull was slaughtered (11) and nobody gave me (any).
(12) As you live, and as do [I], (13) (I swear that) nobody gave [me (any)] (14) and my heart is sick, (15) very much so. MLY[. . .]. (16) *ʾAǵaltēnu* [. . .] (17) ʾALNY in SACRIFICE [. . .].
(18) Now as concerns the letter (regarding) a *ḫipânu*-garment and a pair of leggings (that you sent me): (19) Some remain (made) (of) purple wool, (20) partially. If I KǴ (21) any purple wool, I will certainly put (some of those) with them. (22) When *Biniʾilu* is sent off, (23) he will take your reply (i.e., my reply to your letter).

(24) Whatever is said (there), send (me) back a report (25) through$^{!}$ *Biniʾilu*—he/it is/will be (in$^{?}$) ʿKD. (26) Now, you know the heart of your sister, (27) how sick it will be if there is any (more) enmity. I'll give (28) two ne⟨w⟩$^{?}$ *ḫipānu*-garments (29) (for$^{?}$) the wine from the provisions that were not given to me. (30) The cup ? (31) As for the money that you granted me, (32a) send it (to me) so I may cause (you) to sleep (32b) where your "soul" is going. (33) Why do you delay sending your messenger (34) to me? Don't you know my heart, how sick it is?

Vocalized Text

(1) taḥmu ʾABNY (2) lê ʾurtēṯub ʾurtēnu (3) ʾaḫîya rugum halliniya
(4) bîdê bi$^{!}$niʾilu yatanātu (5) ʾIŠPRêma wa ṯalāṯa (6) ʿRMLḤāti wa ʾarbaʿa sappīma
(7) wa libbu ʾaḫâtika maruṣa (8) kīya ḫabatū wa lā ʾušʾalu (9) ʾū kīya bi ḫiyyāri$^{!}$ kī ʾênudū šaʾilannī (10) wa ṭubaḫa ʾalpu marīʾu (11) wa ʾênudū yatana layya
(12) ḥê napšika wa ḥê na[pšiya] (13) himma ʾiṯu dū yatana la[yya . . .]
(14) wa maruṣa libbīya [. . .] (15) maʾda MLY[. . .] (16) ʾaǵaltēnu [. . .]
(17) ʾALNY bi dabḥi[. . .]
(18) wa lūḥatu ḫipâni wa kiblêma (19) ʾiqnaʾūma ʾištaʾirū (20) bihumu wa himma ʾAK⌜Ǵ⌝ (21) ʾiqnaʾa šātātu bihumu (22) wa gurаša biniʾilu (23) wa yiqqaḫu taʿnâka
(24) wa mannama rigmu wa ṯaṯib (25) bîd$^{!}$ê biniʾilu halli ʿKD (26) wa ʾattama yadaʿāta libba ʾaḫâtika (27) kī maruṣa himma ʾêbatu wa ʾatinu (28) ṯinê ḫipânêma ḥada⟨ṯê⟩ma$^{?}$ (29) hayyêna (?) dā zānati layya lā yatana (30) wa kāsu ? (31) hanna kaspu dū yatanāta layya (32a) laʾakahu ʾašahkiru (32b) lê dī hālikat napšuka (33) wa malʾaktuka lêma tašâḫiru (34) ʿimmaya lā yadaʿāta libbaya kī maruṣa

Notes

(3) {hlny} either the first word of the formula of well-being intended as an abbreviation thereof or else the first word of the body ("Here . . ."); the two small wedges on the right edge are amenable to either interpretation ('abbreviated formula' or 'this word is to be understood as pertaining to the following paragraph').

(4) {bdnỉl} read {bd ⟨b⟩nỉl}; {bḫ.yr} read{b ḫyr}.

(8) {ủšảl} 1c.s. imperfective, Gp-stem, √ŠʾL (the imperfective here expresses the duration of the events to which the writer refers).

(9) {ỉnd} the head of the small vertical wedge is not clearly visible, which gives the impression of a sign consisting of three wedges only (normally {h}).

(12) probably restore {n[pšy]}.

(14) {lby} common noun + pronominal suffix 1c.s. + *y*-enclitic.
(20) {åk⸢ǵ⸣} grammatical identification and meaning both unknown.
(21) {ỉqnå} just above the center of the {q} a small wedge is visible which appears to be unintentional—it appears too small to require the reading of {ṭ}, which in any case does not provide an intelligible text.
(25) {bb} read {bd}.
(26) {åtm} independent personal pronoun 2m.s. + *m*-enclitic.
(28) {ḥdm} mistake for {ḥdṯm}?
(29) {hyn} presentative particle + common noun (← /han/ + /yêna/)?
(32) the "a" section of this line is written in the direction of the top of the tablet, the "b" section in the opposite direction (a writing strategy previously unattested in Ugaritic).
(33) {tšẖr} ← /*taša'ẖiru/.

Text 35: *'Iwriḏēnu* Asks to Be Named before the King (RS [Varia 4])

Bordreuil 1982: 5–9; *KTU* 2.14; Pardee 2002b: 114.

Text

Obverse

(1) tḥm . ỉwrḏ⸢n⸣ (2) l ỉwrpzn (3) bny . åẖy . rgm (4) ỉlm . tǵrk (5) tšlmk

---

(6) ỉky . lḥt (7) spr . d lỉkt (8) ʿm . ṯryl (9) mhy . rgmt

---

(10) w ht . åẖy (11) bny . yšål (12) ṯryl . p rgmt (13) l mlk . šmy (*Lower edge*) (14) w l ỉytlm

---

(*Reverse*) (15) w h[- .] åẖy (16) bny . yšål (17) ṯryl . w rgm (18) ṯṯb . l åẖk (19) l ådnk

Translation

(1) Message of *'Iwriḏēnu*: (2) To *'Iwripuzini*, (3) my son, my brother, say: (4) May the gods guard you, (5) may they keep you well.
(6) How is it with the message-tablet (7) that I sent (8) to *Ṯarriyelli*? (9) What has she said (about it)?
(10) Now may my brother, (11) my son, inquire of (12) *Ṯarriyelli* and may she in turn mention (13) my name to the king (14) and to *'Iyyatalmi*.
(15) No[w] may my brother, (16) my son, make this inquiry of (17) *Ṯarriyelli* and return (18) word to your brother, (19) your father.

Vocalized Text

(1) taḥmu ʾiwriḏēna (2) lê ʾiwripuzini (3) biniya ʾaḫîya rugum (4) ʾilūma taǵǵurūka (5) tašallimūka
(6) ʾêkaya lūḥatu (7) sipri dā laʾiktu (8) ʿimma ṯarriyelli (9) mahhiya ragamat
(10) wa hatti ʾaḫûya (11) binîya yišʾal (12) ṯarriyelli pa ragamat (13) lê malki šumaya (14) wa lê ʾiyyatalmi
(15) wa ha[tti] ʾaḫûya (16) binîya yišʾal (17) ṯarriyelli wa rigma (18) ṯaṯib lê ʾaḫîka (19) lê ʾadānika

Notes

(3, 10–11, 15–16, 18–19) {bn-}, {ảḫ-}, {ảdn-} the social relationship of the correspondents is expressed as existing on two levels, equality ("brothers") and superiority-inferiority ("father . . . son"), but the text does not provide the data necessary to determine what the real-life relationship was (for example, an older brother who has acted as father to a younger brother since the death of their father . . .).

(9) {mhy} ← /mah + hiya/.

(10) {ảḫy} in the French edition, the copy incorrectly read {ảzy}.

(11, 16) {bny} common noun m.s.n. + pronominal suffix 1c.s. + *y*-enclitic.

(15) {h[-]} restore {h[t]} or {h[m]}.

VI. Legal Texts

Text 36: A Suzerainty Treaty between *Ṯuppiluliuma* and *Niqmaddu* (RS 11.772+)

Virolleaud 1940a: 260–66; *CTA* 64; *KTU* 3.1; Pardee 2001b.

Text

Obverse

(1′) ⸢-⸣[. . .] (2′) ʿm[. . .] (3′) mǵ[. . .] (4′) šp[š . . .] (5′) ql . [. . .]

(6′) w ml⸢k⸣[. . .]šḫ (7′) ʿmn . [. . .] (8′) ỉky ⸢.⸣[. . .] (9′) w l ⸢-⸣[. . .]

(10′) ⸢w⸣ nqmd . [. . .] (11′) [-] ʿmn . šp[š . . .] (12′) bʿlh . šlm . ⸢-⸣[. . .] (13′) mlk . rb . bʿlh[. . .] (14′) nqmd . mlk . ủgr[t . . .] (15′) phy

---

(16′) w ṯpllm . mlk . ⸢r⸣[b] (17′) mṣmt . l nqmd . ⸢-⸣[---(-)]št (18′) h⸢l⸣ny . årgmn . d[--(-) n]qmd (19′) l špš . årn . ṯn[---(-)]mn (20′) ʿšrm . ṯql . kbd [. k]s . mn . ḫrṣ (21′) w å⸢rbʿ⸣ . ktnt . w [.?] ⸢ủṭ⸣b (*Lower edge*) (22′) [--]š . måt pḥm (23′) [--]⸢š⸣ [.] ⸢må⸣t . ỉqnủ (*Reverse*) (24′) årgmn . nqmd . mlk (25′) ủgr⸢t .⸣ d ybl . l špš (26′) ⸢m⸣lk . rb . bʿlh

---

(27′) ks . ḫrṣ . ktn . mỉt . pḥm (28′) ⸢m⸣ỉt . ỉqnỉ . l mlkt

(29′) ks . ḫrṣ . kt⸢n⸣ . mỉt . pḥm (30′) mỉt . ỉqnỉ ⸢.⸣ l ủṯryn

---

(31′) ks . ksp . ktn . mỉt . pḥm (32′) m⸢ỉ⸣t . ỉqnỉ .! l ⸢tp⸣nr

---

(33′) [kt]⸢n . m⸣ỉt pḥ⸢m⸣ (34′) [ ] ḫbrtn[r]

(35′) [pḥ]⸢m⸣ (36′) [ḫbrtn]⸢r⸣ ṯn

(37′) [ ] (38′) [ ] ỉ . l skn . [ ]

(39′) [ ]⸢m⸣ỉt pḥm . l ⸢š⸣[. . .]

(40′) [ ]⸢å-⸣[ ]⸢. --⸣[. . .]

. . . .

Translation

Obverse

(1′) ⸢-⸣[. . .] (2′) to[. . .] (3′) ARRIVED[. . .] (4′) the Su[n . . .] (5′) FALLEN [. . .]
(6′) And KING[. . . *Muk*]*ish* (7′) to [. . .] (8′) how [. . .] (9′) and to ⸢-⸣[. . .]
(10′) *Niqmaddu* [. . .] (11′) [-] with the Su[n, great king,] (12′) his lord, remained at peace. [The Sun,] (13′) great king, his lord, [the fidelity of] (14′) *Niqmaddu*, king of Ugari[t], (15′) did see.
(16′) *Ṯuppilulûma*, gr[eat] king, (17′) set up a covenant for *Niqmaddu* [. . .].
(18′) Here is the tribute that[*Ni*]*qmaddu* [will bring] (19′) to the Sun (goddess) of *Arinna*: tw[elve] minas, (20′) twenty shekels (of gold) and a [gob]let of gold (weighing) a mina; (21′) four *kutunu*-garments and a *ʾuṭbu*-garment; (22′) [fi]ve hundred (shekels' weight) of red-dyed cloth; (23′) [fiv]e hundred (shekels' weight) of blue-dyed cloth. (24′) (This is) the tribute of *Niqmaddu*, king of (25′) Ugarit, that he is to bring to the Sun, (26′) great king, his lord.
(27′) A goblet of gold, a *kutunu*-garment, one hundred (shekels' weight) of red-dyed cloth, (28′) one hundred (shekels' weight) of blue-dyed cloth, for the queen;
(29′) a goblet of gold, a *kutunu*-garment, one hundred (shekels' weight) of red-dyed cloth, (30′) one hundred (shekels' weight) of blue-dyed cloth, for the crown prince;
(31′) a goblet of silver, a *kutunu*-garment, one hundred (shekels' weight) of red-dyed cloth, (32′) one hundred (shekels' weight) of blue-dyed cloth, for the *Tupanuru*;
(33′) [a goblet of silver, a *kutu*]*nu*-garment, one hundred (shekels' weight) of red-dyed cloth, (34′) [one hundred (shekels' weight) of blue-dyed cloth, for] the *Ḫuburtanu*[*ru*];
(35′) [a goblet of silver, a *kutunu*-garment, one hundred (shekels' weight) of re]d[-dyed cloth], (36′) [one hundred (shekels' weight) of blue-dyed cloth, for the] second [*Ḫuburtanur*]*u*;
(37′) [a goblet of silver, a *kutunu*-garment, one hundred (shekels' weight) of red-dyed cloth,] (38′) [one hundred (shekels' weight) of blu]e-[dyed cloth], for the governor of [. . .];
(39′) [ ] one hundred (shekels' weight) of red-dyed cloth, for the ⸢Š⸣[. . .].
(40′) [ ]⸢ʾA-⸣[ ]⸢. --⸣[. . .]

. . . .

Vocalized Text

(1′) ⸢-⸣[. . .] (2′) ʿimma[. . .] (3′) MǴ[. . .] (4′) šap[š- . . .] (5′) qāla [. . .]
(6′) wa malku[. . . mugi]šḫi (7′) ʿimmānu [. . .] (8′) ʾêkaya [. . .] (9′) wa

lê⌈ . . .]
(10′) wa niqmaddu [. . .] (11′) [-] ˤimmānu šap[ši . . .] (12′) baˤlihu šalima [wa šapšu] (13′) malku rabbu baˤluhu [. . .] (14′) niqmaddi malki ʾugāri[t . . .] (15′) pahaya
(16′) wa ṯuppilulûma malku ra[bbu] (17′) maṣmatta lê niqmaddi [. . .] šāta (18′) halliniya ʾargamanu dū [yabilu ni]qmaddu (19′) lê šapši ʾarinna ṯinâ [ˤašrihu] manû (20′) ˤašrāma ṯiqlu kubda [kā]su manû ḫurāṣu (21′) wa ʾarbaˤu kutunātu wa ⌈ʾuṭ⌉bu (22′) [ḫami]šu miʾātu paḥmu (23′) [ḫami]šu miʾātu ʾiqnaʾu (24′) ʾargamanu niqmaddi malki (25′) ʾugārit dū yabilu lê šapši (26′) malki rabbi baˤlihu
(27′) kāsu ḫurāṣu kutunu miʾtu paḥmi (28′) miʾtu ʾiqnaʾi lê malkati
(29′) kāsu ḫurāṣu kutunu miʾtu paḥmi (30′) miʾtu ʾiqnaʾi lê ʾuṯriyani
(31′) kāsu kaspu kutunu miʾtu paḥmi (32′) miʾtu ʾiqnaʾi lê tupanuri
(33′) [kāsu kaspu kutu]nu miʾtu paḥmi (34′) [miʾtu ʾiqnaʾi lê] ḫuburtanu[ri]
(35′) [kāsu kaspu kutunu miʾtu paḥ]mi (36′) [miʾtu ʾiqnaʾi lê ḫuburtanu]ri ṯanî
(37′) [kāsu kaspu kutunu miʾtu paḥmi] (38′) [miʾtu ʾiqna]ʾi lê sākini [ ]
(39′) [ ]miʾtu paḥmi lê ⌈Š⌉[. . .]
(40′) [ ]⌈ʾA-⌉[ ]⌈. --⌉[. . .]
. . . .

Notes

General: the restorations indicated primarily in the translation are the result of comparison with several Akkadian texts of the same type (RS 17.227, etc.).
(6′) {[. . .]šḫ} restore {[. . . mg]šḫ}.
(12′) restore {[w špš]} at the end of the line.
(13′) a word expressing fidelity is to be restored at the end of the line.
(18′) restore {[ybl]} in the lacuna (see line 25′).
(19′) restore {[ˤšrh]} in the lacuna.
(21′) recent collation has shown the reading {⌈ủṭ⌉b}, a type of garment, to be likely.
(22′, 23′) restore {[ḫm]š} at the beginning of the line.
(23′, 28′–39′) {ỉqnủ} and {ỉqnỉ} show that the plural form /miʾātu/ is followed by the nominative, whereas the singular /miʾtu/ is followed by the genitive.
(31′–40′) the restorations indicated in the translation of lines 31′-38′ are based on the parallel texts in Akkadian; these texts do not, however, provide good parallels for the restoration of lines 39′-40′.

Text 37: A Real-Estate Transfer (RS 16.382)

Virolleaud 1957, text 8; *KTU* 3.5; Hawley and Pardee 2002–3.

Text

Obverse

Impression of dynastic seal (with syllabic inscription)
(1) l . ym . hnd (2) ˁmṯtmr . bn (3) nqmpˁ . ml⸢k⸣ (4) ủgrt . ytn (5) šd ⸢.⸣ kḏǵdl (6) d ⸢.⸣ š⸢tn .⸣ d . b šd (7) ⸢-mt⸣ [.] ⸢y⸣d . gth (*Lower edge*) (8) [-]⸢d⸣ [.] z⸢t⸣h ⸢.⸣ yd . (9) [-]rmh . yd (10) [-]lklh (*Reverse*) (11) ⸢w .⸣ ytn . nn (12) l ⸢.⸣ bˁln . bn . (13) kltn . w l (14) bnh . ˁ⸢d⸣ [.] ˁlm (15) šḥr . ṯl⸢ṯ⸣t (16) bnš bnšm . (17) l . yqḥnn . bd (18) bˁln . bn . kltn (19) w bd . bnh . ˁd (20) ˁlm . w ủnṯ ⸢.⸣ (21) ⸢ỉ⸣n [.] bh

---

(*Upper edge*) (22) [m(ỉ)š]⸢mn⸣ (23) [ˁmṯtmr .] b⸢n⸣ (*Obverse, above seal impression*) (24) [nqmpˁ . ml]⸢k⸣ (25) [ủgrt]

Translation

(1) On this day, (2) *ʿAmmiṯtamru*, son of (3) *Niqmêpaʿ*, king of (4) Ugarit, has given (5) the land of *Kuḏuǵadal*, (6) which was (previously) transferred (to him), which is situated in the fields of (7) ⸢-MT⸣, with its buildings, (8) [wi]th its olive orchard, with (9) its [vine]yard, with (10) [ever]ything pertaining to it— (11) (all) this he has given (12) to *Baʿlānu*, son of (13) *Kilitēnu*, and to (14) his sons forever. (15) In the future, (16) no member of the (royal) personnel (17) may take (this property) from the possession of (18) *Baʿlānu*, son of *Kilitēnu*, (19) nor from the possession of his sons for(20)ever. As for the *ʾunuṯṯu*-tax, (21) there is none on this (land).
(22) [Se]al of (23) [*ʿAmmiṯtamru*], son of (24) [*Niqmêpaʿ*, kin]g of (25) [Ugarit].

Vocalized Text

(1) lê yômi hannadī (2) ˁammiṯtamru binu (3) niqmêpaˁ malku (4) ʾugārit yatana (5) šadâ kuḏuǵadal (6) dā šutana dā bi šadî (7) ⸢-MT⸣ yada gittihu (8) [ya]da zêtihu yada (9) [ka]rmihu yada (10) [ku]lkulihu (11) wa yatānunnannu (12) lê baˁlīna bini (13) kilitēna wa lê (14) banīhu ˁadê ˁālami (15) šaḥra ṯalāṯata (16) bunušu bunušuma (17) lā yiqqaḥannannu bîdê (18) baˁlāna bini kilitēna (19) wa bîdê banīhu ˁadê (20) ˁālami wa ʾunuṯṯu (21) ʾênu bihu
(22) [ma(ʾ)ša]mānu (23) [ˁammiṯtamri] bini (24) [niqmêpaˁ mal]ki
(25) [ʾugārit]

Notes

(6) {štn} 3m.s. perfective, Šp-stem, √YTN.

(7) perhaps read {⸢hmt⸣} and identify this place name with the one attested once in syllabic script in the form {AN.ZA.GÀR um-ma-ti} (Nougayrol 1955: 80), which would indicate the vocalization /hummati/.

(8) restore {[y]⸢d⸣} in this series of terms referring to the components of the property.

(9) restore {[k]rmh}, for vineyards are often mentioned in the Akkadian contracts of this type and the term is found here below in Ugaritic (text 39:17, RS 94.2965).

(10) restore {[k]lklh} on the pattern of the Akkadian contracts, where a reference to "everything else" often appears at the end of the list of specific components (for example, {qa-du gáb-bi mi-me-šu} RS 16.250:9 [*PRU* III, p. 85]); the term is well preserved here below in text 39:18 (RS 94.2965).

(11) {ytn . nn} infinitive (/yatānunnannu/) or perfective (/yatanannannu/).

(16) {bnš bnšm} singular + singular + *m*-enclitic.

(22) {[m(ỉ)š]⸢mn⸣} the word for 'seal' is attested in three forms ({mỉšmn}, {måšmn}, and {mšmn}) and which of those possibilities is to be restored here is uncertain because the space available is about midway between what is expected for one of the longer or shorter forms.

Text 38: How *ˤAbdimilku* May Bequeath His Property (RS 94.2168)

Bordreuil and Pardee forthcoming: text 56.

Text

Obverse

(1) l . ym . hnd (2) l ⸢.⸣ pn . ˤmṯtmr (3) bn . nqmpˤ (4) mlk . ủgrt

---

(5) bhtm . šdm . d . ytn (6) mlk l . ˤbdmlk (7) w . l . bnh . ủ . l (8) bn . bt . mlk (9) ủ . l . bn . ṣrdth (10) ủ . l . bn . åmhth

---

(11) d . ỉhb . ˤbdmlk (12) b . bnh . l . bnh . hwt (13) ytn . ˤbdmlk (14) bhth . šdh (15) ⸢m⸣rˤh (*Lower edge*)

---

(16) ⸢w⸣ . ˤbdmlk (17) bnh . km (*Reverse*) (18) lbh . yškn . l⸢h⸣m (19) hm . lb . ˤbdmlk (20) bhl . bnh . w . km (21) lbh . ybhl . hm

---

(22) hm . lbh . bhl (23) bnh bn . bt . mlk (24) w . km . lbh (25) ybhl . hm . w . hm (26) lbh . bhl . bn . ṣrdth (27) ủ . bn . åmhth (28) w . km . lbh (29) ybhl . hm

Translation

(1) On this day, (2) in the presence of *ʿAmmiṯtamru*, (3) son of *Niqmêpaʿ*, (4) king of Ugarit (the following decision was handed down):
(5) (As regards) the houses (and) the fields that the king (6) has given to *ʿAbdimilku* (7) and to his sons, whether to (8) sons by the daughter of the king, (9) or to sons by his free-born wives, (10) or to sons by his female servants,
(11) the one whom *ʿAbdimilki* will prefer (12) among his sons, to that son (13) *ʿAbdimilku* may give (14) his houses, his fields, (15) and his pasture lands.
(16) Moreover *ʿAbdimilku*, (as regards) (17) his sons, as (18) he wishes he may dispose (of his property) to them. (19) If *ʿAbdimilku* wishes (20) to dismiss his sons, as he wishes (21) he may dismiss them.
(22) If he wishes to dismiss (23) his sons by the daughter of the king, (24) as he wishes (25) he may dismiss them. If (26) he wishes to dismiss his sons by his free-born wives (27) or his sons by his female servants, (28) as he wishes (29) he may dismiss them.

Vocalized Text

(1) lê yômi hannadī (2) lê panî ʿammiṯtamri (3) bini niqmêpaʿ (4) malki ʾugārit
(5) bahatūma šadûma dū yatana (6) malku lê ʿabdimilki (7) wa lê banīhu ʾô lê (8) banī bitti malki (9) ʾô lê banī ṣaradātihu (10) ʾô lê banī ʾamahātihu
(11) dā ʾihhaba ʿabdimilku (12) bi banīhu lê binihu huwati (13) yatinu ʿabdimilku (14) bahatīhu šadîhu (15) marʿîhu
(16) wa ʿabdimilku (17) banīhu kama (18) libbihu yašakkinu lêhumu
(19) himma libbu ʿabdimilki (20) bahala banīhu wa kama (21) libbihu yibhaluhumu
(22) himma libbuhu bahala (23) banīhu banī bitti malki (24) wa kama libbihu (25) yibhaluhumu wa himma (26) libbuhu bahala banī ṣaradātihu (27) ʾô banī ʾamahātihu (28) wa kama libbihu (29) yibhaluhumu

Notes

(10–11) the horizontal dividing line marks the passage from the protasis to the apodosis.

(11) {ỉhb} the writing with {ỉ} shows the base of the D-stem to have been /qittala/ (or that there was regressive vowel harmony in the G-stem /ʾahiba/ → /ʾihiba/, less likely because such vowel harmony usually occurs when the second vowel is long).

(20 *et passim*) BHL, 'dismiss, set free', used to express the possibility open to the father of dismissing one or more of his sons, usually with a gift, while preferring another as the principal heir to the paternal estate (the

term used in the Akkadian of Ugarit to describe the process is *zukkû*, lit., 'to purify, i.e., to declare free of further obligations', while *zakû*, lit., 'to be pure', is used to describe the state of the sons concerning whom decisions of this type have been carried out).

Text 39: *Yabninu* Acquires Real Estate (RS 94.2965)

Bordreuil and Pardee forthcoming: text 57.

Text

Obverse

(1) ǵr . ảgny (2) d . ptḥ . ybnn (3) yd . ʿpsh (4) yd . nḫlh (5) yd . ǵrh (6) w . ʿpŝh (7) ⸢n⸣pk . kwr (8) d . hlk . b . nḫl (9) w . ʿpŝ . bʿl (10) ảlmg (*Lower edge*) (11) bnš . l . yqḥ (12) ʿpsm . hnmt (*Reverse*) (13) bd . ybnn (14) ʿd . ⸢ʿl⸣m

---

(15) w . gt . ảrt (16) yd . šdh (17) yd . krmh (18) yd . klklh

---

(19) w . y . bnn (20) b . šdm . hnmt (21) ủnṯ . mhkm (22) l . ybl (*Upper edge*) (23) ủnṯm . bth (24) ybl

Translation

(1) Regarding the "mountain" of *ʾAganāyu* (2) that *Yabninu* opened up, (3) with its boundary stones, (4) its water course, (5) its upland section: (6) its boundaries are (7) the spring of KWR (8) which runs into the watercourse (9) and the boundary with the owners of (10) ʾALMG-trees; (11) no member of the (royal) personnel may remove (12) these boundary stones (that is, the property that they mark off) (13) from the possession of *Yabninu* (14) forever.

(15) And the farming installation (associated with the village) of *ʾArutu*, (16) with its fields, (17) with its vineyards, (18) with everything pertaining to it (has also become the property of *Yabninu*).

(19) *Yabninu* (20) for these fields (21) is not required to pay (22) any *ʾunuṯṯu*-tax. (23) Nevertheless (for) his (principal) house (24) he must continue to pay the *ʾunuṯṯu*-tax.

Vocalized Text

(1) ǵūru ʾaganāyi (2) dū pataḥa yabninu (3) yada ʿupasīhu (4) yada naḫlihu (5) yada ǵūrihu (6) wa ʿupaŝūhu (7) napku KWR (8) dū halaka bi naḫli (9) wa ʿupaŝū baʿalī (10) ʾalmuggi (11) bunušu lā yiqqaḥu (12) ʿupasīma hannamati (13) bîdê yabninu (14) ʿadê ʿālami

(15) wa gittu ʾaruti (16) yada šadîha (17) yada karamīha (18) yada kulkuliha

(19) wa yabninu (20) bi šadîma hannamati (21) ʾunuṯṯa mahakama (22) lā yabilu (23) ʾunuṯṯama bêtihu (24) yabilu

Notes

19) {y . bnn} the word-divider is an error.

20) {šdm} apparently refers to the second property only because no "fields" were mentioned in connection with the first.

23) {ủnṯm} the *-m* is enclitic and marks the contrast between this stipulation and the preceding one.

Text 40: A *marziḥu*-Contract (RS [Varia 14])

Miller 1971; *KTU* 3.9; Friedman 1979–80.

Text

Obverse

(1) mrzḥ

---

(2) d qny (3) šmmn (4) b . btw

---

(5) w št . ỉbsn (6) lwm . wm . ảg(7)rškm . (8) b . bty (9) ksp ḫmšm (*Lower edge*) (10) ⸢ỉ⸣sʿ (*Reverse*) (11) w šm.mn (12) rb . ảl . ydd (13) mt . mrzḥ (14) w yrgm . l (15) šmmn . tn . (16) ksp . ṯql d ʿmnk (17) ṯqlm . ysʿ (18) ypḥ . ỉḫršp (19) bn . ủḏrnn (20) w . ʿbdn (*Upper edge*) (21) bn . sgld

Translation

(1) *Marziḥu*-association
(2) founded by (3) *Šamumānu* (4) in his house.
(5) He has set aside his storeroom (6) for them. "If I (7) expel you (8) from my house, (9) fifty (shekels) of silver (10) I must pay." (11) *Šamumānu* (12) is the president. No member (13) of the *marziḥu* may arise (14) and say to (15) *Šamumānu*: "Give (back) (16) the shekel of silver that you're holding." (17) (Should this happen, the member) must pay two shekels (of silver). (18) Witness(es): *ʾIḫîrašap*, (19) son of *ʾUḏurnana*, (20) and *ʿAbdīnu*, (21) son of *Sigilda*.

Vocalized Text

(1) marziḥu
(2) dū qanaya (3) šamumānu (4) bi bêtiwu (or: bêtihu !)
(5) wa šāta ʾibūsāna (6) lêwumu (or: lêhu!mu) wimma (or: wa ‹ʾi›mma) ʾag(7)rušukumu (8) bi bêtiya (9) kaspa ḫamišīma (10) ʾissaʿu (11) wa šamumānu (12) rabbu ʾal yiddad (13) mutu marziḥi (14) wa yargum lê (15) šamumānu tin (16) kaspa ṯiqla dā ʿimmānuka (17) ṯiqlêma yissaʿu (18) yāpiḥu ʾiḫîrašap (19) binu ʾuḏurnana (20) wa ʿabdīnu (21) binu sigilda

Notes

(4) {btw} either phonetic writing (/bêtiwu/ ← /bêtihu/) or scribal error for {bth}.

(5) {št} probably 3m.s. (one would expect the 1c.s. form to be written {štt} for /šātāti/).

(6) {lwm} either phonetic writing (/lêwumu/ ← /lêhumu/) or scribal error for {lhm} 'to them' (if taken as an error for {lkm}, 'to you', the sentence would be in the form of direct speech, unlikely for the reason indicated in the previous note); {wm} either phonetic writing (/wimma/ ← /waʾimma/ or /wahimma/) or scribal error for {whm/wỉm}.

(10) {ỉsʿ} 1c.s. imperfective, G-stem, √NSʿ.

(11) {šm . mn} the word-divider is an error.

(12) {ydd} 3m.s. jussive, N-stem, √DD.

(18) {ỉḫršp} the first vowel of this personal name has assimilated by vowel harmony to the second (/ʾaḫî/ → /ʾiḫî/) as may occur also in the common noun (see above, text 31, RS 94.2406:32).

VII. Administrative Texts

Text 41: Wine for Royal Sacrificial Rites (RS 19.015)

Virolleaud 1965: text 4; *KTU* 1.91; Pardee 2000a: 489–519.

	Text	***Translation***
Obverse		
(1)	yn . d . ykl . bd . ⸢r⸣[. . .]	Wine that is to be consumed under the supervision of [. . .]
(2)	b . dbḥ . mlk ———[. . .]	during the royal sacrificial rites:
(3)	dbḥ ṣpn	the sacrifices (for the gods of Mount) *Ṣapunu*;
(4)	⸢t⸣zǵm	the TZǴ-sacrifices;
(5)	⸢ỉ?⸣lỉb	(the sacrifices for) *ʾIluʾibî*;
(6)	⸢ỉ?⸣l bldn	(the sacrifices for) the Gods-of-the-Land;
(7)	[p]dry . bt . mlk	(the sacrifices for) *Pidray* (in) the royal palace;
(8)	[-]lp . ỉzr	(the sacrifices for/of) [-]LP ʾIZR;
(9)	[-]rz	(the sacrifices for/of) [-]RZ;
(10)	k . tʿrb . ʿṯtrt . šd . bt ⸢. m⸣lk	(the sacrifices for) when *ʿAṯtaru-Šadî* enters the royal palace;
(11)	k . tʿrbn . ršpm . bt . mlk	(the sacrifices for) when the *Rašapūma* enter the royal palace;
(12)	ḫlủ . dg	(the sacrifices for/of) ḪLʾU DG;
(13)	ḥdṯm	(the sacrifices of) the new moons;
(14)	dbḥ . bʿl----. k . tdd . bʿlt . bhtm	the sacrifices for *Baʿlu*; (the sacrifices for) when *Baʿlatu-Bahatīma* arises;
(15)	b . ǵb . ršp . ṣbỉ	(the sacrifices) in the sacrificial pit of *Rašap Ṣabaʾi*;
(16)	[ ]⸢m⸣m	[ ]⸢M⸣M;
Lower edge		
(17)	[ ]⸢-⸣ . ỉln	[ ]⸢-.⸣ ʾILN;
(18)	[ ] . ṣmd [.] r[-]⸢š⸣pd⸢--⸣[. . .]	[ ] . ṢMD [.] R[-]⸢Š⸣PD⸢--⸣[. . .];
(19)	[ ]⸢-⸣	[ ]⸢-⸣;
(20)	[-]⸢-⸣[--]ʿlt	[-]⸢-⸣[--]ʿLT.

Reverse

(21)	lb⸢n⸣m —— [.] ˁšr . yn	*Labnuma*: ten (*kaddu*-measures of) wine,
(22)	ḫlb . gngnt . ṯlṯ . y[n]	*Ḫalbu Ganganati*: three (*kaddu*-measures of) wine,
(23)	bṣr . ˁšr . yn	*Baṣiru*: ten (*kaddu*-measures of) wine,
(24)	nnủ —— [.] ảrbˁ . yn	*Nanuʾu*: four (*kaddu*-measures of) wine,
(25)	šql ——— ṯlṯ . yn	*Šuqalu*: three (*kaddu*-measures of) wine,
(26)	šmny —— . kdm . yn	*Šamnāyu*: two *kaddu*-measures of wine,
(27)	šmgy —— . kd . yn	*Šammigāyu*: one *kaddu* of wine;
(28)	hzp ——— . tšˁ . yn	*Hizpu*: nine (*kaddu*-measures) of wine;
(29)	⸢b⸣ỉr ———. ˁšr [.] ⸢mṣ⸣[b]⸢-⸣m ḥsp	*Biʾiru*: ten (*kaddu*-measures of) *mṣb*-wine, X *kaddu*-measures of *ḥsp*-wine;
(30)	⸢ḫ⸣pty —— . kdm ⸢. mṣ⸣[b . . .]	*Ḫupatāyu*: two *kaddu*-measures of *mṣb*-wine . . . ;
(31)	⸢ả⸣gm —— . ảrbˁ ⸢.⸣ m⸢ṣ⸣[b . . .]	*ʾAgimu*: four (*kaddu*-measures of) *mṣb*-wine . . . ;
(32)	šrš ——— . šbˁ . mṣb[. . .]	*Šurašu*: seven (*kaddu*-measures of) *mṣb*-wine . . . ;
(33)	rqd ——— . ṯlṯ . mṣb . ⸢w⸣ . ⸢-⸣[. . .]	*Raqdu*: three (*kaddu*-measures of) *mṣb*-wine and . . . ;
(34)	ủḫnp —— . ṯṯ — . mṣb	*ʾUḫnappu*: six (*kaddu*-measures of) *mṣb*-wine.
(35)	tgmr . ⸢y⸣n . mṣb . š[. . .]	Total: wine (and) *mṣb*-wine: seventy-four (*kaddu*-measures);
(36)	w . ḥs[p .] ṯn . kbd[. . .]	*ḥsp*-wine: X-TENS and two (*kaddu*-measures).

Vocalized Text

(1) yênu dū yiklû bîdê ⸢R⸣[. . .] (2) bi dabaḥī malki
(3) dabḥu ṣapuni (4) tazuǵǵūma (5) ʾiluʾibî (6) ʾilū bildāni (7) [pi]dray bêta malki (8) [-]LP ʾIZR (9) [-]RZ (10) kī tiˁrabu ˁaṯtartu šadî bêta malki (11) kī tiˁrabūna rašapūma bêta malki (12) ḪLʾU DG (13) ḥudaṭūma (14) dabḥu baˁli---- kī tiddādu baˁlatu bahatīma (15) bi ǵabbi rašap ṣabaʾi (16) [ ]⸢M⸣M (17) [ ]⸢-⸣ ʾILN (18) [ ] ṢMD[-]R[-]⸢Š⸣PD⸢--⸣[. . .] (19) [ ]⸢-⸣ (20) [-]⸢-⸣[--]ˁLT
(21) labnuma ˁašru yênu (22) ḫalbu ganganati ṯalātu yê[nu] (23) baṣiru ˁašru yênu (24) nanuʾu ʾarbaˁu yênu (25) šuqalu ṯalāṯu yênu (26) šamnāyu kaddāma yênu (27) šammigāyu kaddu yênu (28) hizpu tišˁu yênu (29) biʾiru ˁašru ⸢MṢ⸣[B]⸢-⸣M ḤSP (30) ḫupatāyu kaddāma ⸢MṢ⸣[B . . .] (31) ʾagimu ʾarbaˁu M⸢Ṣ⸣[B . . .] (32) šurašu šabˁu MṢB [. . .] (33) raqdu ṯalāṯu MṢB wa

[. . .] (34) ʾuḫnappu ṯiṯṯu MṢB
(35) tagmaru yêni MṢB ša[bʿūma ʾarbaʿu kubda] (36) wa ḪS[P] ṯinâ kubda [. . .]

Notes

(2) lit., 'sacrifices of the king'—*dbḥ* refers to the sacrifices in the narrow sense of the word and to the accompanying feast.

(3–20) each entry refers to a royal sacrificial rite.

(21–34) list of the towns that sent wine and the type and quantity from each.

(35) working from the numbers in the preceding list, it appears necessary to restore {š[bʿm]} + {[årbʿ]} + {[kbd]}, though the order of the last two terms is uncertain since *kbd* may either precede or follow the second element of a compound number.

Text 42: An Account Text for *Yabninu* (RS 15.062)

Virolleaud 1957: text 127; *KTU* 4.158; Pardee 2000b: 24–41.

Text

Obverse

(1) ṯṯ . måt . ksp (2) ḥṯbn . ybnn

---

(3) årbʿm . l . mỉt . šmn (4) årbʿm . l . mỉt . tỉšr (5) ṯṯ . ṯṯ . b . ṯql . ṯlṯt . l . ʿšrm . ksphm (6) ššstm . b . šbʿm (7) ṯlṯ . måt . trm . b . ʿšrt (8) mỉt . ådrm . b . ʿšrt (9) ʿšr . ydt . b . ʿšrt (10) ḫmš . kkrm . ṣml⌜l⌝ (*Lower edge*) (11) ʿšrt . ksph (12) ḫmš . kkr . qnm (13) ṯlṯt . w . ṯlṯt . ksph (*Reverse*) (14) årbʿ . kkr (15) ålgbṯ . årbʿt (16) ksph (17) kkr . šʿrt (18) šbʿt . ksph

---

(19) ḫmš . mqdm . d nyn (20) b . ṯql . dprn . åḥd (21) b . ṯql (22) ḫmšm . ʿrgz . b . ḫmšt

Translation

(1) Six hundred (shekels) of silver: (2) the *Yabninu* account:
(3) one hundred and forty (pieces) of pine-wood, (4) one hundred forty (pieces) of cypress-wood, (5) six of each for (one) shekel (so that) their (total price in) silver is twenty-three (shekels) of silver; (6) two mares for seventy (shekels each); (7) three hundred doves for ten (shekels per hundred); (8) one hundred pins (?) for ten (shekels); (9) ten "handles" for ten (shekels each); (10) five talents (of the aromatic plant) *ṣumlalû*, (11) its (total price in silver being) ten (shekels); (12) five talents of reeds, (13) three (shekels per talent for one kind) and three (shekels per talent for another kind being) the (price of each talent in) silver; (14) four talents (15) of (local) green stone (?) four

(shekels) (16) (being) its (total price in) silver; (17) (one) talent of wool, (18) seven (shekels) (being) its (total price in) silver;
(19) five MQDM DNYN (20) for (one) shekel (per piece); one (piece) of juniper-wood (21) for (one) shekel; (22) fifty (pieces) of walnut-wood for five (shekels per piece).

Vocalized Text

(1) ṯiṯṯu miʾāti kaspu (2) ḥiṯbānu yabnini
(3) ʾarbaʿūma lê miʾti šamnu (4) ʾarbaʿūma lê miʾti tiʾiššaru (5) ṯiṯṯu ṯiṯṯu bi ṯiqli ṯalāṯatu lê ʿašrêma kaspuhumā (6) s̀ūsatāma bi šabʿīma (7) ṯalāṯtu miʾāti turrūma bi ʿašrati (8) miʾtu ʾadarūma bi ʿašrati (9) ʿašru yadātu bi ʿašrati
(10) ḫamišu kakkarūma ṣumlalû (11) ʿašratu kaspuhu (12) ḫamišu kakkarū qanîma (13) ṯalāṯatu wa ṯalāṯatu kaspuhu (14) ʾarbaʿu kakkarū (15) ʾalgabaṯi ʾarbaʿatu (16) kaspuhu (17) kakkaru šaʿarti (18) šabʿatu kaspuha
(19) ḫamišu MQDM D NYN (20) bi ṯiqli diprānu ʾaḥḥadu (21) bi ṯiqli
(22) ḫamišūma ʿirguzu bi ḫamišati

Notes

(3 *et passim*) the unit of sale of the various items mentioned in this text is only indicated in the case of the talent (*kkr*).

(3–5) the phrase *ṯṯ ṯṯ* is to be taken as indicating that the pine and cypress pieces were saplings exchanged in bundles of six.

(5, 6) *ksp* + pronominal suffix indicates the total price for a given entry while *b* followed by a figure indicates the unit price.

(8) these pins (if that is indeed the meaning of the word) were, like doves (line 7), sold by the hundred.

(12–13) as is shown by the singular pronominal suffix on *ksp*, referring to the talent rather than to *qnm*, which is a plural, and the repetition of the number (*ṯlṯt w ṯlṯt*), the price formula here is mixed, apparently reflecting the presence in this lot of several kinds of reeds: this peculiar way of stating the price, by the total price of a talent of each type of reed, leads to the conclusion that the total silver equivalence for these reeds was fifteen shekels.

Text 43: An Account Text for Bronzeworkers (RS 18.024)

Virolleaud 1965: text 101; *KTU* 4.337; Pardee 2000b: 41–56.

Text

Obverse

(1) ⸢s⸣pr . ḥṯbn . sbrdnm

(2) ḫmš- . kkrm . ảlp- ⸢.⸣ kb⸢d⸣ (3) ṯlṯ . l . nskm . bỉrtym (4) bd . ủrtn . w . ṯṯ . mảt . brr (5) b . ṯmnym . ksp ṯlṯt . kbd

---

(6) ḫmš . ảlp . ṯlṯ . l . ḫlby (7) bd . tlmỉ . b . ʿšrm . ḫmšt (8) kbd . ksp

---

(9) kkrm . šʿrt . štt . bd . gg[. . .] (10) b . ʿšrt . ksp

---

(11) ṯlṯ . ủṭbm . bd . ảlḫn . b . ʿšr⸢t⸣ [.] ⸢k⸣sp

---

(12) rṭ . l . ql . d . ybl . prd .(*Lower edge*) (13) b . ṯql . w . nṣp . ksp

---

(14) ṯmn . lbšm . w . mšlt (15) l . ủdmym . b . ṯmnt . ʿšrt . ks⸢p⸣

(*Reverse*) (16) šbʿm . lbš . d . ʿrb . bt . mlk (17) b . mỉt . ḫmšt . kbd . ksp

---

(18) ṯlṯ . ktnt . bd . ản⸢r⸣my (19) b . ʿšrt . ksp . b . ả⸢r⸣

---

(20) ṯqlm . ḫrṣ . b . ṯmnt . ksp

---

(21) ʿšrt . ks⸢p⸣ . b . ảlp . ⸢b⸣d . ⸢b⸣n . m[. . .]

---

(22) tšʿ . ṣỉn . b . tšʿt . ksp

---

(23) mšlt . b . ṯql . ksp

---

(24) kdwṯ . l . grgyn . b . ṯq⸢l⸣[. ksp]

---

(25) ḫmšm . šmt . b . ṯq⸢l⸣[. ksp]

---

(26) ⸢k⸣kr . w . ⸢ml⸣tḥ . tyt . ⸢-⸣[. . .] (27) [b .] šbʿ[t . w .] ⸢n⸣ṣp . ksp

---

(*Upper edge*) (28) [tg]⸢m⸣r . ⸢k⸣[sp .] ṯlṯ . mảt

Translation

(1) Bronzeworkers' account text:
(2) five talents, one thousand (shekels) (3) of copper for the founders of *Biʾirātu*, (4) entrusted to *ʾUrtēnu*, and six hundred (shekels) of tin, (5) for eighty-three (shekels) of silver;
(6) five thousand (shekels) of copper for a man from (the town of) *Ḫalbu*, (7) entrusted to *Talmiʾu*, for twenty-five (shekels) (8) of silver;
(9) two talents of wool cloth, entrusted to GG[. . .], (10) for ten (shekels) of silver;

(11) three *ʾuṭbu*-garments, entrusted to *ʾAliḫanni*, for ten (shekels) of silver;
(12) (one) *rīṭu*-garment, for the messenger who travels on mule-back,
(13) for one and a half shekels of silver;
(14) eight *lubūšu*-garments and (one) *mašallatu*-garment, (15) for persons from (the town of) *ʾUdmu*, for eighteen (shekels) of silver;
(16) seventy *lubūšu*-garments, which were delivered to the royal palace,
(17) for one hundred and five (shekels) of silver;
(18) three *kutunu*-garments, entrusted to *ʾAnnarummiya*, (19) for ten (shekels) of silver, (*ʾAnnarummiya* being established) in (the town of) *ʾAru*;
(20) two shekels of gold for eight (shekels) of silver;
(21) ten (shekels) of silver for (one) male bovid, (which was) entrusted to *bn m*[. . .];
(22) nine (heads) of caprovids for nine (shekels) of silver;
(23) (one) *mašallatu*-garment for (one) shekel of silver;
(24) (one *kiddawaṯṯu*-garment, for *Girgiyannu*, for (one) shekel [of silver];
(25) fifty ropes (or straps) for (one) shekel [of silver];
(26) (one) talent and one *maltaḥu*-measure of the *asa foetida*-plant[. . .]
(27) [for] sev[en (shekels) and a h]alf of silver;
(28) [tot]al si[lver]: three hundred (shekels).

Vocalized Text

(1) sipru ḥiṯbāni sabardennīma
(2) ḫamišu kakkarūma ʾalpu kubda (3) ṯalṯu lê nāsikīma biʾirātiyyīma
(4) bîdê ʾurtēna wa ṯiṯṯu miʾāti barūru (5) bi ṯamāniyīma kaspi ṯalāṯati kubda
(6) ḫamišu ʾalpu ṯalṯu lê ḫalbiyyi (7) bîdê talmiʾi bi ʿašrêma ḫamišati
(8) kubda kaspi
(9) kakkarāma šaʿartu šatûtu bîdê GG[. . .] (10) bi ʿašrati kaspi
(11) ṯalāṯu ʾuṭbūma bîdê ʾaliḫanni bi ʿašrati kaspi
(12) rīṭu lê qāli dī yabala pirdu (13) bi ṯiqli wa naṣpi kaspi
(14) ṯamānû lubūšūma wa mašallatu (15) lê ʾudmiyyīma bi ṯamānati ʿašrati kaspi
(16) šabʿūma lubūšu dū ʿarabū bêta malki (17) bi miʾti ḫamišati kubda kaspi
(18) ṯalāṯu kutunātu bîdê ʾannarummiya (19) bi ʿašrati kaspi bi ʾari
(20) ṯiqlāma ḫurāṣu bi ṯamānati kaspi
(21) ʿašratu kaspu bi ʾalpi bîdê bini M[. . .]
(22) tišʿu ṣaʾnu bi tišʿati kaspi
(23) mašallatu bi ṯiqli kaspi
(24) kiddawaṯṯu lê girgiyanni bi ṯiqli [kaspi]
(25) ḫamišūma šummattu bi ṯiqli [kaspi]
(26) kakkaru wa maltaḥu tiyātu [. . .] (27) [bi] šabʿa[ti wa] naṣpi kaspi
(28) [tag]maru ka[spi] ṯalāṯu miʾāti

Note

(12) {d ybl prd} lit., 'whom a mule bears'.

Text 44: A Ration List for Royal Workers (RS 19.016)

Virolleaud 1965: text 11; *KTU* 4.609; Pardee 1999: 30–58.

	Text	***Translation***
	Obverse	
(1)	spr . ḫpr . bnš mlk . b yrḫ ỉṯ⸢t⸣[bnm]	Ration text of the royal personnel (in service) during the month of ʾIṮTBNM.
(2)	ršpảb . rb ʿšrt . mryn	*Rašapʾabû*, decurion, (and his men:) *Maryānu*,
(3)	pǵḏn . ỉlbʿl . krwn . lbn . ʿdn	*Puǵiḏenni*, *ʾIlîbaʿlu*, *Kurwānu*, *Labnu*, *ʿAdânu*,
(4)	ḫyrn . mdṯ	*Ḫiyyārānu*, MDṮ.
(5)	šmʿn . rb ʿšrt . kkln . ʿbd . ảbṣn	*Šamʿānu*, decurion, (and his men:) *Kukulanu*, *ʿAbdu*, *ʾAbîṣanu*,
(6)	šdyn . ủnn . dqn	*Šaduyānu*, *ʾUnenna*, *Diqnu*.
(7)	ʿbdʿnt . rb ʿšrt . mnḫm . ṯbʿm . sḫ⸢r⸣ . ʿzn . ỉlhd	*ʿAbdiʿanatu*, decurion, (and his men:) *Munaḫḫimu*, *Ṯubʿammu*, *Saḫuru*, *ʿUzzīnu*, *ʾIlîhaddu*.
(8)	bnỉl . rb ʿšrt . lkn . ypʿn . ṯ[ ]	*Biniʾilu*, decurion, (and his men:) *Lukanu*, *Yapʿānu*, Ṯ[. . .].
(9)	yṣḥm . bd . ủbn . krwn . tǵd . ⸢m⸣nḥm	YṢḤM under *ʾUbinu*: *Kurwānu*, *Tēǵida*, *Munaḥḥimu*.
(10)	ʿpṯrm . šmʿ rgm . skn . qrt . ---	ʿPṮRM, "who listens to the word of" the prefect of the city.
(11)	ḥgbn . šmʿ . skn . qrt	*Ḥagbānu*, "who listens to ‹ the word of›?" the prefect of the city.
(12)	nǵr krm . ʿbdảdt . bʿln . ypʿmlk	Vineyard guards: *ʿAbdiʾadattu*, *Baʿlānu*, *Yapaʿamilku*.
(13)	ṯǵrm . mnḥm . klyn . ʿdršp . ǵlmn	Doormen: *Munaḥḥimu*, *Kiliyanu*, *ʿAdîrašapu*, *Ǵalmānu*,

(14)	[å]⸢b⸣ǵl . ṣṣn . ǵrn	*ʾAbîǵilu*, *Ṣīṣānu*, *Ǵūrānu*.
(15)	šỉb . mqdšt . ʿdmlk . ṯṯpḥ . mrṭn	Drawers of water for the sanctuaries: *ʿAdîmilku*, ṮṮPḤ, *Marṭānu*.
(16)	ḫḏǵlm . ỉ [ ]n . pbn . nḏbn . sbd	Arrow-makers: ʾI[ ]N, *Pabnu*, NḎBN, SBD.
(17)	šrm . ṯ[ ]⸢-⸣ . gpn	Singers: Ṯ[ ]⸢-⸣, *Gupanu*.
(18)	ḥrš ⸢b⸣[htm .]⸢-⸣[-]⸢-⸣n . ʿbdyrḫ . ḥdṯn . yṯr	House-builders: [ ]N, *ʿAbdiyariḫu*, *Ḥudṯānu*, *Yaṯru*,
(19)	ådbʿl[ ]ḥdṯn . yḥmn . bnỉl	*ʾAdîbaʿlu*, [ ], *Ḥudṯānu*, *Yaḥminu*, *Biniʾilu*.
(20)	ʿdn . w . ỉldgn . ḥṭbm	*ʿAdânu* and *ʾIlîdaganu*: wood-cutters.
(21)	tdǵlm . ỉln . bʿ⸢l⸣n . ⸢k⸣lḏy	TDǴLM: *ʾIlānu*, *Baʿlānu*, *Kiliḏēyu*.
(22)	tdn . ṣrǵ[ ]⸢-⸣t . ʿzn . mtn . å[--]⸢m⸣g	TDN ṢRǴ[:]T, *ʿUzzīnu*, *Mattēnu*, ʾA[ ]⸢M⸣G
(23)	ḥrš qṭn[ ]dqn . bʿln	Makers of "small objects": [ ], *Diqnu*, *Baʿlānu*,
(24)	ǵltn . ʿbd . ⸢-⸣[ ]⸢-⸣n	*Ǵaltēnu*, *ʿAbdu*, ⸢-⸣[ ]N.
(25)	nsk . ḥḏm . klyn[.] ⸢-⸣[-]qn . ʿbdỉlt . btl	Casters of arrowheads: *Kiliyanu*, ⸢-⸣[-]QN, *ʿAbdiʾilatu*, *Batūlu*,
(26)	ånnmn . ʿdy . klby . dqn	*ʾAnanimennu*, *ʿAdāyu*, *Kalbiya*, *Diqnu*.
(27)	ḥrṯm . ḥgbn . ʿdn . ynḥm[.]⸢-⸣	Plowmen: *Ḥagbānu*, *ʿAdânu*, *Yanḥamu*, [ ]⸢-⸣.
(28)	ḥrš . mrkbt . ʿz⸢n⸣ [.] ⸢b⸣ʿln . ṯ⸢b⸣[ ]⸢p⸣ . ⸢b⸣nbḏ [.] årtn	Chariot-makers: *ʿUzzīnu*, *Baʿlānu*, ṮB[ ]⸢P⸣, ⸢B⸣NBḎ, *ʾArtēnu*.

Lower edge

(29)	[-]⸢k⸣mm . klby . kl[-]⸢y⸣ . dqn[. . .]	[-]KMM: *Kalbiya*, KL[-]Y, *Diqnu* [ ],
(30)	⸢ủ⸣ntn . årtn . bd ⸢.⸣ nr⸢-⸣ [. . .]	*ʾUntēnu*, *ʾArtēnu* under NR⸢-⸣[ ],
(31)	ʿzn . w ymdšr . bd . ånsny	*ʿUzzīnu* and *Yamudšarru* under ʾANSNY.

Reverse

(32)	nsk . ks⸢p⸣ [.] ⸢t⸣mrtn . kṯrmlk	Silversmiths: *Tamartēnu*, *Kôṯarmalku*,
(33)	yḥmn . ảḫm⸢l⸣k . ʿbdrpủ . ảdn [.] ⸢ṯ--(-)⸣	*Yaḥminu*, *ʾAḫîmilku*, *ʿAbdirapaʾu*, *ʾAdānu*, Ṯ⸢--(-)⸣
(34)	bdn ⸢.⸣ qln . mtn . ydln	*Badunu*, QLN, *Mattēnu*, *Yadlinu*.
	———	
(35)	bʿl ⸢ʿ⸣dtt . tlgn . ytn	Makers of ⸢ʿ⸣DTT: TLGN, *Yatanu*.
	———	
(36)	bʿl tǵpṯm . krwn . ỉlšn . ảgyn	Makers of TǴPṮM: *Kurwānu*, *ʾIlišānu*, *ʾAgiyanu*.
	———	
(37)	mnn . šr . ủgrt . ḏkr . yṣr	*Muninu*, singer of Ugarit. *Ḏakaru*, potter.
	———	
(38)	tgǵln . ḫmš . ddm	*Taguǵlinu*: five *dūdu*-measures.
	———	
(39)	[-(-)]⸢-r⸣ . ḫmš . ddm	[-]⸢-R⸣: five *dūdu*-measures.
	———	
(40)	[ ]⸢y⸣[. . .]	[ ]⸢Y⸣[. . .]
	[———]	
(41)	[ ]	
	[———]	
(42)	[ ]lhm	[ ]LHM
	[———]	
(43)	[ ]	
	[———]	
(44)	[ ]	
	[———]	
(45)	[ ]⸢-⸣n	[ ]⸢-⸣N
	[———]	
(46)	[ ]	
	[———]	
(47)	[ ]	
	[———]	
(48)	[ ]dd ⸢m⸣[ ]	[X] *dūdu*-measures.
	[———]	

Left edge

(49)	ṯṯ . l . ʿšrm . bn[š mlk . -] . ḫzr . lqḥ . ḥ⸢p⸣[r]	Twenty-six (types of) royal personnel[ ] (who are) in service ? (and who) have received rations.

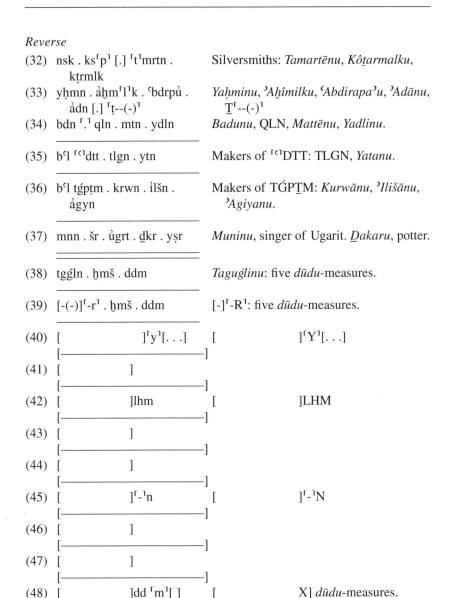

(50) ˤšt . ˤšrh . bn[š mlk . - .] ẖzr . Eleven (persons belonging to) the royal personnel [ ] (who are) in service ?
(51) bˤl . šd (and who are) land owners.

Notes

General remark: the vocalized text of the introduction and of the colophon, the only sections for which the presentation of a separate vocalized text is worth-while, is indicated below in these notes.

(1) vocalized text: /sipru ḥipri bunušī malki bi yarẖi ʾIṮT[BNM]/.

(11) {šmˤ . skn} perhaps emend to {šmˤ ‹rgm› . skn}.

(20) {ḥṭbm} the scribe first wrote {ḥḥbm} then erased the lower wedge of the second {ḥ} but without completely effacing the left part of this wedge.

(35) {⌜ˤ⌝dtt} the form of the first sign is somewhere between {ˤ} and {t}.

(49–51) vocalized text: /ṯiṯṯu lê ˤašrêma bunu[šū malki -] ẖZR lāqiḥū ḥipri | ˤaštê ˤašrihu bunu[šū malki -] ẖZR | baˤalū šadî/.

Text 45: A Ration List with Village Names (RS 86.2213)

Bordreuil and Pardee 2001: text 36.

Text	*Translation*	*Vocalized Text*
Obverse		
(1) mlk ——— ṯn . ḥprm	*Mulukku*: two (units) of rations;	mulukku ṯinâ ḥiprâma
(2) ảr ——— ṯlṯ	*ʾAru*: three;	ʾaru ṯalāṯu
(3) gbˤly ——— ảḥd	*Gibˤalāya*: one;	gibˤalāya ʾaḥḥadu
(4) ủlm ——— ảḥd	*ʾUllamu*: one;	ʾullamu ʾaḥḥadu
(5) mˤrby ——— ảḥd	*Maˤrabāyu*: one;	maˤrabāyu ʾaḥḥadu
(6) ủbrˤy ——— ṯn	*ʾUburˤāyu*: two;	ˤuburˤāyu ṯinâ
(7) mˤr ——— ảḥd	*Muˤaru*: one;	muˤaru ʾaḥḥadu
(8) ảrny ——— ảḥd	*ʾAraniya*: one;	ʾaraniya ʾaḥḥadu
(9) šˤrt ——— ảḥd	*Šaˤartu*: one;	šaˤartu ʾaḥḥadu
(10) bqˤt —— ṣˤq — ảḥd	*Baqˤatu*, *Ṣaˤaqu*: one;	baqˤatu ṣaˤaqu ʾaḥḥadu
(11) ˤ⌜n⌝q⌜p⌝ảt —— ảḥd	*ˤÊnuqapʾat*: one;	ˤênuqapʾat ʾaḥḥadu
(12) ủškn ——— ảrbˤ	*ʾUškanu*: four;	ʾuškanu ʾarbaˤu
Lower edge		
(13) šbn ——— ảḥd	*Šubbanu*: one;	šubbanu ʾaḥḥadu
(14) ṭbq ——— ảḥd	*Ṭibaqu*: one;	ṭibaqu ʾaḥḥadu
Reverse		
(15) rqd ——— ṯn	*Raqdu*: two;	raqdu ṯinâ
(16) šrš ——— ảḥd	*Šurašu*: one.	šurašu ʾaḥḥadu

Text 46: Leaders of Ten and Their Men (RS 94.2050+)

Bordreuil and Pardee forthcoming: text 24.

Text	***Translation***	***Vocalized Text***
Column I		
Upper edge		
(1) [b]⸢n⸣ [.] glʿd . ---- ⸢5⸣	*Binu-Galʿadi* five,	binu galʿadi ḫamišu
Obverse		
(2) ⸢w⸣ nḥlh . ---------- ⸢-⸣	and his heir X,	wa naḥaluhu X
(3) [b]⸢n⸣ . špšm . ----- ⸢-⸣	*Binu-Šapšuma* X;	binu šapšuma X
(4) [b]⸢n⸣ . ảmdn . ------ 2	*Binu-ʾAmmadāni* two,	binu ʾammadāni ṯinâ
(5) [b]⸢n⸣ . ṣnnr . ------- 5	*Binu-Ṣānunūrī* five,	binu ṣānunūrī ḫamišu
(6) [bn] . yrm . ---------- 2	*Binu-Yarimmi* two,	binu yarimmi ṯinâ
(7) [bn .] ⸢ả⸣rpšḫ . ------ 2	*Binu-ʾAripšaḫi* two,	binu ʾaripšaḫi ṯinâ
(8) [ ]bʿn . ----------- 2	*Binu-Gabʿāna* two,	binu gabʿāna ṯinâ
(9) [ ]šy . ---------- 1	[ ]ŠY one,	[ ]ŠY ʾaḥḥadu
(10) [ ]⸢-⸣y . ------------ 1	[ ]⸢-⸣Y one,	[ ]⸢-⸣Y ʾaḥḥadu
(11) [b]⸢n⸣ [.] brzn . ----- 1	*Binu-Burzani* one,	binu burzani ʾaḥḥadu
(12) ⸢w .⸣ nḥlh . ---------- 1	and his heir one,	wa naḥaluhu ʾaḥḥadu
(13) ⸢b⸣n . kdn . ---------- 1	*Binu-Kudūna* one,	binu kudūna ʾaḥḥadu
(14) ⸢b⸣n . ṣbṭn . --------- 1	*Binu-Ṣabṭāna* one,	binu ṣabṭāna ʾaḥḥadu
(15) ⸢b⸣[n .] ṯlgn . -------- 2	*Binu*-ṮLGN two,	binu ṮLGN ṯinâ
(16) bn . ảrsw . ----------- 2	*Binu-ʾArsuwa* two,	binu ʾarsuwa ṯinâ
(17) ʿbd . mlk . ----------- 4	*ʿAbdimilku* four,	ʿabdimilku ʾarbaʿu
(18) bn . ủlb . ------------ 2	*Binu-ʾUllubi* two,	binu ʾullubi ṯinâ
(19) bn . rt . -------------- 2	*Binu*-RT two;	binu RT ṯinâ
(20) ⸢b⸣n . ḫrmln . ------- 1	*Binu*-ḪRMLN one,	binu ḪRMLN ʾaḥḥadu
(21) [b]⸢n⸣ . qṭn . --------- 6	*Binu-Quṭani* six,	binu quṭani ṯiṯṯu
(22) [b]⸢n⸣ . tgḏn . ------- 4	*Binu-Tagiḏāna* four,	[bi]nu tagiḏāna ʾarbaʿu
(23) [b]⸢n⸣ . ỉšbʿl . ------- 3	*Binu-ʾIšibaʿli* three,	[bi]nu ʾišibaʿli ṯalāṯu
Lower edge		
(24) bn . ksd . ------------ 1	*Binu*-KSD one,	binu KSD ʾaḥḥadu
(25) bn . ḫnyn . ---------- 2	*Binu-Ḫanyani* two,	binu ḫanyani ṯinâ
Reverse		
(26) bn . mmy . ---------- 2	*Binu-Mamīya* two,	binu mamīya ṯinâ
(27) bn . gpn . ------------ 1	*Binu-Gupani* one,	binu gupani ʾaḥḥadu
(28) bn . plwn . ---------- 1	*Binu*-PLWN one,	binu PLWN ʾaḥḥadu
(29) bn . ǵrgn . ----------- 1	*Binu-Ǵurgāna* one;	binu ǵurgāna ʾaḥḥadu
(30) bn . ảptn . ----------- 1	*Binu-ʾAputēna* one,	binu ʾaputēna ʾaḥḥadu
(31) bn . ủbyn . ----------- 2	*Binu-ʾUbbiyani* two,	binu ʾubbiyani ṯinâ

(32) bn . šty . ------------- 2	*Binu-Šattuya* two,	binu šattuya ṯinâ
(33) klttb . ---------------- 2	*Kilitēṯub* two,	kilitēṯub ṯinâ
(34) [b]⸢n⸣ . bdn . -------- 1	*Binu-Baduni* one,	binu baduni ʾaḥḥadu
(35) [b]⸢n⸣ . ḫdmn . ------ 6	*Binu-Ḫudmuni* six,	binu ḫudmuni ṯiṯṯu
(36) [b]⸢n⸣ . s⸢b⸣l -------- 2	*Binu-Sibili* two,	binu sibili ṯinâ
(37) [bn] . ṣpr . ----------- 1	*Binu-Ṣupari* one,	binu ṣupari ʾaḥḥadu
(38) [ ]yngrn . -------- 3	[ ]YNGRN three,	[ ]YNGRN ṯalāṯu
(39) [b]⸢n⸣ [.] btry . ------ 4	*Binu*-BTRY four	binu BTRY ʾarbaʿu
(40) ⸢w⸣ [.] nḥlh . -------- 1	and his heir one;	wa naḥaluhu ʾaḥḥadu
(41) [b]⸢n⸣ . šyn . -------- 1	*Binu-Šuyānu* one,	binu šuyāna ʾaḥḥadu
(42) [b]⸢n .⸣ ʿbd . ḫmn . 2	*Binu-ʿAbdiḫamanu* two,	binu ʿabdiḫamani ṯinâ
(43) [b]n . ddy . ---------- 1	*Binu-Dudāya* one,	binu dudāya ʾaḥḥadu
(44) [b]⸢n⸣ . ṭbrn . -------- 3	*Binu-Ṭabrāna* three,	binu ṭabrāna ṯalāṯu
(45) [b]n . ỉlṯr . ----------- 1	*Binu-ʾIluṯarru* one,	binu ʾiluṯarru ʾaḥḥadu
(46) [b]n . ṭ⸢-⸣d . --------- 1	*Binu*-Ṭ⸢D⸣D one,	binu Ṭ⸢D⸣D ʾaḥḥadu

Column II
Obverse

(47) bn . ḥrpt . ------------ 1	*Binu*-ḤRPT one,	binu ḤRPT ʾaḥḥadu
(48) bn . sgryn . ---------- 1	*Binu-Sugriyāna* one,	binu sugriyāna ʾaḥḥadu
(49) bn . nʿmn . ---------- 1	*Binu-Nuʿmāna* one,	binu nuʿmāna ʾaḥḥadu
(50) bn . trnn . ------------ 1	*Binu-Turanana* one;	binu turanana ʾaḥḥadu
(51) brdd . ---------------- 2	BRDD two,	BRDD ṯinâ
(52) w ủ⸢db⸣rh . ---------- 1	and his heir by oath one,	wa ʾUDBRuhu ʾaḥḥadu
(53) bn . mlkym . -------- 1	*Binu-Milkiyama* one,	binu milkiyama ʾaḥḥadu
(54) bn . ntp . ------------- 3	*Binu-Natappi* three,	binu natappi ṯalāṯu
(55) bn . šmtr . ----------- 1	*Binu*-ŠMTR one,	binu ŠMTR ʾaḥḥadu
(56) w ủdbrh . ------------ 1	and his heir by oath one,	wa ʾUDBRuhu ʾaḥḥadu
(57) bn . ḫnzr . ----------- 1	*Binu-Ḫanizarri* one,	binu ḫanizarri ʾaḥḥadu
(58) bn . ʿlmyn . ---------- 1	*Binu-ʿālamiyyāna* one,	binu ʿālamiyyāna ʾaḥḥadu
(59) w nḥlh . ------------- 1	and his heir one,	wa naḥaluhu ʾaḥḥadu
(60) w . nḥlh . ------------ 1	and his heir one,	wa naḥaluhu ʾaḥḥadu
(61) bn . mglb . ---------- 3	*Binu-Maglibi* three.	binu maglibi ṯalāṯu

---

Column III
Reverse

(62) rb . ʿšrt	Leaders of ten:	rabbū ʿašarti

(63) bn . špšm	*Binu-Šapšuma,*	binu šapšuma
(64) bn . trnn	*Binu-Turanana,*	binu turanana
(65) bn . mglb	*Binu-Maglibi,*	binu maglibi
Column IV		
(66) b⸢n⸣ [.] ǵrgn	*Binu-Ǵurgāna,*	binu ǵurgāna
(67) bn . btry	*Binu*-BTRY,	binu BTRY
(68) bn . rt	*Binu*-RT.	binu RT

Notes

General note on the structure of this text: comparison with RS 94.2064 indicates that the figure in each line refers to the number of persons under the control of the individual named, either as his personal assistants (*nʿrm*) or as the quota of men that he is providing to perform service-duty to the king; the six names of "leaders of ten" in lines 62–68 appeared earlier in the text, though the order of mention is different in the two sections, and we have set off each of these names in lines 1–61 with a semicolon on the hypothesis that the text consists of a list of groups of "ten" (an administrative fiction, given that the actual number of persons named per group varies from three to sixteen) with the name of the leader placed at the end of each list of members.

(8) restore {[bn . g]bʿn} on the basis of RS 94.2064:29.

(17) in spite of the word-divider, this is a compound personal name ("servant of [the god] Milku"), not an administrative title ("servant of the king"), as is shown by line 42, where a word-divider separates the two elements of a personal name preceded by *bn*.

(38) {yngrn} finds no parallel in the onomasticon of Ugarit, and we must consider the possibility that it is the beginning of the name that is lost in the lacuna rather than the word *bn* 'son'.

(46) the traces remaining of the second sign appear to indicate the reading {ṭ⸢d⸣d}, though this personal name is presently unknown.

(51) the {r} of the personal name contains an extra wedge, which appears to be a simple error.

(52, 56) {w ủdbr} appears to fill the slot of {w nḫlh} and may designate someone who has been chosen and sworn to heirship because the patron has no natural heir.

Text 47: A Sale of Ebony-Wood (RS 94.2392⁺)

Bordreuil and Pardee forthcoming: text 40.

Text

Obverse

(1) [ ]kr . hbn . d . mkr (2) [ ]ṯ . måt kbd (3) ⸢b⸣ årbʿm . šmn (4) w . krsỉm

(5) kkr . hbnm . ṯn (6) d mnḥt (7) ⸢b⸣ šbʿ . šm⸢n⸣

(8) ṯt . ktnm . b [å]rbʿ (9) šmn w . krsỉ

(10) tgmr . šmn (11) ḫmšm . kd . kbd (12) w . ṯlṯ . krsåt (13) l . åṯqlny

(*Lower edge*) (14) ⸢w⸣ ʿšrm . ṯmn (15) [k]bd . šmn (*Reverse*) (16) [l .] ⸢å⸣lṯy

Translation

(1) [Six$^{?}$ t]alents of ebony, (belonging to the) merchant(-category), (2) (plus) [si]x$^{?}$ hundred (shekels), (3) in exchange for forty (*kaddu*-measures) of (olive) oil (4) and two *kurrusaʾu*(-measures) (of olive oil).
(5) One talent of ebony, (in) two (pieces), (6) (belonging to the) tribute(-category), (7) in exchange for seven (*kaddu*-measures) of (olive) oil.
(8) Two *kutunu*(-garments) in exchange for [f]our (9) *kaddu*(-measures) of (olive) oil and one *kurrusaʾu*(-measure) (of olive oil).
(10) Total of (olive) oil: (11) fifty-one *kaddu*(-measures) (12) and three *kurrusaʾu* (-measures) (of olive oil) (13) to the ʾAshqelonite.
(14) And twenty-eight (15) *kaddu*(-measures) of (olive) oil (16) [to] the Alashian.

Vocalized Text

(1) [ṯiṯṯu ki]kkarū habūni dī makkāri (2) [ṯi]ṯṯu miʾātu kubda (3) bi ʾarbaʿīma šamni (4) wa kurrusaʾêma
(5) kikkaru habūnêma ṯinê (6) dī manaḥāti (7) bi šabʿi šamni
(8) ṯittā kutunāma bi [ʾa]rbaʿi (9) šamni wa kurrusaʾi
(10) tagmaru šamni (11) ḫamišūma kaddu kubda (12) wa ṯalāṯu kurrusaʾātu (13) lê ʾaṯqalāniyyi
(14) wa ʿašrāma ṯamānû (15) [ku]bda šamni (16) [lê] ʾalaṯiyyi

Notes

General note on the structure of this text: the first four paragraphs appear to deal with a three-part transaction (pieces of ebony-wood for resale, two trunks of ebony for tribute, and two *kutunu*-garments, all this exchanged for fifty-one *kaddu*-measures of olive oil, about 560 liters) whereas the fifth deals with a second transaction in which the medium of exchange for the olive oil is not indicated (perhaps silver at a standard rate).

(1, 2) judging from the available space, restore {[ṯṯ . k]kr} and {[ṯ]ṯ} rather than *ṯlṯ* in each case.

(1, 5) the practical distinction between the categories of wood is not clear, perhaps simply that the "tribute"-category was intended to serve as tribute to the Hittite sovereign.

(4, 9, 12) the three principal forms of the common noun *kurrusaʾu* are encountered in this text: {krsỉm} the dual in the oblique case after the preposition *bi*, {krsỉ} the singular in the genitive after the same preposition, {krsảt} the plural in the nominative (or the genitive).

Text 48: Provisions for a Month (RS 94.2600)

Bordreuil and Pardee forthcoming: text 49.

Text	***Translation***	***Vocalized Text***
Obverse		
(1) ṯṯ . dd . šʿrm	Six *dūdu*(-measures) of barley	ṯiṯṯu dūdū šiʿārūma
(2) w . mṯlṯm	plus two-thirds (of a measure);	wa maṯlaṯāma
(3) ḫmš . ʿšr . yn	fifteen *kaddu*(-measures) of wine;	ḫamišu ʿašru yênu
(4) šbʿ . dd . gdl	seven *dūdu*(-measures) of GDL	šabʿu dūdū GDL
(5) w . prš	plus one half (of a measure);	wa parīšu
(6) mṯlṯm . nʿr	two-thirds of a *dūdu*(-measure) of NʿR;	maṯlaṯāma NʿR
Lower edge		
(7) ḫmš . ṣỉn	five caprovids;	ḫamišu ṣaʾnu
Reverse		
(8) ḫmš . ydt . ủṣqm	five 'portions ?' of ʾUṢQM;	ḫamišu yadātu ? ʾUṢQM
(9) ṯlṯm . prqt tyt	thirty PRQT of *asa foetida*;	ṯalāṯūma PRQT tiyātu
(10) kṯ . kmn	one *kīṯu*(-vessel) of cumin;	kīṯu kamūnu

(11) kṯ . sbbym	one *kīṯu*(-vessel) of black cumin;	kīṯu sibibiyyūma
(12) mlȧ . ḥpnm	two handfuls of	malāʾā ḥupnêma
(13) ḫswn . ḫrb	dried thyme;	ḫaswannu ḫaribu
Upper edge		
(14) kršů . w . ṯʿt . šmn	one *kurrušaʾu*(-measure) and one *ṯaʿittu*(-measure) of (olive) oil	kurrušaʾu wa ṯaʿittu šamnu
(15) k . kšm	as KŠM.	ka KŠM
Left edge		
(16) b . yrḫ	In the month of	bi yarḫi
(17) ỉbʿlt . ṯb	*ʾibʿalatu* (which?) repeats.	ʾibʿalati ṯābi

Notes

Right edge: on the photograph, one sees several partially erased remnants of a previous text.

(2) the fraction refers to the measure named in the preceding line.

(12) lit., 'two fulnesses of two cupped hands'.

(17) the meaning of the phrase '(which?) repeats' is unknown, though the reference may be to an intercalary month.

Texts 49–51: Debit Accounts Owing to *Muninuya*

Text 49: RIH 84/04

Bordreuil 1995: 3–5; cf. *CAT* 4.791.

Text	***Translation***	***Vocalized Text***
Obverse		
(1) spr . ksp	Document of silver	sipru kaspi
(2) mnny	of *Muninuya*:	muninuya
(3) ṯṯm . ksp	sixty (shekels) of silver	ṯiṯṯūma kaspu
(4) ʿl . yrmn	owed by *Yarimānu*;	ʿalê yarimāna
(5) šbʿm . ṯqlm	seventy-two shekels	šabʿūma ṯiqlāma
(6) kbd . ksp	of silver	kubda kaspu
(7) ʿl . ȧnntn	owed by *ʾAnantēnu*,	ʿalê ʾanantēna
(8) bn . yrm	son of *Yarimmu*;	bini yarimmi

(9) ảrbʿm . ksp	forty (shekels) of silver	ʾarbaʿūma kaspu
(10) ʿl . tmrtn	owed by *Tamartēnu*,	ʿalê tamartēna
(11) bn . ủrmy	son of *ʾUrumiya*;	bini ʾurumiyi
(12) ảrbʿm . ksp	forty (shekels) of silver	ʾarbaʿūma kaspu
Lower edge		
(13) ʿl . bnỉl	owed by *Biniʾilu*,	ʿalê biniʾili
(14) bn . krwn	son of *Kurwānu*;	bini kurwāna
Reverse		
(15) ṯṯm . ksp	sixty (shekels) of silver	ṯiṯṯūma kaspu
(16) ʿl . ảbǵl . bn . ṯdny	owed by *ʾAbîǵilu*, son of *Ṯidinaya*;	ʿalê ʿabîǵili bini ṯidinaya
(17) ảrbʿm . ksp	forty (shekels) of silver	ʾarbaʿūma kaspu
(18) ʿl . tlmyn . bn . ỉly	owed by *Talmiyānu*, son of *ʾIliya*;	ʿalê talmiyāna bini ʾiliya
(19) ṯṯ . kbd . ṯlṯm	thirty-six (shekels)	ṯiṯṯatu kubda ṯalāṯūma
(20) ksp . ʿl . yʿḏrn	of silver owed by *Yaʿḏirānu*,	kaspu ʿalê yaʿḏirāna
(21) bn ˹.˺ ytrm . šlmy	son of *Yatarmu*, from *Šalmāyu*;	bini yatarmi šalmiyyi
(22) ʿšrm . ksp	twenty (shekels) of silver	ʿašrāma kaspu
(23) ʿl . ršpmlk . šlmy	owed by *Rašapmalku*, from *Šalmāyu*;	ʿalê rašapmalku šalmiyyi
(24) ả˹r˺bʿt . ʿšrt	Fourteen (shekels)	ʾarbaʿatu ʿašratu
(25) ˹k˺sp . ʿl . gln	of silver owed by *Gallānu*,	kaspu ʿalê gallāna
(26) ˹bn˺ . ảmdn . šlmy	son of *ʾAmmadānu*, from *Šalmiyā*.	bini ʾammadāna šalmiyyi

General Note

In these three texts that represent extracts from accounts of a certain *Muninuya*, *ʿl* expresses the existence of a debt (‘on’ = ‘debit account of’), *ʿm* the repayment of a loan (‘with’ = ‘credited to’—apparently the idea is that the money has reached the creditor ‘with’ the debtor); this usage of *ʿl* is well attested in the administrative texts whereas *ʿm* in the meaning of ‘credited to’ is very rare.

Text 50: RIH 84/06

Bordreuil 1995: 3–5; *CAT* 4.792.

Text	***Translation***	***Vocalized Text***
Obverse		
(1) [mỉt .] ⸢k⸣sp [.] ʿm .	One hundred (shekels) of silver, credited to	miʾtu kaspu ʿimma
(2) [bn . r]⸢q⸣dn .	*Binu-Raqdāna*;	bini raqdāna
(3) [ʿšrt] . ksp . ʿm	ten (shekels) of silver credited to	ʿašratu kaspu ʿimma
(4) [s̀zn .] ḫbty	*S̀uzīnu*, from *Ḫubatāyu*;	s̀uzīna ḫubatiyyi
(5) [ʿšr]⸢m⸣ . ksp . ʿm	twenty (shekels) of silver credited to	ʿašrāma kaspu ʿimma
(6) [špš]⸢n⸣ . ủ⸢šk⸣ny	*Šapšānu*, of *ʾUškanu*;	šapšāna ʾuškaniyyi
Lower edge		
(7) [ʿšrt .] ksp [.] ʿm	ten (shekels) of silver credited to	ʿašratu kaspu ʿimma
(8) [--]n . bn . drt	[--]N, son of DRT,	[--]N bini DRT
Obverse		
(9) [ủš]⸢k⸣ny	from *ʾUškanu*.	ʾuškaniyyi

Text 51: RIH 84/33

Bordreuil 1995: 3–5; *CAT* 3.10.

Text

Obverse

(1) sprn mnḥ . ủd . mnny

(2) mỉt . ksp . ʿl . bn . rqdn

(3) ʿšrt . ksp . ʿl . s̀zn . ḫbty

(4) ʿšrm . ksp . ʿl . špšn (5) ủškny .

(6) ʿšrt . ksp . ʿl . bn . (7) drt . ủškny

(8) ḫmšt . ˁšrt . ksp (9) ⌜ˁ⌝l . ˁmy . biry

Lower edge

(10) [ḫm]št . ksp . ˁl . ṯngb (11) [b]⌜ i⌝ry

Reverse

(12) [ṯ]ṯm . ksp . ˁl . ⌜bˁ⌝lyn . ḥṭb

---

(13) šbˁm . ṯqlm [.] kbd . ksp . ˁl (14) ånntn . bn . yrm

---

(15) årbˁm ksp . ˁl . tmrtn (16) bn . ůrmy

---

(17) årbˁm ksp . ˁl . bnil (18) bn . krwn

---

(19) ṯṯm . ksp . ˁl . åbǵl (20) bn . ṯdny

Upper edge

(21) årbˁm . ksp . ˁl . tlmyn (22) bn . ily

Translation

(1) Document of loans of (= made by) *Muninuya*:
(2) one hundred (shekels) of silver owed by *Binu-Raqdānu*;
(3) ten (shekels) of silver owed by *Šuzīnu*, from *Ḫubatāyu*;
(4) twenty (shekels) of silver owed by *Šapšānu*, (5) from *ʾUškanu*;
(6) ten (shekels) of silver owed by *Binu*-(7)DRT, from *ʾUškanu*;
(8) fifteen (shekels) of silver (9) owed by *ˁAmmiya*, from *Biʾiru*;
(10) [fi]ve (shekels) of silver owed by ṮNGB, (11) from [*Bi*]*ʾiru*;
(12) [si]xty (shekels) of silver owed by *Baˁliyānu*, wood-cutter;
(13) seventy-two shekels of silver owed by (14) *ʾAnantēnu*, son of *Yarimmu*;
(15) forty (shekels) of silver owed by *Tamartēnu*, (16) son of *ʾUrumiya*;
(17) forty (shekels) of silver owed by *Biniʾilu*, (18) son of *Kurwānu*;
(19) sixty (shekels) of silver owed by *ʾAbîǵilu*, (20) son of *Ṯidinaya*;
(21) forty (shekels) of silver owed by *Talmiyānu*, (22) son of *ʾIliya*.

Vocalized Text

(1) siprānu minḫi ʾūdi muninuya
(2) miʾtu kaspu ˁalê bini raqdāna
(3) ˁašratu kaspu ˁalê šuzīna ḫubatayyi
(4) ˁašrāma kaspu ˁalê šapšāna (5) ʾuškaniyyi
(6) ˁašratu kaspu ˁalê bini (7) DRT ʾuškaniyyi
(8) ḫamišatu ˁašratu kaspu (9) ˁalê ˁammiya biʾiriyyi

(10) [ḫami]šatu kaspu ʿalê ṮNGB (11) [bi]ʾiriyyi
(12) [ṯi]ṯṯūma kaspu ʿalê baʿliyāna ḥāṭibi
(13) šabʿūma ṯiqlāma kubda kaspu ʿalê (14) ʾanantēna bini yarimmi
(15) ʾarbaʿūma kaspu ʿalê tamartēna (16) bini ʾurumiya
(17) ʾarbaʿūma kaspu ʿalê biniʾili (18) bini kurwāna
(19) ṯiṯṯūma kaspu ʿalê ʾabîǵili (20) bini ṯidinaya
(21) ʾarbaʿūma kaspu ʿalê talmiyāna (22) bini ʾiliya

Notes

(1) {ủd} Gp participle, √ʾD, 'borne by': {mnḥ ủd} 'amount given to and owed by someone = loan'.

(6–7) {bn drt} the debtor is designated here by his patronym alone whereas in RIH 84/06:8 (text 50), the person's own name is partially preserved before the patronym.

General Note on the Accounts of MNNY:

These three texts may plausibly be arranged in the following order: according to RIH 84/33, *Muninuya* loaned money to twelve persons who are identified by name or patronym along with the amount of the loan. RIH 84/06:1–9 records the repayment of the first four debts of RIH 84/33 (lines 2–7). The tablet recording the repayment of the loans recorded in RIH 84/33:8–12 (ʿMY, ṮNGB and BʿLYN) has not been recovered. RIH 84/04 is the latest text for it contains records both of new loans and, in lines 5–18, of debts still outstanding, for the five names and amounts of these lines correspond to those set down in RIH 84/33:13–21.

Text 52: Boats to Carchemish (RIH 83/22)

Bordreuil in Bordreuil et al. 1984: 431–32; *CAT* 4.779.

Text	***Translation***	***Vocalized Text***
Obverse		
(1) tšʿm . ṯlṯt	Ninety-three (shekels)	tišʿūma ṯalāṯatu
(2) w nṣp . kbd	and a half,	wa naṣpu kubda
(3) ksp . ḥbl . rỉšym	silver of the boatmen of *Raʾšu* —	kaspu ḥābilī raʾšiyyīma
(4) l ytn . ksphm	they have indeed given their sum;	la yatanū kaspahumu

(5) ḫmšt . l ʿšrm	twenty five (shekels of this amount in the form of)	ḫamišatu lê ʿašrêma
(6) d ỉqnỉ . ảrbʿm	bluish purple (worth that amount), forty	dū ʾiqnaʾi ʾarbaʿūma

Lower edge

(7) d ktn	(shekels in the form) of *kutunu*(-garments).	dū kutuni

Reverse

---

(8) ảrbʿ . mảt . ḫmšm	Four hundred fifty-	ʾarbaʿu miʾātu ḫamišūma
(9) šbʿt . w nṣp . kbd	seven (shekels) and a half,	šabʿatu wa naṣpu kubda
(10) ksp . d . lqḥ . bdn	silver that *Badunu* has taken	kaspu dū laqaḥa badunu
(11) d mlk . w ʿl	from the king; it has not been	dā malki wa ʿalê
(12) ḥwt . l ḥṯb .	debited to the national account:	ḥuwwati lā ḥuṯiba
(13) d ảnyt . grgmšh	(this is the price) of boats (going) to Carchemish.	dū ʾaniyyāti gargamišaha

Notes

(1–7) The first two paragraphs may be interpreted as recording the payment of an account by the boatmen of the port city of *Raʾšu*, partly in silver (28.5 shekels), partly in two types of cloth (25 and 40 shekels); this amount may correspond either to the repayment of a debt or to these boatmen's participation in the transaction recorded in the following paragraph. In the latter case, the total price of the boats would have been 551 shekels (93.5 + 457.5).

(3) {ḥbl rỉšym} the absence of morphological agreement between the noun and the adjective may be owing to scribal error (read {ḥbl<m> rỉšym}), to {ḥbl} functioning as a collective, or to the structure being that of the genitive of identification (according to the vocalization proposed above, 'the boatmen of the inhabitants of *Raʾsu*' = 'the boatmen who are inhabitants of *Raʾšu*').

VIII. Abecedaries

Text 53: An Abecedary (RS 12.063)

Virolleaud 1951: 22–23; 1957: text 184; *KTU* 5.6

Text

(1) ả b g ḫ d h w z ḥ ṭ y k š l
(2) m ḏ n ẓ s ʿ p ṣ q r ṯ
(3) ǵ t ỉ ủ s̀

Text 54: A Double Abecedary (RS 24.281)

Herdner 1978a: 63–64; *KTU* 5.20

Text

Obverse → Reverse → Obverse

(1a) ả b g ḫ ⸢d⸣ h w z ḥ ṭ y k š l m ḏ n ẓ s ʿ p ṣ
(1b) q ⸢r⸣ ṯ ǵ t ỉ ủ s̀
(2b) q r ⸢ṯ⸣ ǵ t ỉ ủ s̀
(2a) ả b g ḫ d h w [z ḥ ṭ y k] ⸢š l⸣ m ḏ n ẓ s ʿ p ṣ

General Note: the two alphabets on this tablet were inscribed by different hands. The first is more regular and seems to have been that of the teacher while the second would be the student's copy. The latter began writing the signs at the bottom of the tablet and when he had followed around the tablet to where he met the first signs inscribed on the obverse he had to place the last eight signs above the previously inscribed line rather than below as the teacher had done.

Text 55: A Double Abecedary with Place Names (RS 94.2440)

Bordreuil and Pardee forthcoming: text 81.

Text

Obverse → Reverse

(1) ả b g ḫ d h w z ḥ ṭ y k š l m ḏ n ẓ s ʿ p ṣ q r ṯ ǵ t ỉ ủ s̀

Obverse → Reverse → Obverse

(2) ả b g ḫ d h w z ḥ ṭ y k š l m ḏ n ẓ s ʿ p ṣ q r ṯ ǵ t ỉ ủ s̀

Obverse

(3) åtlg

Reverse

(4) mlk . år

(5) ḫ̮lb rpš

Upper edge

(6) ḫ̮lb krd

General Note: these two inscriptions of the alphabet appear to have been inscribed by the same person who, judging from the irregularities, would have been a student. In the first abecedary as well as in the place names, there are four examples of the {r} written with an extra wedge (lines 1, 4, 5, 6).

Concordance of Text Numbers

Text number with excavation number	**Edition**	***KTU/CAT***
1. RS 3.367 i	*CTA* 2 iv	1.2 iv
2. RS 2.[014]+ iii–iv	*CTA* 3 iii–iv	1.3 iii-iv
3. RS 2.[003]+ i	*CTA* 14 i	1.14 i
4. RS 2.[004] i	*CTA* 17 i	1.17 i
5. RS 2.002	*CTA* 23	1.23
6. RS 24.244	*Ugaritica* V 6	1.100
7. RS 24.258	*Ugaritica* V 1	1.114
8. RS 1.001	*CTA* 34	1.39
9. RS 1.002	*CTA* 32	1.40
10. RS 24.260	*Ugaritica* V 11	1.115
11. RS 24.266	*Ugaritica* VII, p. 31–39	1.119
12. RS 24.643	*Ugaritica* V 9	1.148
13. RS 34.126	RSO VII 90	1.161
14. RS 6.021	*Syria* 16 (1935), p. 177–80	6.13
15. RS 6.028	*Syria* 16 (1935), p. 177–80	6.14
16. RS 25.318	*Ugaritica* VII, p. 147–54	6.62
17. RIH 78/20	*Syria* 57 (1980) 346–50	1.169
18. RS 92.2014	RSO XIV 52	
19. RS 17.120	RSO II	1.85
20. RS 24.247+	*Ugaritica* VII, p. 44–60	1.103 + 1.145
21. RS 4.475	*CTA* 53	2.10
22. RS 8.315	*CTA* 51	2.11
23. RS 11.872	*CTA* 50	2.13
24. RS 15.008	*PRU* II 15	2.16
25. RS 16.379	*PRU* II 13	2.30
26. RS 18.031	*PRU* V 59	2.38
27. RS 18.040	*PRU* V 63	2.40
28. RS 29.093	*Ugaritica* VII, p. 75–78	2.70
29. RS 34.124	RSO VII 88	2.72
30. RS 92.2010	RSO XIV 50	
31. RS 94.2406	unpublished	
32. RS 94.2479	unpublished	
33. RS 96.2039	unpublished	
34. RS 94.2284	unpublished	
35. RS [Varia 4]	*Semitica* 32 (1982), p. 5–9	2.14

Text number with excavation number	Edition	*KTU/CAT*
36. RS 11.772+	*CTA* 64	3.1
37. RS 16.382	*PRU* II 8	3.5
38. RS 94.2168	unpublished	
39. RS 94.2965	unpublished	
40. RS [Varia 14]	AnOr 48 (1971), p. 37–49	3.9
41. RS 19.015	*PRU* V 4	1.91
42. RS 15.062	*PRU* II 127	4.158
43. RS 18.024	*PRU* V 101	4.337
44. RS 19.016	*PRU* V 11	4.609
45. RS 86.2213	RSO XIV 36	
46. RS 94.2050+	unpublished	
47. RS 94.2392+	unpublished	
48. RS 94.2600	unpublished	
49. RIH 84/04	*Umwelt*, p. 3–5	cf. 4.791
50. RIH 84/06	*Umwelt*, p. 3–5	4.792
51. RIH 84/33	*Umwelt*, p. 3–5	3.10
52. RIH 83/22	*CRAI* 1984, p. 431–32	4.779
53. RS 12.063	*PRU* II 184	5.6
54. RS 24.281	*Ugaritica* VII, p. 63–64	5.20
55. RS 94.2440	unpublished	

Excavation no.	Text no.	Edition	*KTU/CAT*
RIH 78/20	17	*Syria* 57 (1980) 346–50	1.169
RIH 83/22	52	*CRAI* 1984, p. 431–32	4.779
RIH 84/04	49	*Umwelt*, p. 3–5	cf. 4.791
RIH 84/06	50	*Umwelt*, p. 3–5	4.792
RIH 84/33	51	*Umwelt*, p. 3–5	3.10
RS 1.001	8	*CTA* 34	1.39
RS 1.002	9	*CTA* 32	1.40
RS 2.002	5	*CTA* 23	1.23
RS 2.[003]+ i	3	*CTA* 14 i	1.14 i
RS 2.[004] i	4	*CTA* 17 i	1.17 i
RS 2.[014]+ iii-iv	2	*CTA* 3 iii-iv	1.3 iii–iv
RS 3.367 i	1	*CTA* 2 iv	1.2 iv
RS 4.475	21	*CTA* 53	2.10
RS 6.021	14	*Syria* 16 (1935), p. 177–80	6.13
RS 6.028	15	*Syria* 16 (1935), p. 177–80	6.14
RS 8.315	22	*CTA* 51	2.11

Excavation no.	Text no.	Edition	*KTU/CAT*
RS 11.772+	36	*CTA* 64	3.1
RS 11.872	23	*CTA* 50	2.13
RS 12.063	53	*PRU* II 184	5.6
RS 15.008	24	*PRU* II 15	2.16
RS 15.062	42	*PRU* II 127	4.158
RS 16.379	25	*PRU* II 13	2.30
RS 16.382	37	*PRU* II 8	3.5
RS 17.120	19	RSO II	1.85
RS 18.024	43	*PRU* V 101	4.337
RS 18.031	26	*PRU* V 59	2.38
RS 18.040	27	*PRU* V 63	2.40
RS 19.015	41	*PRU* V 4	1.91
RS 19.016	44	*PRU* V 11	4.609
RS 24.244	6	*Ugaritica* V 6	1.100
RS 24.247+	20	*Ugaritica* VII, p. 44–60	1.103 + 1.145
RS 24.258	7	*Ugaritica* V 1	1.114
RS 24.260	10	*Ugaritica* V 11	1.115
RS 24.266	11	*Ugaritica* VII, p. 31–39	1.119
RS 24.281	54	*Ugaritica* VII, p. 63–64	5.20
RS 24.643	12	*Ugaritica* V 9	1.148
RS 25.318	16	*Ugaritica* VII, p. 147–54	6.62
RS 29.093	28	*Ugaritica* VII, p. 75–78	2.70
RS 34.124	29	RSO VII 88	2.72
RS 34.126	13	RSO VII 90	1.161
RS 86.2213	45	RSO XIV 36	
RS 92.2010	30	RSO XIV 50	
RS 92.2014	18	RSO XIV 52	
RS 94.2050+	46	unpublished	
RS 94.2168	38	unpublished	
RS 94.2284	34	unpublished	
RS 94.2392+	47	unpublished	
RS 94.2406	31	unpublished	
RS 94.2440	55	unpublished	
RS 94.2479	32	unpublished	
RS 94.2600	48	unpublished	
RS 94.2965	39	unpublished	
RS 96.2039	33	unpublished	
RS [Varia 4]	35	*Semitica* 32 (1982), p. 5–9	2.14
RS [Varia 14]	40	AnOr 48 (1971), p. 37–49	3.9

KTU/CAT	**Text no.**	**Excavation no.**	**Edition**
1.2 iv	1	RS 3.367 i	*CTA* 2 iv
1.3 iii-iv	2	RS 2.[014]+ iii–iv	*CTA* 3 iii–iv
1.14 i	3	RS 2.[003]+ i	*CTA* 14 i
1.17 i	4	RS 2.[004] i	*CTA* 17 i
1.23	5	RS 2.002	*CTA* 23
1.39	8	RS 1.001	*CTA* 34
1.40	9	RS 1.002	*CTA* 32
1.85	19	RS 17.120	RSO II
1.91	41	RS 19.015	*PRU* V 4
1.100	6	RS 24.244	*Ugaritica* V 6
1.103 + 1.145	20	RS 24.247+	*Ugaritica* VII, p. 44–60
1.114	7	RS 24.258	*Ugaritica* V 1
1.115	10	RS 24.260	*Ugaritica* V 11
1.119	11	RS 24.266	*Ugaritica* VII, p. 31–39
1.148	12	RS 24.643	*Ugaritica* V 9
1.161	13	RS 34.126	RSO VII 90
1.169	17	RIH 78/20	*Syria* 57 (1980) 346–50
2.10	21	RS 4.475	*CTA* 53
2.11	22	RS 8.315	*CTA* 51
2.13	23	RS 11.872	*CTA* 50
2.14	35	RS [Varia 4]	*Semitica* 32 (1982), pp. 5–9
2.16	24	RS 15.008	*PRU* II 15
2.30	25	RS 16.379	*PRU* II 13
2.38	26	RS 18.031	*PRU* V 59
2.40	27	RS 18.040	*PRU* V 63
2.70	28	RS 29.093	*Ugaritica* VII, p. 75–78
2.72	29	RS 34.124	RSO VII 88
3.1	36	RS 11.772+	*CTA* 64
3.5	37	RS 16.382	*PRU* II 8
3.9	40	RS [Varia 14]	AnOr 48 (1971), pp. 37–49
3.10	51	RIH 84/33	*Umwelt*, p. 3–5
4.158	42	RS 15.062	*PRU* II 127
4.337	43	RS 18.024	*PRU* V 101
4.609	44	RS 19.016	*PRU* V 11
4.779	52	RIH 83/22	*CRAI* 1984, p. 431–32
4.791	49	RIH 84/04	*Umwelt*, p. 3–5
4.792	50	RIH 84/06	*Umwelt*, p. 3–5
5.6	53	RS 12.063	*PRU* II 184
5.20	54	RS 24.281	*Ugaritica* VII, p. 63–64
6.13	14	RS 6.021	*Syria* 16 (1935), pp. 177–80

KTU/CAT	Text no.	Excavation no.	Edition
6.14	15	RS 6.028	*Syria* 16 (1935), pp. 177–80
6.62	16	RS 25.318	*Ugaritica* VII, pp. 147–54

Edition	Text no.	Excavation no.	*KTU/CAT*
AnOr 48 (1971), p. 37–49	40	RS [Varia 14]	3.9
CRAI 1984, p. 431–32	52	RIH 83/22	4.779
CTA 2 iv	1	RS 3.367 i	1.2 iv
CTA 3 iii-iv	2	RS 2.[014]+ iii–iv	1.3 iii–iv
CTA 14 i	3	RS 2.[003]+ i	1.14 i
CTA 17 i	4	RS 2.[004] i	1.17 i
CTA 23	5	RS 2.002	1.23
CTA 32	9	RS 1.002	1.40
CTA 34	8	RS 1.001	1.39
CTA 50	23	RS 11.872	2.13
CTA 51	22	RS 8.315	2.11
CTA 53	21	RS 4.475	2.10
CTA 64	36	RS 11.772+	3.1
PRU II 8	37	RS 16.382	3.5
PRU II 13	25	RS 16.379	2.30
PRU II 15	24	RS 15.008	2.16
PRU II 127	42	RS 15.062	4.158
PRU II 184	53	RS 12.063	5.6
PRU V 4	41	RS 19.015	1.91
PRU V 11	44	RS 19.016	4.609
PRU V 59	26	RS 18.031	2.38
PRU V 63	27	RS 18.040	2.40
PRU V 101	43	RS 18.024	4.337
RSO II	19	RS 17.120	1.85
RSO VII 88	29	RS 34.124	2.72
RSO VII 90	13	RS 34.126	1.161
RSO XIV 36	45	RS 86.2213	
RSO XIV 50	30	RS 92.2010	
RSO XIV 52	18	RS 92.2014	
Semitica 32 (1982) 5–9	35	RS [Varia 4]	2.14
Syria 16 (1935) 177–80	14	RS 6.021	6.13
Syria 16 (1935) 177–80	15	RS 6.028	6.14
Syria 57 (1980) 346–50	17	RIH 78/20	1.169
Ugaritica V 1	7	RS 24.258	1.114
Ugaritica V 6	6	RS 24.244	1.100

Edition	**Text no.**	**Excavation no.**	***KTU/CAT***
Ugaritica V 9	12	RS 24.643	1.148
Ugaritica V 11	10	RS 24.260	1.115
Ugaritica VII, pp. 31–39	11	RS 24.266	1.119
Ugaritica VII, pp. 44–60	20	RS 24.247+	1.103 + 1.145
Ugaritica VII, pp. 63–64	54	RS 24.281	5.20
Ugaritica VII, pp. 75–78	28	RS 29.093	2.70
Ugaritica VII, pp. 147–54	16	RS 25.318	6.62
Umwelt, pp. 3–5	49	RIH 84/04	cf. 4.791
Umwelt, pp. 3–5	50	RIH 84/06	4.792
Umwelt, pp. 3–5	51	RIH 84/33	3.10
unpublished	31	RS 94.2406	
unpublished	32	RS 94.2479	
unpublished	33	RS 96.2039	
unpublished	34	RS 94.2284	
unpublished	38	RS 94.2168	
unpublished	39	RS 94.2965	
unpublished	46	RS 94.2050+	
unpublished	47	RS 94.2392+	
unpublished	48	RS 94.2600	
unpublished	55	RS 94.2440	

Glossary*

ʾU conjunction ‘and’ /ʾū/ **11** (RS 24.266):13bis; **13** (RS 34.126):12, 26; **17** (RIH 78/20):5; **18** (RS 92.2014):1; **29** (RS 34.124):42′; **34** (RS 94.2284):9

ʾU conjunction ‘or’ /ʾô/ ← /*ʾaw/ **5** (RS 2.002):63, 64; **9** (RS 1.002):2′ et passim in this text; **38** (RS 94.2168):7, 9, 10, 27

ʾAB common noun ‘father’ /ʾabû/ ← /*ʾabawu/$^{?}$ **3** (RS 2.[003]$^{+}$) i:37, 41, 43; **4** (RS 2.[004]) i:23′; **7** (RS 24.258):14; **9** (RS 1.002):[24′], 33′, 41′

ʾABṢN personal name /ʾabîṣanu/ **44** (RS 19.016):5

ʾABǴL personal name /ʾabîǵilu/ **44** (RS 19.016):14; **49** (RIH 84/04):16; **51** (RIH 84/33):19

ʾIB common noun ‘enemy’ /ʾêbu/# ← /*ʾaybu/ **1** (RS 3.367) i:8′, 9′, 39′; **2** (RS 2.[014]$^{+}$) iii:37′, iv:4, 5; **20** (RS 24.247^{+}):[7], 9, 10, 16, 17, [35′], 37′, [50′], 51′, 54′, 58′, 59′

ʾIBT common noun ‘enmity’ /ʾêbatu/ **34** (RS 94.2284):27

ʾBD verb ‘perish’ (Gt-stem) **3** (RS 2.[003]$^{+}$) i:8$^{!}$, 24

D-stem ‘destroy’ **1** (RS 3.367) i:3′; **6** (RS 24.244):5, 11, 16, 22, 27, 32, ⟨34c⟩, 37, 42, 47, 54, 60

[*ʾBY]: ʾABYN adjective ‘destitute, poor’ /ʾabyānu/ **4** (RS 2.[004]) i:16′

ʾUBYN personal name /ʾubbiyanu/ **46** (RS 94.2050^{+}):31

ʾABYNN: see ʾBY

ʾABN common noun ‘stone’ /ʾabnu/ **2** (RS 2.[014]$^{+}$) iii:23′; **5** (RS 2.002):66; **6** (RS 24.244):1; **20** (RS 24.247^{+}):1

ʾUBN personal name /ʾubinu/ **44** (RS 19.016):9

ʾABNY personal name, feminine, vocalization and etymology unknown **34** (RS 94.2284):1

* The order of alphabetization is that used at Ugarit for the 27 principal consonantal phonemes. As for the 3 additional signs, roots and words beginning with *alif* are always in first position irrespective of which *alif*-sign is used, and words written with both {s} and {ś} are under a single heading at {s}. Because the glossary is organized by roots, root lemmas are provided when only derived forms are attested in the Selection of Texts. The consonantal root is to be taken as an abstraction when primitive forms, nouns or particles, are listed under a lemma that reflects the consonantal substructure of a word, e.g., [ʾMM] for the primitive noun /ʾummu/. Hollow roots are listed under their biconsonantal form, usual in Ugaritic. Vocalizations attested by a syllabic vocabulary entry or in another type of syllabic text are followed by #; vocalized proto-Ugaritic nominal forms are marked with an asterisk (e.g., /ʾêbu/# ← /*ʾaybu/). All attestations of all words attested in the Selection of Texts are included, but only these words—this is not a glossary of the Ugaritic language.

ʾIBSN common noun ‘storehouse, storeroom’ /ʾibūsānu/ **40** (RS [Varia 14]):5

ʾIBʿLT month name (fourth of the lunar year = December–January) /ʾibʿalatu/ **11** (RS 24.266):1, 11; **48** (RS 94.2600):17

ʾABṢN: see ʾAB

ʾIBR common noun ‘bull’ /ʾibbīru/ (← /ʾabbīru/?) **11** (RS 24.266):29′

ʾUBRʿY: see BRʿ

ʾABǴL: see ʾAB

ʾAGZR: see GZR

ʾAGYN personal name /ʾagiyanu/ **44** (RS 19.016):36

ʾAGM place-name /ʾagimu/ **41** (RS 19.015):31

ʾAGN common noun ‘cooking pot’ /ʾagannu/ **5** (RS 2.002):15, 31, 36

ʾAGNY place-name /ʾaganāyu/ **39** (RS 94.2965):1

ʾAGPṮR personal name /ʾagapṯarri/ **16** (RS 25.318):1

ʾUGR part of compound divine name (see GPN W ʾUGR) ‘field’ /ʾugāru/ **2** (RS 2.[014]$^{+}$) iii:36′

ʾUGRT place-name ‘Ugarit’ /ʾugārit/ (rarely /ʾugārītu/) **9** (RS 1.002):10′, [18′], 26′, ⟨26′⟩, 35′, 36′; **11** (RS 24.266):3, 10 ({ủ!grt}), 12, 22′; **13** (RS 34.126):33; **24** (RS 15.008):5; **26** (RS 18.031):1; **31** (RS 94.2406):23, 40; **36** (RS 11.772^{+}):14′, 25′; **37** (RS 16.382):4; **38** (RS 94.2168):4; **44** (RS 19.016):37

ʾḪ: ʾAḪ common noun ‘brother (either familial or social)’ /ʾaḫû/ ← /*ʾaḫawu/$^{?}$, pl. /ʾaḫḫûma/ **3** (RS 2.[003]$^{+}$) i:9; **4** (RS 2.[004]) i:19′, 20′; **26** (RS 18.031):2, 3, 26; **31** (RS 94.2406):32 ({ỉḫy}); **33** (RS 96.2039):3 ({ỉḫy}); **34** (RS 94.2284):3; **35** (RS [Varia 4]):3, 10, 15, 18

ʾAḪMLK personal name /ʾaḫîmilku/ (‘my brother is [the god] *Milku*’) **44** (RS 19.016):33

ʾIḪRŠP personal name /ʾiḫîrašap/ (‘my brother is [the god] *Rašap*’) **40** (RS [Varia 14]):18

ʾAḪT common noun ‘sister’ /ʾaḫâtu/ ← /*ʾaḫawatu/$^{?}$ **34** (RS 94.2284):7, 26

ʾAḪTMLK personal name, feminine /ʾaḫâtumilku/ (‘sister of [the god] *Milku*’) **22** (RS 8.315):4

ʾḪD verb ‘take, hold, seize’ **4** (RS 2.[004]) i:30′, 34′; **19** (RS 17.120):12, 15; **20** (RS 24.247^{+}):7, 17; **31** (RS 94.2406):37; **33** (RS 96.2039):14

ʾAḪMLK: see ʾAḪ

ʾUḪNP place-name /ʾuḫnappu/ **41** (RS 19.015):34

[ʾḪR verb ‘be behind, late’]: Š-stem ‘cause delay’ **34** (RS 94.2284):33 ({tšḫr})

ʾUḪRY common noun ‘posterity’ /ʾuḫrāyu/ **20** (RS 24.247^{+}):39′–40′

ʾIḪRŠP: see ʾAḪ

ʾAḪTMLK: see ʾAḪ

ʾD verb ‘bend, load (with)’ **51** (RIH 84/33):1

ʾAD common noun ‘father, papa’ /ʾadu/ **5** (RS 2.002):32bis, 43bis

ʾADBʿL personal name /ʾadîbaʿlu/ ('[the god] *Baʿlu* is my father') **44** (RS 19.016):19

ʾADN common noun 'father, lord' /ʾadānu/# **33** (RS 96.2039):13

ʾADN personal name /ʾadānu/ ('[god-X is the] father [of this child]') **35** (RS [Varia 4]):19; **44** (RS 19.016):33

ʾADT common noun 'lady' /ʾadattu/ ← /*ʾadān(a)tu/ **22** (RS 8.315):1, 5, 15; **32** (RS 94.2479):1, 3, 4, 8, 20

ʾUDN common noun 'power (← paternal power)' /ʾudānu/ **2** (RS 2.[014]⁺) iv:2

ʾID : see D

ʾUDBR: see DBR

ʾIDK: see D

ʾADM common noun 'man, humanity' /ʾadamu/ **3** (RS 2.[003]⁺) i:37, 43; **17** (RIH 78/20):14, 15

[ʾUDM place-name]: ʾUDMY gentilic /ʾudmiyyu/ **43** (RS 18.024):15

ʾUDMʿT: see DMʿ

ʾUDN (← ʾḎN) common noun 'ear' /ʾudnu/ **20** (RS 24.247⁺):35′, 37′

ʾDN verb 'listen, give ear' **18** (RS 92.2014):8

ʾADNY place-name /ʾadaniya/ **31** (RS 94.2406):8

[ʾDR 'be/become powerful']: ʾADR adjective 'powerful' /ʾaduru/# **26** (RS 18.031):14

ʾADR common noun 'pin (?)' /ʾadaru/ **42** (RS 15.062):8

ʾIDRP: see RŠP ʾIDRP

ʾHB verb 'love' **29** (RS 34.124):44′ ({[?]hbk})

D-stem 'love intensely' **38** (RS 94.2168):11

ʾAHBT common noun 'love' /ʾahbatu/ **2** (RS 2.[014]⁺) iii:7′

ʾIWRḎN personal name /ʾiwriḏēnu/ **35** (RS [Varia 4]):1

ʾIWRḎR personal name /ʾiwriḏarri/ **21** (RS 4.475):1

ʾIWRPZN personal name /ʾiwripuzini/ **35** (RS [Varia 4]):2

ʾZR verb 'gird' **4** (RS 2.[004]) i:2′, [3′], [6′], [7′], 7′ , [9′], 9′, 10′, 11′, 12′, [13′], 21′, 22′

MʾIZRT common noun 'belted garment' /maʾzaratu/ **4** (RS 2.[004]) i:[5′], 15′

ʾAḤD number adjective 'one' /ʾaḥḥadu/ **10** (RS 24.260):14; **31** (RS 94.2406):16; **42** (RS 15.062):20; **45** (RS 86.2213):3–5, 7–11, 13–14, 16

ʾAḤDH adverb 'together (← as one)' /ʾaḥḥadaha/ **7** (RS 24.258):31′; **19** (RS 17.120):6, 8, 11, [22], 28, 32

ʾUṬB common noun '(type of garment)' /ʾuṭbu/ **43** (RS 18.024):11

ʾAY emphatic particle /ʾāya/ **5** (RS 2.002):6bis

ʾAYMR proper name /ʾāyamiri/ **1** (RS 3.367) i:19′^{bis}

ʾIYTLM personal name /ʾiyyatalmi/ **35** (RS [Varia 4]):14

ʾIK adverb 'how? how is it that?' /ʾêka/ ← /*ʾayka/ **2** (RS 2.[014]⁺) iii:36′

ʾIKY extended form /ʾêkaya/ **35** (RS [Varia 4]):6; **36** (RS 11.772⁺):8′

[ʾKL verb ‘eat’]: ʾAKL common noun ‘food’ /ʾaklu/ **14** (RS 6.021):3; **19** (RS 17.120):12, 15; **26** (RS 18.031):21; **28** (RS 29.093):22

[ʾŠ common noun ‘fire’]: ʾIŠT common noun ‘fire’ /ʾištu/# **5** (RS 2.002):14, 41, 44, 48

ʾIŠT divine name (ditto) **2** (RS 2.[014]$^{+}$) iii:45′

[ʾŠ verb ‘give’]: ʾIŠBʿL personal name /ʾišibaʿlu/ (‘gift of [the god] *Baʿlu*’) **46** (RS 94.2050^{+}):23

ʾUŠḪR(Y) divine name, feminine /ʾušḫarâ/ʾušḫaraya/ **8** (RS 1.001):13; **10** (RS 24.260):2, 12$^{!}$; **12** (RS 24.643):8, [37]

ʾIŠD common noun ‘leg’ /ʾišdu/# **2** (RS 2.[014]$^{+}$) iii:20′

ʾUŠK common noun ‘testicle’ /ʾušku/ **20** (RS 24.247^{+}):14

ʾUŠKN place-name /ʾuškanu/ **45** (RS 86.2213):12

ʾUŠKNY gentilic /ʾuškaniyyu/ **50** (RIH 84/06):6, 9; **51** (RIH 84/33):5, 7

ʾAŠKR: see ŠKR

ʾAŠKRR: see ŠKR

ʾŠM: MʾIŠMN, MʾAŠMN or MŠMN common noun ‘seal’ /maʾšamānu/ (→/maʾ^{a}šamānu/, /mašamānu/ ?) **37** (RS 16.382):22 (it is uncertain which form is to be restored in this text)

ʾIŠPR common noun, meaning unknown **31** (RS 94.2406):26; **34** (RS 94.2284):5

ʾUŠPǴT common noun ‘(type of garment)’ /ʾušpaǵǵatu/ **12** (RS 24.643):21

ʾUŠR common noun ‘penis’ /ʾušaru/ **20** (RS 24.247^{+}):47′

ʾAL particle: see L negative particle

ʾIL common noun ‘god’ /ʾilu/# **2** (RS 2.[014]$^{+}$) iii:29′, 32′, 39′; **4** (RS 2.[004]) i:2′, 6′, [7′], 9′, [10′], [12′], 12′, 21′; **5** (RS 2.002):1, 13, 19, 23, 28, 29, 58, 60, 67; **7** (RS 24.258):2, 3, 6; **12** (RS 24.643):9, 23; **17** (RIH 78/20):13bis; **20** (RS 24.247^{+}):41′, 56′; **21** (RS 4.475):12; **22** (RS 8.315):7; **23** (RS 11.872):7; **24** (RS 15.008):4; **25** (RS 16.379):6; **26** (RS 18.031):4; **28** (RS 29.093):6; **29** (RS 34.124):[5]; **30** (RS 92.2010):4; **35** (RS [Varia 4]):4; **41** (RS 19.015):6

ʾIL divine name /ʾilu/ **2** (RS 2.[014]$^{+}$) iii:39′, 43′, 44′, 45′, 46′; **3** (RS 2.[003]$^{+}$) i:36, 41; **4** (RS 2.[004]) i:23′, 32′, 34′; **5** (RS 2.002):31, 33, 34bis, 35bis, 37bis, 39, 42bis, 45bis, [48], 49, 52, 53, [56], 59, 60; **6** (RS 24.244):3; **7** (RS 24.258):1, 12, 14bis, 15, 17, 21, 22; **8** (RS 1.001):2, 7; **9** (RS 1.002):7′, [24′], 25′^{bis}, 33′, 34′, 〈34′〉, 41′, [42′], 42′; **11** (RS 24.266):6, 14; **12** (RS 24.643):2, 10, 25

ʾILʾIB common noun ‘god of the father, ancestral deity’ /ʾiluʾibî/ **4** (RS 2.[004]) i:26′, 44′

ʾILʾIB divine name (same vocalization) **12** (RS 24.643):[1], 10, 23; **41** (RS 19.015):5

ʾILBʿL personal name /ʾilîbaʿlu/ (‘my god is [the god] *Baʿlu*’) **44** (RS 19.016):3

ʾIL BT divine name 'the god of the house/palace' /ʾilu bêti/ **8** (RS 1.001):13; **10** (RS 24.260):3, 7, 9

ʾILDGN personal name /ʾilîdagan/ ('my god is [the god] Dagan') **44** (RS 19.016):20

ʾIL DDMM compound divine name /ʾilū dadmima/ 'the gods of Dadmuma' **12** (RS 24.643):42–43

ʾILHD personal name /ʾilîhaddu/ ('my god is [the god] Haddu') **44** (RS 19.016):7

ʾILY personal name /ʾiliya/ (← /ʾili + ya/) **49** (RIH 84/04):18; **51** (RIH 84/33):22

ʾIL LB[-]N compound divine name /ʾilī LB[-]N/ 'the gods of Labana' **12** (RS 24.643):43

ʾILMLK personal name /ʾilîmilku/ ('my god is [the god] *Milku*') **31** (RS 94.2406):31

ʾILN personal name /ʾilānu/ **44** (RS 19.016):21

ʾIL QRT compound divine name 'the gods of the city' /ʾilū qarîti/ **12** (RS 24.643):40 ({[ʾil q]⸢r⸣t})

ʾILṮR personal name /ʾiluṯarru/ ('*ʾIlu* is ruler') **46** (RS 94.2050^{+}):45

ʾIL TʿḎR BʿL compound divine name 'Auxiliary-Gods-of-*Baʿlu*' /ʾilū taʿḏiri baʿli/ **12** (RS 24.643):8

ʾILT ʾASRM compound divine name 'the goddess/ʾIlatu of ʾASRM (the meaning of the second element is uncertain)' **8** (RS 1.001):11

ʾILT MGDL compound divine name 'the goddess/ʾIlatu of the tower' /ʾilatu magdali/ **8** (RS 1.001):11

ʾILTM ḪNQTM compound divine name 'the strangling goddesses' /ʾilatāma ḫāniqatāma/ **8** (RS 1.001):18

[ʾL verb 'be/become strong']: ʾULNY common noun ← adjective 'the strong one' /ʾūlāniyyu/ **1** (RS 3.367) i:5′

ʾALʾIY(N): see LʾY

ʾULB personal name /ʾullubu/ **46** (RS 94.2050^{+}):18

ʾALGBṮ common noun '(type of soft stone, perhaps local green stone)' /ʾalgabaṯu/ **42** (RS 15.062):15

ʾALḪN personal name /ʾaliḫannu/ **43** (RS 18.024):11

ʾILH divine name /ʾilāhu/ **8** (RS 1.001):5

ʾILHM divine name, plural, 'offspring of *ʾIlu*' /ʾilāhūma/ **8** (RS 1.001):3, 5bis, 9

ʾULKN divine name (ancestor of the kings of Ugarit), vocalization unknown **13** (RS 34.126):4

ʾILŠN personal name /ʾilišānu/ ('pertaining to [the god] ʾIlišu') **44** (RS 19.016):36

ʾALYY personal name /ʾalliyaya/ **29** (RS 34.124):13

[ʾLM]: ʾALMT ‘widow’: ʾULMN common noun ‘widowhood’ /ʾulmānu/ **5** (RS 2.002):9
ʾULM place-name /ʾullamu/ **45** (RS 86.2213):4
ʾALMG common noun ‘(type of tree)’ /ʾalmuggu/ **39** (RS 94.2965):10
ʾILN: see ʾIL
ʾALP common noun ‘bovid’ /ʾalpu/ **8** (RS 1.001):2, 5; **11** (RS 24.266):12; **12** (RS 24.643):[1], 2, [2bis], 3, [3bis], 4bis, [4], 9, 10, 26, 27, 28, 44bis, [44], 45; **14** (RS 6.021):3; **15** (RS 6.028):3; **34** (RS 94.2284):10; **43** (RS 18.024):21
ʾALP number noun ‘thousand’ /ʾalpu/ **2** (RS 2.[014]$^{+}$) iii:[1]; **43** (RS 18.024):2, 6
ʾALṮY gentilic ‘Cypriot’ /ʾalaṯiyyu/ **9** (RS 1.002):[20′], 29′, 37′; **47** (RS 94.2392^{+}):16
ʾM: ʾAMT common noun ‘female servant’ /ʾamatu/, pl. /ʾamahātu/ **28** (RS 29.093):12, 19; **38** (RS 94.2168):10, 27
ʾIM conjunction ‘or’ /ʾimma/ (see also HM) **29** (RS 34.124):12, 13bis, 20; **40** (RS [Varia 14]):6$^{?}$
ʾUM: see ʾMM
ʾAMDN personal name /ʾammadānu/ **46** (RS 94.2050^{+}):4; **49** (RIH 84/04):26
[ʾMM]: ʾUM common noun ‘mother’ /ʾummu/ **3** (RS 2.[003]$^{+}$) i:6, 9, 15; **5** (RS 2.002):33bis; **6** (RS 24.244):1, 2, 8bis, 14$^{!}$, 14, 19bis, 25bis, 30bis, ⟨34a^{bis}⟩, 35bis, 40bis, 45bis, 51bis, 57bis; **22** (RS 8.315):1; **23** (RS 11.872):2, 5, 6, 11; **24** (RS 15.008):2, 6, 10, 18; **25** (RS 16.379):1, 4, 5, 9, 21; **29** (RS 34.124):[1], 4, 5, 18, 34
ʾAMR place-name ‘Amurru’ /ʾamurru/ **29** (RS 34.124):17, 24, 26, 29, 32
ʾIMR common noun ‘lamb’ /ʾimmiru/ **11** (RS 24.266):10
ʾUḎR: see NDR/NḎR
ʾUḎRNN personal name /ʾuḏurnana/ **40** (RS [Varia 14]):19
ʾIN particle expressing absence or non-existence /ʾênu/ ← /*ʾayn-/ **4** (RS 2.[004]) i:18′; **20** (RS 24.247^{+}):4, 7, 9, 10, 12, 14, 15, 26′, 27′, 28′, 30′, 31′, 35′, 37′, [52′], 55′, 59′; **33** (RS 96.2039):18; **37** (RS 16.382):21
ʾIND indefinite pronoun, negative ‘no one’ /ʾênudū/ **34** (RS 94.2284):9, 11
ʾINMM doubly extended form of the basic particle /ʾênumama/ **21** (RS 4.475):9
ʾINN extended form of the basic particle /ʾênuna/ **29** (RS 34.124):12
ʾINBB mountain name /ʾinbubu/ **6** (RS 24.244):20
ʾNḪ verb ‘groan, sigh’ **4** (RS 2.[004]) i:17′
ʾANHB common noun ‘(beauty product from the sea)’ /ʾanhabu/ **2** (RS 2.[014]$^{+}$) iii:1
[ʾNY]: ʾANY common noun ‘group of boats’ /ʾanayyu/ **26** (RS 18.031):10, 24
ʾANYT common noun ‘boat’ /ʾaniyyatu/ **52** (RIH 83/22):13

[ʾNY verb 'to meet']: TʾANT common noun 'communication, meeting' /taʾ^a^natu/ ← /*taʾnatu/ ← /*taʾnayatu/ **2** (RS 2.[014]⁺) iii:24′
ʾANK independent personal pronoun 1c.s. /ʾanāku/# ← /*ʾan + ʾāku/ **2** (RS 2.[014]⁺) iii:28′; **18** (RS 92.2014):2; **22** (RS 8.315):13; **24** (RS 15.008):13; **26** (RS 18.031):18, 23; **28** (RS 29.093):14; **29** (RS 34.124):23, 44′; **31** (RS 94.2406):3, 6, 25, 35; **33** (RS 96.2039):6
ʾNŠ verb 'be/become weak, sick' **2** (RS 2.[014]⁺) iii:35′
ʾANŠT common noun 'weakness, sickness' /ʾanašatu/ **17** (RIH 78/20):15
[ʾINŠ common noun 'man']: ʾINŠ ʾILM collective divine name 'men (who have become) gods' /ʾināšu ʾilīma/ **8** (RS 1.001):22
ʾUNN personal name /ʾunenna/ **44** (RS 19.016):6
ʾANNḪ common noun 'mint' /ʾananiḫu/ **5** (RS 2.002):14
ʾANNMN personal name /ʾananimennu/ **44** (RS 19.016):26
ʾANNTN personal name /ʾanantēnu/ **30** (RS 92.2010):3; **49** (RIH 84/04):7; **51** (RIH 84/33):14
ʾANSNY personal name, vocalization and etymology unknown **44** (RS 19.016):31
[ʾNP]: ʾAP common noun 'nose, nostrils (in the dual), tip (whence) nipple, (whence also) anger (← the redness/heat of the angry person's nose)' /ʾappu/# ← /*ʾanpu/ **5** (RS 2.002):24, 59, 61; **9** (RS 1.002):22′, 31′, 39′; **19** (RS 17.120):4, 6, 8, 11, 14, 17, 19, [22], 29, [32]; **20** (RS 24.247⁺):6, 30′, 41′bis
ʾINR common noun 'puppy, hound' /ʾināru/ **7** (RS 24.258):13
ʾANRMY personal name /ʾannarummiya/ **43** (RS 18.024):18
[ʾNṮ]: ʾAṮT common noun 'woman, wife' /ʾaṯṯatu/ ← /*ʾanṯatu/ **3** (RS 2.[003]⁺) i:12, 14; **4** (RS 2.[004]) i:39′; **5** (RS 2.002):39bis, 42tris, 43, 46, 48, 49, 52, 60, 64; **9** (RS 1.002):36′; **10** (RS 24.260):8; **33** (RS 96.2039):6, 11
ʾUNṮ common noun '(type of tax or service)' /ʾunuṯṯu/# **37** (RS 16.382):20; **39** (RS 94.2965):21, 23
ʾUNǴ place-name /ʾunuǵu/ **31** (RS 94.2406):10
ʾUNTN personal name /ʾuntēnu/ **44** (RS 19.016):30
ʾSP verb 'gather' (Gt-stem) **3** (RS 2.[003]⁺) i:18
ʾASRM: see ʾILT ʾASRM
ʾAP common noun: see ʾNP
ʾAP adverb: see P
ʾAPHM ditto
ʾAPK ditto
ʾAPN(K) ditto
[ʾPQ denominal verb 'block (like a stream)']: N-stem 'be blocked up (like a stream)' **17** (RIH 78/20):12
ʾAPQ common noun 'stream, canal' /ʾapīqu/ **17** (RIH 78/20):12

ʾAPTN personal name /ʾaputēnu/ **46** (RS 94.2050^{+}):30

ʾUṢBʿ: see ṢBʿ

ʾUṢQM common noun, meaning unknown **48** (RS 94.2600):8

ʾIQNʾU common noun 'lapis-lazuli, (whence) wool dyed in a shade of blue' /ʾiqnaʾu/ **5** (RS 2.002):21; **34** (RS 94.2284):19, 21; **36** (RS 11.772^{+}): 23′, 28′, 30′, 32′, [34′], [36′], 38′ ({[ỉqn]ỉ}); **52** (RIH 83/22):6

[ʾR verb 'burn, shine']: ʾUR common noun 'fire, flame' /ʾūru/ **8** (RS 1.001):8; **11** (RS 24.266):13

[ʾR]: ʾIRT common noun 'heart, breast' /ʾiratu/# **1** (RS 3.367) i:3′; **2** (RS 2.[014]$^{+}$) iii:5′

ʾAR divine name, feminine, daughter of *Baʿlu*, 'Shower' /ʾarû/ **2** (RS 2.[014]$^{+}$) iii:6′

ʾAR place-name /ʾaru/ **43** (RS 18.024):19; **45** (RS 86.2213):2; **55** (RS 94.2440):4

ʾRB: ʾURBT '(latticed) window' /ʾurubbatu/ **17** (RIH 78/20):3

ʾARBDD: see RBD

ʾARBʿ: see RBʿ

ʾARGMN common noun 'tribute' /ʾargamanu/ **36** (RS 11.772^{+}):18′, 24′

ʾARW common noun 'lion' /ʾarwu/ **16** (RS 25.318):2

ʾARY common noun 'clan' /ʾaryu/ **4** (RS 2.[004]) i:19′, 21′

ʾRK verb 'be/become long, extend' **5** (RS 2.002):33, 34

ʾRŠ verb 'ask' **3** (RS 2.[003]$^{+}$) i:42

  ʾARŠ divine name in the form of a G-participle /ʾārišu/ **2** (RS 2.[014]$^{+}$) iii:43′

  ʾIRŠT common noun 'desire' /ʾirištu/# **31** (RS 94.2406):15

ʾARŠḪ place-name (← Hurrian name for the Tigris) /ʾaraššiḫu/ **6** (RS 24.244):63, 64

ʾURMY personal name /ʾurumiya/ **49** (RIH 84/04):11; **51** (RIH 84/33):16

ʾARN place-name, Anatolian /ʾarinna/ **36** (RS 11.772^{+}):19′

ʾIRN common noun '(species of animal)' vocalization unknown **20** (RS 24.247^{+}):33′

ʾARNY place-name /ʾaraniya/ **45** (RS 86.2213):8

ʾARSW personal name /ʾarsuwa/ **46** (RS 94.2050^{+}):16

ʾARPŠḪ personal name /ʾaripšaḫu/ **46** (RS 94.2050^{+}):7

ʾARṢ (← *ʾRḌ) common noun 'earth' /ʾarṣu/# **1** (RS 3.367) i:5′, 23′, 26′; **2** (RS 2.[014]$^{+}$) iii:14′, 16′, 24′, 28′; **3** (RS 2.[003]$^{+}$) i:29; **4** (RS 2.[004]) i:27′, 45′; **5** (RS 2.002):62; **7** (RS 24.258):22; **13** (RS 34.126):2, 9, 21bis; **17** (RIH 78/20):11; **18** (RS 92.2014):12

  ʾARṢY divine name, feminine, daughter of *Baʿlu*, 'Earthy' /ʾarṣay/ **2** (RS 2.[014]$^{+}$) iii:7′; **12** (RS 24.643):7

  ʾARṢ W ŠMM divine name, binomial, 'earth and heaven' /ʾarṣu wa šamûma/ **12** (RS 24.643):5, 24

ʾIRǴN common noun ‘fennel’ /ʾirǵānu/ **19** (RS 17.120):17, 28
ʾART place-name /ʾarutu/ **39** (RS 94.2965):15
ʾIRT: see ʾR
ʾARTN personal name /ʾartēnu/ **44** (RS 19.016):28, 30
ʾURTN personal name /ʾurtēnu/ (diminutive of ʾURTṮB) **18** (RS 92.2014):14; **31** (RS 94.2406):2, 32; **34** (RS 94.2284):2; **43** (RS 18.024):4
ʾURTṮB personal name /ʾurtēṯub/ **34** (RS 94.2284):2
ʾIṮ particle expressing existence ‘be’ /ʾiṯu/ **5** (RS 2.002):74; **31** (RS 94.2406):18
  ʾIṮ + L (preposition) = ‘have, possess’ /ʾiṯu lê/ **2** (RS 2.[014]$^{+}$) iii:21′; **4** (RS 2.[004]) i:20′; **5** (RS 2.002):[71], 72; **28** (RS 29.093):29; **34** (RS 94.2284):13
ʾUṮḪT divine name, ‘incense burner’ /ʾuṯḫatu/ **12** (RS 24.643):43 ({⸢ủ⸣[ṯḫt]})
ʾIṮM: see ŠGR-W-ʾIṮM
ʾAṮQLNY: see ṮQL
ʾAṮR common noun ‘place’ /ʾaṯru/ **4** (RS 2.[004]) i:28′, 46′; **20** (RS 24.247^{+}):2$^{?}$
  ʾAṮR preposition ‘after, behind (← in the place of)’ /ʾaṯra/ **6** (RS 24.244):77; **13** (RS 34.126):20bis
  ʾUṮRYN common noun ‘crown prince’ /ʾuṯriyanu/# **36** (RS 11.772^{+}):30′
  ʾAṮRT common noun ‘place’ /ʾaṯratu/ **20** (RS 24.247^{+}):49′
  ʾAṮRT divine name, feminine /ʾaṯiratu/# **5** (RS 2.002):13, 24, 28; **8** (RS 1.001):6; **12** (RS 24.643):7, 31; **17** (RIH 78/20):16
[ʾṮṮ]: ʾIṮṮ common noun ‘offering, gift’ /ʾiṯṯatu/ **23** (RS 11.872):15; **25** (RS 16.379):14
ʾAṮṮ: see ʾNṮ
ʾIṮṮBNM month name, eleventh of the lunar year, vocalization unknown **44** (RS 19.016):1 ({ỉṯ⸢ṯ⸣[bnm]})
ʾAǴLTN personal name /ʾaǵaltēnu/ **34** (RS 94.2284):16
ʾAT independent personal pronoun ‘you’ /ʾatta/# (← /*ʾan + ta/) (2m.s.), /ʾatti/ (← /*ʾan + ti/) (2f.s.) **1** (RS 3.367) i:11′, 19′; **25** (RS 16.379):20; **30** (RS 92.2010):19; **31** (RS 94.2406):11, 21, 37, 39; **33** (RS 96.2039):13, 22; **34** (RS 94.2284):26
ʾTY verb ‘arrive, come’ **2** (RS 2.[014]$^{+}$) iii:28′
ʾATLG place-name /ʾatalligu/ **55** (RS 94.2440):3
ʾITNN: see YTN

B preposition ‘in, within, by (means of), from (within)’ /bi/# **1** (RS 3.367) i:3′^{bis}, [4]′, 6′^{bis}, 14′, 16′, 21′, 24′, 28′, 30′, 38′; **2** (RS 2.[014]$^{+}$) iii:2, 14′, 15′, 29′, 30′^{bis}, 31′^{bis}, 32′, iv:1; **3** (RS 2.[003]$^{+}$) i:20, 24, 25, 26, 27, 32, 35, 36, 38; **4** (RS 2.[004]) i:15′, 16′, 25′^{bis}, 26′, 30′, 32′, 33′, 40′, [43′], 43′, 44′; **5** (RS 2.002):4, 6bis, 14bis, 24, 27, 36, 38, 51, 56, 59, 61, 62, 63,

64bis, 74; **6** (RS 24.244):3, 61, 64, 65; **7** (RS 24.258):1bis, 11, 14, 15, 21, 27′; **8** (RS 1.001):8; **9** (RS 1.002):$22'^{bis}$, [22′], $31'^{tris}$, $39'^{bis}$, [39′]; **10** (RS 24.260):3, 7, 10, 11; **11** (RS 24.266):1bis, 4, 9, 11, $20'^{bis}$, $22'^{bis}$; **15** (RS 6.028):3; **17** (RIH 78/20):7bis, 8^{tris}, 15, 16; **19** (RS 17.120):3, 4bis, 6, 8, 11, 14, 17, 19, [22], 29, [32]; **20** (RS 24.247^{+}):1, 3, 5, 9, [11], 12, 14, 26′, 27′, 31′, 35′, 37′, 48′, 49′, 51′, 52′, 54′, 55′, [57′], 58′, 59′; **21** (RS 4.475):19; **23** (RS 11.872):18; **24** (RS 15.008):10; **25** (RS 16.379):13, 23; **26** (RS 18.031):12, 27; **27** (RS 18.040):9; **29** (RS 34.124):20, 30, 43′; **30** (RS 92.2010):24; **31** (RS 94.2406):3, 5, 6, 8, 9, 21, 25, 28, 39; **32** (RS 94.2479):5; **33** (RS 96.2039):9; **34** (RS 94.2284):9, 17, 20, 21; **37** (RS 16.382):6, 21; **39** (RS 94.2965):8, 20; **40** (RS [Varia 14]):4, 8; **41** (RS 19.015):2, 15; **42** (RS 15.062):5, 6, 7, 8, 9, 20, 21, 22; **43** (RS 18.024):5, 7, 10, 11, 13, 15, 17, 19bis, 20, 21, 22, 23, 24, 25, [27]; **44** (RS 19.016):1; **47** (RS 94.2392^{+}):3, 7, 8; **48** (RS 94.2600):16; **52** (RIH 83/22):10

BD compound preposition ‘in the hand(s) of’ /bîdi/bîdê/ (B + D [← YD]) **1** (RS 3.367) i:13′, 15′, 21′, 23′; **4** (RS 2.[004]) i:⟨34′⟩; **5** (RS 2.002):8bis; **26** (RS 18.031):21; **28** (RS 29.093):19; **33** (RS 96.2039):17, 22; **34** (RS 94.2284):4, 25!; **37** (RS 16.382):17, 19; **39** (RS 94.2965):13; **41** (RS 19.015):1; **43** (RS 18.024):4, 7, 9, 11, 18, 21; **44** (RS 19.016):9, 30, 31

BDN extended form /bîdêna/ **26** (RS 18.031):18

BY extended form /biya/ **26** (RS 18.031):13, 25

BM extended form /bima/ **3** (RS $2.[003]^{+}$) i:31; **4** (RS 2.[004]) i:⟨34′⟩, 39′; **5** (RS 2.002):51, 56; **23** (RS 11.872):14

BN extended form /bina/ **5** (RS 2.002):[23], 59, 61

Bʾ verb ‘enter’ **6** (RS 24.244):72; **17** (RIH 78/20):18bis

BʾIR place-name /biʾiru/ (‘well’) **41** (RS 19.015):29

BʾIRY gentilic **51** (RIH 84/33):9, 11

[BʾRT place-name /biʾirātu/ (‘wells’)]: gentilic BʾIRTY /biʾirātiyyu/ **43** (RS 18.024):3

BBT place-name, Anatolian /bibitta/ **6** (RS 24.244):31

BD: see B

BDN personal name /badunu/ **44** (RS 19.016):34; **46** (RS 94.2050^{+}):34; **52** (RIH 83/22):10

BHL verb ‘liberate, allow to leave freely’ **38** (RS 94.2168):20, 21, 22, 25, 26, 29

BHTM see BT

[BHM]: BHMT common noun ‘cattle’ /bahimatu/ **20** (RS 24.247^{+}):2, 8, 15, 16, 34′

BKY verb ‘weep’ **3** (RS $2.[003]^{+}$) i:26, 31, 39; **13** (RS 34.126):15

N-stem ‘be bewept’ **13** (RS 34.126):13

BKR common noun 'firstborn' /bikāru/ **11** (RS 24.266):31′
BL: see BLY
BLDN common noun 'land, country' /bildānu/ **41** (RS 19.015):6
BLY: BL negative particle 'not' /balû/ (← common noun 'nothingness') **4** (RS 2.[004]) i:20′
[BLL verb 'mix']: BL common noun 'mix, (whence) drink' /billu/ **17** (RIH 78/20):7, 16
BLN common noun '(plant name)' /billānu/ **19** (RS 17.120):18
BLʿ verb 'swallow' **13** (RS 34.126):16
BM: see B
BN common noun 'son' /binu/, pl. /banūma/ **3** (RS 2.[003]$^{+}$) i:9; **4** (RS 2.[004]) i:3′, 8′, 10′, 13′, 18′, 20′, 22′, 25′, 42′; **5** (RS 2.002):2, 65; **6** (RS 24.244):74, 75; **9** (RS 1.002):7′, [24′], 25′^{bis}, 26′, 33′, 34′, ⟨34′⟩, 41′, [42′], 42′; **16** (RS 25.318):1; **17** (RIH 78/20):15; **18** (RS 92.2014):10; **23** (RS 11.872):4; **25** (RS 16.379):3; **28** (RS 29.093):11, 17; **29** (RS 34.124):[3], 12, 13; **35** (RS [Varia 4]):3, 16; **37** (RS 16.382):2, 12, 14, 18, 19, 23; **38** (RS 94.2168):3, 7, 8, 9, 10, 12bis, 17, 20, 23bis, 26, 27; **40** (RS [Varia 14]):19, 21; **43** (RS 18.024):21; **46** (RS 94.2050^{+}):1 et passim in this text; **49** (RIH 84/04):8, 11, 14, 16, 18, 21, 26; **50** (RIH 84/06):[2], 8; **51** (RIH 84/33):2, 6, 14, 16, 18, 20, 22
  BNʾIL personal name /biniʾilu/ ('son of [the god] *ʾIlu*') **34** (RS 94.2284):4$^{!}$, 22, 25; **44** (RS 19.016):8, 19; **49** (RIH 84/04):13; **51** (RIH 84/33):17
  BT common noun 'daughter' /bittu/ ← /*bintu/ **2** (RS 2.[014]$^{+}$) iii:6′, 7′, 8′, 46′; **5** (RS 2.002):45^{tris}; **6** (RS 24.244):1^{tris}; **9** (RS 1.002):35′; **29** (RS 34.124):17, 24, 32; **38** (RS 94.2168):8, 23
BN preposition 'between, among' /bêna/ ← /*bayna/ **1** (RS 3.367) i:14′, 16′, 22′, 25′, 40′
BN verb 'understand' **2** (RS 2.[014]$^{+}$) iii:26′, 27′
  Lt-stem 'recognize' **17** (RIH 78/20):17
BNʾIL: see BN
BNY verb 'build, create' **4** (RS 2.[004]) i:24′
  BNWT common noun 'creatures, descendants' /bunuwwatu/ **4** (RS 2.[004]) i:24′; **6** (RS 24.244):62
  YBNN personal name /yabninu/ **29** (RS 34.124):25; **39** (RS 94.2965):2, 13, 19$^{!}$; **42** (RS 15.062):2
BNŠ common noun '(member of) the (royal) personnel' /bunušu/# **33** (RS 96.2039):4, 8, 10, 15; **37** (RS 16.382):16bis; **39** (RS 94.2965):11; **44** (RS 19.016):1, 49, 50
BʿD preposition 'with respect to an opening, (whence) behind, (or) with respect to' /baʿda/ **5** (RS 2.002):70; **6** (RS 24.244):70bis, 71
  BʿDN extended form /baʿdāna/ **2** (RS 2.[014]$^{+}$) iii:33′

Bˁ L common noun 'master, owner' /baˁlu/# **7** (RS 24.258):20; **13** (RS 34.126):20, 21; **15** (RS 6.028):2; **17** (RIH 78/20):2; **20** (RS 24.247^{+}):34′, 39′; **27** (RS 18.040):1, 5, 18; **28** (RS 29.093):1, 6, 8, 28; **30** (RS 92.2010):2, 6, 12, 21; **36** (RS 11.772^{+}):12′, 13′, 26′; **39** (RS 94.2965):9; **44** (RS 19.016):51

Bˁ L divine name (weather god) /baˁlu/ **1** (RS 3.367) i:8′, 9′, 13′, 15′, 21′, 23′, 27′, 28′, 31′, 32′, 36′ {bˁlm}; **2** (RS 2.[014]$^{+}$) iii:6′, 13′, 37′, 47′, iv:4, 6; **4** (RS 2.[004]) i:16′, 31′; **6** (RS 24.244):9; **8** (RS 1.001):6, 7, 14; **11** (RS 24.266):9, 15, 25′, 27′, 28′, 30′^{bis}, 31′, 32′^{bis}, 33′^{bis}, 34′; **12** (RS 24.643):3, [3bis], 4bis, [4] ({bˁlm} all six times), 8, 11^{quadris} ({bˁlm}), 12bis ({bˁlm}), [43] ({bˁlm}), 44, [44bis] ({bˁlm}^{bis}); **41** (RS 19.015):14

Bˁ L ʾUGRT divine name '*Baˁlu* of Ugarit' /baˁlu ʾugārit/ **11** (RS 24.266):3, 12, 21′–22′

Bˁ L ḪLB divine name '*Baˁlu* of Aleppo' /baˁlu ḫalbi/ **12** (RS 24.643):26

BˁLYN personal name /baˁliyānu/ **51** (RIH 84/33):12

BˁLM divine name (plural expressing the various manifestations of *Baˁlu* as a collectivity) /baˁalūma/ **8** (RS 1.001):9; **11** (RS 24.266):6

BˁLN personal name /baˁlānu/ **37** (RS 16.382):12, 18; **44** (RS 19.016):12, 21, 23, 28

Bˁ L ṢPN divine name 'the *Baˁlu* of (the mountain) *Ṣapunu*' /baˁlu ṣapuni/ **8** (RS 1.001):10; **12** (RS 24.643):[2], 10$^{!}$, 27

Bˁ L RˁKT divine name, hypostasis of *Baˁlu*, identification, meaning, and vocalization of second element unknown **11** (RS 24.266):2

BˁLT BHTM divine name, feminine 'the lady of the houses = of the palace$^{?}$' /baˁlatu bahatīma/ **8** (RS 1.001):21; **41** (RS 19.015):14

Bˁ L (← PˁL) verb 'manufacture (a garment)' **28** (RS 29.093):27

Bˁ L ˁDTT common noun, profession name, substantivized participle, 'maker of ˁDTT (meaning unknown)' /bāˁilu ˁDTāti/ **44** (RS 19.016):35

Bˁ L TǴPṮM common noun, profession name, substantivized participle, 'maker of TǴPṮM (meaning unknown)' /bāˁilu TǴPṮīma/ **44** (RS 19.016):36

[BˁR verb 'burn']: D-stem 'destroy' **20** (RS 24.247^{+}):41′, 56′, 58′; **30** (RS 92.2010):23

BṢQL common noun '(green) outer layer, shell' /biṣqalu/ **19** (RS 17.120):5

BṢR verb 'observe' **27** (RS 18.040):11

BṢR place-name /baṣiru/ **41** (RS 19.015):23

BQL common noun 'groats' /buqlu/ **19** (RS 17.120):32

BQˁT place-name /baqˁatu/ **45** (RS 86.2213):10

BRDD personal name, vocalization and etymology unknown (perhaps /baraddaddu/, ← /barad + hadd-/, 'by the hail of [the god] Haddu') **46** (RS 94.2050^{+}):51

BRZN personal name /burzanu/ **46** (RS 94.2050^{+}):11
BRK verb 'bless' (D-stem?) **4** (RS 2.[004]) i:23′, ⟨34′^{bis}⟩, 34′
BRLT common noun 'throat' /būrālatu/ **4** (RS 2.[004]) i:37′
BRʿ: ʾUBRʿY place-name /ʾuburʿāyu/ **45** (RS 86.2213):6
BRQ common noun 'lightning' /baraqu/ **2** (RS 2.[014]$^{+}$) iii:26′
BRR verb 'be/become pure, clean' **11** (RS 24.266):5
  BRR common noun 'tin' /barūru/ **43** (RS 18.024):4
BṮN common noun 'serpent' /baṯnu/ **2** (RS 2.[014]$^{+}$) iii:41′; **6** (RS 24.244):74, 75; **17** (RIH 78/20):3; **18** (RS 92.2014):4, 6
BṮṮ verb 'scatter, make fly in all directions' **1** (RS 3.367) i:28′, 29′, 31′
BǴY verb 'explain' **2** (RS 2.[014]$^{+}$) iii:29′
BT common noun 'house, household' /bêtu/ ← /*baytu/; pl. BHTM /bahatūma/ **1** (RS 3.367) i:5′; **3** (RS 2.[003]$^{+}$) i:7; **4** (RS 2.[004]) i:25′, 31′, 32′, [43′]; **5** (RS 2.002):36; **6** (RS 24.244):67, 70bis, 71, 72; **7** (RS 24.258):1, 12, 17; **8** (RS 1.001):12, 21; **10** (RS 24.260):3bis, 7, 9, 11; **11** (RS 24.266):3, 8, 9, 14, 22′; **12** (RS 24.643):18; **13** (RS 34.126):32$^{!}$, 33; **17** (RIH 78/20):18; **28** (RS 29.093):16, 24; **30** (RS 92.2010):17, 21; **31** (RS 94.2406):16, 37; **32** (RS 94.2479):6; **33** (RS 96.2039):12; **38** (RS 94.2168):5, 14; **39** (RS 94.2965):23; **40** (RS [Varia 14]):4, 8; **41** (RS 19.015):7, 10, 11, 14; **43** (RS 18.024):16
  BT verb 'stay, lodge' **31** (RS 94.2406):7
BT common noun 'daughter': see BN 'son'
[BTL common noun 'young man']: BTL personal name /batūlu/ ('young man') **44** (RS 19.016):25
  BTLT common noun 'girl of marriageable age' /batūlatu/ **2** (RS 2.[014]$^{+}$) iii:11′
BTRY personal name, vocalization and etymology unknown **46** (RS 94.2050^{+}):39, 67

G common noun 'voice' /gû/ (← /*gVyu/) **1** (RS 3.367) i:6′; **2** (RS 2.[014]$^{+}$) iii:36′; **3** (RS 2.[003]$^{+}$) i:27 ({gmm}: G); **5** (RS 2.002):14
GB common noun 'goblet' /gūbu/ **7** (RS 24.258):5
[GBB]: GB common noun 'back, (whence) body' /gabbu/ **17** (RIH 78/20):5; **18** (RS 92.2014):14
GBʿ common noun 'hill' /gabʿu/ **2** (RS 2.[014]$^{+}$) iii:31′
GBʿN personal name /gabʿānu/ **46** (RS 94.2050^{+}):8 ({[g]bʿn})
GBʿLY place-name /gibʿalāya/ **45** (RS 86.2213):3
GG common noun 'roof' /gaggu/ **4** (RS 2.[004]) i:32′
GD common noun 'coriander' /giddu/ **5** (RS 2.002):14; **19** (RS 17.120):20, 25
[GDL verb 'be/become big']: GDLT common noun 'cow (← large female [animal])' /gadulatu/ **8** (RS 1.001):3, 5, 8bis, 13^{tris}, 14bis, 15^{tris}, 18, 19, 21; **11** (RS 24.266):6bis, 7, 7 {g⟨d⟩lt}; **12** (RS 24.643):9

GDL common noun '(food product, perhaps a type of flour)' vocalization unknown **32** (RS 94.2479):14; **48** (RS 94.2600):4
GHR verb 'sound aloud' **18** (RS 92.2014):11
[GZR verb 'cut']: GZR common noun 'delimitation' /gazaru/ **5** (RS 2.002):63bis!
ʾAGZR common noun 'something that cuts off, delimits' /ʾagzaru/ **5** (RS 2.002):[23], 58, 61
GŠM common noun 'storm' /gišmu/ **26** (RS 18.031):14
GLB: MGLB personal name /maglibu/ **46** (RS 94.2050+):61, 65
GLN personal name /gallānu/ **49** (RIH 84/04):25
GLʿD personal name /galʿadu/ **46** (RS 94.2050+):1
GMŠ adjective 'smooth, hairless' /gamīšu/ **20** (RS 24.247+):3
GMR: TGMR common noun 'total' /tagmaru/ **41** (RS 19.015):35; **43** (RS 18.024):28 ({[tg]⌜m⌝r}); **47** (RS 94.2392+):10
[GN]: GT common noun '(wine/oil press, whence) farming installation with its buildings' /gittu/ ← /*gintu/ **33** (RS 96.2039):9; **37** (RS 16.382):7; **39** (RS 94.2965):15
GN divine name element: see RŠP GN
GʿR verb 'cry out, yell, rebuke, make a loud noise (said of a sick horse)' **1** (RS 3.367) i:28′; **7** (RS 24.258):11, 14; **19** (RS 17.120):2, 23
GP common noun 'edge' /gīpu/ **5** (RS 2.002):30bis
GP common noun, meaning unknown **31** (RS 94.2406):27
GPN common noun 'vine' /gapnu/ **5** (RS 2.002):9, 10, 11
GPN-W-ʾUGR divine name, binomial, messengers of *Baʿlu*, /gapnu wa ʾugāru/ 'Vine and Field' **2** (RS 2.[014]+) iii:36′
GPN personal name /gupanu/ **44** (RS 19.016):17; **46** (RS 94.2050+):27
GR verb 'sojourn, live in a place as a resident alien' **5** (RS 2.002):66bis
GR common noun 'resident alien' /gêru/ **9** (RS 1.002):18′, [26′], 35′
GR verb 'attack' **11** (RS 24.266):26′
GRGMŠ place-name 'Carchemish' /gargamiš/ **52** (RIH 83/22):13
GRGYN personal name /girgiyannu/ **43** (RS 18.024):24
GRDŠ verb 'crush, destroy' **3** (RS 2.[003]+) i:11, 23
GRŠ verb 'drive away, send away' **1** (RS 3.367) i:12′bis; **2** (RS 2.[014]+) iv:2; **4** (RS 2.[004]) i:29′, 47′; **17** (RIH 78/20):9; **34** (RS 94.2284):22; **40** (RS [Varia 14]):6–7
YGRŠ proper name /yagrušu/ **1** (RS 3.367) i:12′bis
GRN common noun 'threshing floor' /gurnu/ **19** (RS 17.120):13, 16
GṮR divine name, god of war, 'the Strong One' /gaṯaru/# **12** (RS 24.643):[38?]
GT: see GN

[ḪBL verb ‘mutilate’]: ḪBLY divine title (attributed to the goddess *ʿAnatu*, lit., ‘mutilated’) /ḫablay/ **8** (RS 1.001):17

ḪBRTNR title of a Hittite official /ḫuburtanuru/ **36** (RS 11.772^{+}):34′, 36′ ({[ḫbrtn]⸢r⸣})

ḪBṮ verb ‘belong to the *ḫupṯu*-class, serve as a *ḫupṯu*’ **33** (RS 96.2039):9

ḪPṮ (← ḪBṮ) common noun ‘member of the *ḫupṯu*-class (in service, civil or military)’ /ḫupṯu/ ← /*ḫubṯu/ **20** (RS 24.247^{+}):57′; **29** (RS 34.124):10

ḪBT verb ‘oppress’ **9** (RS 1.002):21′, 30′, 38′; **34** (RS 94.2284):8

[ḪBT place-name /ḫubatāyu/ = /ḫupatāyu/$^{!}$]: ḪBTY gentilic /ḫubatiyyu/ **50** (RIH 84/06):4; **51** (RIH 84/33):3

ḪDMN personal name /ḫudmunu/ **46** (RS 94.2050^{+}):35

ḪZR common noun ‘(type of service)’ vocalization unknown **44** (19.016):49, 50

ḪṬ common noun ‘stick, staff’ /ḫaṭṭu/ **5** (RS 2.002):8, 9, 37, 40, 43, 47; **7** (RS 24.258):8; **17** (RIH 78/20):1, 2, 5bis, 14

ḪṬʾ verb ‘sin, act improperly’ **9** (RS 1.002):19′, 22′, 23′; **17** (RIH 78/20):5

ḪṬʾ common noun ‘sin, misdeed’ **29** (RS 34.124):33 ({ḫ⸢ṭ⸣[?]})

ḪYR month name /ḫiyyāru/ **12** (RS 24.643):23; **34** (RS 94.2284):$9^{!}$

ḪYRN personal name /ḫiyyārānu/ (‘born in the month of Ḫiyyāru’) **44** (RS 19.016):4

ḪLʾU DG name of a sacrificial rite, meaning unknown **41** (RS 19.015):12

ḪLB place-name ‘Aleppo’ /ḫalbu/ **12** (RS 24.643):26; **19** (RS 17.120):20

ḪLB GNGNT place-name /ḫalbu ganganati/ **41** (RS 19.015):22

ḪLBY gentilic, person from one of the towns named ḪLB /ḫalbiyyu/ **43** (RS 18.024):6

ḪLB KRD place-name /ḫalbu karradi/ **55** (RS 94.2440):6

ḪLB RPŠ place-name /ḫalbu rapši/ **55** (RS 94.2440):5

ḪLMẒ nominal epithet of the divinity ʾUŠḪR ‘(kind of reptile)’ /ḫulmiẓẓu/ **10** (RS 24.260):2, 4, 12

ḪLṢ common noun ‘oppression’ /ḫulṣu/ **17** (RIH 78/20):7

ḪLQ verb ‘perish’ **20** (RS 24.247^{+}):4, [6], 18, 59′; **31** (RS 94.2406):30

D-stem ‘destroy’ **20** (RS 24.247^{+}):15, 16

ḪMʾAT common noun ‘melted butter’ /ḫimʾatu/ **5** (RS 2.002):14

ḪMŠ cardinal number ‘five’ /ḫamišu/; pl. ‘fifty’ /ḫamišūma/ **5** (RS 2.002):57; **8** (RS 1.001):9; **12** (RS 24.643):20; **13** (RS 34.126):29; **32** (RS 94.2479):13, 14; **36** (RS 11.772^{+}):22′ ({[ḫm]š}), 23′ ({[ḫm]⸢š⸣}); **40** (RS [Varia 14]):9; **42** (RS 15.062):10, 12, 19, 22bis; **43** (RS 18.024):2, 6, 7, 17, 25; **44** (RS 19.016):38, 39; **47** (RS 94.2392^{+}):11; **48** (RS 94.2600):3, 7, 8; **51** (RIH 84/33):8, 10; **52** (RIH 83/22):5, 8

ḪMŠ ordinal number ‘fifth’ /ḫamīšu/ **4** (RS 2.[004]) i:11′; **11** (RS 24.266):20′

ḪMŠ verb 'do five times' (D-stem) **3** (RS 2.[003]⁺) i:18 (Dp-participle)
ḪMŠM plural of /ḫamišu/ 'fifty' /ḫamišūma/
ḪMŠT common noun 'five(-shekel) weight' /ḫamišatu/ **3** (RS 2.[003]⁺) i:30

ḪMR common noun 'wine (← ferment, bubble)' /ḫamru/ **5** (RS 2.002):6
ḪD̲MRT personal name /ḫid̲miratu/ **30** (RS 92.2010):1
ḪD̲Ǵ L common noun (← Hurrian), 'arrow maker' (← Ugaritic *ḥẓ/ḥd̲*, 'arrow', + Hurrian /ḫuli/ occupational designation) /ḫid̲d̲iǵulu/ **44** (RS 19.016):16
ḪNDRT̲ common noun '(plant name: grown in the place Ḫundurašu)' /ḫunduraṯu/ **19** (RS 17.120):7
ḪNZR personal name /ḫanizarru/ **46** (RS 94.2050⁺):57
ḪNYN personal name /ḫanyanu/ **46** (RS 94.2050⁺):25
ḪSWN common noun 'thyme' /ḫaswannu/ **48** (RS 94.2600):13
[ḪPY]: ḪPN common noun '(type of garment)' /ḫipânu/ **12** (RS 24.643):19; **28** (RS 29.093):28; **34** (RS 94.2284):18, 28
ḪPN: see ḪPY
ḪPT̲: see ḪBT̲
ḪPTY place-name /ḫupatāyu/ (= /ḫubatāyu/!) **41** (RS 19.015):30
[ḪṢY]: ḪṢT common noun 'half' /ḫaṣâtu/ ← /*ḫaṣayatu/ **8** (RS 1.001):10
ḪR verb 'whinny (unnaturally when the horse is sick)' **19** (RS 17.120):5, 7
[ḪR place-name 'the Hurrian land']: ḪRY gentilic 'person of Hurrian origin' /ḫurriyyu/ **9** (RS 1.002):[20′], 29′, 37′
ḪR: see ḪRR
ḪRʾ verb 'defecate' **19** (RS 17.120):9
ḪRʾU common noun 'feces' /ḫurʾu/ **7** (RS 24.258):21
ḪRB adjective 'dry, dried' /ḫaribu/ **48** (RS 94.2600):13
ḪRD common noun 'troops, army' /ḫurādu/ **20** (RS 24.247⁺):39′, 46′, 52′; **24** (RS 15.008):13
ḪRṬ verb 'pluck (feathers)' **5** (RS 2.002):38
ḪRY: see ḪR place-name
ḪRMLN personal name, vocalization and etymology unknown **46** (RS 94.2050⁺):20
[ḪRP]: ḪRPN adjective 'autumnal' /ḫurpānu/ **7** (RS 24.258):31′ ({ḫrpn!})
ḪRṢ common noun 'gold' /ḫurāṣu/# **2** (RS 2.[014]⁺) iii:47′; **29** (RS 34.124):28; **36** (RS 11.772⁺):20′, 27′, 29′; **43** (RS 18.024):20
ḪRṢP common noun '(a body part, perhaps a tendon)' /ḫarṣuppu/ (if the word means 'tendon') **20** (RS 24.247⁺):27′
[ḪRR]: ḪR common noun '(hole, whence) nostril' /ḫurru/ **20** (RS 24.247⁺):6, 30′
ḪT place-name 'Ḫatti' /ḫatti/ **25** (RS 16.379):16
ḪTY gentilic 'person from Ḫatti' /ḫattiyyu/ **9** (RS 1.002):20′, 29′, 37′

[Ḫ̮T' verb 'strike']: N-stem **21** (RS 4.475):8, 10
Ḫ̮T'U common noun 'blow' /ḫataʾu/ **21** (RS 4.475):7

D form of the common noun YD 'hand' that appears with the preposition B /bîdi/ ← /bi yadi/: see B and YD

D/DT determinative/relative pronoun /dū/# **1** (RS 3.367) i:10′; **2** (RS 2.[014]⁺) iii:[1], 26′, 35′, 42′; **3** (RS 2.[003]⁺) i:8; **4** (RS 2.[004]) i:18′, 29′, 47′; **5** (RS 2.002):74; **6** (RS 24.244):62; **7** (RS 24.258):6, 7, 29′; **14** (RS 6.021):1; **15** (RS 6.028):1; **16** (RS 25.318):2; **17** (RIH 78/20):1; **18** (RS 92.2014):1; **19** (RS 17.120):3; **21** (RS 4.475):17; **26** (RS 18.031):10; **31** (RS 94.2406):17, 18; **32** (RS 94.2479):20; **33** (RS 96.2039):5; **34** (RS 94.2284):13, 29, 31, 32b; **35** (RS [Varia 4]):7; **36** (RS 11.772⁺):18′, 25′; **37** (RS 16.382):6bis; **38** (RS 94.2168):5, 11; **39** (RS 94.2965):2, 8; **40** (RS [Varia 14]):2, 16; **41** (RS 19.015):1; **42** (RS 15.062):19?; **43** (RS 18.024):12, 16; **47** (RS 94.2392⁺):1, 6; **52** (RIH 83/22):6, 7, 10, 11, 13

DM extended form that functions as a conjunction 'for' /dāma/ **2** (RS 2.[014]⁺) iii:20′

ʾID adverb 'at that time' /ʾida/ **10** (RS 24.260):1

ʾIDK adverb 'then' /ʾidaka/ **6** (RS 24.244):63

DʾY verb 'fly (away)' **20** (RS 24.247⁺):42′

[DB ← *D̲B verb 'flow']: MDB common noun 'flow(ing waters)' /madūbu/ ← /*mad̲ūbu/ **5** (RS 2.002):34, 35

[DBB verb 'speak']: DBB common noun 'tormenter (← who speaks evil of)' /dābibu/ **17** (RIH 78/20):1, 9; **18** (RS 92.2014):9, 13

DBḤ verb 'slaughter, sacrifice' **7** (RS 24.258):1; **10** (RS 24.260):1; **11** (RS 24.266):8, 13; **27** (RS 18.040):16

N-stem **9** (RS 1.002):15′ ({[ndb]ḥ}), 23′ ({[ndb]⌜ḥ⌝}), 32′, 41′

DBḤ common noun 'sacrifice' /dabḥu/# **5** (RS 2.002):27; **8** (RS 1.001):17; **9** (RS 1.002):23′ ({‹d›bḥ⌜m⌝}), 23′ ({d[bḥn]}), 32′bis, [40′], 40′; **12** (RS 24.643):1; **13** (RS 34.126):1; **34** (RS 94.2284):17; **41** (RS 19.015):2, 3, 14

MDBḤ common noun 'altar' /madbaḥu/, pl. MDBḤT /madbaḥātu/ **8** (RS 1.001):20

DBLT common noun 'clump of dried figs' /dabilatu/ **19** (RS 17.120):31

[DBR verb 'speak, lead']: D-stem 'speak' **29** (RS 34.124):18

ʾUDBR common noun 'sworn (heir, i.e., he who has been made to speak)'? /ʾudbaru/? **46** (RS 94.2050⁺):52, 56

MDBR common noun 'steppe-land (← where one leads herds of caprovids)' /madbaru/ **5** (RS 2.002):4, 65, 68

DG common noun 'fish' /dagu/ **5** (RS 2.002):63

[DGL]: MDGL BʿL ʾUGRT divine name, meaning of first element uncertain, perhaps 'place of observation' (or correct to MGDL 'tower') **11** (RS 24.266):12

DGN divine name /dagan/ ← 'grain' **6** (RS 24.244):15; **12** (RS 24.643):[2], 10, 26; **14** (RS 6.021):2; **15** (RS 6.028):2

DD (← *ḎḎ) verb 'arise' (N-stem) **5** (RS 2.002):63; **40** (RS [Varia 14]):12; **41** (RS 19.015):14

DD common noun 'love' /dādu/ **2** (RS 2.[014]$^{+}$) iii:5′, 7′

DDYM common noun '(offerings that produce) love' /dādāyūma/ **2** (RS 2.[014]$^{+}$) iii:15′

DD common noun '(dry measure [perhaps about fifty liters])' /dūdu/ **32** (RS 94.2479):12, 13, 15; **44** (RS 19.016):38, 39, 48; **48** (RS 94.2600):1, 4

DDY personal name /dudāyu/ **46** (RS 94.2050^{+}):43

DDMŠ divine name /dadmiš/ **12** (RS 24.643):8, [34]

DDMM **12** place-name 'the region around Aleppo' /dadmuma/ **12** (RS 24.643):43

DDMY gentilic 'person from Dadmuma' /dadmiyyu/ **9** (RS 1.002):20′, 28′ ({[ddm]y}), 37′

DDN divine name (ancestor of the kings of Ugarit) /didānu/ **13** (RS 34.126):3, 10

DḤṢ verb 'suffer distress' **25** (RS 16.379):21

DK(K) verb 'bray, pulverize' **19** (RS 17.120):3, 6, 8, 11, 14, 17, 19, 22, 28

DLY: YDLN personal name /yadlinu/ ('he [a divinity] drew [this child] as in the act of drawing water') **44** (RS 19.016):34

DLP verb 'slump' **1** (RS 3.367) i:17′, 26′

[DLL verb 'be/become poor, destitute']: D-stem 'impoverish, cast down' **9** (RS 1.002):21′, 30′, 38′; **20** (RS 24.247^{+}):7, 46′$^{!}$

DLT common noun 'destitution, feebleness' /dullatu/ **5** (RS 2.002):25

DM common noun 'blood, (whence) juice (liquid from a plant)' /damu/# **7** (RS 24.258):31′

DMʿ verb 'shed tears' **3** (RS 2.[003]$^{+}$) i:27, 32, 40; **13** (RS 34.126):14

DMʿT common noun 'tear' /dimʿatu/ (pl. ʾUDMʿT /ʾudmaʿātu/) **3** (RS 2.[003]$^{+}$) i:28; **13** (RS 34.126):16

DNʾIL personal name 'ʾ*Ilu* is my judge' /dānîʾilu/ **4** (RS 2.[004]) i:[1′], 6′, 9′, 12′, 14′, 17′, 35′, 36′

[DNY verb 'be near, approach']: D-stem 'make near' **11** (RS 24.266):22′

DʿT: see YDʿ

DPRN common noun 'juniper' /diprānu/# **19** (RS 17.120):[23]; **42** (RS 15.062):20

DQN personal name /diqnu/ **44** (RS 19.016):6, 23, 26, 29 ({dqn[. . .]})

[DQQ verb 'be/become fine']: DQT common noun 'ewe/nanny (← small female [animal])' /daqqatu/ **8** (RS 1.001):1bis, 3, 4bis, 16bis, ⟨16⟩, 18; **11** (RS 24.266):7

DQT divine name, feminine /daqqītu/ **8** (RS 1.001):15

[DR verb ‘form a circle, dwell’]: DR ‘circle, generation (period of time)’ /dāru/ **1** (RS 3.367) i:10′^{bis}

DR ʾIL W PḪR BʿL compound divine name ‘the Circle of *ʾIlu* and the Assembly of *Baʿlu*’ /dāru ʾili wa puḫru baʿli/ **8** (RS 1.001):7

DR BN ʾIL compound divine name ‘the Circle of the Sons of *ʾIlu*’ /dāru banī ʾili/ **9** (RS 1.002):7′, 25′, 33′–34′, 42′ ({⸢d⸣[r . bn ỉl]})

YDRM personal name /yadurma/ **28** (RS 29.093):1

[DRK verb ‘stride, step on’]: DRKT common noun ‘sovereignty, dominion’ /darkatu/ **1** (RS 3.367) i:10′, 13′, 20′; **2** (RS 2.[014]$^{+}$) iv:3; **3** (RS 2.[003]$^{+}$) i:42

DRʿ/ḎRʿ common noun ‘seed’ /darʿu/ḏarʿu/ **19** (RS 17.120):[24]; **20** (RS 24.247^{+}):14, 43′, 55′; **26** (RS 18.031):17, 19

MDRʿ common noun ‘sown (place)’ /madraʿu/ **5** (RS 2.002):69bis, 73

DRT personal name, vocalization and etymology unknown **50** (RIH 84/06):8; **51** (RIH 84/33):7

[DṮʾ]: DṮT ‘(vegetal offering)’ /daṯâtu/ ← /*daṯaʾatu/ **8** (RS 1.001):9

DǴṮ common noun ‘(type of offering)’ **5** (RS 2.002):15 ({dǵ[. . .]})

DT: see D

[H presentative particle /ha/]

H(N) extended form ‘here (is), look, behold’ /han/ (the /n/, if it was present, has assimilated to the following consonant) **28** (RS 29.093):16; **34** (RS 94.2284):29

HN extended form ‘here (is), look, behold’ /hanna/ **4** (RS 2.[004]) i:5′; **5** (RS 2.002):46, 50, 55; **7** (RS 24.258):28′; **9** (RS 1.002):17′, 25′, 34′, 43′; **11** (RS 24.266):24′; **17** (RIH 78/20):16; **20** (RS 24.247^{+}):2, 34′; **33** (RS 96.2039):4, 8, 10, 15; **34** (RS 94.2284):31

HND extended form functioning as a demonstrative pronoun/adjective /hannadū/ ← /hanna + dū/ **31** (RS 94.2406):5; **37** (RS 16.382):1; **38** (RS 94.2168):1

HNDN extended form functioning as a demonstrative pronoun/adjective /hannadūna/ ← /hanna + dū + na/ **29** (RS 34.124):10

HNDT extended form functioning as a demonstrative pronoun/adjective /hannadūti/ ← /hanna + dū + ti/ **26** (RS 18.031):12

HNMT extended form functioning as a demonstrative pronoun/adjective /hannamati/ ← /hanna + ma + ti/ **39** (RS 94.2965):12, 20

HNN extended form ‘here (is), look, behold’ /hannana/ ← /*ha + n + na + na/ **30** (RS 92.2010):9; **32** (RS 94.2479):5

HNNY extended form of HNN /hannaniya/ ← /*ha + n + na + ni + ya/ **22** (RS 8.315):10; **26** (RS 18.031):6; **29** (RS 34.124):7

HL extended form ‘here (is), look, behold’ /halli/ ← /*ha + n + li/ **5** (RS 2.002):41, 44, 47; **34** (RS 94.2284):25

HLH extended form /halliha/ ← /*ha + n + li + ha/ **5** (RS 2.002):32^{tris}, 33

HLM extended form /hallima/ ← /*ha + n + li + ma/ **2** (RS 2.[014]$^{+}$) iii:32′; **6** (RS 24.244):6, 11, 17, 22, 28, 33, 〈34d〉, 38, 43, 48, 54

HLN extended form /hallina/ ← /*ha + n + li + na/ **32** (RS 94.2479):11

HLNY extended form ‘look, behold, here’ /halliniya/# ← /*ha + l + li + ni + ya/ **23** (RS 11.872):9; **25** (RS 16.379):8, 12; **28** (RS 29.093):11; **31** (RS 94.2406):3; **32** (RS 94.2479):5; **34** (RS 94.2284):3; **36** (RS 11.772^{+}):18′

HT extended form ‘here (is), look, behold’ /hatti/ ← /ha + n + ti/ **1** (RS 3.367) i:8′, 9′^{bis}; **21** (RS 4.475):8; **25** (RS 16.379):14; **27** (RS 18.040):13; **29** (RS 34.124):20; **31** (RS 94.2406):35; **33** (RS 96.2039):8, 10; **35** (RS [Varia 4]):10, 15 ({h⸢t⸣})

HBN common noun ‘ebony wood’ /habūnu/ **47** (RS 94.2392^{+}):1, 5

HBR verb ‘bow down’ **2** (RS 2.[014]$^{+}$) iii:9′; **5** (RS 2.002):49, 55

[HDD divine name /hadad/ (absolute form); HD divine name /haddu/ (cased form)]: YRMHD personal name /yarmihaddu/ (‘[the god] Haddu has laid the foundations [of this child]’) **28** (RS 29.093):4; **33** (RS 96.2039):2

HDM common noun ‘footstool’ /hidāmu/ **13** (RS 34.126):14

HW independent/demonstrative personal pronoun, 3m.s. /huwa/# **4** (RS 2.[004]) i:38′; **5** (RS 2.002):70, 75; **9** (RS 1.002):24′^{bis}, 32′, 33′, 41′, [41′]; **29** (RS 34.124):27, 29, 31; **33** (RS 96.2039):8, 10, 15

HWT oblique form /huwati/ **20** (RS 24.247^{+}):43′; **31** (RS 94.2406):6; **38** (RS 94.2168):12

HY independent/demonstrative personal pronoun, 3f.s. /hiya/ **35** (RS [Varia 4]):9 ({mhy} ← /mah + hiya/)

HYT oblique form /hiyati/ **2** (RS 2.[014]$^{+}$) iii:10′; **20** (RS 24.247^{+}):45′, 55′, 56′

HM independent personal pronoun, 3c.du. /humā/ **5** (RS 2.002):68, 69, 71

[HM independent personal pronoun 3m.pl.]: HMT independent personal pronoun, 3m.pl., oblique form /humati/ **1** (RS 3.367) i:36′

[HW]: HWT common noun ‘word, speech’ /huwātu/# **1** (RS 3.367) i:6′; **2** (RS 2.[014]$^{+}$) iii:13′, 22′; **18** (RS 92.2014):9, 10

HZP place-name /hizpu/ **41** (RS 19.015):28

HY: see HW personal pronoun

HYT: see HW personal pronoun

HKL common noun ‘palace’ /hēkalu/ **4** (RS 2.[004]) i:26′, 43′; **6** (RS 24.244):72; **7** (RS 24.258):2

[HKR verb 'sleep deeply']: Š-stem, 'cause/allow to sleep', **34** (RS 94.2284):32a
HL, HLH: see H
HLK verb 'go' (without /h/ in /YQTL/ forms) **5** (RS 2.002):16, 27, 67; **7** (RS 24.258):17; **29** (RS 34.124):15, 25; **33** (RS 96.2039):18; **34** (RS 94.2284):32b; **39** (RS 94.2965):8
  Gt-stem **11** (RS 24.266):34′
HLM verb 'strike' **1** (RS 3.367) i:14′, 16′, 21′, 24′; **7** (RS 24.258):8
HLM (particle), HLN, HLNY: see HL under H
HM independent pronoun 3c.du.: see HW personal pronoun
HM conjunction 'either/or' /himma/ (see also ʾIM) **3** (RS 2.[003]⁺) i:42; **5** (RS 2.002):39, 42, 71, 72; **11** (RS 24.266):28′; **19** (RS 17.120):3, 4; **21** (RS 4.475):9, 14; **25** (RS 16.379):16, 18; **34** (RS 94.2284):13, 20, 27; **38** (RS 94.2168):19, 22, 25
HMLT common noun 'throng, crowd, horde' /hamul(l)atu/ **2** (RS 2.[014]⁺) iii:28′
HMT: see HW personal pronoun
HN, HND, HNDN, HNDT, HNMT, HNN, HNNY: see H
[HPK verb 'turn over/around']: N-stem 'turn' **20** (RS 24.247⁺):52′
HRY verb 'conceive, be/become pregnant' **4** (RS 2.[004]) i:[40′] ({[hrt]} verbal noun), [41′] ([hr] verbal noun); **5** (RS 2.002):51, 56
[HRNM place-name]: HRNMY gentilic /harnamiyyu/ **4** (RS 2.[004]) i:[2′], 18′, 36′, 37′
HT: see H

W conjunction /wa/ **1** (RS 3.367) i:3′ et passim
WTḤ: see YTḤ

ZBB verb 'foam (of serpents' venom)' **18** (RS 92.2014):1
[ZBL verb 'bear, support']: ZBL common noun 'Highness (as title), prince' /zabūlu/ **1** (RS 3.367) i:7′, 8′, 14′, 16′, 22′, 24′, 29′
  ZBLN common noun 'illness' /zabalānu/ **3** (RS 2.[003]⁺) i:17
ZBR verb 'prune' **5** (RS 2.002):9bis
ZD common noun 'breast' /zadû/ ← /d̲adû/ (see D̲D) ← /*t̲adayu/ **5** (RS 2.002):24
[ZN verb 'feed']: ZNT common noun 'food, provisions' /zānatu/ **32** (RS 94.2479):20; **34** (RS 94.2284):29
[ZRM verb 'flow']: ZRM common noun 'flow' /zarmu/ **17** (RIH 78/20):14
ZT common noun 'olive, olive tree, olive orchard' /zêtu/ **7** (RS 24.258):31′; **32** (RS 94.2479):19; **37** (RS 16.382):8
ZTR common noun 'monument (with inscribed figures)' /zittaru/ **4** (RS 2.[004]) i:27′, [45′]

Ḥ: see ḤYY
ḤBY divine name, identification uncertain **7** (RS 24.258):19
[ḤBL verb 'bind']: ḤBL common noun 'boatman' /ḥābilu/ **52** (RIH 83/22):3
ḤBQ verb 'hug' **4** (RS 2.[004]) i:40′; **5** (RS 2.002):51, 56
ḤBR common noun 'companion' /ḥabiru/ **5** (RS 2.002):76; **17** (RIH 78/20):10
ḤGBN personal name /ḥagbānu/ **44** (RS 19.016):11, 27
ḤGR verb 'gird' **5** (RS 2.002):17
ḤDR common noun '(private) room' /ḥuduru/# **3** (RS 2.[003]+) i:26
ḤDṮ common noun 'new moon, new moon festival' /ḥudṯu/ **41** (RS 19.015):13
  ḤDṮ adjective 'new' /ḥadaṯu/ **34** (RS 94.2284):28!
  ḤDṮN personal name /ḥudṯānu/ ('born at the time of the new moon') **44** (RS 19.016):18, 19
[ḤW]: ḤWT common noun 'country, land' /ḥuwwatu/# **20** (RS 24.247+):1, 3, 4, 5, 6, 7, 16, 35′, 37′, 41′, 45′, 50′, 51′, 53′, 55′, 56′, 59′; **52** (RIH 83/22):12
[ḤWY verb 'live']: D-stem 'repair' **28** (RS 29.093):15
  Št-stem 'bow down' **2** (RS 2.[014]+) iii:10′
ḤṬB common noun, profession name, substantivized participle, 'wood gatherer' /ḥāṭibu/ **44** (RS 19.016):20; **51** (RIH 84/33):12
ḤYY verb 'live' **4** (RS 2.[004]) i:36′
  Ḥ common noun 'life', /ḥayyu/ in the absolute case (*/ḥayy/ → /*ḥay/ → /ḥê/) **34** (RS 94.2284):12bis
ḤŠ verb 'hasten' **2** (RS 2.[014]+) iii:18′; **31** (RS 94.2406):34
ḤLB common noun 'milk' /ḥalabu/ **5** (RS 2.002):14
ḤLL verb 'be/become clean, pure, absolved of cultic responsibility' **11** (RS 24.266):4, 24′
  D-stem 'purify → restore to non-cultic state' **11** (RS 24.266):23′
  Š-stem 'cause to be purified' **10** (RS 24.260):6
ḤLM common noun 'dream' /ḥulumu/ **3** (RS 2.[003]+) i:35
[ḤMY verb 'protect']: YḤMN personal name /yaḥminu/ **44** (RS 19.016):19, 33
  ḤMT common noun 'wall, rampart' /ḥāmîtu/ ← /ḥāmiyatu/, pl. ḤMYT /ḥāmiyātu/ **9** (RS 1.002):[18′], 36′; **11** (RS 24.266):27′, 29′, 36′
[ḤMM verb 'be/become hot']: ḤMḤMT common noun 'conception (← heat)' /ḥamḥamatu/ **4** (RS 2.[004]) i:40′, 41′; **5** (RS 2.002):51, 56
ḤMṢ common noun 'vinegar' /ḥamiṣu/ **32** (RS 94.2479):18
ḤMR common noun '(plant name)' **19** (RS 17.120):17, 28
ḤMT: see YḤM
ḤḎ (← ḤẒ) common noun 'arrow' /hiḏḏu/ **44** (RS 19.016):25

ḤḎRT: common noun '(plant of the lettuce category)' /ḥaḏratu/ **19** (RS 17.120):14, 27
ḤNN verb 'favor, have pity on' **4** (RS 2.[004]) i:16′ (verbal noun ḤNT)
ḤẒR common noun 'court(yard)' /ḥaẓiru/ **6** (RS 24.244):68; **7** (RS 24.258):18
ḤSL verb 'devour, consume' **20** (RS 24.247⁺):36′, 38′, 55′
ḤSP common noun '(type of wine)' (precise meaning and vocalization unknown) **41** (RS 19.015):29, 36
ḤPN common noun 'handful' /ḥupnu/ **48** (RS 94.2600):12
ḤPR common noun 'rations' /ḥipru/ **44** (RS 19.016):1, 49; **45** (RS 86.2213):1
ḤR common noun '(part of the body)' (precise meaning and vocalization unknown) **20** (RS 24.247⁺):58′
ḤRB common noun 'sword' /ḥarbu/ **1** (RS 3.367) i:4′
ḤRYT place-name, vocalization unknown **6** (RS 24.244):36
[ḤRŠ verb 'make, manufacture']: ḤRŠ common noun 'artisan' /ḥarrāšu/# **28** (RS 29.093):14
  ḤRŠ BHTM common noun, profession name 'house builder' /ḥarrāšu bahatīma/ **44** (RS 19.016):18 ({ḥrš ⌜b⌝[htm]})
  ḤRŠ MRKBT common noun, profession name 'chariot maker' /ḥarrāšu markabāti/ **44** (RS 19.016):28
  ḤRŠ QṬN common noun, profession name 'maker of "small objects" (basically of wood)' /ḥarrāšu qaṭuni/ **44** (RS 19.016):23
ḤRN divine name /ḥôrānu/ (← /*ḥawrānu/) **6** (RS 24.244):58, 61, 67; **17** (RIH 78/20):9
ḤRPT personal name, vocalization and etymology unknown **46** (RS 94.2050⁺):47
[ḤRR verb 'be/become hot']: L-stem 'heat up, cook, roast' **5** (RS 2.002):41, 44, 48
[ḤRṮ verb 'plow']: ḤRṮ common noun, profession name 'plowman' /ḥarrāṯu/ **44** (RS 19.016):27
  MḤRṮT common noun /maḥraṯatu/ 'plow' **15** (RS 6.028):3
ḤṮB verb 'count, calculate' **52** (RIH 83/22):12
  ḤṮBN common noun 'account' /ḥiṯbānu/ **42** (RS 15.062):2; **43** (RS 18.024):1
[ḤTK verb 'exercise paternal power']: ḤTK 'family (of the father)' /ḥatku/ **3** (RS 2.[003]⁺) i:21, 22
  ḤTKN same /ḥatkānu/ **3** (RS 2.[003]⁺) i:10
ḤTP common noun '(type of sacrifice)' /ḥitpu/ **11** (RS 24.266):32′

ṬB adjective 'good' /ṭābu/# **5** (RS 2.002):14
ṬBḪ verb 'slaughter' **34** (RS 94.2284):10
ṬBQ verb 'shut' **4** (RS 2.[004]) i:28′, [47′]
ṬBQ place-name /ṭibaqu/ **45** (RS 86.2213):14

ṬBRN personal name /ṭabrānu/ **46** (RS 94.2050^{+}):44

ṬḪ verb 'reconstitute surface of a mud roof (with a stone roof roller)' **4** (RS 2.[004]) i:32′

ṬDD personal name, vocalization and etymology unknown **46** (RS 94.2050^{+}):46 ({ṭ⌜d⌝d})

ṬḤL common noun 'spleen' /ṭiḥālu/ **20** (RS 24.247^{+}):12

[ṬLL: common noun 'dew']: ṬLY divine name, feminine, daughter of *Baʿlu*, 'Dewy' /ṭallay/ **2** (RS 2.[014]$^{+}$) iii:7′

ṬRD verb 'drive away' **2** (RS 2.[014]$^{+}$) iii:47′

Y particle, vocative 'O' /yā/ **5** (RS 2.002):40, 43, 46, 64, 65, 69; **11** (RS 24.266):28′, 29′

YBL verb 'carry, bring' **5** (RS 2.002):52, 59; **6** (RS 24.244):2, 8, 14, 19, 25, 30 ({b⟨l⟩}), ⟨34a⟩, 35, 40, 45, 51, 57, 66–67, 67; **29** (RS 34.124):27; **36** (RS 11.772^{+}):[18′], 25′; **39** (RS 94.2965):22, 24; **43** (RS 18.024):12

YBMT common noun 'sister-in-law' /yabimtu/ **2** (RS 2.[014]$^{+}$) iii:12′ (!)

YBNN: see BNY

[YGY verb 'suffer']: TG common noun 'pain' /tôgû/ ← /*tawgayu/ **17** (RIH 78/20):1, 2

YGRŠ proper name: see GRŠ

YD common noun 'hand, forearm (with hand), foreleg (of animal)' /yadu/ **1** (RS 3.367) i:14′, 16′; **4** (RS 2.[004]) i:30′; **5** (RS 2.002):33, 34bis, 35, 37, 40, 44, 47; **10** (RS 24.260):6; **20** (RS 24.247^{+}):15, 28′, 46′, 48′, 59′; **21** (RS 4.475):11; **30** (RS 92.2010):24

D form of YD used with the preposition B in the contracted form BD: see B

YD preposition 'with (← as regards the hand, perhaps a pun on Akkadian *qadu* 'with', similar to *qātu* 'hand') /yada/ **37** (RS 16.382):7, 8bis, 9; **39** (RS 94.2965):3, 4, 5, 16, 17, 18

YD common noun '(type of handle)'$^{?}$, pl. /yadātu/ **42** (RS 15.062):9; **48** (RS 94.2600):8

[YDD 'love' (← *WDD)]: YD common noun 'love' /yaddu/ **2** (RS 2.[014]$^{+}$) iii:6′

MDD 'beloved' /môdadu/ ← /*mawdadu/ **2** (RS 2.[014]$^{+}$) iii:38′, 43′

YDY verb 'throw down, out' **6** (RS 24.244):5, 11, 17, 22, 27, 32, ⟨34c⟩, 38, 42, 48, 54, 60, 64; **11** (RS 24.266):28′, 35′; **17** (RIH 78/20):1

YDLN: see DLY

YDʿ verb 'know' **2** (RS 2.[014]$^{+}$) iii:26′, 27′; **7** (RS 24.258):6, 7; **18** (RS 92.2014):1; **24** (RS 15.008):7; **27** (RS 18.040):19; **31** (RS 94.2406):10, 38; **34** (RS 94.2284):26, 34

DʿT common noun 'knowledge (particularly of magic)' /daʿtu/ **17** (RIH 78/20):10

YDʿ (← *WḎʿ) verb 'perspire' **2** (RS 2.[014]$^{+}$) iii:34′

YDRM: see DR

[YḤL (← *WḤL) verb ‘be/become discouraged’]: N-stem **24** (RS 15.008):12

[YḤM verb ‘be/become hot’]: ḤMT common noun ‘venom (← heat)’ /ḥimatu/ **6** (RS 24.244):6, 11, 17, 22, 28, 33, ⟨34d⟩, 38, 43, 48, 54, 60, 68 ({ḥ⟨m⟩t})

YḤMN: see ḤMY

YḪR common noun ‘(type of) venomous lizard’ /yaḫaru/ **6** (RS 24.244):73

YŠN verb ‘sleep’ **3** (RS 2.[003]$^{+}$) i:31

ŠNT common noun ‘sleep’ /šinatu/ **3** (RS 2.[003]$^{+}$) i:33

[YŠR verb ‘be/become straight’]: YŠR common noun ‘legitimacy’ /yušru/ **3** (RS 2.[003]$^{+}$) i:13

MŠR common noun ‘rectitude’ /mêšaru/ ← /*mayšaru/ **9** (RS 1.002):26′^{bis}, 35′^{bis}

YLD verb ‘give birth’ **4** (RS 2.[004]) i:41′; **5** (RS 2.002):52, ⟨52⟩, 53bis, 58bis, 60bis; **20** (RS 24.247^{+}):1$^{!}$, 2$^{?}$

Š-stem ‘engender’ **5** (RS 2.002):65

YLD common noun ‘child’ /yaldu/ **5** (RS 2.002):53

YLK: see HLK

YM common noun ‘day’ /yômu/# **4** (RS 2.[004]) i:5′, 8′, 11′, 15′, 32′, 33′; **5** (RS 2.002):23$^{[bis]}$, 58, 59, 61bis; **10** (RS 24.260): 14; **11** (RS 24.266):1; **20** (RS 24.247^{+}):34′; **31** (RS 94.2406):5; **37** (RS 16.382):1; **38** (RS 94.2168):1

YM common noun ‘sea’: see YMM

YMʾAN place-name, vocalization unknown **9** (RS 1.002):27′

YMDŠR: see MDD

[YMM]: YM common noun ‘sea’ /yammu/ **2** (RS 2.[014]$^{+}$) iii:2; **5** (RS 2.002):30, 33, 34, 63; **31** (RS 94.2406):3

YM divine name (same form and meaning) **1** (RS 3.367) i:3′^{bis}, 7′, 12′^{bis}, 14′, 16′, 17′, 19′^{bis}, 22′^{bis}, 25′^{bis}, 27′ [29]′, 32′, 34′; **2** (RS 2.[014]$^{+}$) iii:39′; **3** (RS 2.[003]$^{+}$) i:20; **8** (RS 1.001):13; **12** (RS 24.643):9, [41]

YMN common noun ‘right hand’ /yamīnu/ **4** (RS 2.[004]) i:⟨34′⟩; **5** (RS 2.002):63; **20** (RS 24.247^{+}):26′, [28′], 35′

verb, /qatlal/-stem, ‘take in the right hand’ **5** (RS 2.002):37, 40, 44, 47

[YN]: YNT common noun ‘dove’ /yônatu/ ← /*yawnatu/ **8** (RS 1.001):1; **11** (RS 24.266):10

YN common noun ‘wine’ /yênu/ ← /*yaynu/ **4** (RS 2.[004]) i:31′; **5** (RS 2.002):6, [72], 74, 75, 76; **7** (RS 24.258):3 ({y⟨n⟩}), 16; **34** (RS 94.2284):29; **41** (RS 19.015):1, 21, 22, 23, 24, 25, 26, 27, 28, 35; **48** (RS 94.2600):3

YNḤM: see NḤM

YNQ verb ‘suck, nurse’ **5** (RS 2.002):24, 59, 61

YSM adjective ‘beautiful’ /yasīmu/ **5** (RS 2.002):2

YʿBDR: see ʿB

[YʿD verb 'assemble']: ʿDT common noun 'assembly' /ʿidatu/ **6** (RS 24.244):3

YʿL common noun 'mountain goat' /yaʿlu/ **17** (RIH 78/20):4

YʿD̲RN: see ʿD̲R

YPḤ common noun, substantivized participle, 'witness' /yāpiḥu/ **40** (RS [Varia 14]):18

[YPY verb 'be/become beautiful']: Rt-stem 'make oneself beautiful' **2** (RS 2.[014]$^{+}$) iii:1

YP common noun 'beauty (whence) well-being' /yupû/ ← /*yupyu/ **9** (RS 1.002):28′, 30′, 32′, 36′, 39′, 40′

NPY 'manifesting beauty (whence) well-being' /nôpayu/ ← /*nawpayu/ **9** (RS 1.002):1′ et passim in this text

YPʿ verb 'arise, come forth' **2** (RS 2.[014]$^{+}$) iii:37′, iv:4, 5

YPʿMLK personal name /yapaʿamilku/ ('[the god] *Milku* has arisen') **44** (RS 19.016):12

YPʿN personal name /yapʿānu/ **44** (RS 19.016):8

YṢʾ/YẒʾ verb 'exit, go/come forth' **1** (RS 3.367) i:6′, 30′; **17** (RIH 78/20):2; **20** (24.247^{+}):45′, 51′; **31** (RS 94.2406):22, 38, 39

Š-stem **1** (RS 3.367) i:2′; **4** (RS 2.[004]) i:27′, 45′

ẒʾU common noun 'exiting, extent' /ẓiʾu/ **2** (RS 2.[014]$^{+}$) iii:2

YṢḤ common noun, profession name, meaning unknown **44** (RS 19.016):9

YṢQ verb 'pour out' **19** (RS 17.120):4, 6, 8, 11, 14, 17, 19, 22, 29, 32; **29** (RS 34.124):31

YṢR common noun, profession name, substantivized participle, 'potter (he who forms)' /yāṣiru/# **44** (RS 19.016):37

YRḪ common noun 'moon (whence) month' /yarḫu/ **11** (RS 24.266):1; **44** (RS 19.016):1; **48** (RS 94.2600):16

YRḪ divine name, 'moon deity' /yariḫu/ **6** (RS 24.244):26; **7** (RS 24.258):4; **8** (RS 1.001):14; **12** (RS 24.643):5, 29

YRḪ KT̲Y divine name 'the Kassite moon deity' /yariḫu kat̲t̲iyyu/ **8** (RS 1.001):19

YRD verb 'descend, come/go down' **3** (RS 2.[003]$^{+}$) i:36; **7** (RS 24.258):22; **8** (RS 1.001):20; **13** (RS 34.126):21, 22; **17** (RIH 78/20):14$^{!}$

YRY verb 'cast, shoot' **5** (RS 2.002):38bis

YRM: see RM

YRMN: see RM

YRMHD: see RMY and HD

YRT̲ verb 'take possession of, inherit' (Gt-stem) **2** (RS 2.[014]$^{+}$) iii:47′

YRT̲ 'heirship' /yurt̲u/ **3** (RS 2.[003]$^{+}$) i:25

YT̲B verb 'sit (down), dwell, stay' **5** (RS 2.002):8, 29, 56; **6** (RS 24.244):7, 13, 18, 24, 29, 34, 〈34e〉, 39, 44, 50, 56; **7** (RS 24.258):14, 15; **29** (RS 34.124):21

ṮBT common noun 'the act of sitting or dwelling' /ṯibtu/ **3** (RS 2.[003]$^{+}$) i:23

MṮBT common noun 'seat' /môṯabatu/ ← /*mawṯabatu/ **5** (RS 2.002):19

YṮN adjective 'old' /yaṯana/ **19** (RS 17.120):31bis

YṮQ verb 'tie (up)' **6** (RS 24.244):6, 11, 17, 22, 28, 33, ⟨34d⟩, 38, 43, 48, 54

YṮR personal name /yaṯru/ **44** (RS 19.016):18

YTḤ ← WTḤ verb 'hasten' (D-stem) **2** (RS 2.[014]$^{+}$) iii:20′

YTN verb 'give' **1** (RS 3.367) i:6′; **5** (RS 2.002):3, 71, 72; **6** (RS 24.244):63, 73bis, 75; **28** (RS 29.093):22; **31** (RS 94.2406):4; **33** (RS 96.2039):7; **34** (RS 94.2284):4, 11, 13, 27, 29, 31; **37** (RS 16.382):4, 11; **38** (RS 94.2168):5, 13; **40** (RS [Varia 14]):15; **52** (RIH 83/22):4

Š-stem 'send, have delivered, transfer' **32** (RS 94.2479):21; **33** (RS 96.2039):16, 24; **37** (RS 16.382):6

ʾITNN common noun 'gift (at marriage)' /ʾitnānu/ **6** (RS 24.244):74, 76

YTN personal name /yatanu/ ('he [a god] has given') **44** (RS 19.016):35

[YTR verb 'be/become abundant']: YTRM personal name /yatarmu/ **49** (RIH 84/04):21

K preposition 'like' /ka/ **2** (RS 2.[014]$^{+}$) iv:1; **3** (RS 2.[003]$^{+}$) i:43; **5** (RS 2.002):33, 34bis, 35, 50, [55]; **7** (RS 24.258):22; **17** (RIH 78/20):3bis, 4bis; **20** (RS 24.247^{+}):41′; **48** (RS 94.2600):15

KM extended form /kama/ **1** (RS 3.367) i:13′, 15′, 21′, 24′; **3** (RS 2.[003]$^{+}$) i:29, 30; **4** (RS 2.[004]) i:19′^{bis}, 20′$^{!}$, 21′; **5** (RS 2.002):11; **6** (RS 24.244):68, 69, 73bis; **7** (RS 24.258):5, 21; **38** (RS 94.2168):17, 20, 24, 28

KM extended form functioning as adverb 'then' /kama/ **2** (RS 2.[014]$^{+}$) iii:8′

KM extended form, vocalically and consonantally, 'thus' /kāma/ **18** (RS 92.2014):8

KMM doubly extended form functioning as adverb 'also' /kamāma/ **12** (RS 24.643):11^{quadris}, 12bis; **18** (RS 92.2014):12

K conjunction /kī/ **1** (RS 3.367) i:29′, [29′]; **3** (RS 2.[003]$^{+}$) i:39; **4** (RS 2.[004]) i:[31′]; **5** (RS 2.002):39; **11** (RS 24.266):26′; **12** (RS 24.643):18; **19** (RS 17.120):2, 5, 7, 9, [12], 15, 18, 20, 23, 30; **20** (RS 24.247^{+}):[1]; **21** (RS 4.475):12; **28** (RS 29.093):23, 25; **31** (RS 94.2406):4, 24, 33, 38; **33** (RS 96.2039):18; **34** (RS 94.2284):9, 27, 34; **41** (RS 19.015):10, 11, 14

KY extended form /kīya/ **24** (RS 15.008):7; **29** (RS 34.124):18, 34; **31** (RS 94.2406):34; **34** (RS 94.2284):8, 9

KM extended form /kīma/ **7** (RS 24.258):28′

[KBD verb 'be/become heavy, important']: D-stem 'honor' **2** (RS 2.[014]$^{+}$) iii:10′

KBD common noun 'liver (whence) within' /kabidu/# **2** (RS 2.[014]$^{+}$) iii:16′, 17′; **8** (RS 1.001):2; **11** (RS 24.266):21′

KBD adverb used to link elements of compound numbers /kubda/ **36** (RS 11.772^{+}):20′; **41** (RS 19.015):[35], 36; **43** (RS 18.024):2, 5, 8, 17; **47** (RS 94.2392^{+}):2, 11′; **49** (RIH 84/04):6, 19′; **51** (RIH 84/33):13; **52** (RIH 83/22):2, 9

KBKB common noun 'star' /kabkabu/ **2** (RS 2.[014]$^{+}$) iii:25′; **5** (RS 2.002):54

KBL common noun 'legging' /kiblu/ **34** (RS 94.2284):18

KD common noun '(liquid measure [about eleven liters])' /kaddu/# **32** (RS 94.2479):16, 17, 18, 19; **41** (RS 19.015):26, 27, 30; **47** (RS 94.2392^{+}):11

KDWṮ common noun '(type of garment)' /kiddawaṯṯu/ **43** (RS 18.024):24

KDN personal name /kudūnu/ **46** (RS 94.2050^{+}):13

KHP verb 'be/become bent down, prostrate' **19** (RS 17.120):30

KWR place-name, vocalization unknown **39** (RS 94.2965):7

[KḤD verb 'hide']: D-stem 'refuse, reject' **28** (RS 29.093):13

KḤṮ common noun 'seat, chair, throne' /kaḥṯu/ **1** (RS 3.367) i:13′, 20′; **2** (RS 2.[014]$^{+}$) iv:3

KKLN personal name /kukulanu/ **44** (RS 19.016):5

KKR common noun 'talent (unit of weight [about twenty-eight kilograms])' /kakkaru/# **42** (RS 15.062):10, 12, 14, 17; **43** (RS 18.024):2, 9, 26; **47** (RS 94.2392^{+}):1 ({[k]kr}), 5

KŠM common noun, form and meaning unknown (may be a plural form) **48** (RS 94.2600):15

KŠP common noun 'sorcerer' /kaššāpu/ **17** (RIH 78/20):9; **18** (RS 92.2014): 9, 13

[KŠR (← *KŚR) verb 'break']: MKŠR 'something that has been broken up' /makšaru/ **19** (RS 17.120):12, 16

KL: see KLL

KLʾ: KLʾAT common noun 'pair' /kilʾatu/ **5** (RS 2.002):57

KLB(T) common noun 'dog, bitch' /kalbu/kalbatu/ **2** (RS 2.[014]$^{+}$) iii:45′; **7** (RS 24.258):5, 12 ({k$^{!}$lb}), 29′

KLBY personal name /kalbiya/ **21** (RS 4.475):6; **44** (RS 19.016):26, 29

KLY verb 'be used up, disappear' **31** (RS 94.2406):13$^{?}$; **41** (RS 19.015):1

D-stem 'finish off, bring to an end' **1** (RS 3.367) i:27′; **2** (RS 2.[014]$^{+}$) iii:39′, 46′; **20** (RS 24.247^{+}):40′; **29** (RS 34.124):43′$^{?}$

KLYN personal name /kiliyanu/ **44** (RS 19.016):13, 25

[KLL]: KL common noun 'all' /kullu/ **3** (RS 2.[003]$^{+}$) i:24; **10** (RS 24.260): 10; **26** (RS 18.031):17, 19, 20

KLKL common noun 'all' /kulkulu/ **31** (RS 94.2406):11; **37** (RS 16.382):10; **39** (RS 94.2965):18

KLL common noun 'all' /kalīlu/ **22** (RS 8.315):11; **23** (RS 11.872):10; **24** (RS 15.008):15; **29** (RS 34.124):7 ({[kl]⌜l⌝]}); **32** (RS 94.2479):6, 21

KLT common noun 'all' /kullatu/ **28** (RS 29.093):22

KLḎY personal name /kiliḏēyu/ **44** (RS 19.016):21
KLTN personal name /kilitēnu/ **37** (RS 16.382):13, 18
KLTṮB personal name /kilitēṯub/ **46** (RS 94.2050^{+}):33
KM: see K, conjunction and preposition
KMM: see K, preposition
KMN common noun 'cumin' /kamūnu/ **48** (RS 94.2600):10
KMṮ divine name: see ẒẒ-W-KMṮ
KḎǴDL personal name /kuḏuǵadal / **37** (RS 16.382):5
KN verb 'to be' **3** (RS 2.[003]$^{+}$) i:15; **4** (RS 2.[004]) i:25′, 42′; **20** (RS 24.247^{+}):3, 5
  Š-stem 'establish' **4** (RS 2.[004]) i:41′
  KN adjective 'solid, unmovable' /kīnu/ **5** (RS 2.002):54
  MKNT common noun 'place, establishment' /makānatu/ **3** (RS 2.[003]$^{+}$) i:11
[KNR common noun 'lyre' /kinnāru/#]: divine name **12** (RS 24.643):9, 43$^{?}$
KS common noun 'cup' /kāsu/ **4** (RS 2.[004]) i:[34′]; **34** (RS 94.2284):30; **36** (RS 11.772^{+}):20′, 27′, 29′, 31′, [33′], [35′], [37′]
KSʾU common noun 'chair, throne' /kussaʾu/ **1** (RS 3.367) i:7′, 12′, 20′; **2** (RS 2.[014]$^{+}$) iv:2; **6** (RS 24.244):7, 12, 18, 23, 29, 34, ⟨34e⟩, 39, 44, 49, 56; **13** (RS 34.126):13, 20
KSD personal name, vocalization and etymology unknown **46** (RS 94.2050^{+}):24
KSL common noun '(collective) sinews of the back, back' /kislu/ **2** (RS 2.[014]$^{+}$) iii:33′, 35′
KSM/KS̀M common noun 'emmer wheat' /kussumu/# **4** (RS 2.[004]) i:31′; **8** (RS 1.001):9
KSP common noun 'silver, money' /kaspu/# **2** (RS 2.[014]$^{+}$) iii:46′; **28** (RS 29.093):19; **34** (RS 94.2284):31; **40** (RS [Varia 14]):9, 16; **42** (RS 15.062):1, 5, 11, 13, 16, 18; **43** (RS 18.024):5, 8, 10, 11, 13, 15, 17, 19, 20, 21, 22, 23, [24], [25], 27, 28 ({⌜k⌝[sp]}); **44** (RS 19.016):32; **49** (RIH 84/04):1, 3, 6, 9, 12, 15, 17, 20, 22, 25; **50** (RIH 84/06):1, 3, 5, 7; **51** (RIH 84/33):2, 3, 4, 6, 8, 10, 12, 13, 15, 17, 19, 21; **52** (RIH 83/22):3, 4, 10
KPR verb 'expiate' **29** (RS 34.124):43′
KPTR place-name, 'Crete' /kaptāru/ **6** (RS 24.244):46
KRWN personal name /kurwānu/ **44** (RS 19.016):3, 9, 36; **49** (RIH 84/04):14; **51** (RIH 84/33):18
KRY verb 'give a feast' **7** (RS 24.258):14
KRM common noun 'vine, vineyard' /karmu/ **37** (RS 16.382):9; **39** (RS 94.2965):17; **44** (RS 19.016):12
KRSʾU common noun '(container and measure [smaller than the *kaddu*])' /kurrusaʾu/ **47** (RS 94.2392^{+}):4, 9, 12; **48** (RS 94.2600):14

KRˁ common noun ‘middle part of lower leg’ /karaˁu/ **20** (RS 24.247^{+}):15, 28′

KRPN common noun ‘drinking vessel, goblet’ /karpānu/ **4** (RS 2.[004]) i:〈34′〉

KRR verb ‘return, come/go back, retrace one’s steps’ **6** (RS 24.244):62

KRT proper name /kirta/ **3** (RS 2.[003]$^{+}$) i:1, 10, 11, 22, 38, 39

KṮ common noun ‘(small container and measure)’ /kīṯu/ **12** (RS 24.643):22bis; **48** (RS 94.2600):10, 11

[KṮR ‘be/become healthy, able’]: KṮR common noun ‘health’ /kiṯru/ **3** (RS 2.[003]$^{+}$) i:16

KṮR divine name (artisan deity, ‘the skilled one’) /kôṯaru/# **1** (RS 3.367) i:11′, 18′; **8** (RS 1.001):〈14〉; **12** (RS 24.643):6, 30

KṮR-W-ḪSS divine name, binomial, ‘skilled and intelligent’ /kôṯaru wa ḫasīsu/) **1** (RS 3.367) i:7′; **6** (RS 24.244):46

KṮRMLK personal name /kôṯarmalku/ (‘[the god] Kôṯaru is king’) **44** (RS 19.016):32

KṮRT compound divine name, seven goddesses who deal with procreation from conception to birth (‘midwives’) /kôṯarātu/ **12** (RS 24.643):5, 25

KTN common noun ‘(type of garment)’ /kutunu/; pl. KTNT /kutunātu/ **36** (RS 11.772^{+}):21′, 27′, 29′, 31′, 33′ ({[kt]⌜n⌝}), [35′], [37′]; **43** (RS 18.024):18; **47** (RS 94.2392^{+}):8; **52** (RIH 83/22):7

KTP common noun ‘shoulder, cut of meat (from the shoulder)’ /katipu/ **1** (RS 3.367) i:14′, 16′; **7** (RS 24.258):11, 13

Š common noun ‘ram (of sheep)’ /šû/ (← /*śayu/) **8** (RS 1.001):2, 5, 6^{tris}, 7bis, 10, 11^{tris}, 19; **9** (RS 1.002):17′, 25′; **10** (RS 24.260):4, 9, 12; **11** (RS 24.266):2, 21′;**12** (RS 24.643):[1], 2, [2bis], 3, [3bis], 4, [4bis], 5^{tris}, [5], 6^{quadris}, 7^{quintis}, 8^{quadris}, 9^{tris}, 10bis, [10bis], 23, 24, 25bis, 26bis, 27, 28, 29bis, 30bis, 31bis, 32bis, 33, [34], 34, [37], [38bis], [39], 39, 40, [40], [41bis], 42, [42bis], 43bis, [43$^{\text{(bis)}}$], 44, [44bis], 45

Šʾ IB common noun, profession name, substantivized participle ‘drawer of water’ /šāʾibu/ **44** (RS 19.016):15

ŠʾL verb ‘ask (a question)’ **3** (RS 2.[003]$^{+}$) i:38; **28** (RS 29.093):23; **34** (RS 94.2284):8, 9; **35** (RS [Varia 4]):11, 16

tD-stem ‘make repeated demands’ **28** (RS 29.093):12

ŠʾR verb ‘remain behind’ (Gt-stem) **29** (RS 34.124):42′ ({[?]štỉr}); **34** (RS 94.2284):19

ŠʾIR common noun ‘flesh’ /šiʾru/# **20** (RS 24.247^{+}):11

[ŠBY verb ‘capture’]: ŠBY common noun ‘captive’ /šabyu/ **1** (RS 3.367) i:29′, 30′

ŠBM verb ‘muzzle’ (Gt-stem) **2** (RS 2.[014]$^{+}$) iii:40′

ŠBN place-name /šubbanu/ **45** (RS 86.2213):13

ŠBʿ cardinal number 'seven' /šabʿu/; pl. 'seventy' /šabʿūma/ **2** (RS 2.[014]$^{+}$) iii:42′; **3** (RS 2.[003]$^{+}$) i:8; **5** (RS 2.002):20, 66; **11** (RS 24.266):4; **12** (RS 24.643):19; **13** (RS 34.126):30; **41** (RS 19.015):32, 35 ({š[bʿm]}); **42** (RS 15.062):6, 18; **43** (RS 18.024):16, 27; **47** (RS 94.2392^{+}):7; **48** (RS 94.2600):4; **49** (RIH 84/04):5; **51** (RIH 84/33):13; **52** (RIH 83/22):9

ŠBʿ ordinal number 'seventh' /šabīʿu/ **4** (RS 2.[004]) i:15′; **11** (RS 24.266):1, 22′

ŠBʿ verb 'do seven times' (D-stem) **3** (RS 2.[003]$^{+}$) i:20 (Dp-participle)

ŠBʿD adverb, multiplicative, 'seven times' /šabʿida/ (← /šabʿaʾida/) **5** (RS 2.002):12, 14, 15 ({šbʿdm}); **27** (RS 18.040):6bis; **28** (RS 29.093):9; **30** (RS 92.2010):7bis

ŠBʿ (← *ŚBʿ) verb 'be/become satiated' **4** (RS 2.[004]) i:31′

ŠBʿ common (or verbal) noun 'satiety' /šubʿu/ **7** (RS 24.258):3, 16

ŠBʿN common noun 'satiety' /šabʿānu/ **5** (RS 2.002):64

ŠGR-W-ʾIṮM divine name, binomial, god of the mixed herds of sheep and goats /šaggar wa ʾiṯum/ **12** (RS 24.643):31

[ŠḪN verb 'be/become hot']: N-stem 'grow hot' **13** (RS 34.126):18bis

ŠD common noun 'field, arable land, country-side' /šadû/# (← /*šadVyu/) **2** (RS 2.[014]$^{+}$) iii:17′; **5** (RS 2.002):13^{tris}, 28bis, 68; **12** (RS 24.643):18; **37** (RS 16.382):5, 6; **38** (RS 94.2168):5, 14; **39** (RS 94.2965):16, 20; **41** (RS 19.015):10; **44** (RS 19.016):51

ŠDYN personal name /šaduyānu/ **44** (RS 19.016):6

ŠDMT compound common noun 'field-of-a-man' /šadûmuti/ **5** (RS 2.002):10

[ŠD:] ŠT common noun 'lady' /šittu/ ← /*šidtu/ ← /*šīd(a)tu/ **5** (RS 2.002):61

[ŠDD verb 'ruin']: D-stem 'ruin' **20** (RS 24.247^{+}):35′, 37′

[ŠDD]: ŠD common noun '(surface measure)' /šiddu/ **2** (RS 2.[014]$^{+}$) iii:[1]

ŠḤ common noun 'bush' /šīḥu/, pl. /šīḥātu/ **6** (RS 24.244):65

[ŠḤR common noun 'dawn']: divine name, in binomial ŠḤR-W-ŠLM 'Dawn-and-Dusk' /šaḥru wa šalimu/ **5** (RS 2.002):52, 53; **6** (RS 24.244):52

ŠḤR ṮLṮT adverbial phrase 'in the future (← at dawn [= tomorrow] and on the third [day] [= day after tomorrow])' /šaḥra ṯalāṯata/ **37** (RS 16.382):15

ŠḤT: see ŠḤ

ŠYN personal name /šuyānu/ **46** (RS 94.2050^{+}):41

ŠKB verb 'lie down' **3** (RS 2.[003]$^{+}$) i:34; **4** (RS 2.[004]) i:4′, 14′, [39′]

[ŠKḤ verb 'find']: N-stem 'be located (← be found/find oneself)' **26** (RS 18.031):15

[ŠKN verb 'settle']: D-stem 'put, establish' **38** (RS 94.2168):18

[ŠKR verb 'be/become drunk']: ŠKR common noun 'drunkenness' /šukru/ **7** (RS 24.258):4, 16

ŠKRN common noun 'drunkenness' /šikkarānu/ **4** (RS 2.[004]) i:30′

ʾAŠKR common noun ‘drinking party’ /ʾaškaru/ **7** (RS 24.258):15
ʾAŠKRR common noun ‘henbane’ /ʾaškuraru/ **19** (RS 17.120):13
ŠLḤ common noun ‘sword’ /šilḥu/ **3** (RS 2.[003]⁺) i:20
ŠLYṬ: see LṬ
[ŠLL (← ŚLL)]: MŠLT ‘(type of garment)’ /mašallatu/ **12** (RS 24.643):19; **43** (RS 18.024):14, 23
ŠLM verb ‘be/come well, at peace with’ **20** (RS 24.247⁺):54′; **21** (RS 4.475):4; **22** (RS 8.315):12; **23** (RS 11.872):7, 10; **24** (RS 15.008):4, 14; **25** (RS 16.379):6, 8; **26** (RS 18.031):4, 7; **28** (RS 29.093):26; **29** (RS 34.124):5!, 7; **30** (RS 92.2010):11; **31** (RS 94.2406):33; **32** (RS 94.2479):4, 7; **36** (RS 11.772⁺):12′
D-stem ‘provide with well-being’ **5** (RS 2.002):7bis, 26; **22** (RS 8.315):9; **23** (RS 11.872):8; **24** (RS 15.008):6; **25** (RS 16.379):7; **26** (RS 18.031):5; **28** (RS 29.093):7; **29** (RS 34.124):6; **30** (RS 92.2010):5; **35** (RS [Varia 4]):5
ŠLM common noun ‘well-being, peace’ /šalāmu/ **2** (RS 2.[014]⁺) iii:16′; **11** (RS 24.266):24′; **13** (RS 34.126):31bis, 32bis, 33bis, 34; **22** (RS 8.315):16; **23** (RS 11.872):12; **24** (RS 15.008):17; **25** (RS 16.379):10; **26** (RS 18.031):8; **28** (RS 29.093):5; **29** (RS 34.124):9; **30** (RS 92.2010):13, 14, 16, 17; **32** (RS 94.2479):8 ({〈šlm〉})
ŠLM divine name, ‘the ultimate, the last (whence) Dusk’ (see ŠḤR-W-ŠLM) /šalimu/# **8** (RS 1.001):8
[ŠLM(Y) place-name /šalmāyu/]: ŠLMY gentilic /šalmiyyu/ **49** (RIH 84/04):21, 23, 26
ŠLMM common noun, *plurale tantum* ‘sacrifice of well-being’ /šalamūma/ **8** (RS 1.001):4; **10** (RS 24.260):9; **12** (RS 24.643):10
ŠM common noun ‘name’ /šumu/ (pl. ŠMT) **1** (RS 3.367) i:11′bis, 18′, 19′, 28′; **5** (RS 2.002):18; **31** (RS 94.2406):12; **35** (RS [Varia 4]):13
[ŠM]: ŠMT common noun ‘carnelian (the stone and the color)’ /šamtu/ **5** (RS 2.002):21
ŠMʾAL common noun ‘left (hand)’ /šamʾalu/ ← /*śamʾalu/ **5** (RS 2.002):64; **20** (RS 24.247⁺):[9], 10, 11, 37′, 59′
ŠMGY place-name /šammigāyu/ ← /*šamnigāyu/ **41** (RS 19.015):27
[ŠMḪ verb ‘rejoice’]: D-stem ‘put in a state of rejoicing’ **24** (RS 15.008):11
ŠMD verb ‘destroy’ (Gt-stem) **2** (RS 2.[014]⁺) iii:40′
[ŠMY]: ŠMM common noun pl. ‘heavens’ /šamûma/# ← /*šamayūma/ **2** (RS 2.[014]⁺) iii:24′, 26′; **5** (RS 2.002):38bis, 62bis; **6** (RS 24.244):1, 52
ŠMM divine name: see ʾARṢ-W-ŠMM
ŠMMN personal name /šamumānu/ **40** (RS [Varia 14]):3, 11!, 15
ŠMN common noun ‘oil (usually olive oil)’ /šamnu/ **11** (RS 24.266):24′; **12** (RS 24.643):21; **29** (RS 34.124):30; **32** (RS 94.2479):16, 17; **47** (RS 94.2392⁺):3, 7, 9, 10, 15; **48** (RS 94.2600):14

ŠMN common noun '(species of pine or fir)' /šamnu/ **42** (RS 15.062):3
ŠMNY place-name /šamnāyu/ **41** (RS 19.015):26
[ŠMN]: ŠMT common noun 'cord, strap, tether' /šummattu/ (← */šummantu/) **43** (RS 18.024):25
ŠMᶜ verb 'hear, listen' **11** (RS 24.266):34′; **21** (RS 4.475):7, 17; **31** (RS 94.2406):24
ŠMᶜN personal name /šamᶜānu/ **44** (RS 19.016):5
ŠMᶜ RGM common noun, profession name, substantivized participle 'he who listens to the word of X' /šāmiᶜu rigmi/ **30** (RS 92.2010):18; **44** (RS 19.016):10, 11 ({šmᶜ ⟨rgm⟩$^{?}$})
MŠMᶜT common noun 'royal guard (← those who listen and obey)' /mašmaᶜtu/ **29** (RS 34.124):11, 14
ŠMT common noun 'carnelian': see ŠM
ŠMT common noun 'cord': see ŠMN
ŠMTR personal name, vocalization and etymology unknown **46** (RS 94.2050^{+}):55
[ŠN]: ŠNT common noun 'year' /šanatu/# **5** (RS 2.002):66
ŠNʾ (← *ŚNʾ) verb 'hate, be the enemy of' **29** (RS 34.124):45′ ({[š]ni͗tk})
ŠNY verb 'change (for the worse)' **9** (RS 1.002):28′, 30′, 32′, 36′, 39′, 40′
[ŠNN:] ŠNT adjective 'in a liquid state' /šannatu/ **12** (RS 24.643):22
ŠNPT: see NP
ŠNT common noun 'sleep': see YŠN
ŠNT common noun 'year': see ŠN
ŠNT common noun 'liquid': see ŠNN
ŠᶜR (← ŚᶜR) common noun 'hair' /šaᶜru/ **7** (RS 24.258):29′; **20** (RS 24.247^{+}):3 ({š[ᶜr]})
ŠᶜR common noun 'barley' /šiᶜāru/; attested only in the plural, expressing '(multiple) grains of barley' **32** (RS 94.2479):12; **48** (RS 94.2600):1
ŠᶜRT common noun 'wool' /šaᶜartu/# **12** (RS 24.643):20 ({˹š˺[ᶜrt]}); **42** (RS 15.062):17; **43** (RS 18.024):9
ŠᶜRT place-name /šaᶜartu/ **45** (RS 86.2213):9
[*ŠP]: ŠPT common noun 'lip' /šapatu/ **1** (RS 3.367) i:6′; **5** (RS 2.002):49, 50, 55bis, 61, 62; **18** (RS 92.2014):11; **20** (RS 24.247^{+}):32′
ŠP common noun 'barren hilltop' /šapû/ ← /*šapayu/ **5** (RS 2.002):4
ŠPḤ common noun 'offspring, family' /šapḥu/# **20** (RS 24.247^{+}):13, 29′
ŠPḤ common noun, 'family (as an abstract concept)' /šupḥu/ **3** (RS 2.[003]$^{+}$) i:24
ŠPK verb 'pour out' **18** (RS 92.2014):12
ŠPŠ common noun 'sun' /šapšu/# **11** (RS 24.266):4, 23′
ŠPŠ divine name, feminine, 'sun-deity' **5** (RS 2.002):25, 54; **6** (RS 24.244):2bis, 8bis, 14bis, 19bis, 25bis, 30bis, ⟨34a^{bis}⟩, 35bis, 40bis, 45bis, 51bis, 57bis; **12** (RS 24.643):7, 32; **13** (RS 34.126):18, 19; **20** (RS 24.247^{+}):45′

ŠPŠ title of the Sun-king, Hittite or Egyptian /šapšu/ **24** (RS 15.008):8, 9; **36** (RS 11.772^{+}):4′, 11′, 19′, 25′

ŠPŠM personal name /šapšuma/ (‘pertaining to [the goddess] Šapšu’) **46** (RS 94.2050^{+}):3, 63

ŠPŠN personal name /šapšānu/ (‘pertaining to [the goddess] Šapšu’) **50** (RIH 84/06):6; **51** (RIH 84/33):4

ŠPŠ PGR divine name ‘Šapšu of the corpse’ (expresses function as psychopomp) /šapšu pagri/ **8** (RS 1.001):12, 17

ŠPL verb ‘be/become low’ **5** (RS 2.002):32; **13** (RS 34.126):22

ŠQ common noun ‘thigh’ /šāqu/ **20** (RS 24.247^{+}):9, 26′

[ŠQY verb ‘drink (or give to drink)’]: D-stem ‘serve drink’ **4** (RS 2.[004]) i:[3′], [8′], 10′, 13′, 22′

ŠQY common noun ‘libation (or libator$^{?}$)’ **10** (RS 24.260):11

ŠQL place-name /šuqalu/ **41** (RS 19.015):25

[ŠR verb ‘sing’]: ŠR common noun, profession name, substantivized participle, ‘singer’ /šāru/ **5** (RS 2.002):22; **44** (RS 19.016):17, 37

MŠR common noun ‘song’ /mašīru/ **2** (RS 2.[014]$^{+}$) iii:5′

ŠR common noun ‘prince’: see ŠRR

ŠR common noun ‘stalk’: see ŠRR

ŠRŠ common noun ‘root (whence) scion’ /šuršu/ **4** (RS 2.[004]) i:19′, 20′, 25′, [43′]

ŠRŠ place-name /šurašu/ **41** (RS 19.015):32; **45** (RS 86.2213):16

ŠRʿ common noun, meaning unknown **12** (RS 24.643):21

ŠRP (← *ŚRP) common noun ‘burnt-offering’ /šurpu/ **8** (RS 1.001):4, 17; **11** (RS 24.266):21′; **12** (RS 24.643):9

[ŠRR]: ŠR common noun ‘prince’ /šarru/ divine name, in binomial MT-W-ŠR ‘Man and Prince’ /mutu wa šarru/ **5** (RS 2.002):8

[ŠRR]: ŠR common noun ‘stalk, shoot’ /šurru/ **7** (RS 24.258):30′

ŠRR adjective ‘true’ /šarrīru/ **1** (RS 3.367) i:33′, 35′, 37′

ŠT verb ‘put, place, establish’ **2** (RS 2.[014]$^{+}$) iii:15′; **5** (RS 2.002):36 ({yš‹t›}), 38; **7** (RS 24.258):29′; **17** (RIH 78/20):13bis; **21** (RS 4.475):18; **25** (RS 16.379):24; **26** (RS 18.031):27; **34** (RS 94.2284):21; **36** (RS 11.772^{+}):17′; **40** (RS [Varia 14]):5

MŠT common noun ‘putting, where one puts’ /mašītu/ **2** (RS 2.[014]$^{+}$) iii:4′

ŠT common noun ‘(dry measure)’ /šūtu/ **19** (RS 17.120):2, 10bis, 12, 13, 15, 16bis, 18, 26, [26]

ŠT common noun ‘lady’: see ŠD

ŠTY verb ‘drink’ **5** (RS 2.002):6, 72; **7** (RS 24.258):3bis, 16, 31′; **17** (RIH 78/20):7

ŠTY verb ‘weave’ **43** (RS 18.024):9

ŠTY personal name /šattuya/ **46** (RS 94.2050^{+}):32

ŠTT (← ŚTT) verb ‘scatter, dismember’ **1** (RS 3.367) i:27′

L particle, emphatic, ‘certainly’ /la/ **1** (RS 3.367) i:2′, 3′, 7′, 32′, 33′, 34′, 35′, 37′; **2** (RS 2.[014]$^{+}$) iii:38′, 39′, 40′ ; **4** (RS 2.[004]) i:23′; **6** (RS 24.244):63; **10** (RS 24.260): 10; **11** (RS 24.266):11, 13; **23** (RS 11.872):16; **28** (RS 29.093):27; **52** (RIH 83/22):4

L particle, negative ‘not’ /lā/# **1** (RS 3.367) i:6′, 17′^{tris}; **2** (RS 2.[014]$^{+}$) iii:26′, 27′^{bis}, iv:5; **3** (RS 2.[003]$^{+}$) i:12; **5** (RS 2.002):64; **7** (RS 24.258):7; **18** (RS 92.2014):1, 3, 5, 6, 7, 8; **19** (RS 17.120):9bis; **20** (RS 24.247^{+}):13, 29′; **25** (RS 16.379):19; **31** (RS 94.2406):24, 28bis; **33** (RS 96.2039):19; **34** (RS 94.2284):8, 29, 34; **37** (RS 16.382):17; **39** (RS 94.2965):11, 22; **52** (RIH 83/22):12

ʾAL particle, negative /ʾal/ **17** (RIH 78/20):11bis, 12, 18, 19; **24** (RS 15.008):12; **25** (RS 16.379):21, 23; **26** (RS 18.031):27; **30** (RS 92.2010):22; **31** (RS 94.2406):21, 39; **40** (RS [Varia 14]):12

L preposition ‘at, towards, (from) at’ /lê/# (← /*lay(a)/) **1** (RS 3.367) i:5′^{bis}, 8′, 12′, 13′, 20′^{bis}, 23′, 26′; **2** (RS 2.[014]$^{+}$) iii:5′^{bis}, 9′, 11′, 12′, 16′, 17′, 21′, 37′, 38′, iv:2, 3bis, 4bis, 6bis; **3** (RS 2.[003]$^{+}$) i:1, 9, 15; **4** (RS 2.[004]) i:18′, 20′, 27′, 28′, 38′, [42′], [45′], [46′]; **5** (RS 2.002):3, 5, 31, 36, 39, 41bis, 44, 45, 48bis, 52, 54bis, 57bis, 59, 62bis, 63, 66bis, [71], [72]; **6** (RS 24.244):2, 8, 14, 19, 25, 30, 〈34a〉, 35, 40, 45, 51, 57, 67, 68; **7** (RS 24.258):2, 7, 10, 13, 17, 18, 29; **8** (RS 1.001):2, 12, 19, 21, 22; **9** (RS 1.002):3′ et passim in this text; **10** (RS 24.260):2, 3, 4, 5, 9, 11, 12, 13; **11** (RS 24.266):2, 6, 7, 8, 12, 14, 15, 16, 21′, 27′, 28′, [29′], 34′, 35′, 36′; **13** (RS 34.126):20; **14** (RS 6.021):2, 3; **15** (RS 6.028):2; **16** (RS 25.318):2; **17** (RIH 78/20):5, 6, 10, 14bis, 15, 17; **18** (RS 92.2014):14bis, 15; **20** (RS 24.247^{+}):43′, 52′, 54′; **21** (RS 4.475):2, 4, 5, 6; **22** (RS 8.315):1, 5, 18; **23** (RS 11.872):1, 5, 6, 13; **24** (RS 15.008):2, 4, 8; **25** (RS 16.379):1, 4, 5, 11; **26** (RS 18.031):1, 4, 23; **27** (RS 18.040):1, [5]; **28** (RS 29.093):1, 6, 8, 13, 22, 26, 28, 29; **29** (RS 34.124):[1], [4], 9, 19, 20, 28, 31; **30** (RS 92.2010):1, 6; **31** (RS 94.2406):2, 12, 32, 33, 36, 37; **32** (RS 94.2479):1, 3, 4; **33** (RS 96.2039):2, 7; **34** (RS 94.2284):2, 11, 13, 29, 31, 32b; **35** (RS [Varia 4]):2, 13, 14, 18, 19; **36** (RS 11.772^{+}):9′ $^{?}$, 17′, 19′, 25′, 28′, 30′, 32′, [34′], [36′], 38′, 39′; **37** (RS 16.382):1, 12, 13; **38** (RS 94.2168):1, 2, 6, 7bis, 9, 10, 12, 18; **40** (RS [Varia 14]):6, 14; **42** (RS 15.062):3, 4, 5; **43** (RS 18.024):3, 6, 12, 15, 24; **44** (RS 19.016):49; **47** (RS 94.2392^{+}):13, [16]; **52** (RIH 83/22):5

LY extended form /lêya/ **29** (RS 34.124):5 ({[l]⸢y⸣})

LM extended form /lêma/ **7** (RS 24.258):12

LM extended form functioning as interrogative adverb ‘why?’ /lêma/ (L + M) **28** (RS 29.093):16; **29** (RS 34.124):10; **34** (RS 94.2284):33

LN extended form /lêna/ **4** (RS 2.[004]) i:29′, [48′]; **6** (RS 24.244):5bis, 10, 11, 16bis, 21, 22, 27bis, 32bis, ⟨34c^{bis}⟩, 37bis, 42bis, 47, 48, 53, 54, 59, 60

L PN compound preposition /lê panî/ **13** (RS 34.126):15; **17** (RIH 78/20):2; **24** (RS 15.008):8; **29** (RS 34.124):19; **31** (RS 94.2406):36; **38** (RS 94.2168):2

L particle, vocative, may be formally identical to the preposition **1** (RS 3.367) i:8′^{bis}, 28′, 29′; **4** (RS 2.[004]) i:23′, 24′

LʾY verb 'be/become able, powerful; overpower' [D-stem$^{?}$] **3** (RS 2.[003]$^{+}$) i:33

ʾALʾIY adjective 'most powerful' (title of *Baʿlu*) /ʾalʾiyu/ **2** (RS 2.[014]$^{+}$) iii:14′

ʾALʾIYN same /ʾalʾiyānu/ **1** (RS 3.367) i:28′, 31′; **2** (RS 2.[014]$^{+}$) iii:5′, 13′

TLʾIYT common noun 'power, victory' /talʾiyatu/ **2** (RS 2.[014]$^{+}$) iii:31′

LʾY (← *LʾW$^{?}$) verb 'be/become weak' **6** (RS 24.244):68

LʾK verb 'send (whence) send a message/messenger' **21** (RS 4.475):10; **25** (RS 16.379):17, 19, 20; **26** (RS 18.031):11; **28** (RS 29.093):13; **29** (RS 34.124):23; **31** (RS 94.2406):23, 25, 29, 33, 34, 36; **33** (RS 96.2039):19, 21; **34** (RS 94.2284):32a; **35** (RS [Varia 4]):7

D-stem 'send (intensively)' **29** (RS 34.124):10

MLʾAKT common noun 'embassy, messenger party' /malʾaktu/ **33** (RS 96.2039):17, 23; **34** (RS 94.2284):33

LʾIM divine name /liʾmu/ **2** (RS 2.[014]$^{+}$) iii:12′ {lỉmm}

LB common noun 'heart': see LBB

LB[-]N place-name, precise form uncertain **12** (RS 24.643):43

LBʾU common noun 'lion' /labaʾu/ **17** (RIH 78/20):4

[LBB]: LB common noun 'heart' /libbu/ **8** (RS 1.001):8; **25** (RS 16.379):23; **26** (RS 18.031):27; **29** (RS 34.124):16; **34** (RS 94.2284):7, 14, 26, 34; **38** (RS 94.2168):18, 19, 21, 22, 24, 26, 28

LBŠ verb 'dress' **17** (RIH 78/20):12

LBŠ common noun 'garment' /lubūšu/ **43** (RS 18.024):14, 16

LBN personal name /labnu/ **44** (RS 19.016):3

LBNM place-name /labnuma/ **41** (RS 19.015):21

[LGG]: LG common noun '(small container and liquid measure)' /luggu/ **5** (RS 2.002):75; **12** (RS 24.643):21

[LḪŠ verb 'whisper']: D-stem 'charm (serpents)' **6** (RS 24.244):5, 11, 16, 21–22, 27, 32, ⟨34c⟩, 37, 42, 47, 53, 59

LḪŠT common noun 'whispering' /laḫaštu/ **2** (RS 2.[014]$^{+}$) iii:23′

LWSND place-name /lawasanda/ **27** (RS 18.040):10

LHN verb 'serve food/drink' (D-stem) **5** (RS 2.002):75

LḤ: LḤT common noun 'tablet' /lūḥatu/ **29** (RS 34.124):17, 23; **33** (RS 96.2039):4; **34** (RS 94.2284):18; **35** (RS [Varia 4]):6

[LḤ(Ḥ) verb ‘flow (of sap)’]: LḤT common noun ‘sap, liquid’ /liḥḥatu/ **19** (RS 17.120):3

[LḤY]: LḤT common noun ‘cheek, jaw’ /laḥatu/ (← laḥayatu/) **4** (RS 2.[004]) i:28′, [47′]

LḤM common noun ‘bread’ /laḥmu/ **5** (RS 2.002):6, 71; **7** (RS 24.258):7; **17** (RIH 78/20):6

LḤM verb ‘eat’ **5** (RS 2.002):6, 72; **7** (RS 24.258):2; **10** (RS 24.260):8, 10; **17** (RIH 78/20):6

D-stem ‘serve with food’ **4** (RS 2.[004]) i:2′, 7′, 10′, 12′, 21′

Š-stem ‘cause to eat’ **6** (RS 24.244):6, 12, 17, 23, 28, 33, ‹34d›, 38, 43, 49, 55

MLḤMT common noun ‘bread offering’ /malḥamatu/ **2** (RS 2.[014]$^{+}$) iii:15′

[LṬ ‘roll (up)’ ← LYṬ]: ŠLYṬ common noun ’who produces coils, rolls up’ /šalyaṭu/ **2** (RS 2.[014]$^{+}$) iii:42′

LKN personal name /lukanu/ **44** (RS 19.016):8

[LŠY verb ‘fall, be debased’]: verb ‘bring low’ (D-stem) **7** (RS 24.258):20

LŠN common noun ‘tongue’ /lašānu/# **17** (RIH 78/20):12; **20** (RS 24.247^{+}):31′, 53′

LL common noun ‘night’ /lêlu/ ← /*laylu/ **8** (RS 1.001):12

LM: see L preposition

LN verb ‘spend the night’ **4** (RS 2.[004]) i:5′$^{!}$, 15′

LN preposition: see L

[LẒY verb ‘burn, be very hot’]: LẒT common noun ‘heat’ /luẓatu/ ← /*luẓayatu/ **17** (RIH 78/20):11

LSM verb ‘run, leg it’ **2** (RS 2.[014]$^{+}$) iii:19′

LṢB common noun ‘forehead’ /liṣbu/ **7** (RS 24.258):29′; **20** (RS 24.247^{+}):49′, 57′

LQḤ verb ‘take, receive’ **1** (RS 3.367) i:10′; **5** (RS 2.002):35, 36; **23** (RS 11.872):17$^{!}$; **26** (RS 18.031):17, 22; **28** (RS 29.093):15, 18; **29** (RS 34.124):29; **33** (RS 96.2039):5; **34** (RS 94.2284):23; **37** (RS 16.382):17; **39** (RS 94.2965):11; **44** (RS 19.016):49; **52** (RIH 83/22):10

LRGT place-name /larugatu/ **6** (RS 24.244):26

LRMN common noun ‘pomegranate’ /lurmānu/ **5** (RS 2.002):50, [55]

[LTḤ common noun ‘(fraction of a greater measure)’ /litḥu/]: MLTḤ common noun ‘(LTḤ-container and measure$^{?}$, perhaps 1/15th)’ /maltaḥu/ **43** (RS 18.024):26

[*M interrogative/indefinite pronoun]

[M interrogative/indefinite personal pronoun ‘who?, whoever’ /mī/]

MN extended form /mīna/ **2** (RS 2.[014]$^{+}$) iii:37′; **3** (RS 2.[003]$^{+}$) i:38$^{!}$;

MNM extended form /mīnama/ **2** (RS 2.[014]$^{+}$) iv:4

[*M interrogative/indefinite impersonal pronoun ‘what?, whatever’ /ma/]

LM interrogative adverb ‘why?’ /lêma/ (L + M): see L

MH extended form /mah(a)/ ← /*ma + ha/ **5** (RS 2.002):53, 60; **35** (RS [Varia 4]):9 ({mhy} ← /mah + hiya/)

MHK extended form functioning as indefinite pronoun /mahaka/ **26** (RS 18.031):26; **31** (RS 94.2406): 40

MHKM extended form functioning as indefinite pronoun /mahakama/ **25** (RS 16.379):22; **39** (RS 94.2965):21

MK extended form functioning as adverb ‘then’ /maka/ **4** (RS 2.[004]) i:15′

MN extended form of the interrogative pronoun ‘why?’ /mana/ **29** (RS 34.124):22

MNK extended form functioning as indefinite pronoun /mannaka/ ← /*ma + h + na + ka/ **31** (RS 94.2406):22

MNM extended form functioning as indefinite pronoun /mannama/ ← /*ma + h + na + ma/ **21** (RS 4.475):16; **22** (RS 8.315):16; **23** (RS 11.872):12; **24** (RS 15.008):16; **25** (RS 16.379):10; **26** (RS 18.031):8; **28** (RS 29.093):29; **29** (RS 34.124):8, 33; **32** (RS 94.2479):8; **34** (RS 94.2284):24

[Mʾ]: MʾIT number noun ‘(one) hundred’ /miʾtu/# **12** (RS 24.643):20; **29** (RS 34.124):27; **36** (RS 11.772$^+$):22′, 23′, 27′, 28′, 29′, 30′, 31′, 32′, 33′, [34′], [35′], [36′], [37′], [38′], 39′; **42** (RS 15.062):1, 3, 4, 7, 8; **43** (RS 18.024):4, 17, 28; **47** (RS 94.2392$^+$):2; **50** (RIH 84/06):[1]; **51** (RIH 84/33):2; **52** (RIH 83/22):8

MʾAB personal name /maʾʾabû/ **24** (RS 15.008):11

MʾID adverb ‘completely, utterly, very’ /maʾda/ **3** (RS 2.[003]$^+$) i:23; **19** (RS 17.120):30; **21** (RS 4.475):13; **22** (RS 8.315):11; **24** (RS 15.008):10; **30** (RS 92.2010):11; **34** (RS 94.2284):15

MʾADT common noun ‘much, many’ /maʾadatu/ **20** (RS 24.247$^+$):1

MʾIZRT: see ʾZR

MʾIYT common noun ‘well watered place’ /māʾiyyatu/ **17** (RIH 78/20):8

MBK: see NBK

MGDL: see ʾILT MGDL

MGŠḪ place-name ‘Mukish’ /mugišḫi/ **36** (RS 11.772$^+$):6′ ({[mg]šḫ})

MGLB: see GLB

MḪ common noun ‘brain’ /muḫḫu/ **4** (RS 2.[004]) i:38′

MḪṢ verb ‘strike, smite’ **1** (RS 3.367) i:9′; **2** (RS 2.[014]$^+$) iii:38′, 41′, 43′, 45′

Gt-stem **2** (RS 2.[014]$^+$) iii:46′

MDB: see DB

MDBḤT: see DBḤ

MDBR: see DBR

MDGL: see DGL

[MDD verb 'measure']: YMDŠR personal name /yamudšarru/ ('the [divine] prince measured out [this child]') **44** (RS 19.016):31
MDD: see YDD
MDRʿ: see DRʿ
MDṮ personal name, vocalization and etymology unknown **44** (RS 19.016):4
MH: see M
MHR common noun 'bride-price' /muhru/ **6** (RS 24.244):73 ({<mhry>}), 74, 75
MḤRṮT: see ḤRṮ
MṬT: see NṬY
[MY common noun 'water']: MM /mêma/ **32** (RS 94.2479):19
MK (*MWK or *MKK) verb 'sag, collapse' **1** (RS 3.367) i:17′; **17** (RIH 78/20):11
MK particle: see M
MKŠR: see KŠR
MKNT: see KN
MKR common noun 'merchant' /makkāru/ **47** (RS 94.2392^{+}):1
MŠLT: see ŠLL
MŠMN: see ʾŠM
MŠMʿT: see ŠMʿ
MŠR common noun 'song': see ŠR
MŠR common noun 'rectitude': see YŠR
MŠT: see ŠT
[MLʾ 'be/become full']: D-stem 'fill' **5** (RS 2.002):76; **11** (RS 24.266):31′, 32′
  MLʾU common noun 'fullness' /malāʾu/ **8** (RS 1.001):10; **48** (RS 94.2600):12
MLʾAKT: see LʾK
MLWM place-name, identification and vocalization unknown **31** (RS 94.2406):6
MLḤMT: see LḤM
MLK verb 'reign' **1** (RS 3.367) i:32′
  MLK common noun 'king' /malku/# **3** (RS 2.[003]$^{+}$) i:8; **5** (RS 2.002):7; **8** (RS 1.001):12; **10** (RS 24.260):1; **11** (RS 24.266):4, 5, 14, 24′, 25′; **12** (RS 24.643):18; **13** (RS 34.126):11, 12, 15, 25, 26; **20** (RS 24.247^{+}):7bis, 9, 10, 13, 17, 37′, 43′, 46′, 47′, 52′, 54′, 57′, 58′; **23** (RS 11.872):3, 18; **25** (RS 16.379):3, 13; **26** (RS 18.031):1, 3; **27** (RS 18.040):1, 12, 14, 18; **29** (RS 34.124):3 (⸢m⸣[lk]), 11, 14, 17, 24, 26, 29, 32; **31** (RS 94.2406):29; **32** (RS 94.2479):6; **33** (RS 96.2039): 20; **35** (RS [Varia 4]):13; **36** (RS 11.772^{+}):6′ ({ml⸢k⸣[. . .]}), 13′, 14′, 16′, 24′, 26′; **37** (RS 16.382):3; **38** (RS 94.2168):4, 6, 8, 23; **41** (RS 19.015):2, 7, 10, 11; **43** (RS 18.024):16; **44** (RS 19.016):1, [49], [50]; **52** (RIH 83/22):11

MLK common noun ‘reign, kingship, kingdom’ /mulku/ **1** (RS 3.367) i:10′; **2** (RS 2.[014]$^{+}$) iv:2; **3** (RS 2.[003]$^{+}$) i:41
MLKT common noun ‘queen’ /malkatu/ **5** (RS 2.002):7; **23** (RS 11.872):1, 15; **25** (RS 16.379):1; **29** (RS 34.124):[1]; **31** (RS 94.2406):1, 36, 38; **32** (RS 94.2479):1; **33** (RS 96.2039):1; **36** (RS 11.772^{+}):28′
MLK divine name /milku/ **6** (RS 24.244):41
ʾAḪTMLK personal name, feminine /ʾaḫâtumilki/ **22** (RS 8.315):4
MLKYM personal name /milkiyama/ (← /milki + ya + ma/) (‘pertaining to [the god] *Milku*’) **46** (RS 94.2050^{+}):53
MLK place-name /mulukku/ **45** (RS 86.2213):1; **55** (RS 94.2440):4
MLǴǴ meaning unknown, type of sacrifice? **27** (RS 18.040):17
MM: see MY
MMY personal name /mamīya/ **46** (RS 94.2050^{+}):26
MḎR divine name, identification unknown /maḏara/ **12** (RS 24.643):39
MḎR: see NDR/NḎR
MN interrogative pronoun ‘who?’: see M
[MN:] TMN common noun ‘body (← form), members of the body’ /tamūnu/ **1** (RS 3.367) i:18′, 26′
TMNT feminine variant /tamūnatu/ **17** (RIH 78/20):6; **18** (RS 92.2014):15
MN common noun: see MNY
MNDǴ common noun ‘(plant name)’ **19** (RS 17.120):4
[MNḤ ‘bring, present (a gift), transfer’]: MNḤ common noun ‘what has been transferred (to someone)’ /minḥu/ **51** (RIH 84/33):1
MNḤT common noun ‘tribute’ /manḥatu/ **47** (RS 94.2392^{+}):6
MNḤM: see NḤM
[MNY verb ‘count’]: MN common noun ‘mina’ /manû/ ← /*manVyu/ **36** (RS 11.772^{+}):19′, 20′
MNT common noun ‘portion’ /manatu/ ← /*manayatu/ **4** (RS 2.[004]) i:32′
MNT common noun ‘recitation, incantation’ /minûtu/ ← /*minūyatu/ **6** (RS 24.244):4, 9 ({mnty}), 15, 20, 26, 31, ⟨34b⟩, 36, 41, 46, 52, 58, 70, 71, 79
MNK: see M
MNM: see M
MNN personal name /muninu/ **44** (RS 19.016):37
MNNY personal name /muninuya/ **49** (RIH 84/04):2; **51** (RIH 84/33):1
[MSK verb ‘mix’]: MSKT common noun ‘mixture’ /maskatu/ **19** (RS 17.120):3
[MSS verb ‘dissolve’]: D-stem **19** (RS 17.120):3, 10
MʿN: see ʿNY
MʿR place-name /muʿaru/ **45** (RS 86.2213):7

MʿRBY: see ʿRB
MPḪRT: see PḪR
MṢB common noun '(type of wine)' (precise meaning and vocalization unknown) **41** (RS 19.015):29, 30, 31, 32, 33, 34, 35
MṢD place-name, identification and vocalization unknown **6** (RS 24.244):58
MṢD common noun 'prey': see ṢD
MṢMT: see ṢMD
MṢQT: see ṢQ
MṢRM place-name 'Egypt' /miṣrāma/ (dual) **26** (RS 18.031):11
MQDM common noun, meaning unknown **42** (RS 15.062):19
MR place-name (town on the middle Euphrates) 'Mari' /mari/ **6** (RS 24.244):〈34b〉, 78
MR verb 'provide for the needs (of someone) (← supply with provisions)' **4** (RS 2.[004]) i:24′, 35′
MRʾ adjective 'fattened' /marīʾu/ **34** (RS 94.2284):10
MRDT: see RDY
MRZḤ: see RZḤ
[MRḤ]: MRḤY common noun 'weapon' /murḥay/ **20** (RS 24.247^{+}):7, 47′
MRḤQT: see RḤQ
[MRṬ]: MRṬN personal name /marṭānu/ **44** (RS 19.016):15
MRY verb 'expel, drive out' **1** (RS 3.367) i:2′, 19′^{bis}
MRYM: see RM
MRYN personal name /maryānu/ **44** (RS 19.016):2
MRKBT: see RKB
MRMT: see RM
MRʿ: see RʿY
MRṢ verb 'be/become ill' **34** (RS 94.2284):7, 14, 27, 34
[MRR verb 'be/become bitter']: MR adjective 'bitter' /marru/ **19** (RS 17.120):7, [24]
  MRR common noun 'myrrh' /murru/ **32** (RS 94.2479):16
  ŠMRR common noun 'venom (← causing bitterness)' /šamriru/ **6** (RS 24.244):4, 10, 15, 21, 26, 31, 〈34b〉, 36–37, 41, 47, 53, 59
[MRR verb 'pass']: R-stem, 'move (something) back and forth, agitate' **18** (RS 92.2014):2
MṮBT: see YṮB
[MṮL]: TMṮL common noun '(a container/measure)' /tamṯīlu/ **19** (RS 17.120):25bis, [27]
MṮN: see ṮNY
MǴY verb 'arrive' **2** (RS 2.[014]$^{+}$) iii:36′; **5** (RS 2.002):75; **6** (RS 24.244):67; **7** (RS 24.258):9; **28** (RS 29.093):25; **31** (RS 94.2406):14, 22 ({m⸢ǵ⸣[?]}); **36** (RS 11.772^{+}):3′ ({mǵ[?]})
MǴMǴ common noun '(plant name)' /maǵmaǵu/ **19** (RS 17.120):5, [25], 27

MT verb ‘die’ **1** (RS 3.367) i:32′, 34′; **3** (RS 2.[003]$^{+}$) i:16; **7** (RS 24.258):21; **26** (RS 18.031):13
  MT common noun ‘death’ /môtu/ ← /*mawtu/ **6** (RS 24.244):65; **21** (RS 4.475):12
  TMTT common noun ‘(death →) shipwreck’ /tamūtatu/ **26** (RS 18.031):16, 22
MT common noun ‘man’ /mutu/ **4** (RS 2.[004]) i:[1′], [2′], 17′, 18′, 35′, [36′], [37′], 37′, [42′]; **5** (RS 2.002):40bis, 46bis, 48; **40** (RS [Varia 14]):13
  MT-W-ŠR divine name ‘Man-and-Prince’ /mutu wa šarru/ **5** (RS 2.002):8
MTK: see NTK
[MTN common noun ‘loin’]: MTNT common noun ‘loin, kidney’ /matunatu/ **8** (RS 1.001):2
MTN personal name /mattēnu/ (of Hurrian origin?) **44** (RS 19.016):22, 34
MTQ adjective ‘sweet’ /matuqu/ **5** (RS 2.002):50bis, 55, [55]

ḎBB divine name ‘Spark’ /ḏabību/ **2** (RS 2.[014]$^{+}$) iii:46′
ḎD common noun ‘breast’ /ḏadû/ ← /*ḏadayu/ (see also ZD) **5** (RS 2.002):59, 61
ḎHRT common noun ‘dream, vision’ /ḏahratu/ **3** (RS 2.[003]$^{+}$) i:36
ḎKR personal name /ḏakaru/ **44** (RS 19.016):37
ḎMR verb ‘make music, sing’ **4** (RS 2.[004]) i:28′, 46′
ḎNB common noun ‘tail’ /ḏanabu/ **7** (RS 24.258):20
ḎRʿ: see DRʿ

NʾṢ verb ‘denigrate’ **4** (RS 2.[004]) i:29′, [47′]
[NB]: NBT common noun ‘honey’ /nūbatu/ **12** (RS 24.643):22
[NBK common noun ‘spring’ /nabaku/]: NPK common noun ‘spring’ /napku/ (← /*nabku/) **39** (RS 94.2965):7
  MBK common noun ‘spring’ /mabbaku/ ← /*manbaku/ **6** (RS 24.244):3
NGŠ verb ‘approach’ **5** (RS 2.002):68; **7** (RS 24.258):19
NḪ verb ‘rest’ **22** (RS 8.315):14
  MNḪ common noun ‘resting place’ /manūḫu/ **1** (RS 3.367) i:3′
  NḪT common noun ‘rest → chair, throne’ /nāḫatu/ **2** (RS 2.[014]$^{+}$) iv:3
NḪL common noun ‘stream bed (with or without water)’ /naḫalu/ **6** (RS 24.244):68; **39** (RS 94.2965):4, 8
NDY verb ‘throw down, off’ **4** (RS 2.004)$^{+}$ i:3′, 4′, 13′, 14′, [15′]
NDR (← NḎR) verb ‘vow’ **23** (RS 11.872):14; **25** (RS 16.379):13
  ʾUḎR common noun ‘vow’ /ʾuḏḏaru/ ← /*ʾunḏaru/ **25** (RS 16.379):15!
  MḎR common noun ‘that which is vowed’ /maḏḏaru/ **11** (RS 24.266):30′
[NHM verb ‘slumber’]: NHMMT common noun ‘slumber’ /nahamāmatu/ **3** (RS 2.[003]$^{+}$) i:32, 34
NHR common noun ‘river’ /naharu/ **3** (RS 2.[003]$^{+}$) i:6; **6** (RS 24.244):3

NHR divine name 'River' **1** (RS 3.367) i:4′, 13′, 15′, 17′, 20′, 22′, 25′, 27′, 30′; **2** (RS 2.[014]$^{+}$) iii:39′

NḤŠ common noun 'serpent' /naḥašu/ **6** (RS 24.244):4bis, 6, ⟨6⟩, 10bis, 12bis, 15, 16, 17, 18, 21bis, 23bis, 26, 27, 28bis, 31, 32, 33bis, ⟨34b⟩, ⟨34c⟩, ⟨34d^{bis}⟩, 36, 37, 38bis, 41, 42, 43bis, 46, 47, 48, 49, 52, 53, 55bis, 58, 59, 73, 75, 79

NḤL common noun 'heir' /naḥalu/ **46** (RS 94.2050^{+}):2, 12, 40, 59, 60

NḤLT common noun 'inheritance, personal possession' /naḥlatu/ **2** (RS 2.[014]$^{+}$) iii:30′

[NḤM verb 'have pity on'; D-stem 'comfort']: MNḤM personal name /munaḥḥimu/ ('he who comforts' ← D-stem participle) **44** (RS 19.016):7, 9, 13

YNḤM personal name /yanḥamu/ ('he has had pity' [Amorite form]) **44** (RS 19.016):27

NḤT verb 'prepare' **5** (RS 2.002):37, 40, 43, 47

D-stem functioning as intensive **1** (RS 3.367) i:11′, 18′

NṬṬ verb 'tremble, shake' **2** (RS 2.[014]$^{+}$) iii:33′

[NṬY verb 'stretch out']: MṬ common noun 'rod, staff' /maṭṭû/ ← /*manṭayu/ **5** (RS 2.002):37, 40, 44, 47

MṬT common noun 'bed' /maṭṭatu/ ← /*manṭayatu/ **3** (RS 2.[003]$^{+}$) i:30

NYN common noun, meaning unknown **42** (RS 15.062):19

NYR: see NR

[NKL divine name]: NKLY personal name /nikkaliya/ **30** (RS 92.2010):15

[NKT 'slaughter']: N-stem **9** (RS 1.002):24′, 33′, 41′

NKT common noun 'slaughter' /nakatu/ **9** (RS 1.002):24′, 33′, [41′]

NŠ common noun (attested as pl.) 'men, humanity, mankind' /našūma/# **2** (RS 2.[014]$^{+}$) iii:27′; **18** (RS 92.2014):10

NŠʾ (← NŚʾ) verb 'lift up, carry, bear' **2** (RS 2.[014]$^{+}$) iii:35′; **5** (RS 2.002):37, 54, 65; **11** (RS 24.266):27′

Gt-stem **9** (RS 1.002):16′, 24′, 25′, 33′^{bis}, 41′, 42′

N-stem **20** (RS 24.247^{+}):47′

NŠB common noun '(a cut of meat)' **7** (RS 24.258):10, 13

NŠQ verb 'kiss' **4** (RS 2.[004]) i:39′; **5** (RS 2.002):49, 51, 55, 56

NŠQ ← *NŚQ verb (D-stem) 'destroy by burning' **1** (RS 3.367) i:4′

NŠR common noun '(bird of prey, type of hawk or eagle)' /našru/ **1** (RS 3.367) i:13′–14′, 15′, 21′, 24′

ND̠BN personal name, vocalization and etymology unknown **44** (RS 19.016):16

NNʾU common noun 'ammi' (type of plant) /nīniʾu/ **19** (RS 17.120):15, 26

NNʾU place-name /nanuʾu/ **41** (RS 19.015):24

NS verb 'flee, depart in haste' **27** (RS 18.040):15

NSY verb 'banish' **6** (RS 24.244):66

Gt-stem **1** (RS 3.367) i:4′

NSK verb ‘pour out’ **2** (RS 2.[014]$^{+}$) iii:16′

NSK common noun, profession name, substantivized participle ‘founder, metalworker’ /nāsiku/# (substantivized participle) **43** (RS 18.024):3

NSK ḪD̠M common noun, profession name, ‘arrowhead maker’ /nāsiku ḫid̠d̠īma/ **44** (RS 19.016):25

NSK KSP common noun, profession name, ‘silversmith’ /nāsiku kaspi/ **44** (RS 19.016):32

NSʿ verb ‘pay’ **40** (RS [Varia 14]):10, 17

[NʿM verb ‘be/become good’] : D-stem ‘make good’ **19** (RS 17.120):1

NʿM adjective ‘good’ /naʿīmu/ **2** (RS 2.[014]$^{+}$) iii:31′; **5** (RS 2.002):1, 23, 58, 60, 67; **30** (RS 92.2010):19

NʿMN adjective ‘good’ /naʿmānu/ **3** (RS 2.[003]$^{+}$) i:40

NʿMN personal name /nuʿmānu/ (‘goodness [of a given deity]’) **46** (RS 94.2050^{+}):49

NʿMT common noun ‘goodness’ /nuʿmatu/ **5** (RS 2.002):27

NʿR verb ‘expel’ (D-stem) **6** (RS 24.244):65 ({ynʿrnˈh})

NʿR common noun ‘(food product—perhaps a type of flour)’ vocalization unknown **32** (RS 94.2479):15; **48** (RS 94.2600):6

[NP verb ‘wave, wield’]: ŠNPT common noun ‘presentation offering (presented in up-lifted hands)’ /šanūpatu/ **8** (RS 1.001):10; **11** (RS 24.266):13

NPY verb ‘expel, banish’ **20** (RS 24.247^{+}):19

NPY common noun: see YPY

NPK: see NBK

NPŠ common noun ‘throat, neck (whence) life (whence) human being’ /napšu/ **4** (RS 2.[004]) i:36′; **9** (RS 1.002):22′, 31′, 39′; **11** (RS 24.266):14, 15; **17** (RIH 78/20):16; **26** (RS 18.031):20; **34** (RS 94.2284):12bis, 32b

NPL verb ‘fall’ **1** (RS 3.367) i:5′

Gt-stem **3** (RS 2.[003]$^{+}$) i:21

NPṢ common noun ‘outfit, uniform, garment’ /nipṣu/ **4** (RS 2.[004]) i:33′

NṢB verb ‘erect’ **4** (RS 2.[004]) i:26′, [44′]

NṢP common noun ‘half-shekel (weight)’ /naṣpu/ **43** (RS 18.024):13, 27; **52** (RIH 83/22):2, 9

[NṢṢ verb ‘fly’]: Š-stem ‘cause to fly/flee’ **2** (RS 2.[014]$^{+}$) iv:1

NQH verb ‘recover from illness’ **17** (RIH 78/20):5

NQMD personal name, king of Ugarit /niqmaddu/ ← /*niqmîhaddu/ (‘[the god] Haddu is my retribution’) or /*niqmihaddu/ (‘[this child represents] retribution of [= from] [the god] Haddu’) **9** (RS 1.002):28′; **13** (RS 34.126):12, 13, 26; **36** (RS 11.772^{+}):10′, 14′, 17′, 18′, 24′

NQMPʿ personal name, king of Ugarit /niqmêpaʿ/ ← /*niqmîyapaʿa/ (‘my retribution has arisen’) **37** (RS 16.382):3; **38** (RS 94.2168):3

[NQP verb ‘go around’]: NQPT common noun ‘circuit, circle’ /niqpatu/ **5** (RS 2.002):67

NR verb ‘burn (said of flames), shine’ **23** (RS 11.872):18; **24** (RS 15.008):9

L-stem ‘make fire, make light’ **11** (RS 24.266):9

NYR common noun ‘light producing’ /nayyāru/ **13** (RS 34.126):19

NR common noun ‘fire’ /nīru/ **32** (RS 94.2479):17

NRN personal name /nūrānu/ **16** (RS 25.318):2

[NṮK verb ‘bite’]: NṮK common noun ‘(snake-)bite’ /niṯku/ **6** (RS 24.244):4, 9, 15, 20, 26, 31, ⟨34b⟩, 36, 41, 46, 52, 58, 79

NǴṢ (← NǴḎ) verb ‘shake’ **2** (RS 2.[014]$^{+}$) iii:34′

N-stem ‘tremble, go slack’ **1** (RS 3.367) i:17′, 26′

NǴR ← *NẒR verb ‘guard’ **22** (RS 8.315):8; **23** (RS 11.872):8; **24** (RS 15.008):5; **25** (RS 16.379):7; **26** (RS 18.031):5; **28** (RS 29.093):7; **29** (RS 34.124):6; **30** (RS 92.2010):5; **35** (RS [Varia 4]):4

NǴR common noun, profession name, substantivized participle, ‘guard’ /nāǵiru/# **5** (RS 2.002):68, 69bis, 70, 73; **44** (RS 19.016):12

[NTB]: NTBT common noun ‘path’ /natībatu/ **11** (RS 24.266):33′

[NTK verb ‘pour (out)’]: N-stem ‘pour forth (intransitive)’ **3** (RS 2.[003]$^{+}$) i:28

MTK common noun ‘libation’ /mattaku/ ← /*mantaku/ **11** (RS 24.266):25′

NTP personal name /natappu/ **46** (RS 94.2050^{+}):54

Ẓ’U: see YṢ’

[ẒHR]: ẒR common noun ‘back(bone), top’ /ẓûru/ ← /*ẓuhru/ **2** (RS 2.[014]$^{+}$) iii:35′; **17** (RIH 78/20):4

ẒẒ-W-KMṮ divine name, binomial /ẓiẓẓu wa kamāṯu/ **6** (RS 24.244):36

[ẒLL]: ẒL ‘shadow, shade (whence) shade (of an ancestor)’ /ẓillu/ **13** (RS 34.126):1; **17** (RIH 78/20):8

[ẒMY]: ẒM common noun ‘the state of being brown, faded, hard (of bread)’ /ẓumû/ **17** (RIH 78/20):7

ẒR: see ẒHR

ẒRW common noun ‘gum’ /ẓurwu/ **12** (RS 24.643):22

SBBYN common noun ‘black cumin’ /sibibiyyānu/; pl. SBBYM ‘grains of black cumin’ /sibibiyyūma/ **48** (RS 94.2600):11

SBD personal name, vocalization and etymology unknown **44** (RS 19.016):16

SBL personal name /sibilu/ **46** (RS 94.2050^{+}):36

SBRDN common noun ‘bronzeworker’ /sabardennu/ **43** (RS 18.024):1

SGLD personal name /sigilda/ **40** (RS [Varia 14]):21

SGR verb ‘close’ **6** (RS 24.244):70

SGRYN personal name /sugriyānu/ **46** (RS 94.2050^{+}):48

SḪR personal name /saḫuru/ **44** (RS 19.016):7
SDN-W-RDN divine name (ancestor of the kings of Ugarit), vocalization and etymology unknown **13** (RS 34.126):6, 23
S̀ZN personal name /s̀uzīnu/ **50** (RIH 84/06):[4]; **51** (RIH 84/33):3
SYR mountain name /sēyēra/ **27** (RS 18.040):14
SK common noun '(type of cloth)' /sakku/ **12** (RS 24.643):19
SK common noun 'thicket, lair' /sukku/ **17** (RIH 78/20):4
SKN common noun 'stela' /sikkannu/ **4** (RS 2.[004]) i:26′, [44′]; **14** (RS 6.021):1
SKN common noun 'governor, prefect' /sākinu/# **32** (RS 94.2479):2; **36** (RS 11.772+):38′; **44** (RS 19.016):10, 11
[SNY verb 'be/become great, high']: D-stem 'increase, augment'? **25** (RS 16.379):15
SNǴR place-name /sunnaǵara/ **31** (RS 94.2406):9
S̀S̀W common noun 'horse' /s̀ūs̀awu/ **19** (RS 17.120):1, 2, 5, 7, 9, 12, 15, 18, 20, 23, ⟨30⟩
S̀ST common noun 'mare' /s̀ūsatu/ **42** (RS 15.062):6
SSN common noun 'fruit stalk of a date palm' /sissinnu/ **6** (RS 24.244):66
SP common noun '(container and liquid measure)' /sappu/ **34** (RS 94.2284):6
SPʾ verb 'serve food' **4** (RS 2.[004]) i:31′
N-stem 'eat' **20** (RS 24.247+):51′
SPR verb 'count' **5** (RS 2.002):57
MSPR common noun 'account, recitation' /masparu/ **9** (RS 1.002):35′
SPR common noun 'account (whence) written document' /sipru/ **13** (RS 34.126):1; **19** (RS 17.120):1; **21** (RS 4.475):19; **31** (RS 94.2406):4; **35** (RS [Varia 4]):7; **43** (RS 18.024):1; **44** (RS 19.016):1; **49** (RIH 84/04):1
SPRN common noun 'document' /siprānu/ **51** (RIH 84/33):1

[ʿB verb 'be/become broad'] : YʿBDR: divine name, feminine, daughter of *Baʿlu*, 'the circle/generation is broad', /yaʿību + dāru/ **2** (RS 2.[014]+) iii:8′
ʿBD common noun 'servant' /ʿabdu/# **4** (RS 2.[004]) i:34′; **22** (RS 8.315):4, 18; **27** (RS 18.040):4, 9; **28** (RS 29.093):5, 20, 24, 26, 29; **30** (RS 92.2010):4, 10, 20, 22; **32** (RS 94.2479):2, 10
ʿBD personal name /ʿabdu/ ('servant [of god-X]') **44** (RS 19.016):5, 24
ʿBDʾADT personal name /ʿabdiʾadattu/ ('servant of [the goddess who bears the title of] Lady') **44** (RS 19.016):12
ʿBDʾILT personal name /ʿabdiʾilatu/ ('servant of the goddess') **44** (RS 19.016):25
ʿBDḪMN personal name /ʿabdiḫamanu/ ('servant of [the god] *Ḫamanu*') **46** (RS 94.2050+):42 ({ʿbd . ḫmn})

ˤBDYRḪ personal name /ˤabdiyariḫu/ ('servant of [the god] *Yariḫu*') **44** (RS 19.016):18

ˤBDMLK personal name /ˤabdimilku/ ('servant of [the god] *Milku*') **38** (RS 94.2168):6, 11, 13, 16, 19; **46** (RS 94.2050^{+}):17 ({ˤbd . mlk})

ˤBDN personal name /ˤabdīnu/ ('servant') **40** (RS [Varia 14]):20

ˤBDˤNT personal name /ˤabdiˤanatu/ ('servant of [the goddess] *ˤAnatu*') **44** (RS 19.016):7

ˤBDRPˀU personal name /ˤabdirapaˀu/ ('servant of [the divine] ancestor') **44** (RS 19.016):33

ˤBK common noun '(plant name)' (precise meaning and vocalization unknown) **19** (RS 17.120):26

ˤBṢ verb 'hurry' **2** (RS 2.[014]$^{+}$) iii:18′

ˤGL common noun 'calf' /ˤiglu/ **2** (RS 2.[014]$^{+}$) iii:44′

ˤD common noun 'throne room (of king or god)' /ˤādu/ **5** (RS 2.002):12; **11** (RS 24.266):9

ˤD common noun: see ˤDY

ˤD preposition and conjunction: see ˤDY

ˤDB verb 'prepare, arrange, place' **5** (RS 2.002):63; **6** (RS 24.244):7, 12 ({y⟨ˤ⟩db}), 18, 23, 29, 34, ⟨34e⟩, 39, 44, 49, 55, 71; **7** (RS 24.258):4, 7, 10, 12, 13; **31** (RS 94.2406):27

ˤDB common noun 'gift, offering (← something prepared, arranged, placed [before the recipient])' /ˤadūbu/ **5** (RS 2.002):54, 65

ˤDY (← *ˤDW$^{?}$) verb 'pass (by, on)' **6** (RS 24.244):66

ˤD common noun 'duration, time' /ˤadû/ ← /*ˤadyu/ **5** (RS 2.002):67

ˤD preposition and conjunction 'near, unto, to, until' /ˤadê/ ← /*ˤaday/ **7** (RS 24.258):3, 4, 16bis; **31** (RS 94.2406):22; **37** (RS 16.382):14, 19; **39** (RS 94.2965):14

[ˤDY verb 'ornament oneself']: ˤDY personal name /ˤadāyu/ ('ornament') **44** (RS 19.016):26

ˤDN personal name /ˤadânu/ ('ornament') **44** (RS 19.016):3, 20, 27

ˤDMLK personal name /ˤadîmilku/ ('[the god] *Milku* is my ornament' or '[this child is] the ornament of [the god] *Milku*') **44** (RS 19.016):15

ˤDRŠP personal name /ˤadîrašap/ ('[the god] *Rašap* is my ornament' or '[this child is] the ornament of [the god] *Rašap*') **44** (RS 19.016):13

ˤDM common noun 'misery' /ˤudmatu/ **13** (RS 34.126):17^{tris}

ˤDN : see ˤDY

ˤDT common noun 'heart of a reed' /ˤadattu/ **6** (RS 24.244):66

ˤDT common noun '(type of garment or cloth)' (precise meaning and vocalization unknown) **44** (RS 19.016):35

ˤDT common noun 'assembly' : see YˤD

[ˤZZ verb 'be/become strong']: D-stem 'strengthen' **20** (RS 24.247^{+}):20

L-stem: 'be very strong' **20** (RS 24.247^{+}):57′

ˤZ adjective ‘strong’ /ˤazzu/ **1** (RS 3.367) i:17′; **11** (RS 24.266):26′, 28′, 35′; **21** (RS 4.475):13

ˤZ common noun ‘strength, force’ /ˤuzzu/ **20** (RS 24.247^{+}):17

ˤZN personal name /ˤuzzīnu/ **15** (RS 6.028):2; **44** (RS 19.016):7, 22, 28, 31

ˤYN personal name /ˤayānu/ **28** (RS 29.093):11, 17

ˤKD meaning unknown, place-name? **34** (RS 94.2284):25

ˤKY place-name ‘Acco’ /ˤakkāyu/ **26** (RS 18.031):25

ˤŠY verb ‘do (harm to someone)’ **4** (RS 2.[004]) i:29′, 47′

ˤŠR verb ‘put on a sacrificial feast’ **11** (RS 24.266):32′–33′

ˤŠRT common noun ‘sacrificial feast’ /ˤašratu/ **11** (RS 24.266):32′

*ˤŠR (← ˤŚR) cardinal number ‘ten’ /ˤašru/; dual ‘twenty’ /ˤašrāma/ **5** (RS 2.002):57; **11** (RS 24.266):5, 11; **32** (RS 94.2479):11; **36** (RS 11.772^{+}):20′; **41** (RS 19.015):21, 23, 29; **42** (RS 15.062):5, 7, 8, 9bis, 11; **43** (RS 18.024):7, 10, 11, 15, 19, 21; **44** (RS 19.016):49; **47** (RS 94.2392^{+}):14; **48** (RS 94.2600):3; **49** (RIH 84/04):22, 24; **50** (RIH 84/06):[3], 5 ({[ˤšr]⌜m⌝}), [7]; **51** (RIH 84/33):3, 4, 6, 8; **52** (RIH 83/22):5

ˤŠRH extended form, used in numbers from eleven to nineteen /ˤašrihu/ **8** (RS 1.001):10; **36** (RS 11.772^{+}):[19′]; **44** (RS 19.016):50

ˤŠRT common noun ‘group of ten (administrative unit)’ /ˤašartu/ **44** (RS 19.016):2, 5, 7, 8; **46** (RS 94.2050^{+}):62

ˤŠTY cardinal number ‘one’ /ˤaštayu/ **13** (RS 34.126):27

ˤŠT ditto /ˤaštê/ **44** (RS 19.016):50

ˤLG verb ‘stutter’ **17** (RIH 78/20):11

ˤLY verb ‘ascend, go/come up’ **4** (RS 2.[004]) i:[4′], 14′, 38′; **11** (RS 24.266):33′; **18** (RS 92.2014):4, 6bis; **25** (RS 16.379):17, 19

Š-stem ‘present (a gift or offering)’ **14** (RS 6.021):1; **15** (RS 6.028):1; **16** (RS 25.318):2

Št-stem ‘present (a gift) for the purpose of acquiring a benefit for oneself’ **5** (RS 2.002):31bis, 35, 36

ˤL preposition ‘on, above, to the debit of’ /ˤalê/ ← /*ˤalay/ **5** (RS 2.002):12, 14, 15; **18** (RS 92.2014):3, 6; **20** (RS 24.247^{+}):57′; **49** (RIH 84/04):4, 7, 10, 13, 16, 18, 20, 23, 25; **51** (RIH 84/33):2, 3, 4, 6, 9, 10, 12, 13, 15, 17, 19, 21; **52** (RIH 83/22):11

ˤLY common noun ‘height’ /ˤalliyu/ **5** (RS 2.002):3

ˤLM adverb ‘on the next day’ /ˤalâma/ **31** (RS 94.2406):7

ˤLN adverb ‘on high, above’ /ˤalâna/ ← /*ˤalayāna/ **2** (RS 2.[014]$^{+}$) iii:34′; **13** (RS 34.126):19

ˤLLMN: see T̠R ˤLLMN

ˤLM common noun ‘undefined period of time’ /ˤālamu/ **1** (RS 3.367) i:10′; **5** (RS 2.002):42, 46, 49; **37** (RS 16.382):14, 20; **39** (RS 94.2965):14

ˤLMYN personal name /ˤālamiyyāna/ **46** (RS 94.2050^{+}):58

ʿLM adverb: see ʿLY
ʿLN adverb: see ʿLY
ʿM preposition 'with, toward, to the credit of' /ʿimma/ **2** (RS 2.[014]⁺) iii:19′bis, 24′; **5** (RS 2.002):69; **6** (RS 24.244):2, 9, 14, 19 ({ʿm!}), 25, 30, ‹34a›, 35, 40, 45, 51, 58, 78; **21** (RS 4.475):11, 19; **22** (RS 8.315):15; **23** (RS 11.872):11; **24** (RS 15.008):17, 19; **25** (RS 16.379):9, 18; **26** (RS 18.031):8; **27** (RS 18.040):12; **28** (RS 29.093):12, 27; **29** (RS 34.124):8, 16, 26; **30** (RS 92.2010):10, 20; **31** (RS 94.2406):5, 29, 34; **32** (RS 94.2479):8, 10; **33** (RS 96.2039):11 ({ʿmm}), 20, 21; **34** (RS 94.2284):34; **35** (RS [Varia 4]):8; **36** (RS 11.772⁺):2′ ({ʿm[. . .]}); **50** (RIH 84/06):1, 3, 5, 7
ʿMN extended form /ʿimmānu/ **2** (RS 2.[014]⁺) iii:25′; **22** (RS 8.315):10; **23** (RS 11.872):9, 15; **24** (RS 15.008):14; **25** (RS 16.379):8, 12; **26** (RS 18.031):6; **28** (RS 29.093):21; **29** (RS 34.124):7; **36** (RS 11.772⁺):7′, 11′; **40** (RS [Varia 14]):16
ʿMD common noun 'pillar, column' /ʿammūdu/ **17** (RIH 78/20):3
ʿMY personal name: see ʿMM
[ʿMM]: ʿM common noun '(paternal uncle →) clan, people' /ʿammu/ **4** (RS 2.[004]) i:27′, [45′]
ʿMY personal name /ʿammiya/ **51** (RIH 84/33):9
ʿMS verb 'bear (on the shoulder), bear up, support' **4** (RS 2.[004]) i:30′; **7** (RS 24.258):18
ʿMRPʾI personal name, king of Ugarit /ʿammurāpiʾ/ ('the [divine] uncle is a healer') **13** (RS 34.126):31
ʿMṮTMR personal name, king of Ugarit /ʿammiṯtamru/ ← /ʿammīyiḏtamiru/ ('the [divine] uncle has protected') **13** (RS 34.126):11, 25; **37** (RS 16.382):2; **38** (RS 94.2168):2
[ʿḎR verb 'help']: YʿḎRN personal name /yaʿḏirānu/ **49** (RIH 84/04):20
TʿḎR common noun 'help' /taʿḏiru/: see ʾIL TʿḎR BʿL
ʿN common noun 'eye, spring' /ʿênu/ ← /*ʿaynu/ **1** (RS 3.367) i:22′, 25′, 40′; **6** (RS 24.244):1; **11** (RS 24.266):27′; **20** (RS 24.247⁺):49bis, 57′
ʿN denominal verb 'see, look at' **3** (RS 2.[003]⁺) i:21, 22
ʿNQPʾAT place-name /ʿênuqapʾat/ **45** (RS 86.2213):11
ʿNY verb 'answer, respond, speak up' **1** (RS 3.367) i:7′, 34′, 35′; **2** (RS 2.[014]⁺) iv:5; **5** (RS 2.002):12, 73
MʿN common noun 'reply' /maʿnû/ **2** (RS 2.[014]⁺) iv:5; **21** (RS 4.475):15
TʿN common noun 'reply' /taʿnû/ **34** (RS 94.2284):23
ʿNT divine name, feminine /ʿanatu/# **2** (RS 2.[014]⁺) iii:9′, 11′, 32′; **7** (RS 24.258):9, 11, 22, 26′; **8** (RS 1.001):7; **12** (RS 24.643):7
ʿNT ḪBLY divine name, feminine /ʿanatu ḫablay/ ('*ʿAnatu* [who has been] mutilated') **8** (RS 1.001):17
ʿNT-W-ʿṮTRT divine name, feminine, binomial /ʿanatu wa ʿaṯtartu/ **6** (RS 24.244):20

[ʿẒM verb 'be/become powerful']: ʿẒMNY common noun ← adjective 'the powerful one' /ʿaẓūmāniyyu/ **1** (RS 3.367) i:5′

ʿPS/ʿPŠ common noun 'boundary stone' /ʿupsu/ **39** (RS 94.2965):3, 6, 9, 12

ʿPR common noun 'dust' /ʿaparu/ **1** (RS 3.367) i:5′; **2** (RS 2.[014]$^{+}$) iii:15′; **4** (RS 2.[004]) i:28′, [46′]; **13** (RS 34.126):22

ʿPṮRM personal name, vocalization and etymology unknown **44** (RS 19.016):10

ʿṢ common noun 'wood, tree, tree trunk' /ʿiṣu/# **2** (RS 2.[014]$^{+}$) iii:23′; **5** (RS 2.002):66; **6** (RS 24.244):64, 65; **18** (RS 92.2014):3; **20** (RS 24.247^{+}):2

ʿṢY (or ʿṢṢ) verb 'to hurry, press on' **2** (RS 2.[014]$^{+}$) iii:18′

ʿṢR common noun 'bird' /ʿuṣṣūru/# **2** (RS 2.[014]$^{+}$) iv:1; **5** (RS 2.002):38, 41, 44, 47, 62; **8** (RS 1.001):21; **11** (RS 24.266):20′, 20′–21′; **12** (RS 24.643):9; **13** (RS 34.126):30; **20** (RS 24.247^{+}):41′

[ʿQL verb 'be/become crooked, twisted']: ʿQLTN adjective 'twisting, twisted' /ʿaqallatānu/ **2** (RS 2.[014]$^{+}$) iii:41′

ʿQŠR adjective 'scaly (lit., that has sloughed its skin)' /ʿaqšaru/ **6** (RS 24.244):5, 6, 10, 12, 16, 18, 21, 23, 27, 29, 32, 33–34 ({ʿqš⟨r⟩}), ⟨34c⟩, ⟨34e⟩, 37, 39 ({ʿq⟨⟨.⟩⟩šr}), 42, 44, 47, 49, 53, 55, 59

ʿQRB common noun 'scorpion' /ʿaqrabu/ **18** (RS 92.2014):5, 7

ʿQRBN common noun '(plant name)' /ʾuqrubānu/ **19** (RS 17.120):2, [26$^{!}$]

ʿR verb 'awake' **7** (RS 24.258):28′

ʿR common noun 'town, city' /ʿīru/ **6** (RS 24.244):62

ʿR common noun 'donkey' /ʿêru/ ← /*ʿayru/ **9** (RS 1.002):26′, 34′, 43′; **11** (RS 24.266):16

ʿRB verb 'enter (whence) set (said of the sun), (also whence) stand as surety for, guarantee (+ B)' **2** (RS 2.[014]$^{+}$) iii:9′; **3** (RS 2.[003]$^{+}$) i:26; **5** (RS 2.002):7, 12, 18, 26, 62, 71, 74; **11** (RS 24.266):4, 23′; **12** (RS 24.643):18; **24** (RS 15.008):7; **31** (RS 94.2406):24, 28bis; **41** (RS 19.015):10, 11; **43** (RS 18.024):16

MʿRBY place-name /maʿrabāyu/ **45** (RS 86.2213):5

ʿRGZ common noun 'walnut (tree, wood, nut)' /ʿirguzu/ **19** (RS 17.120):5, 10; **42** (RS 15.062):22

ʿRY adjective 'naked, stripped' /ʿarīyu/ **26** (RS 18.031):25

ʿRŠ common noun 'bed' /ʿaršu/ **4** (RS 2.[004]) i:38′

ʿRM adjective 'naked' /ʿarumu/ **17** (RIH 78/20):13

ʿRMLḤT common noun, formation and meaning unknown **34** (RS 94.2284):6

ʿRMT place-name, vocalization unknown **9** (RS 1.002):27′

ʿRʿR common noun 'tamarisk' /ʿarʿaru/ **6** (RS 24.244):64, 65

[ʿRP]: ʿRPT common noun 'cloud' /ʿurpatu/ **1** (RS 3.367) i:8′, 29′; **2** (RS 2.[014]$^{+}$) iii:38′, iv:4, 6

ʿṮRB common noun '(plant name)' (precise identification and vocalization unknown) **19** (RS 17.120):24

ʿṮR divine name, masculine, designating the evening star /ʿaṯtaru/# **12** (RS 24.643):5 ({[ʿṯt]⌜r⌝}), 30
ʿṮRT divine name, feminine, designating the morning star /ʿaṯtartu/ **1** (RS 3.367) i:28′; **6** (RS 24.244):⟨34b⟩, 77, 78; **7** (RS 24.258):9, 10, 23, 26′ ({[ʿṯ]⌜t⌝rt}) (cf. ʿNT-W-ʿṮRT); **12** (RS 24.643):7, 38 ({[ʿṯ]⌜tr⌝[t]})
ʿṮRT ŠD divine name, feminine, '*ʿAṯtartu* of the field' /ʿaṯtartu šadî/ **12** (RS 24.643):18; **41** (RS 19.015):10
ʿṮRT place-name (town to the northeast of the Sea of Galilee) /ʿaṯtartu/ **6** (RS 24.244):41
[ʿTK verb 'tie (up)'] : ʿTK divine name in the form of a G-participle /ʿātiku/ **2** (RS 2.[014]+) iii:44′
ʿTN verb 'guard, protect' **24** (RS 15.008):13

P common noun 'mouth (whence) declaration' /pû/ (/*pVyu/) **1** (RS 3.367) i:6′; **5** (RS 2.002):62, 64; **9** (RS 1.002):3′ et passim in this text; **18** (RS 92.2014):11; **20** (RS 24.247+):51′; **31** (RS 94.2406):21, 39
P conjunction 'and' /pa/ **4** (RS 2.[004]) i:5′, 15′; **28** (RS 29.093):5, 27; **29** (RS 34.124):11, 22, 42′; **31** (RS 94.2406):14; **35** (RS [Varia 4]):12
ʾAP adverb 'also, moreover' /ʾapa/ **1** (RS 3.367) i:2′; **22** (RS 8.315):13; **25** (RS 16.379):22; **31** (RS 94.2406):38
ʾAPHM extended form 'then, next' /ʾapahama/ **17** (RIH 78/20):8
ʾAPN extended form 'then, next' /ʾapana/ **4** (RS 2.[004]) i:1′
ʾAPNK extended form /ʾapanaka/ **4** (RS 2.[004]) i:[0′]
PN conjunction 'lest, that . . . not' /pana/ **7** (RS 24.258):12
P adverb 'here' /pā/ **21** (RS 4.475):12
[Pʾ]: PʾIT common noun 'edge, border, temple (body part)' /piʾtu/# **5** (RS 2.002):68; **20** (RS 24.247+):11, 54′
PʾM: PʾAMT common noun 'time (number of repetitions)' /paʾmatu/ **5** (RS 2.002):20; **8** (RS 1.001):20
PBN personal name /pabnu/ **44** (RS 19.016):16
[PGR common noun 'cadaver']: PGR common noun 'mortuary offering/feast' /pagrû/ ← /*pagraʾu/ **14** (RS 6.021):2; **15** (RS 6.028):1
PḪR common noun 'union, assembly' /puḫru/ **5** (RS 2.002):57
PḪR ʾILM compound divine name 'the Assembly of the gods' /puḫru ʾilīma/ **12** (RS 24.643):9
PḪR BʿL: see DR ʾIL W PḪR BʿL
PḪYR common noun 'totality' /puḫayyiru/ [vocalization uncertain] **3** (RS 2.[003]+) i:25
MPḪRT common noun 'assembly' /mapḫartu/ **9** (RS 1.002):17′ ({[mpḫ]⌜r⌝t}), 25′, ⟨34⟩′, 42′

[PDR common noun 'fat']: PDRY divine name, feminine, daughter of *Baʿlu*, 'Fatty' /pidray/ **2** (RS 2.[014]$^+$) iii:6′; **8** (RS 1.001):15; **12** (RS 24.643):6; **41** (RS 19.015):7

PHY verb 'see, perceive, contemplate' **2** (RS 2.[014]$^+$) iii:32′; **36** (RS 11.772$^+$):15′

PḤL common noun 'male (as reproductive agent) → stallion' /paḥlu/ **6** (RS 24.244):1

PḤLT 'female' (feminine of preceding) **6** (RS 24.244):1

PḤM common noun 'glowing coal, wool dyed to a reddish hue' /paḥmu/ **5** (RS 2.002):39, 41, 45, 48; **36** (RS 11.772$^+$):22′, 27′, 29′, 31′, 33′, 35′ ({[pḥ]⌜m⌝}), [37′], 39′

[PŠL verb 'oppress']: D-stem 'oppress, abase' **20** (RS 24.247$^+$):45′$^!$

PLG verb 'divide, split' **6** (RS 24.244):69

PLG common noun 'canal, stream (of water)' /palgu/ **6** (RS 24.244):69

PLD common noun '(type of garment)' /palidu/# **12** (RS 24.643):21 (p⌜l⌝[d])

PLWN personal name, vocalization and etymology unknown **46** (RS 94.2050$^+$):28

PLSY personal name /pilsiya/ **21** (RS 4.475):2

PNḤṮ personal name, Egyptian origin /pinḥaṯu/ **28** (RS 29.093):3

[PNY verb 'turn']: PNM common noun (plural only) 'face' /panûma/ **2** (RS 2.[014]$^+$) iii:34′; **6** (RS 24.244):61, 63; **13** (RS 34.126):15; **16** (RS 25.318):2; **17** (RIH 78/20):2; **20** (RS 24.247$^+$):33′^{bis}; **23** (RS 11.872):17; **24** (RS 15.008):8, 9; **29** (RS 34.124):19; **31** (RS 94.2406):36; **38** (RS 94.2168):2

[PNN]: PNT common noun 'joint' /pinnatu/ **1** (RS 3.367) i:17′, 26′; **2** (RS 2.[014]$^+$) iii:34′

PẒL verb 'save': N-stem 'be saved' **17** (RIH 78/20):15

PʿN common noun 'foot' /paʿnu/ **2** (RS 2.[014]$^+$) iii:9′, 19′, 32′; **13** (RS 34.126):14; **20** (RS 24.247$^+$):39′, 52′; **22** (RS 8.315):5; **23** (RS 11.872):5; **25** (RS 16.379):4; **27** (RS 18.040):5; **28** (RS 29.093):8; **29** (RS 34.124):4; **30** (RS 92.2010):6; **32** (RS 94.2479):3

PʿR verb 'proclaim' **1** (RS 3.367) i:11′, 18′

PQ verb 'acquire, possess' **3** (RS 2.[003]$^+$) i:12; **20** (RS 24.247$^+$):13, 29′

PQQ common noun '(plant name)' (identification and vocalization unknown) **7** (RS 24.258):30′

PRD common noun 'mule' /pirdu/ **43** (RS 18.024):12

PRY: PR common noun 'fruit (whence) seeds (of certain plants)' /pirû/ (← /*piryu/) **19** (RS 17.120):14, 24, 26, 27

PRS/Ś common noun ('dry measure [half of the *dūdu*-measure])' /parīsu/ **48** (RS 94.2600):5

PRSḤ verb 'lose equilibrium' (N-stem) **1** (RS 3.367) i:22′, 25′

PRṢ common noun 'breach, opening' /parṣu/ **5** (RS 2.002):70

PRŠ (← *PRŚ) verb 'disperse, scatter' **20** (RS 24.247$^+$):53′

PRQ: PRQT common noun '(container/measure)' (identification and vocalization unknown) **48** (RS 94.2600):9
PǴḎN personal name /puǵiḏenni/ **44** (RS 19.016):3
PTḤ verb 'open' **5** (RS 2.002):70bis; **6** (RS 24.244):71, 72; **39** (RS 94.2965):2
PTY verb 'charm, convince, seduce' (D-stem) **5** (RS 2.002):39

Ṣ'IN common noun 'caprovids' /ṣaʾnu/ **20** (RS 24.247^{+}):1; **43** (RS 18.024):22; **48** (RS 94.2600):7
ṢBʾU common noun 'army' /ṣabaʾu/ **41** (RS 19.015):15
ṢBṬ personal name /ṣabṭānu/ ('the state of being held in the hand [of a god]') **46** (RS 94.2050^{+}):14
ṢBʿ: ʾUṢBʿ common noun 'finger' /ʾuṣbaʿu/ **1** (RS 3.367) i:14′, 16′, 21′, 24′
ṢD verb 'hunt' **5** (RS 2.002):16, 68; **7** (RS 24.258):23
ṢD common noun 'game' /ṣêdu/ **7** (RS 24.258):1
MṢD common noun 'prey' /maṣūdu/ **7** (RS 24.258):1
ṢDQ common noun 'justice, right, legitimacy' /ṣidqu/ **3** (RS 2.[003]$^{+}$) i:12
ṢḤ verb 'cry out' **2** (RS 2.[014]$^{+}$) iii:36′; **5** (RS 2.002):32, 33, 39, 43, 46, 69; **7** (RS 24.258):2; **13** (RS 34.126):19; **18** (RS 92.2014):1, 2
[ṢḤR verb 'be/become yellow, golden (in color)']: L-stem 'become golden brown (as a result of roasting)' **5** (RS 2.002):41, 45, 48
[ṢLY verb 'pray']: ṢLT common noun 'prayer' /ṣalîtu/ ← /*ṣaliytu/ **11** (RS 24.266):34′
ṢMD verb 'bind' **5** (RS 2.002):10bis
ṢMD common noun 'mace' /ṣimdu/ **1** (RS 3.367) i:11′, 15′, 18′, 23′
MṢMT common noun 'treaty' /maṣmattu/ ← /*maṣmadtu/ **36** (RS 11.772^{+}):17′
ṢML common noun 'dried figs' /ṣamlu/ **17** (RIH 78/20):7
ṢMLL common noun '(kind of aromatic plant)' /ṣumlalû/ **42** (RS 15.062):10 ({ṣml⌜l⌝})
ṢMQ common noun 'raisins' /ṣimmūqu/ **19** (RS 17.120):31
ṢMT verb 'destroy' (D-stem) **1** (RS 3.367) i:9′; **2** (RS 2.[014]$^{+}$) iii:44′
ṢNNR personal name /ṣānunūrî/ ('my light is [the god] ṢN' [cf. ʾABṢN]) **46** (RS 94.2050^{+}):5
ṢʿQ place-name /ṣaʿaqu/ **45** (RS 86.2213):10
ṢPN mountain name /ṣapunu/ **2** (RS 2.[014]$^{+}$) iii:29′, iv:1; **6** (RS 24.244):9; **12** (RS 24.643):1, [2], 10, 27; **41** (RS 19.015):3
ṢPN divine name derived from former **12** (RS 24.643):6, 29
ṢPR verb 'help, support, care for' (D-stem) **5** (RS 2.002):25
ṢPR personal name /ṣuparu/ **46** (RS 94.2050^{+}):37
ṢṢN personal name /ṣīṣānu/ **44** (RS 19.016):14
[ṢQ verb 'be/become narrow']: MṢQT common noun 'anguish, distress, difficult situation' /maṣūqatu/ **20** (RS 24.247^{+}):19; **29** (RS 34.124):21
ṢR place-name 'Tyre' /ṣurru/ **26** (RS 18.031):3, 12

ṢRD adjective '(pure, whence) of noble birth' /ṣardu/ **38** (RS 94.2168):9, 26

[ṢRR verb 'be/become hostile']: ṢRT '(state of being an) adversary' /ṣarratu/ **1** (RS 3.367) i:9′; **2** (RS 2.[014]$^{+}$) iii:37′, iv:4, 6

ṢĠD verb 'walk with long steps, take a walk' **5** (RS 2.002):30

ṢT common noun '(type of garment)' /ṣītu/ **4** (RS 2.[004]) i:[4′], 13′, 14′

QBʾ verb 'summon, invite' **13** (RS 34.126):3, 10

QBṢ common noun 'assembly' /qibūṣu/ **13** (RS 34.126):3, 10

QDQD common noun 'pate, head' /qudqudu/ **1** (RS 3.367) i:21′–22′, 24′

[QDŠ 'be/become holy']: Š-stem 'sanctify, give to a divinity' **11** (RS 24.266):30′, 31′

QDŠ common noun 'holiness, holy thing' /qudšu/ **2** (RS 2.[014]$^{+}$) iii:30′; **4** (RS 2.[004]) i:3′, 8′, [11′], 13′, 22′, 26′, 44′; **18** (RS 92.2014):3

QDŠ common noun 'holy place, sanctuary' /qidšu/ **10** (RS 24.260):7; **11** (RS 24.266):6, 33′; **17** (RIH 78/20):8

QDŠ place-name 'Qadesh (on the Orontes)' /qidšu/ **5** (RS 2.002):65

MQDŠ common noun 'sanctuary' /maqdašu/; pl. MQDŠT /maqdašātu/ **44** (RS 19.016):15

[QDM verb 'go before']: D-stem 'present (as an offering)' **13** (RS 34.126):30

QDM common noun 'east' /qidmu/ **6** (RS 24.244):62

QDMY adjective 'ancient' /qadmiyyu/ **13** (RS 34.126):8, 24

QṬ place-name /qaṭi/ **19** (RS 17.120):18

QṬY gentilic 'person from (the town of) Qaṭi' /qaṭiyyu/ **9** (RS 1.002): [19′], 28′ ({q[ṭy]}), 36′

QṬṬ verb 'commit turpitude' (L-stem) **9** (RS 1.002):23′, 31′, 40′

QṬT common noun 'turpitude' /quṭṭatu/ **9** (RS 1.002):[22′], 31′, 39′

[QṬN 'be/become small']: QṬN common noun 'small object' /qaṭunu/: see ḤRŠ QṬN

QṬN personal name /quṭanu/ **46** (RS 94.2050^{+}):21

QṬR common noun 'smoke, incense' /quṭru/ **4** (RS 2.[004]) i:27′, [46′]; **17** (RIH 78/20):3

QL verb 'fall' **1** (RS 3.367) i:23′, 25′; **2** (RS 2.[014]$^{+}$) iii:10′; **7** (RS 24.258):21; **20** (RS 24.247^{+}):1; **22** (RS 8.315):7; **23** (RS 11.872):6; **25** (RS 16.379):5; **27** (RS 18.040):8; **28** (RS 29.093):10; **29** (RS 34.124):[4]; **30** (RS 92.2010):9; **32** (RS 94.2479):3; **36** (RS 11.772^{+}):5′

Š-stem 'cause to fall' **5** (RS 2.002):10

Št-stem 'arrive' **6** (RS 24.244):68, 72; **7** (RS 24.258):17

QL common noun 'voice, message, messenger' /qālu/ **6** (RS 24.244):2, 8, 14, 19, 25, 30, 〈34a〉, 35, 40, 45, 51, 57; **17** (RIH 78/20):2; **43** (RS 18.024):12

QLḤ divine name (identification unknown) **10** (RS 24.260):5, 13

QLN personal name, vocalization and etymology unknown **44** (RS 19.016):34

QLQL common noun ‘cardamom’ /qulqullu/# **19** (RS 17.120):10

QMḪ common noun ‘flour’ /qamḫu/ **19** (RS 17.120):32

QMṢ verb ‘shrink up, assume the fetal position’ **3** (RS 2.[003]$^{+}$) i:35

[QNY]: QN common noun ‘reed’ /qanû/ ← /*qanVyu/ **42** (RS 15.062):12

QNY verb ‘acquire, make, possess’ **40** (RS [Varia 14]):2

QNN verb ‘stand erect’ (L-stem) **18** (RS 92.2014):5, 7bis

QNṢ verb ‘crouch’ (Gt-stem) **5** (RS 2.002):51, 58

QṢ: see QṢṢ

QṢR verb ‘be/become short’ **20** (RS 24.247^{+}):33′

QṢR adjective ‘short’ /qaṣiru/ **20** (RS 24.247^{+}):39′

QṢRT common noun ‘shortness’ /quṣratu/ + NPŠ ‘throat’ = ‘impatience’ **9** (RS 1.002):22′, 31′, [39′]

QṢRT common noun ‘lower part of the leg’ /qiṣratu/ **20** (RS 24.247^{+}):10

[QṢṢ verb ‘to cut’]: QṢ common noun ‘feast (← cutting [of meat])’ /quṣṣu/ **7** (RS 24.258):2

QRʾ verb ‘call, summon, invite’ **5** (RS 2.002):1, 23; **6** (RS 24.244):2, 8, 14, 19, 25, 30, ⟨34a⟩, 35, 40, 45, 51, 57; **13** (RS 34.126):2, 4, 5, 6, 7, 8, 9, 11, 12

QRB verb ‘be near, approach’ **3** (RS 2.[003]$^{+}$) i:37; **4** (RS 2.[004]) i:16′; **17** (RIH 78/20):5

Š-stem ‘bring near’ **9** (RS 1.002):26′

QRB common noun ‘middle, midst’ /qirbu/; B QRB ‘in the midst of, within, in’ **4** (RS 2.[004]) i:25′, 43′; **7** (RS 24.258):1

QRD common noun ‘warrior, hero’ /qarrādu/ **2** (RS 2.[014]$^{+}$) iii:14′; **11** (RS 24.266):26′, 29′, [35′]

QRZBL identification unknown **9** (RS 1.002):21′ ({q[rzbl]}), 30′, 38′

[QRY verb ‘meet’]: D-stem ‘present’ **2** (RS 2.[014]$^{+}$) iii:14′

QRT common noun ‘town, village’ /qarîtu/# ← /*qariytu/ **5** (RS 2.002):3; **11** (RS 24.266):10; **12** (RS 24.643):40; **29** (RS 34.124):19, 22; **44** (RS 19.016):10, 11

QRN common noun ‘horn’ /qarnu/ **7** (RS 24.258):20; **20** (RS 24.247^{+}):11; **29** (RS 34.124):30

QRT: see QRY

QṮṮ verb ‘drag (to/for oneself)’ **1** (RS 3.367) i:27′

R-stem same **7** (RS 24.258):5

[RʾIM common noun ‘wild bovid’]: RʾIMT common noun ‘lyre partially in the form of a bull’s head’ /riʾmatu/ **2** (RS 2.[014]$^{+}$) iii:4′

RʾIŠ common noun ‘head’ /raʾšu/ **1** (RS 3.367) i:38′; **2** (RS 2.[014]$^{+}$) iii:42′; **5** (RS 2.002):5, 31, 36; **7** (RS 24.258):30′; **17** (RIH 78/20):19; **20** (RS 24.247^{+}):43′; **29** (RS 34.124):31; **31** (RS 94.2406):30

[Rʾ IŠ place-name]: Rʾ IŠY gentilic ‘from (the town of) Raʾšu’ /raʾšiyyu/ **52** (RIH 83/22):3

Rʾ IŠYT common noun ‘first, best’ /raʾšiyyatu/ **11** (RS 24.266):25′

Rʾ Š denominal verb ‘have an illness of the head’ **19** (RS 17.120):18, 30

[RBB verb ‘be/become great (particularly: in number)’]: RB adjective ‘numerous, great’; as a substantive ‘chief, leader’ /rabbu/# **2** (RS 2.[014]⁺) iii:39′; **5** (RS 2.002):54; **6** (RS 24.244):63; **13** (RS 34.126):19; **17** (RIH 78/20):16; **26** (RS 18.031):16, 22; **36** (RS 11.772⁺):13′, 16′; **40** (RS [Varia 14]):12; **44** (RS 19.016):2, 5, 7, 8; **46** (RS 94.2050⁺):62

RB divine name, feminine, daughter of *Baʿlu*, ‘rain (as many drops)’ /rabbu/ **2** (RS 2.[014]⁺) iii:7′

[RBD verb ‘be calm’]: ʾARBDD common noun ‘calm’ /ʾarbadādu/ **2** (RS 2.[014]⁺) iii:17′

[RBʿ]: ʾARBʿ cardinal number ‘four’ /ʾarbaʿu/; pl. ‘forty’ /ʾarbaʿūma/ **12** (RS 24.643):19; **13** (RS 34.126):28; **34** (RS 94.2284):6; **36** (RS 11.772⁺):21′; **41** (RS 19.015):24, 31, [35]; **42** (RS 15.062):3, 4, 14, 15; **45** (RS 86.2213):12; **47** (RS 94.2392⁺):3, 8; **49** (RIH 84/04):9, 12, 17, 24; **51** (RIH 84/33):15, 17, 21; **52** (RIH 83/22):6, 8

RBʿ ordinal number ‘fourth’ /rabīʿu/ **4** (RS 2.[004]) i:8′; **11** (RS 24.266):20′; **31** (RS 94.2406):9

RBʿ verb ‘do four times’ (D-stem) **3** (RS 2.[003]⁺) i:17 (Dp-participle)

RGM verb ‘say’ **1** (RS 3.367) i:7′; **2** (RS 2.[014]⁺) iii:11′, 21′; **5** (RS 2.002):12; **21** (RS 4.475):3; **22** (RS 8.315):2; **23** (RS 11.872):2; **24** (RS 15.008):3; **25** (RS 16.379):2; **26** (RS 18.031):2; **27** (RS 18.040):2; **28** (RS 29.093):2; **29** (RS 34.124):[2]; **30** (RS 92.2010):2; **31** (RS 94.2406):2, 32; **32** (RS 94.2479):1; **33** (RS 96.2039):3; **34** (RS 94.2284):3; **35** (RS [Varia 4]):3, 9, 12; **40** (RS [Varia 14]):14

RGM common noun ‘word’ /rigmu/ **1** (RS 3.367) i:6′; **2** (RS 2.[014]⁺) iii:20′, 22′, 27′; **5** (RS 2.002):52, 59; **20** (RS 24.247⁺):6, [12], 18; **21** (RS 4.475):17; **22** (RS 8.315):17; **23** (RS 11.872):13, 16; **24** (RS 15.008):20; **25** (RS 16.379):11; **26** (RS 18.031):9; **29** (RS 34.124):9; **30** (RS 92.2010):18; **31** (RS 94.2406):35 ({rgt}); **32** (RS 94.2479):9; **34** (RS 94.2284):24; **35** (RS [Varia 4]):17; **44** (RS 19.016):10

[RDY]: MRDT common noun ‘(type of cloth)’ /mardêtu/# ← /*mardaytu/ **29** (RS 34.124):28

RDN: see SDN-W-RDN

[RZḤ]: MRZḤ ‘(societal group devoted to the drinking of wine)’ /marziḥu/# **7** (RS 24.258):15; **40** (RS [Varia 14]):1, 13

RḤM divine name ← common noun ‘womb’ /raḥmu/ **5** (RS 2.002):13

RḤMY ditto /raḥmay/ **5** (RS 2.002):16, 28

RḤQ verb ‘be/become far off’

D-stem ‘expel’ **17** (RIH 78/20):1 ({r[ḥq]})

MRḤQT common noun 'far-off place, distance' /marḥaqtu/ **22** (RS 8.315):6; **27** (RS 18.040):7; **28** (RS 29.093):10; **30** (RS 92.2010):8
RḤṢ verb 'wash' **4** (RS 2.[004]) i:33′
Gt-stem 'wash oneself' **11** (RS 24.266):5
D-stem 'clean, cleanse' **31** (RS 94.2406):20
RṬ common noun '(type of garment)' /rīṭu/ **43** (RS 18.024):12
RKB verb 'mount, be/get astride' (active participle as a title of *Baʿlu*) **1** (RS 3.367) i:8′, 29′; **2** (RS 2.[014]+) iii:38′, iv:4, 6
RKB common noun, meaning unknown **12** (RS 24.643):20
MRKBT common noun 'chariot' /markabtu/# **44** (RS 19.016):28
RŠŠ verb 'crush' **3** (RS 2.[003]+) i:10, 22
RŠʿ verb 'do evil' **17** (RIH 78/20):6
RŠʿ adjective 'evil' /rašaʿu/ **18** (RS 92.2014):10
RŠP divine name, head of the netherworld /rašap/ **3** (RS 2.[003]+) i:19; **6** (RS 24.244):31, 77; **8** (RS 1.001):4, 7, ‹16›; **12** (RS 24.643):8; **20** (RS 24.247+):40′; **41** (RS 19.015):11 (pl.)
RŠPʾAB personal name /rašapʾabû/ ('*Rašap* is the father [of this child]') **44** (RS 19.016):2
RŠP ʾIDRP manifestation of *Rašap*, identification unknown /rašap ʾidrippi/ **12** (RS 24.643):32
RŠP GN compound divine name '*Rašap* of [the place] Guni' /rašap guni/ **16** (RS 25.318):2
RŠPMLK personal name /rašapmalku/ ('*Rašap* is king') **49** (RIH 84/04):23
RŠP ṢBʾI divine name '*Rašap* of the army' /rašap ṣabaʾi/ **41** (RS 19.015):15
RM verb 'be/become high' **5** (RS 2.002):32
YRM personal name /yarimmu/ (← /yarim + ma + u [case-vowel]/ '[god-X] is up-lifted') **46** (RS 94.2050+):6; **49** (RIH 84/04):8; **51** (RIH 84/33):14
YRMN personal name /yarimānu/ (← /yarim + ān + u/ '[god-X] is up-lifted') **49** (RIH 84/04):4
MRMT common noun 'height' /marāmatu/ **17** (RIH 78/20):7
MRYM common noun 'height' /maryamu/ **2** (RS 2.[014]+) iv:1; **6** (RS 24.244):9
[RMY 'cast (foundations)']: YRMHD personal name /yarmihaddu/ **28** (RS 29.093):4; **33** (RS 96.2039):2
[RMṢ verb 'roast']: RMṢT common noun 'roast (offering)' /ramaṣatu/ **8** (RS 1.001):9
[RʿY verb 'lead flocks to pasture']: MRʿ common noun 'pasture-land' /marʿû/ **38** (RS 94.2168):15
RʿK: see BʿL RʿKT

[Rʿʿ verb 'be/become bad']: RʿT common noun/substantivized adjective 'evil' /raʿʿatu/ **17** (RIH 78/20):20

RPʾ verb 'heal' **7** (RS 24.258):28′

RPʾU common noun 'shade (ancestor) (← healthy one)' /rapaʾu/ **13** (RS 34.126):2, 4, 5, 8, 9, 24

RPʾU divine name (same form and meaning) **4** (RS 2.[004]) i:1′, 17′, 35′, 37′, 42′

RPS verb 'tread under' **20** (RS 24.247+):50′

RQD place-name /raqdu/ **41** (RS 19.015):33 ; **45** (RS 86.2213):15

RQDN personal name /raqdānu/ **50** (RIH 84/06):2; **51** (RIH 84/33):2

RQḤ common noun 'perfume' /ruqḥi/ **12** (RS 24.643):21

RQṢ verb 'dance' (Gt-stem) **1** (RS 3.367) i:13′, 15′, 20′, 23′

[RṮṮ]˙: RṮ common noun 'dirt' /raṯṯu/ **4** (RS 2.[004]) i:33′

RǴ verb 'turn (back)' **6** (RS 24.244):61 ({trǵn⟨⟨w⟩⟩})

[RǴB 'be/become hungry']: RǴB common noun 'famine' /raǵabu/ **20** (RS 24.247+):5, 19

RT personal name, vocalization and etymology unknown **46** (RS 94.2050+):19, 68

RTN common noun, meaning unknown **12** (RS 24.643):20

[Ṯʾ]: ṮʾAT common noun 'ewe/nanny' /ṯuʾatu/ **20** (RS 24.247+):1 (pl. /ṯuʾatātu/)

ṮʾIṬ common noun 'mud' /ṯaʾṭu/ **4** (RS 2.[004]) i:33′ ({[ṯỉ]ṭ})

ṮʾAR common noun 'blood relationship' /ṯaʾaru/ **3** (RS 2.[003]+) i:15

ṮB verb 'return, come/go back' **9** (RS 1.002):35′; **28** (RS 29.093):16; **33** (RS 96.2039):12; **48** (RS 94.2600):17

L-stem 'turn' **17** (RIH 78/20):19

Š-stem (ṮṮB ← *ŠṮB) 'cause to return' **7** (RS 24.258):27′; **22** (RS 8.315):17; **23** (RS 11.872):13; **24** (RS 15.008):19; **25** (RS 16.379):[11]; **26** (RS 18.031):9, 23; **29** (RS 34.124):9!; **30** (RS 92.2010):19; **32** (RS 94.2479):9; **34** (RS 94.2284):24; **35** (RS [Varia 4]):18

ṮBʿM personal name /ṯubʿammu/ ('return, O [divine] paternal uncle') **44** (RS 19.016):7

ṮBR verb 'break' **2** (RS 2.[014]+) iii:33′; **29** (RS 34.124):16

ṮBT: see YṮB

ṮDNY personal name /ṯidinaya/ **49** (RIH 84/04):16; **51** (RIH 84/33):20

[ṮDṮ]˙: ṮṮ cardinal number 'six' /ṯiṯṯu/ ← /*ṯidṯu/; pl. 'sixty' /ṯiṯṯūma/ (← /*ṯidṯūma/) **13** (RS 34.126):29; **41** (RS 19.015):34; **42** (RS 15.062):1, 5bis; **43** (RS 18.024):4; **44** (RS 19.016):49; **47** (RS 94.2392+):[1], 2 ({[ṯ]ṯ}); **48** (RS 94.2600):1; **49** (RIH 84/04):3, 15, 19; **51** (RIH 84/33):12, 19

ṮDṮ ordinal number ‘sixth’ /ṯadīṯu/ **4** (RS 2.[004]) i:11′

ṮDṮ verb ‘do six times’ (D-stem) **3** (RS 2.[003]$^{+}$) i:19 (Dp-participle)

ṮH common noun ‘disaster’ (etymology unknown) **31** (RS 94.2406):14

ṮWY verb ‘receive (as guest), feed, take care of; stay as guest, lodge’ **26** (RS 18.031):24

ṮT common noun ‘care’ /ṯâtu/ ← /*ṯawayatu/ **17** (RIH 78/20):17

ṮY common noun ‘tribute’ /ṯayyu/ **23** (RS 11.872):14; **25** (RS 16.379):13

ṮKL verb ‘be bereaved (lose a child)’ **6** (RS 24.244):61

ṮKL common noun ‘bereavement’ /ṯuklu/ **5** (RS 2.002):8

ṮKMN-W-ŠNM divine name, binomial (two sons of *ʾIlu*) /ṯukamuna wa šunama/ **7** (RS 24.258):18–19; **8** (RS 1.001):3, 6; **9** (RS 1.002):17′ ({[ṯkmn w šn]m}), 25′ ({[ṯkmn . w š]nm}), 34′, 43′ ({ṯkm⌜n⌝ [. w šnm]})

[ṮKP verb ‘overcome’]: N-stem ‘be overcome’ **21** (RS 4.475):14

ṮLGN personal name, either /ṯalgānu/ (‘[child born when it had] snow[ed]’ ← /ṯalgu/ ‘snow’) or /ṯelligani/ (Hurrian) **46** (RS 94.2050^{+}):15

ṮLḪN common noun ‘table’ /ṯulḫanu/; pl. ṮLḪNT /ṯulḫanātu/ **7** (RS 24.258):6, 8; **13** (RS 34.126):15

ṮLṮ cardinal number ‘three’ /ṯalāṯu/; pl. ‘thirty’ /ṯalāṯūma/ **8** (RS 1.001):20; **12** (RS 24.643):20bis; **13** (RS 34.126):28; **34** (RS 94.2284):5; **37** (RS 16.382):15; **41** (RS 19.015):22, 25, 33; **42** (RS 15.062):5, 7, 13bis; **43** (RS 18.024):5, 11, 18, 28; **45** (RS 86.2213):2; **47** (RS 94.2392^{+}):12; **48** (RS 94.2600):9; **49** (RIH 84/04):19; **52** (RIH 83/22):1

MṮLṮ fraction ‘third’ /maṯlaṯu/ **48** (RS 94.2600):2, 6

ṮLṮ ordinal number ‘third’ /ṯalīṯu/ **4** (RS 2.[004]) i:8′; **31** (RS 94.2406):8

ṮLṮ verb ‘do three times’ (D-stem) **3** (RS 2.[003]$^{+}$) i:16 (Dp-participle)

ṮLṮ common noun ‘copper, bronze’ /ṯalṯu/# **6** (RS 24.244):71; **43** (RS 18.024):3, 6

ṮM adverb ‘there’ /ṯamma/ **1** (RS 3.367) i:4′; **5** (RS 2.002):66

ṮMN extended form /ṯammāna/ **25** (RS 16.379):9

ṮMNY extended form /ṯammāniya/ ← /ṯam + m(a) + ān + i + ya/ **22** (RS 8.315):14; **23** (RS 11.872):11; **26** (RS 18.031):7; **27** (RS 18.040):15; **29** (RS 34.124):8; **32** (RS 94.2479):7

ṮMT extended form /ṯammati/ ← /ṯam + ma + ti/ **21** (RS 4.475):18; **28** (RS 29.093):21

ṮMNY: ṮMN cardinal number ‘eight’ /ṯamānû/ ← /*ṯimāniyu/; fem. ṮMNT /ṯamānatu/ ← /*ṯamāniyatu/; pl. ‘eighty’ /ṯamāniyūma/ **3** (RS 2.[003]$^{+}$) i:9; **5** (RS 2.002):19bis, 67; **11** (RS 24.266):11; **43** (RS 18.024):5, 14, 15, 20; **47** (RS 94.2392^{+}):14

ṮMRG common noun ‘(plant name)’ **19** (RS 17.120):25

ṮN verb ‘urinate’ (Gt-stem) **19** (RS 17.120):9

ṮNT common noun ‘urine’ /ṯênātu/ ← /*ṯaynātu/ **7** (RS 24.258):21

ṮNGB personal name, vocalization and etymology unknown **51** (RIH 84/33):10

[ṮNY]: ṮN cardinal number ‘two’ /ṯinâ/ **5** (RS 2.002):22; **12** (RS 24.643):19; **13** (RS 34.126):[27]; **28** (RS 29.093):20; **34** (RS 94.2284):28; **36** (RS 11.772^{+}):19′; **41** (RS 19.015):36; **45** (RS 86.2213):1, 6, 15; **47** (RS 94.2392^{+}):5, 8

ṮN ordinal number ‘second’ /ṯanû/ **4** (RS 2.[004]) i:[6′]; **36** (RS 11.772^{+}):36′

ṮNʾID adverb, multiplicative ‘twice’ /ṯinêʾida/ **28** (RS 29.093):9

ṮNY verb ‘say, announce, repeat’ **1** (RS 3.367) i:8′; **2** (RS 2.[014]$^{+}$) iii:12′, 22′; **3** (RS 2.[003]$^{+}$) i:27; **12** (RS 24.643):22′$^{?}$; **29** (RS 34.124):15bis

MṮN common noun ‘response, return (to a recitation), repetition’ /maṯnû/# **20** (RS 24.247^{+}):6, 12, 18

ṮNN common noun ‘archer, soldier, guard’ /ṯannānu/# **5** (RS 2.002):7, 26; **20** (RS 24.247^{+}):17

[ṮʿD]: ṮʿT common noun ‘(liquid measure [smaller than the *kaddu*])’ /ṯaʿittu/# ← /*ṯaʿidtu/ **48** (RS 94.2600):14

ṮʿY verb ‘(offer a *ṯaʿû*-sacrifice)’ **13** (RS 34.126):27bis, 28bis, 29bis, 30

N-stem **9** (RS 1.002):6′ ({[nṯʿ]⸢y⸣}), 24′, 32′, 41′ ({n[ṯʿy]})

Ṯʿ common noun ‘(type of sacrifice) [function unknown]’ /ṯaʿû/ **8** (RS 1.001):1^{tris}; **9** (RS 1.002):[6′], 23′, 24′, 32′^{bis}, 40′, 41′; **11** (RS 24.266):11

ṮʿY common noun ‘(offerer of the *ṯaʿû*-sacrifice)’ /ṯaʿʿāyu/ **11** (RS 24.266):8; **17** (RIH 78/20):2

ṮʿT: see ṮʿD

[ṮPṬ verb ‘rule (clan or tribe)’]: common noun ‘ruler’ /ṯāpiṭu/ (substantivized G-participle) **1** (RS 3.367) i:4′ ({[ṯp]⸢ṭ⸣}) 15′, 16′, 22′, 25′, 27′, 30′

ṮPṬBʿL personal name /ṯipṭibaʿlu/ (‘[this child is owing to] the decision of [the god] *Baʿlu*’) **27** (RS 18.040):3

ṮPLLM royal name (Hittite) /ṯuppilulûma/ **36** (RS 11.772^{+}):16′

ṮQD common noun ‘almond’ /ṯuqdu/# **19** (RS 17.120):7, 24

ṮQL common noun ‘shekel (weight [about 9.5 grams])’ /ṯiqlu/ **3** (RS 2.[003]$^{+}$) i:29; **28** (RS 29.093):18; **36** (RS 11.772^{+}):20′; **40** (RS [Varia 14]):16, 17; **42** (RS 15.062):5, 20, 21; **43** (RS 18.024):13, 20, 23, 24, 25; **49** (RIH 84/04):5; **51** (RIH 84/33):13

ʾAṮQLNY gentilic ‘person from (the town of) Ashqelon’ /ʾaṯqalāniyyu/ **47** (RS 94.2392^{+}):13

ṮR common noun (title of *ʾIlu*) ‘bull’ /ṯôru/ ← /*ṯawru/ **3** (RS 2.[003]$^{+}$) i:41; **4** (RS 2.[004]) i:23′

ṮRYL personal name (Hurrian) (queen and queen-mother of Ugarit) /ṯarriyelli/ **13** (RS 34.126):32; **14** (RS 6.021):2; **24** (RS 15.008):2; **35** (RS [Varia 4]):8, 12, 17

ṮRMN divine name /ṯarrummanni / **8** (RS 1.001):12, 15
ṮR ʿLLMN divine name (ancestor of the kings of Ugarit), vocalization unknown **13** (RS 34.126):7, 23–24
ṮRR adjective 'well watered' /ṯarīru/ **6** (RS 24.244):64
ṮRṮY divine name, a manifestation of the weather deity (≈ *Baʿlu/Haddu*), precise identification unknown /ṯarraṯiya/ **12** (RS 24.643):28
ṮṮ: see ṮDṮ
ṮṮPḤ personal name, vocalization and etymology unknown **44** (RS 19.016):15
ṮǴR common noun 'gate, gateway' /ṯaǵru/# **11** (RS 24.266):26′, 28′–29′, 35′; **13** (RS 34.126):34
ṮǴR common noun, profession name, substantivized participle 'door-keeper' /ṯāǵiru/ **7** (RS 24.258):11; **44** (RS 19.016):13

ǴB common noun 'sacrificial pit' /ǵabbu/ **41** (RS 19.015):15
ǴBR identification unknown **9** (RS 1.002):4′, 20′, [29′], 38′
ǴZR common noun 'young man, hero' /ǵazru/ **4** (RS 2.[004]) i:1′, 17′, 35′, 37′; **5** (RS 2.002):14, 17; **17** (RIH 78/20):1
ǴLM common noun 'boy' /ǵalmu/ **2** (RS 2.[014]+) iii:8′, iv:5; **3** (RS 2.[003]+) i:19, 40; **17** (RIH 78/20):10
ǴLM divine name /ǵalmu/ **11** (RS 24.266):7
ǴLMN personal name /ǵalmānu/ **44** (RS 19.016):13
ǴLMT divine name, feminine /ǵalmatu/ **8** (RS 1.001):19; **11** (RS 24.266):8
ǴLTN personal name /ǵaltēnu/ **44** (RS 19.016):24
ǴNB common noun 'bunch of grapes' /ǵanabu/ **5** (RS 2.002):26
ǴR common noun 'mountain' /ǵūru/ **2** (RS 2.[014]+) iii:29′, 30′; **39** (RS 94.2965):1, 5
ǴRM-W-THMT divine name, binomial 'Mountains and Waters-of-the-Abyss' /ǵūrūma wa tahāmātu/ **12** (RS 24.643):6, 41
ǴRN personal name /ǵūrānu/ **44** (RS 19.016):14
ǴR (← *ǴWR?) verb 'go lower, dive' **1** (RS 3.367) i:6′
ǴR (← *ǴYR?) verb 'confront' (Gt-stem) **20** (RS 24.247+):39′
ǴRGN personal name /ǵurgānu/ **46** (RS 94.2050+):29, 66

Tʾ IŠR common noun '(species of cypress)' /tiʾiššaru/ **42** (RS 15.062):4
TʾANT: see ʾNY
TBʿ verb 'leave, go away' **3** (RS 2.[003]+) i:14
TG: see YGY
TGMR: see GMR
TGḎN personal name /tagiḏānu/ **46** (RS 94.2050+):22
TGǴLN personal name /taguǵlinu/ **44** (RS 19.016):38

TDǴL common noun, profession name, 'maker of TD (meaning unknown)' **44** (RS 19.016):21

TDN (+ ṢRǴ[. . .]$^{?}$) common noun, profession name, meaning unknown **44** (RS 19.016):22

THM common noun 'abyss (of the fresh waters)' /tahāmu/ ← /*tihāmu/ **5** (RS 2.002):30; **6** (RS 24.244):1

THMT feminine variant of the same /tahāmatu/# ← /*tihāmatu/ **2** (RS 2.[014]$^{+}$) iii:25′; **6** (RS 24.244):3

THMT divine name: see ǴRM-w-THMT

TZǴ common noun '(type of sacrifice)' /tazuǵǵu/ **41** (RS 19.015):4

TḤM common noun 'message' /taḥmu/ **2** (RS 2.[014]$^{+}$) iii:13′, iv:7; **21** (RS 4.475):1; **22** (RS 8.315):3; **23** (RS 11.872):3; **24** (RS 15.008):1; **25** (RS 16.379):2; **26** (RS 18.031):3; **27** (RS 18.040):3; **28** (RS 29.093):3; **29** (RS 34.124):[3]; **30** (RS 92.2010):3; **31** (RS 94.2406):1, 31; **32** (RS 94.2479):2; **33** (RS 96.2039):1; **34** (RS 94.2284):1; **35** (RS [Varia 4]):1

TḤT preposition 'under' /taḥta/ **1** (RS 3.367) i:7′; **7** (RS 24.258):5, 8; **13** (RS 34.126):22, 23, 24, 25, 26$^{!}$; **18** (RS 92.2014):4, 8

TḤTY adjective 'lower' /taḥtiyyu/ **20** (RS 24.247^{+}):32′$^{!}$

TYT common noun '(name of plant and medication derived therefrom)' /tiyātu/ **43** (RS 18.024):26; **48** (RS 94.2600):9

TK preposition 'midst' /tôka/ ← /*tawku/ (substantive) **2** (RS 2.[014]$^{+}$) iii:29′; **5** (RS 2.002):65; **6** (RS 24.244):63

TŠʿ cardinal number 'nine' /tišʿu/; pl. 'ninety' /tišʿūma/ **41** (RS 19.015):28; **43** (RS 18.024):22bis; **52** (RIH 83/22):1

TLʾIYT: see LʾY

TLGN personal name, vocalization and etymology unknown **44** (RS 19.016):35

TLMʾ personal name /talmiʾu/ **43** (RS 18.024):7

TLMYN personal name /talmiyānu/ **22** (RS 8.315):3; **24** (RS 15.008):1; **49** (RIH 84/04):18; **51** (RIH 84/33):21

TLʿ common noun 'neck' /talaʿu/ **1** (RS 3.367) i:4′

[TMM]: TM adjective 'mature, complete' /tammu/ **5** (RS 2.002):67

TMN(T): see MN

TMRTN personal name /tamartēnu/ **44** (RS 19.016):32; **49** (RIH 84/04):10; **51** (RIH 84/33):15

TMṮL: see MṮL

TMT: see MT

TNN common noun 'sea monster, dragon' /tunnanu/# **2** (RS 2.[014]$^{+}$) iii:40′

TʿḎR: see ʿḎR

TʿN: see ʿNY

TPNR title of Hittite official /tupanuru/ **36** (RS 11.772^{+}):32′

TR common noun 'dove' /turru/ **10** (RS 24.260):5, 13; **42** (RS 15.062):7

TRḪ verb 'marry (said of bridegroom)' **3** (RS 2.[003]⁺) i:14; **5** (RS 2.002):64
D-stem 'marry (said of bride's father)' **3** (RS 2.[003]⁺) i:13
TRMN divine name (ancestor of the kings of Ugarit), vocalization unknown **13** (RS 34.126):5
TRNN personal name /turanana/ **46** (RS 94.2050⁺):50, 64
TRṮ common noun '(type of wine)' /tirāṯu/ **7** (RS 24.258):4, 16
TRṮ divine name (ditto) **8** (RS 1.001):11, 16; **12** (RS 24.643):[39]
TRǴDS personal name /tarǵuddassi/ **21** (RS 4.475):5
TǴD personal name /tēǵida/ **44** (RS 19.016):9
TǴPṮ common noun '(type of garment or cloth)' **44** (RS 19.016):36
TTL place-name (town on the Baliḫ) /tuttul/ **6** (RS 24.244):15

green press INITIATIVE

Eisenbrauns is committed to preserving ancient forests and natural resources. We elected to print this title on 30% post consumer recycled paper, processed chlorine free. As a result, for this printing, we have saved:

3 Trees (40' tall and 6-8" diameter)
1,484 Gallons of Wastewater
1 million BTU's of Total Energy
90 Pounds of Solid Waste
308 Pounds of Greenhouse Gases

Eisenbrauns made this paper choice because our printer, Thomson-Shore, Inc., is a member of Green Press Initiative, a nonprofit program dedicated to supporting authors, publishers, and suppliers in their efforts to reduce their use of fiber obtained from endangered forests.

For more information, visit www.greenpressinitiative.org

Environmental impact estimates were made using the Environmental Defense Paper Calculator. For more information visit: www.papercalculator.org.